PHYSICAL ANTHROPOLOGY AND ARCHAEOLOGY

SELECTED READINGS

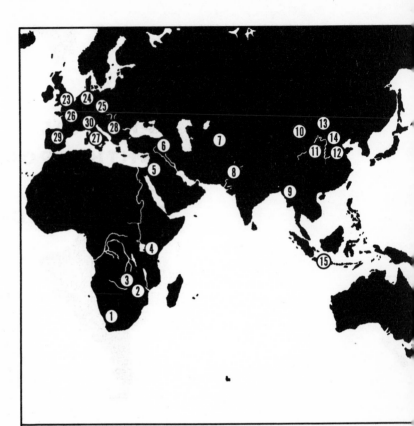

EARLY MAN AND ANCIENT CULTURES

AFRICA

❶ Saldanha man
❷ Australopithecus and
   Paranthropus
❸ Rhodesian man
❹ Proconsul, Australopithecus,
   and Zinjanthropus

ASIA

❺ Mt. Carmel, Bir Abu Matar,
   and Bir es-Safadi
❻ Karim Shahir
❼ Teshik-Tash

❽ Mohenjo-Daro
❾ Anyathian
❿ Sjara-osso-gol
⓫ Yang-shao, Hsiao-t'un,
   Lung-shan, and Gobi
⓬ Anyang
⓭ Shui-tung-kou
⓮ Choukoutien, Pekin man

SOUTHEAST ASIA

⓯ Java man

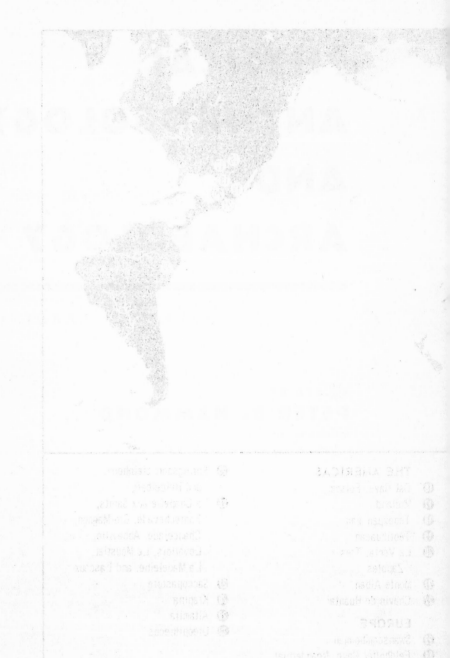

PHYSICAL ANTHROPOLOGY AND ARCHAEOLOGY

SELECTED READINGS

EDITED BY
PETER B. HAMMOND
Indiana University

THE MACMILLAN COMPANY, NEW YORK
COLLIER-MACMILLAN LIMITED, LONDON

Third Printing, 1964

Library of Congress catalog card number: 64–17381

THE MACMILLAN COMPANY, NEW YORK

COLLIER-MACMILLAN CANADA, LTD., TORONTO, ONTARIO

Printed in the United States of America

DESIGNED BY ANDREW P. ZUTIS

PREFACE

The basic subject of anthropology is man—all that he has been, is, and can become. In planning a book on a topic of such vast and divergent dimensions, the chronological beginning seemed the best place to start. And that is what I have done: an article that introduces the objectives of physical anthropology is followed by a series of selections that illustrate the story of our own evolution. In making these selections I tried to choose articles in which the presentation of facts was complemented by a consideration of concepts—ideas that make the facts seem important and worth remembering. The conceptual theme for the first section relates to the evolution of man's capacity for culture. As anthropology develops, whatever concepts we now have will—we hope—be replaced by better ones. But for the present I find the idea of an evolving ability to make use of culture as a means of survival important for an understanding of our past and compelling in its implications for our future.

A further intriguing conceptual problem in physical anthropology concerns our present evolutionary status—and our prospects for evolving still more. Several articles on this subject have been included. They are followed by a series on human variation. Here the problem of "race"—what the term does and does *not* mean— provides the theme.

The second half of the text—on archaeology—follows a parallel pattern. It begins with an introduction to archaeology as a subject of study. There follows a series of articles that present in chronological order some important statements on the early phases of the development of culture itself.

Although I grant the obvious possibility that the book might have been arranged in other ways, I hope the reader will find this organization reasonable and helpful. Ten years from now I would *not* expect him to remember the specifics of Sinanthropus' dentition or the style of any particular Peruvian pot, but I *do* hope he will remember, at least generally, the important ideas about human evolution and human races, and some of the problems involved in understanding the development of culture. I also hope that he will have been able to use some of these concepts to achieve a better understanding of himself as a human animal and of his own changing way of life.

At the beginning of each section and just before each article, I have made some brief editorial notes. They are included to provide continuity. It would be presumptuous to use them to synthesize the articles themselves, and I have not tried to do this. Most of the essential facts and ideas the authors are dealing with are clear enough by themselves. However, if the reader is occasionally baffled by a hyperpolysyllabic technical term or what seems to be an unwarrantedly windy phrase, he should check the glossary. It is printed at the back of the book and provides simple definitions for the special terms anthropologists must sometimes use. There is also an index. When the reader finds what seems to be an arguable idea, he can check the index and quickly locate what other scholars have said on the same subject.

Most of the articles reprinted here appeared first in somewhat specialized scientific publications. Originally, most of them had footnotes and long bibliographies that, unfortunately, it has not been possible to reproduce. Whenever a reader encounters an article that especially interests him, I urge him to track down the original source. There he will find footnotes citing relevant related works, bibliographical references to background reading, and occasionally a word or phrase that has been deleted here.

I wish to thank first of all the men whose work gives this book its substance and value. I am also grateful to the Graduate School, the Anthropology Department, and the Program of African Studies at Indiana University for their cooperation. The duplicating service at the university library processed my material with alacrity and unfailing good cheer. Two of my students, Alan G. Fix and Edwin S. Segal, attended with interest and care to many of the details involved in a work of this sort. Mr. Segal did the index. The steady support of my wife, Fatmeh Isfahani-Zadeh Hammond, made the endeavor possible and pleasurable. She provided the text design that appears on page 328; the others are mine, and so, of course, are whatever errors of commission, omission, or organization the reader may encounter here.

My small part in this book is dedicated to my mother.

PETER B. HAMMOND

CONTENTS

PHYSICAL ANTHROPOLOGY AND ARCHAEOLOGY

SELECTED READINGS

PART ONE

PHYSICAL ANTHROPOLOGY

In most ways man is very much like the rest of the animals. His similarity to other mammals—particularly the primates, the monkeys and apes—is especially striking. His physique and physiology are quite like theirs. And he shares with them a common set of biologically determined needs. However, there is a sense in which man is absolutely unique; he has one essential attribute that sets him apart from all the others: his capacity for culture.

Culture can be defined as the learned behavior that is generally shared, together with its consequences, by all the members of a human group. The Chinese have a culture. So do the Russians, the Americans, the Pygmies, and the Eskimos. And so did our Stone Age ancestors. All people, but only people, have culture. None of the other animals do.

Learning is intended as a key word in this definition. Not because the ability to learn is exclusively human, but because man relies on learning far more than any of the other animals to solve the problems of being alive. In contrast, instinct plays a much more important part in the behavior of the nonhuman animals. A newborn puppy, for example, will grow up to behave like a dog even if it is separated from its mother at birth and raised exclusively among humans. The way it behaves will be largely determined by its canine heredity. In contrast, a human infant separated from his

1

parents and all other humans would probably die. But if, however, he were to survive, he certainly would not be a human being in any really significant sense. For without the company of other humans, and the chance to learn from them how to be human, the potential of his capacity for culture could not be realized. Without culture he would not be importantly different from any other animal. In fact, without culture and without developed instincts, he would be considerably worse off than most.

Because the human infant comes into the world uncultured, he is completely unable to care for himself. He has to be taught—and at first he learns very slowly—how to survive. At the beginning his parents provide for his biological needs. Then gradually, through infancy and childhood, they teach him how to meet them himself. He learns to satisfy his hunger pangs with certain kinds of foods; he learns he must perform his excretory functions in particular ways; and he learns from his parents' response to his first childish attempts at sexuality how he must deal with such feelings. His need for nurture, protection, love, and comfort are met so long as he is successful at this learning. When he violates the rules and regulations of his parents, his first "community," love and comfort, and possibly protection and even food, may be temporarily withdrawn. Slowly, by this process of trial and error, punishment and reward, he begins to learn the culture of his group, that is, the particular system of behavior its members have developed for meeting their needs.

Of course, what culture he learns depends on what culture he is raised in. Americans, for example, behave like Americans because, unsurprisingly, they are raised in America and learn American culture. But if, for example, they had American parents but were separated from them at birth and raised among Congo Pygmies, or Greenland Eskimos, they would not automatically grow up behaving like Americans, speaking English, playing baseball, and enjoying hot dogs. Their culture would be that of the people who raised them, those who taught them how to be human beings: the Pygmies or the Eskimos. In other words, what all men possess in common is the capacity to acquire culture and to rely on culture as a means of meeting their needs. The particular culture they acquire, American, Pygmy, or Eskimo, depends on the particular culture in which this capacity is developed.

As important as the role of learning is the fact that culture is readily transmitted. Again the distinction is relative, but it has profound implications. Man is far more efficient in communicating his knowledge, discoveries, and speculations than are the other animals. Neither individual animals nor generations of animals can transmit their ideas and experience from one to the other. Consequently, the record of whatever knowledge they acquire cannot be cumulative. For this reason there can be no significant progress, or change, in their behavior patterns except through the genetically determined modification of their instincts.

It was the gradual emergence of the capacity for culture that assured the survival of man's ancestors throughout the course of their evolution. Otherwise they were relatively weak creatures living in a harsh environment among other animals much stronger and fiercer than themselves. Just as this capacity for culture made it possible for man to become the dominant and most widely dispersed species on our planet, and an animal like, yet very different, from all the rest, so does this faculty unite all men. For all of us, in contrast to all the other animals, share this unique ability.

This concept of the capacity for culture is fairly simple, but its implications are enormous. The readings collected here provide a beginning exploration of these implications. They start with physical anthropology, the special field in anthropology that is concerned with understanding the biological basis of man's ability to use culture, the evolution, of this ability, its present development, and its future.

Physical anthropology is concerned, at least potentially, with all aspects of man's biological being. But whatever the specific human aspect under study, evolution, the pattern of growth from conception through maturity to senescence and death, or the superficial differences that distinguish varieties of modern men, one basic question persists—how do we explain man's humanness? How did we become human and what does being human mean?

The following article provides an introduction to the field in anthropology that deals with the many dimensions of this compelling question.

The Objectives of Physical Anthropology [1]

The word anthropology is employed at the present time to express two distinct concepts: (a) In the broadest sense, it is the science of man, or rather the comparative science of man. It treats of his differences and their causes with reference to structure, function and other manifestations according to time, place and condition. Because of this broadness and as data accumulated, anthropology gradually became divided into various branches, until it now embraces such independent disciplines as: archaeology, ethnology and ethnography, linguistics, physical anthropology, paleoanthropology, etc. It is thus understood and defined on the American continent. (b) On the other hand, in the Old World, the term anthropology is limited exclusively to physical anthropology.

Paul Broca, one of the founders of our science, defines it as the "natural history of the genus Homo" and more concretely as the "science whose objective is the study of humanity considered as a whole, in its parts, and in relationship to the rest of nature."

It could be defined more briefly as the "science which studies human variations," "comparative study of the human body and its inseparable functions," "exposition of the causes and courses of human evolution, transmission and classification, effects and tendencies in the functional and organic differences," etc.

The solution of the problem of a concrete definition, classification and determination of the objectives of physical anthropology is neither easy nor conclusive as has been demonstrated in some very recent cases. For example, there is R. Martin's statement on this matter or the interesting international survey carried out by S. Sergi in 1932 in which, among other points, he requested a definition of the terms "anthropology" and "ethnology" and the boundary between their respective fields of investigation. Replies were received from 71 specialists in anthropological sciences. The heterogeneity

[1] JUAN COMAS, from *Manual of Physical Anthropology*, Chapter 1, pp. 27–39, 1960. Courtesy of the author and Charles C. Thomas, Publisher, Springfield, Ill.

Dr. Comas is Professor of Anthropology at the National University of Mexico.

of their opinions makes clear to what extent precision is still lacking in this respect. This is so, precisely because its field of action and need for cooperation from other sciences are growing every day.

Physical anthropology has sometimes been confused with human biology, anatomy and physiology, but there is no reason for this.

The three latter sciences deal essentially with the structure and function of the contemporary *average man,* while physical anthropology undertakes the study of all that refers to the chronological, racial, social, and even pathological groupings of human nuclei. However, an intimate relationship does exist between both groups of sciences although it is obvious that they differ in working methods and techniques as well as in their goals.

According to Vallois, the special property of anthropology and that which distinguishes it essentially from human anatomy and physiology, is that it does not study man as a standard being, identical in all epochs and places. On the contrary, it tries to point out his differences, using these as a basis for establishing natural groups which it attempts to define by a precise determination of their characteristics. Moreover, it does not restrict itself to specifying such traits, but tries to investigate their origin and recognize their significance.

While anatomy and physiology deal with the standard individual, anthropology is the science of the group. That is, the important elements for the anthropologist are exactly those traits which distinguish individuals within the species. Those characteristics which to date have provided the greatest information in this respect belong to three distinct fields: differential physiology of the blood, color and structure of the skin and adnata areas, and morphology of the skeleton. Other differential elements in the somatic structure of man are of secondary

value in comparison with those just cited.

An additional element of basic importance is the analysis of exterior form, i.e. height, proportions among the different body segments, etc., which has acquired sufficient importance to constitute a new science, biotypology (structural types, constitutional types, psychosomatic types, etc.).

It has already been seen that physical anthropology became an independent science at a time when human anatomy was still imperfectly known, consequently, it had to undertake the difficult task of establishing or improving the bases for future comparisons. As a result of this situation, a large number of anthropological works are purely anatomical even at the present time. A century ago very few human characteristics had been fully studied and comprehended, and even today it would perhaps not be an exaggeration to state that there are some bones and organs whose structure and degree of variation are still not perfectly understood.

Anatomy texts provide generalities, since this is their primary objective, but omissions and at times errors abound, with regard to differential traits and details which are absolutely indispensable for anthropological comparisons.

In the not too distant past, physical anthropology was considered to be, primarily, a technique. Instruction consisted almost exclusively of learning to take carefully defined measurements and to classify indices and compute statistics.

Methods of observation, measurement and comparison were essentially the same, regardless of the object of study (evolution, races, growth, criminal and constitutional types, selection of military personnel, etc.). The measurements were used for various purposes, but body measurement, classification and correlation continued to be the basic objectives of the anthropologist, and the techniques of physical anthropology were applied to a limited number of problems. It may be stated that the prevailing approach was static, with emphasis on taxonomy, because of the fact that a large part of the method was developed before the evolutionary thesis had been accepted and, naturally, before the development of the science of genetics.

Since classical physical anthropology was in this sense fundamentally a technique, the core of this science was for a long period of time the measurement of body form, that is, anthropometry.

For many years physical anthropology did not change. This is easily explained by the fact that the specialists interested in human evolution or races employed measurements as their primary technique, and their basic training consisted of learning to take such measurements as exactly as possible. Consequently, one of the greatest concerns of the profession was to reach an agreement upon the techniques employed. It was assumed that if the metric values were correct and sufficient in number all problems could be solved.

Initial knowledge of the Primates and of the races within the genus *Homo* had already been gained in the nineteenth century. Since that time, the most conspicuous progress made is represented by the discovery of fossils and the notable improvement in the quantity and quality of descriptive material taken from life. Naturally, many problems of a secondary nature have been solved but neither the new data nor the improvement of techniques has provided any effective advance in the understanding of the evolutionary process. It is a fact that among scientists today there is less agreement than there was fifty years ago concerning the phylogenetic links between man and the rest of the Primates. This however, is due not only to a lack of adequate methods of investigation but also to the greater complexity presented by the problem in the light of constant paleonto-

logical discoveries and the progress of genetic studies.

The same may be said of races, for an obvious discrepancy exists among the various taxonomic systems proposed, above all with regard to their biogenetic relationship.

Measurements and indices may determine the degree of brachycephaly but do not tell us if all brachycephalics should be placed in a single biological category. A photograph may show that a person is fat, but it does not indicate the causes of the obesity. A grouping of fat people may be just as arbitrary as one of brachycephalics.

A previous background knowledge of the varieties of cranial forms, pigmentation, somatic structure, growth process, etc., is of course, necessary before we can approach and understand the problems of evolution, race, and constitution. Yet such initial descriptive information permits no more than preliminary understanding and tentative classification.

A reorientation of methodology is necessary in order to go forward: *After the first descriptive phase, Physical Anthropology enters the analytical stage.*

But the general approach has gradually undergone a change. Four studies, among others, deserve special atention in this respect, because, in our opinion, they effectively set forth the objectives of the new orientation in physical anthropology.

Washburn points out certain contrasts between what he calls classical physical anthropology and the new physical anthropology, even though it should not be expected to find precise limits dividing the two. Both are necessary stages in the beginnings of a science and, as will be seen, in no way imply radical changes and much less a negative balance of past achievements. Here are a few examples:

1. It is natural enough that the field of interest or the final aims should be the same for both. The comprehension and interpretation of human evolution con-

tinue to be the main objectives, However, while the investigator today is more concerned with the problems of race, constitution, fossil man and other similar questions, the principal aim of the majority in the past was to classify rather than interpret phenomena.

For example, it has long been known that the browridges vary in size and shape. Cunningham has classified these variations. But, what do these differences mean and how are they related to other features? Simply setting the shapes in order does not answer these questions. If we say that an individual has browridges of type 2 and another of type 3, it does not explain the meaning behind such a difference, nor can we make deductions concerning their relationship. In general, big browridges correspond to large faces but their size also depends upon the size and shape of the skull among other factors. We may then ask what percentage of browridge variation is due to facial and how much to cranial differences.

Such descriptions are undoubtedly valuable and necesary, but the attempt to draw conclusions fails because the supraorbital ridges are anatomically complex and the same general form may be due to a diversity of different conditions. No description of ridge types gives us the reasons for their shape but only states their existence and the circumstances under which they have been encountered.

Analysis is, accordingly, indispensable and is made possible by the use of methods which until a few years ago were not included in the anthropologist's equipment.

Another example is the classical procedure of taking a series of measurements of the nose (length, breadth, shape of profile, etc.). This data is analyzed under the assumption that the nose is an independent entity whose attributes may be compared. But the concept of adaptation suggests other possibilities. Benninghoff

and Seipel have shown that the facial region is highly organized in response to the stresses of mastication. The margins of the piriform aperture become thick or thin according to the extent of muscular tension or relaxation. Moreover, the breadth of the aperture corresponds approximately to the intercanine distance, or breadth of the incisor teeth which in man develop in the subnasal area. As Baker has demonstrated, developing teeth exert a positive force which increase the size of the surrounding bone. Gans and Sarnat have proved that the growth in the region of the premaxillary suture is accelerated at the time of eruption of the permanent canine teeth. This fact complements Seipel's observations on how the eruption of the canines in the chimpanzee causes modifications over an extended facial area.

Far from being an independent structure that may be described by itself the nose is an integral part of the face. Variations in its form may only be interpreted as a part of the face in function. The form of the nose is the result of very diverse factors. The number of these and their relationship to each other can only be determined by research, but apparently, we repeat, the teeth and forces of mastication are among the most important elements. Nevertheless neither factor is included in traditional descriptions of the nose.

These examples show how simple description and classification served not only as the instruments but also as the goal of physical anthropology. Consequently, (a) it was vitally important to obtain complete uniformity and accuracy in the technique of measurement and description and because of this, books on physical anthropology allotted ample space to instructions on this technique and very little to the significance and interpretation of the results. (b) The attempt to solve new problems complicates the systematization still further. Race studies offer a classic example. During the first half of the nineteenth century, several simple classifications of races existed and causal explanations had been offered. Races were due to climate, isolation, etc. Today, the taxonomy of human groups has grown extremely complex generally without any new causal theory in justification.

The new physical anthropology is separated from the old, not by any difference in the desire to know causes but by a very real difference in belief as to the extent to which classification can reveal causes. We cannot and should not deny the need for classification as the first step in ordering the data of a specific area of knowledge. After this preliminary stage, however, we must tackle the problem of process. Otherwise, the data is useless without adequate technique and theories for its interpretation.

2. At the beginning, physical anthropology like other sciences did not consider theory important, but theory acquires value as the field of knowledge is broadened and problems are more clearly formulated. For a long time after the idea of organic evolution had been accepted, comparisons were still being made with no concern for general theory as long as the compared parts were homologous, which was not even always the case. Later, a controversy arose as to whether biological relationship shold be based upon adaptive or non-adaptive characteristics. This raised the question of whether it was better to compare many features or whether the comparison of a few critical ones might not give more reliable results.

In spite of this, physical anthropologists continued their work without any great concern for its theoretical foundations. The situation was analogous in other sciences (zoology, ethnology, archaeology). Points for theoretical discussion did exist, but they were not considered very important. The main emphasis was on collection of specimens and data and the description of facts. Only during the last few decades has it been possible to make any headway with the idea that facts alone cannot solve fundamental questions.

3. As we shall see further on, evolution is considered to be the history of genetic systems in which changes are due, among other factors, to mutation and selection. Selection includes a number of mechanisms and their implications in relation to man are many and intricate. The chief task of the anthropologist is to understand the nature and kind of adaptation or selection. Therefore, since evolution is a sequence of the most effective behavior systems, in order to understand behavior, we must first study living subjects.

Next, we should attempt to interpret the differences among fossil hominid remains aided by our knowledge of living forms, keeping in mind that fossils were once animate and adapted to their time and as such, should be studied within their proper environment. It is a difficult and uncertain task because the materials are fragmentary, but this inherent difficulty does not change the methodological problem.

4. Traditional physical anthropology based on the study of the skeleton and especially the skull places particular emphasis upon the elaboration of measurements for describing the characteristics of bones.

When the technique was extended to the living, the new measurements used followed the preceding ones as closely as possible. This was reasonable enough for that age and for comparative and taxonomic purposes, but it brought the limitations of death to a study of the living.

The new physical anthropology, on the contrary, aims to enrich knowledge of the past by study of the present. That is, it explains the bone in terms of function and life. Similarities of measurements or combinations of measurements do not prove genetic affinity. Some individuals of similar genotype are metrically comparable, but it is a mistake to assume that similar measurements necessarily mean genetic resemblance.

The following example comes from Washburn also. The lower jaw is classically considered to be a unit comparable in its metric values. But, on the contrary, the mandible is apparently a complex the different parts of which evolve independently of each other, but in relation to other facial regions; (a) the coronoid processes which vary with the temporal muscle; (b) the angle of the jaw varies with the masseter and internal pterygoid muscle; (c) the tooth-supporting area varies with the teeth; (d) the main core of the jaw is affected by hormones which do not affect the other parts. If this is true, we are confronted with a bone complex whose different segments are modified independently. This must be considered in establishing comparisons, especially if we mean to draw conclusions of a phylogenetic type.

If the somatic or osteologic features are for the most part complex and adaptive, this obviously presents interpretational problems which the measuring stick alone cannot solve. Investigation along these lines must employ other methods. For example, measurements and statistics tell us that roundheads have become more common, but they do not tell us if roundheads are genetically similar or why roundheads have become more common. From an anatomical point of view we may ask if brachycephalization is due to changes in the brain, dura mater, sutures or base of the skull. Then, from the viewpoint of evolution, is the change due to adaptation or genetic drift?

The simple statement that a trait does or does not exist, is methodologically complemented by an attempt to understand under what conditions it might be present. For example, if the simian shelf (the bony plate found on the mesial-inferior-ventral segment of the lower jaw in many Primates) is developed in monkeys and great apes when the jaws are long and the anterior teeth large, we cannot expect to find it among the South African man-apes (*Australopithecinae*). The simian shelf does not exist in any fossil or living human types because their dentition does not have the necessary size and strength to make it appear.

Understanding the process or mechanism which creates a specific trait is something very different from and of far greater importance than the simple statement of the presence or lack of such a trait even though the first would barely be possible without the second.

The development of appropriate quantitative and descriptive methods is merely a matter of time and technique. The sequence might be as follows: (a) to diagnose the complex; (b) to establish proper methods for describing its variations; and (c) to make an effort to discover the genetic antecedents of these variations. Actually, we have not yet passed much beyond the first stage.

The new concept of physical anthropology also differs from the old in the field of raciology. Even though the anthropologist has little or nothing to contribute to the modern evolutionary theory in the field of mutation, he can, on the other hand, make useful contributions with regard to migration, genetic drift and selection.

The confused human genetic picture is due precisely to migrations which were made possible by culture. Prior to an investigation of selection it is necessary to know how long a people has been in an area and under what conditions they have been living. An interpretation of the genetic situation demands a previous understanding of the history. Thus, the distribution of physical traits will be interpreted differently depending on whether the population has become adapted to cold by selection or by change in their way of life. This fact, fully recognized by physical anthropologists, shows that a solution of a given difficulty requires the active collaboration of archaeologists, ethnologists and linguists.

The foregoing considerations indicate the broad horizons now opening to physical anthropology, which imply new objectives and consequently the development of new work methods. Perhaps these may be achieved if agreement can be reached on the following points:

(a) The necessity for a consistent and carefully formulated theoretical framework in physical anthropology; (b) the application of available genetic and evolutionary theories to the problems of human evolution; (c) the abandonment of certain untenable classical concepts; (d) that we are in a period of transition during which great differences in personal opinion are to be expected, which should be settled by research.

A good orientation in physical anthropology, therefore, depends on both its theoretical concept and the techniques employed in the solution of the problems raised. As the latter change, the former should also be modified since they exist solely as a means and not as an end in themselves. The traditional techniques failed to solve the problems of process as is proved by the fact that there are now more different theories of man's origin and differentiation than there were fifty years ago. This is partly due to the use of unsuitable techniques for dealing with the question. Evidently, in this case we must resort to the genetic, paleontological, geological and cultural methods best adapted to the particular ends of our science.

In summary: it was possible at one time for the physical anthropologist to believe that his task was restricted to measuring, classifying and speculating. That time, however, has passed. Now, he also needs methods to test the accuracy or inaccuracy of theories. *The best of the past should be combined with new techniques to obtain proofs rather than simple assumptions.*

The new anthropological orientation does not solve problems, but it does suggest a different and better way to approach them. The change affects the various branches of physical anthropology very differently. In growth studies and applied anthropology, where measurements have a direct use, there have been few changes, while the approaches to problems of evolution and heredity have been profoundly affected.

If, during the first decades of the twentieth century, traditional physical anthropology may be said to have been compounded of three quarters measurement and the remainder concerned with the evolutionary process, heredity, etc., in the new physical anthropology the proportions may be approximately reversed. One of the main implications of the new point of view is that a much more concrete interrelationship exists between the different subdivisions of anthropology. Thus, a dynamic analysis of the form of the jaw to which reference has been made, will clarify problems of evolution, fossil man, race, growth, constitution and medical application.

It should not be forgotten that some problems of human evolution are unique to man and do not exist in other mammals. They derive from the adaptation brought about by his way of life and in this respect, a knowledge of human evolution is *inseparable* from the study of ethnology and archaeology. Human migrations, adaptations, marriage systems, population density, diseases, ecology, etc., are biological factors increasingly influenced by the way of life. Therefore, to understand the process of evolution it is necessary to complement the new and dynamic orientation in physical anthropology with a profound appreciation of the history and the mechanism of culture.

It is this exigency that gives anthropology -lato sensu- *unity as a science*.

There are, however, two obstacles, among others, which even today seriously impede the rapid realization of a broad study of physical anthropology as outlined:

1. A lack of specialized experts. There is an urgent need for prepared personnel, preferably with biological training. Furthermore, we find a general lack of understanding of the social importance of such investigators and when they are available, the material rewards are less than those received by other scientists of the same rank. Anthropology was not considered important for application to industry, but this situation has changed somewhat during the last decades.

2. Sentimentality, superstitions and certain religious beliefs, etc., often impose barriers which prevent access to the basic materials of anthropological study. People must be educated to appreciate the positive benefits that living humanity may receive in the future from a better understanding of its anthropological features. Unless we acquire more information and a comprehension of man's nature and the human societies he forms, we may find ourselves involved in another world crisis.

Conditions in anthropology contrast unfavorably with research facilities available to the zoologist, the botanist and even the biologist.

HUMAN EVOLUTION

The focus of interest in physical anthropology is changing. The cautious disinterment of old bones, their careful measurement, and the classification of living peoples according to physical type are no longer regarded as sufficient to provide the answers we need.

Neither measurement nor classification has been abandoned, but now both are regarded as no more than the important first step in understanding process: how we became human and what being human means. An approach to such understanding must begin with the study of our own evolution.

We have become men by a process that is presently estimated to have taken nearly two million years. Ours is a story in which such factors as a physique facilitating erect bipedal locomotion, tool-use, and intellect have acted upon one another to achieve the gradual but persistent evolution of our apelike ancestors that resulted, ultimately, in the emergence of us.

11

1. Human Evolution and Culture [1]

In *The Descent of Man* Darwin (1871) outlined the structural-functional complexes which distinguish man from the anthropoid apes. He attributed the differences in skull structure to the great size of the brain of man. He noted that "nearly all the other and more important differences between man and the quadrumana are mainfestly adaptive in their nature, and relate chiefly to the erect posture of man; such as the structure of his hand, foot, and pelvis, the curvature of his spine, and the position of his head." This led Darwin to speculate that:

As the progenitors of man became more and more erect, with their hands and arms more and more modified for prehension and other purposes, with their feet and legs at the same time transformed for firm support and progression, endless other changes of structure would have become necessary. . . . The early male forefathers of man were, as previously stated, probably furnished with great canine teeth; but as they gradually acquired the habit of using stone, clubs, or other weapons, for fighting with their enemies or rivals, they would use their jaws and teeth less and less. In this case, the jaws, together with the teeth, would become reduced in size, as we may feel almost sure from innumerable analogous cases.

Darwin recognized the great importance of language and its relation to the size of the human brain. He stressed the importance of reason, social life, and the moral order in the selective process which led to man. He believed that the anthropomorphous apes—gorilla, chimpanzee, orang, and gibbon—constituted a natural group and that "some ancient member of the anthropomorphous sub-group gave birth to man."

A large number of primate fossils have been discovered since 1871. Only the Neandertal skull cap and the Naulette lower jaw were known to Darwin. Although Darwin did mention the discoveries of Boucher de Perthes in the Somme River in connection with the antiquity of man, almost the whole science of prehistoric archeology has developed since the writing of *The Descent of Man*. As did Huxley, Darwin had to build his theory primarily from the comparsion of living forms, since a fossil record was lacking and there was an absence of archeological specimens associated with human fossils. However, he did caution that "we must not fall into the error of supposing that the early progenitors of the whole Simian stock, including man, was identical with, or even closely resembled, *any existing ape or monkey.*"

At that time it was impossible to do more than speculate about the order of the actual events in human evolution. Perhaps one of the main reasons why Darwin did not trust his own theory of natural selection further but tried to support it with various subsidiary theories was simply that he did not have sufficient data to see how well it applies in accounting for human origins.

Darwin did express the hope that the necessary fossils of man would be found; surely he would have been delighted to see the extent to which his prophecy has been fulfilled. Equally surely, with his usual caution, he would have reminded us that many of the problems raised by him nearly a century ago are still unanswered. On which continent did man originate? How rapidly did the evolution

[1] S. L. WASHBURN and F. CLARK HOWELL, "Human Evolution and Culture," in *The Evolution of Man*, Sol Tax (ed.) (Chicago: 1960), pp. 33–57. Reprinted by permission of the authors and The University of Chicago Press, © 1960 by The University of Chicago Press.

Dr. Washburn is Professor of Anthropology at the University of California, Berkeley; Dr. Howell is Professor of Anthropology at the University of Chicago.

of man proceed? Why did man lose his body hair? What was the nature of the social life of early man? If progress continues at the present rate in human evolutionary studies, it will be another hundred years before answers are provided to many of the queries posed by Darwin.

This paper will present an interpretation of man's evolution during the Pleistocene. Our contention will be that the actual events follow very closely the order postulated by Darwin, except that the human brain seems to have been a secondary development which evolved later rather than the primary factor in the differentiation of ape and man. The authors recognize that certain points in the interpretation are debatable. However, it is felt that there is sufficient new information to make an attempt at synthesis.

SEQUENCE OF EVOLUTIONARY EVENTS

A schematic view of the order of events in human evolution during the Pleistocene is presented in Figure 1 (page 14). Certain of these materials may be summarized, as follows.

1. Neither fossils of the Hominidae nor stone implements are known from the terminal Pliocene nor from the basal Pleistocene (earliest Villafranchian stage).

2. The oldest known bipedal Hominidae, capable of using and manufacturing stone implements, were certain australopithecines (genus *Australopithecus*) of late Villafranchian age.

3. A variety of fossil men (genus *Homo,* probably with several species) appears during the earlier Middle Pleistocene associated with types of stone implements that were prepared according to clearly defined traditions of manufacture. Some tools of the Chelles-Acheul tradition (hand-axes, cleavers, and various flake tools) are distributed over Africa, southwestern Europe, and most

of India (but not east of the Ganges flood-plain). The Far East, including southeastern Asia, is characterized by a different tradition, the chopper/chopping-tool tradition.

4. Anatomically modern man (*Homo sapiens*) appeared very late in the Pleistocene and always with a great variety of implements in stone (and other materials) which changed very rapidly in comparison with those of earlier traditions.

Australopithecine Stage. BIPEDAL LOCOMOTION. Darwin and many workers after him stressed development of bipedal locomotion as a factor in differentiating man from ape. This process freed the hands, made possible the use and manufacture of tools, and led to reduction in the size of the teeth and the facial skeleton. The australopithecines in general represent such a stage in human evolution. Portions of the pelvis of four different individuals from three different sites are now known. This is most important for the interpretation of locomotion since the pelvis of a bipedal hominid is very different from that of either apes or monkeys. The australopithecine ilium is short, broad, and conforms very closely to the human pattern. It should be stressed that the human ilium is a very specialized and peculiar bone and that, among all known mammals, the only ilium approximating man's is that of the australopithecines. It is in just those special features related to bipedal locomotion that the ilia of man and the australopithecines are alike. As nearly as we can tell from the ilium and the small fragments of the proximal end of the femur, the hip musculature must have functioned as in man; that is, *gluteus medius* functioned as an abductor and *gluteus maximus* as an extensor. Likewise, judging from the femur, the *quadriceps femoris,* so important in human bipedal locomotion, must have been large (the authors are grateful to Dr. J. T. Robinson for permission to examine these

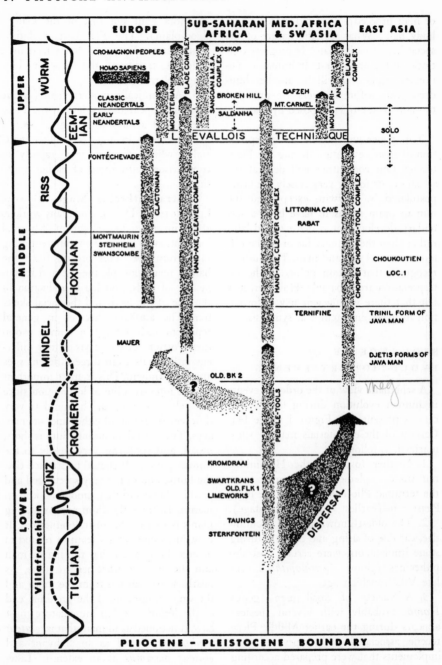

Figure 1. Temporal and spacial distribution of Pleistocene Hominid skeletal remains. (After Washburn and Howell)

specimens, still in part unpublished). Unfortunately, only fragments of the limb bones are preserved, and these are so short that reconstruction of proportions is impossible.

On the basis of the geological evidence and the associated fauna it is evident that the australopithecines lived in open grassland country, either somewhat drier or not unlike that of southern Africa at present. This habitat is very different from that of the living arboreal apes and supports the interpretation of locomotion based on the morphology of the pelvis.

REDUCED DENTITION. Darwin suggested that the reduction in size of the canine teeth of man was the result of tool use. The canines of all the australopithecines are small and of human conformation. These fossils support Darwin's contention, which in turn suggests that the use of implements may very well be considerably older than the earliest known artifacts. Perhaps, as Darwin suggested, tool use is both the cause and effect of hominid bipedalism, and the evolution of erect posture occurred simultaneously with the earliest use of tools. Primitive apes that were bipedal part-time and were capable of employing objects as implements must have lived in the woodlands or on the margins of forested areas. The ancestral populations of such apes were possibly like *Proconsul,* a form fully capable of bimanual locomotion through the trees in riverine gallery forests, although it probably also spent much of its waking life in the adjacent, open grasslands. It seems most probable that the australopithecines represent a subsequent evolutionary stage in which such creatures are already essentially bipedal, fully plains-living, and utilizing selected raw materials for the manufacture of stone tools. The preceding anthropoid or protohominid stage may very well have occurred at the beginning of the Villafranchian stage; if so, there may be no need to postulate a distinct, fully hominid

line prior to the Pleistocene. The great gap in the hominid fossil record is now terminal Pliocene and early Pleistocene. And in Africa at least, sites of such age are extremely rare.

CRANIAL CAPACITY. The brains of the australopithecines were surprisingly small. The capacity in the best preserved specimens ranges between approximately 450 and 600 cc. Prior to the discovery of the australopithecine pelvis, the small size of the brain led a number of scientists to dismiss the australopithecines as fossil apes. Some remarks on the evolution of the human brain will be made later on, but it is worth noting here that many scientists, including Darwin, have viewed the large brain as the essential factor in the diagnosis of man. For a time some workers even denied that Pekin man was an implement-maker because of the size of his brain. However, at least some australopithecines, with less cranial capacity than that of Pekin man, were already fashioning implements from stone. Consequently, it would appear that after acquisition of bipedalism and the beginnings of tool use new selection pressures led to the expanded brains of the Middle and later Pleistocene.

EARLIEST EVIDENCE OF CULTURE. The oldest stone implements, referred to the Pre-Chelles-Acheul industrial stage, have been known for some time from open sites; they have been found in Africa both north and south of the Sahara and are of Lower Pleistocene age, according to the associated Villafranchian fauna. Such evidence is not forthcoming from Villafranchian sites in either Europe or Asia, nor have any such extra-African sites yielded hominid skeletal remains. Hence it is likely that hominids were still restricted to continental Africa for this extended period.

Remains of australopithecines are associated with tools at Sterkfontein, Swartkrans and Olduvai Gorge (Bed I).

At Sterkfontein no Pre-Chelles-Acheul

implements have been found in the lower and main australopithecine-bearing pink breccia. The first such association with fragmentary australopithecine remains has come from the overlying red-brown breccia. Over two hundred specimens are now known, entirely fresh and unweathered and largely in raw materials (quartz, quartzite, diabase, and chert) which do not occur naturally in the cave deposits, but must have been collected and brought to the site. These include pebble-choppers, core-choppers, rough but retouched flakes, and quantities of fractured and utilized pebbles. An incomplete, longitudinally split and pointed bone implement, worn smooth at one end by use, has also been reported.

A new discovery by Dr. and Mrs. L. S. B. Leakey has proved australopithecine tool-making abilities and determined the makers of the Oldowan implements. At an open-air occupation site (FLK) in Olduvai Gorge Bed I, where the Oldowan industry was first recognized, a beautifully preserved hominid skull with excellent associations has been recovered. This new australopithecine (termed *Zinjanthropus boisei* Leakey) is very similar to the large and later form (*Paranthropus*) so abundantly represented at Swartkrans. Stone implements, including choppers and chopping-tools, flakes and flake implements, and cores are associated on the partially-excavated habitation horizon, an old land surface between clays (below) and sands (above), some three meters below the top of Bed I. Fossil remains of animals are also present, including broken bones of numerous rodents, immature larger mammals (e.g., pigs, antelopes), various reptiles and birds.

A number of attempts have been made previously to reconstruct the life habits of the australopithecines. The most useful general framework for such a reconstruction has been given by Bartholomew and Birdsell. In southern Africa the remains of australopithecines occur in ancient calcite-cemented soils infilling caves. They are typically found in association with a varied but characteristic mammalian fauna of the open grasslands, including very numerous antelopes (mostly medium to small varieties), numerous carnivores (including various hyaenids and sabretooths), suids, equids, and other primates (largely baboons); a microfauna includes numerous rodents, insectivores, hyracoids, and lagomorphs. Very large mammals are rare. The bones are generally broken; however, some well-preserved skulls do occur, and there is a fairly high proportion of skull fragments.

The central question has been whether the australopithecines were the hunters or the hunted. The vast majority of the animal bones show no clear use as tools, but merely represent the remains of meals by animals. Did these creatures already have the human hunting habit? Or were they scavengers? Hyena coprolites occur in the cave deposits, and it seems extremely likely that some broken bones represent remains of their meals (since some hyenas accumulate bones as part of their eating habits). It is by no means certain, however, that this accounts for all the bone accumulations. The southern African sites were worked extensively for lime by commercial firms so that much necessary evidence of detailed stratigraphy and associations has been lost.

The extraordinary new discovery at Olduvai Gorge has clarified some of these important questions concerning australopithecine behavior. It affords clear-cut evidence that these primitive hominids were to some extent carnivorous and predaceous, augmenting their basically vegetal diet with meat, particularly from small animals and the young of some larger species. It is very unlikely that the early and small-bodied australopithecines did much killing, whereas the later and larger forms, which probably replaced them, could cope with small and/or immature mammals. There is no evidence to suggest such creatures were capable of preying on the large herbivorous mammals so characteristic of the African Pleistocene.

Indirect evidence on the habits of the australopithecines will ultimately be gained from their distribution and classification. Unfortunately, several such matters are still under debate. Robinson has attributed to the australopithecines several hominid jaw fragments from the Putjang beds of Java. This hominid falls fully outside the range of variation of the other Javanese "pithecanthropine" forms, whether from the same Putjang beds or the later Kabuh beds. The scant evidence available supports Robinson's conclusion that the dental and jaw morphology of this hominid is generally similar to that of certain australopithecines. It is premature, however, to say that this was certainly a *Paranthropus,* since the cranial morphology is still wholly unknown.

In the southern African sites several types of hominids are represented. These have been treated as genera (*Australopithecus, Paranthropus,* and *Telanthropus*) by Robinson. The new australopithecine from Olduvai Gorge indicates a still broader distribution of the larger and later form. Such differences are not found among later fossil hominids. The existence of morphological differences of this magnitude within the same geographic region, and supposely within relatively short intervals of time, is the strongest evidence that the way of life of these forms was also different from that of later hominids. If these creatures had been fully effective hunters, as was the case among later Pleistocene peoples, the presence of two species from a single site would be most improbable.

Since the australopithecines occupied the same ecological position as the men of the Middle Pleistocene, it is no surprise that they were in due course completely replaced by early members of the genus *Homo.* However, the earliest men may very well have been contemporary with the latest australopithecines for a short time. This situation was quite different from that of such forms as the chimpanzee or gorilla, which could co-exist with men in a different ecological zone, or the baboon, which could easily escape from man until the development of firearms.

The Early *Homo* Stage. The early Middle Pleistocene, perhaps even the terminal Villafranchian, seems to have been a time of hominid dispersal into extra-African areas. Hominids were more widely distributed following the end of the Lower Pleistocene (Cromerian interglacial stage). Their stone implements or fragmentary fossilized skeletal remains occur in deposits of early Middle Pleistocene age in Sundaland of southeastern Asia and in southwestern Europe. Paleogeographic conditions would appear to have been particularly favorable for such expansion and the occupation of new habitats; there was maximum continentality as a result of uplift plus greatly lowered sea levels accompanying the expansion of the first continental ice sheets in North Temperate latitudes. The morphological evidence suggests the attainment of advanced evolutionary status for such early men. There were also undoubtedly behavioral differences, including enhanced cultural capacities, in comparison with the australopithecines of the Villafranchian.

STRUCTURAL ADVANCES. The bipedal hominids of the Middle Pleistocene are larger-brained and indicate major structural and behavioral advances beyond the australopithecine stage. However, there is no morphological evidence to preclude their having evolved from an australopithecine group. The locomotor skeleton, or what is known of it, of all the subsequent Pleistocene hominids is remarkably similar to that of anatomically-modern human races. In fact, the femur of Java man (from the Kabuh beds) or that of Pekin man is considerably more like the femur of *Homo sapiens* than it is like that of European (early or classic) Neandertal peoples. This fact would suggest that all variation in limb-bone morphology manifest in the latter half of the Pleistocene may be racial variation rather than illustrative of any major evolutionary trend.

In comparison with the australopithecines the brains of Middle Pleistocene men were very much larger, and the masticatory apparatus, particularly the molar dentition, was much reduced.

CULTURAL ADVANCES. Fossils of Middle Pleistocene peoples are associated with well-planned stone implements and weapons manufactured according to complex and clearly-defined traditions. These peoples, especially in Africa and Europe, where the evidence is best, hunted and killed large herbivorous animals in some quantity. There is no longer any question that men of the Middle Pleistocene —and even the earlier Middle Pleistocene —were capable and effective hunters. The earliest evidence has been largely provided by the very careful and extensive excavations of Leakey in two Chellean occupation horizons at Olduvai Gorge, west of the Crater Highlands in northern Tanganyika. One such horizon (BKII), on an old land surface adjoining a small, natural clay-filled depression representing a former marsh, has provided a rich assemblage of very early Chellean implements: choppers and chopping-tools, utilized flakes and flake-tools, rough polyhedral stones, a few bifacially-worked, picklike hand-axes, and many natural pebbles and stones, all brought to the site. These implements were found in association with articulated animal remains, sometimes whole skeletons but usually only skulls (and horn cores), vertebral columns, and limbs. Most of the bones and the skulls show clear signs of having been broken open to obtain the marrow and brains. This situation provides the earliest and clearest evidence that the primitive folk of the Chellean were meat-eaters, and were sufficiently skilled hunters to kill giant pigs, sheep, oxen, baboons, horses, hippos, and elephants.

One of the strongest indirect arguments that the australopithecines carried on at least a limited amount of hunting is that the hunting of such larger game in the Middle Pleistocene must have been preceded by the development of a taste for meat, probably through scavenging and the occasional killing of lesser game. The earliest use of fire is reported from the cave lair of Pekin man (at Choukoutien Locality 1). There is also evidence of fire on some open sites of broadly similar age, e.g., in the Swanscombe Middle Gravels of the Thames Valley, and at Cagny-la-Garenne in the Somme Valley. This very important development plus the increased dependence on the use of implements—of stone as well as other raw materials—probably accounts for the altered selection pressures that resulted in smaller molar teeth.

DISTRIBUTION OF MIDDLE PLEISTOCENE HOMINIDS. There are still relatively few hominid fossils from the Middle Pleistocene. The best preserved early Middle Pleistocene remains, including portions of the cranium, are from Java, either from the earlier Putjang beds (Djetis fauna) or the later Kabuh beds (Trinil fauna). In the former horizon at least two distinctive hominids are present. Only hominid mandibles and teeth are represented in either western Europe (Mauer) or northwestern Africa (Ternifine) at a comparable time. However, slightly later, at a time broadly corresponding to the middle of the Middle Pleistocene of Europe, a good population sample is present from northern China (Choukoutien Locality 1). Two skulls, one only half preserved, provide the only evidence in Europe. Only fragmentary jaws and teeth are known from the end of this time in northwest Africa (Morocco).

There appear to be rather marked differences between the fossil men of the Far East and Europe during the Middle Pleistocene, although the evidence is admittedly scanty and incomplete. These differences may be evidence of two distinctive phyletic lineages worthy of species status. Some workers, like Vallois and Le Gros Clark, although dealing with the problem in a quite different manner, would give such differences full generic rank. Howell regards the evidence as indicative of differential dispersal within the early hominid lineage (cf. Table 1). The Asian lineage is conceived of as representing an early, essentially subtropical, primary dispersal, linked with the spread of chopper/chopping-tool tradition, of late Villafranchian age, and persisting in the Far East; it apparently did not extend into Europe mainly due to the high sea levels of the Lower Pleistocene (the Calabrian and especially, the main Sicilian transgressions). The other dispersal, whose center of origin remains unknown but which may very well have been largely equatorial African, was later and was probably linked with the spread of the Chelles-Acheul hand-axe industries of the Middle Pleistocene.

By last interglacial times in Europe there appear larger-brained hominids, already of distinctive morphology, such as those from Ehringsdorf and Saccopastore, which are already recognizable as the populations ancestral to the later classic and other Neandertal peoples of the early Last Glacial in Europe. The last of these more ancient human groups indicate a considerable variety of raciation during the earlier Upper Pleistocene (as evidenced by Solo in Java, Broken Hill and Saldanha in southern Africa, the various European Neandertals, the southwest Asian Neandertals, and very

likely many more not yet discovered). There is little evidence of any great structural modifications over the immediately preceding forms. However, there was considerable progress in the technique of implement manufacture as well as in the diversity of stone implements and the development of special tool types.

Homo Sapiens Stage. During the middle of the Last Glaciation, commencing some thirty-five to forty thousand years ago, men structurally like ourselves (*Homo sapiens*) spread rapidly over much of the Old World. This form of man, particularly in Europe and southwestern Asia where the evidence is most complete, is associated with greatly accelerated change, apparently due to both the cumulative effects of culture and the specific biology of *Homo sapiens*. Human material culture changed rapidly and there were extraordinary regional differences, undoubtedly related to specific ecological adaptations. Expanded human populations with enhanced hunting capabilities and specialized equipment, crossed large bodies of water and populated Australia. Such populations conquered the sub-arctic, living in front of caves or shelters, or in huts and larger semi-subterranean communal dwellings, with food storage facilities, in the open loess lands. Such groups, from an unknown Asian source, peopled the New World. Art made its appearance, in both naturalistic and stylized forms, with engraving, carving (in both bas relief and the round), painting (both monochrome and, subsequently, polychrome) and personal decoration and adornment. Within a span of some twenty thousand years there was more technological change than in the preceding half million years. This is, of course, the record of culture as we know it. It is the evidence of the presence of the restless creator, *Homo sapiens*.

According to the view of evolution of the Hominidae outlined here, at least three major evolutionary stages are rec- ognizable during the course of the Pleis- tocene: (1) an australopithecine stage, in some cases associated with the earliest stone implements ("pebble-tools"); (2) an early human (*Homo*) stage, during which there was wide dispersal, develop- ment and maintenance of significant tra- ditions of stone-implement manufacture, but very slow cultural change; (3) an anatomically-modern (*H. sapiens*) stage associated with major cultural innova- tions and rapid technological change. It is necessary to stress that such stages were not static, but that change occurred within each and that each represented evolutionary transformation from the preceding stage. Moreover, the relation- ships of particular stages to one another are not necessarily simple. Thus, although some members of the earlier and more generalized australopithecines may have been directly ancestral to ancient human forms, some populations of the latter may very well have replaced later and more specialized australopithecine populations. Similarly, populations such as those rep- resented in the southwest Asian Upper Pleistocene caves of Qafzeh and Mt. Car- mel (Palestine) may have evolved into *Homo sapiens,* but *H. sapiens* forms may have then replaced numerous other popu- lations (such as some Neandertal folk, the Broken Hill-Saldanha peoples of sub- Saharan Africa, and the Solo people of southeastern Asia).

As technical efficiency increases, the structural diversity among hominids at any given time level decreases. Among those at the australopithecine stage, at least three distinct groups are known from the present geographically restricted material (or four groups, if the Javan form, referred to *Meganthropus,* is in- cluded). Presumably there must have been even more, especially among later representatives of the group and espe- cially if such populations eventually in- habited much of the tropical Old World.

The differences between such forms as Pekin man and Steinheim man, or be- tween the Solo people and European Neandertal populations, suggest very con- siderable isolation and, correspondingly, distinct races or even, in some cases, species. It is especially interesting that *H. sapiens,* although inhabiting a far wider area and very diverse ecological zones, shows only racial differences.

INTERPRETATION OF HUMAN EVOLUTIONARY SEQUENCE

If the foregoing is a reasonable state- ment of the order of human evolutionary events, then an interpretation can be suggested and examined to see how closely it parallels Darwin's theories.

The australopithecines were plains- living, bipedal hominids. Their locomo- tor-skeleton morphology, in particular, their pelvic structure, is far more similar to that of later human forms than is their cranial morphology. (This same contrast is evident in the femur and skull remains of Java man and leads to the same con- clusion.) The autralopithecines merely belong to an earlier evolutionary stage in which the contrast between the locomotor skeleton and the skull was even greater. It is interesting that although Weiden- reich regarded the australopithecines as essentially apes because of the size of their brains, he was always convinced that bipedalism evolved prior to any major changes in the brain and skull. However, the australopithecine canine teeth were of essentially human size and form and thus depart widely from the canine teeth of the anthropoid apes. Moreover, the evidence would now sug- gest that some such forms were already stone-implement makers. Darwin postu- lated that the reduction in the size of the canines of the "early male forefa- thers" was the consequence of employing stones and clubs for fighting. This interpretation may be correct, and it now appears reasonable that forms ancestral to the australopithecines were probably the earliest to employ and even, to some extent, to manufacture stone and other implements. Since the canine teeth were already small and of the human type, the substitution of the use of implements for canines in fighting (and defense in general) must have taken place still earlier. It has been suggested that only after the development of weapons for protection could anatomically unprotected and slow-moving hominids have lived successfully in the African plains.

Selective Value of Bipedalism. Presumably the proto-hominids living on the edge of forested areas or in transitional woodland-grassland zones were neither fully erect nor efficiently bipedal. This would support Darwin's suggestion that "the free use of arms and hands, partly the cause and partly the result of man's erect posture, appears to have led in an indirect manner to other modifications of structure."

It may well be that the basis for the hominid adaptive radiation was *both* bipedalism and the use of implements. Each is so intimately, causally associated with the origin of man that it is perhaps meaningless to speak of one without consideration of the other. Even partially liberating the forelimbs from locomotor functions could have led to some use of implements, and this would have been of such survival value that enhanced bipedalism and further implement use would have evolved together. It must be recalled that the hands which began to be freed with the beginnings of bipedalism were those of an intelligent, manipulative, curious, and playful ape. Such an animal is eminently pre-adapted to implement use and manufacture, as numerous studies have shown.

What were the factors which initiated and made biologically advantageous the shift from incipient, occasional, inefficient bipedalism to an habitual, efficient, terrestrial bipedalism? Extraordinarily little is known about the necessary background, including environmental situations and the particular structures, physiological mechanisms, or behavior patterns, which formed the basis for the transition of some proto-hominid group to an early (australopithecine) grade. Certainly much more might be learned of these basic, important behavioral and structural pre-adaptations from field studies of African-ape behavior in particular ecological situations.

Significance of Dental Reduction. Darwin discussed the reduction of the dentition and the facial skeleton as if it had been a single and relatively simple event. The fossil record clearly indicates that the actual events were considerably more complex. Whereas the whole canine-premolar complex is reduced in the australopithecines, and hence closely comparable to the typical human condition, the molar teeth are large and, in many respects, primitive in their morphology. The later form of australopithecine (from the geologically younger sites of Swartkrans and Kromdraai) has still larger molar (and premolar) teeth compared with the earlier form (from the sites of Sterkfontein, Makapan and Taungs). In correlation with such large teeth the australopithecine face is massive; there is, however, some reduction of the anterior portion related to the incisor and canine teeth. In all Middle Pleistocene and later human forms the entire face is very markedly reduced in size. The evidence would favor the conclusion that those selection pressures which maintained large canine teeth seem to have changed long before those which favored large molar teeth. One interpretation of this situation is that implements were first and primarily employed for protection, hence as weapons, and only to a lesser extent in the food quest. Or perhaps, and this seems extremely likely, their earliest use was in obtaining food, but not preparing it since extracting food from the earth would greatly enhance the food supply, but abrasive roots and tubers would increase tooth wear and favor selection for large molar teeth.

In the Middle Pleistocene there is abundant evidence that men fashioned excellent stone implements in standardized forms by well-defined traditions, knew the use of fire, used fire-hardened wooden spears, and killed some large animals. It seems likely that there was some preparation of food, and, with some variation, a trend began toward reduction in molar dentition which continued throughout the remainder of the Pleistocene. However these events may be interpreted ultimately, the authors feel that different rates of evolution in various parts of the hominid dentition, combined with a study of dental wear, masticatory muscle size, and careful appraisal of the associated implements and animal bones will lead toward a much richer understanding of the habits of early man. Even now it seems certain that Darwin was essentially correct in attributing decreases in the dentition, facial skeleton, and masticatory muscles to the use of implements by hominids. This point of view has been criticized as essentially Lamarckian, but there is no suggestion that such changes were the consequence of the inheritance of acquired characteristics. As implements and tools assumed a greater importance and performed functions formerly carried out by muscles, bone, and teeth, it seems clear that selection pressures would have shifted. A correlation between form and function may be produced by selection, and the use of implements and tools has altered the whole life of man, resulting in changed selection pressures leading toward many more changes than those already briefly discussed here.

The Expanding Braincase. When the existing anthropomorphous apes are compared with living man, one of the greatest differences is in the size of the brain. Thus, the area of cerebral cortex in the chimpanzee is only about one-fourth that of the surface area in man, although in the former the convolutions are well marked and have a disposition similar to man's and the cyto-architecture is nearly identical in both. Not only is the brain of man approximately three to four times as large but it is the particular pattern of cortical development, and relations with diencephalic structures, which makes human life as we know it possible. Language, memory, motor skills, foresight, complex social organization, and art are all specific human attributes related to the structure and function of the brain. Although almost nothing was known of the latter when he wrote, Darwin stressed the human brain, its mental powers, and the attributes of reason, language, moral sense, sense of beauty, religion, and social virtues. In fact, far more of *The Descent of Man* is devoted to such topics than to the origin of human morphology. Considering this fact, and their original close agreement regarding man, it is indeed rather strange that Darwin and Wallace eventually disagreed on this very point.

All verified human fossils discovered up to the 1920's, with the exception of the earlier Middle Pleistocene form from the Kabuh beds in Java, had large braincases. With the exception noted, all such remains were of Upper Pleistocene age. The brains of these peoples, the form and proportions of which could be studied from endocranial casts, were not particularly different in size from those of living *Homo sapiens*. For this reason, and because many scientists accepted the validity of either faked or wrongly-dated human skeletal remains as evidence that large-brained, anatomically-modern man (*Homo sapiens*) existed throughout the Pleistocene, man was often defined on the basis of brain size. It was also often implied that such forms had discovered culture as we know it bit by bit. It would now appear, however, that the large size of the brain of certain hominids was a relatively late development and that the brain evolved due to new selection pressures *after* bipedalism and consequent upon the use of tools. The tool-using, ground-living, hunting way of life created the large human brain rather than a large-brained man discovering certain new ways of life. The authors believe this conclusion is the most important result of the recent fossil hominid discoveries and is one which carries far-reaching implications for the interpretation of human behavior and its origins.

The approximate changes in gross size of the hominid brain, as measured by cranial capacity (in cubic centimeters), during the Pleistocene are summarized in Table 1.

TABLE 1. REPRESENTATIVE CRANIAL
CAPACITIES

Homo sapiens	1200–1500 cc.
Java and Pekin man	900–1100 cc.
Australopithecines	400–550 cc.
Chimpanzee	350–450 cc.

The figures cover the most common capacities and indicate moderately well the general tendency for an increase in size. In nearly all cases the samples are so small and the difficulties of reconstruction are often so great that these approximate figures are adequate. The significance of the figures is essentially clear and would not be changed by any minor alterations. The important point is that size of brain, insofar as it can be measured by cranial capacity, has increased some threefold *subsequent to* the use and manufacture of implements. Erect, bipedal hominids, capable of making and employing tools, existed early in the Pleistocene when the brain was no larger than that of the existing apes. It can be maintained (if the gorilla is excluded from comparison because of great body size)

that the australopithecines had slightly larger capacities on the average, but the difference, if any, is small. I, could also be argued that if the australopithecines had been employing and manufacturing implements sufficiently long for the canine complex to be reduced by new selective pressures, then portions of the cerebral cortex may already have increased to some extent. However, in the absence of hominoid skulls of any sort from the upper Pliocene or earliest Pleistocene it is clearly impossible to ascertain certainly whether australopithecine cranial capacities were already augmented.

In the expansion of an apelike protohominid brain into a hominid brain, there was not equal expansion of the various parts. For example, the area of the cortex associated with the hand and thumb is greatly expanded compared to the bulk of the motor and sensory areas. This is a reflection in the cortex of motor skills related to tool use. In the same manner as altered selection after tool use favored shorter fingers and a larger, fully mobile thumb, so a much enlarged area of cortex was favored to guide the skilled hand of the implement maker. From the fossil record of the hominids it is evident that there were differential modifications in the form and proportions of the brain. Various functional areas, as delimited by modern investigations through electrical stimulation, were affected unequally and at different times, including those relating to motor skills (particularly the hand), patterns of memory, and the elaboration of thought. Notable in man is the extent of cortex which is associational compared with that which represents motor and sensory projection areas.

The evidence of the cerebral cortex strongly supports the conception that cortical expansion followed the acquisition of tool use. The areas of the cortex associated with human vocalization are very large and the control of the flow of speech is situated in various areas in the dominant hemisphere. Vallois notes that the brains of apes are essentially symmetrical while that of man is larger on the dominant side. This asymmetry is customarily ascribed to handedness, but hand preference is also present in monkeys with symmetrical brains. Hence it is possible that the asymmetrical condition is correlated with speech and its control by the dominant hemisphere. Should this prove to be the case, it might be possible to determine whether some of the early men whose skulls are well preserved were capable of speech. In any case it is clear that the reason a chimpanzee cannot learn to talk is that the necessary special cortical areas are either not present or not sufficiently differentiated. Those areas of the cortex associated with persistent motivation, memory, anticipation, and imagination are greatly expanded in the human brain. These abilities are essential to complicated social life. In the future it may become possible to demonstrate that this social brain is the outcome of new selection pressures which came with increasingly complex society. The general pattern of the human brain is in many ways like that of a chimpanzee or even a monkey; its uniqueness lies especially in its great size and in the enlargement of particular areas. From the immediate point of view this brain structure makes possible a complicated technical-social life; but from the long term evolutionary point of view, it was altered selection pressures of the new technical-social life which gave the brain its peculiar size and form.

At the time Darwin wrote there was great emphasis upon instinct. Subsequently, especially among sociologists and anthropologists, the main emphasis shifted to learning. It is now possible to see some of the interrelationships between learning and the structural base. A person can learn any language, but only a human being is capable of learning language. An ease of learning is built in, so to speak (no pun intended), and man can learn thousands of words as easily as a chimpanzee can learn a few sounds. Language must have been of such great importance to our distant ancestors that those capable of learning easily were greatly favored by selection, until learning ability became a distinctive human characteristic. However, this inherited ability in no way determines which language will be learned, and *both* inherited ability and learning are essential for speech, human nature is a product of man's evolution and man does easily the things for which he has been prepared by situations now long past. The crowded, industrialized world in which we live bears little relation to the sparsely populated world of ancient hunters and gatherers. Yet it was in that world in which early man evolved, and much of what men are required to do today is made difficult because selection has not yet had sufficient time to alter the biological base to make the learning easy.

SUMMARY

If comparisons are made now between ape and man and if one speculates upon the reasons for the differences, much the same conclusions are arrived at as those reached by Darwin. The brain and the behavior which it makes possible are all-important. Erect bipedalism frees the hands and facilitates the use of tools. What is new and truly significant is the hominid fossil record that reveals something of the actual stages through which man has evolved and that affords an understanding which comes only from the history of the actual events. The uniqueness of modern man is seen as the result of a technical-social life which tripled the size of the brain, reduced the face, and modified many other structures of the body. When one looks upon the skull of

Homo sapiens, with its great braincase and small face, one gazes upon the results of cultural and natural selection as they are ossified in the bone.

Darwin was essentially correct about the evolution of man. But at the time he lacked the evidence necessary to check his brilliant guess; such evidence has since been found—in quantity and quality sufficient to satisfy all but the most intransigent. It is provided by a careful examination of the chronological order of appearance of our fossil antecedents.

2. The Crucial Evidence for Human Evolution [1]

It has been remarked that it is never possible ultimately to prove a scientific hypothesis—the most that one can hope to do is to disprove it. Except possibly to the more metaphysically minded, this is no doubt an extreme proposition, for plenty of examples could be adduced to illustrate a prediction based on a scientific hypothesis which has subsequently been verified. In the whole field of evolutionary studies, however, the situation is rather different. Here, past events which can never be subjected to direct observation have to be inferred from the data provided by material which is presently existing (even when it consists of relics of the past). In *The Origin of Species* Darwin did, of course, refer to the geological and fossil evidence for evolution, but at that time he had to stress the imperfection of the geological record, and he realized well enough that critics of his theory of evolution by natural selection would "ask in vain where are the numberless transitional links which must formerly have connected closely allied and representative species." In fact, Darwin's evidence for his theory was derived almost entirely from his observations on living organisms—their variation in nature and under domestication, the tendency of their populations to increase rapidly in numbers and the inference that they are necessarily exposed to what he termed the "struggle for existence," their geographical distribution, and so forth. All this kind of evidence (some of his critics argued), however formidable it might be in its collective and mutual reinforcement, was no more than circumstantial, or presumptive, evidence. Now, it is an interesting question, but one which is not easily answered—just at what point in the gradual accumulation of circumstantial evidence can the latter be accepted as adequate for demonstrating the truth of a proposition? Perhaps the most we can say is that, in practice, this point is mainly determined by the multiplicity of independent sources from which this evidence is derived; if several lines of argument based on apparently unrelated data converge on, and mutually support, the same general conclusion, the probability that this conclusion is correct may appear so high as to carry conviction to the mind of unbiased observers.

Let us adventure on a journey backward in time and follow in retrospective order the antecedents of *Homo sapiens* so far as they have been displayed by their fossilized relics. We have not at our disposal any Wellsian time-machine, but we have an excellent substitute for it in

[1] WILFRID E. LE GROS CLARK, "The Crucial Evidence for Human Evolution," in *Proceedings of the American Philosophical Society,* Vol. 103, No. 2, pp. 159–172 (1959), © American Philosophical Society. Reprinted by permission of the author and the publisher. This article also appeared in condensed form in the *American Scientist,* Vol. 47, pp. 299–313 (1959).
Sir Wilfrid is Professor of Anatomy at Oxford University.

the established succession of geological deposits which contain fossilized remains. In recent years, the methods and techniques of estimating the chronological order of these deposits have been greatly elaborated, to the extent that their relative dating can often be determined with considerable assurance. This may be done by reference to relative levels of deposits superimposed the one on the other, to the varying thickness of the geological strata (which provides some indication of the relative length of time required for their deposition), to the succession of climatic changes which are known to have followed in rather regular sequence in different parts of the world and which have left their traces in the soil, and to the slow and gradual accumulation in the fossils themselves of certain chemical elements such as fluorine and uranium. These elements, it may be noted, tend to be taken up by bones which are undergoing fossilization from traces which may be present in percolating waters of the soil, and they accumulate in greater and greater quantity with the passage of time. A chemical analysis of fossils may thus provide important information for their *relative* dating. There are also methods for the determination of an *absolute* dating in terms of years. These methods are difficult of application and they are also limited in the periods of time to which they can be applied. From our present point of view it is particularly unfortunate that they are not (with techniques so far available) applicable to just that period of geological time which evidently saw some of the most significant stages in the evolution of Hominidae. Thus, the radioactive carbon method permits the estimation of the absolute antiquity of fossils (or associated organic material) not much further back than about 50,000 years. The uranium-helium method, on the other hand, can only be used for estimating the age of much more ancient

deposits, and, as far as I am aware, the most recent geological period which has been dated by this method is a stage of the Miocene period, which was about 30 million years ago. But even this distant period has some relevance to our present subject, for it was during the Miocene that many interesting types of primitive and generalized anthropoid apes flourished in the Old World (particularly in the central regions of Africa), and it has been surmised from their anatomical structure that some of these types may have provided the evolutionary material for the subsequent development of the earliest representatives of the Hominidae. Be that as it may, the earliest fossil remains so far discovered which can with certainty be termed "hominid," that is to say, which had already developed anatomical characters which are known to be quite distinctive of the Hominidae as contrasted with the related family Pongidae, occur in geological deposits laid down in the early part of the Pleistocene period. Now, methods of relative dating based on purely geological considerations show a fair agreement that the beginning of this period began somewhere about one million years ago. Obviously, we should like to have estimates of the absolute antiquity of the early hominids which lived during this period, but it will be necessary first to discover some technique similar to the radioactive carbon method which will carry the chronological estimates a long way beyond 50,000 years ago. Until such techniques have been developed, we have to rely for estimates of antiquity during most of the Pleistocene on the methods of relative dating, and it is well to recognize that these methods can only give approximate results.

I may note here that the Pleistocene can be subdivided on a relative chronological basis by reference to its climatic fluctuations. The latter half of the period (or perhaps rather more) was marked by a series of very cold cycles when much of the temperate regions of the earth became covered by glaciers and ice sheets. There were four of these glaciations, separated by three interglacial periods during each of which the climate became much warmer. The last glaciation reached its initial climax probably about 50,000 years ago, and the first glaciation is reckoned to have occurred almost half a million years ago.

Today the family Hominidae is represented by one genus only, *Homo*, and by only one species of this genus, *Homo sapiens*—that is to say, modern mankind. The geographical varieties of this species, or "races" as they are commonly termed, show considerable differences in superficial features such as skin color, hair texture, and so forth, but they are much less easily distinguished by their skeletal characters. Nevertheless, the latter do show differences, and it is well to recognize the extent of these skeletal variations in modern man when the problem arises whether a fossil human skeleton is that of *Homo sapiens*, or of some different and extinct species of *Homo*. For it has happened from time to time, by failing to recognize the wide range of individual and racial variability in our own species, some authorities have claimed that the human remains which they have discovered are those of a hitherto unknown species, and have even christened them with a new specific name. This has had the unfortunate effect of confusing and distorting the perspective of the latter-day prehistory of mankind (so far as it has been revealed by fossil remains) to a quite ridiculous degree.

More careful and systematic comparisons have now made it clear that *Homo sapiens* has a quite respectable antiquity. For example, during the time when the Palaeolithic (Old Stone Age) culture known as the Magdalenian flourished in Western Europe, the local population was composed of people who, judging from their skull and skeleton, were similar in physical characters to modern Europeans. The Magdalenians had developed a quite rich culture, and they were responsible for some of the most beautiful examples of cave paintings and sculptures such as those found in the famous caves at Lascaux in France. They lived during the latter phases of the last glaciation in what is sometimes called the Reindeer Age (for the reason that reindeer herds occupied Europe in large numbers at that time). Now, pieces of charcoal left by the Magdalenians in one of the Lascaux caves have been analyzed for their content of radioactive carbon, and this has given an antiquity of about 15,000 years. We can go back further into the Aurignacian period which immediately preceded the Magdalenians, and still we find from a number of fossilized remains that the local population was apparently not distinguishable from modern populations of *Homo sapiens*. A radioactive carbon dating of 27,000 years has recently been reported for the period of the Aurignacian culture, and if the species *Homo sapiens* was already fully differentiated at that time the final stages of its evolutionary emergence must have occurred still earlier. We know also from fossil evidence that the species had spread widely over the earth many thousands of years ago. For example, *Homo sapiens* had certainly reached Australia, and even North America, about 10,000 years ago, and at Florisbad in South Africa there was found in 1933 a human skull, also not to be distinguished from the *Homo sapiens* type, whose antiquity has been estimated by the radioactive carbon method to have been at least 40,000 years.

The question now arises—is there any concrete evidence from the fossil record that *Homo sapiens* was actually in existence before the last glaciation of the Ice Age? Preceding the Aurignacian period in Europe there was a prolonged cultural period of the Palaeolithic termed the Mousterian, which can be conveniently divided into an Early Mousterian phase and a Late Mousterian phase (though this is really an over-simplification of the cultural sequences which followed, and partly overlapped, each other during those times). The Early Mousterian covered the latter part of the last interglacial period and extended into the onset of the last glacial period, while the Late Mousterian coincided with the climax of the first part of the last glaciation. A fair number of fossil remains of Early Mousterian man have been found in Central Europe and also in Palestine so that we know a good deal about their cranial and dental anatomy. A striking character is their wide variability, for while many individuals show primitive features such as strongly developed brow ridges, a somewhat retreating forehead, prominent jaws, and a feebly formed or absent chin eminence, others are very similar in their skull structure to the more primitive races of modern mankind. Further, the limb bones (so far as they are known) appear to be of quite modern type. Opinions vary on the question whether in some of their skull characters the Early Mousterians exceed the limits of variation found in *Homo sapiens*. Even if this is the case, I myself am not convinced that they exceed the limits to the extent that they can properly be assigned to another species altogether. Probably it is wise to defer a decision on this point for the present—if they are not *Homo sapiens* in the strict sense, they represent the immediate precursors of modern *Homo sapiens* and may be conveniently designated as such. But their great variability is of particular interest from another point of view.

In later Mousterian times, characterized archaeologically by the full development of the typical stone-tool industry to which the term "Mousterian" is properly attached, there existed in Europe and neighboring regions the distinctive type of man now so well-known as Neanderthal man. The outstanding features of this type are the massive brow ridges, retreating forehead, large projecting jaws, absence of a chin eminence, and certain peculiarities of the occipital region and base of the skull. Some of the limb bones, also, are unusual in the thickness and curvature of their shafts and the relative size of their articular extremities. In curious contrast, the size of the brain of Neanderthal man—as indicated by the cranial capacity—was surprisingly large, on the average even larger than that of modern *Homo sapiens*. A sufficient number of Neanderthal skulls have been collected to permit of their study by statistical analysis; this has not only demonstrated their homogeneity as a local European population, it has also shown that in a number of dimensions (and proportional indices constructed therefrom) they lie outside the known range of variation of *Homo sapiens*. All these facts have led to the assumption, maintained by many (but not all) anthropologists, that Neanderthal man constitutes a distinct species, *Homo neanderthalensis*. At one time it was generally supposed that this extinct type was directly ancestral to modern man. But, as I have already mentioned, we now know that it was preceded by earlier types, and these, though showing a number of primitive features, were much more akin to *Homo sapiens*. Moreover, the fossil and archaeological record makes it clear that, at the end of the Mousterian period, Neanderthal man disappeared from Europe quite abruptly, to be replaced by a population of the modern *Homo sapiens* type. Presumably, the latter spread into Europe from a neighboring area, perhaps the Middle East, and by replacement led to the extinction of *Homo neanderthalensis*.

Let us now return to the Early Mousterian populations and reconsider them in the light of their wide range of variability. At one end of this range are individuals which appear to presage the more extreme features of Neanderthal type; at the other end are individuals which approach so closely to primitive races of *Homo sapiens* that it is difficult to decide whether they can be taxonomically separated from this species. In other words, it seems that this degree of variability would readily have provided the raw material, so to speak, for the evolutionary diversification of what were evidently two terminal types—*Homo neanderthalensis* which became extinct, and the modern forms of *Homo sapiens*. Such a conclusion fits in quite well with the evidence relating to the temporal sequence. Some authorities, it may be noted, have been tempted to interpret the variability of Early Mousterians in terms of the coexistence of genetically different types, some of which may have interbred. But this is to complicate the picture unnecessarily and somewhat arbitrarily. The high variability of the Early Mousterians—considered as a single general population composed of regional variants—was probably related to their dispersal over Europe in small hunting communities, their exposure to changing climatic extremes, and the increasing intergroup competition for the means of survival. Such circumstances are particularly favorable for the diversifying action of the selective processes in evolution.

We now come to the problem of "pre-Mousterian man," that is to say, the nature of the populations which immediately preceded the Early Mousterians. Here we are faced with the difficulty that their fossil record is still too meager to allow firm conclusions. A fairly complete and well-preserved skull found at Steinheim in Germany dates from the last interglacial period, or perhaps even earlier from the second interglacial period. It closely resembles the Early Mousterians

and shows pronounced brow ridges of the skull, but the forehead region is quite well developed and the occipital region is full and rounded as in modern man. The cranial capacity is estimated to be less than 1100 cc; this comes well within the range of variation of *Homo sapiens* but is considerably below the mean value (1350 cc). Two fragments of skulls found at Fontéchevade in France, also reckoned to be of pre-Mousterian date, show a much closer resemblance to modern *Homo sapiens,* for the brow ridges are only moderate in size. Finally, a most important discovery was made of portions of a skull at Swanscombe in Kent in 1935—important because their antiquity may be assigned with considerable assurance to the second interglacial period which, by methods of relative dating, can hardly have been less than 100,000 years ago and may well have been more. Unfortunately, only three of the main bones forming the roof and back of the skull (the two parietals and the occipital) were found, and, although they are excellently preserved, they do not tell us very much. But careful anatomical and statistical studies have shown that, while in some respects they are certainly unusual, as far as can be ascertained they do not exceed the range of variation of *Homo sapiens* in their dimensions, shape, and individual structural features. They are unusual in the thickness of the skull wall and in the width of the occipital region. There is also definite evidence that the air sinuses of the face region were extensively developed, and this suggests the probability that the facial skeleton was rather massive, and that the frontal region may have had large brow ridges like the Steinheim skull. Until further remains of the contemporary population are discovered, all we can say, therefore, is that, *on the evidence of the three skull bones available,* Swanscombe man was probably similar to the Steinheim man, and at least very closely akin to *Homo sapiens*. The brain, incidentally, was quite large (the cranial capacity has been estimated at about 1320 cc), and the impressions on the inner surface of the skull bones also show that it was richly convoluted.

In our journey back in time, we have now traced primitive representatives of *Homo sapiens,* or at any rate the immediate precursors of this species, to the second interglacial period, that is to say the Middle Pleistocene. Moreover, there is no structural break in continuity through which these early types are linked in gradational series with modern *Homo sapiens.* If we now continue our journey into still greater antiquity, we come to a period, the early part of the Middle Pleistocene, when a much more primitive type of hominid was distributed over wide areas of the Old World, and at a time when (so far as we can say from the available evidence) *Homo sapiens* had not yet come into existence. So different from *Homo* was this primitive type, and so apelike in certain features of the skull and jaws, that it is usually regarded not only as a separate species of mankind, but as a separate genus, *Pithecanthropus.* The first relics of *Pithecanthropus* to be discovered were found in Java as long ago as 1891. For many years after this, in spite of expeditions which were planned to search for more remains, nothing else was found. Then, in 1937 and the following years, further fossils were brought to light, consisting of a few skulls, some jaw fragments, and a number of teeth. More extensive fossil material representing the same genus has been excavated from caves near Pekin. This was at first regarded as a separate and distinct type and was called *Sinanthropus,* but careful comparisons later made it clear that it is not to be distinguished generically from *Pithecanthropus.* The antiquity of these fossils is very great, but since their age can only be estimated by methods of relative dating,

it can only be estimated to a rough approximation—probably somewhere between 200,000 and half a million years. Some of the Javanese representatives of *Pithecanthropus* are more ancient than the Chinese and (as might be anticipated from the time differential) they are in several respects more primitive in their anatomical structure.

Perhaps the most striking feature of the skull of *Pithecanthropus* is the small size of the braincase. The average cranial capacity of all known specimens taken together is only about 1000 cc, and only about 900 cc in the Javanese specimens considered separately. The latter actually include a skull with a capacity as low as 775 cc, which is only about 90 cc greater than the largest so far recorded for anthropoid apes. At the same time, the brain size was evidently very variable, for in one of the skulls from Pekin the cranial capacity reached 1200 cc, which is well within the range of variation of *Homo sapiens.* Apart from its average small size, the braincase shows a number of other characters which are obtrusively simian. For example, the cranial roof is flattened and the side walls slope downwards and outwards so that the brain case as a whole is much broader towards the skull base; the forehead is markedly retreating—indeed, in some skulls a forehead can hardly be said to exist in the ordinary sense of the term; the brow ridges project to form a prominent and uninterrupted shelf of bone overhanging the eye sockets; the jaws are not only massive—they project in muzzle fashion and the lower jaw lacks any trace of chin eminence; the teeth are large, and in some individuals (though this seems to have been unusual) the canines project and partly interlock when the jaws are closed; the occipital region of the skull is marked by strong transverse crests of bone for the attachment of what must have been powerful neck muscles; the nasal aperture is low and broad; and a number of minor features in the construction of the base of the skull also approximate in some degree to the conditions generally regarded as more characteristic of the ape's than the human skull. It is interesting to note, however, that, in spite of the lowly appearance of the skull, jaws, and teeth, the limb bones of *Pithecanthropus* are quite similar to those of *Homo sapiens*. Now, this serves to illustrate a most important principle of evolution—that an ancestral species or genus does not become gradually transformed *as a whole* into a descendant species or genus. It commonly happens that different parts or systems of the body evolve at different rates so that transitional stages of evolution show a mosaic of primitive and advanced characters and not an "all round" halfway stage of development. As far as the Hominidae are concerned, it is clear from the fossil record of *Pithecanthropus* that the limbs reached the final stage of their evolutionary development long before the brain, skull, and teeth had done so.

In brief, then, we may picture members of the genus *Pithecanthropus* as rather small-brained individuals with retreating forehead, beetling brows, and big jaws, but with limbs fashioned like our own. But, in spite of their relatively small brains, they were evidently quite advanced culturally, for we know from the traces they have left of the remains of their feasts and of their cooking hearths that those which inhabited China were skilled hunters and even knew the use of fire. They were also capable of fabricating stone implements, though of a rather crude character. It is of considerable importance for the question whether *Pithecanthropus* could have provided the ancestral basis for the subsequent evolutionary development of *Homo* to note that the remains discovered in the Far East show a fairly wide range of variation. I have already mentioned that the cranial capacity, at its upper limits,

reaches close to the mean value of *Homo sapiens,* and there are similar degrees of variability in the size of the jaws, the development of the forehead region, and so forth. In fact, at one end of the range, *Pithecanthropus* approaches quite closely to the Early Mousterian or Pre-Mousterian populations which I have already mentioned, and the morphological "gap" between them is almost insignificant. Unfortunately, as has so often happened in the subject of palaeo-anthropology, the variants of *Pithecanthropus* have been labelled by different specific or generic names on the unwarranted assumption (or, at any rate, unwarranted on the present evidence) that they actually represent quite different types. There may be some justification for accepting the suggestion, at least provisionally, that the Javanese and Chinese populations represent different species (*P. erectus* and *P. pekinensis*), though even this distinction is doubtful. It is a well-established fact that both the genus *Homo* and also the modern genera of anthropoid apes show a high degree of variability, and, if this is duly recognized, the variability within the genus *Pithecanthropus* no longer appears exceptional and any further taxonomic subdivision of the genus loses its validity.

It is probable that some local representatives of *Pithecanthropus* persisted in some parts of the world after the evolutionary appearance of the genus *Homo* in other parts, but the fact remains that the earliest representatives so far known appear to have preceded the appearance of *Homo*. Thus, the temporal sequence fits in with the evidence of the graded morphological series which they present, and supports the proposition that the one was probably ancestral to the other.

The most abundant remains of *Pithecanthropus* which have been discovered are those of the local populations which lived in the Far East, but there is now fossil evidence that this ancient type was by no means confined to that region of the world. For example, there have recently been found in Algeria three fossil jaws and a parietal bone of the skull which so closely resemble those of Pekin man that they are not really distinguishable in the generic sense. In spite of this, these remains have been given a new name, *Atlanthropus,* an appellation which is unfortunate not only because it seems unjustified, but also because it introduces an unnecessary complication and may obscure their real significance for human evolution. These Algerian remains were found in association with stone implements referable to the Early Acheulian phase of Palaeolithic culture, and there is reason to suppose that they date from the early part of the second interglacial period, probably more or less contemporaneously with the later Javanese fossils but antedating Swanscombe man. Another possible representative of *Pithecanthropus* is "Heidelberg man," known only from a massive lower jaw discovered in 1908, and probably of somewhat greater antiquity than the Algerian fossils. But the dentition of this species shows certain features which have led some authorities to think that its relation to *Pithecanthropus* may not be very close. Obviously, a decision on this question can only be reached when further fossil material of Heidelberg man is available for comparative study.

Thus far, it seems, we have a fossil record which, though still by no means as well-documented as we could wish, does suggest a high degree of probability that, from the beginning of the Middle Pleistocene onwards, there has been a progressive sequence of hominid types leading almost insensibly from the primitive, small-brained *Pithecanthropus* through pre-Mousterian and Early Mousterian man to *Homo sapiens* as this species exists today. If Darwin's line of reasoning from the indirect evidence at his disposal is sound, it might be pre-

dicted that the genus *Pithecanthropus* would itself have been preceded by a type showing even more primitive and apelike features, such as a still smaller brain, jaws of more simian dimensions, and so forth. Until 1924, we had no direct knowledge at all that any such connecting link had actually existed. In that year, there was found a remarkably fine and well-preserved specimen of a new type of hominid which conformed in a most remarkable way with expectations and thus, once again, provided a verification of the predictions implied by less direct evidence. In more recent years, great quantities of the fossilized remains of these creatures have been collected from cave deposits at widely different sites in the Transvaal, so that it is possible to speak with considerable assurance about their anatomical characters. Of the latter, undoubtedly the most striking is the size of the braincase, for this is not only much smaller when compared with *Pithecanthropus,* it actually overlaps the range of the modern large apes. The small braincase, combined with huge jaws, gives the whole skull a very simian appearance indeed, and it was for this reason that, on their first discovery, they were given the name *Australopithecus* (which means the "southern ape"). As we know now, however, they were not apes in the strict taxonomic sense of zoological nomenclature; they were exceedingly primitive hominids which in a number of fundamental features had already developed a considerable way along the direction of hominid evolution and quite opposite to the direction of evolution which characterized the anthropoid ape family (Pongidae). In fact, they provide another excellent example of "mosaic evolution" in their combination of relatively advanced hominid features with the continued retention of primitive features inherited in common with the Pongidae from a common ancestral stock. The range of variation of the cranial capacity in *Australopithecus* has not been determined with any certainty; most of the skulls so far discovered are too incomplete, or distorted by crushing, to allow of direct estimates. Probably, however, they ranged from about 450 cc up to about 700 cc. The higher estimates of much over 700 cc which have been suggested for some of the specimens are too insecure to be reliable, and it is likely that they are overestimates.

It is perhaps not surprising that the earlier reports of these South African fossils were received with some scepticism and gave rise to a good deal of controversy. Because of the intense interest which they arouse, it seems almost inevitable that every discovery of fossil hominids which appears to confirm Darwin's anticipation of connecting links should be followed by controversies, and these have often been of rather a contentious and polemical character; indeed, opposing views still tend to be expressed with a vehemence which is rather unusual in scientific discussions today. No doubt this is to be explained by the fact that the problem of our own origin is by its very nature a peculiarly personal problem, so much so that even scientists may sometimes find it difficult to free their minds entirely of an emotional bias and to view the evidence quite dispassionately. In the case of *Australopithecus,* it has been the distinctly hominid characters which formed the main center of controversy, for the obviously primitive (and therefore apelike) general proportions of the skull have never been in dispute. Let me enumerate some of the most fundamental of these hominid characters very briefly, in order to emphasize their significance for the correct interpretation of the evolutionary position of *Australopithecus.*

Australopithecus conforms to the hominid pattern of dentition. The differences from the pongid type of dentition are sufficiently abrupt and clear-cut to be readily apparent simply by direct visual comparison, but they have also been abundantly confirmed by statistical analyses.

When the first australopithecine skull was found, attention was called to certain, not very conspicuous, features in which it appeared to approximate to the hominid type of skull. Later discoveries considerably reinforced the inferences drawn from these similarities, in particular an adult skull, complete except for the lower jaw and unusually well-preserved, excavated in a cave at Sterkfontein near Johannesburg. This exceptional specimen has provided the opportunity for making satisfactory comparisons with extensive series of apes' skulls, and has thus served to demonstrate some rather impressive contrasts. For example, the height of the braincase in relation to the eye sockets exceeds the range of variation found in any of the apes, and so does the low position of the muscular ridge on the back of the skull for the attachment of the neck muscles. Similarly, the relatively forward position of the occipital condyles on the base of the skull (for articulation with the upper end of the vertebral column) indicates a significant approach towards the hominid condition. Together with other characters of the skull such as the conformation of the articular socket for the condyle of the lower jaw, certain structural details of the lower jaw, and the consistent presence in all the known skulls (young as well as adult) of a prominent mastoid process of typical human shape, all these anatomical details comprise a total pattern of construction which is not found in ape skulls, but which is found in hominid skulls. Thus, in spite of the simian appearance of the *general* proportions of the skull, the structural details of the latter add further support to the evidence of the dentition that the australopithecines represent an early phase in the hominid sequence of evolution.

On the basis of the early discoveries, it had been inferred from some of the features of the skull base that the australopithecines quite probably were erect, bipedal creatures, for these features appeared to indicate that the head was poised more or less evenly on the top of a vertical spinal column, and not held up by powerful neck muscles on a forwardly sloping spine as it is in apes. This indirect evidence could not by itself, of course, amount to a final proof of erect bipedalism; while it certainly justified a strong presumption that such was the case, it was at that time no more than predictive and therefore depended for its corroboration on the accession of more direct evidence. In fact, confirmatory evidence was later supplied by a detailed study of the thigh bone, and the earlier predictions finally received the most remarkable verification when specimens of the pelvis were found. Now, there is no element of the skeleton which is more distinctive of the Hominidae as compared with the large apes than the bony pelvis. In the two families it has very different proportions, which are evidently associated mainly with radical differences in posture and gait. Altogether, four different specimens of the australopithecine pelvis have been found at widely different sites in South Africa, and they all conform in their fundamental characters to the hominid pattern of construction. There can be no reasonable doubt, therefore, that the australopithecines had already achieved an erect, bipedal posture. But it should be emphasized that the pelvis shows certain differences in detail from that of *Homo sapiens,* and it may be assumed from a consideration of these differences that they had not developed the erect posture to the perfection found in modern man.

Morphologically speaking, the genus *Australopithecus* conforms so closely to theoretical postulates for the connecting link which must be presumed to have been immediately ancestral to *Pithecanthropus,* that a true ancestral relationship seems extremely probable. The important question arises whether this inference fits into the time relationships. As the result of intensive studies of the australopithecine deposits in South Africa based on several collateral lines of evidence, it now appears certain that the most ancient remains of *Australopithecus* so far discovered did antedate *Pithecanthropus.*

The time sequence conforms with the morphological gradations represented by these fossil hominids. Of course, this general statement must not be taken to imply that the local varieties of *Australopithecus* found in South Africa were *themselves* the ancestral stock, for the genus may have had a much wider geographical distribution, and it may be that the South African types were local variants which persisted there for some time after other populations of the same genus in another part of the world had already given rise to the more advanced hominids of the *Pithecanthropus* stage of evolution.

An important aspect of *Australopithecus* is the great variability shown by different individuals and local groups, even in the circumscribed regions of South Africa in which their remains have been found. Again, as in the case of *Pithecanthropus,* there has been a tendency to interpret this variability in terms of different genera and species, and it seems to me that this has introduced the same sort of unnecessary complication into the picture. It may be emphasized again that it is the genetic fluctuation within populations that provides the basis for the selective action of the environment, and herein lies the real importance of the range of variation within the genus *Australopithecus.*

The hominid status of *Australopithecus* has been conclusively demonstrated by extensive anatomical studies, and quite recent discoveries have now given rise to the suggestion that, in spite of the small size of the brain, the South African representatives of this genus may even have been sufficiently advanced culturally to have been capable of fashioning crude stone implements. At any rate, definite artifacts have been found embedded in breccia which also contained remains of *Australopithecus,* but which has not been found to contain any remains of a more advanced type of hominid. Clearly, this is a most exciting discovery, but perhaps not altogether unexpected. For attention had previously been drawn to quantities of baboon skulls associated with australopithecine remains, most of which show depressed fractures of the roof of the skull which suggest the possibility that they had been killed by skilful blows with an implement of some sort. The obvious inference from the discovery of the stone artifacts is that they were actually fabricated by the australopithecine individuals whose remains were found close alongside them. But there still remains the possibility that there *was* a more advanced type of hominid occupying the same region which may have been the actual tool maker, even though it has to be admitted that, so far, no remains of this problematical type have come to light. If, as the result of further search, it should be established that similar crude artifacts are to be found at several independent sites in association with australopithecine remains (but with no remains of any more advanced type), this would no doubt be acceptable as sufficiently good evidence of the tool-making capacity of *Australopithecus.* Naturally, the question has also been raised whether a creature with so small a brain could have possessed the intelligence required for tool-making. This is a question which cannot at present be answered with any assurance. Taking into account the extraordinarily wide range of variation in the cranial capacity of modern man—

from less than 900 cc to about 2300 cc in people of apparently "normal" intelligence—and taking into account also the fact that no marked correlation has been discovered between intellectual ability and cranial capacity in normal people, it seems that, within very wide limits, the absolute size of the brain gives no indication of degrees of intelligence. It has to be remembered, further, that while the cranial capacity of fossil hominids can give information on the brain volume, it provides no information of the complexity of organization of the nervous tissue of which it was composed.

We have now traced in retrospect a graded morphological series, arranged in an ordered time sequence, linking *Homo sapiens* through Early Mousterian man, pre-Mousterian man, and the small-brained *Pithecanthropus,* with the still smaller-brained *Australopithecus.* This sequence comprises a remarkable confirmation of the connecting links postulated and predicted by Darwin's hypothesis of the descent of man, at any rate as far back as the Early Pleistocene. There is no conspicuous gap in the sequence, but there still remains a serious gap covering the preceding period of the Pliocene. We know that, during the early part of the Pliocene, and throughout the Miocene period before then, many interesting varieties of anthropoid apes were distributed over wide areas of the Old World, in Europe, Asia, and Africa. It is also the case that some of these fossil apes show generalized features of the skull, dentition and limb bones which might well have provided the structural basis for the subsequent emergence and differentiation of the hominid line of evolution. But as yet we have no objective evidence to show just when, or how, the emergence of this new line took place.

Darwin in his time found it necessary to emphasize the imperfection of the geological record to account for the absence of many of the connecting links demanded by his conception of the evolutionary process. Since then, of course, the continual accession of fossil remains of all kinds has amplified the record enormously, and has provided much of the crucial evidence for the succession of intermediate types. But, so far as human evolution is concerned, we in our time still find it necessary to emphasize its imperfection, and to re-emphasize Darwin's words, "The crust of the earth with its embedded remains must not be looked at as a well-filled museum, but as a poor collection made at hazard and at rare intervals."

In view of the hazards which must always attend the preservation of fossilized remains, even under the most favorable circumstances, it is not a little remarkable that our record of the later phases of hominid evolution is as good as it is. A sequence of fossils in any other mam-

malian group equivalent in their close gradation to the sequence *Australopithecus → Pithecanthropus → Homo* would be regarded by most vertebrate palaeontologists as a highly satisfactory record. For even if it should prove not to represent a linear sequence of evolution (which it most probably does), it at least provides the concrete and objective evidence of a general evolutionary trend. It is an interesting fact that each discovery of a possible connecting link in human ancestry seems always to arouse more contentious and more prolonged disputation than equivalent discoveries relating to the ancestry of other mammalian species. Indeed, considered in retrospect, some of these argumentations may appear to us to savor of the ridiculous and comical, if only for the reason that such unlikely interpretations seem often to have been based on evidence the real purport of which we now accept as reasonably well assured.

The problem of dating, both absolute and relative, is of first importance in validating the record of our evolution. It is also a source of continuing controversy.

3. Dating Human Evolution [1]

Ever since it became apparent that man did not originate by a sudden act of creation, but rather by the normal process of speciation, one of the primary goals of paleoanthropological research has been to date the various stages of human evolution. The different ways by which such dating may be attempted and the complex problems arising therefrom have been discussed by Oakley. This author carefully distinguishes between relative and absolute dating methods, and

he lists four different (and often complementary) methods under each one of these two categories. The four methods listed by Oakley for absolute dating of fossil hominids are the following: (1) direct age determination of the bones; (2) age determination of the source bed by determining the age of material (charcoal, shells, and so forth) associated with the bones; (3) age determination of the source bed by correlating such bed with a deposit of known age; (4) age deter-

[1] CESARE EMILIANI, "Dating Human Evolution," in *The Evolution of Man,* Sol Tax (ed.), (Chicago: 1960). Reprinted by permission of the author and The University of Chicago Press, © 1960 by The University of Chicago Press.

Dr. Emiliani is Professor of Marine Biology at the University of Miami.

mination of the source bed by correlating such bed with certain geophysical parameters (the Milankovitch curve, for instance), under the assumption that these parameters have a bearing on the history of the Pleistocene. The fourth method is actually an integral part of the third, insofar as it has been used to establish Pleistocene chronologies or, in other words, to estimate the ages of deposits with which source beds are to be correlated. Its value is limited to the validity of the assumption upon which it is based.

The first and second methods have been applied extensively by means of radiocarbon techniques. I will not discuss radiocarbon here, which is a topic familiar to everybody today, but I will rather deal with current possibilities of dating fossil hominids beyond the range of radiocarbon. These possibilities fall largely under Oakley's methods 2 and 3.

Important steps in the evolutionary process leading to the development of modern man took place between a million and fifty thousand years ago. Unfortunately, this time interval is perhaps the most difficult one to date. Suitable material formed at earlier and later times can be rather accurately dated by various methods based on radioactive isotopes, such as U^{238}, U^{235}, Th^{232}, Rb^{87}, K^{40}, and C^{14}. Twenty induced or secondary radioisotopes with half-lives ranging from 30,000 to 2×10^6 years are known. Some of these are artificial; others exist in nature, being formed either by the disintegration of long-lived parent isotopes or by nuclear bombardment in continuous natural processes; none is a leftover of the primordial formation of the elements (being too short-lived). In order for any of these radioisotopes to be useful for dating, it is necessary that either the radioisotope itself or its parent element be incorporated into the material to be dated at the time that this material was formed. It is also essential that no subsequent losses or additions have occurred.

In the particular case of human evolution, the material most desirable to date is bone. Unfortunately, bone is physically and chemically very active, so that fossil bone is likely to be contaminated with all sorts of additions and losses. A recent attempt by Sackett (1958) to date bones using the U^{238}/Th^{230} ratio has given uncertain results, because uranium and thorium seem to migrate quite freely into the bone material.

If bone does not seem suitable for dating purposes beyond the range of C^{14}, other material closely associated with fossil bones or artifacts may be more appropriately used. Dating of shells occurring in caves (food refuse), using the U^{238}/Th^{230} or the Pa^{231}/Th^{230} ratios, seems feasible, and measurements should become available in the near future. These two dating methods might be usable for shell material formed during the time interval between 10,000 and 200,000 years ago. For the time interval between 200,000 and 2×10^6 years ago it does not seem likely, at present, that suitable methods of dating human evolution *directly* will be developed in the near future. Refinements in K^{40}/A^{40} dating techniques indicate that this method may become useful for dating potassium-bearing minerals as young as a few tens of thousands of years. Significant ages of less than 500,000 years have already been published. Particularly important is the dating of Zinjanthropus at 1.75×10^6 years. Man, however, developed during a period of the earth's history when repeated glaciations occurred, so that human and prehuman fossils which can be closely correlated with glacial and interglacial events may be indirectly dated if such events are dated.

Studies of Pleistocene history have been based mainly upon the continental record in glaciated areas and especially upon till and loess sheets, fossil soils, and terminal moraines. On that basis, Calvin, working in the North American mid-continent, recognized five successive glaciations separated by four interglacials. In Europe the classic work of Penck and Brückner recognized four glaciations separated by three interglacials. The discrepancy between the European and North American classifications was believed eliminated when the Iowan stage of Calvin was reduced to a substage of the last glacial age, the classical Wisconsin. However, recent C^{14} measurements by Rubin have shown that the Iowan deposits of Iowa are much older than the earliest classical Wisconsin deposits. It is now believed that, as Calvin proposed, five major glaciations occurred, with the last two glaciations (Early and Main Würm in European terminology, Early and Main Wisconsin in North American terminology) separated by a "cool" interglacial.

The above difficulty and many others encountered by geologists in their attempts to unravel the history of the Pleistocene epoch on the basis of the continental record stem from the fact that that record, especially in glaciated areas, is always discontinuous and fragmentary. A cursory look at the enormous literature is sufficient to make anyone marvel at both the complexity of the record and the ingenuity of the scholars who have coped with it. The task of these scholars would have been incomparably easier if some stratigraphic section covering the entire Pleistocene were available, showing, for instance, a complete sequence of alternating tills and soils. Unfortunately, such a section seems to be available nowhere in the glaciated areas.

In order to obtain a complete section of sediments covering the whole Pleistocene, one has to turn to deposits formed under water in periglacial or non-glacial areas or in the ocean. Complete sections of Pleistocene deposits may exist on the bottom of certain lakes, such as, for instance, the lakes of northern Florida. Coring of such lake beds and pollen analysis of the cores may yield important information on the climatic changes caused by glaciation, and, if the sections of lake deposits are complete, the climatic pattern of the Pleistocene might be reconstructed rather easily. Work along these lines has been and is being done by, among others, Sears and Clisby, Clisby, Foreman, and Sears, and Maarleveld and Van der Hammen on the lake beds of Mexico City, San Augustin Plains (New Mexico), and the Sabana de Bogotá (Colombia).

While lake sediments offer interesting opportunities, the best sections of continuous Pleistocene sediments have been found on the ocean floor. About 40 per cent of the ocean floor is carpeted with a type of sediment called *"Globigerina ooze."* This sediment consists essentially of clay with imbedded test of planktonic protophyta and Foraminifera, the latter representing 30 per cent or more of the dry weight of the bulk sediment. *Globigerina* ooze accumulates on the ocean floor at rates ranging from a few to several centimeters per thousand years. Following the development of the piston corer by Kullenberg, deep-sea sediments can be sampled as far down as 20 meters below the surface of the ocean floor. Thus *Globigerina*-ooze sections covering the whole Pleistocene time have become available in recent years. The study of these sections, especially by the modern method of oxygen isotopic analysis developed by Urey and co-workers, has shown that the surface water of the ocean underwent numerous and apparently periodic temperature variations in the recent past. These temperature oscillations are best evidenced by deep-sea cores from the equatorial and North Atlantic and adjacent seas, a probable result of the fact that the Atlantic Ocean, being surrounded by large ice sheets at its northern end during the glacial ages, was subjected to more marked temperature variations than were the other oceans. The temperature curves obtained from various deep-sea cores were combined into a single, generalized temperature curve (Figure 1), which is believed to have more than regional significance. Radiocarbon measurements on the upper portions of some of the deep-sea cores have proved that the last temperature minimum of the deep-sea cores corresponded in time to the Wisconsin glaciation. Extrapolations of the radiocarbon data, together with inferences from ionium-radium data by Urry (1949) on other deep-sea cores, provided a basis for a tentative time scale of the temperature variations. According to this time scale, the Early Würm glaciation occurred about 65,000 years ago. This figure has been substantiated recently by a radiocarbon date from the Groningen laboratory. A reliable, absolute time scale for the deep-sea stratigraphy back to 200,000 years ago, based on the changing Pa^{231}/Th^{230} ratio, should become available in the very near future.

The Pa^{231}/Th^{230} ratio has been used to date three Caribbean cores and one from the North Atlantic. The Caribbean cores yielded ages which are internally consistent and in good agreement with the C^{14} ages over the common range. The resulting time scale is essentially the same as that previously predicted. Discrepant ages were obtained from the North Atlantic core, a result which was attributed to reworking. Preliminary measurements by Rosholt appear to substantiate the time scale of Figure 1. Altogether, one may presently venture to say that the time scale of Figure 1 is probably correct within 10 per cent all the way back to 300,000 years ago.

The older portion of the generalized temperature curve is based on two deep-sea cores from the Caribbean, both of which are less than 10 meters long. Longer, undisturbed cores of *Globigerina*-ooze facies are not yet available from the Atlantic and adjacent seas, so that a clear picture of the temperature variations before 300,000 years ago cannot yet be presented. Some deep-sea cores from the Pacific Ocean extend back in time much more than 300,000 years. The surface temperature variations of the Pacific Ocean, however, were much smaller than those of the Atlantic and adjacent seas, so that the Pacific cores are not so suitable for a clear reconstruction of the temperature variations during the Pleistocene epoch. In spite of this difficulty, isotopic analysis of a long core from the eastern equatorial Pacific (core 58 of the Swedish Deep-Sea Expedition, 1947–48) clearly revealed a broad trend of decreasing temperature from the Late Pliocene into the Early Pleistocene.

The percentage of $CaCO_3$ varies remarkably throughout the Pacific core in question, as well as in other cores from the same general area. This variation is believed to have been caused, ultimately, by climatic changes. In particular, high-carbonate layers are thought to have been deposited during glacial ages, and low-carbonate layers during interglacial ages. Since the temperature cycles revealed by the deep-sea cores from the Atlantic and adjacent seas apparently lasted about 40,000 years each, a similar duration would obtain for each carbonate cycle of the Pacific cores. The Plio-Pleistocene boundary was tentatively placed at about 610 cm. below the top of core 58, because this level immediately follows a high-temperature level and immediately precedes a marked carbonate maximum. About 15 carbonate cycles occur above this level, so that a duration of about 600,000 years may be calculated for the whole Pleistocene epoch. Officially, however, the Plio-Pleistocene boundary is not defined on the basis of the deep-sea sea stratigraphy, but on the Late Cenozoic stratigraphy of Italy. Specifically, this boundary is placed at the time when certain northern species of marine invertebrates entered the Mediterranean. It is not known at present whether this event corresponds in time to the level of core 58 mentioned above, so that no estimate can be given for the age of the officially established Plio-Pleistocene boundary.

There seems to be no generally accepted agreement on the definition of Pleistocene and of Plio-Pleistocene boundary. According to different definitions currently in use, the age of the Plio-Pleistocene boundary could be as little as 350,000 years and as great as three million years. As a consequence, the "Pleistocene" of some authors may be only 10 per cent of the "Pleistocene" of others. Confusion arises from the fact that authors of Pleistocene topics generally do not define their Pleistocene. Perhaps the soundest definition so far available is that based on the Late Cenozoic marine sections of Italy, which follows classic stratigraphic practice. The boundary is paleoecological insofar as it is defined by the first appearance in the Mediterranean of certain northern species of Foraminifera and marine mollusks. These species appear suddenly and, usually, in abundance. While some species arrived earlier than others (notably *Cyprina islandica*), the boundary, as defined, is generally sharp and easy to recognize in the field. O^{18}/O^{16} analysis of pelagic and benthonic Foraminifera and benthonic mollusks collected at close stratigraphic intervals across the Plio-Pleistocene boundary at Le Castella, Calabria, southern Italy, showed that appreciable temperature fluctuations were already occurring in the Late Pliocene; that the amplitude of the fluctuations increased from the Late Pliocene to the Early Pleistocene, and from this to the Late Pleistocene; that the values of the secular temperature maxima and minima decreased in the same direction; and that no especially important temperature drop occurred across the paleoecological boundary. The age of the boundary is not

known, but the occurrence, in areas of the Po Valley, of Pleistocene sediments 2,000 m. thick suggest that the age might range from at least several hundred thousand years to perhaps one or two million years.

Attempts have been made to redefine the Plio-Pleistocene boundary in terms of deep-sea sediments, thus giving to this boundary a wider geographical significance. Riedel and Riedel *et al.* informally redefined the Plio-Pleistocene boundary as the time when the two radiolarians *Pterocanium prismatium* and *Eucyrtidium elongatum peregrinum* and some other Protista disappeared in the Pacific. These extinctions take place between 7 and 8 m. below the top of the eastern equatorial Pacific core 58. Using the age estimates given by Emiliani for core 58, the extinctions would date from 700–800,000 years ago. Ericson *et al.* have proposed a redefinition of the Plio-Pleistocene boundary based on abrupt micropaleontological changes in seven deep-sea cores from the Atlantic and one from the Indian Ocean. The age of the changes has been estimated to be at least 800,000 years. While the sharp and conspicuous micropaleontological changes described would provide a very good "Plio-Pleistocene boundary," it cannot yet be excluded that they may have been produced by unconformities.

Another definition of Plio-Pleistocene boundary, generally used by Pleistocene geologists working in former glacial and periglacial regions, is that based on the onset of the first major glaciation. The "first major glaciation" is usually understood to be the Günz of Europe and the Nebraskan of North America. The sediments of the jüngere Hauptterrasse of the Rhine, correlated with the Günz glaciation by Woldstedt, have been dated at about 350,000 years by the K/A method. This age is close to that of 300,000 years estimated by Emiliani. It is apparent that the onset of the Günz-Nebraskan glacian

TABLE 1

Definition of Plio-Pleistocene Boundary	Probable Age (Years)
1. Onset of first major glaciation (Günz-Nebraskan)	350,000
2. Micropaleontological changes in pelagic organisms	800,000+
3. Arrival of *Anomalina baltica* in the Mediterranean	1,000,000?
4. First appearance of Villafranchian fauna	3,200,000+

postdates considerably both the micropaleontological changes noticed in the deep-sea cores and the arrival of the northern species in the Mediterranean.

Finally, a definition of Plio-Pleistocene boundary which is generally used by paleoanthropologists and vertebrate paleontologists is that based on the first appearance of the so-called "Villafranchian fauna." The age of this event is not known, but ages as great as 3.2×10^6 years have been obtained for Villafranchian assemblages using the K/A method.

It is clear, from the above discussion, that the age of the Pleistocene varies greatly depending on which definition is used for the Plio-Pleistocene boundary. This conclusion is stressed in Table 1.

As previously mentioned, the temperature variations of the Pleistocene are best studied in the deep-sea cores from the Atlantic and adjacent seas. The stratigraphic record of these deep-sea cores has been divided in stages identified by positive integers, following a system introduced by Arrhenius. No. 1 is the present, high-temperature age; No. 2 is the preceding low-temperature age; No. 3 is the high-temperature age preceding age 2; etc. Thus odd numbers refer to high-temperature ages and stages, even numbers to low-temperature ages and stages. A tentative correlation between temperature stages and the glacial and interglacial stages of the continents is shown in Figure 1. This correlation is supported by C^{14} age measurements on both continental and pelagic material, reaching back to about 70,000 years and, therefore, including the Early

Würm glaciation. A reasonable extrapolation, together with a comparison between the generalized temperature curve of the deep-sea cores (Figure 1) and the continental record worked out by Brandtner in Austria and Moravia, strongly suggests that stage 5 is the last interglacial (Riss/Early Würm), and stage 6 at least part of the Riss glaciation. The correlations for older stages are more uncertain. If the suggested correlation is correct all the way back to stage 14, the Günz glaciation would be dated at about 280,000 years ago. Although this age may seem relatively young to Pleistocene scientists accustomed to older estimates which placed the Günz glaciation at about 600,000 years ago, it is nevertheless in agreement with such older estimates if these are corrected for the now generally accepted shorter duration of the postglacial time.

Although neither the chronology of the deep-sea deposits nor their correlation with the glacial and interglacial events of the Pleistocene epoch are yet well established beyond about 100,000 years ago, that is, beyond the last interglacial, the chronology and correlations of older deep-sea deposits afford time estimates for continental events which are undoubtedly superior to previous estimates.

Some important human and prehuman fossils and groups of fossils are rather surely correlated with glacial and interglacial stages of the continental stratigraphy. These, as discussed above, may be correlated, with various degrees of confidence, with the stages of the deep-sea deposits. The latter can be dated, or

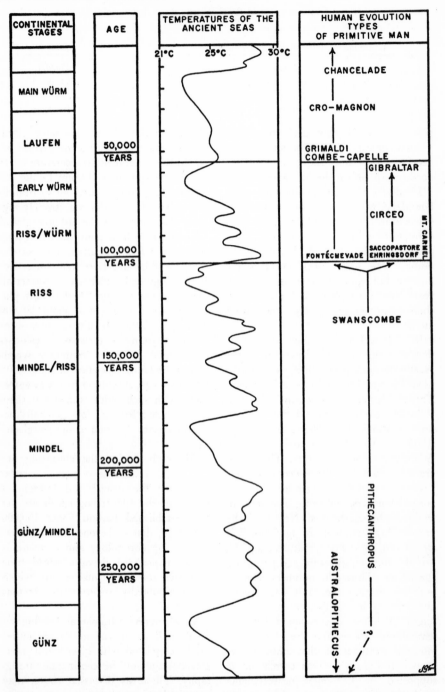

Figure 1. Time scale of temperature variation in the Pleistocene, based on the method of analyzing deep-sea sediment. Tentative dates are then attributed to the human and prehuman fossils according to the glacial and interglacial events with which they are associated. (After Emiliani)

ages can be reasonably estimated. The above relationship results in estimates of the ages of selected human and prehuman fossils. Although this method of dating human evolution may seem rather devious, it nevertheless provides age estimates which, at the present time, would be otherwise impossible to make. This method is based on the following three requirements: (1) the stages of the deep-sea stratigraphy must be dated; (2) the stages of the continental glacial stratigraphy must be correlated with the deep-sea stratigraphy; (3) the fossil hominids to be dated must be correlated with the continental glacial stages.

The first requirement is strictly fulfilled only back to 70,000 years ago, by radiocarbon measurements. Older deep-sea deposits are tentatively dated by extrapolations and inferences, as discussed above. Until recently the second requirement was strictly met again only back to 20,000 years ago, by radiocarbon measurements. It is now fulfilled to about 150,000 years ago by the Pa^{231}/Th^{230} measurements mentioned above. Beyond this age, the work by Brandtner on the loess and soil profiles of Austria and Moravia rather strongly suggest that the correlation shown in Figure 1 is probably correct at least back to the Riss glaciation. The third requirement is met only by the selected fossils shown in Figure 1. Some fossil hominids, in fact, have not yet been surely correlated with given stages of the Pleistocene continental stratigraphy. These are omitted from Figure 1.

Some interesting, though tentative, conclusions may be drawn from Figure 1. Modern man (*Homo sapiens sapiens*) appears already to have been present on the earth 50,000 years ago. The Fontéchevade remains are about 100,000 years old, and the Swanscombe skull bones about 125,000 years old. If these are assigned to an ancestral subspecies of *H. sapiens sapiens,* the latter appears to have

originated between 100,000 and 50,000 years ago. *Pithecanthropus* extended through the Günz/Mindel interglacial. If *Pithecanthropus* is ancestral to *Homo,* the first Homininae may have appeared sometime between 200,000 and 125,000 years ago. The older limit is uncertain, however, because the early Homininae may have been contemporaneous with the late Pithecanthropinae. A similar relationship exists between the Australopithecinae and the Pithecanthropinae. If the former are ancestral to the latter, speciation might have occurred substantially earlier than the time when the late Australopithecinae were in existence.

Homo sapiens neanderthalensis may have originated between 125,000 and 100,000 years ago. In any case, the Neanderthals were already in existence 100,000 years ago. Recent paleotemperature analyses of marine shells associated with the neanderthaloid jaw discovered in the deep layers of the Haua Fteah cave of Cyrenaica have unmistakably given fully interglacial temperatures, which result in indirect dating of the jaw at about 100,000 years. This date is probably correct within 10,000 years, because the high temperatures shown by the shells existed in the Mediterranean for only a relatively short time around 100,000 years ago. The Neanderthals appear to have existed for only about 50,000 years, a time interval which may represent a total of only about 2,000 generations.

The Pleistocene glaciations undoubtedly had a profound significance for the evolution of man. One may even venture the opinion that, if glaciations had not occurred, modern man might have failed to develop. *Pithecanthropus,* which was already in existence before the beginning of the major Pleistocene glaciations, was, in fact, a remarkably evolutionary type. He was apparently quite capable of taking care of himself and of disposing suitably of his enemies.

If glaciations had not created uncomfortable conditions, *Pithecanthropus* might have developed into a large, interbreeding population, occupying the whole earth. Glaciation favored migrations and the splitting-up of populations into small groups. Conditions for efficient evolutionary processes were thus created.

These resulted, ultimately, in the production of modern man. Today, modern man is a very large, interbreeding population, with strict laws protecting and even favoring the misfits. No further evolution seems likely, except by artificial means or by isolation on planets outside the solar system.

The ability to use language is probably as old as the capacity for culture. The two evolved together by a process in which tool-making and tool-use, communication and cooperative endeavor, and abstract thought and inventiveness were all inextricably linked.

4. The Evolution of Man's Capacity for Language [1]

The spate of criticism which followed the publication a hundred years ago of the *Origin of Species* often included the protest that Darwin in his argument had ignored man's higher mental faculties. This was perhaps true in fact, though captious in spirit. A recent critic, Leslie Paul, has written: "There is therefore through the invention of speech the entry into and the exploration of a new dimension of human activity. I think it was rather provincial and dull-witted of Darwin not to have shown a glimmer of interest in all this." In any event the gap was filled four years later when his geological colleague, Lyell, devoted a chapter in his classical *Antiquity of Man* to a comparison between the origin and growth of languages and of species. Schleicher, a botanist as well as a professional philologist, had called attention, three years before ever reading Darwin's book, to the struggle for existence among words, the disappearance of primitive forms, and the immense expansion and differentiation which may be produced by ordinary causes in a single family of

speech. He looked upon languages as natural organisms, which, according to definite physical influences and independently of human will, take origin and mature, grow old and die, and therefore manifest the series of phenomena to which are given the name of "life." In 1863, Schleicher issued his pamphlet *Die Darwinsche Theorie und die Sprachwissenschaft,* which was the expansion of a letter he had written to Professor Häckel acknowledging a copy of the *Origin of Species.* Herein he argued that the inception of species is notably paralleled in the genealogy of language, and particularly of the Aryan and Semitic tongues. Analogous with the struggle for life among the more or less favoured species in the animal and vegetable kingdoms, a struggle for survival occurs among individual languages.

This analogy between the evolution of species and of language was discussed in contemporary scientific literature. F. W. Farrar believed that comparative philology supported Darwin's hypotheses in two important respects, viz., the effect of

[1] MACDONALD CRITCHLEY, "The Evolution of Man's Capacity for Language," in *The Evolution of Man,* Sol Tax (ed.) (Chicago: 1960), pp. 289–308. Reprinted by permission of the author and The University of Chicago Press, © 1960 by The University of Chicago Press.

Dr. Critchley is Senior Physician at the National Hospital, London.

infinitesimal modifications in gradually bringing about great changes; and the preservation of the best and strongest elements in the struggle for existence. Just as very many primordial cells, closely resembling each other, may have been the earliest rudiments of all living organisms, so in philology different linguistic families may have sprung from multitudes of "speech cells" or "sound cells," that is, the fundamental roots of language. Like an extinct species, a language—once extinct—can never reappear. Intermediate linguistic forms also die out. Thus external factors disturb the primitive relationship of languages, and consequently one may find radically different languages existing side by side. Farrar said, "All this, as every naturalist is well aware, represents a condition of things precisely similar to that which prevails in animated nature."

Darwin's contemporary, Max Müller, who occupied the Chair of Comparative Philology at Oxford, was also interested in this parallelism between the struggle for existence in the biological sense and in the case of languages. He laid stress on an important difference, however. It is not on account of inherent defects that languages gradually become extinct, but rather because of external causes; that is to say, the physical, moral, and political weaknesses of those who speak the languages concerned. Müller considered that a much more pertinent linguistic analogy with Darwinism lay in the struggle for survival among words and grammatical forms which is constantly going on in every language, whereby shorter and easier forms gain the upper hand.

Views of this kind were of topical interest a century ago, but since then philologists, with the possible exception of Jespersen, have been largely out of sympathy with the application of Darwinian ideas to their own subject.

In 1871 Darwin himself dealt in some detail with the human faculties which he had rightly omitted from his earlier monograph; in *Descent of Man* the problem of speech was specifically discussed. The faculty of articulate speech, he wrote, in itself offers no insuperable objection to the belief that man had evolved from some lower form. The mental powers in some early progenitor of man must have been more highly developed than in any existing ape, before even the most imperfect form of speech could have come about. The continued advancement of this power would have reacted on the mind itself, by enabling and encouraging it to pursue long trains of thought. Complex reflection can no more be carried on without the aid of words, whether spoken or silent, than can a long abstraction without the use of figures or algebra.

Darwinian theories and ideas pervaded every aspect of scientific and philosophic thought, and Max Müller was also caught up in the current excitement. Leaving aside his purely linguistic considerations, we may examine his views upon the evolution of the speech faculties in man. After detailing *seriatim* the characters of mind and body which are shared by man and animal, he went on to inquire in 1861:

Where, then, is the difference between brute and man? What is it that man can do, and of which we find no signs, no rudiments, in the whole brute world? I answer without hesitation: the one great barrier between the brute and man is *language*. Man speaks, and no brute has ever uttered a word. Language is our Rubicon, and no brute will dare to cross it. This is our matter-of-fact answer to those who speak of development, who think they discover the rudiments at least of all human faculties in apes, and who would fain keep open the possibility that man is only a more favoured beast, the triumphant conqueror in the primeval struggle for life. Language is something more palpable than a fold of the brain or an angle of the skull. It admits of no cavilling, and no process of natural selection will ever distil significant words out of the notes of birds or the cries of beasts.

Professor Müller's views were, on the whole, opposed to those of Darwin, and their differences of opinion were studied and discussed at length by the German linguist Noiré. Strongly critical of "Darwinian foibles, incompleteness and one-sidedness," Noiré proclaimed in 1879 that Max Müller was the only equal, not to say superior, antagonist who had entered the arena against Darwin. "Here is reason, here language, here humanity. None shall pass here; none penetrate into the sanctuary who cannot tell me first how reason, how speech, was born. And the shouting bands of the assailants were struck dumb, for they could give no answer."

Although Professor Müller was, in the main, out of sympathy with Darwin, nevertheless he proclaimed in 1873: "In language, I was a Darwinian before Darwin." As early as 1861 he was trying to reconcile Darwin's doctrines with linguistic phenomena. He compared Darwin with Epicurus, and he spoke of the origins of language in terms of natural selection, or—as he preferred to call it —natural elimination.

ANATOMICAL BASIS FOR LANGUAGE

Any discussion of the evolution of man's capacity for language must entail an inquiry, not only into the appropriate intellectual equipment, but also into the necessary and actual anatomical substratum. This latter is a twofold problem. In the first place, a physiological cerebral mechanism exists peculiar to man. In addition, the faculty of speech requires certain peripheral instrumentalities, which can fulfill a complex co-ordinated activity of the lips, palate, tongue, pharynx, larynx, and respiratory apparatus. Herein lies the structural basis for the achievement of an audible motor-skill of the utmost delicacy. In the course of both phylogeny and ontogeny it is often possible to observe that anatomical structures are present even before they are actually utilized. Structure, in other words, antedates function. Consequently, within the animal series it may be expected that both cerebral and peripheral mechanisms will stand ready for use, though not yet productive of mature speech.

Even in the anthropoid there is no valid morphological reason, at a peripheral level, why speech should not occur. At any rate, most authorities would agree with this opinion. The relative coarseness of the tissues would no doubt impart a certain unmusical quality to the articulation, but the phonemic range would probably be not inconsiderable. As Max Müller said, there is no letter of the alphabet which a parrot will not learn to pronounce, and the fact that the parrot is without a language of his own must be explained by a difference between the *mental,* not between the *physical,* faculties of animal and man.

It must be stressed that language is a function which can be looked upon as overlaid, or even parasitic. There are no specific cerebral structures which are peculiar to the faculty of speech. It would be difficult—if not, indeed, impossible—to decide merely from a study of the brain, however meticulous, whether the subject had been a polyglot, an orator, a writer, or even an illiterate or a deaf-mute. Simply by microscopical examination of the cerebral cortex it would not be easy to distinguish gorilla from man. In other words, no essentially human cerebral speech centre can yet be confidently identified as an anatomical entity. Speech likewise makes use of predetermined bucco-laryngeal structures which were primarily destined to serve for acts of feeding and respiration. Certain teleological advantages accrued when the function of communication took over structures which were also being utilized for other purposes. Man did not develop *de novo* some entirely novel means for subserving the novel faculty of language. Linguistic precursors, anatomical, physiological, psychological, and cultural, must obviously have existed in the subhuman animal series. In some creatures like bees, simple communicative acts operate by dint of global movements. In birds and primates, elaborate combinations of cries, intention movements, and pantomimic displays fulfill the role of primitive sign-making or communication. Some birds possess the faculty of mimicking human utterances in a plausible and even startling fashion, but it must be remembered that this is a learned, artificial performance and that their innate instinctive calls are crude, raucous, stereotyped—indeed, anything but human in quality.

We recall Buffon's speculation as to what would happen if the ape had been endowed with the voice of a parrot and its faculty of speech. The talking monkey would, he said, have struck dumb with astonishment the entire human race and would have so confounded the philosopher that he would have been hard put to prove—in the face of all these human attributes—that the monkey was still an animal. It is, therefore, just as well for our understanding that Nature has separated and relegated into two very different categories the mimicry of speech and the mimicry of our gestures.

Koehler has put the question why it is, if there are so many precursors of our own language in the animal kingdom, no known animal speaks like man. It is because no animal possesses all those *initia* of our language at one and the same time. They are distributed very diffusely, this species having one capacity, that species another. We alone possess all of them, and we are the only species using words.

CRITERIA OF LANGUAGE

Among the prerogatives of *Homo sapiens* the faculty of speech is the most obvious. Other members of the animal kingdom, not excluding the higher primates, are not so endowed, however vocal may be the individuals. By contrast, it can be asserted that no race of mankind is known, however lowly, which does not possess the power of speech. Nay more, the linguistic attainments may be subtle, complex, flexible, and eloquent —even though the cultural level be primitive in the extreme. It is indeed difficult to identify among the races of man anything which can be justly termed a "primitive" tongue.

At the very outset it is important to be clear in what way the cries, utterances, calls, and song of birds and subhuman mammals can so readily be deemed as lying outside the category of language attainment. On inquiry, it is found that no one touchstone of distinction is entailed, but rather a co-ordination of factors, some of which may be present in this or that animal, but which do not come together in integration until the stage of *Homo sapiens* is achieved.

Doubtless the most weighty single criterion of human speech is the use of symbols. Animals betray abrupt fluctuations in their emotional state by making sounds. To this extent they may be said to utilize signs. Whether the sign be perceived and identified as such by other members of the same species is arguable. An alarm-call may act as a signal of danger, and others within earshot may take flight. This effect may be an instance of direct signaling between one bird or mammal and another. Or, possibly, the frightened creature's cry may be interjectional rather than purposeful, and others within call may thereupon be made merely partners in alarm rather than the recipients of a directed message. Be that as it may—and the possibility that both types of concerted action occur in nature cannot be gainsaid—the animal's cry cannot strictly be looked upon either as language or as speech. At most, it is communication. The communicative act may be deliberate, willed, directed encoding, while the comprehending recipients who act upon the signal may be looked upon as decoders. Here, then, is communication in the accepted sense of the term. Or it may be that the communicative act is merely incidental, and no true encoding and decoding can be said to take place.

"Animal communication" is therefore the term which carries with it the fewest drawbacks. In essence it can be said to comprise a series of signs which refer to ideas or feelings within immediate awareness. They do not and cannot apply to circumstances within past or future time. Herein lies an all-important distinction. Man's utterances entail the use of symbols or signs of signs and consequently possess the superlative advantage of applying to events in time past, present, and future and to objects *in absentia*. This endowment has been called the "time-binding" property of human language. It also possesses the merit of beginning the process of storage of experience, a process which eventually reaches fruition with the subsequent introduction of writing.

THE EVOLUTION OF BEHAVIOR

Most of the early arguments concerning the problem of the origin of speech in man have been either theological or linguistic. In the former case the doctrine of a divine creation was accepted, but many controversies arose, including such questions as monogenesis versus polygenesis. The purely linguistic theories rejected altogether the idea of a special creation of a mature system of language, and while some process of

transition between the communication of animals and the beginnings of speech in *Homo sapiens* was assumed, there was disagreement as to the *modus operandi*. The sources of argument included the relative importance of the role of imitation, of interjectional utterances, of associated motor-vocal phenomena, of gesture and still other factors, none of which nowadays excites serious comment or concern.

Attention became focussed more upon the mysterious evolutionary changes which are believed to have taken place between the behavioral systems of the highest primates and those of earliest man. The beginnings of speech, in the strict sense of the term, rank among these changes. However striking in character and fundamental in importance, speech certainly cannot be looked upon as man's sole perquisite, singling him out from the rest of the animal kingdom. Several other important developments took place at more or less the same period of evolution, any one or any combination of which may actually prove to be supremely significant in the genesis of speech.

The principal clash of opinion turns around the debate whether the difference between animal communication and the speech of early man entail factors which are qualitative or merely quantitative. Expressed somewhat differently, the question has been raised whether the distinction between man and animals is one of kind or merely of degree, as far as the communicative act is concerned.

Within that stage between the most complex of animal communication and the speech-efforts of earliest man lies the core of our problem. Obviously, this transition from animal cries to human articulation is but an item in a much bolder process of evolution. Instinctive responses no longer prove biologically adequate, and more and more complicated vocal reactions gradually emerge. Linguistics alone can never afford the whole solution, and other realms of thought and endeavor will need exploring.

Social Factors Favoring Language. COMMUNAL LIVING. Attempts which have been made to identify these important steps in the evolution of human language fall roughly into two classes. Thus one can distinguish sociological from intellectual hypotheses, the former envisaging some modification in behavior, the latter implying a change in the mode of thinking as between animals and man. These two attitudes are not mutually irreconcilable, and both types of change may well have operated together.

Many would agree that the ancestry of language lay within the prehominid stages, at the same time denying the existence of anything that can be strictly termed "animal language."

Révész spoke of "contact reactions" as being important in the genesis of speech in man. By this expression he understood the basic, innate tendency of social animals to approach one another, establish rapport, co-operate, and communicate. Contact reactions are a necessary precondition of linguistic communication. In a rather unconvincing fashion, Révész seems to have equated the essential differences between human speech and the cries and directed calls of the animal world with an elaboration of this "contact reaction" in the domain of articulate utterance.

Much earlier, Lord Monboddo realized the critical role of communal existence. To convert man into a speaking animal, the factor of society is essential. He posed the question: which is the more important—language for the institution of society, or society for the invention of language. In his view, society came first and had existed perhaps for ages before language developed, for man is by nature a political as well as a speaking animal.

Biologists realize that communal existence is an important factor in survival, which can be traced as a principle throughout the animal kingdom, even in the lowliest species. Indeed, the physiological value of coexistence can perhaps be better demonstrated in the invertebrate phyla. In the higher ranks of Mammalia, there is perhaps a greater co-ordination of group activity, whereby there is a limited degree of sharing of function and a deputing of special tasks increasingly becomes the rule. Allee has shrewdly asked at what stage can an animal group be said to have become truly social: is it at the point when animals behave differently in the presence of others than they would if alone? If this is the case, then we witness in an interesting fashion the first hint of ethical or moral factors in animal behavior.

One of the principal functions of speech is to co-ordinate the behavior of the individual members of a group. Grace de Laguna stressed the progressively elaborate communal life which synchronizes with the development of speech. Planned hunting forays, the need for securing safety by night, the indoctrination of the young—all these are among the activities of early *Homo sapiens,* and they must have been considerably assisted by the faculty of speech. The power of speech thus confers an important survival value upon its owner.

TOOL-USING: TOOL-MAKING. Allied to this notion is the role of an increasing utilization of tools, as an immediate precursor of speech. *Homo sapiens* has often been identified not only with *Homo loquens* but also with *Homo faber.* An animal achieves its purposes by modifying its own bodily structure, that is, by making a tool out of some part of itself. Man ventures further by making use of instruments outside his own body.

As L. S. Amery said, man also began to employ a "sound-tool"; that is to say, he made use of differentiated sounds as an instrument of precision, in order to indicate not only emotions but also specific objects, qualities, actions, and judgments. Both language and tools are instruments which humans alone employ to achieve definite and concrete actions. "Language, like the tool, and unlike the limb, is something objective to, and independent of, the individual who uses it".

We now approach a critical point in the argument. The term *Homo faber* is ambiguous, for it can be interpreted in two very different ways. It can be read as meaning either the "tool-maker" or the "tool-user." This distinction is important and is not to be glossed over. Mere tool-taking or tool-utilizing is quite consistent with anthropoid behavior; tool-making is not. The higher apes are not infrequently to be seen making use of a convenient stick as an implement with which to draw a delicacy within reach. But deliberately to choose and to set it carefully aside, against the contingency of finding at some possible future date an edible morsel just inaccessible, is outside the capacity of the anthropoid. To select an instrument and keep it for future use can be reckoned as analogous to fashioning a tool out of sticks or stones to attain an immediate need or desire.

When the species can do these latter things, it steps over the frontier and qualifies as *Homo sapiens.* Similarly, in the most primitive communal groups of man's ancestors, a piece of sharp stone, a stick, a shell might have been picked up and used straightway as a weapon to fell an object of prey, as a weapon of self-defence, or as a tool for decorticating a tree-trunk or skinning a beast. This sort of activity is consistent with primate behavior, and speech acquisition is unnecessary. But when the apelike creature breaks a stick in two or pulls it out of a bush or if he puts it aside for another occasion, it is beginning this apprenticeship for qualifying as *Homo sapiens,* and here the first beginnings of speech may be detected.

With the art of knapping of flint core-tools or flake-tools or by shaving down a stake, we have the unmistakable marks of attainment of man's stature, and speech can doubtless be assumed as a concomitant. For here we have the earliest mastery over purely perceptual thinking, the dawn of conceptual thought, and release from the shackles of time-present.

DELEGATION OF LABOR. Closely linked with an elaborate communal life and the construction of tools, delegation of labor can also be reckoned as a factor in the ancestry of speech. Greater efficiency in hunting and in the acquisition and preparation of food for the group follows upon the use of speech and leads to the beginnings of a simple form of specialization. This is an aspect of linguistics which has naturally appealed particularly to Soviet writers. Soviet philosophers of language believe that language began when man—a new species of animal—began to use tools and to co-operate with others in order to produce the means of subsistence. Human labor is a new form of social activity and gives rise to a new phenomenon, articulate speech, and to a new characteristic of the mind, the conscious reflection of objective reality. Stalin—himself a dabbler in linguistics—looked upon language not only as a tool of communication but also as a means of struggle and development of society. Language is connected with man's productive activity and also with every other human activity. Seppe, a Russian neurologist, went further. Work appeared to him as a main factor in the development of higher and abstract thinking of man. Speech functions are created from work. Furthermore, we find Stalin declaring: "In the history of mankind, a spoken language has been one of the forces which helped human beings to emerge from the animal world, unite into communities, develop their faculty of thinking, organize social production, wage a successful struggle against the forces of nature, and attain the stage of progress we have today."

Such were the progressive elaborations in animal behavior which immediately antedated and perhaps accelerated the development of speech in man. The alternative group of hypotheses puts the emphasis more upon the elaboration of certain ways of thinking, as bridging the gap between animal communication and human speech.

Intellectual Behavior. ABSTRACT THINKING. Since Aristotle, many philosophers have stressed man's gift of conceptual thought, whereby he is enabled to deal with general ideas as well as the particular or the concrete. Man's unique power of coping with "abstractions," "universals," "generalizations," has been associated with his endowment of speech. Geiger, a contemporary of Darwin's, was one of the most eloquent advocates of conceptual thought as a human perquisite. In his *Ursprung der Sprache* he wrote:

It is easy to see that blood is red and milk is white; but to abstract the redness of blood from the collective impression, to find the same notion again in a red berry and, in spite of its other differences, to include under the same head the red berry and the red blood—or the white milk and the white snow—this is something altogether different. No animal does this, for *this, and this only, is thinking.*

Noiré inquired how man's power of abstraction came about. He attributed it to man's manual dexterity coupled with his ingenuity. More than any other creature, man has the power of selecting objects from his environment and then modifying them to suit his own purposes. Thus he became master of his environment. He learned to create things, and these creations were for him the first "things." Such "things" became endowed with independent existence, and from this point to the endowment of names for the things was quite an easy step.

Terminology readily misleads, however. We now believe that the older, narrow views upon the essentially human nature of conceptual thinking are not warranted by the facts. As Darwin showed, it is not possible to deny that in some animals, as judged by their behavior, indications of a kind of abstract thinking can at times be traced. Although perhaps an exceptional state of affairs, it occurs often enough to cast doubts upon any notion of a Rubicon separating the brute beasts from man.

Let us recall the very beginnings of philology as a science, which can be said to date from 1772, when J. G. Herder wrote his essay on the *Origin of Language*. Herder rejected the doctrine that language was a divine creation and also the idea that it might be a willed invention on the part of men. Nor did he believe that the difference between man and animals was one of degree. He considered that there had taken place in man as he emerged from the subhuman state a development of all of his powers, in a totally different direction. This abrupt exploration led to the appearance of speech. Language sprang, of necessity, out of man's innermost nature. Herder likened the birth of language to the irresistible strivings of the mature embryo within the egg. In particular, man possessed a keener faculty of "attention" than any other animal, and he was thereby enabled to seize hold of isolated impressions from out of a mass of detail surrounding him. In this way man became able to identify the most arresting feature within his environment. For example, the distinguishing property of a lamb would be its vocalization; that is, its bleating. Thereafter the lamb would be recollected, and referred to, as a "bleater." So, according to Herder, primitive nouns stemmed from verbs (as indeed we know to be the case in the sign-language of the deaf-and-dumb).

PERCEPTION AND CONCEPTION. Herder's theory, couched in somewhat different terms by Noiré, reappeared a century later. And fifty-five years after that, contemporary animal psychologists state this theory anew. Professor E. S. Russell warned us not to assume that an animal's perceptual world would be like our own: on the contrary, judging from its behavior, we must conclude that every animal has its own perceptual world, one which is very different from ours. Animals do not ordinarily perceive their environment in the same "articulated" fashion as we do. They perceive things only as ill-distinguished parts of a general complex. Isolated from its habitual context, an object may not be recognized for what it is. Animals respond only to perception-complexes and not to simple and solitary stimuli.

We have already referred to the philologist Max Müller as in many ways an antagonist of Darwin. This would be to do an injustice to both writers, for —as we have stated earlier—in 1861 we find Müller aligning Darwin with Epicurus. The latter believed that primitive man's uncouth instinctive ejaculations were fundamental in the origins of language. In addition, there must have been an important second stage, whereby agreement is made in associating certain words with certain conceptions. For the "agreement" of Epicurus, Müller would offer his doctrine of natural selection, or natural elimination. The phenomenon of the origin of language would then be visualized as follows: Sensuous impressions would produce a mental image or *perception;* a number of perceptions would bring about a general notion or *conception.* A number of sensuous impressions might also occasion a corresponding vocal expression—a cry, an interjection, or an imitation of the sound in question. A number of such vocal expressions might be merged with one general expression and leave behind the root as the sign belonging to a general notion. The gradual formation of roots and of natural cries or onomatopoeia is a product of rational control. Rational selection is natural selection, not only in nature but also in thought and language. "Not every random perception is raised to the dignity of a general notion, but only the constant recurring, the strongest, the most useful." Of the multitudinous general ideas, those and only those which are essential for carrying on the work of life survive and receive definite phonetic expression.

SYMBOLIC BEHAVIOR

Another way of looking upon the development of human speech out of animal vocalizations is to regard speech as the utilization of symbols. The sounds emitted by animals are in the nature of signs, while man's speech is made up of symbols. Signs *indicate* things, while symbols *represent* them. Signs are announcers of events; symbols are reminders. In other words, symbols are not restricted to the confines of immediate time and place. As "substitute" signs, symbols can refer to things out of sight and outside present experience. When an ape utters a cry of hunger, it can be looked upon as perhaps making a declaration, perhaps an imperative utterance, or even an exclamation of discomfort. No ape, however, has ever uttered the word "banana," for such a word is a concrete symbol, a tool of thought which only man can employ, and he can do so in a variety of ways, irrespective of the barriers of time and space. Man can refer to a banana in past or future tense, as well as the present. Man can talk about a banana *in absentia*. No animal can do these things, the task being far beyond its system of thought and therefore of expression. Likewise no monkey can emit a word meaning "hunger," for this term would constitute, or refer to, an abstract or universal idea.

In Pavlovian modes of thought the use of symbols is regarded as a hallmark of man's cerebral function—although other terminologies are used. Pavlov taught that when the developing animal world reached the human stage, an extremely important addition came about, namely, the functioning of speech. This signified a new principle in cerebral activity. Sensations and ideas from the outer world constitute the first system of signals (concrete signals; signals of reality). Speech, however, constitutes a second set of signals—or "signals of signals." These make possible the formation of generalizations, which, in turn, constitute the higher type of thinking, specific for man.

Man's capacity for dealing with symbols rather than signs or things has been visualized by Korzybski as a specific "time-binding" faculty, peculiar to mankind. Pumphrey has described as many as three considerations which are attached to the human employment of verbal symbols as opposed to the sign-making cries of animals. These properties are (1) *detachment,* whereby man is able to use language to describe events in a wholly dispassionate fashion, if he should so desire; (2) *extensibility,* whereby a proposition can be made and discussed in terms of past, present, or future time; and (3) *economy,* whereby symbols enable man to abbreviate what would otherwise be a long-winded description or declaration.

Many writers view the origins of speech as merely part of a large developing faculty, namely, the beginnings of symbolic behavior. As Sapir put it, language is primarily a vocal actualization of the tendency to see reality symbolically, a property which renders it a fitting medium for communication. The problem, therefore, really resolves itself into a search for the earliest indications of symbolic behavior, as the immediate precursor of speech. S. Langer believes that these beginnings of symbolic thought can be detected when an animal—the highest of the primates, in fact—behaves as if significance were being attached to certain objects or sounds. This attitude may be seen in the anthropoid in capitivity, in its attachment toward some inanimate and favored plaything—a piece of wood, a toy, a rag, or a pebble. Here, then, we are attempting to discern the dawn of symbolic thought; and here, too, we may perhaps descry the remote ancestry of human speech. In other words, the chimpanzee, although devoid of speech, begins to show a rudimentary capacity for speech—an opinion which reminds us of Müller's uneasy feeling that the gorilla is "behind us, close on our heels."

Some of the nineteenth century philosophers who were critical of Darwin, compared the appearance of language in man with the beginnings of religious belief. Certainly, at a very early date in man's emergence we find that there are indications of primitive magical practices, with evidences of ritual or ceremonial. It can safely be concluded that, at such a cultural level, primitive man was surely endowed with the faculty of speech. Noiré believed that the two aptitudes grew up in concert, the rise of mythology being an important and necessary stage in the development of language. This can be looked upon as a period when objects began to mark themselves off from the indefiniteness of the total perceptual processes and to form themselves into independent existence.

EMERGENCE OF SPEECH

The intriguing question naturally arises: At which point in the evolution of primitive man did speech, in the strictest sense of the word, first make its appearance? When did the ululations of the anthropoids give way to the use of verbal symbols, disciplined by phonetic and syntactical rules? Obviously, it is not possible—nor is it ever likely to be possible—to answer this question with confidence. The evidence, such as it is, is meager, indirect, and oblique. But speculation on this interesting matter is quite permissible.

Anthropological data are of great importance here. They comprise arguments which are of a cultural order and which discriminate clearly between anthropoid and human communities. They also include the weighty evidence which lies within the domain of comparative anatomy. Here are to be found the impressive distinctions between ape and man in respect to the crania and the problems which arise from a study of the fossil skulls of man's immediate ancestors. Here, too, are marshaled the anatomical features in the crania which are to be regarded as specific for *Homo sapiens*. The size of the cranial cavity will naturally indicate brain-volume. This is an important point in that, ordinarily speaking, the human brain differs from anthropoid brain in its greater size, while the cranial capacity of prehistoric man occupies an intermediate position. But the rule is not invariable: one or two prehistoric specimens are characterized by megalencephaly. More valuable than sheer size is the question of the shape and proportions of the cranial cavity. In addition, the endocranial markings may be taken as a likely index of the convolutional pattern of the cerebral hemisphere. In assigning a fossil specimen to its evolutionary rank, the development of such specifically "human"

areas of the brain as the frontal lobes and the parietal eminences are all-important. Obviously, clues such as these may be followed when discussing the problem of when in prehistory man developed speech.

L. S. Palmer, a dental surgeon as well as paleontologist, has approached the question of the development of speech in man from a somewhat unusual angle. He distinguishes between human speech and animal noises, the former being regarded as being effected by delicate and voluntary variation in the size and shape of the oral cavity. The power of articulation (as exemplified in human speech) depends upon a specific morphology of the jaws, and here man differs in an important manner from the ape. In man the two rami of the mandibles are splayed apart, whereas in apes they are parallel. There results a difference in the shape of the posterior ends of the mandibles, together with an increased width between the condyles at the upper ends of the rami. In man there is consequently ample space for the free movement of the tongue, in this way facilitating articulate speech.

Another difference between the jaws of apes and men consists in the presence of a bony ledge connecting the anterior ends of the mandibles in apes. This "simian shelf" serves as an attachment for the genioglossus muscles. The range of lingual movement is rather restricted. In man, however, the tongue muscles are attached to a series of small genial tubercles, which, taking up but little room, permit freer movement of the tongue within a broader intermandibular space.

The same author (Palmer) also associates himself with L. A. White (*The Science of Culture*) and believes that there was an important connection in prehistory between favorable climatic factors and cultural acceleration, which naturally includes the origin of the faculty of speceh. Palmer set out the chain of causes as follows:

A rigorous ameliorating climate → appropriate gene mutation → expansion of the skull → development of brain → increased mental ability → development of articulate speech and the introduction of written words.

Thus we can surmise with no little confidence that Cro-Magnon man must surely have been endowed with speech, even though no firm evidence exists that written language was ever in use at that period. The refinement of the skeletal structure and the large cranial capacity point to a quite highly evolved type of *Homo sapiens*. But the weightiest arguments are of a cultural order. The skilful cave-paintings of the Aurignacian, Solutrean, and Magdalenian periods obviously must have been the work of individuals endowed with symbolic and conceptual thinking. The frequency with which hand-prints occur on the cavern walls may also be taken as suggestive of individual personal awareness. Furthermore, the relative preponderance of left hands over right at El Castillo (4 to 1) must indicate that cerebral dominance obtained at that period. Perhaps, too, the appearance of obscure linear markings—red blobs and dots—adjacent to these hand-prints may be looked upon as the very first modest indications of written communication. The fashioning of elaborate tools, the use of fire and of clothing, and the evidence of ceremonial burials as well as religious or magical practices cannot be reconciled with a speechless state. Even the Negroid variant of Cro-Magnon civilization, known as the Grimaldi man, as well as the Eskimo-like Chancelate man, is no exception to these arguments. These fragmentary clues take the story of language back to the last Ice Age of late Paleolithic times, that is between 25,000 and 10,000 years B.C.

Can language be assumed in even ear-lier man? European *Homo neanderthalensis (or mousteriensis)* constitutes a less straightforward problem. Some anatomists are tempted to explain some of the contradictory characteristics of Neanderthal skulls by suggesting that they were out on a side line, away from the main stream of evolution. Thus the anthropoid characters of the supraciliary and occipital ridges, the massive jaw, and the wide orbits and nasal apertures contrast with the large cranial capacity, which actually exceeds that of average modern man. The African Neanderthaloids, including the *Homo rhodesiensis,* and the *Homo soloensis* of Java, present essentially the same problem.

A. Keith believed that the faculty of speech could be traced back as far as Neanderthal man, but no further. His evidence was wholly anatomical, and not very convincing. The left hemisphere was apparently more massive than the right, indicating cerebral dominance. Tilney also believed that Neanderthal man was "possessed of linguistic capabilities not far below the standard of *Homo sapiens.*" His conclusion was based upon the depth of the parietal fossae in the skulls, suggesting a well-developed "auditory area," i.e., the abutment of the parietal lobe upon the outer occipital and upper temporal lobes. This postero-inferior part of the parietal lobe is commonly regarded as a true and specific human perquisite. L. S. Palmer, however, is impressed by the poor temporal lobe development in the brain of Rhodesian man, and he doubts very much whether this specimen of Hominidae ever could speak.

Cultural evidence is more convincing than the morphological. The coexistence of eoliths in the way of sharpened flints and arrow-heads, and signs of the use of fire and the practice of cooking, all point to Neanderthal man's possessing a degree of conceptual and symbolic thinking consistent with the possession of language, just as in the case of Cro-Magnon man. If this argument is admitted, then the story of language can be taken back to about 50,000 years B.C., that is, to the post-Acheulian Paleolithic period, or the last glacial era.

Let us now turn to the early and middle Pleistocene periods. The hominid representatives of this time are exemplified by *Pithecanthropus pekinensis* (*erectus*) or *sinanthropus,* by *Homo heidelbergensis,* and perhaps also by *ternifine man.* Possibly, too, the Swanscombe and the Steinheim skulls belong here, though admittedly they may represent a transitional or intermediate type between *Pithecanthropus* and *Homo sapiens.* Later specimens within this same period include the skulls associated with Ehringsdorf, Fontéchevade, Florisbad, Krapina, and Mount Carmel.

According to Tilney, the left frontal area of the brain was larger than the right, a fact which he was tempted to associate with a state of right-handedness. The same author pointed out the development of the inferior frontal convolutions, a feautre which suggested to him that *Pithecanthropus* could speak. He went on to assert: "Doubtless the linguistic attainments were extremely crude." It is difficult to comprehend exactly what Tilney implied by this statement, for present-day linguistics has no knowledge of a language system which can be designated as "extremely crude," even among the most primitive and uncultured communities.

Upon other grounds, too, there is evidence that speech was an endowment of *Pithecanthropus.* Implements of quartz have been found in the caves alongside the human remains, obviously fabricated with some skill. There is evidence also that *Pithecanthropus* knew how to produce fire and that at times he produced cooking. Again it is almost useless to conjecture what manner of speech was employed by *Pithecanthropus.* Oakley

was merely guessing when he surmised that the earliest mode of expression of ideas was perhaps by gesticulation, mainly of mouth and hands, accompanied by cries and grunts to attract attention.

By such suggestive paleontological clues, we can refer the faculty of speech to a period at least as far back as 100,000 years B.C., that is, the middle Pleistocene period. On the evidence of the Javanese and Chinese skulls (*P. soloensis* and *pekinensis*) the date might even be relegated as far back as the early Pleistocene era, that is, perhaps 500,000 years B.C.

Few would venture to seek the pioneers of speech at any more remote period. There arises for serious discussion, however, an interesting series of fossil skulls found in South Africa, small in size and of an interesting morphology. These are associated with an extinct series of pygmy man-apes, originally called the fossil Taung's ape, but more often nowadays as *Australopithecus.* Where these specimens rightly belong is debatable; Le Gros Clark regards them as exceedingly primitive representatives of the family which includes modern and extinct types of man. Leakey called them "near-men." The recent findings of a number of crude stone artifacts in proximity to the bones and the associated fractured skulls of the fossil bones makes is possible that *Australopithecus* utilized stones as weapons, even though it did not, strictly speaking, manufacture weapons.

L. S. Palmer believes that *Australopithecus* was perhaps endowed with speech. He bases his opinion upon the anatomical characteristics of the mandible. The absence of a simian shelf and of diastema (or gap between the incisor and the canine) and the convergence angle of the teeth are all features which correspond with a hominoid morphological pattern. Recently it has been suggested that *Australopithecus* had the ability to make fire. If this is really the case, it should be taken as an additional piece of evidence to suggest that speech might have been within its capacity. Obviously, the answer to the question awaits the production of further findings.

The date of *Australopithecus* is remote indeed—probably beyond the earliest Pleistocene era and back into the end of the Pliocene. This means anything from one to fifteen million years B.C.

There is one aspect about the beginnings of speech in man which is only too often completely overlooked. Was speech a consistent endowment in the case of early man? When man first appeared on the earth, as in the middle and late Pleistocene periods, perhaps only some of the newly evolved *Homo sapiens* were endowed with speech. Speech in those remote times might have constituted an exceptional phenomenon or aptitude, one which was within the competency of only a few highly favored individuals.

In the case of hand-skills, too, maybe only comparatively few members of *Pithecanthropus* were able to fashion arrow-heads or flints, this expertise being a rare and no doubt highly accorded accomplishment. Then again, skill in handicrafts might perhaps have correlated closely with the faculty of speech. Such especially gifted members of the community probably also had an expectation of life above the average, and therefore speech and the art of tool-making may well have had considerable survival value.

EVOLUTION AND THE ORIGIN OF LANGUAGE

On rereading these remarks, it appears that perhaps insufficient attention has been paid to the difficulties inherent in a purely Darwinian conception of the origin of language.

It was implicit in this particular hypothesis as to evolution that differences between human and animal structure and function are matters of degree. Were this principle to be firmly established, then it would be difficult to avoid the idea that animal communication leads by insensible gradations to the faculty of speech in man. There are numerous linguistic objections to this view, however. It is important to realize, too, that language does not stand alone in this matter and that there are other weighty considerations which lead to the well-nigh inescapable conclusion that some potent qualitative change occurs at a point somewhere between the anthropoid and *Homo sapiens*.

Animals, at best, may possess a limited store of vocal sounds. These are innate, instinctive, or "natural." Under appropriate circumstances, internal or external, they are emitted. They may happen to possess communicative action in respect to other animals mainly of the same species. It is doubtful, however, whether these cries are always communicative in intent. In ordinary circumstances the adolescent animal does not increase its vocabulary of sounds, except that in one or two strictly delimited circumstances the vocal repertoire may be extended. Thus some animals in states of domestication may amplify their stock of cries and calls. Other animals, particularly certain birds, may elaborate their performance by dint of imitation. In this way the innate and instinctive bird song or call is overlaid by dint of learning from other birds, not necessarily of the same species. Finally, certain animals, particularly a small group of birds and a few higher apes in captivity, may be taught to mimic human articulate speech, the specific cries of quadrupeds, or even inanimate noises.

The foregoing recounts the sum-total of achievement in the domain of animal sounds. Between these and human articulate speech lies a very considerable gulf. Even in the case of the most untutored, primitive, and savage human communities the language-system is so far removed in its complexity from the crude and simple utterances of the primates as to be scarcely comparable. And nowhere and at no time has there been any hint of an approximation between these two extremes. No "missing link" between animal and human communication has yet been identified.

Can it be, therefore, that a veritable Rubicon does exist between animals and man after all, as Professor Müller insisted when discussing the origins of language? Has a new factor been abruptly introduced into the evolutionary stream at some point between the Hominoidea and the Hominidae, constituting a true "barrier"? Can it be that Darwin was in error when he regarded the differences between man and animals as differences merely in degree?

The lessons gained from comparative linguistics would certainly suggest that there are serious differences "in kind" which interpose themselves at a late stage in evolution. We have been told that the contrasting of differences in kind and in degree is in itself an outmoded attitude. However that may be—and such argument is not easy to follow—it is tempting to doubt whether anything like a smooth gradation has occurred. Outside the domain of language there are other human endowments which are not readily traced in the animal series. As such, they scarcely pertain to our present subject-matter, unless it can be shown that their very existence depends upon the presence of a language system. Here, for example, may be placed the advent in man of what we might loosely term the various "moral faculties." Darwin was not oblivious of this problem, and he believed that a moral sense had been evolved from prehuman ancestors. This aspect of evolution was not mediated by a process of natural selection, however, but it arose from man's newly acquired power of reasoning. So then it is a mechanism of evolution additional to the ordinary natural selection. When early man became endowed with reason and when to that mental accomplishment was added the power of speech, then the way lay open for the operation of conscious purpose or the psychosocial factor. In this way there develops—again indirectly out of the beginnings of language—the beginnings of choice as to conduct. This also implies the power of doing harm as well as the power of doing good. So arise ethical and altruistic considerations. The earlier stages of these aspects of behaviour can be visualized in the animal kingdom in the instinct of maternal solicitude. This instinct is restricted—be it noted—in both time and place. With the achievement of adulthood, the young animal no longer receives maternal solicitude. The instinct, too, is limited to the immediate family group. Altruism extends from beyond the family circle to the clan only with the attainment of human status; and thence, with the growth of social conscience, it expands to embrace the tribe and eventually the nation. This act of stepping outside the strict family circle may doubtless be assisted—if not mediated—by the faculty of language.

Despite apparent superficial similarities between animal and human societies, the difference between them is profound: "Human social life is culturally, not biologically, determined." The triumph of intellect over instinct—of altruism over individualism—was demonstrably basic to our evolution.

5. The Origin of Society [1]

This discussion of the early phases of human society considers events that occurred a million years ago, in places not specifically determined, under circumstances known only by informed speculation. It will therefore be an exercise in inference, not in observation. This means juxtaposing the social life of man's closest relations—monkeys and apes—on the one side, with the organization of known primitive societies on the other. The gap that remains is then bridged by the mind.

No living primate can be directly equated with man's actual simian ancestor, and no contemporary primitive people is identical with our cultural ancestors. In both instances only generalized social traits—not particular, specialized ones—can be selected for historical comparison. On the primate side one must rely primarily on the few field reports of free-ranging groups and on certain pioneer studies of captive animals. These have covered the anthropoid apes, especially the gibbon and the chimpanzee (which are more closely related to man) as well as the New and Old World monkeys. On the human side the nearest contemporary approximations to the original cultural condition are societies of hunters and gatherers, preagricultural peoples exacting a meager livelihood from wild food resources. This cultural order dominated the Old Stone Age (one million to 10,000 or 15,000 years ago). Confidence in the comparative procedure which equates modern hunters and gatherers with the actual protagonists of the Stone Age is fortified by the remarkable social congruence observed among these peoples, even though they are historically as separated from one another as the Stone Age is distant from modern times. They include the Australian aborigines, the Bushmen of South Africa, the Andaman Islanders, the Shoshoni of the American Great Basin, the Eskimo, and Pygmy groups in Africa, Malaya and the Philippines.

Comparison of primate sociology with the findings of anthropological research immediately suggests a startling conclusion: The way people act, and probably have always acted, is not the expression of inherent human nature. There is a quantum difference, at points a complete opposition, between even the most rudimentary human society and the most advanced subhuman primate one. The discontinuity implies that the emergence of human society required some suppression, rather than a direct expression, of man's primate nature. Human social life is culturally, not biologically, determined.

This is not to slander the poor apes, to suggest that their social behavior is necessarily innate and unlearned. Yet it is clearly the product of their nature, of animal needs and reactions, physiological processes and psychological responses.

[1] MARSHALL D. SAHLINS, "The Origin of Society," in *Scientific American*, 203, No. 3 (1960), pp. 76–86. Reprinted with permission of the author and the publisher. Copyright © 1960 by Scientific American, Inc. All rights reserved.

Dr. Sahlins is Associate Professor of Anthropology at the University of Michigan.

Their social life therefore varies directly with the organic constitution of the individual and the horde. In an unchanging environment the social characteristics of a given subhuman primate species are unchanging, unless or until the species is organically transformed. The same cannot be said about human social arrangements. We are all one species, but our social orders grow and diversify, even within a constant environment, and they do so quite apart from the minor biological (racial) differences that develop among different peoples.

This liberation of human society from direct biological control was its great evolutionary strength. Culture saved man in his earliest days, clothed him, fed him and comforted him. In these times it has become possible to pile form on form in great social edifices that undertake to secure the survival of millions of people. Yet the remarkable aspect of culture's usurpation of the evolutionary task from biology was that in so doing it was forced to oppose man's primate nature on many fronts and to subdue it. It is an extraordinary fact that primate urges often become not the secure foundation of human social life, but a source of weakness in it.

The decisive battle between early culture and human nature must have been waged on the field of primate sexuality. The powerful social magnet of sex was the major impetus to subhuman primate sociability. This has long been recognized. But it was the British anatomist Sir Solly Zuckerman—whose attention to the matter developed from observation of the almost depraved behavior of baboons in zoos—who made sexuality the key issue of primate sociology. Subhuman primates are prepared to mate at all seasons, and although females show heightened receptivity midway through the menstrual cycle, they are often capable of sexual activity at other times.

Most significantly for the assessment of its historic role, year-round sex in higher primates is associated with year-round heterosexual social life. Among other mammals sexual activity, and likewise heterosexual society, is frequently confined to a comparatively brief breeding season.

Of course other important social activities go on in the subhuman primate horde. Group existence confers advantages, such as defense against predation, which transcend the gratification of erotic urges. In the evolutionary perspective the intense, long-term sexuality of the primate individual is the historic complement of the advantages of horde life. Nor, in considering subhuman primate sexuality, should attention be confined to coitus. The evidence grows that certain Old World monkeys—the closely related baboon, rhesus monkey and Japanese monkey—do have seasonal declines in breeding without cessation of horde life. But sex enters into subhuman primate social relations in a variety of forms, and heterosexual copulation is only one of them. Sexual mounting is involved in the establishment of dominance, which grows out of chronic competition for food, mates, and other desirable objects. It is a common element of youthful play; indeed, the female higher primate is unique among female mammals in displaying the adult sexual pattern prior to puberty. The familiar primate trait of mutual grooming—the pulling and licking out of parasites and other objects from the coat of another animal—often appears to be a secondary sexual activity. Sex is more than a force of attraction between adult males and females; it also operates among the young and between individuals of the same sex. Promiscuity is not an accurate term for it; it is indiscriminate. And while we might deem some of the forms perversions, to a monkey or an ape they are all just sociable.

Sex is not an unmitigated social blessing for primates. Competition over partners, for example, can lead to vicious, even fatal, strife. It was this side of primate sexuality that forced early culture to curb and repress it. The emerging human primate, in a life-and-death economic struggle with nature, could not afford the luxury of a social struggle. Co-operation, not competition, was essential. Culture thus brought primate sexuality under control. More than that, sex was made subject to regulations, such as the incest tabu, which effectively enlisted it in the service of co-operative kin relations. Among subhuman primates sex had organized society; the customs of hunters and gatherers testify eloquently that now society was to organize sex—in the interest of the economic adaptation of the group.

The evolution of the physiology of sex itself provided a basis for the cultural reorganization of social life. As Frank Beach of Yale University has pointed out, a progressive emancipation of sexuality from hormonal control runs through the primate order. This trend culminates in mankind, among whom sex is controlled more by the intellect— the cerebral cortex—than by glands. Thus it becomes possible to regulate sex by moral rules; to subordinate it to higher, collective ends. The consequent repression of primate sexuality in primitive as well as more developed societies has taken striking forms. In every human society sex is hedged by tabus: on time, place (the human animal alone demands privacy), on the sex and age of possible partners, on reference to sex in certain social contexts, on exposing the genitalia (particularly for females), on cohabitation during culturally important activities which range in different societies from war and ceremony to brewing beer. By way of an aside, it is notable that the repression of sex in favor of other ends is a battle which, while won for the spe

cies, is still joined in every individual to this day. In Sigmund Freud's famous allegory, the conflict between the self-seeking, sexually inclined id and the socially conscious superego re-enacts the development of culture that occurred in the remote past.

The design of many of these tabus is obvious: the disconcerting fascination of sex and its potentially disruptive consequences had to be eliminated from vital social activities. Thus the incest tabu is a guardian of harmony and solidarity within the family—a critical matter for hunters and gatherers, for among them the family is the fundamental economic as well as social group. At the same time, the injunction on sexual relations and marriage among close relatives necessarily forces different families into alliance and thus extends kinship and mutual aid.

It has been said that kinship, with its economic aspect of co-operation, became the plan for primitive human society. "Kinship" here means a cultural form, not a biological fact. Apes are of course genetically related to each other. But apes do not and cannot name and distinguish kinsmen, and they do not use kinship as a symbolic organization of behavior. On the other hand, cultural kinship has virtually nothing to do with biological connection. No one, for example, can be absolutely certain who his father is in a genetic sense, but in all human societies fatherhood is a fundamental social status. Almost all societies adhere, implicitly or explicitly, to the dictum of the Napoleonic code in this respect: the father of the child is the husband of the mother.

Many hunters and gatherers carry kinship to an extreme that is curious to us. By a device technically known as classificatory kinship they ignore genealogical differences between collateral and lineal kin at certain points, lumping them terminologically and in social be havior. Thus my father's brother may be "father" to me, and I act accordingly. Close kinship may be extended indefinitely by the same logic: My father's brother's son is my "brother," my grandfather's brother is my "grandfather," his son is my "father," his son my "brother," and so on. As one observer remarked of the Australian aborigines: "It is impossible for an Australian native to have anything whatever to do with anyone who is not his relative, of one kind or another, near or distant."

The subhuman primate horde varies in size among different species, ranging from groups in the hundreds among certain Old World monkeys to the much smaller groups, often smaller than 10, characteristic of anthropoid apes. The horde may stay together all the time, or it may scatter during daytime feeding into packs of various sorts—mate groups of males and females, females with young, males alone—and come together again at night resting places. Monkeys seem inclined to scatter in this way more than apes.

There are typically more adult females than adult males within the horde, sometimes, as in the case of the howler monkey, three times as many. This may be in part due to a faster maturation rate for females. It may also reflect the elimination of some males in the course of competition for mates. These males are not necessarily killed. They may lead a solitary life outside or on the fringes of the horde, attempting all the while to attach themselves to some group and acquire sexual partners.

The progressive emancipation of sex from hormonal control in the primate order that was noted by Beach seems to be paralleled by a progressive development from promiscuous mating to the formation of exclusive, permanent heterosexual partnerships between specific animals. Among certain New World monkeys, females with their young comprise a separate pack within the horde, and only when a female is in heat does she forsake this group for males. She does not become attached to a specific male, but, wearing them out in turn, goes from one to another. The Old World rhesus horde and mate relations are similar except that a receptive female is taken over primarily by dominant males, a step in the direction of exclusiveness. In the anthropoid gibbon the trend toward exclusiveness is fully developed: the entire horde is typically composed of an adult male, a permanent female consort and their young. As yet it is not safe to state unequivocally that such progressive change runs through the entire primate order. It does appear that the higher subhuman primates presage the human family more than do the lower.

The primate horde is practically a closed social group. Each horde has a territory, and local groups of most species defend their ground (or trees) against encroachment by others of their kind. The typical relation between adjacent hordes is that of enmity, especially, it seems, if food is short. Their borders are points of social deflection, and contact between neighbors is often marked by belligerent vocal cries, if it does not erupt into fatal violence.

Territorial relations among neighboring human hunting-and-gathering bands (a term used technically to refer to the cohesive local group) offer an instructive contrast. The band territory is never exclusive. Individuals and families may shift from group to group, especially in those habitats where food resources fluctuate from year to year and from place to place. In addition, a great deal of interband hospitality and visiting is undertaken for purely social and ceremonial reasons. Although bands remain autonomous politically, a general notion of tribalism, based on similarity in language and custom and on social collaboration, develops among neighboring groups. These tendencies are powerfully reinforced by kinship and the cultural regulation of sex and marriage. Among all modern survivors of the Stone Age, marriage with close relatives is forbidden, while marriage outside the band is at least preferred and sometimes morally prescribed. The kin ties thereby created become social pathways of mutual aid and solidarity connecting band to band. It does not seem unwarranted to assert that the human capacity to extend kinship was a necessary social condition for the deployment of early man over the great expanses of the planet.

Another implication of interband kinship deserves emphasis: Warfare is limited among hunters and gatherers. Indeed, many are reported to find the idea of war incomprehensible. A massive military effort would be difficult to sustain for technical and logistic reasons. But war is even further inhibited by the spread of a social relation—kinship—which in primitive society is often a synonym for "peace." Thomas Hobbes's famous fantasy of a war of "all against all" in the natural state could not be further from the truth. War increases in intensity, bloodiness, duration and significance for social survival through the evolution of culture, reaching its culmination in modern civilization. Paradoxically the cruel belligerence that is popularly considered the epitome of human nature reaches its zenith in the human condition most removed from the pristine. By contrast, it has been remarked of the Bushmen that "it is not in their nature to fight."

The only permanent organization within the band is the family, and the band is a grouping of related families, on the average 20 to 50 people altogether. Bands lack true government and law; the rules of good order are synonymous with customs of proper behavior toward kinsmen. In certain ways this system of etiquette is even more effective than law. A breach of etiquette cannot go undetected, and punishment in the form of avoidance, gossip and ridicule follows hard upon offense.

The primitive human family, unlike the subhuman primate mate group, is not based simply on sexual attraction. Sex is easily available in many band societies, both before and outside marriage, but this alone does not necessarily create or destroy the family. The incest tabu itself implies that the human family cannot be the social outcome of erotic urges. Moreover, sexual rights to a wife may even be waived in the interest of securing friendly relations with other men, as in the famous Eskimo custom of wife lending. This, incidentally, is only one cultural device among many for enlisting marriage and sex in the creation of wide social alliance. In remarkable contrast to subhuman primate unions, often created and maintained in violence, marriage is in band society a means of securing peace. Adultery and quarrels over women are not unknown among primitive peoples. But such actions are explicitly considered antisocial. Among monkeys and apes, on the other hand, comparable events create the social order.

Marriage and the family are institutions too important in primitive life to be built on the fragile, shifting foundations of "love." The family is the decisive economic institution of society. It is to the hunter and gatherer what the manor was to feudal Europe, or the corporate factory system is to capitalism: it is the productive organization. The primary division of labor in band economy is that between men and women. The men typically hunt and make weapons; the women gather wild plants and take care of the home and children. Marriage then is an alliance between the two essential social elements of production. These factors complement each other—the Eskimos say: "A man is the hunter his wife makes him"—and they lock their possessors in enduring marital and familial relations. Many anthropologists have testified that in the minds of the natives the ability to cook and sew or to hunt are much more important than is beauty in a prospective spouse.

The economic aspect of primitive marriage is responsible for many of its specific characteristics. For one thing, it is the normal adult state; one cannot economically afford to remain single. Hence the solitary subhuman primate male has no counterpart in the primitive band. The number of spouses is, however, limited by economic considerations among primitives. A male ape has as many mates as it can get and defend for itself; a man, no more than he can support. In fact, marriage is usually monogamous among hunters and gatherers, although there are normally no rules against polygamy. Culture, reflecting the compulsions of economics, thus dramatically altered human mating and differentiated the human family from its nearest primate analogues.

"Peck orders" of dominance and subordination are characteristic of subhuman primate social relations. Chronic competition for mates and perhaps food or other desirable objects establishes and maintains such hierarchies in every grouping of monkeys and apes. Repeated victory secures future privileges for a dominant animal; subordinates, by conditioned response, withdraw from or yield access to anything worth having. As Henry W. Nissen of the Yerkes Laboratories of Primate Biology has observed, "the bigger animal gets most of the food; the stronger male, most of the females." In most species males tend to dominate over females, although in certain anthropoid apes, notably the chimpanzee and the gibbon, the reverse can occur. A difference in what has been called dominance quality seems to arise between primate suborders: in New World monkeys, dominance is "tenuous"; in Old World monkeys it may become "rough" and "brutal"; in apes, while clearly apparent, it is not so violently established or sustained. In all species, however, dominance affects a variety of social activities, including play, grooming and interhorde relations as well as sex and feeding.

Compared both to subhuman primate antecedents and to subsequent cultural developments, dominance is at its nadir among primitive hunters and gatherers. Culture is the oldest "equalizer." Among animals capable of symbolic communication, the weak can always collectively connive to overthrow the strong. On the other side, political and economic means of tyranny remain underdeveloped among hunters and gatherers.

There is some evolutionary continuity in dominance behavior from primate to primitive; among hunters and gatherers leadership, such as it is, falls to men. Yet the supremacy of men in the band as a whole does not necessarily mean the adject subordination of women in the home. Once more the weapon of articulate speech must be reckoned with; the Danish anthropologist Kaj Birket-Smith observes: "A census would certainly show a higher percentage of henpecked husbands among the Eskimos than in a civilized country (except, perhaps, the U. S.!); most Eskimos have a deeply rooted respect for their wives' tongues."

The men who lead the band are the wiser and older. They are not, however, respected for their ability to commandeer limited supplies of desired goods. On the contrary, generosity is a necessary qualification for prestige; the man who does most for the band, who sacrifices most, will be the one most loved and heeded by the rest. The test of status among hunters and gatherers is usually the reverse of that among monkeys and apes;

it is a matter of who gives away, not who takes away. A second qualification for leadership is knowledge—knowledge of ritual, tradition, game movements, terrain and the other things that control social life. This is why older men are respected. In a stable society they know more than the others, and to be "old-fashioned" is a great virtue.

Knowledge of itself breeds little power. The headmen of a band can rule only by advice, not by fiat. As a Congo Pygmy leader bluntly remarked to an anthropologist, there is just no point in giving orders, "as nobody would heed them." The titles of reference given leaders of hunting and gathering bands speak eloquently of their powers: the Shoshoni leader is "the talker," and his Eskimo counterpart is "he who thinks." In a primitive band each family is a more cohesive, stronger polity than the band as a whole, and each is free to manage its own affairs. Birket-Smith said: "There is no rank or class among the Eskimos, who must therefore renounce that satisfaction, which Thackeray calls the true pleasure of life, of associating with one's inferiors." The same may be said of other primitive societies.

The leveling of the social order that accompanied the development of culture is related to the fundamental economic change from the selfish—literally rugged —individualism of the primate to cooperative kin dealings. Monkeys and apes do not co-operate economically; monkeys cannot even be taught by humans to work together, although apes can. Nor is food ever shared except in the sense that a subordinate animal may be intimidated into handing it over to a dominant one. Among primitives, on the other hand, food sharing follows automatically from the division of labor by sex. More than that, the family economy is a pooling of goods and services—"communism in living" as a famous 19th-century anthropologist called it. Mutual aid is extended far beyond the family. It is a demand of group survival that the successful hunter be prepared to share his spoils with the unsuccessful. "The hunter kills, other people have," say the Yukaghir of Siberia.

In a band economy goods commonly pass from hand to hand, and the circulation gains momentum in proportion to the degree of kinship among households and the importance of the goods for survival. Food, the basic resource, must always be made available to others on pain of ostracism; the scarcer it becomes, the more readily it must be given away, and for nothing. In addition, food and other things are often shared to promote friendly relations, utilitarian considerations notwithstanding. There was a time in human affairs when the only right of property that brought honor was that of giving it away.

The economic behavior of primitives obviously does not conform to the stereotype of "economic man" by which we organize and analyze our own economy. But it does conform to a realm of economics familiar to us, so familiar that no one bothers to talk about it and it lacks an economic science: kinship-friendship economics. There is much to be learned about primitive economics here, and it would not be a mere exercise in analogy, for our kin life is the evolutionary survival of relations that once encompassed society itself.

In selective adaptation to the perils of the Stone Age, human society overcame or subordinated such primate propensities as selfishness, indiscriminate sexuality, dominance and brute competition. It substituted kinship and co-operation for conflict, placed solidarity over sex, morality over might. In its earliest days it accomplished the greatest reform in history, the overthrow of human primate nature, and thereby secured the evolutionary future of the species.

SECTION **II**

THE FOSSIL RECORD

Becoming fully human has taken a long time—very nearly two million years. We know that we humans are, in a sense, ex-apes. But we have not yet identified with certainty all the apes, man-apes, and ape-men from whom we are descended. It is likely that the sequence of our evolutionary egression has not been so conveniently unilinear. As a consequence our problem is probably not to discover a single "missing link" but to get a better idea of the particular crowd from which we are descended—one comprised first of varying kinds of apes coexisting and occasionally inter-breeding, some of whom were the parents of the varying kinds of man-apes coexisting and occasionally interbreeding, some of whom produced the vary-ing kinds of ape-men who also coexisted and occasionally interbred, for thousands and thousands of years, producing among their descendants some individuals rather like ourselves. They were more nearly "human" than their fellows. They were more clever and cultured, and thus better able to survive, and, ultimately, to produce our own more immediate *sapient* human ancestors.

Although we still lack a neat serial listing of all the prehuman beings from whom we are descended, we have found the fossil remains of several

66

apes and a number of near men and men who were clearly ancestral to our own genus and species.

On this fossil record, our Pliocene pongid progenitors—the apes living just prior to the beginning of the Pleistocene—have so far been elusive. However, we strongly suspect that they lived in Africa, like our earliest hominid ancestors. And we have a good general idea of what they must have been like.

1. Reconstructing Man's Pliocene Pongid Ancestor [1]

Although the time span during which the ape to man transition took place is not known today with any precision, several lines of evidence seem to indicate the place as somewhere in Africa. One of the strongest lines of evidence is the fact that, since the time of Huxley, it has been generally recognized that man is closest anatomically to the great apes of Africa, the gorilla and the chimpanzee. More recently it has been shown that he is also serologically closest to these two apes. If these similarities indicate a close common ancestry, then the problem arises as to how such a generalized ape could have adapted to the bipedal, carnivorous ecological niche which the early hominids appear to have occupied and which distinguishes them sharply from all known apes. This paper will attempt to reconstruct this transition from ape to man by a consideration of certain ecological, behavioral, and anatomical evidence. This evidence seems to imply that an ape with a way of life similar to that of the mountain gorilla would have been the most plausible ancestor.

One of the basic assumptions of this paper is that an open grassland or woodland environment was a necessary prerequisite for the development of bipedalism. A second assumption, which has considerable evidence in its favor, is that

geographic isolation was another necessary prerequisite for the speciation and ecological divergence of this ape population from its neighbors. The gradual decrease in the area covered by tropical forest was also one of the necessary factors, but the development of bipedalism would probably not have occurred on the fringe of the forest since this area would not be separated from the forest. Hence, a tract of forest and a group of forest-living apes must have been cut off from their relatives by some natural phenomenon. Two such natural phenomena during the Pliocene in Africa which may have been implicated are the spread of the Kalahari Desert and the tectonic activity in the Rift Valley region.

The question of which ape was so cut off, or really which modern ape is closest to that one which was cut off, can be best answered by a consideration of the ecology of these modern apes. For a statement of the ecological principles which I think bear on this question, I can do no better than to quote extensively from Audy:

Another type is due to the fact that the edge is frequently itself a distinct community, differing significantly from the vegetation on either side—this is a fringe-habitat.

Edge-specific, edge preferring, and edge-avoiding species can be recognized.

[1] FRANK B. LIVINGSTONE, "Reconstructing Man's Pliocene Pongid Ancestor," in *American Anthropologist*, 64 (1962), pp. 301–305, © American Anthropological Association. Reprinted by permission of the author and the publisher.

Dr. Livingstone is Associate Professor of Anthropology at the University of Michigan.

The application of these principles to the apes of Africa indicates that the gorilla is not adapted to the tropical forest but is an edge-specific—or at least an edge-preferring—species which occupies the fringe habitat around the tropical forest. On the other hand, the chimpanzee with its wide distribution throughout the tropical forest is well-adapted to this vegetational zone. The coastal and mountain gorillas are now in areas which are covered by a great deal of tropical forest, but in the center of the distribution of each of these sub-species is a large montane area which is a fringe-habitat. The expansion of these animals into the tropical forest seems to have been for the most part the result of man's cutting down and destroying large areas of tropical forest and thus creating a fringe-habitat out of much of this area. However, gorillas have also spread extensively along rivers in the tropical forest, but this too is a fringe-habitat. The preceding view of the ecology of the mountain gorilla is demonstrated rather conclusively by Emlen and Schaller's recent study of the distribution of this species.

The fact that the mountain gorilla is adapted to this fringe-habitat is reflected in its anatomical characteristics. In contrast to the brachiating ability of the chimpanzee, the gorilla is more of a terrestrial animal, and its foot with its elongated calcaneum and less opposable great toe approaches most closely in these respects to the human foot. In addition, the greater size and sexual dimorphism of the gorilla indicate that it relies to a greater extent on defending itself against enemies rather than escaping to the trees. When these characteristics of the gorilla are considered in conjunction with certain behavioral characteristics, these adaptations to the fringe-habitat around the tropical forest can be viewed as pre-adaptations to the open savanna and the carnivore niche in that habitat. In addition, an animal which occupies a fringe-habitat, which is more unstable, is more likely to get cut off from the tropical forest and its surrounds.

Although the gorilla's basic mode of locomotion is quadrupedal, there are occasions when the animal is bipedal. These usually occur in its behavior toward other animals. The gorilla is famous for its chest-thumping and even the females of the species participate in this behavior at times. During this chest-thumping the gorilla will be standing on its hind legs or perhaps squatting. Chest-thumping has been observed in many circumstances but one of the most common is in threatening other animals. This activity is accompanied by charging, but contact is rather rare since the gorilla is generally more of a bluffer than an aggressor. During the chest-thumping the gorilla is bipedal, and in addition the gorilla charges on its hind legs and then grasps or hits its enemy with its forelimbs and also bites. Thus, although some observers have seen gorillas charging over long distances on all fours, just prior to attacking the gorilla is always bipedal. The gorilla bites frequently when attacking but its most effective weapon is the tremendous strength of its forelimbs, one swipe of which can kill a man. This is also true of many carnivores whose major lethal weapon is a blow of the forepaws. The fact is that the gorilla is strikingly bipedal when attacking. His behavior is thus remarkably pre-adapted to the carnivorous, bipedal, open grassland ecological niche which the early hominids appear to have occupied. Since the gorilla's major weapon is his forelimbs, and in this he contrasts with the chimpanzee who usually bites, he would also seem to be pre-adapted to the tool-using habits of the hominids.

Washburn has postulated that the Australopithecines probably were not fully bipedal since they could not walk or balance efficiently. Instead, they probably would squat, get up and run, and then squat again. It can be seen that the gorilla in his attacks on other animals is very close to this mode of locomotion even today, although, of course, time, tool-making, and a very hominid skeleton separate the Australopithecines from the gorilla. More importantly, these two species are widely separated by their very distant ecological niches. However, the adaptation of an ape population with a way of life similar to that of the gorilla to one like that of the Australopithecines seems a very distinct possibility.

When, in the absence of its normal food supply, a gorilla-like ape first began carnivorous practices, it had to rely on its charging ability and powerful forearms to obtain food. As natural selection for this altered way of life began to change the hindquarters, it would also most likely result in the use of tools, and particularly stones, carried in the hand to increase the efficiency of the forelimbs for predation. Natural selection would have also acted on the mental characteristics of this ape population, since modern gorillas and apes in general are ill-suited psychologically to a carnivorous way of life. The gorilla's aggresive behavior is mostly bluff and when he attacks he is a very inefficient killer con-

sidering his strength. Raven's account of an attack on a native by a gorilla illustrates this inefficiency and inability to "follow through." Although the gorilla has a formidable bite and powerful jaws, it does not rely on these as its primary weapons of defense and offense against *other* species. The powerful jaws appear to be more of an adaptation to the cracking of very hard nuts and the peeling and crushing of wood to get at the pith and heart of many shrubs. The increasing reliance on "soft" meat for food and on the forearms for predation would most likely result in the reduction of the jaws, and this has certainly been the trend from the Dryopithecines to Gigantopithecus to the Australopithecines. In this way natural selection for this changed way of life could have produced the hominids and the trend of hominid evolution from a generalized ape similar to the mountain gorilla. One further possible implication of this reconstruction is that prior to the use of wooden spears, which appear early in the Pleistocene, the forelimbs of the early hominids should have been comparatively longer and stronger. Thus, the finds of forelimb bones from either Gigantopithecus or the early Australopithecines may settle this question.

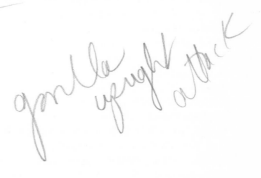

The first of our known ancestors to develop the capacity for culture was an African—a tool-maker and user—and a member of the Australopithecine subfamily of the Hominidae, the family of man. His body apparently looked rather like ours, and some fascinating things were happening in his head. Questions about the details of his pedigree and the extent of his ability to use culture are the subject of an important and persistent controversy.

2. The Australopithecines [1]

South Africa has played a significant part in the piecing together of the story of the evolution of man by providing a large proportion of the known evidence relating to the very early chapters of this story. The evidence has been of several sorts, but here I refer chiefly to fossil remains of early members of the family of man. In this paper I shall be concerned to outline some of the major features of what has so far been learned about the australopithecines and how they fit into the evolutionary story of man.

The first australopithecine specimen came into scientific hands 36 years ago— the story of this and later discoveries has been told often and will not be repeated here. For roughly thirty of those years considerable controversy existed as to the nature of these creatures. In the last few years fairly general agreement has been reached that the australopithecines truly belong with the family of man and not among the apes. Emphasis has now shifted to attempts to evaluate the nature of the relationship to true man and from the early majority view that they were nothing but apes, the pendulum has now swung almost to the other extreme with the rapidly growing tendency to regard them as the earliest true man. I shall put before you a view which is less extreme than either of these.

THE MAJOR PREHOMININE FEATURES

The australopithecines are roughly intermediate in grade of organization between the small-brained pongids and the large-brained, bipedal hominines. They were erect-walking but had small brains. Well over 300 specimens, representing nearly a hundred individuals, are now known from South Africa. A small amount of material; less than a dozen specimens, is known from East Africa and the Far East. This is a good sample, palaeontoolgically speaking, and has given much information about variation and other population characteristics. This is important since it is not individuals that evolve but populations and it is the business of the palaeontologist to try to get back from the bits of individuals which comprise his material to the charcteristics of the populations to which those individuals belonged.

The evidence for erect posture in the prehominines is good. The pelvis is known from one almost complete specimen as well as a number of incomplete ones and it differs markedly from the pongid or monkey type but only very insignificantly from the hominine type. The lumbar region of the spinal column, the proximal and distal ends of the

[1] J. T. ROBINSON, "The Australopithecines and Their Bearing on the Origin of Man and of Stone Tool-Making," in *South African Journal of Science*, 57 (1961), pp. 3–13, © South African Association for the Advancement of Science. Reprinted by permission of the author and the publisher.

Dr. Robinson is Professor of Anthropology and Zoology at the University of Wisconsin.

685

femur, and the nature and orientation of the occiput all add to the evidence which shows that the australopithecines were functionally and structurally well adapted to erect posture and locomotion.

The dentition provides considerable evidence of hominid affinity. The anterior teeth are small and compact and built closely on the hominine pattern. Even the canines are within the size range of hominines. Other teeth which are especially diagnostic are the first lower premolar, first lower deciduous molar, and deciduous canine. In pongids the first two are semisectorial teeth usually having one prominent cusp, though a second may be partially developed. In the prehominines and hominines the premolar is bicuspid and the deciduous molar well molarized, with five cusps, as in the permanent molars. Sophisticated statistical analysis of the deciduous canines has shown that the prehominine teeth are easily and sharply distinguished from the pongid form while they closely resemble, and in some cases are indistinguishable from, the hominine form.

These—and other—telling morophological features clearly indicate close affinity with hominines. But the small brain indicates a more primitive condition. The endocranial volume appears to be only about 500 cm^3—I know of no sound evidence at present indicating a brain significantly larger than this. The range was evidently about 450–550 cm^3 and therefore well below the pongid maximum of 685 cm^3. The early hominines appear to have had endocranial volumes averaging from about 900–1100 cm^3, though estimated volumes as low as 755 cm^3 have been given.

Along with this small endocranial volume in the prehominines the braincase is relatively small and the face relatively prognathous. It is therefore evident that an important feature of hominines—the enlarged brain and the consequent modifications in skull architecture—was not yet significantly developed in the known prehominines.

TAXONOMIC DIFFERENTIATION WITHIN THE PREHOMININES

It is common at present to regard the prehominines as comprising a single rather variable group without any significant differentiation. A considerable volume of evidence exists which shows that this is not the case. Two different forms are known in South Africa at present: *Australopithecus* occurs at Taung, Sterkfontein, and Makapansgat, and *Paranthropus* at Kromdraai and Swartkrans. It is important to realize that the largest *Paranthropus* sample, 160 specimens from Swartkrans, occurs less than a mile from Sterkfontein which yielded the largest sample of *Australopithecus*—108 specimens. Geographic variation can therefore be disregarded in this case.

Australopithecus has a dolichocephalic skull with a good hominine shape. A distinct, low forehead is present and the vertex rises well above the level of the brow ridges. The latter are poorly developed and the postorbital constriction is moderately developed. The face is fairly wide, the nasal region is slightly raised above the surrounding level of the face, which is distinctly prognathous. The skull is gracile, without any heavy bone or strong development of ridges or crests. The mandible is robust with a moderately high ramus and an almost vertical chin region. The dentition is morphologically very similar to that of early hominines. Molars and premolars are well developed and the canines are fairly large but do not protrude because they are recessed into the jaw to a greater extent than the other teeth. The proportions along the tooth row are typical of early hominines.

Paranthropus is very different. Although the endocranial volume appears to differ insignificantly from that of *Australopithecus,* the skull architecture is markedly dissimilar. The skull is brachycephalic, with no trace of a forehead; the frontal passes straight back from the well developed supraorbital torus in a manner reminiscent of the condition in the gorilla. The vertex rises very little above the upper level of the orbits. Le Gros Clark devised an index to measure this feature in primate skulls and it places *Paranthropus* right in the middle of the pongid range while *Australopithecus* is well outside this position and very near to modern man. In all known adults with the appropriate area preserved a sagittal crest is present—occupying roughly the middle third of the distance from glabella to inion. The degree of postorbital constriction is relatively greater than in *Australopithecus* and the zygomatic arches stand out well away from the braincase. The face is massive and wide. The enormously robust cheek bones actually project further forward than does the nose, which is completely flat. The face is appreciably less prognathous than in *Australopithecus.* The lower jaw is massive with a very high and vertical ramus. A most curious situation is found to exist in the dentition. The postcanine teeth are massive, being distinctly more robust than those of *Australopithecus,* but the canines and incisors are distinctly smaller than in the latter form. There is thus a sharp change in proportion between the anterior teeth and the postcanine teeth which is unique in the hominids.

Paranthropus thus has a very robust skull with enormous development of bone and a curiously spheroidal braincase with strong development of rugosites and crests, a very wide, dished face, and the dentition is specialized quite differently to that in *Australopithecus.* These descriptions are based on female skulls in both cases, but sexual dimor-phism does not appear to be well developed. Furthermore *Paranthropus* was a very heavily built, muscular animal which probably stood over five feet in height and must have weighed a few hundred pounds. *Australopithecus* clearly was very small and slenderly built—the female apparently being no more than about four feet in height and weighing only some 40–50 lbs.

Besides these differences—which are obvious enough—there are other important dental differences. The first lower deciduous molar in *Australopithecus* is of the same type as is found in all known hominines, having a characteristic specialization of the anterior half of the crown. *Paranthropus* is unique in the primates in having a completely molarized deciduous first lower molar without any trace of the specializations seen in *Australopithecus* and all hominines. The deciduous canines also differ considerably in the two forms.

The differences in skull architecture can be explained primarily in terms of differences of dental and dietary specialization. *Paranthropus* has very heavy crushing and grinding cheek teeth and the anterior teeth are less important, being appreciably reduced in size. This implies a vegetarian diet which requires considerable bulk to provide the necessary nutritive value. Much chewing is required to comminute the often tough plant material. Enlargement of cheek teeth with specialization for crushing and grinding are common features of creatures adapted to vegetarian diet. *Paranthropus* apparently also ate roots and bulbs since there is clear evidence of grit in the diet, in the form of small chips and flakes of enamel which have broken off from the occlusal margins of the tooth crowns. The powerful chewing forces which must have been involved have resulted in great thickening of the bone in which the cheek teeth are set and along the avenues through which the

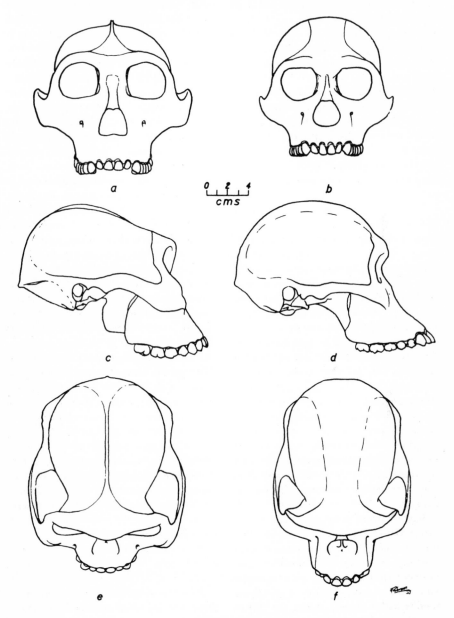

Figure 1. Comparison between skulls of females of *Paranthropus* (*a, c, e*) and *Australopithecus* (*b, d, f*). The former series is based largely on SK 48 from Swartkrans; the latter on Sts 5 from Sterkfontein.

chewing forces are dissipated—such as the palate, the cheek bones, and jugal arches, lateral parts of the supraorbital torus and the pterygoids. Also the heavy jaws needed powerful muscles, hence there is further robustness introduced in such areas as the origin and insertion of the masseter and pterygoid muscles. The relation of large temporal muscles to small braincase was such that even females apparently normally had a sagittal crest. On the other hand the very small anterior teeth result in a face which does not protrude forwards at all markedly.

Australopithecus, on the other hand, has none of these extreme modifications. Both skull shape and structure and especially dental morphology are closely comparable to the early hominine condition. It therefore seems reasonable to conclude that the diet of this form was essentially the same as that of early hominines—i.e., they were omnivores eating both flesh and vegetable matter. This was probably the sort of diet still found in hunters and food-gatherers of today.

The adaptive difference between these two forms is thus considerable. Their ecological requirements and direction of evolution were quite different. The degree of difference between them in these respects was of a distinctly greater order than that between any two of the living pongids. This is precisely the sort of difference which is regarded by modern mammalian systematists as excellent grounds for generic separation. It is interesting to notice that there is good evidence indicating that the vegetarian *Paranthropus* was present in the Sterkfontein valley in times when the climate was apparently significantly wetter than when the more carnivorous *Australopithecus* lived there.

Recently Leakey has found a fine australopithecine skull at Olduvai in East Africa and has given it a new generic name, "Zinjanthropus." He regards it as more advanced than either of the australopithecines already dealt with. However it is very clear that this form has all the major features already described for *Paranthropus*. The same pattern of modification of the skull architecture as a consequence of a specialized vegetarian diet is clearly developed. No valid grounds appear to exist for regarding this form as anything other than a typical *Paranthropus*.

Some mandibular fragments from Sangiran in Java, which have been called "Meganthropus" and regarded as members of the Pithecanthropus group, seem to me manifestly also to belong to the genus *Paranthropus*. They agree very closely with the equivalent parts of *Paranthropus* from South Africa—in almost every known feature the morphology is identical with that in *Paranthropus*—up to and including the greatly reduced anterior teeth coupled with very large cheek teeth.

Paranthropus therefore appears to have been spread across the width of the Old World with little modification. *Australopithecus* is not known from quite so far afield yet, but it is also known from near Olduvai and probably from Olduvai as well. One specimen found in 1938 by Kohl-Larsen in the Laetolil beds near Lake Eyassi is fairly clearly an *Australopithecus*. Some recent finds by Leakey at Olduvai, especially the adolescent mandible from the bottom of Bed I, appear also to belong to this genus.

TELANTHROPUS

From among the large number of *Paranthropus* remains which have come from Swartkrans I found a fragmentary upper and lower jaw of apparently the same individual and another almost complete mandible with a few other fragments of what clearly is a different type of hominid. This has been called *Telan-*

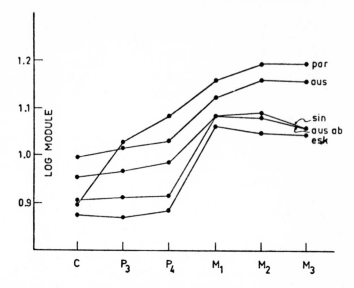

Figure 2. Size comparison of some mandibular teeth in five hominids. *par = Paranthropus*, aus = *Australopithecus*, sin = Pekin man, aus ab = Australian aborigine, and esk = East Greenland Eskimo. This illustrates very clearly the aberrant nature of the *Paranthropus* dentition in which a marked change of proportion between the anterior and postcanine teeth occurs between the canine and first premolar. (After Robinson)

thropus and in my opinion represents a hominine, not an australopithecine.

The teeth are distinctly smaller than those of either australopithecine and agree in size very closely with those of the hominine from Java and Pekin now generally known as *Pithecanthropus*. The canine crowns were about the size of those of *Paranthropus,* but the roots were much reduced compared to those of either of the australopithecines. As well there are a few important characters which are found only among hominines but not among australopithecines. These are: (1) the structure of the nasal cavity floor and the premaxillary face of the maxilla, (2) the wide U-shape of the mandibular contour with wide interramal distance, (3) the small distance between the occlusal plane and the mandibular articulation with the skull, and (4) the slender construction of the man-

dible. None of these features can be matched in the australopithecines. In some respects *Telanthropus* is actually more advanced than the Pekin hominine. On the other hand, in no known feature is *Telanthropus* less advanced than the australopithecines. If the science of comparative morphology means anything, then *Telanthropus* must be classed with that group with which it shows closest and most fundamental resemblance, the hominines. *Telanthropus* is often passed over lightly on the grounds that since so few specimens are known its affinities cannot be determined. It should be remembered that these few specimens occur right among the two largest australopithecine samples known and therefore in the most favorable possible situation for determining whether this form is an australopithecine or not. Here again geographic variation does not

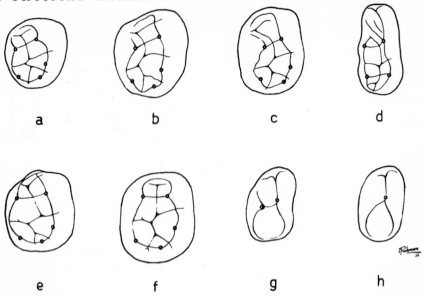

a   b   c   d

e   f   g   h

Figure 3. Basic cusp and fissure patterns in mandibular first deciduous molars of (*a*) European (Netherlands); (*b*) Bantu; (*c*) Bush; (*d*) baboon (*Papio*); (*e*) *Australopithecus;* (*f*) *Paranthropus;* and (*g, h*) chimpanzee. All to same scale. The specialized pattern of the hominines (*a, b, c*) is also present in *Australopithecus* but not at all in *Paranthropus.* The pongid teeth (*g, h*) are very different from those of hominids.

enter into the matter and apparently time differences are also not involved. Furthermore, although not much is known about the variation in *Telanthropus,* a great deal is known about that of both *Paranthropus* and *Australopithecus* from that locality.

STONE TOOLS ASSOCIATED WITH AUSTRALOPITHECINES

The cultural level attained by the australopithecines is of great interest. Professor Dart has argued that much evidence points to the australopithecines having used bones, horns, and teeth as implements and weapons. One may, I think, accept this in principle, but with two reservations: (a) the case should not be carried beyond the legitimate evi-

dence; (b) the evidence so far available is primarily concerned with *Australopithecus* and does not necessarily apply equaly to *Paranthropus.* It seems fair to conclude, therefore, that at least *Australopithecus,* and possibly also *Paranthropus,* were tool-users, bearing in mind that upon occasion the distinction between tool-using and tool-making can be rather fine.

But in 1956 Dr. Brain found some evidence of a stone industry in loose breccia at Sterkfontein and in 1957-8, in two seasons of excavation there, I was able to demonstrate for the first time the direct association of an australopithecine (*Australopithecus*) and a true stone industry. This placed a different complexion on the matter; most students accepted that *Australopithecus* must have been a stone toolmaker. The recent discovery by Dr.

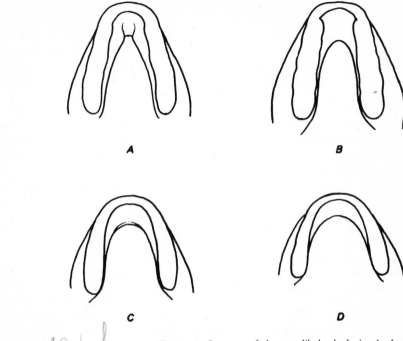

Figure 4. Contours of the mandibular body in *A, Australopithecus*; *B, Paranthropus*; *C,* "Telanthropus" (*Homo erectus*); and *D, Homo sapiens* (modern American white). Both australopithecines have a narrow interramal distance anteriorly; "Telanthropus" has the hominine condition in this respect. (After Robinson)

Leakey of a stone industry with his Olduvai *Paranthropus* seems to have clinched the matter in the minds of most workers, who are now convinced that the australopithecines were stone toolmakers and state so without reservation.

However it seems to me, as I have pointed out elsewhere, that this is far too facile a view of the situation. At Sterkfontein there is a considerable depth of deposit, which has yielded a hundred specimens of *Australopithecus* and not a trace of stone artifacts or even foreign stone. Unconformably overlying this is breccia which is demonstrably more recent by both faunal and lithological evidence. It nevertheless still contains *Australopithecus* but also a genuine stone industry, mainly in rock foreign to the immediate neighborhood of the excavation. Furthermore, this industry is not of extreme primitiveness—it is not the very beginnings of tool-making, but appears to belong to the earliest levels of the handaxe culture, as Dr. R. Mason of the Archaeological Survey, Johannesburg, has shown. So at the same site we have evidence of considerable depth of deposit with the largest sample of *Australopithecus* specimens known but no evidence of a stone industry, followed by a small time gap, after which *Australopithecus* still occurs but with a fully fledged stone industry. The time gap appears to correspond closely in age with the *Australopithecus* deposit at Makapansgat, where tons of breccia have so far yielded no such stone industry as that at Sterkfontein. So roughly 96 per cent. of the known South African material of

Australopithecus is not associated with stone implements, but suddenly a clear stone industry, representing an early stage of the Chelles-Acheul culture, appears towards the close of Sterkfontein time. Where did it come from? It seems to me that the only explanation can be that a toolmaker invaded the Sterkfontein valley during the time represented by the unconformity—and that invader could not have been *Australopithecus* as he had already been there for a long time.

It seems anything but coincidence that the stone artifacts turn up in the Sterkfontein valley at just about the time that the remains of *Telanthropus* also appear in the valley, less than a mile away at Swartkrans. As we have seen, *Telanthropus* has some major features which can be matched only among tool-making hominines, but not among the australopithecines. What more logical than that *Telanthropus* was the invading toolmaker? It is of interest to note that at Sangiran in Java, *Pithecanthropus*, a toolmaker, occurs side-by-side with *Paranthropus*, the vegetarian and least manlike australopithecine. At Swartkrans we find *Telanthropus*, also a hominine and in my opinion a toolmaker, side-by-side with *Paranthropus*. In North Africa at Ternifine *Pithecanthropus* is again present with a slightly more advanced form of the Chelles-Acheul culture than that at Sterkfontein. This is the opinion of Dr. Mason, who has examined both industries.

What, then, of the Olduvai specimen and the stone artifacts found with it? This site is directly on the migration route south to the Transvaal and the Sterkfontein valley and it seems impossible for the tool-making hominine, *Telanthropus*, to be present down here without it having been present at some stage in East Africa also. If *Australopithecus* occurs with stone tools and is not their maker, then this can as easily be true of the Olduvai individual. A powerful argument, in my opinion, against the Olduvai *Paranthropus* being a stone toolmaker is that it is a specialized vegetarian and vegetarians have little need for manufactured stone tools. If either of the australopithecines were to be toolmakers it is far more likely to be the partly carnivorous *Australopithecus*. If *it* is not, as clearly seems the case from the Sterkfontein evidence, it is improbable in the extreme that the vegetarian *Paranthropus* would be. Australopithecines, it will also be recalled, had small brains well within the pongid size range. Finally, a characteristic feature of the earlier levels of the stone age culture sequence is the exasperating fact that remains of the makers of the tools are so exceedingly rare. Why then, if the australopithecines were toolmakers, should their remains be so common and stone tools rare when the normal experience is exactly the reverse? This seems a further argument against any of the australopithecines being toolmakers. On the other hand *Telanthropus* remains *are* very rare and this fits in with the general picture.

I submit therefore, that there is no good evidence in support of the thesis that australopithecines were stone toolmakers but that there is very pertinent evidence against it, favoring the idea that this group consisted essentially of tool-users.

One may conclude that *Australopithecus* occupied the Sterkfontein valley over a long period when the climate was rather arid. Then *Telanthropus* moved into the valley, already a toolmaker. Since the ecological adaptations of these two forms were very similar, the more advanced *Telanthropus* will presumably have displaced or eliminated *Australopithecus*. Meanwhile the climate was becoming appreciably wetter, as has been

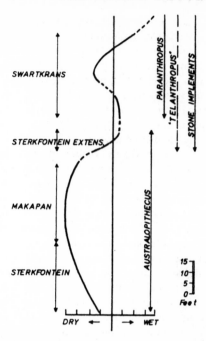

Figure 5. Climatic curve for Sterkfontein, Makapan (Limeworks), Sterkfontein Extension, and Swartkrans sites, modified after Brain. The curve is based on porosity, reflecting degree of rounding of the sand grains in the breccia from these sites. Central line indicates present rainfall conditions. The distribution of *Australopithecus*, *Paranthropus*, and "Telanthropus" is shown along with that of stone implements.

shown by analysis of the breccia itself, and soon the vegetarian *Paranthropus* moved into the valley. Since the *ecological* requirements of *Paranthropus* and Telanthropus differed far more than those of the latter and *Australopithecus*, there will have been much less competition between them and they could occupy the same area as successfully as the gorilla and man have for long enough in Central Africa. This is demonstrated also by just the same sort of association from roughly the same time period at Sangiran in Java, right at the other end of the Old World from the Sterkfontein area, where *Pithecanthropus* and *Paranthropus* occur together.

TELANTHROPUS AND THE HOMININES

We have seen that *Paranthropus* and *Australopithecus* are very different creatures, ecologically quite differently adapted and morphologically very distinct. *Telanthropus* must be classed with the hominines, not the australopithecines, on morphological grounds. But is the genus *Telanthropus* valid? Answering that question involves a reconsideration of the whole hominine group. It seems to me clearly impossible to make the sort of distinction within the hominines that is so clear in the australopithecine group. There is no evidence of which I am aware which suggests that any major adaptational differences existed which could conceivably be of a generic magnitude. The morphological differences also are of a low order. Probably the chief variable is brain size, the early *Pithecanthropus* forms being relatively small-brained and hence with slightly differently shaped braincases. The dentition was also relatively robust in the early forms and so the face was still fairly robust and prognathous. But the known range in brain size of the earliest hominines can be accommodated within the observed range of variation in modern man. The dental and facial changes appear to be part of a continuous sequence of modification of no great magnitude. These differences and the lack of any significant divergence of ecological requirements, fit well into the picture of species differences within a good and well defined genus among modern vertebrates. Furthermore, it is clear that as soon as hominines were well launched on their path of cultural development, the character of their evolutionary mechanism would have been modified. As Mayr has pointed out, man occupies a wider range of environments than any other animal. This is a result of his capacity for artificial adaptation. He can adapt himself to arctic conditions or to tropical conditions without significant change in his morphology or physiology —which is what occurs in other animals in such cases.

This capacity for artificial adaptation reduces his capacity to speciate. Natural adaptation, under the control of natural selection, to different environmental conditions is the normal basis of speciation and hence also of the achievement of any greater level of taxonomic distinction. Reduced rate of speciation and the more recent increasing tendency to interbreed over a wider area, have reduced appreciably the possibilities of significant adaptive radiation within the hominines. This

and the very short time in which hominines have existed argue against such radiation.

For all of these reasons it seems to me that the hominines must all be included within a single genus, *Homo.* This was suggested a few years ago by Mayr as part of a taxonomic scheme which included other aspects which do not appear to me to be valid. It therefore appears that *Pithecanthropus* should be reduced simply to a species of *Homo-H. erectus. Homo sapiens* appears to be the only other valid species, including Neandertal man as no more than a subspecies. However, there is no time now to go further into this aspect of the matter save only to say that in this scheme *Telanthropus* would become *Homo erectus* and I therefore now formally sink the genus *Telanthropus* (originally created by Broom and me in 1949) and transfer the specimens hitherto contained in that genus to *Homo erectus.*

This scheme reduces the contents of the whole family Hominidae to three genera only, *Paranthropus, Australopithecus,* and *Homo*—and I trust that university students of the future will be grateful for this nomenclatural simplification! But is should be clearly recognized that these genera are not all of the same sort. *Paranthropus* and *Australopithecus* are validly distinct on any grounds. They were divergent, adaptively well separated stocks which represented an adaptive radiation within the prehominines and could successfully have occupied the same territory for a long time. But *Australopithecus* and *Homo* are probably two phases of the same phyletic sequence, though evidently at least one species of *Australopithecus* was contemporaneous for a short time with an early *Homo erectus* in the Sterkfontein valley. But there is no sharp discontinuity between *Australopithecus* and *Homo,* except, in the known specimens, in brain size. But clearly there was at least one phyletic line

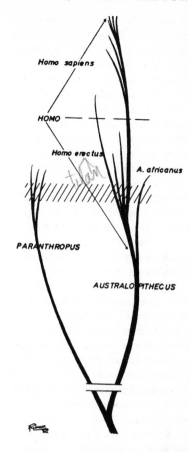

Figure 6. Schematic representation of relationship between *Paranthropus*, *Australopithecus*, and *Homo*. The hatched zone represents approximately the time period from which the australopithecines and "Telanthropus" are known. This period appears to be entirely in the Middle Pleistocene.

in which this gap was bridged. So while it is convenient to keep a generic distinction between the two groups, it should be recognized that this is not a distinction of the same type as that between *Paranthropus* and *Australopithecus*. This "vertical" type of arbitrary taxonomic distinction within a single evolutionary sequence is one of the troublesome things which the palaeontologist has learned to live with, about which the neozoological taxonomist with his "horizontal" distinctions does not have to worry.

HOMINID EVOLUTION

Hominids apparently arose from an apelike form more closely related to pongids than to any other known primates. This was probably a vegetarian stock. The dentition of the early Miocene pongids is closely similar to that of the modern ones, and presumably therefore there has been no major change in diet during that time. The monkeys and pongids of today are, with very minor exceptions, vegetarians of one sort or another and carnivorousness is not characteristic of them. In such a stock, then, an adaptive shift of enormous importance occurred—the acquisition of erect posture. It seems likely that changes in the pelvic region, especially in the innominate, occurred for some reason not primarily concerned with erect posture. But when this change had, as a prospective adaptation, got to the point where gluteus maximus could function as an extensor of the thigh rather than as an abductor, the animals would find that erect posture became far more easy to use than is the case in pongids. The nature of selection would then have changed markedly and this would probably have led to what has been called quantum evolution—the rapid readaptation of a group, producing a very distinct change in the population.

This would have given rise to the prehominid group and the first primate bipeds. I visualize these as more nearly *Paranthropus*-like with an essentially vegetarian diet, perhaps with an insectivorous element as well. But a second adaptive shift must have occurred, probably in a more arid environment—the adoption of a more specifically carnivorous element in the diet. This resulted in the emergence of the *Australopithecus* line. Definite carnivorousness would have placed a premium on tools in the absence of large canines and this probably led to a well developed phase of tool-using—sticks, stones, bones—whatever came to hand conveniently. But freed hands resulting from erect posture and the premium on tools resulting from carnivorousness, would certainly have resulted in appreciable selection pressure in favor of increased intelligence. This would result in increase of brain size, with consequent skull changes, a shift from tool-using to tool-making, etc.—in short, in the emergence of *Homo*. Meanwhile *Paranthropus*, a large animal, perhaps as expert at intimidation tactics as is the gorilla, and probably a moderate tool-user—e.g., digging "stick"—lost its previously larger canines, which reduced to modern size, while selection maintained the size of the dietarily more important cheek teeth. *Paranthropus* is basically less distinct from the hominid ancestor than is the more progressive *Australopithecus*.

The study of this phase of the evolution of man is of relatively recent origin and I hope that we shall have the opportunity to learn as much in the next 25 years as we have in the last 25.

The paleontological evidence makes it clear that we cannot—at least not yet—arrange our fossil progenitors in a single line running from man-like apes to men like ourselves. Our lines of descent are neither pure nor simple. Africa is important to understanding the complex problems of our early evolution, but so is Asia.

3. Java Man, Pekin Man, and Early Man in the West [1]

JAVA MAN

Here is the greatest story of serene confidence I have ever heard. The confidence belonged to Eugene Dubois, who at nineteen began to specialize in anatomy and natural history at the University of Amsterdam in 1877, under such men as

[1] WILLIAM W. HOWELLS, "Java Man," "Pekin Man," and "Early Man in the West," from *Mankind in the Making* by William Howells. Copywright © 1959 by William Howells. Reprinted by permission of the author, Doubleday & Company, Inc., and Martin Secker & Warburg, Ltd.

Dr. Howells is Professor of Anthropology at Harvard University.

Hugo de Vries and Max Fürbringer. A few years later, starting a promising career in teaching as Professor Fürbringer's assistant, he became engrossed with the notion of finding a really primitive and ape-like fossil of man, and he concluded that the East Indies might be the place to search for it.

He tried to get the Netherlands government to give him an expedition. But if you were a Hollander whose official business it was to disburse money on the prospect of finding a purely imaginary creature in the vast islands of the Indies, just because a young professor's-assistant asserted that it would be a likely place to look, you could have but one answer, and that would be "No."

The dauntless Dubois, however, sought and was given a post as army surgeon in the colonial service in the Netherlands Indies. He told his associates in so many words that he was going out to find the missing link and, to their dismay, resigned his Amsterdam appointments. Professor Fürbringer shrugged his shoulders and muttered to another of his assistants: "Hans im Glück." He was thinking of silly Hans, in Grimm's fairy tale, who kept exchanging the thing he owned for something of less worth, until he ended with nothing. But Dubois gave up his nice little job and made one of the greatest discoveries in all the past of man.

He was not being quite as woolly-headed as he seemed. True, a main source of his excitement was the German naturalist Haeckel, a florid writer who had drawn up a provisional ancestry for man and had put in, as the latest ancestor, a phantasmic missing link for whom he had selected the designation *Pithecanthropus alalus* (Speechless Ape-man). The zoologists have since passed a law against giving linnaean names to dream creatures. You now must have an actual animal or part of one, and you must provide a description, along with

your proposed name, to show wherein it differs from its closest relatives and thus deserves a name of its own. True also, Dubois' project called for twice the assurance of Columbus and for at least as much perseverance, and as much luck, as the man who finds a needle in a haystack.

Nevertheless, Dubois' ideas were clear in his mind, and he wrote them down in an article. He followed Darwin's suggestion that man had probably lost his hairy covering in a hot country. He accepted Wallace's belief that looking for early human remains should be done where apes still lived today. He noted Virchow's remark that vast regions, particularly in the tropics, were totally unknown as far as fossils went. Furthermore, Dubois was aware that suggestive animal remains were coming to light in northern India and that there were caves in Central Sumatra which might also yield the object he was after. So, for the knowledge of the time, he was adding things up pretty well. He had the determination. And he certainly had the luck.

Dubois and *Pithecanthropus*. He took himself to Sumatra and began poking around in caves in his free time. When the authorities grasped his purpose they freed him for research, and he went at it in earnest. But his only finds were orang teeth, with certain other fossils, which convinced him that the cave material was too recent. At any rate, no men. Here luck made her first entrance: a Mr. van Rietschoten found a fossilized skull at Wadjak in neighboring Java. It was passed on by the Royal Society in Batavia to Dubois, who got permission to include Java in his territory. He went to Wadjak and found another of the same sort himself! They were interesting and like the living natives of Australia in appearance. But they were no missing links—not what he was seeking.

Three years had now gone by, but at last, working in Central Java, he came

Haeckel

across a small piece of human jaw, late in 1890. The next year he found a promising place in the bank of the Solo River, near the small village of Trinil, where a fossil-bearing bed lies close to the present level of the water. In the course of one month he exposed a few ape-like teeth, and then the treasure he was looking for: a brain pan (the top and part of the sides and back of the skull) too large to be that of an ape and too small to be that of a man, but just exactly right to be an "Übergangsform," a "missing link." The next year, forty-five feet away but in precisely the same level, he brought to light the femur, or thighbone, of a man. In 1894 he published a full description of the Java Man. Borrowing Haeckel's old name, he christened him *Pithecanthropus erectus* and put him in a new family, Pithecanthropidae, between the Pongidae and the Hominidae (because he felt the skull so crude as to be still subhuman). Apart from this last gesture, his diagnosis is the one which still prevails, of an upright, human walker with a very primitive cranium. The whole thing was a brilliant feat and an astonishing triumph.

It was, for obvious reasons, a sensation in Europe. The first really primitive kind of man, the being so long talked about in the abstract, had suddenly appeared, if not in the flesh, at least in the bone. And yet his reception was not a glad ovation but a fierce controversy, and indeed during the next forty years *Pithecanthropus* underwent some embarrassing moments. In 1896, Dubois himself assembled the opinions of nineteen other authorities on the find: five of them thought the skull to be an anthropoid ape, seven thought it human, and seven considered it intermediate. To the anti-evolutionists, of course, the whole thing was an illusion, and even those who were willing to gaze upon it all were able to find at least fifteen grounds on which to quarrel. Some said the skull was that of an idiot, others that it was normal. Some said it was human; others said it was a monkey, a chimpanzee, or a gibbon. The Java Man could speak. The Java Man could not speak. Perhaps the sorest question was whether the skull and the leg bone were actually parts of the same creature, because of the apparently more "human" status of the leg, because of differences in the amount of abrasion the two bones had undergone, and because they were separated, when found, by a distance of forty-five feet.

And *Pithecanthropus* was not the only sufferer. In a strange way, as von Koenigswald has put it, the Java Man became Dubois' own fate. The two brought glory to one another, and then sorrow. Dubois began to feel an identity with the fossil. Its detractors were his own enemies; his anthropological colleagues all became suspect, and Dubois was not at home to them any longer. And at last he withdrew the bones from scientific contact. He took them to his house at Zijlweg 77, Haarlem; he put them in a box; he took up his dining-room floor and buried the box in the ground below it; he put back boards, liner, and carpet; and he ate his meals above the Java Man for many long years. Jealous adversaries, he had come to think, might even steal the precious fossils. For all these years, too, he kept the Wadjak skulls in a glass case, but with newspaper pasted to the inside of the glass, so that the skulls could not see out, and nobody else could see in. Only in the 1920's did he relent and expose the Wadjak crania to science. Later still, he was persuaded to put the remains of *Pithecanthropus* in the museum at Leiden, in a small safe inside a larger safe.

In the meanwhile the original controversy had died away, and Dubois' first judgment had come to be broadly accepted. One voice alone now cried that the Java Man was no near-man at all, but a super-gibbon whose principal occupation was walking about in the trees. A big-brained gibbon, said the voice, whose leg bone showed lines of stress which meant that it was not used like a man's. And here it was that *Pithecanthropus* felt the unkindest cut of all. For the voice was that of Dr. Dubois himself.

This was a strange thing. Dubois, steadfast while others argued, began to vacillate when everyone agreed with him. Shortly after restoring Java Man to society, Dubois changed opinion of his status, making him more human. But he changed again and came to the belief that his beloved fossil was not a sub-man but a super-ape, supporting his bizarre argument by several new fragments of femurs which had turned up in collections made in the year 1900 and also by ingenious hypotheses regarding evolution which found no favor among his colleagues. He changed his mind one last time, admitting a mistake in interpreting the stress lines on the femur, but by now confusion was complete.

Dubois died during the last war, to be forever honored for his brilliance and energy in finding Java Man. Before this time the fossil had been vindicated, and its place was more important than ever. The ancient uproar had been replaced by a peace of unanimity wherein the rest of the world watched apathetically while the elder Dubois broke lances against the younger. At last, any doubts about the association of skull and leg bone (and after all, it had never been necessary to suppose they had come from the same individual, but only from the same kind of being) vanished when the fluorine test eventually showed the femurs and the skull to be of the same—considerable—age.

But for forty years no more of the Java Man had ever come to light. A mighty expedition went out from the Academy of Science in Berlin in 1907 to the Solo River, where it dug hard and systematically; according to von Koenigs-

wald, the scene of its labors is still readily detected by the litter of broken beer bottles. The one result was a collection of mammalian fossils to define the "Trinil fauna"; Dubois' own collections had left much to be desired for exactness. But not a sign of *Pithecanthropus* did it discover, which only goes to emphasize how much Dubois, like Broom, was luck's companion.

Von Koenigswald and More Skulls. When at last Java yielded more pieces of her ape-man, this was due almost entirely to the persistence and the intelligent organization of a newly appeared paleontologist, G. H. R. von Koenigswald. He worked for the Geological Survey of the islands, lost his job in 1935 but made a comeback in 1937, and served as a paleontologist till 1948. He spotted a most likely area in Central Java for useful fossils in 1935, and taught local villagers to collect and keep fossil remains as they washed out of the ground. These he purchased, necessarily at a very low rate per piece. For to get occasional significant pieces, he had to buy vast numbers of unimportant ones, as well as a great deal of plain trash. Just as things were going well, however, he found himself out of a job. He was rescued and sustained by the Carnegie Institution of Washington, when he wrote and described the promising prospects of his work, supported by Father Teilhard de Chardin.

Actually the first new find came by another route. Geological mapping near Surabaya in eastern Java had just disclosed a new layer of the Pleistocene, with a new fauna, the Djetis, older than the Trinil fauna, when a native collector of the Survey discovered the brain case of a human infant within this same layer, at Modjokerto. Here, because of its youth, was the problem of Dart's young skull from Taung all over again: what did its father look like? Although it was more ancient than Dubois' find, von Koenigswald concluded it must be a *Pithecanthropus*. But he gave it a different name, *Homo modjokertensis*, simply to avoid a wrangle with the elderly Dubois and his imaginary giant gibbon. The maneuver was only partly successful.

This was in 1936. And then von Koenigswald's preparations began to pay off. In 1937 from his most important new locality, Sangiran in Central Java, and apparently from Djetis bed, came a lower jaw, long, strong, and primitive. Then at last a skull, in pieces. Von Koenigswald himself found one part, and the natives found others. They had begun to appreciate a good thing, and they appreciated their piecework very well; they broke the pieces they found into still smaller pieces, until there were forty of them to be bought and paid for—at ten cents a piece. But the harm was small, financial and otherwise; the breaks of nature and of art were easily repaired. Here was a skull, still baseless and faceless, but much more perfect than the first and almostly exactly like it. Certainly on the night of the great find, forty-six years after Trinil, von Koenigswald decided it was time to pass around rice and salt and have a party, complete with gamelan orchestra and the local dancing girls.

Late in the next year another skull top turned up, that of a young person, and less complete. It was like the first two in shape and came, like them, from the Trinil zone. And in January 1939, this time from the earlier Djetis zone, came the first upper jaw, just as von Koenigswald was going to pay a visit to the laboratory of Dr. Weidenreich in Pekin, where the specimens of Pekin Man were being studied. These two men looked the new fragment over and saw signs of recent breakage. Von Koenigswald sent a message to his collector to search carefully at the place where the jaw had come from, and sure enough the major portions of the back of the skull were dis-

covered, showing signs that the head had been shattered by a heavy blow at or about the time of death. This heavier, cruder individual seems to supply the missing father of the Modjokerto baby.

Before war interrupted his work, von Koenigswald found the first *Meganthropus* jaw (another was discovered in 1952). But Java Man has not appeared again. Nonetheless, four of his skulls, three of them fairly good, together with several pieces of the jaws, large and small, tell us a good deal. They say the Java Man was no ape, no freak, no imbecile, but a brutish early human being, and indeed a euhominid. They say Dubois was right the first time, as von Koenigswald finally tried to suggest to the old man without success. There is some difference, in other words, between an isolated fossil, and a creature known from several individuals, so that one can be certain of the average or typical form. The moral? Do not try to make an ape out of *Pithecanthropus*, or *Pithecanthropus* may make a monkey out of you.

The Nature of Java Man. This most ancient man was about the same size as ourselves, judging from his thighbones. These bones cannot really be distinguished from our own, Dubois to the contrary; and to try finding signs of special primitiveness is probably to run the risk of being fooled, as Keith was fooled by Galley Hill. There is really nothing more to be said. There used to be serious discussion as to whether Java Man was really erect, but now that we know about the australopithecines, we should be more than surprised if he were anything else. His femur shows he walked upright, and his head shows the same, by the position of its base and of the *foramen magnum*.

Nevertheless his neck was stout and strong, with its muscles spread well across and up the back of his skull. And no wonder, for they had work to do. The

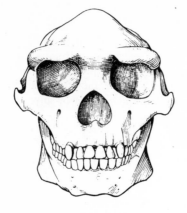
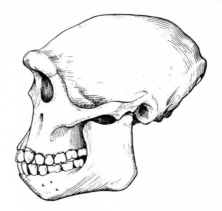

Figure 1. Java Man. Drawn from Weidenreich's restoration, based on skull IV and mandible B. One-fourth natural size. (After Cirulis)

skull itself was tremendously heavy and thick, in contrast to the South African man-apes; and the still-large face and jaw threw the skull forward, much further off balance than in our own head. The jaws, generous in size, contained the largest teeth yet found in the skull of any kind of "man" (euhominid), and still these teeth were not crowded together but often had slight spaces between them. The dentition was rather more like ours than in the man-apes; the molars were not of such exaggerated size, nor were the incisors by contrast so greatly reduced. And, while the lower molars grew steadily larger from the first to the wisdom tooth (a primitive trait), in the upper jaw the last molar had become relatively diminished in size, as it has in us but not in the man-apes. In the latter, the upper molar size in order is three, two, one; in us it is one, two, three; in *Pithecanthropus* it was two, one, three.

To everyone's astonishment, the front of the upper jaw revealed a diastema, a gap between the canine and incisors like that into which an ape's lower canine fits when he shuts his mouth. It is no illusion—the diastema is the size of an orang's and was found in two different specimens. Java Man is the one and only hominid with such a gap; none of the australopithecines displayed this mark of the beast, nor did our strange little relative from the Italian Pliocene, *Oreopithecus*.

If this feature of *Pithecanthropus* had been known in the old days much would have been made of its ape-like appearance. But now we had better be restrained. Java Man cannot possibly be closely related to pongid apes, and his canine teeth, though not dainty, are not the strongly projecting kind which need such an open space. Probably he had the space because of the generally broad front of his face and the open nature of his forward tooth row. These are traits in which he is in extreme contrast with the man-apes, whose dental arches were compact forward and much enlarged behind. Probably, also, the gap was a property of males—a sex difference—since some of the pithecanthropi had it and some did not.

Java Man's face was fairly projecting, as the above might suggest, although his lower jaw was long, rather than deep, with its more human, smaller, molar teeth. He could probably chew better than he did most things, for his brain was very small. It stood at an approximate size of some 850 cubic centimeters, males higher, females lower (the second skull found having a probable capacity of 775). Compare this figure with apes at some 500, australopiths at a little more, and European males today with 1450. That is to say, if Java Man had 200 cubic centimeters more than a man-ape— and even this is dubious—he was still some 500 below ourselves. Housed above a long face and a long platform for neck muscles at the rear, this meager tissue of intellect made a poor job of filling out the skull. The skull was widest just above the ears and sloped rapidly in toward a low peak or ridge, leaving no forehead behind the beetling bony brows.

The Age of Java Man. So Java Man was the earliest of humankind— barring the man-apes—about whom we have satisfactory knowledge. And he looks it. He probably lived, in fact, at much the same time as the later man-apes, and at any rate we know his dates better than theirs. His oldest remains were from the beds of the Djetis fauna and his later (actually the first found) from the Trinil fauna immediately above. Now the Trinil beds are Middle Pleistocene, that is, Second Glacial and later. However, the Djetis zone (Oakley calls this a "paleontologists' battle zone") is late Lower or early Middle Pleistocene; in any case it is post-Villafranchian and probably very late First Interglacial.

By majority opinion this coincides with the general time span of the later australopithecines (*Paranthropus*) of South Africa, although such connections between continents are not entirely certain. And, do not forget, the jaws of *Meganthropus,* a possible australopithecine, lay cheek by jowl, to make a horrible pun, with the bones of Java Man in the Djetis zone. So, over and over, it is indicated that the late man-apes and the early "men" overlapped.

No tools have turned up in direct association with the bones in Java. However, we should never suppose that the Man was not able to make them. In any case crude flake tools of a definite kind, called Patjitanian, are known from southern Java, from deposits just later than the latest of the bones, and it is not likely that the tools were made by anyone except *Pithecanthropus* himself.

He must have lived in Java (and doubtless other places in the Far East where he has not been so fortunate as to be found) for many thousands of years. Did he change during this time? Dr. Weidenreich insisted that he did: that the exceptionally thick, low, and heavy skull (number four, he of the split brain case) from the earlier Djetis level was distinctly more primitive than the other three adult skulls, all of which came from the later Trinil beds. But it seems equally likely that the most ancient individual happened to be a male and the other three happened to be female. Males are more "primitive" than that other sex, with thicker, larger, heavier (and fuller) skulls, and with larger teeth, jaws, and brow ridges. And so this last explanation will have to be disproved, by finds of more Java men and Java women, before the other one becomes more probable.

The Solo Cannibals. But still Dr. Weidenreich may have been part right. For *Pithecanthropus, Meganthropus,* and the almost modern Wadjak men were not the only interesting fossils from the opulent island of Java. Above the Trinil beds in many places, and of much later age, lies another set of beds, with another set of animals, the Ngandong fauna. So there is a series: Djetis, Trinil, Ngandong, which is basic to the dating of the Pleistocene of Java.

The discovery of the last fauna came in a great stroke of good fortune. A member of the Geological Survey, ter Haar by name, had lately made his quarters in the village of Ngandong, on the banks of the same Solo River and only six miles from Trinil. One evening he had stepped out to enjoy the sunset when he realized that the river bank here had preserved a distinct terrace remnant, twenty meters above the water, and thus different from the older deposits. His first quick search revealed the horns of a giant water buffalo, and so the Geological Survey fell to work on the terrace in earnest. It turned out to be very rich, with many thousands of animal bones. Not only that; it yielded two shinbones and eleven fragmentary skulls of a new kind of man.

The skulls were found one after another by various workers between September 1931 and November 1932. Von Koenigswald, then young and newly arrived, went with ter Haar to take out the best one, with von Koenigswald doing the photography in such a state of excitement that he underexposed many of his films. These bones have a grisly story to tell. Except for the two leg bones, only heads were found, and these lay in every position, upside down or otherwise. And from each skull a large piece had been knocked out below, usually almost the whole base. From every one the face was missing entirely. Not a vestige, not a jaw, not a tooth ever turned up. In fact, Solo Man was a cannibal, and this was where he had been eating the last, hardest-to-get part, the brain. There are, it is true, various reasons for eating one's own kind. One is to acquire the virtues of the dead, by ingesting the parts where virtue resides—intelligence, the brain; courage, the heart. Another reason is to keep well fed.

You may choose, but in any case we are left with only Solo Man's brain case to inspect. This was massive and heavy, extremely long, and still relatively low and poorly filled out. The brain was much larger than in Java Man, but still rather small. There is, withal, a sort of family resemblance to Java Man. It is this on which Dr. Weidenreich relied, believing that Solo Man was a direct descendant of the Java Man, hundreds of thousands of years later, on the same spot. Evolution, he believed, had gone its own way within this little parish, almost throughout the Pleistocene.

This is a broad and general problem, and we must hold Solo Man over for the time being. His skulls are now in Holland. Von Koenigswald had a complicated and unpleasant time during the war. German-born, but a Dutch national,

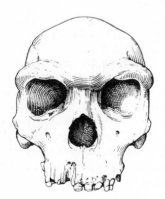 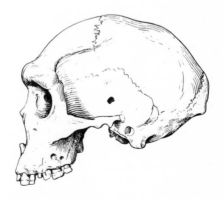

Figure 2. Solo Man. Left, skull XI from Ngandong. Right, side view, with hypothetical restoration of the face by Weidenreich. One-fourth natural size. (After cast, Weidenreich and Cirulis)

he was separated from his family and put into a concentration camp by the Japanese, and there were even rumors in the United States that this admired scientist had lost his life. But the fossils did better, even though the Japanese military considered them the property of the expanding Empire and ordered them impounded. They got the Solo skulls, and sent one of them, Number XI, to the Emperor for his birthday. But von Koenigswald hid all the new finds, not yet described and therefore unknown to the conquerors. Swedish and Swiss friends took the *Gigantopithecus* and *Pithecanthropus* teeth, mixed them with a lot of others, and buried them in large milk bottles, and Mrs. von Koenigswald herself kept the new upper jaw. What the Japanese got were mostly fakes— beautifully made casts of the older skulls, with dye and brickdust mixed into the plaster so that even an accidentally broken piece would still look like a proper fossil, at least to the visiting representatives of the Greater East Asia Co-Prosperity Sphere. The latter actually showed them- selves remarkably careful of their booty, real and bogus, and after the war von Koenigswald was reunited with family and fossil alike.

PEKIN MAN

Pekin Man was less fortunate. Java Man went into Dubois' locker for a time. But Pekin Man seems to have gone into Davy Jones' locker, and for good. He disappeared, one of the first casualties of the war in the Pacific, half a million years after he had died the first time.

His story will remind you of the South African man-apes more than a little. His remains lay in the same kind of lime- hardened cave fill, and they emerged in the same kind of peekaboo way. Let us go back two generations, and to the town of Choukoutien, about twenty- seven miles southwest of the present Peiping. Here the plain which runs back from the coast gives way to the Western Hills, limestone bluffs laid down in the sea long ago when the fishes were new. During the Pleistocene, water action ate out caves and fissures in the bluffs, at different times. These caves filled up again with earth and fossilized remains, and in some of them, like Locality 1, the large cave used by Pekin Man, the fill became a hard breccia.

In the year 1900 a human tooth (actu- ally not a very ancient one) turned up in a Pekin drugstore and drew the atten- tion of paleontologists to the region. A long stream of them started coming to Choukoutien. They worked through the government Geological Survey of China, and the first of them were a Swedish geologist, J. G. Andersson, and an Aus- trian associate, O. Zdansky, helped by Swedish philanthropy. In 1921 they were led to Locality 1, and immediately they found bits of quartz. Animals do not use quartz, or eat it or wear it, and so it has no business in a cave in limestone and no natural way of getting there. But it is good for making stone tools. Accord- ing to Roy Chapman Andrews, who was on the scene for much of the early story, Andersson said: "In this spot lies primi- tive man. All we have to do is to find him!"

Find him they did, bit by bit. Two years later, Zdansky discovered a single human tooth there, and in 1926, after taking a mass of animal fossils back to Upsala in Sweden, he recognized an- other human tooth in the collections. Enter now Dr. Davidson Black, Professor of Anatomy at the American-instituted Peiping Union Medical College, who, more than anyone else, was responsible for the discoveries to come. Excited by the teeth Zdansky had found, he per- suaded the Rockefeller Foundation, backer of his college, to come in on the work and to co-operate with the Geo- logical Survey. An able Swedish paleontologist, Birgir Bohlin, was brought to do the field work. This new phase began in 1927, and after six months of toil Bohlin produced one more tooth. This was enough for Black. After concentrated study of the new tooth he announced the find, and felt justified in allotting it a new human genus and species, *Sinanthropus pekinensis* (Chinese man of Pekin). Black took the tooth on a world tour that winter.

The Skulls Appear. All this intensity of purpose was rewarded. As the old cave was dug into more deeply, and its branchings and crannies were traced out, it began to yield less niggardly portions of Pekin Man. In 1928, Bohlin found fragments of two jaws, parts of skull walls, and a number of teeth. In 1929 a Chinese paleontologist, Pei, became director of the work, and on the very last day of the season, December 2, he himself found the first skull and cut it out still embedded in limestone, with only the top showing. This was what everyone had waited for. Shortly after, Black went to dinner at the British Legation. He scribbled a note about the skull and passed it to Andrews; afterward the initiated gathered from all over the city for a skull viewing, Pekin Man's vernissage, followed by an appropriate beer-and-pig's-knuckles party.

And now Pekin Man made his formal debut in the press. Such was the change which one generation had made, in attitudes toward human fossils, that Pekin Man was greeted with nothing like the Donnybrook which broke out upon the first Java discovery. Rather, he was met with deference, enthusiasm, and immediate acknowledgement of his importance. Only Dr. Dubois remained in character, huffing the skull away, abetted somewhat by our own Dr. Hrdlička of the National Museum, who pronounced the find to be a Chinese Neanderthal, nothing more.

Locality 1, now becoming a really large cavity, continued to give up Pekin men, together with their tools and meat bones. In the next two years other skull parts and jaws were recovered. But in 1934, Dr. Black unfortunately died, the result, it is said, of silicosis caused by dust from drilling on the *Sinanthropus* materials. This was a setback to operations. However, a celebrated German anatomist, already well known for his studies of the fossil men of Europe, was asked to come to direct the Laboratory at Peiping Union Medical College, and the work at Choukoutien. This was Dr. Franz Weidenreich, and a fortunate choice, as his great monographs on the remains have proved.

Work started afresh, with better results than ever. In 1936 alone major or minor portions of seven skulls were found; and from beginning to end, parts of well over forty different men, women, and children were taken from this brecciated tomb. But now history of another sort began to interfere: the Japanese took over North China in 1937. At first the handicaps to work at Choukoutien were not severe. Once a Japanese general, on his day off, showed up at Locality 1 and announced that he was about to launch his own personal dig. Weidenreich managed to find and pull the right wires to Tokyo at once, however, and the general was not seen again. But difficulties multiplied, and what was worse, the Japanese command showed a mounting interest in the fossils: these, it evidently thought, had become Japanese citizens with the extension of the Empire to North China. At last, convinced that things had become impossible for fruitful work, Dr. Weidenrecih in 1941 went to New York, taking with him a set of plaster casts of the skulls, fortunately of Chinese execution and extraordinarily good. The originals, always the property of the Geological Survey of China (and under the Japanese shadow), remained in custody of the Peiping Union Medical College.

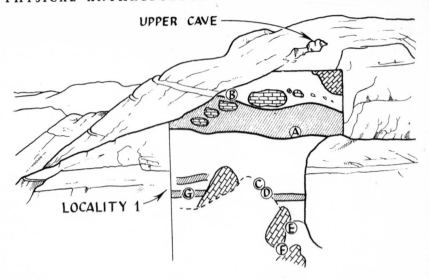

Figure 3. Choukoutien, the site of Pekin Man. The cross section of Locality 1 is from an early stage of the excavations. Shaded bands are zones rich in ashes, tools, and bone. Letters are points where skulls or other bones were found. Limestone blocks (the "brickwork") are partly due to falls from the original cave roof. Position of the Upper Cave is shown above the main section. (After Black and Cirulis)

The Skulls Disappear. But now the director of the Geological Survey, Dr. Wong, became more fearful—and certainly with justice, it turned out—that the Japanese were about to carry off the whole fossil tribe to Tokyo. He decided to forestall this by sending the bones to America, if it were possible. Dr. Wong was also a trustee of the Peiping Union Medical College, and he urged its president, Dr. Henry Houghton, to take charge. Dr. Houghton was quite unwilling to have the United States assume responsibility for the fossils, but Dr. Wong overcame his objections, and the bones were packed up and sent to the U. S. Embassy.

There they were given to Colonel Ashurst, commanding the Marine detachment at the Embassy, just as the Marines were being ordered to evacuate North China. Colonel Ashurst was told to treat the boxes as "secret" material, to be put

with his personal gear. This, and all Marine baggage, equipment, and ammunition, was to be sent on a special train, under the guard of nine Marines, down to the port of Chinwangtao, there to meet the liner *President Harrison,* which was to transport the Marines to the Philippine Islands. So far so good. The train left Peiping at five in the morning on December 5, 1941. It arrived in Chinwangtao on December 7.

We know what happened next, to everyone except Pekin Man. We know what happened to the *Harrison:* her crew appraised the situation and grounded her to prevent the Japanese from making immediate use of her; the Japanese refloated her, renamed her *Kachidoki Maru,* and used her as a transport until she was sunk in 1944 by the U. S. submarine *Pampanito.* We know what happened to the nine Marines; they were captured, sent back to Peiping, and put in prison camps along with Colonel Ashurst and the rest of his command. We even know what happened to the ammunition and equipment; they were later seen in Japanese possession.

But what happened to the bones is anyone's guess. And it has been almost everyone's guess. That they were actually put on a lighter, which capsized in the harbor. That local Chinese got them and ground them up for medicine. There is even an opium-scented story that they were smuggled safely away by sinister international merchants of the China coast and finally tracked down and purchased by an American medical man who lives in California and guards the hoard like Fafnir, the great worm. At any rate, the press in Japan and in Hong Kong periodically erupted with developments of this tale for some years.

It is quite clear that the Japanese—meaning actual officials—never got the ancient Pekinese. For the Japanese in Peiping immediately started looking for the bones, and they went over the United States Embassy "with a fine-toothed comb," according to accounts. They were sufficiently interested, in fact, to put the business manager of the Medical College, Trevor Bowen, in a wooden cage too small to lie down in, on rice and water for five days, before they were convinced he did not know Pekin Man's whereabouts. Evidently Dr. Wong was a good prophet. The Japanese took to Tokyo the stone tools found at Choukoutien, all carefully and exactly catalogued, where everything was found to be in good order after the war.

So it is evident that the Japanese would have made no bones about the bones. They wanted quite guilelessly to bring them home, and so they must have conducted the most efficient search one could imagine, at Chinwangtao as well as at Peiping. There is no reason to suppose they might have hidden the bones away. They did not hide Solo Man, nor did they hide the valuable stone tools. And anyhow, a hidden fossil is no more good to the hider than to the seeker; Dr. Dubois proved that.

It is equally clear that the Chinese have never found them. Whatever its shortcomings in some of the primary virtues, the government of Communist China has been strongly in favor of ancient man. It has opened a museum at Choukoutien, and resumed excavations, of which the results have been a few more teeth and bone fragments. It is totally improbable that anyone in authority in China secretly knows where the bones are.

Certainly they were not sent to the United States. The Chinese government was a party to the guessing game I mentioned, its guess being that the fossils had ended up in the American Museum of Natural History in New York. Pekin Man number XI, it said, had been looted by an American soldier from the Imperial Japanese collection. "In other words," declared the New China News Agency in 1952, "the Japanese imperialists stole it from the American imperialists after the latter had stolen it. It was shipped to Japan and kept in the Imperial Japanese collection. After Japan surrendered, the American imperialists stole it again, this time from the Japanese robbers, and put it in the New York Museum."

A fine dish of anti-American propaganda, even if it was not as interesting as the germ-warfare fantasy. But strangely enough the story was not made up out of whole cloth. What seems to have happened is this. A distinguished naturalist from over the Atlantic, a man famous in his own specialty and other fields as well, but not closely acquainted with fossil man, came to call on Dr. Weidenreich, before the latter's death in 1948, at the Natural History Museum in New York. He encountered Weidenreich walking down the hall on the floor reserved for staff. "Look at this," said Weidenreich, holding out a primitive-looking human skull with the number XI painted on it. "It's just been brought back from Japan." "This" was Solo XI, the one which had been sent up from Java during the war for the Emperor's birthday. It was recovered by Lieutenant Walter Fairservis and brought back to von Koenigswald, arriving in New York, in September 1946, with the rest of his fossils.

Von Koenigswald was so busy with Java Man that he turned over the Solo skulls to Dr. Weidenreich, orphaned guardian of Pekin Man, to study and describe. That is how Weidenreich came to be walking in the hall with Solo XI in his hands. His visitor paid no great attention to the fossil but, on getting home, came to suppose he had been looking at one of the Pekin skulls—they have a family likeness to Solo. He said as much to some fellow naturalists at tea one day. One of these shortly afterward went behind the Iron Curtain, taking the "news" with him, and thus an innocent little mistake became a big and beautiful piece of propaganda.

So here we have Pekin Man, world traveler, associate of merchant pirates, or pawn of international politics. His weird experiences since 1941 prove, I fear, that fiction is stranger than truth. It is unlikely that he ever left the environs of Chinwangtao. He is, if there is anything left of him, probably there today. The judgment of men who were in China in 1941 is likely to be the right one. Japanese officialdom was hot on the scent of *Sinanthropus,* but it was not Japanese officials who captured the Marines and looted the train with its secret freight at Chinwangtao. It was ordinary Japanese soldiers. And they doubtless did what ordinary Japanese soldiers, or ordinary American soldiers, would do in a captured train. Expecting something interesting and finding what looked like dog bones, they probably threw the whole lot onto the trash heap or over the dockside. This may be prosaic, but at least it is reasonable. Unfortunately, people have a perverse liking for the improbable and implausible. There were many, for a while, who were certain Hitler had not died in 1945 in Berlin. I think we will see Hitler and Pekin Man again on the same day. Judgment Day.

The Nature of Pekin Man. So, unless and until more skulls are found, we can make no progress with this very important early man. In particular, new ideas, or new chemical tests, can never be applied to the lost material. We are left only with casts and with Dr. Weidenreich's fine descriptions. But this is much better than nothing, because Weidenreich was an extraordinarily gifted describer of fossil man. And such descriptions are all that many anthropologists, unless they are inveterate travelers, usually have at their disposal for their studies of many specimens and types of ancient man.

In fact, though his relics are gone, we actually know more about Pekin Man than about any other fossil hominids, excepting only the australopithecines, because so many specimens were found, and because of Weidenreich's meticulous work. I will describe the Pekin type simply. How simply, or oversimply, you can judge by comparing my few words with more than a thousand large pages published by Weidenreich in the monographs of the Geological Survey of China alone.

Let us say first of all that Pekin Man is Java Man's brainy brother. The two are closely related—very much the same kind of man. Weidenreich said they were merely two races, though most others think this is a slight exaggeration, when it is taken to mean that they differ no more than two of our races of today. Let us say rather that Pekin Man is another edition of Java Man, virtually identical in some respects, but in two very human

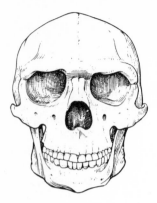
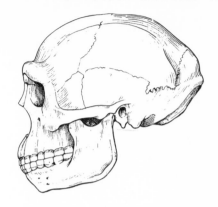

Figure 4. Pekin Man. Restoration of a female skull by Weidenreich. One-fourth natural size. (After Weidenreich and Cirulis)

ways a small advance away from the man-apes and toward ourselves. These two ways are, as you would expect, brains and teeth.

The Pekin and Java men did not differ in the skeleton, for both, as far as we know them, had already arrived at a skeleton indistinguishable from our own. Pekin Man, it is true, had rather thick walls to his thighbones, but he showed none of the distinctions in shape seen in the australopithecines.

Nor did they differ in some basic skull specifications. Both skulls were equally thick—very thick for humanity—and both had equally large and beetling bony brows. And in the base, the most fundamental part of the skull—something for the top of the neck, so to speak—they were alike, with the Pekin men only showing signs of a slightly less massive neck attachment at the very back and in the region of the ears.

But above this base plate Pekin Man's brain was larger than Java Man's, by better than 200 cubic centimeters. This is a significant difference, a rise from Java Man's 85 c.c. to an average, for both sexes, of 1075 c.c. This suggests an average for males of about 1150 c.c., to be compared with modern males having 1450. And the increased volume is evi-

dent in the shape of the skulls. Though still slanting sharply in above the ears, the sides were broader and the central ridge higher; and there was a distinct bump for a forehead, immediately contrasting with the low slope running back from the brows in Java Man. In fact, this greater rise of forehead threw the bony brows into sharper relief, with a deep furrow running across the forehead just behind them. But paradoxically, the primitive look this furrow imparts is actually due to a progressive feature, the angle created by the embryo forehead.

The same degree of progress is seen in the teeth. Robust, and with obvious primitive traits (cingulum, root and cusp arrangements), such as enabled Davidson Black to be sure of his ground in recognizing a new kind of man on three teeth alone, they are nonetheless diminished from those in the Java specimens. And with this, the whole mouth suddenly looks truly human. The dental arch is shorter and more rounded in front, and there is no sign of an opening or diastema in the upper row. The jaw is shorter and more compact, and this is reflected in a real angle at the chin: not a true bony bump such as we have, but not a smooth receding curve either; instead, a somewhat flattened and steeper front. Finally, in the molar teeth, the first upper molar is the largest (the second in the Java Man), but in the lower teeth as well, the third molar—wisdom tooth—is now shorter than the second.

Pekin Man used his teeth on a diet much like our own in essence, a mixture of meat and vegetables. And he had tools to cut his food up with and fire to cook it. So any demand by natural selection for powerful jaws was probably already a thing of the past. All this is known from the fill in the cave in which his bones lay.

Locality 1 and Its Contents. It may not be true that he "lived" in the cave. More likely he "frequented" it, as did bears, hyenas, and many other carnivores, including no less than six members of the cat family, not counting a sabertooth. These frequenters and predators, man among them, are probably responsible for bringing in the bones of many other animals: big horses, big camels, buffaloes, elephants, rhinos, and a very large number of deer, as well as sheep and antelopes. Much of this must have been Pekin Man's own leavings, judging from the other kinds of rubbish he left. There were also quantities of bird cherry seeds, signs of the vegetable side of his diet.

High and low in the fill were layers of ash and burned bones, hearths where the men had sat and cooked. Now this is the first solid evidence of using fire in human history, and it is important. Its meaning for early man is not warmth mainly, nor even as a weapon in the rivalry with other beasts for use of the cave. Rather, it is that cooking makes meat more edible and digestible for us. Man is a primate and a descendant of primates, and the higher primates are adjusted to a diet which is very largely vegetable. But there is more energy in the proteins and fats of meat, which their omnivorous systems can use, especially if the meat is partly broken down by heat. So fire and cooking unlocked the door, for man, to greater efficiency and economy of diet, by letting him make a much greater use of meat.

A second factor in the success of developing human life was good stone tools. These Pekin Man had. The Cro Magnons of Europe or the North American Indians would have derided his efforts. But for a man whose brains still lacked thirty or forty per cent of our own advance beyond a chimpanzee, these implements were nothing less than praiseworthy. They were by no means the crudest which are known to archaeologists. The characteristic tool of Pekin Man was a pebble trimmed to make an edged chopper. He also had flake scrapers, and points consisting of a crude beak. And he used animal bones as tools a good deal, although he does not appear to have shaped them before using them.

Locality 1 must have been an odorous place in those days. But Pekin Man was worse than a poor tenant. Last but not least in the inventory of the mess he created in the cave is the state of his own remains. Like Solo Man, Pekin Man was a cannibal. The disorder in which human bones lay was no mere lack of funerary fastidiousness. And there is this guilty statistic: few parts of his trunk or limbs lay within the cave, the vast majority of fossil parts being from the head. Plainly, he did his killing and dying outside and brought only the skulls of his fellows indoors, there to eat the brains by breaking through the base of the cranium. A good many pieces of face and jaw were present, but not affixed to the brain case.

But all this is his affair. What's done is done, and we might as well be thankful that he was unwittingly packing away skulls for future science. If Pekin Man had had any latter-day compunctions about anthropophagy, Dr. Weidenreich would have had far less to dig up and write about.

Those grisly wakes must have gone on

for many thousands of years. While Pekin Man picked bones, pecked flint, and dug out his colleagues' brains, the floor of the cave rose higher and higher, until earth and bones had filled its whole great space, over 100 feet high, and as much as 500 feet long in one direction. There was no sign of changes—of different periods of weather, or of animals, or of human types and tools. Nevertheless, the animals are so varied that they do not tell a precise story of either cool times or warm, except that the climate was not glacial; and this fact also allows one to suppose that a long span of time may be represented. Taken altogether, the animal life indicates that this time was the Middle Pleistocene, and specifically the Second Interglacial, which is known to have been of particularly long duration. Therefore we may safely say that Pekin Man appeared at the cave in that major period which followed on the last known Java men and that he used the cave for a substantial part of the Second Interglacial.

Does this signify a little tribe or clan, hanging about the spot, faithful to it for two or three thousand generations? Surely not. It means that, as in the case of South Africa, Locality 1 was a place favorable, during the Middle Pleistocene, for occupation and fossilization, within a much larger sphere populated by Pekin Man. Other caves of his will sooner or later be found. Indeed von Koenigswald, in his apothecary-shop hunts among the dragon bones, where he found Gigantopithecus, has already turned up a few teeth which are almost the same as those from Choukoutien, but slightly larger. He has named this relative Sinanthropus oficinalis (drugstore Sinanthropus). These teeth came from somewhere in South China. Slight though such evidence is, it looks strong enough to extend Pekin Man up and down most of China, which is a lot of territory.

Even without this indication, we would be inclined to suppose that he was in truth a major form of early man, and probably the only one in the continental Far East in the Middle Pleistocene. The Choukoutien animals indicate a kinship in time with those living in South China. This suggests, not so much that man was the same throughout this zone as that, if a significantly different kind of man had been present, some sign of him might have intruded at Choukoutien. We might judge this better if we knew more about the history of stone-working in China generally. We know very little.

If we consider the whole Far East, we find in any case only one general kind of man for most of the Pleistocene (disregarding possible surviving Asiatic australopithecines like Meganthropus). The Java and Pekin men are so alike that writers who are concerned with names now call them both Pithecanthropus, sinking the genus Sinanthropus as a scientific designation (and Dr. Weidenreich called them only races, not even species). The Javanese branch looks like a slightly more primitive offshoot, entering Indonesia late in the Lower Pleistocene. At the moment, of course, we know nothing about the mainland at the same time, or whether the ancestors of Pekin Man were already a little more advanced, within the same mold, or not. Long afterward we find Solo Man on Java, perhaps a later development of the same stock, and really rather primitive for this late part of the Ice Age (Fourth Glacial?). At any rate, with these three well-known, related forms constituting a major human stock, we have a clear and simple picture of Eastern Asia, which will serve until something comes along to change it.

EARLY MAN IN THE WEST

When we turn to the west of the Old World, and the well-studied continents

Hell - end Jfl

of Europe and Africa, there is a curious reversal in the nature of our information. In Asia stone tools of man have not been traced back into the Lower Pleistocene, nor even to Java Man, though I am morally certain he made and used them. But in Europe tools may be followed down into the First Interglacial, and even into the First Glacial (Pluvial) in Africa, where they become barely recognizable as raw pebbles, split for use or crudely flaked with a few chips. It is these implements which were succeeded, probably before the Second Glacial phase, by the long-enduring hand-axes.

With this richer, older body of human tools, do we find in the west a more impressive list of human ("euhominid") fossils? We do not. To represent the whole late Lower and Middle Pleistocene—for all the time of Java Man and Pekin Man in the Far East—there have been found, not fine sets of skulls, but only isolated jaws and fragments of jaws. With a couple of exceptions to come later, which hardly vitiate this statement, that is the size of it. It is not until the Upper Pleistocene (beginning with the Third Glacial) that we have more, with the remains of the Neanderthal and Rhodesian men. Oddest of all, Europe, with so much archaeology, and so much careful searching, is fossilwise almost a blank, with the major exception of the Heidelberg jaw.

Heidelberg Man. Even this find goes back to 1907, leaving us over half a century of disappointment. The jaw did not thrust itself forward; it was found because Dr. Otto Schoetensack of Heidelberg University was looking for it and had been looking for twenty years. About seven miles southeast of Heidelberg, at the village of Mauer, a huge sand pit had been dug against the side of a long series of Pleistocene deposits of clay, sand, and gravel. Cut vertically to a great height, this fine ladder of strata, with its fossil animals, was more beautiful to the eye

of a geologist than a garden of flowers, and Dr. Schoetensack was one of the professorial bees who buzzed around it. He felt certain that somewhere in the face of the vast exposure the remains of man would sooner or later come to light, and he infected the owner of the pit with the same feeling. It finally happened: a big human jaw, quite by itself, was found in the sand, well down at the base of the bank and nearly eighty feet below the top of the deposit.

No convincing stone tools have been found in the Mauer beds. The animals at Mauer (archaic horses, a straight-tusked elephant, and the Etruscan rhino, as well as a variety of bears, deer, bison, etc.) are clearly early, being a group which comes soon after the fauna which introduces the Pleistocene itself, the Villafranchian. So the Heidelberg Man may be about as old as the earlier Java men, overlapping with the last of the manapes of South Africa. A very ancient man indeed, belonging to the end of the First Interglacial or the beginning of the Second Glacial.

This jaw is well preserved, having most of its teeth in a state of moderate wear, except for four left molars and premolars, broken at the time of discovery and only partly repaired. Before the manapes and the later finds of Java Man, the jaw was alone in its great size, and it is still impressive. It is perhaps a shade heavier than the jaw known as Pithecanthropus B.

Compared to other human jaws, the most striking thing about its shape is the great breadth of the ascending ramus, or branch. This is the vertical blade which underlies the back part of your cheek and which carries the condyle, or knob for the joint, at its hinder corner. To the forward corner, the coronoid process, there attaches one of the main muscles which close the jaw. This is the temporal muscle, which fans out on the side of

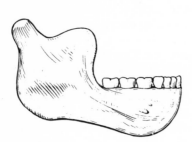

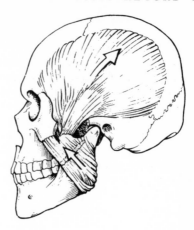

Figure 5. The Heidelberg jaw (left) in profile. After Schoetensack. One-fourth natural size. Right, the main muscles of the jaw in biting. From the angle, the *masseter,* partly cut away, which pulls up and slightly forward, being attached to the under edge of the cheek arch (zygomatic arch). From the coronoid process, or forward point of the upright branch, the *temporal* muscle, pulling up and slightly back, being attached to the side of the skull. (Drawing not to scale.) (After Cirulis)

the skull. To the outer surface of the lower portion of the ramus there attaches the other main muscle, the masseter, a short broad muscle which runs up to the under edge of the cheek bone. This is easily felt: it stands out sharply when you grit your teeth, and so may be used for dramatic effect as well as for chewing. Therefore, while the width of this ascending ramus may be related in part to the length of the whole jaw, it also suggests jaw muscles of power and efficiency. The Heidelberg jaw is in the class of the great *Paranthropus* jaws from Swartkrans, though not on a par with the larger ones. It is not as high, suggesting a less massive face. While the face was probably projecting (since the jaw is certainly long), its upright and forwardly directed coronoid process suggests that the skull above the face, where the temporal muscle lay, also extended well forward, so the face as a whole probably did not have a markedly protruding mouth region.

Nonetheless, the width of the whole jaw, and the generous expanse of ascending ramus, indicate big muscles, and wide-flaring, strong cheek arches on the vanished skull. All this power is peculiar, because the teeth, the real business edge of the whole machine, are not very large. They are not small, but they are not in proportion with the jawbone, so to speak (the same can be said of the Swartkrans jaws, to a degree). In size the teeth do not approach those of australopithecines. They are in fact nearer to modern man than they are to Java Man; the dental arch is even distinctly smaller than Pekin Man's. The teeth are rather modern in character, as well, though of good size, and with crowns which are robust right down to the base, and with big roots. Their upper surfaces are worn flat. The canines are well reduced in size and have been ground level with the other teeth, as one would expect. And the molars are of recent proportions, with the hindmost being

somewhat smaller than the one in front of it.

Beyond guessing that he had a wide, not strongly projecting face, we cannot reconstruct the Heidelberg Man's skull nor get any worth-while idea as to the size of his brain. But we can pass remarks about his relations to other hominids. The jaw suggests the australopithecines somewhat, in its breadth, size, and chunky, non-pongid look. It is entirely chinless, certainly a primitive trait. It is of course greatly inferior to the man-apes in thickness, and apparently also in height. And considering the teeth—size may be considered a particular mark of difference between australopithecines and euhominids—the jaw could not for a minute be put with the man-apes. It is clearly a euhominid, though an early and primitive one.

At the same time, it cannot be classed with those early and primitive euhominids of the Far East, Java and Pekin Man. The Heidelberg teeth are smaller and are less primitive in detail. The jaw is of a different shape, and I should venture to guess that the skull was somewhat more vertical. So, before the end of the First Interglacial at least two different kinds of men were in existence, in the east and in the west, along with the last of the man-apes.

Early Jaws in Africa. I say "at least two." Judging whether there were more depends just now on some African remains of the same period. The first of these looks like a relative of Heidelberg Man. He is *Telanthropus,* found and named by Broom and Robinson. They discovered three scraps of lower and upper jaw, all at Swartkrans and in the same deposit as *Paranthropus.* These are primitive remnants, providing no great contrast with the man-apes who, of course, are also hominids. But *Telanthropus'* teeth are smaller, in a class with the Pekin and Java men, and in fact seem more advanced in their nature than those of the latter types. The lower jaw itself resembles the Heidelberg specimen a little, and certain details in the region of the nose and bony upper gum on one fragment point to a face different from the man-apes and more vertical. Sir Wilfrid Le Gros Clark, always a sober and judicious observer, thinks it is possible that *Telanthropus* is simply a female *Paranthropus.* But Robinson finds too wide a distinction in tooth size from his many specimens of *Paranthropus,* and sticks by his guns. In any case, it is almost certain that pebble-tool-making hominids were present in South Africa by this time, and there is nothing implausible in the presence at Swartkrans of a Heidelberg-like human being to make them.

In East Africa, L. S. B. Leakey brought to light one of the most puzzling of all the fossils. He found it in 1932 close to the shore of Lake Victoria, at Kanam. It is the chin part of a jaw, quite massive, with two premolars and the

 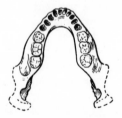 

Figure 6. Jaws of *Telanthropus* (left and center) and Ternifine Man. One-fourth natural size. (After Robinson, Arambourg, and Cirulis)

roots of the other front teeth. Its age has been accepted as Lower Pleistocene, though Oakley has tested it for accumulated uranium (a test like fluorine) and found it unexpectedly low, raising a query as to its true antiquity. Supposedly it is about as old as the Heidelberg Man and the first of the Java men. But it looks like a third kind of ancient human being: the jaw seems to have a real protruding chin on the front, like ours. In fact, the fossil gives the appearance of a huge edition of the forepart of a modern jaw.

Unfortunately, this astonishing possibility is far from clear-cut. The fragment has other material adhering to it, and the whole is densely fossilized and hard as marble. Cut in sections, it shows that the swollen lower portion, the "chin," is at least partly due to a bony tumor which grew during life, so that where tumor stops and chin begins has never been settled and perhaps cannot be. Nevertheless, Ashley Montagu has pointed out that the tooth-bearing part, at the top, is itself entirely modern in shape, showing the kind of curvature below the incisors which is only found with true chin prominences and not seen in the jaws of such fossils as the Pekin, Heidelberg, or Neanderthal men.

So we are left with an enigma, and an important one. This raises the curtain, in fact, on one of the great problems in our history. Did our own kind of man exist (naturally, in a relatively primitive, probably overgrown form) in the early Pleistocene? That is what the Kanam jaw seems to be trying to say. Certainly if you were questioning a fossil for admission to our strictly modern circle of mankind, you would ask to see his chin. Fortunately, this is the part of Kanam Man which was discovered. Unfortunately, it is the part which cannot be properly seen. The riddle remains. Kanam Man lives in a box at the British Museum, where he is subject to constant further questioning by Dr. Kenneth Oakley.

Our procession of jaws now takes us to North Africa and the beginning of the Middle Pleistocene (about the time of the Second Glacial of Europe, and of the later Java men). In Algeria, a little southeast of Oran, when the sea was beginning to fall with the onset of the Second Glacial, there existed a spring-fed pond at Ternifine. Men frequented the pond, and, like the people at Choukoutien, they were untidy. They let their tools and meat bones get into their water supply, along with the bones of other beasts of prey. A familiar picture: the men were simply a large species of primate, living among a plenitude of other Ice Age mammals, of which the great African fauna we are busily destroying today is only the last faded copy. To the springs at Ternifine came zebras, giraffes, and many antelopes; elephants, rhinos and all the kinds of carnivore; an ancient form of sabertoothed cat, giant wart hogs, and giant baboons, all these being archaic species, early Pleistocene types. And here and there in the debris in the pond there came to rest hand-axes, heavy and of an early variety but well made for their time, better than anything from the hands of the men we have reviewed so far.

Finally, thick beds of sand filled and buried the whole depression. In our own times it came into use as a sand pit, tools were discovered, and archaeologists dug there in 1931. They stopped work partway down, however, because of striking water and also from fear of undercutting Moslem graves next to one side of the pit. But the government enabled Professor Camille Arambourg to work in 1954 and 1955, with special equipment and pumps. He made a major excavation: he was able to go fifteen feet lower, down to the clay of the ancient pond. Part of his reward was three human jaws and a parietal bone, all right at the bottom.

The parietal bone, a young person's, does not tell us much. While not extremely thick, it has features like Pekin Man's, suggesting a low, poorly filled skull. The jaws, large and thick, are well preserved. In size and shape their best match is Pekin Man, and this appears to hold for traits of the teeth as well (a cingulum or collar of enamel is present on the premolars). But the total size of the molar teeth goes further and matches Java Man. Perhaps the ascending ramus of the jaw was as broad as Heidelberg Man's, but the latter's teeth are different in nature. Arambourg pointed out the likenesses to the Far Easterners but believed that the differences were enough to grant Ternifine Man a genus of his own, *Atlanthropus*. It seems probable that most people will accept Professor Arambourg's assertion that the Ternifiners are closely related to Pekin and Java Man, and will therefore reject his new genus.

At any rate, we are confronted with a being who must have been a good deal like the Pekin and Java men, occupying North Africa at about the same time. However, he was making tools of the western hand-axe variety, not of the eastern chopper school. As if to confirm the proposition, recent years have also brought to light other broken jaws from three places on the Atlantic coast of Morocco, from the other end of the Middle Pleistocene, or even a little later. The owner of the jaw fragment found at Casablanca (Sidi Abderrahman) lived at the very beginning of the Third Glacial, and of those from Rabat and Temara somewhat later, perhaps the start of the Third Interglacial. All, at any rate, were also associated with hand-axes of a later stage of the same sequence.

These jaws, with their teeth, are less primitive than the Ternifine examples, but they have various characteristics which recall the latter and, beyond them, the Far Eastern fossils. Remnants of a primitive cingulum are developed on the molar teeth, but on the premolars only of the Rabat specimen. Patterns of the cusps are like the Ternifiners. All in all, they suggest a later and less crude stage of the Ternifine family with the specimen youngest in time, that from Temara, apparently the least crude of the lot.

Does this mean that the Java-Pekin (*Pithecanthropus*) family line was actually the ruling one all over the Old World? Was Heidelberg Man only an exceptional, aberrant individual, with his smaller teeth? Is Kanam Man a booby trap? I think the answer is no, all round. For one thing, the australopithecines of the Transvaal differed considerably among themselves, and you would expect early euhominids to do likewise. It is very plain that we need fossils for the Lower and Middle Pleistocene badly, and I can only apologize for the foregoing boring display of mandibles.

Rhodesian Man. We emerge at last into much more recent times, the Upper Pleistocene, with Rhodesian Man, a later citizen of Africa and perhaps a contemporary of Solo Man of Java. Evidently he lived throughout southern Africa. At any rate, he certainly inhabited or used a cave in what is now Northern Rhodesia, not very far north of the Zambesi River. This was a long, tunnel-like affair running into a kopje, or small hill, standing above the generally flattish country. This cave started at the base of the kopje and sloped gently into its middle, a hundred and twenty feet away. The kopje itself consisted of limestone richly impregnated with ores of lead, zinc, and vanadium.

At some time it appears that ground water deep below, leaching out the soil, caused the kopje's peak to subside, leaving a saddle-like depression at the top and making the innermost end of the cave take a sudden steep dip, to a final point ninety feet below the level of the entrance. The cave, long though it was, filled up in a relatively short period with

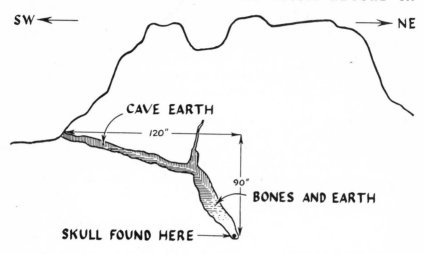

SW ← → NE

CAVE EARTH

120"

90"

BONES AND EARTH

SKULL FOUND HERE →

Figure 7. The cave at Broken Hill, in cross section. (After Clark and Cirulis)

earth containing bones and stone tools. Among the animal species represented some are extinct, but the majority are still living, which shows the comparative recency of the group. The tools belong to a recognized set of rather late, smallish cutting and scraping tools, the "Rhodesian Proto-Still Bay" culture. This is the first phase of the Middle Stone Age of Africa, known to have flourished here in the latter part of the Upper Pleistocene. Far back in the cave were a few random bones of human beings, including an upper jaw. Down at the very bottom of the last slope, where it had rolled or been thrown, was a skull.

A ninety-foot grave should have made a good hiding place, after the cave had filled and its entrance was no longer to be seen. Nonetheless, the skull came back into the light. For the hill itself, being made of ores, became useful to man when civilization arrived. The Europeans appeared, founded a mine and a town, and named them both Broken Hill after a famous mine in Australia. They dug away at the kopje, until now there is only a colossal crater in the ground where the hill stood, and the mining has

moved a mile or so away to another part of the lode.

In 1921 the miners had come unknowingly to the deep part of the lost cave. One day a Swiss miner named Zwigelaar and his African "boys" were working here. Mr. Zwigelaar loosened some ore with a small explosive charge, and when the dust cleared, there was the skull, sitting all by itself on a little shelf in the cut, right side up and looking Zwigelaar in the eye. The Africans ran off and did not come back that afternoon; and Zwigelaar was so pleased with the little drama that he stuck the skull on a pole for a day or so to awe the Africans further. Then it was taken to the mine office and came into the hands of the doctor, who saw its importance. Also, general curiosity had led to a search of the mine dumps for other remains, which produced several arm, leg, and pelvic bones and another upper jaw. Luckily, collections had and have been made of animal bones and tools as well.

The same year the bones were sent off to London to the British Museum (Natural History), where Rhodesian Man was gladly welcomed as an important new member of the then short list of fossil ancestors. At that time even Pekin Man was unknown. The skull is still a source of pride to the people of Broken Hill, who have given it a place of honor on the city's coat of arms. However, far away from home, absurd fables for some reason began to attach to Rhodesian Man, especially about his discovery. By one account, an entire body had been found, preserved even to the skin by natural embalming in zinc salts. But it was thrown into the smelter except for the skull and a few bones, because it was considered worth more as ore than as anthropology. And a staff member of the Museum (actually more of a popular writer than a scientist) looked at the pelvic bones and conceived the bizarre idea that Rhodesian Man had walked about with a stoop, and so he christened the fossil *Cyphanthropus* (Bent-over Man). Other fictions were picked up around the mine by different visitors, until more than thirty years had gone by, when Oakley and J. D. Clark thought it worth while to look up Mr. Zwigelaar, still living in Lusaka, to ask him for the simple facts. The above is his story, by courtesy of Drs. Oakley and Clark.

The Rhodesian men may have had to stoop in their cave, but out in the daylight they stood as straight as any hominid. There is nothing to say about the skeleton bones except that they can be distinguished in no particular from ours. As to the skull, it is a fine specimen, excellently preserved except for a break the size of your palm low behind the right ear, and for the teeth, which in life were all badly worn, decayed, abscessed, or lost. It is a low skull, though not like the older Far Eastern men. Actually, it is rather large, with a bigger and much more primitive face than ours, though not a very projecting one. The Rhodesian Man must have had a lower jaw verging in width on the one from Heidelberg, though not as large altogether, and higher in its ascending ramus.

But he was a new kind of man. His brain size was about 1300 c.c., still below the modern average but at the level of some living races of today. Furthermore, the skull has none of the thickness of those of Java and Pekin or of the Solo Man. His actual primitive traits were his enormous bony brow ridges above his eyes—a really spectacular development—and his large dental arch and teeth. Even these last were not primitive, the arch being very broad and the wisdom tooth much reduced in size. Also, the second upper jaw found is smaller than that on the skull, suggesting that the average size may have been less impressive than the skull suggests.

For many years this was the only discovery of Rhodesian Man. He was long something of a mystery. In the first place, nothing was known about Rhodesian archaeology when he was found, and no one had the least idea where he belonged in time, until recent years and the further development of knowledge. Secondly, because the skull was an only find there were mutterings of "pathology," meaning that disease might have been responsible for the great brows and large face, as in pituitary giantism. Java Man, you will remember, was also considered by some to be a freak. But as in Java Man's case, another Rhodesian skull was eventually found, and it was seen to be entirely like the first.

Dr. Ronald Singer of Cape Town University located a good site for animal fossils, on the barren Atlantic coast of South Africa near Saldanha Bay, some eighty miles north of Cape Town, and fifteen hundred miles away from Broken Hill. Here are the remains of a rich fauna, from a prosperous part of the Ice Age, together with a series of human tools from the latest times back toward the Middle Pleistocene. The spot, however, is now a small sand desert; the wind moves sand dunes and blows away sand

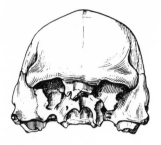

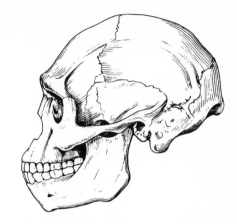

Figure 8. Rhodesian Man. The Broken Hill skull. One-fourth natural size. From cast and photographs. (After Cirulis)

and leaves the heavier fossils sitting on the surface. Here Singer and an associate found, by great good luck, a human skull top in twenty-seven small pieces, picking these up on more than one visit as the wind exposed them. The pieces fit nicely together to make a skull differing in only slight ways from the Broken Hill specimen. Somewhat smaller in size, it may be female. The ridge for neck muscles at the back differs, but not impressively, since the ridge varies somewhat in all populations. The skull is thicker, a more interesting distinction.

A Lesson in Dating. This find is evidence that Rhodesian Man, like Pekin Man, is not the relic of a one-cave band, but belonged to a definite population covering a wide continental space. Did he also stretch over a good span of time? A little while ago a blown-out skull like the Saldanha fragments would have been at loose ends, giving small possibility of telling what fossils or tools it went with. But the fossil hunters are not so helpless now, and the picture seems bright, with what they already know and what they can find out.

Very exact examination of the Saldanha (Hopefield) site shows that the main fossil animals all belong to a single layer of deposition, which contains late hand-axes and which can only fit into the onset of the Gamblian, the last great rainy phase (supposedly the time of the Fourth Glacial in the north). And Oakley, with fluorine tests and with newer tests for radioactive uranium based on the same principle of accumulation, proves that the Saldanha skull goes with the animals and thus with the hand-axes. Later men at the same place left tools of the next culture stage above the hand-axes, called the Still Bay.

Now we know the Broken Hill Man had Proto-Still Bay tools in his cave, but no hand-axes. We also know that the Still Bay sequence followed right on the end of the hand-axes, and the Broken Hill specimens belong to the early phase of that sequence. Other things being equal, this would make the Broken Hill people just later in time than the Saldanha individual. However, one more adjustment is needed, because the Still Bay culture appeared somewhat earlier north of the Zambesi than in South Africa.

So it is safe to say only that these two fossil men lived and died about the same time. Still it is a great advance to know as much as we do, and to have the finds

Figure 9. Africa: sites of the fossil men. The *Australopithecus* sites are included for reference, also that of *Proconsul* (Rusinga Island), and of probable Neanderthal specimens (Tangier, Haua Fteah, Diredawa). (After Cirulis)

corroborate each other. We can conclude with some confidence that the human beings, who lived in southern Africa as the last glacial phase was reaching its peak in Europe, and who were changing from the use of hand-axes to the smaller tools of the Middle Stone Age, were the big-browed kind we know from Broken Hill and Saldanha. This is an improvement; as late as 1949 Professor Zeuner, an authority on dating, could still write

that the Broken Hill bones could not even be placed within one of the main divisions of the Pleistocene.

Perhaps we can stretch things even further. In 1935 and 1938, Kohl-Larsen found a large number of small pieces of at least three human skulls near Lake Eyasi. This is up near the northern border of Tanganyika in East Africa and about nine hundred miles as the crow flies from Broken Hill, in the direction opposite to Cape Town. Some of the pieces were pasted up into a very primitive looking "skull," which was baptized *Africanthropus* and believed to be a cousin of the Java and Pekin people. Few anthropologists have exhibited any enthusiasm for this restoration. The individual scraps look more like the Rhodesian type (with the kind of sharp crest for the neck muscles which graces the Broken Hill skull) than like anything else. And other material found at the sites seems to agree in date with the Rhodesian remains found further south. We cannot presume that this is find number three of the Rhodesian type, but we certainly cannot presume the contrary.

All this is a little dry and complicated. But it is really well worth attending to as a fine example of how small facts, and a few skulls, can be put together and, by persistent detective work and new methods of study, be made to say something definite and important to human history.

With the question of man's more recent ancestry—the exact identity and order of relation of our Middle and Upper Pleistocene predecessors—controversy continues. Neanderthal man has been persistently, and perhaps incorrectly, described as too brutish to deserve a position of prominence on our family tree. But this view is changing.

4. The Problem of the Neanderthals [1]

At the time when Darwin and Huxley first claimed that man evolved from a primate similar to the anthropoids of today, little evidence substantiated by palaeontological facts was available. In the meantime, however, quite a number of fossil forms have been recovered all of which may justifiably be claimed as "missing links." Yet, strangely enough, the more such intermediate types came to light, the less was the readiness of acknowledging them as ancestors of *Homo sapiens*. In many cases the scepticism apparently was the last bastion from which the final acceptance of Darwin's theory could be warded off with a certain air of scientism.

Interpretation of the hominid fossil record has inevitably been colored by the climate of opinion prevalent at the time of the discovery of the major pieces of evidence. What are now recognized as being the earliest known hominids were not the earliest fossil hominids to be known, which may account in large measure for the fact that their essential humanity was not recognized at the time of their discovery. When the first Australopithecine was found in 1924 there already were candidates for all the postulated stages of human evolution, and the suggestion that this was anything more than just another fossil ape was greeted with a notable lack of enthusiasm.

At this time, the earliest known hominid was *Pithecanthropus* (now properly considered *Homo* by Weidenreich and Mayr) *erectus,* and even the most enthusiastic proponents of the human status of this fossil had to concede that if culture had indeed been associated with the population of which it was a member,

[1] C. LORING BRACE. Parts of this paper, originally entitled "The Fate of the 'Classic' Neanderthals," were read at the 1962 meeting of the American Anthropological Association, Chicago, Ill., November 18, 1962. Printed here by permission of the author. A revised version later appeared in *Current Anthropology* (February 1964), Vol. 5, No. 1, pp. 3–19.

Dr. Brace is Assistant Professor of Anthropology at the University of California, Santa Barbara.

then that culture must have been of the crudest recognizable sort. *Pithecanthropus* was widely hailed as Haeckel's "missing link," and considered to exist on the very borderline of human and subhuman stages in evolution. With the bottommost rung in the scale of human evolution presumably occupied, it took some thirty years and an abundance of evidence before the hominid status of the Australopithecines became generally acceptable. Opinion is still far from being unanimous, and, despite the necessary relationship between Australopithecine anatomy and tool use, and the clear unbroken sequence of cultural evolution from the Oldowan to the atomic bomb, many authorities prefer to reserve judgment or to deny them lineal precedence to morphologically more modern hominids on geological grounds alone, ignoring the fact that the geological placement of the Australopithecines is so fluid that even absolute dating techniques differ in the age assigned by more than 100 per cent.

If the climate of opinion prevalent at the time of discovery has had such a profound and lasting effect on the interpretation of fossil material found within the last forty years, it should be instructive to consider the effects exerted by the climate of opinion on the interpretation of the first hominid fossils to be discovered more than a century ago. The first publicized discovery of skeletal remains now attributable to an earlier stage in human evolution occurred in Germany in 1856 just three years prior to the publication of Darwin's *Origin of Species* (1859). Even in England where Darwin's influence was relatively stronger than elsewhere, sympathy with an evolutionary viewpoint was far from being unanimous as is evident from the record of the conflicts. In Germany, where the Neanderthaler was found, evolution, despite the support of Haeckel met with continued scientific opposition and was much longer

in being accepted. In the absence of stratigraphic evidence for antiquity, the Neanderthaler could have been found some years later and still have been given a similar reception. With no proof for its age, and no morphologically similar skeletal material available for comparison, these remains which clearly differed in form from modern man were judged as being not normal. The power of this judgment was such that later, when datable remains of clearly similar morphology finally did turn up, the interpretation tended to remain the same although the basis changed markedly, and totally different kinds of evidence were offered in its support.

The nineteenth century view was summarized by Virchow in 1872 when he enumerated the pathological characteristics of the remains. Neanderthal was regarded as being peculiar from that point on, and the peculiarities were at first thought to be pathological in origin. Circumstantial evidence in favor of his interpretation was offered by the fact that fossil man was already known to exist and his form was not radically different from that of modern man. As yet, degrees of antiquity were but dimly perceived, and, in addition, the resemblance of the so-called Old Man of Cro-Magnon to modern man has been enthusiastically stressed with greater confidence than its edentulous condition properly warrants. With a restored set of teeth occluded in characteristic Upper Palaeolithic fashion, his face would look far more like that of Combe Capelle, and the supposed paradox of its short wide form would be eliminated, Virchow's final denial of the antiquity of the Neanderthal find was based on the assumed age of the individual. Because of suture closure, it was assumed that he was elderly, and Virchow's claim was that no one could live to such an advanced age in a nomadic or hunting and gathering society, therefore he must have belonged to a sedentary group and great antiquity would not have been possible.

By the end of the century, however, much more was known concerning the relative placement of the various subdivisions of prehistory. At Spy, the two individuals of Neanderthal-like morphology had been found in a Mousterian layer definitely prior to the Upper Palaeolithic, and a calva has been found which differed even more from modern man and which belonged to a geological time far earlier even than Spy. Putting these facts together, Gustav Schwalbe tried to support a view of human evolution in three stages starting with Pithecanthropus, developing through Neanderthal into modern man. Schwalbe's views had the advantages of simplicity and logic, although they did run counter to the strong current of thought which was decidedly uncomfortable when suggestions were advanced that man might have evolved from something which looked less man-like than man.

Furthermore, for the next twenty years, the most significant work on fossil man was to come from France because of the fact that relatively extensive remains of Neanderthalers were to be discovered at four different sites: e.g., Le Moustier 1908, La Chapelle-aux-Saints 1908, La Ferrassie 1909, and La Quina 1911. While the Le Moustier skeleton was the first of this group to be found, the somewhat devious activities of the discoverer, the series of unfortunate reconstructions, and the long delay before a description was published combined to deprive it of the notice which it should have received. Because the description of the La Ferrassie skeletons was entrusted to Boule, work on them was delayed by his preoccupation with the previously discovered La Chapelle find, and, in fact, a study of the La Farrassie remains has yet to be published although a half century has elapsed since their discovery. The discovery of the La Quina material was apparently eclipsed by the simultaneous publication of the first major installment of the description of La Chapelle-aux-Saints. Thus, by chance, the La Chapelle find became the center of attention as the most complete Neanderthal to have been discovered, and, as a result, the work which has long been regarded as definitive for the Neanderthal "type" was a product of French scholarship.

After their discovery on August 3, 1908, the Abbés A. and J. Bouyssonie and L. Bardon sought the advice of their friend and colleague l'Abbé Henri Breuil, who suggested that they give the bones to Professor Marcellin Boule at the Museum d'Histoire Naturelle in Paris for detailed study and description. Boule with great industry and dispatch produced a series of works culminating in the tomes of 1911, 1912, and 1913 in which he depicted the Neanderthals in terms which have served journalists and scholars ever since as the basis for the caricature of the cave man. Since he was not prepared to accept such a creature in the human family tree, he settled the question to the general satisfaction by declaring the Neanderthals as well as the Pithecanthropines—the only other nonmodern hominid fossils known—became extinct without issue.

At the time when Boule established the view that Neanderthal could not be the ancestor to subsequent forms of men, he offered two points in support of his conclusion. It is instructive to look at these today since they are both accepted without much question, although the evidence involved has undergone marked changes.

1. Modern forms of man already existed at the time of the Neanderthalers.

2. The Mousterian was suddenly replaced by the Upper Palaeolithic and the very suddenness of the change indicated that the bearers of the Upper Palaeolithic must have been developing their cultural traditions elsewhere for a considerable

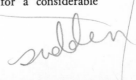

period of time. As a corollary to this, it was claimed that the anatomical differences between the supposed immediately succeeding populations were so great that they precluded the possibility of evolution. Both of these points are offered in support of his claim that modern forms of *Homo sapiens* have an antiquity which extends far back into the Pleistocene, but, even at that time, the evidence in their support was very far from being adequate. Curiously enough, both points persist in anthropological writings of recent years, and, while different evidence is offered, it is equally inadequate, as will be discussed shortly.

Boule's candidates for morphologically modern precursors or contemporaries with Neanderthalers were the Grimaldi skeletons—the so-called "Negroids" from the Grotte des Enfants at Menton—and later the Piltdown skull. These he felt were proof of the early existence of modern forms of man, although he was aware that Cartailhac had already cautioned that the Grimaldi finds were to be associated with Aurignacian cultural material overlying the Mousterian. The reason for Boule's acceptance of Piltdown as valid evidence is not at all clear from the literature, although it may have depended upon the personalities and friendships of the people involved. Previously Boule had examined and rejected the evidence for the antiquity of Galley Hill, Clichy, Denise, Grenelle, Ipswich, Olmo, Bury St. Edmonds, and others, although these could be regarded as at least as reliable as Piltdown.

Boule's position on the replacement of the Mousterian (and hence, Neanderthal Man) by the Upper Palaeolithic (and hence, *Homo sapiens* in the modern sense) is remarkably similar to the theory of Catastrophism supported by Cuvier just a century earlier as an explanation for geological successions. This should not be surprising since Boule was trained as a palaeontologist in midnineteenth

century France where palaeontology, comparative anatomy, and geology were taught by Cuvier's disciples and immediate successors who followed in detail the teachings of their late master. Cuvier's explanation for the apparently sudden changes visible in specific stratigraphic sequences was based on his feeling that stratigraphic columns literally recorded *all* the events which had formerly taken place. A sudden change in faunal content indicated that a corresponding sudden change in the animal populations must have taken place at the past time indicated. The appearance of new forms of animals in succeeding superimposed strata did not necessarily signify creation *de novo,* but rather indicated that these animals had previously existed elsewhere in the world, and, following the catastrophe which had eliminated their predecessors in the area under examination, they swept in as an invasion and suddenly occupied the area of their extinct precursors.

These views have their roots in the eighteenth and early nineteenth centuries when some sort of explanation was needed for the sequences being discovered in the fossil record, but when a theory of evolution was emotionally unacceptable and had not yet been worked out as an encompassing explanatory principle. Cuvier's influence was so strong that many continental scholars, when faced with the development of evolutionary thinking, tried to illustrate every possible way in which it would *not* work instead of examining it rationally and trying to understand how it *could* work. The battle fought by these people has been a defensive one emphasizing negative facets, and the result has largely been a devious and unproductive delaying action.

Boule, following the tradition in which he had been trained, attempted to show that the morphological gap between Neanderthal and modern man was so large

Boule → Vallois *catastrophe*

rTHE FOSSIL RECORD 111

and the temporal gap was so small that the former could not have been the ancestor of the latter. The extinction of the one and the invasion of the other was postulated, and the result was the development of what could be labelled the theory of hominid catastrophism—still vigorously advocated by Boule's disciple Vallois and echoed by many others. In his efforts to give his arguments the greatest possible effect, Boule claimed that Neanderthals exhibited many characters which subsequent unbiased research has failed to substantiate. Thus, despite Boule's claims, there is no trace of evidence that Neanderthalers had exceptionally divergent great toes or that they were forced to walk oranglike on the outer edges of their feet; there is no evidence that they were unable to fully extend their knee joints; there is no evidence that their spinal columns lacked the convexities necessary for fully erect posture; there is no evidence that the head was slung forward on a peculiarly short and thick neck; and there is no evidence that the brain was qualitatively inferior to that of modern man.

One could logically ask, then, in what ways, if any, the Neanderthals do differ from modern men. In general, they convey the impression of skeletal rugosity including the wide epiphyses of the long bones, the relative thickness of the hand and foot bones, and the relative stoutness of the ribs, but primarily their distinctiveness occurs in the size of the face involving gross tooth dimensions and supporting architecture. No one of these differences is outside the range of variation of modern man, but taken together, the face dimensions, especially, indicate a population noticeably distinct from any *populations* existing today, yet there is no good reason why such a population could not have been ancestral to modern man. In fact, given the aggregate human fossil material from the Australopithecines through the Pithecanthropines and

presumably on up, it would be most extraordinary if something like Hrdlička's Neanderthal phase had *not* occurred just prior to the development of more modern forms.

Since the time of Boule's analysis, very few attempts have been made to compare Neanderthals as a group with other human populations. One of these compares individual (mainly La Chapelle-aux-Saints) measurements with the range of modern population means, and, however correct the conclusions may be, this remains highly dubious as a statistical procedure. Another study does not even use measurements but relies on subjective appraisal of morphological features, arbitrarily designated as single gene traits, and does not allow for any population variability at all. These works, as did that of Boule, are not interested in how the characteristics of modern man developed and what they developed from, since their primary purpose is a negative one— to demonstrate that Neanderthal Man could not have had any descendants.

While the morphology and particularly the functional significance of morphological differences, has been left largely unstudied, there has on the other hand been much interest in the question involving the possible contemporaneity of modern man with the Neanderthals. The idea has been that if evidence of a morphologically modern population would be found at the same time as, or earlier than, the Neanderthals, then this would serve as the logical ancestor to modern man, and we need never fear that anything so "brutish" as a Neanderthal would show up in our family tree. The popularity of this approach has been enormous in spite of the fact that, over the years, the candidates offered to represent this supposed population have proved to be a shadowy lot and impossible to pin down.

Boule himself offered the Grimaldi skeletons as contemporaries of Neanderthals although Cartailhac had already noted that they should be considered Aurignacian and hence subsequent to the Mousterian. Boule also regarded Piltdown as a possible early stem from which modern man arose. The famous exposure of the Piltdown remains as fraudulent means that both of the pieces of evidence which he offered in favor of this view must be discarded. Curiously enough, Schwalbe in his extensive review of Boule's work on La Chapelle, noted the Aurignacian status of Grimaldi and the questionable nature of Piltdown, but still was so impressed by Boule's weighty scholarship that he partially changed his former assertion that Neanderthals had been the direct precursors to later forms of men.

Following the capitulation of Schwalbe in 1913, the standard interpretation of the European Neanderthals was that they were a curious and peculiar group of "specialized," squat, clumsy, and unadaptable men doomed to sudden extinction following the first stadial of the Würm glaciation when faced with the invasion of a population of "noble," "handsome," "clean-limbed," fully modern men of superior form and culture. This widespread certainty that a gap in the stratigraphic sequence necessarily indicated a break in the continuity of the local population—catastrophism in the best pre-Darwinian tradition—was momentarily upset by the find of a population at Skhul (Mount Carmel, Palestine) in 1931–1932 which was morphologically intermediate between Neanderthal and modern peoples. Thus there was great relief among the proponents of Neanderthal extinction when Mount Carmel was presumably demonstrated to have been Third Interglacial and hence necessarily prior to the more primitive Neanderthalers. With sapiens occurring earlier than Neanderthal, then the likelihood was considered eliminated that Neanderthal was the ancestor to modern man, and the relief of those who were manifestly un-

easy about the possibility of discovering a Neanderthal skeleton in a sapiens closet was apparent. But it was the uneasy relief of those who had been badly jolted by an uncomfortably near miss, so the attempt to grasp at early sapiens straws continued.

With the existence of fossil skeletal material from various places exhibiting a complete gradation from fully Neanderthal to fully modern morphology, former efforts to deny the Neanderthals ancestral status on the grounds that they were too "specialized" or "peculiar" or just plain "different" have lost their force, although remnants of such arguments still exist. Whereas "thirty years ago it almost became a sport of a certain group of authors to search the skeletal parts of Neanderthal Man for peculiarities which could be proclaimed as 'specialization', thereby proving the deviating course this form had taken in evolution," this has now been abandoned by most scholars and the case has been reduced to one of dating—for instance the primary concern exhibited by Clark Howell for geological relationships rather than for morphological change and the factors influencing it. As Le Gros Clark says, "On purely morphological grounds (and without reference to paleontological sequence), there is no certain argument why H. Neanderthalensis could not be ancestral to H. sapiens. But, in this particular instance, the fossil record shows clearly that such was not the case."

Interestingly enough, in his various works Clark himself apparently has been guilty of three "fallacies," all of which he warns against. He refers to sapiens skulls in Europe prior to the last major glaciation on what he calls "reasonably sound" geological evidence. Since in this particular instance he refers to no specific fossil, one cannot appraise what he means by "reasonably sound," but if, as he implies elsewhere, his reference is to the dating of such finds as Fontéchevade, Mount

Carmel, and Arapine, then he has been guilty first of the fallacy of relying on tentative and inadequately documented dating procedures. Clark himself has recognized the "equivocal" nature of the dating of many hominid fossils but this does not deter him from using such equivocal data to support his previously drawn conclusions.

Second, he is guilty of another fallacy to which he alludes—that of inferring form and taxonomic affiliation on the basis of fragmentary and inadequate evidence. Thus he offers the Fontéchevade fragments as being not demonstrably different from *Homo sapiens,* yet, problems of dating aside, the uncertainties surrounding the form of the major fragment (Fontéchevade II) are clearly apparent despite the extraordinarily poor quality of the illustrations in Vallois' monograph. When tracings are made of these, enlarged to the same size, and superimposed for comparison, the differences between the form of the vault prior to restoration and that claimed following restoration are so great that the only hint that the subject is the same skull is in the rough similarity in outline of the broken margin on the right. With such gross disagreement apparent in the work of the only author who has made a close study of the original, the claim that the reconstruction of the frontal width indicated a lack of brow ridge becomes simply a statement unsupported by any evidence.

Vallois' claims concerning the significance of the placement of the supposed trace of frontal sinus must be taken on faith since it fails to show in the poor photographs. Apparently it is in a part of the frontal devoid of the external bony table, and any cranial contour based on diploe alone—even in a skull which has not spent any time in the ground—is not something which can be used with much confidence. The simple presence of sinus in an otherwise undistinguished piece of frontal is not in itself evidence either for or against the existence of a brow ridge as can be seen from Krapina frontal number 2 in which the sinus extends 27 mm. above the top of the naso-frontal suture and a good 15 mm. above the maximum swelling of a well-developed brow ridge at glabella. The top of the sinus is above any trace of the start of the brow ridge.

Furthermore, the assertion that the presence of a sinus precludes the juvenile status of Fontéchevade I implies a knowledge of the age of development of the frontal sinus in possible Neanderthal populations which we do not possess, in spite of Vallois' reference to the eight year old La Quina child. When it suits their convenience, authors frequently refer to the supposed fact that distinctive Neanderthal morphology develops early in life, yet when an undoubted Neanderthaler is found, such as Le Moustier, which lacks the supposedly typical brow ridge, then there is no hesitation to refer this to the relative youth of the bearer, conveniently ignoring the fact that at age sixteen the Le Moustier "youth" had relatively little growing left to do. It is just possible that in accepting the Fontéchevade remains as representative of a presumed population, Le Gros Clark and others have not been heeding the caution which he advances against utilizing individuals for comparison where size, sex, and particularly age are in doubt, and it would seem that despite Montagu's somewhat indignant expostulations, Clark Howell's initial and repeated cautions against relying too heavily on such fragmentary pieces of evidence as Fontéchevade as the primary prop for radical theories should have had more influence.

In connection with this same fallacy of inferring from inadequate data, Le Gros Clark and many others have stressed the mixture of neanthropic and primitive features in the Steinheim skull, but few such commentators have even mentioned the fact stressed in the descriptive monograph that the skull had undergone a considerable amount of post-mortem deformation. This is clearly visible in the cast. The presence of a canine fossa claimed by Boule and Vallois is not conclusive in either cast or photographs, the claimed absence of prognathism could just as easily be due to the fact that the incisor-bearing part of the face is missing, and furthermore the whole facial skeleton has been badly warped post-mortem. The "laterally compressed" aspect of the skull supposedly indicating *sapiens* form should be taken literally since the whole left side of the skull has been deformed towards the midline as can be seen from the fact that the width of the palate between the third molars is only 35 mm. and the biauricular breadth is only approximately 82 mm. The occipital has apparently been slightly warped underneath creating the supposedly *sapiens* "rounded back and neck region." Finally, the brow ridges and the forehead, as noted in Weinert's description and recently recognized only by Montagu are reminiscent of Pithecanthropus rather than Neanderthal or *sapiens*. The presumably "neanthropic" features of Steinheim, then, would seem to occur mainly in the reconstructions of those who would have them appear that way.

Finally, in considering inferences made from incomplete remains, one must refer to the famous Swanscombe skull. Reference could also be made to Ehringsdorf and Quinzana where the face is likewise missing, but since, excluding the fragmentary and dubious Fontéchevade remains, the greater part of the case for sapiens antiquity rests on Swanscombe, it will be considered by itself. Unlike the Fontéchevade finds, there can be no doubt concerning the late second interglacial age of the Swanscombe remains. If the form of the vault were indistinguishable from modern man this would be most suggestive, although by itself

not conclusive. The original detailed report found no measurements or proportions wherein the remains could be considered distinguishable from recent *Homo sapiens* despite the Neanderthaloid biasterionic breadth. Yet on the other hand, it could not be distinguished from the warped and distorted Steinheim skull.

In connection with the appraisal of unquantifiable characters, Clark quite properly warns against overemphasis of "primitive" features of fossil remains simply because the material is old; however he neglects to warn against the overemphasis of "modern" features by authors whose desire to find clear evidence for the pre-Würm existence of morphologically modern man is so strong that some have expressed it as a "need." Still, with Clark's caution against inferring from inadequate data and his emphasis on the consideration of total morphological pattern, and despite his admission that further finds might show that Swanscombe was quite distinct from modern form, yet he concludes that it is indeed indistinguishable from modern man. He feels that if the face were of a form comparable to the "extreme Neanderthal type" this would be reflected in the anatomy of the preserved vault parts. Since he indicates that this is not the case, he believes that the brow ridges could not have been more pronounced than those of the Steinheim skull, although, as has been indicated above the Steinheim brow is so far from being *sapiens* in form that it is better compared with Pithecanthropus than with the Neanderthals, and yet as Morant has indicated the Steinheim vault differs less from the modern "type" than does the Swanscombe.

To contrast with Clark's confidence in the sapient form of Swanscombe, Weidenreich felt that attempts to classify it were doubtful until proof could be brought forward of the characters of the brow and face. This was a logical recognition of the fact emphasized by Morant that the greatest distinction between Neanderthals and subsequent forms of men occurs in the development of the face. In spite of his good morphological caution and the other solid theoretical reasons for insisting on full documentation before a fossil be accepted which would

Gros Clark in this as in the other instances cited he has failed to follow his own very good advice.

A brief listing of the major authors and their candidates for ancient sapiens should show how the evidence has changed since 1908 without becoming any less nebulous.

Boule 1908	Grimaldi
Boule 1913	Grimaldi and Piltdown
Keith 1915	Galley Hill (Piltdown)
Osborn 1919	No evidence at all except sheer faith
Osborn 1922	Piltdown
Hooton 1931	Piltdown (Galley Hill)
Howells 1944	Mount Carmel (Galley Hill and Swanscombe)
Hooton 1946	Piltdown (Galley Hill and Swanscombe)
Keith 1949	Abandons the view
Le Gros Clark 1955	Swanscombe and Fontéchevade
Boule and Vallois 1957	Fontéchevade
Montagu 1960	Swanscombe and Fontéchevade

[handwritten marginal note: ancient sap]

contradict most of the evidence for human evolution, Weidenreich has been criticized for possible "morphological dating" and for "preferring morphological to geological evidence in the dating of fossils." In retrospect, however, his cautions were well founded. The Piltdown fragments which he refused to believe have been proven fraudulent, and, after some thoughtful scepticism regarding the morphology of the Swanscombe skull, one of the very people who questioned Weidenreich's motives in urging such caution has himself observed that the occipito-mastoid crest of the Swanscombe skull looks much more like that of the known Neanderthals than that of modern man. These observations, showing that the anatomical evidence for pre-Neanderthal *sapiens* is far from secure, suggest the final fallacy which weakens the case of the proponents of such views.

This fallacy might be called that of establishing broad and far-reaching theories of human evolution on poorly documented samples—in many cases single dubious specimens. This has been clearly warned against by Clark Howell, and although it has been recognized by Le

This should suffice to show that the evidence has undergone a complete change while the argument has remained substantially the same. The words of Samuel Butler, uttered in protest to the triumph of Darwinian views, but now peculiarly appropriate in their support, complained that ". . . no matter how much anyone now moves the foundations, he cannot shake the superstructure, which has become so currently accepted as to be above the need of any support from reason. . . ." Evidently the theoretical framework has not altered since the influential works of Boule on La Chapelle-aux-Saints, and a great majority of the students of human evolution have tried to demonstrate on the flimsiest kind of evidence the contemporaneity of modern forms of man with the various nonmodern hominids discovered so far in an apparent attempt to prove that these nonmodern hominids thereby could not be the forerunners of truly modern men. Despite this clearly antievolutionary bias, fully realized twenty years ago by an interested sociologist, no modern work goes so far as to deny that human evolution occurred. It would seem rather to be a case of "out of sight, out of mind" since the crucial events in the development of *sapiens* morphology are generally pushed back in time to a point where "the fossil record dwindles into obscurity" and people are not likely to be disturbed by the sight of a human ancestor who looks rather less than human.

The effect of Boule's work and the immediate and continuing influence which it has had was so powerful that Clark Howell has recently commented that he knew of no "thoughtful worker in the field in the past half century" who has advocated a view involving the evolution of men of modern form from the European Neanderthals. Actually he is forgetting the views of Hrdlička, Weidenreich, Weinert, and others who must be accounted as thoughtful workers however much one may disagree with them on some points. As far as the effect which their opposition to the picture painted by Boule has had, they might just as well have never existed.

It is interesting that the fundamentally antievolutionary, or at least nonevolutionary, tone of palaeoanthropology as represented in the writings of the majority of western European and American authors has been clearly recognized by Russian and Polish anthropologists. The willingness of eastern European students to accept the fossil record as indicative of the evolution of man may stem in part from the prestige which Hrdlička continued to enjoy in the country of his birth and neighboring areas although it would seem that at least part of the reason may be based on sociopolitical ideology and not on basic biology—witness the pointless pregenetic insistence on typology, and the continued fruitless attempts to view the issues of human biological variation as revolving around the long dead conflict of polyphyletism monophyletism. In the "conflict" according to Dambski it is claimed that ". . . it is the Soviet students who now stand in the van" and

exhibit "the correct attitude." It appears however that the "van" stalled before a concern was developed for natural selection and the mechanisms involved in heredity, and it would seem to have remained stationary ever since. This criticism, while primarily directed at the purposeless typologies of the living, can also be made of the great majority of the attempts to interpret the human fossil record. It is hoped that this paper will serve as a preliminary effort to reverse the trend.

In the desire to prove Neanderthal extinction, it would appear as though many recent authors have rejoiced in chronological indications, however shaky, which would tend to confound a logical view of human evolution. Thus both Hrdlička and Weindenreich have been taken to task for putting more reliance on the morphological developments, which they were professionally competent to evaluate in their thinking about evolutionary development than in the tentative orderings which the very incomplete geochronological studies sought to assign to certain fossil specimens. Admittedly the concept of morphological dating, as applied by Hrdlička to the New World, thoroughly deserved the criticism which it received, but condemnation was pushed beyond the specific to the general with the implication that the morphological assessment of evolutionary development and hence possible age is *never* a legitimate procedure. As an indication that the criticism was carried too far, the same source deplored the fact that by 1948 Sir Arthur Keith had finally wavered in his former blind acceptance of the geological appraisal of the Galley Hill skeleton. Ironically in a publication which appeared at the same time as the criticism, it was finally and unassailably demonstrated that the supposedly objective evidence for the antiquity of Galley Hill was worthless.

Subsequent events have shown that

Weidenreich's suspicion of the validity of Piltdown and the sapient form of Swanscombe, while certainly "very close to morphological dating," was suspicion well founded. Other facets of Weidenreich's work such as his claim for giant hominid ancestors, his failure to recognize the significance of the Australopithecines, and his approach to orthogenesis will draw few defenders now.

Whatever the weaknesses in the works of Weidenreich, Hrdlička, and Weinert, their similar approaches to the Neanderthal question deserve careful consideration which, so far, has not been given them. Because Hrdlička published his views extensively before Weidenreich, he will be considered first, while Weinert, as the last major living representative of such an interpretation, will be considered after Weidenreich.

The full development of Hrdlička's ideas can be seen in his Huxley Memorial Lecture for 1927 reprinted in the Annual Report of the Smithsonian Institution for 1928 and repeated and emphasized in 1930. It is not surprising that the perspective of more than thirty years should reveal that Hrdlička cannot be substantiated in some of his ideas, but what *is* surprising is that these turn out to be remarkably few and do not affect his major thesis.

Thus he refused to accept geological indications for a succession of four glacial maxima in Europe during the Pleistocene, although, since he did recognize the evidence for the onset of periglacial conditions at the time of the Neanderthals, he was able to view evolutionary problems where early Würm populations are concerned from the point of view of changes in selective factors. His question concerning the motivation of a supposed *sapiens* population to invade a Europe in the grip of a most unappealing climate might be parried by the postulation that the Neanderthal-*sapiens* change took place during the Göttweiger interstadial,

although both the skeletal and the geological evidence is still not even adequate to frame the question let alone answer it, and such an answer must hence be in the nature of an evasion.

While Hrdlička made a conscientious effort to view the human evolutionary changes he observed in terms of changes in selective pressures, he did not have a sufficient grounding in evolutionary genetics, and, consequently, he misinterpreted the significance of the great morphological variability which his extensive familiarity with the skeletal material had led him to appreciate. Noting Neanderthal skeletal variability and postulating increasing stringency of selective pressures, he inferred that the two were connected in a cause and effect relationship, although he did not tackle the problem of why the ultimate change resulted in a reduction of general muscularity and a reduction in size of the facial skeleton. Weidenreich, faced with similar problems in later years, likewise could see no logical rationale for such reductions and concluded by assigning them in some cryptic way to the enlargement of the brain. It is interesting to note that Clark Howell goes no farther than to assign "Classic Neanderthal" form to "severe selective pressures" but does not say how this works and makes no effort to view *sapiens* evolution from this point of view. Le Gros Clark, for his part, is simply content to quote Clark Howell.

In speaking of an increase in population variability, Thoma noted that according to sound evolutionary theory this should indicate a *decrease* in selective pressures, but since he, like the other authors cited, feels certain that Palaeolithic conditions call for strong selection, he explains the variability (for the Mount Carmel populations) as a result of hybridization. Actually, all of these authors have failed to appreciate the fact that culture, rather than climate, has been the prime factor to be reckoned with in assessing the selective pressures operating on man. If Neanderthal and Neanderthaloid (e.g., Mount Carmel) actually do show unusual variability, then it seems logical to view this as a reduction in the former adaptive significance of the traits in question. With the clear indications of the increase of special tools for special purposes beginning in the Mousterian and continuing without break through the Upper Palaeolithic in Europe and the Middle East, the extreme rounding wear seen on the anterior teeth of earlier populations, indicative of extensive use of the dentition as a tool, gradually reduces, and it can be inferred that developing culture has reduced the adaptive significance of the huge Middle Palaeolithic dentition and its supporting facial architecture. In conjunction with principles recently elaborated, the ultimate result of the reduction of the adaptive significance of a structure will be the reduction of the structure itself. This provides the final reason for the transformation of a Neanderthal into a *sapiens* population which Hrdlička, Weidenreich, and Weinert postulated but could not quite account for.

Aside from these weak points in Hrdlička's reasoning, the rest is quite sound in spite of the fact that it has been almost completely ignored. First of all, he recognized that a view calling for Neanderthal extinction demands that there should be a demonstrable sudden replacement in Europe of one population by the other which had been developing elsewhere. While Hrdlička did not observe, as he might have done to some effect, that this in miniature was precisely the type of stratigraphic explanation which Darwin was up against nearly a century before in refuting the prevailing views of Cuvier and catastrophism, yet he did note that there are a number of problems which views involving extinctions and invasions must face.

1. Invasion and replacement presupposes a long double line of evolution which is so unlikely as to require solid proof before it could be rendered acceptable. Furthermore, an invasion to be successful in the face of an established population presupposes a large invading force, and a large invading force presupposes a still larger mother population elsewhere. As Hrdlička noted, there is no clear evidence for any such large non-Neanderthal population in Europe, and there certainly is none in Asia or Africa. To this one might add that, despite the efforts of a whole subsequent generation of students all anxious to prove *sapiens* antiquity, there is neither cultural nor skeletal evidence for these phantom *sapiens* populations, and the few individuals offered as such (for instance, Steinheim, Swanscombe, Fontéchevade, and Kanjera) are either distorted, fragmentary, of dubious date, or downright un-*sapiens*.

Howell has sought to provide a reason for a long independent period of evolution for two hominid lines by claiming the climatic isolation of Europe during the early Würm, but the marked cultural similarities between Europe and the Middle East as opposed to either one and other parts of the Old World (Africa or eastern Asia) would seem to indicate that the ecological zone stretching from Iran across the northern Mediterranean border to southwest Europe, far from being broken up into cultural isolates, was a zone in which similar cultural elements maintained circulation—i.e., a kind of Middle Palaeolithic or Mousterian culture area. Evidence for claimed isolation is going to have to come from human cultural/physical data and not exclusively from speculations based on climatological information.

2. Differential rates of evolution for postulated different human groups, as Hrdlička noted, need to be justified. Why should one group, the European Neanderthals, cease to evolve? Hrdlička's question might be strengthened by noting

that selective pressures must have been quite similar in their operation on human populations throughout the then north temperate areas of the Old World during the Pleistocene. Certainly the cultural parallels archaeologically evident between Europe, southern Russia, and the Near East are striking evidence that the cultural solution to environmental problems has been quite similar from the time of the third interglacial on up. If, as has been suggested culture is a major determiner of the selective forces operating on human populations, then there is no reason to regard the selection in Europe as having been different in nature from that to the East, and the supposed evolutionary stagnation of the European inhabitants is still unexplained.

3. If invasion and population replacement did occur, presumably due to the superiority of the invading population, Hrdliča asks:

a. Why did the invading population not prevail sooner?

b. Why did they take over the precise caves and sites formerly occupied by the Neanderthals?

c. Why did this supposedly superior population live exactly the same kind of life their predecessors had? Since evidence is accumulating to indicate that the European Upper Palaeolithic may be largely the product of cultural evolution *in situ*, it might be added that the superior new-comers must have arrived cultureless or have abandoned their own so-far undiscovered culture to take over that of the Neanderthalers whom they presumably displaced. This in fact comes close to being the argument used in one of the most strained explanations yet produced.

d. What example can one give from contemporary and historical knowledge of the complete extinction of a whole group of humanity by the action of another one?

Of all the sound and compelling questions asked by Hrdlička, only the last facet of this one, which is relatively trivial, seems to have drawn any response. Howells and Vallois offer the American Indians as an example of the presumed extinction of a whole group of humanity, noting that they will never noticeably affect the physical type of the United States, and, for the purposes of future excavators, they might as well be extinct. This of course assumes that the future anthropologists can ignore the accumulation of evidence from the 60 million inhabitants of Mexico and the countries further south where pre-Columbian genes represent a substantial proportion of the common pool. The previous requirement noted by Hrdlička of a large invading population and an even larger parent population would of course have been met, rendering Howells' and Vallois' example inappropriate even if it were true.

It would seem that any view which attempts to picture the Neanderthalers as "aberrant," "extreme," "special," or "specialized," and as having been a blind end in evolution which became extinct without descendants would have to be able to answer in convincing fashion the points raised by Hrdlička, yet, although such views are practically unanimous among the students of fossil man today, none has attempted such answers.

While Hrdlička was thoroughly familiar with the early human skeletal remains prior to 1930 and had made one of the most significant attempts to interpret them, he does not seem to have been as familiar with the literature as he was with the bones. While he quotes from the published works of five of the most influential scholars of his day, and remarked with what should have been devastating effect that, "they give us *H. sapiens*, without showing why, or how, and where he developed his superior make-up," yet he apparently believed that: "All these opinions can probably be traced, directly or indirectly, to the authoritative notions arrived at during the earlier years of this century, on material less ample than at present, by one of the foremost students of Neanderthal man, Gustav Schwalbe." He cites no reference to back up this accusation, but in a recent although much milder version of the same view, Clark Howell lists as sources Schwalbe's publications in 1901, 1906, and 1923. A check of these and others has not only failed to reveal any evidence for this, but has clearly shown that quite the reverse was true. Prior to his yielding to the influence of Boule in 1913, he had arranged the available fossil men as stages in a linear squence—Pithecanthropus, Neanderthal, and modern—which he believed represented the course of human evolution. Rather than Schwalbe, whose views apparently were basically the same as Hrdlička's, the latter should properly have implicated the views of Boule and the fundamentally antievolutionary ethos of French palaeontology which, via the subsequent espousals by Keith and Osborn and others, have delayed the acceptance of the human fossil record from an avowedly evolutionary point of view from that day to this.

A proper appreciation of the position of Schwalbe is raised since it gives a clue to the background of his pupil and, later, colleague Franz Weidenreich, one of the very few scholars besides Hrdlička to have attempted to view the Neanderthals as a normal facet of human prehistoric development. Weidenreich's views, reflecting the years he spent in China, are less oriented towards the specifically European fossil record, and his attempts to interpret the position of the Neanderthals were always made from the point of view of his larger views of human evolution. As a result, his general thinking was a little more sophisticated, while his specific treatment of European Neanderthal problems is much more sketchy than the above recounted views of Hrdlička.

In general, Weidenreich maintained that no more than one species of man existed at any one time during the Pleistocene. While he recognized that long-standing differences in the selective factors prevalent in different geographical areas would result in local differentiation, yet he believed that interpopulation contacts involving inevitable genetic exchange had always been sufficient to maintain specific unity within the genus *Homo*. This view receives considerable confirmation from the Lower Palaeolithic archaeological record which shows the broad spread of similar culture traits over wide areas of the Old World. Where culture traits have spread, genes must have spread also.

Yet despite Weidenreich's clear reasoning concerning prehistoric population dynamics, one recent work presents a diagram of "the Polyphyletic or Candelabra school, modified (and exaggerated)" purporting to represent Weidenreich's views of human evolution. In this diagram, vertical lines are used to represent evolutionary continuity in four areas of the world, but the horizontal and diagonal lines of Weidenreich's own original diagram indicating genetic interchange between adjacent populations have been eliminated. After decreeing that Weidenreich's areal populations must follow rigid separate grooves, Howells expresses incredulity that these four lines should converge to produce "the same kind of man everywhere." The scheme is then rejected as being too rigid.

This, however, has not done justice to Weidenreich's intent. To take a specific instance, Weidenreich regarded the Pekin group, with which he was most familiar, as a direct ancestor to *Homo sapiens* with a closer relationship ". . . to certain Mongolian groups—than to any other races. . . . *This statement does not mean that modern Mongols derived exclusively from Sinanthropus or that Sinanthropus did not give origin to other races"* [italics added]. Certainly the inhabitants of a given area have a larger proportion of genes derived from the previous inhabitants of that same area than of those from any other area, but there is always going to be a certain amount of genetic interchange with adjacent populations as Weidenreich has indicated, and he has regarded this interchange as sufficient to have maintained the unity of the human species at any given time level during the Pleistocene. To picture his scheme of evolution as consisting of rigid separate grooves is not to exaggerate it, it is to misrepresent it.

The views of Weidenreich, while expressed in the terms of a morphologist and human palaeontologist, correspond quite closely to those expressed by a population geneticist (Dobzhansky) which should not be surprising since, in fact, both types of scholar are concerned with the same problem—human evolution. While they approach it from different directions, they can be expected to agree with each other as they converge.

While Weidenreich, being less familiar with the European stratigraphic and skeletal records than Hrdlička, accepted the view of the supposed 'stratigraphic break between the Neanderthal and *sapiens* inhabitants of Europe which the proponents of hominid catastrophism have advanced, yet he notes that this still does not deny the possibility that evolution from a Neanderthal population to a *sapiens* one did not occur in another part of the world. Recognizing this as a possibility, he was careful to note, in relation to Neanderthal man in Europe, that, "In no case, however, can the capability of his advancing into *Homo sapiens* be denied."

Weidenreich clearly accepted Hrdlička's Neanderthal Phase of Man noting in effect that it is much more reasonable for human palaeontologists to explain

evolution in terms of the fossils already on their desks rather than to engage in the perpetual pursuit of phantom populations of supposedly sapient form. In one of the last things which he wrote, Weidenreich, like Hrdlička (1930:348) asks the question, "If Neanderthal Man, for example, was not an ancestor of modern man, who was this ancestor?"

With such substantial views and challenging questions offered by two of the major figures in American Physical Anthropology in the twentieth century, it is legitimate to wonder why they have received no serious consideration, why the views find no supporters, and why the questions remain unanswered. Certainly it cannot be due exclusively to the demonstrable discrepancies in some of the other issues supported by Hrdlička and Weidenreich, for one can cite the example of Sir Arthur Keith whose conviction of sapiens antiquity sails on without him despite the fact that the major issues for which he stood on race, eugenics, and Piltdown have had to be abandoned.

It would seem that at least part of the failure of the ideas of Hrdlička and Weidenreich to have their deserved impact can be assigned to the positions occupied by both men. Weidenreich, following his introductions to a similar viewpoint, by Schwalbe, taught for a third of a century as an anatomist and physiologist, but the final phase of his career, where he was specifically dealing with fossil man and human evolution and where his evolutionary thinking reached its published expression, was spent in connection with the museum world. Hrdlička's entire career was spent in a museum, and however much a museum environment may encourage research, it does not guarantee the general recognition of the knowledge thus gained.

Meanwhile, Hooton was attempting to build American Physical Anthropology in the image of Sir Arthur Keith, and the success which he had can be seen in the almost unanimous acceptance of Keith's general evolutionary views in spite of the demise of Galley Hill and Piltdown, and in spite of the fact that Keith himself abandoned them at the end of his life. Weidenreich and Hrdlička had no students, and, as a result, their thinking is unrepresented in the current generation of anthropologists. It is an interesting commentary on the strength of academic tradition to note that these two men were among the few physical anthropologists of their generation not specifically trained in the concepts of hominid catastrophism —one having been specifically trained to view the hominid fossil record from an evolutionary viewpoint, and the other having acquired his anthropological training by himself and independent of any established scholar or school of thought.

No discussion of Neanderthal interpretations would be complete without some consideration of Hans Weinert, the only living anthropologist who has actively maintained that the known Neanderthals represent a previous stage in human evolution. Weinert has represented this point of view since the 1920's but has, if anything, drawn even less notice in the French and especially the English speaking worlds than has either Hrdlička or Weidenreich. Part of the tendancy to overlook his work may be due to the language barrier, although his views have been translated into French. While he wrote the section on fossil man in the widely read compendium *Anthropology Today*, it remains in German and one fears that this only serves as an exercise for graduate students boning up for their language exams.

The disruptions suffered by German anthropology as a result of two world wars, and the stiffling influence of the Nazi regime, have meant that few German anthropologists have achieved much

recognition since the 1920's. Writers on fossil man such as Breitinger, Gieseler, and Heberer accept the predominant views of the significance of the Neanderthals advocated by French (and derived English and American) anthropology. In this area, Weinert is the sole perpetuator of German evolutionary views dating from prior to the First World War, and some of the failure of his position to receive recognition may be traceable to the general eclipse of German anthropology.

The other possible reason for his failure to attract serious consideration is his insistence, almost amounting to an obsession, that the human ancestor was a chimpanzee. This, however, should have been put in its proper perspective by his clear recognition that both men and chimpanzees have been pursuing long independent courses of evolution since the Tertiary. Perhaps his acceptance of Piltdown despite the suspicion of German anatomists from Schwalbe to Weidenreich can be traced to this early confusion. In any case, if one reads Australopithecine or even prehominid for chimpanzee wherever it occurs in his earlier writings, then his reasoning makes quite good sense.

If the Pithecanthropus-Sinanthropus skulls can be taken as morphologically intermediate between the immediate prehominids and modern man, and if they do represent a stage in the prehistoric development of the genus *Homo*, then the rest of Weinert's arguments must be given serious attention.

At the outset, he noted the frequent lack of a clear correspondence between the record of archaeology and the geological time scale and the untrustworthiness of absolute time designations. Thus his position is less dependent upon the accuracy of premature time estimates than is the position of those who prefer a catastrophic to an evolutionary explanation for the hominid fossil record. His major arguments run as follows:

1. Neanderthal morphological characteristics fit nicely in between those of Pithecanthropus and those of modern man, and it would be difficult on morphological grounds alone to deny the existence of a Neanderthal stage in the line which developed into modern man.

2. ". . . everywhere we meet Middle Palaeolithic forms of men, only the Neanderthaler and nothing else is to be found." If in fact the Neanderthals became extinct without issue, this would mean that ". . . up to now we have always found in the Middle Palaeolithic only the remains of extinct side lines but never individuals of our own ancestral line."

3. The frequency of Neanderthaloid features visible in Upper Palaeolithic skeletal remains, particularly among those of the earliest known Upper Palaeolithic, is perticularly marked in comparison with their evident descendants, the later Neolithic and modern peoples. Especially notable in this respect are the finds at Brunn, Brux (noted in this same context by Schwalbe, Chwalynsk, Combe Capelle, Lautsch, Mount Carmel (actually a late Mousterian population), Podbaba, Podkumok, and Předmost.

Not since before the last world war has any other established authority specifically recognized the morphological intermediacy of the earliest Upper Palaeolithic populations between the earlier Mousterian and more recent peoples, although a number of authors have apparently been aware of the possible implications since they have taken pains to explain that, in these cases, there is nothing really reminiscent of Neanderthal morphology, or that for reasons of dating this could not be linked in an evolutionary series with the Neanderthals. On the other hand, the recognition of this morphological intermediacy has led a number of authors to seek some sort of explanation, and, being unwilling to concede that "pure" Homo sapiens did not exist in remote antiquity, they have suggested varying degrees of hybridization between a "classic" Neanderthal and one or another sort of "modern" form of man. This, however, becomes exceedingly vague when the "modern" element in the mixture is described as "primitive sapiens" which in turn is considered as differing irrevocably from Neanderthal form by nuances in the degree of brow ridge division, of canine fossa and relative chin development. Since the functional significance of these features is not considered, it is not at all clear why so much importance should be attached to them—particularly when it is realized that the range of variation amongst modern peoples greatly exceeds the difference between for instance Skhūl V and La Ferrassie I (c.f., brow ridges in Australian versus Chinese, canine fossa in Negro versus Eskimo, chin in Tasmanian versus European).

There is no doubt that the available evidence is insufficient to constitute proof in the sense of "highly significant" statistical probability for any given hypothesis as was realized by Hrdlička, although this should not be taken to indicate, as Vallois does, that a catastrophist hypothesis is therefore more likely than an evolutionary one. Before a defense of the evolutionary point of view is undertaken, it should be briefly mentioned that two schools of hominid catastrophism exist at the present. The first is represented solely by Vallois who still maintains the position established by Boule that if there is any relation between Neanderthal and modern forms of man, it was due to common ancestry at a time so remote that there is no fossil evidence for it. This view, entitled Présapiens by Vallois, might be called the position of extreme (or "classic") catastrophism, in opposition to the modified (or "progressive") catastrophism of Sergi, Heberer, Clark Howell, Breitinger, Le Gros Clark, and others (entitled the "Préneanderthal theory" by Vallois). This latter view has relied heavily on the third interglacial status of the Skhūl remains as an indication that a population existed prior to the European Neanderthals of the early

Würm whose morphological features were closer to those of modern man. The removal of Skhūl from the third interglacial and the discovery of early Würm Neanderthals of "classic" form in the Middle East indicate that the sequence and timing of hominid developments in southwest Asia was not significantly different from the picture derived from the European record. This leaves primarily Saccopastore as support for the views of modified hominid catastrophism, and an appreciation of the expression of sexual differences in the Neanderthals and the great but generally ignored range of variation of the "classic" Neanderthals themselves should remove the arguments built on this basis.

Recently Clark Howell has stated, in reference to the possibility of a Neanderthal phase in human evolution, that, "Unfortunately, this point of view has still to be meaningfully stated in terms of modern evolutionary theory," although he regards such a concept as "no longer useful since there was marked variability from one such group to another." This, of course, implies that Hrdlička's definition of Neanderthal was conceived in terms of physical characteristics which, in fact, it was not. Since I believe that some concept of Neanderthal Phase *can* prove to be useful, it should be worthwhile to restate it—I hope meaningfully—and see whether the "marked variability" correctly noted by Howell is indeed a fatal flaw.

While quantities of writing exist on the subject of the Neanderthals, almost no concise definition is offered. Hrdlička's definition, however, is not only concise, it is the only one offered in conjunction with clear evolutionary principles. It is worth quoting it here.

The only workable definition of Neanderthal man and period seems, for the time being, to be, *the man and period of the Mousterian culture.* An approach to a somatological definition would be feasible but might for the present be rather prejudicial. [Italics Hrdlička's.]

Contrary to what one might have expected, Hrdlička's definition, then, was primarily a cultural definition. If culture is ". . . the principal adaptive mechanism employed by man in his so far successful bid for survival," then it makes good sense to view the major stages of human evolution in terms of major changes which culture has undergone. Since major cultural changes have in each case altered the selective pressures operating on the human physique, then there is good reason to expect a correlation between the cultural and the physical changes in the human fossil record, and we should be able to fill in the somatological part of the definition left blank by Hrdlička.

Necessarily the sequence of stages so discovered will depend upon the completeness of the information which we possess, and inevitably our information is sketchy for the earlier part. Here again, culture shows an advantage over skeletal material alone as a guide since the archaeological record, whatever its defects, is far more complete than the record of hominid fossils. Fortunately there are just enough of the latter to make, tentatively, some of the correlations necessary in the construction of such a scheme.

Utilizing the cultural and skeletal evidence available, four stages in human evolution can usefully be postulated which simply constitute a redefinition, with the addition of an Australopithecine stage, of the scheme offered by Schwalbe and defended by Weinert and Weidenreich—realizing of course that future increases in information will show that these are really arbitrary points chosen in what is actually a continuum. The four stages are presented diagrammatically in Figure 1, with an indication of the cultural-biological interactions designated by the arrows. Since this paper is

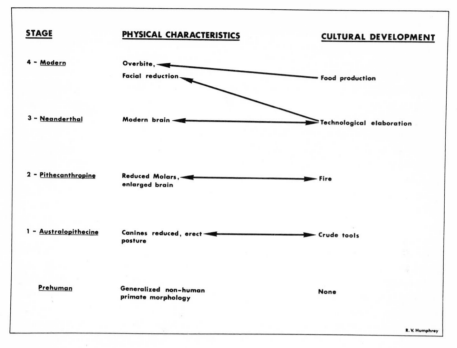

STAGE	PHYSICAL CHARACTERISTICS	CULTURAL DEVELOPMENT
4 - Modern	Overbite, Facial reduction	Food production
3 - Neanderthal	Modern brain	Technological elaboration
2 - Pithecanthropine	Reduced Molars, enlarged brain	Fire
1 - Australopithecine	Canines reduced, erect posture	Crude tools
Prehuman	Generalized non-human primate morphology	None

R. V. Humphrey

Figure 1.

primarily concerned with the Neander-thal problem, and since these designated relationships have been discussed else-where, it need only be added that the biological consequences of the cultural changes indicated in stages 1 and 2 prob-ably were delayed in much the same way that the general facial reduction of stage 4 is the consequence of the cultural elabo-ration of stage 3.

Specifically, reliance on tools for de-fence, characterizing the difference be-tween the Prehumans and the Australo-pithecine stage, meant that projecting canines were no longer necessary equip-ment, and hence free to vary. With the cumulative effect of random mutation inevitably resulting in the reduction of those structures whose adaptive signifi-cance has been reduced or suspended, the canines of the first tool users could be expected to reduce after a sufficient period of reliance on tools (and hence culture in the larger sense) as the primary means

for defence. The same kind of delay can be expected before the reduction of the molars followed the regular utilization of fire (and perhaps the addition of significant and regular quantities of pro-tein to the diet as a result of the develop-ment of effective hunting techniques. Meat does not have to be chewed as much as other foods since protein digestion is primarily in the stomach and there is less requirement to be mixed with sali-vary enzymes).

Among the bearers of the Mousterian cultural traditions assigned to stage 3, "the postcranial skeleton is basically mod-ern human in over-all morphology." The brain has reached its modern size and, despite the attempts of Boule to charac-terize its supposed "structural inferior-ity," there are no indications that the brain was functionally different from that of modern man. Clear differences can be seen only in the metric and morphologic characters relating to the face. With much of the organization of the human face concerned with the supporting role it plays in regard to the dentition, any change in selective factors affecting the teeth will ultimately have effects on total facial morphology. According to published figures, there is no evident difference between the gross tooth dimensions and little between the tooth forms of the Pithecanthropine and the Neanderthal stages shown in Figure 1. It is evident that the greatest difference in the teeth of the Middle Palaeolithic and those of modern man occurs in the anterior part of the dental arch.

In the absence of any other reliable evidence pertaining to the facial morphology of the Pithecanthropine stage (where no complete face is preserved), it can be tentatively assumed that this was not significantly different from that of the Neanderthal stage except in the area of the brow ridge where the face is hafted onto the skull. Selective factors pertaining to the dentition, then, can be presumed to have changed little between the Pithecanthropine and the beginning of the Neanderthal stages, but following the Neanderthals, the reduction, amounting to the transformation into the modern face, is clear evidence of such a change. It has been suggested elsewhere that technological elaboration starting in the Mousterian and proceeding on through the Upper Palaeolithic introduced specialized tools to perform the variety of tasks formerly handled by the teeth—especially the front teeth. The adaptive significance of a large dentition having been thus reduced, it is free to vary, and the probable effect of accumulating random mutations is reduction.

With such an explanation for the significance of the difference between Pithecanthropine, Neanderthal, and modern form, I suggest that a morphological corrollary be added to Hrdlička's cultural definition of Neanderthal as a stage or phase of human evolution.

Neanderthal man is the man of the Mousterian culture prior to the reduction in form and dimension of the Middle Pleistocene face.

This view of human evolution in general, and the problems represented by the interpretation of Neanderthals in particular, is offered in place of the views of hominid catastrophism generally held which apparently had their theoretical bases in the early 19th century doctrines of Georges Cuvier, and which have dominated anthropological thinking for the past fifty years following their application to the extensive French Neanderthal material by the palaeontologist Marcellin Boule. Such views reach an absurd extreme with Weckler's fantastic fabrication involving hypothetical populations tramping to and fro over vast distances "for reasons not as yet ascertained," but perhaps the clearest expression of this view is in the writings of the French prehistorian Teilhard de Chardin who believed that the phases of human development ". . . displace each other rather than pass into each other directly . . . neither Pekin Man . . . nor Neanderthal Man have any direct offspring left today in the living world: they have been swept away by *Homo sapiens.*"

To eliminate the headache concerning the origin of modern man by claiming that he sprang full blown from the mind of a troubled palaeontologist into an early Pleistocene stratum is to propose an explanation which borders on mythology. Instead, it is urged that the orientation based on standard evolutionary theory as developed by Schwalbe, Hrdlička, Weidenreich, and Weinert be re-examined and a systematic attempt be made to view the known hominid fossil record in these terms as modified by more recent theoretical advances in the thinking of genetics and ecology.

Finally, in keeping with the promise inherent in the title of this paper, I suggest that it was the fate of the Neanderthal to give rise to modern man, and, as has frequently happened to members of the older generation in this changing world, to have been perceived in caricature, rejected, and disavowed by their own offspring, *Homo sapiens*.

Members of our own genus and species, *Homo sapiens*, first emerged in Europe and Southeast Asia near the close of the Pleistocene. Expectably, the details of this event—just who they were most closely related to, precisely where and when they appeared, and where they came from— have been the source of heated speculation.

5. The Origins of Modern Man [1]

EARLY MIXTURES OF DIFFERENT TYPES OF MEN

While the populations of early man were very small, there is good reason to believe that whenever such populations met they did exactly what modern populations do, they interbred. Actual evidence of such intermixture was until recently a matter of speculation, but during 1931–32 the evidence became factual. For it was during this period that an assemblage of fossil neanderthaloids were discovered in caves on the slopes of Mount Carmel in Palestine.

Here were found two types, a clearly Neanderthal type, in the caves of Tabūn,

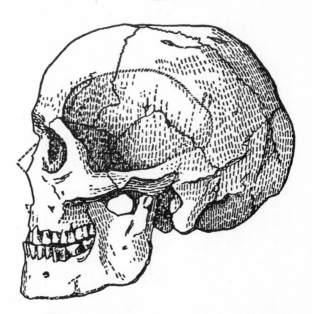

Figure 1. Skull of Cro-Magnon male. (After Gottlieb and Marcelin)

[1] ASHLEY MONTAGU. Reprinted by permission of The World Publishing Company from *Man: His First Million Years* by Ashley Montagu. Copyright © 1957 by Ashley Montagu.

Figure 2. Chronological-cultural table of the divisions of prehistory and of the historic period. In using this table it should be understood that the approximate dates assigned to the different "Ages" refer only in a general way to the areas mentioned. As the table indicates, these "Ages" were not everywhere contemporaneous. The different "Ages" do not afford a measure of time, for they varied in different parts of the world both in the time of their appearance and in their duration, while some of the cultural stages they embrace never appeared at all, but were completely skipped in the progress from one cultural stage to another. These ages are therefore to be regarded as *cultural or technological* rather than as *chronological* periods. It is extremely important to grasp this fact. There was no world-wide evolution from one stage to another; each stage represents an industrial revolution in the manufacture of tools which occurred in different places at different times; nor did the several stages begin and end simultaneously all over the world. Thus, to give a simple example, the Early Iron Age began in Asia Minor about 1200 B.C., in Italy about 1000 B.C., in central Europe about 900 B.C., in China about 700 B.C., in southern England about 600 B.C., in Japan about A.D. 200, and in Fiji about 1872. In the last column names in *italics* refer to types which are uncertainly dated.

Age	Alpine and Scandinavian glacial oscillations with corresponding changes of sea level and climate	Approximate dates	Principal Culture Stages of Europe, Egypt, and the Near East			
			Northwestern Continental Europe	West Central Europe	Egypt and the Near East	Human Types (Persisting Varieties of Homo sapiens)
Power Tools — Steel / New / Old	Present conditions of Mya Period in Baltic area	A.D. 1900	Rise of the Age of Power Tools			
		A.D. 1850	Steel Age Develops			
		A.D. 1700	Steel (carbonized iron)			
		A.D. 1000				
IRON — Late / Middle / Early		A.D. 500	Viking Age			
		50 B.C.	Roman Period of Iron Age	Historic Times		
		500 B.C.	Iron Age Introduced	Iron Age Introduced	Iron Age Begins	
	Final land rise in Baltic area or Late Tapes Period	1000 B.C.				
BRONZE		1500 B.C.	Bronze Age Introduced			
		2000 B.C.	Traces of Copper	Bronze Age Introduced	Bronze Age Begins	
COPPER		2500 B.C.	Late Neolithic with thick poll ax	Copper Age Introduced	Alloys in use	
NEO-LITHIC — Late		3000 B.C.	Middle Neolithic with thin poll ax	Late Neolithic	History Begins / Writing Invented	
		3500 B.C.			Amratian industry	
		4000 B.C.			Use of Iron Begins / Agriculture and the Domestication of Animals	
NEO-LITHIC — Middle	Sea rising, Ragunda retreat, with Littorina Sea (Early Tapes Period) preceded by late Ancylus Lake	4500 B.C.	Early Neolithic: Shell mound or Campignian industry Ertebølle industries	Middle Neolithic or Robenhausian industry	Badarian industry	
		5000 B.C.	Norse industry with petroglyphs	Early Neolithic or Campignian and Asturian industries	Use of Copper Begins	
		5500 B.C.				
MESO-LITHIC — Early		6000 B.C.	Maglemose industry		Tasian industry	
		6500 B.C.	Lyngby industry	Azilian, Tardenoisian, and Capsian industries		
	Ragunda pause with Ancylus Lake	7800 B.C.				

Stage	Glacial geology	Date	Industries	Nile valley and other industries	Chancelade (human fossils)
Upper Palaeolithic	Fini-Glacial pause with Baltic ice-lake	8500 B.C.	Late Magdalenian	Probable beginning of Neolithic culture in Nile valley floor silts	Predmost, Cro-Magnon, Baker's Hole Rhodesian
	Fini-Glacial pause with Baltic ice-lake	13,500 B.C.	Early Magdalenian and Capsian industries		Châtelperron, Grimaldi; Cro-Magnon, Africanthropus, Solo
	Gothi-Glacial retreat with Baltic ice-lake		Solutrean industry. Late Aurignacian industry	Sebilian industry of Nile valley terrace silts	
	Gothi-Glacial pause with Baltic ice-lake	18,500 B.C.	Early Aurignacian or Châtelperronian and Capsian industries		Boskop
	Würm or Achen and Dani-Glacial retreats with Frankfort and Pomeranian pause. Flandrian terrace.		Final Mousterian of the caves	Late Mousterian of the 10 ft. Nile terrace	
Middle Palaeolithic	Würm and Brandenburg or Dani-Glacial advances, 4TH GLACIAL	50,000 B.C.	Mousterian of the caves		Florisbad, Skhūl, Gibraltar II, Wadjak
	Riss retreat with Monastirian terrace. 3RD INTERGLACIAL. Hot summer	75,000 B.C.	Contemporary Acheulian, Early Mousterian, Tayacian, Micoquian, Levalloisian, and Clactonian industries from Somme terrace, etc.	Early Mousterian of the 30 ft. Nile terrace	London, Tabūn, Neanderthal, Ehringsdorf, Fontéchevade, Solo, Montmaurin
Lower Palaeolithic	Riss and Polonian Advances. 3RD GLACIAL	150,000 B.C.	Derived implements		*Steinheim* Swanscombe *Gigantopithecus* Heidelberg Sinanthropus, Atlanthropus Pithecanthropus erectus
	Mindel retreat with Tyrhenian terrace. 2ND INTERGLACIAL	250,000 B.C.	Acheulian and contemporary Abbevillian and Clactonian industries from 2nd Somme terrace. Clacton-on-Sea, Mesvin, etc.	Acheulian industry of the 50 ft. Nile terrace	
	Mindel advance. 2ND GLACIAL	450,000 B.C.	Derived implements		Pithecanthropus robustus
	Günz retreat with Milazzian terrace. 1ST INTERGLACIAL	550,000 B.C.	Proto-Abbevillian industry from below the Cromer forest beds and 3rd Somme terrace	Abbevillian and Early Abbevillian industries of the 100 ft. Nile terrace	Pithecanthropus (Modjokerto) *Meganthropus* *Kanam*
	Günz Advance. 1ST GLACIAL	600,000 B.C.	Pre-Abbevillian or Ipswichian flake industry of East Anglian Crag formations	?	
Archeolithic	PLEISTOCENE		Pre-Abbevillian or Ipswichian flake industry of subcrag formations		
	PLIOCENE — Donau with Sicilian terrace	1,000,000 YRS.	Eolithic stage?	Eolithic stage?	

and another type which closely approached modern man, from the caves of Skūhl. Between the two types there was every variety of intergradation. It is quite clear that there had been an intermixture between a modernlike form of man and Neanderthal men, and that the Mount Carmel population was the product of this intermixture.

There is every reason to believe that similar intermixtures occurred between early human populations throughout the long history of man.

CRO-MAGNON MAN

The Cro-Magnons are the Apollos of the prehistoric world. This form was discovered originally in 1868 in the little village of Les Eyzies in southern central France, in a rock shelter called Cro-Magnon. The remains of thirteen other individuals were uncovered between 1872 and 1902 in the caves of the Red Rocks of the Côte d'Azur, some forty minutes walk from Mentone on the Italian Riviera. A headless, incomplete skeleton found in Paviland Cave in southwestern Wales in 1823 almost certainly belongs to the Cro-Magnon variety of man.

The Cro-Magnons were about 5 feet 11 inches in height, with a brain capacity in the larger representatives of 1660 c.c., a straight face, a well-developed, projecting nose, a high forehead, and a strong jaw. They made the most beautiful bone implements associated with an industry known as Aurignacian (from Aurignac in France where they were first found). Furthermore, the Cro-Magnons are believed to be the people who made some of the masterly paintings on the walls of caves, and the sculptures sometimes found in them, which have been discovered in many different parts of Europe. Perhaps the wall paintings in Lascaux Cave are the most famous of these.

Cro-Magnon man is a modern man in every sense of the word, but where he came from or how he came about we have not the slightest idea.

At one time, things used to be quite simple when anthropologists discussed the origin and evolution of man. Modern man was the last and highest type of man to be evolved. The most primitive type of man was held to be *Pithecanthropus erectus* or possibly *Pithecanthropus robustus*. All the types of men in between the pithecanthropines and modern man were held to be simply intermediate stages in the evolution of man from the most primitive to the most advanced type. However, certain finds of fossil man made in recent years render this earlier and apparently perfectly logical interpretation of the evolution of man seriously open to question.

SWANSCOMBE MAN

In 1935–36 there were found in the Barnfield gravel quarry at Swanscombe in Kent, England, two skull bones, the left parietal and the complete occipital bone, of a single individual in a Middle Pleistocene deposit associated with tools of typically Acheulian industry. In 1955 the right parietal bone was discovered. Except for being slightly thicker, these bones might in every way fit a modern head. Some authorities say that the face might not have been modern. This is a possibility, but a remote one. Were Swanscombe the only example of the kind, we might put it in the "suspense account." But there are others, and therefore we must pay Swanscombe the attention it deserves.

FONTÉCHEVADE MAN

In a cave near the village of Montbrun in the Department of Charente, France, in a deposit of the Third Interglacial period, there the portions of two skulls were discovered, associated with artifacts of Tayacian industry. The Tayacian in-

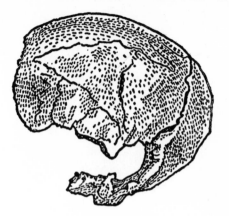

Figure 3. Left lateral view of the Swanscombe skull. (After Lorenc)

dustry always precedes the Mousterian industry which is associated with Neanderthal man. So that we can be fairly certain that Fontéchevade man preceded Neanderthal man.

Fontéchevade I is represented by a beautifully preserved fragment of the region above the nose and the upper margin of the left orbit. This is a critically important part of the skull because it tells us at a glance what the forehead and facial region were like in the complete skull. In this type, almost all authorities are agreed, the face was exactly as in modern man. Fontéchevade I was either of late adolescent age or a young adult female.

Fontéchevade II is represented by an almost complete skullcap. Facial bones and base of skull are missing. But again, except for thickness of bones, this is in every way a modernlike skull. The brain capacity was about 1470 c.c.

In Fontéchevade man we see yet another type with which the forerunners of Neanderthal man, and later Neanderthal man himself, may have intermixed.

KANAM MAN

In 1932 at West Kanam, on the southern shores of the Kavirondo Gulf of Victoria Nyanza, in Kenya, East Africa, the front portion of a human lower jaw was discovered. The importance of this mandible lies in the fact that it is in every way completely modern in appearance, yet it is claimed to have been recovered from a Lower Pleistocene deposit (now unfortunately washed away), which would make the Kanam mandible very old indeed. Kanam man suffered from a cancer of the chin region, which overgrew that structure in the form of a tumor, but there can be little doubt that Kanam man had a well-developed chin before it was obliterated by the tumor.

KANJERA MAN

At Kanjera in Kenya, East Africa, the skeletal remains of three individuals of modern Negroid type were found in a Middle Pleistocene deposit associated with implements of Acheulian industry, that is to say of the same age and industry as Swanscombe man in England.

THE EARLY APPEARANCE OF NEANTHROPIC MAN

Swanscombe, Fontéchevade, Kanam, and Kanjera man are representatives of the modernlike type of man, yet they ap-

Gibbon   *Chimpanzee*   *Gorilla*

Chimpanzee

Pithecanthropus
Face restored
by Prof. J. H. McGregor

Chimpanzee   *Orangutan*

Primitive
Neanderthaloid
(Ehringsdorf)

peared extremely early in the history of man's evolution. It therefore becomes a reasonable theory to assume that the modernlike type of man is much more ancient that was previously supposed, and it is quite possible that Neanderthal man, for example, is the product of admixture between such types as Solo with

Pithecanthropus
Based on a study
of the original skull top
by Prof. J. H. McGregor

Neanderthal Man
(Chapelle-aux-Saints)

Modern Man

Neanderthal Man
(Chapelle-aux-Saints)
By Prof. J. H. McGregor

Cro-Magnon Man
By Prof. J. H. McGregor

Heidelberg Man

Neanderthal Man
(Chapelle-aux-Saints)

Cro-Magnon
Man

Modern
White Man

Figure 4. Comparison of the brains, midsagital sections, and inner sides of lower jaws of anthropoids and man. (After Gottlieb and Marcelin)

neanthropic man, rather than being a descendant of *Pithecanthropus* or Solo man in the direct line.

The older notion of straight-line evolu- tion from ape to increasingly more ad- vanced types of man is essentially sound, though in its oversimplified form of more advanced types appearing in

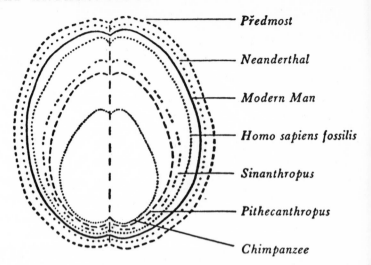

Figure 5. A comparison of brain sizes: chimpanzee, 400 c.c.; Pithecanthropus, 860 c.c.; Sinanthropus, 1075 c.c.; Homo sapiens fossilis; 1300 c.c.; Modern Man, 1400 c.c.; Neanderthal Man 1450 c.c.; Předmost, 1500 c.c. (After Gottlieb and Marcelin)

a continuous straight line from less advanced types, it requires substantial modification.

Evolution is not best likened to a straight line but rather to a reticulum or network, in which all sorts of crisscrossing lines (groups) go in all sorts of directions, with interconnections estab-lished between the different cords.

As a matter of fact, if we want to study the processes which have been operative in the past in giving rise to the varieties of men as we know them today, we can do no better than to observe them as they are occurring at the present time.

ONGOING HUMAN EVOLUTION

Casually, we tend to think of ourselves as standing at the apex of a developmental pyramid—vastly superior to the other animals, and, ex-apes or not, clearly the final and finest product of evolution. Such a view is philosophically untenable, an anthropocentric illusion, and scientifically unsound. We are superior only according to our own standards.

Because we now play such an important part in creating our environment, in considering our evolutionary future we must complement our understanding of natural selection with a comprehension of the processes of social selection. For the consequences of our culturally determined likes and dislikes—standards of beauty and sexual attractiveness—affect our chances of passing on our genetic heritage, thus affecting the biological endowment of populations to come. We must also consider the possible consequences of changes in culture, such as the recent innovations in technology that have resulted in the release of atomic energy and, thereby, of new sources of radiation likely to affect seriously our genes and those of our descendants in ways that are still uncertain. And finally there is the question of selective breeding for human betterment—applying our knowledge of evolution to the improvement of our own stock—creating a man

135

better than most of us, superior in physical strength and resistance to disease, and perhaps more intelligent.

Avoiding for the moment the possibly troublesome ethical implications of controlling our own ongoing evolution, we can see that we might easily profit—even by our own self-satisfied standards—from a little more evolving. For example, the results of our so far imperfectly assumed bipedal locomotion are a frequently aching back, varicose veins, and a tendency to midriff bulge.

Man now evolves by selection for an environment that is largely of his own making. This creates problems: he may be changing his culture at a rate that surpasses his own evolutionary adaptation.

1. The Present Evolution of Man [1]

The evolution of man is a natural process that has transcended itself. Only once before, when life originated out of inorganic matter, has there occurred a comparable event.

After that first momentous step, living forms evolved by adapting to their environments. Adaptation—the maintenance or advancement of conformity between an organism and its surroundings—takes place through natural selection. The raw materials with which natural selection works are supplied by mutation and sexual recombination of hereditary units: the genes.

Mutation, sexual recombination and natural selection led to the emergence of *Homo sapiens*. The creatures that preceded him had already developed the rudiments of tool-using, toolmaking and cultural transmission. But the next evolutionary step was so great as to constitute a difference in kind from those before it. There now appeared an organism whose mastery of technology and of symbolic communication enabled it to create a supraorganic culture. Other organisms adapt to their environments by changing their genes in accordance with the demands of the surroundings. Man and man alone can also adapt by changing his environments to fit his genes. His genes enable him to invent new tools, to alter his opinions, his aims and his conduct, to acquire new knowledge and new wisdom.

The possession of these faculties brought the human species to its present biological eminence. Man has spread to every section of the earth, bringing high culture to much of it. He is now the most numerous of the mammals. By these or any other reasonable standards, he is by far the most successful product of biological evolution.

For better or worse, biological evolution did not stop when culture appeared. In this article we address ourselves to the question of where evolution is now taking man. The literature of this subject has not lacked for prophets who wish to divine man's eventual fate. In our age of anxiety, prediction of final extinction has become the fashionable view, replacing the hopes for emergence of a race of demigods that more optimistic authorities used to foresee. Our purpose is less ambitious. What biological

[1] THEODOSIUS DOBZHANSKY, "The Present Evolution of Man," in *Scientific American*, 203, No. 3 (1960), pp. 206–217. Reprinted with permission of the author and the publisher. Copyright © 1960 by Scientific American, Inc. All rights reserved.

Dr. Dobzhansky is Professor of Genetics at the Rockefeller Institute.

evolutionary processes are now at work is a problem both serious and complex enough to occupy us here.

The impact of human works on the environment is so strong that it has become very hard to make out the forces to which the human species is now adjusting. It has even been argued that *Homo sapiens* has already emancipated himself from the operation of natural selection. At the other extreme are those who still assume that man is nothing but an animal. The second fallacy is the more pernicious, leading as it does to theories of biological racism and the justification of race and class prejudice which are bringing suffering to millions of people from South Africa to Arkansas. Assuming that man's genetic endowment can be ignored is the converse falsehood, perhaps less disastrous in its immediate effects, but more insidious in the long run.

Like all other animals, man remains the product of his biological inheritance. The first, and basic feature of his present evolution is that his genes continue to mutate, as they have since he first appeared. Every one of the tens of thousands of genes inherited by an individual has a tiny probability of changing in some way during his generation. Among the small, and probably atypical, sample of human genes for which very rough estimates of the mutation frequencies are available, the rates of mutation vary from one in 10,000 to one in about 250,-000. For example, it has been calculated that approximately one sex cell in every 50,000 produced by a normal person carries a new mutant gene causing retinoblastoma, a cancer of the eye affecting children.

These figures are "spontaneous" frequencies in people not exposed to any special agents that can induce mutation. As is now widely known, the existence of such agents, including ionizing radia-

tion and certain chemicals, has been demonstrated with organisms other than man. New mutagens are constantly being discovered. It can hardly be doubted that at least some of them affect human genes. As a consequence the members of an industrial civilization have increased genetic variability through rising mutation rates.

There is no question that many mutations produce hereditary diseases, malformations and constitutional weaknesses of various kinds. Some few must also be useful, at least in certain environments; otherwise there would be no evolution. (Useful mutants have actually been observed in experiments on lower organisms.) But what about minor variations that produce a little more or a little less hair, a slightly longer or a slightly shorter nose, blood of type O, or type A? These traits seem neither useful nor harmful. Here, however, we must proceed with the greatest caution. Beneficial or damaging effects of ostensibly neutral traits may eventually be discovered. For example, recent evidence indicates that people with blood of type O have a slightly higher rate of duodenal ulcer than does the general population. Does it follow that O blood is bad? Not necessarily; it is the most frequent type in many populations, and it may conceivably confer some advantages yet undiscovered.

Still other mutants that are detrimental when present in double dose (the so-called homozygous condition, where the same type of gene has been inherited from both parents) lead to hybrid vigor in single dose (the heterozygous condition). How frequently this happens is uncertain. The effect surely operates in the breeding of domestic animals and plants, and it has been detected among X-ray-induced mutations in fruit flies. Only one case is thus far known in man. Anthony C. Allison of the University of Oxford has found that the gene caus-

anemia hetro → resist malaria

ing sickle-cell anemia in the homozygous condition makes its heterozygous carriers relatively resistant to certain forms of malaria. This gene is very frequent in the native population of the central African lowlands, where malaria has long been endemic, and relatively rare in the inhabitants of the more salubrious highlands. Certainly there are other such adaptively ambivalent genes in human populations, but we do not know how many.

Despite these uncertainties, which cannot be glossed over, it is generally agreed among geneticists that the effects of mutation are on the average detrimental. Any increase of mutation rate, no matter how small, can only augment the mass of human misery due to defective heredity. The matter has rightly attracted wide attention in connection with ionizing radiation from military and industrial operations and medical X-rays. Yet these form only a part of a larger and more portentous issue.

Of the almost countless mutant genes that have arisen since life on earth began, only a minute fraction were preserved. They were preserved because they were useful, or at least not very harmful, to their possessors. A great majority of gene changes were eliminated. The agency that preserved useful mutants and eliminated injurious ones was natural selection. Is natural selection still operating in mankind, and can it be trusted to keep man fit to live in environments created by his civilization?

One must beware of words taken from everyday language to construct scientific terminology. "Natural" in "natural selection" does not mean the state of affairs preceding or excluding man-made changes. Artificially or not, man's environment has altered. Would it now be natural to try to make your living as a Stone Age hunter?

Then there are phrases like "the struggle for life" and "survival of the fittest." Now "struggle" was to Darwin a metaphor. Animals struggle against cold by growing warm fur, and plants against dryness by reducing the evaporating leaf surface. It was the school of so-called social Darwinists (to which Darwin did not belong) who equated "struggle" with violence, warfare and competition without quarter. The idea has long been discredited.

We do not deny the reality of competition and combat in nature, but suggest that they do not tell the whole story. Struggle for existence may be won not only by strife but also by mutual help. The surviving fit in human societies may in some circumstances be those with the strongest fists and the greatest readiness to use them. In others they may be those who live in peace with their neighbors and assist them in hour of need. Indeed, co-operation has a long and honorable record. The first human societies, the hunters of the Old Stone Age, depended on co-operation to kill big game.

Moreover, modern genetics shows that "fitness" has a quite special meaning in connection with evolution. Biologists now speak of Darwinian fitness, or adaptive value, or selective value in a reproductive sense. Consider the condition known as achondroplastic dwarfism, caused by a gene mutation that produces people with normal heads and trunks, but short arms and legs. As adults they may enjoy good health. Nevertheless, E. T. Mørch in Denmark has discovered that achondroplastic dwarfs produce, on the average, only some 20 surviving children for every 100 children produced by their normal brothers and sisters. In technical terms we say that the Darwinian fitness of achondroplasts is .2 or, alternatively that achondroplastic dwarfism is opposed by a selection-coefficient of .8.

This is a very strong selection, and the reasons for it are only partly understood. What matters from an evolutionary point of view is that achondroplasts are much less efficient in transmitting their genes to the following generations than are nondwarfs. Darwinian fitness is reproductive fitness. Genetically the surviving fittest is neither superman nor conquering hero; he is merely the parent of the largest surviving progeny.

With these definitions in mind, we can answer the question whether natural selection is still active in mankind by considering how such selection might be set aside. If all adults married, and each couple produced exactly the same number of children, all of whom survived to get married in turn and so on, there would be no selection at all. Alternatively, the number of children, if any, that each person produced might be determined by himself or some outside authority on the basis of the desirability of his hereditary endowment. This would be replacing natural selection by artificial selection. Some day it may come to pass. Meantime natural selection is going on.

It goes on, however, always within the context of environment. As that changes, the Darwinian fitness of various traits changes with it. Thus by his own efforts man is continually altering the selective pressure for or against certain genes.

The most obvious example, and one with disturbing overtones, is to be found in the advance of medicine and public health. Retinoblastoma, the eye cancer of children, is almost always fatal if it is not treated. Here is "natural" selection at its most rigorous, weeding out virtually all of the harmful mutant genes before they can be passed on even once. With proper treatment, however, almost 70 per cent of the carriers of the gene for retinoblastoma survive, become able to reproduce and therefore to transmit the defect to half their children.

More dramatic, if genetically less clear-cut, instances are afforded by advances in the control of tuberculosis and malaria. A century ago the annual death rate from tuberculosis in industrially advanced countries was close to 500 per 100,000. Improvement in living conditions and, more recently, the advent of antibiotic drugs have reduced the death rate to 7.5 per 100,000 in the U. S. today. A similarly steep decline is under way in the mortality from malaria, which used to afflict a seventh of the earth's population.

Being infectious, tuberculosis and malaria are hazards of the environment. There is good evidence, however, that individual susceptibility, both as to contracting the infection and as to the severity of the disease, is genetically conditioned. (We have already mentioned the protective effect of the gene for sickle-cell anemia. This is probably only one of several forms of genetic resistance to malaria.) As the prevalence of these diseases decreases, so does the threat to susceptible individuals. In other words, the Darwinian fitness of such individuals has increased.

It was pointed out earlier that one effect of civilization is to increase mutation rates and hence the supply of harmful genes. A second effect is to decrease the rate of discrimination against such genes, and consequently the rate of their elimination from human populations by natural selection. In thus disturbing the former genetic equilibrium of inflow and outflow, is man not frustrating natural selection and polluting his genetic pool?

The danger exists and cannot be ignored. But in the present state of knowledge the problem is tremendously complex. If our culture has an ideal, it is the sacredness of human life. A society that refused, on eugenic grounds, to cure children of retinoblastoma would, in our eyes, lose more by moral degradation than it gained genetically. Not so easy, however, is the question whether a person who knows he carries the gene for retinoblastoma, or a similarly deleterious gene, has a right to have children.

Even here the genetic issue is clear, although the moral issue may not be. This is no longer true when we come to genes that are harmful in double dose, but beneficial in single. If the central African peoples had decided some time ago to breed out the sickle-cell gene, they might have succumbed in much larger numbers to malaria. Fortunately this particular dilemma has been resolved by successful methods of mosquito control. How many other hereditary diseases and malformations are maintained by the advantages their genes confer in heterozygous carriers, we simply do not know.

Conversely, we cannot yet predict the genetic effect of relaxing selection pressure. If, for example, susceptibility to tuberculosis is maintained by recurrent mutations, then the conquest of the disease should increase the concentration of mutant genes as time goes on. On the other hand, if resistance arises from a single dose of genes that make for susceptibility in the double dose, the effects of eradication become much less clear. Other selective forces might then determine the fate of these genes in the population.

In any case, although we cannot see all the consequences, we can be sure that ancient genetic patterns will continue to shift under the shelter of modern medicine. We would not wish it otherwise. It may well be, however, that the social cost of maintaining some genetic variants will be so great that artificial selection against them is ethically, as well as economically, the most acceptable and wisest solution.

If the evolutionary impact of such biological tools as antibiotics and vaccines is still unclear, then computers and rockets, to say nothing of social organizations as a whole, present an even deeper puzzle. There is no doubt that human survival will continue to depend more and more on human intellect and technology. It is idle to argue whether this is good or bad. The point of no return was passed long ago, before anyone knew it was happening.

But to grant that the situation is inevitable is not to ignore the problems it raises. Selection in modern societies does not always encourage characteristics that we regard as desirable. Let us consider one example. Much has been written about the differential fertility that in advanced human societies favors less intelligent over more intelligent people. Studies in several countries have shown that school children from large families tend to score lower on so-called intelligence tests than their classmates with few or no brothers and sisters. Moreover, parents who score lower on these tests have more children on the average than those who get higher marks.

We cannot put our finger on the forces responsible for this presumed selection against intelligence. As a matter of fact, there is some evidence that matters are changing, in the U. S. at least. People included in *Who's Who in America* (assuming that people listed in this directory are on the average more intelligent than people not listed there) had fewer children than the general population during the period from 1875 to 1904. In the next two decades, however, the difference seemed to be disappearing. L. S. Penrose of University College London, one of the outstanding human geneticists, has pointed out that a negative correlation between intelligence and family size may in part be corrected by the relative infertility of low-grade mental defectives. He suggests that selection may thus be working toward maintaining a constant level of genetic conditioning for intelligence in human populations. The evidence presently available is insuffi-cient either to prove or to contradict this hypothesis.

It must also be recognized that in man and other social animals qualities mak-ing for successful indivduals are not necessarily those most useful to the so-ciety as a whole. If there were a gene for altruism, natural selection might well discriminate against it on the individual level, but favor it on the population level. In that case the fate of the gene would be hard to predict.

If this article has asked many more questions than it has answered, the purpose is to suggest that answers be sought with all possible speed. Natu-ral selection is a very remarkable phe-nomenon. But it does not even guaran-tee the survival of a species. Most living forms have become extinct without the "softening" influence of civilization, sim-ply by becoming too narrowly special-ized. Natural selection is opportunistic; in shaping an organism to fit its sur-roundings it may leave the organism un-able to cope with a change in environ-ment. In this light, man's explosive ability to change his environment may offer as much threat as promise. Techno-logical evolution may have outstripped biological evolution.

Yet man is the only product of bio-logical evolution who knows that he has evolved and is evolving further. He should be able to replace the blind force of natural selection by conscious direc-tion, based on his knowledge of nature and on his values. It is as certain that such direction will be needed as it is questionable whether man is ready to provide it. He is unready because his knowledge of his own nature and its evolution is insufficient; because a vast majority of people are unaware of the necessity of facing the problem; and because there is so wide a gap between the way people actually live and the values and ideals to which they pay lip service.

It is frequently contended that the ethical problems and practical dangers involved in controlled breeding for human "betterment" are so dan-gerous that they far outweigh the possible advantages of trying to im-prove our species. Who will have the power to determine fitness for parent-hood, and to deny the right to those judged unfit? But scientifically based knowledge is always potentially dangerous—everything depends on how it is used, and, of course, that depends on us.

2. The Guidance of Man's Future Evolution [1]

Even though natural selection has been the great guiding principle that has brought us and all other higher organ-isms to their present estate, every respon-sible student of evolution knows that natural selection is too opportunistic and shortsighted to be trusted to give an ad-vantageous long-term result for any single group of organisms. Mankind constitutes one of those relatively rare, fabulously lucky lines whose ancestors did happen to win out—else we would not be here—while the incalculably vast majority of species sooner or later vanished—that is,

[1] HERMANN J. MULLER, "The Guidance of Human Evolution," in *The Evolution of Man*, Sol Tax (ed.) (Chicago: 1960), pp. 423–462. Reprinted by permission of the author and The University of Chicago Press, © 1960 by The University of Chicago Press.

Dr. Muller is Distinguished Service Professor of Zoology at Indiana University.

there are no living descendants now. Of all the species existing at any one time, only a relatively few ever function as conveyors of germ plasm that is to continue indefinitely, but most of these few branch and rebranch to more than compensate for the far greater number that are lost. Do we have reasons for believing that our species belongs in that very limited category that is to continue into the geologically distant future?

In examining this question we may first note that man is virtually excluded from ever again splitting into diversified species on this earth, so long as his technological culture remains. For that culture has the effect of shrinking the earth and removing ever more effectively the barriers to migration and interbreeding. Moreover, besides lacking the multiple chances for success which multiple speciation confers, our single species is undergoing, genetically, something analogous to an increase in entropy within itself. For its diverse sublines—hitherto numerous, partly isolated, and to some extent subject to ultimate competition with one another—are increasingly dissipating their separate individualities by merging genetic combinations, so that ever less opportunity is afforded for the intraspecies selection among many small groups that has been so potent an evolutionary force. Finally, the remaining intragroup selective processes are becoming subject to modification in their direction of operation through the influence of social processes which, left to themselves, tend to preserve and in some ways even to aid the multiplication of characteristics that are disserviceable to the welfare of the group as a whole—that is, of the species. For all these reasons it seems to follow that the one final remaining line of man will, if he retains or amplifies his technological culture, meet with biological extinction long before the earth grows too hot or too cold to support him.

The question arises here, May not this very culture that man has made effect some further alterations in the working of the principles of selection or add features to them that will, after all, permit man's indefinite survival as a civilized being? The answer seems clear. Cultural interference can bring about the survival of man and his culture only if it makes consummate use of man's most distinctive characteristic, his foresight, so as *consciously* to evade the otherwise inevitable decline.

GENETIC BENEFITS RESULTING FROM PAST CULTURAL EVOLUTION

Before discussing what such purposeful action would imply, we may first acknowledge that cultural factors, operating *without* man's realization of the evolutionary effects they would ultimately produce—that is, without long-range foresight—have in fact exerted major influences on human evolution in the past. And most, although not all, of the changes wrought thereby were of kinds that we would nowadays classify as good.

Prime examples are man's facility in using tools, permitting better manipulation of the environment, and his facility in communicating, mainly through speech. Tools and speech themselves are, of course, cultural developments, improved through many generations of extragenically transmitted experience. The possession of these aids to living, even in their more primitive forms, gave increasing scope for the exercise of the faculties that produced them and thereby strengthened and sharpened the selection that elaborated further the genetic bases of these faculties. Involved here, primarily, were mental abilities and proclivities of diverse kinds, including the very drives to engage in such activities. For example, the invention of numerical terms and methods of measuring afforded more abundant means whereby mathematical aptitudes could be utilized advantageously and thus enabled selection to be more effective in developing the biological basis of these aptitudes; the latter process, in turn, paved the way for still more cultural advance in these directions. Thus cultural and biological evolution were mutually reinforcing in their effects on intellectual development.

Similar considerations apply to other psychological aspects of culture that were made practicable and advantageous as a result of cultural advance, such as the wider gregariousness and the impulses to comradeliness and co-operation within larger groups than the family. Susceptibility to group experiences of the type called "religious" is a part of this genetic pattern that has developed in response to culture, one of the major advantages in this case being the group solidarity that it fosters. At the same time, the cultural development of hunting and its derivative activity, warfare, served as the foundation for the intensified selection of predispositions to combativeness, xenophobia, and related impulses, which made intergroup antagonism an active complement to intragroup cohesion. And so, despite the radically different methods that underlie the cultural process of acceptance of communicated lessons derived from experience and the genetic process of multiplication of genes arising by mutation, one can no longer disentangle the influence of these two interwoven sets of factors in changing both human culture and the human genotype.

When we turn to visible morphological features, the story is in principle the same. Among the human morphological traits that have probably developed in considerable measure as a result of selective conditions that were promoted by cultural features, we must, of course, set in the first place the enlargement of the brain and features that were directly subsidiary to increased cranial size, such as the widening of the pelvis. Another

obvious morphological development that was promoted by cultural advance was the recession of the jaws and the converse relative prominence of the chin and perhaps also of the nose. For these changes were surely selective consequences of cooking, cutting, scraping, clubbing, and stabbing, by the use of the fire, knives, scrapers, weapons, etc., as substitutes (by means of culture) for the operations of biting and mangling. Likewise, the cultural development of coverings for the body made it advantageous for the body hair to be genetically reduced, since temperature regulation became more refined thereby, external parasites could be brought under better control, and cleanliness in general was enhanced.

Specific features of given cultures have also led to distinctive bodily changes in given subgroups—such as those in adaptation to climates where men were enabled to live only after cultures suitable for these climates were developed. A well-known case in point is that of the narrower eyes, shorter intestines, and other adjustments to arctic and almost purely carnivorous ways of life in groups which have long complied with such conditions. Another obvious case is that of the light pigmentation of groups which, by reason of the climate they live in and types of clothing, shelter, and food they have adopted, receive a minimum of ultraviolet on their skin and at the same time relatively little vitamin D in their diet. Moreover, long-term cultural emphasis on given features of bodily form, such as steatopygy among the Hottentots and Bushmen of South Africa or a retreating forehead among some Amerindians, has evidently favored a reproductive selection that intensified the genetic factors for these traits. To what extent long-continued fashions in behavior limited to given groups have correspondingly exerted effective selection for given psychological propensities is a question to which only speculative answers can at present be given. But there can be little doubt that such a widespread practice, common to many cultures, as living by routine labor must have resulted in some selection, even though largely unconscious, of the proclivities conducive to it.

GENETIC INADEQUACIES OF CULTURAL EVOLUTION

The examples of physical deformities (as we would think of them) that have been consciously selected within certain groups show that the influence of culture on selection has not always been in advantageous and wholesome directions. Numerous are the instances in which cultures have gone off on tangents by inertias of their own, as in the squandering of people's efforts on useless work among ancient Egyptians and Sumerians and modern Tibetans, the sacrificial excesses of the Aztecs, and (though in lesser degree) the puritanical excesses of the forefathers of some of us. In each such case there must have been repercussions on the workings of genetic selection, and it is evident that the resulting influences were likely to be detrimental to the advancement of some genetic traits most desirable for human welfare. In early times such tendencies must have been held in check to a considerable extent by intergroup selection. The groups were small and numerous, and, other things being equal, those with harmful cultural developments must have tended to dwindle in competition with the sounder ones. With the merging of many small into few large groups, intergroup selection, whether of culture or of genes, loses its force, and, with the formation of the all-inclusive, virtually panmictic society, it practically ceases to exist. Thereafter there remains no mechanism for the rectification of harmful practices except the conscious recognition of them

for what they are and resultant socially adopted reform based on that recognition.

Certainly, as Darwin pointed out, the family, long before the arrival of man, must have afforded the primary unit for intergroup selection whereby the genetic basis of altruistic proclivities became developed. Then, as the groups came to include a number of families, they were still small enough and numerous enough to allow effective selection for the traits that predisposed their members for the wider co-operation and altruism here in order. Even if the individual sacrificed himself for the small group, he tended to foster the multiplication, through the others of that group, of genes like those that had predisposed him to this behavior. With the formation of towns and large civil units in general, this kind of influence on selection tended to disappear.

It is doubtless true that, even today, co-operation *within* the family results in some positive selection in favor of genes conducive to intrafamilial aid. In the setting of large-scale communities, the operation of these same genes can to some extent be adapted through cultural practices for the purposes of mutual aid in these larger communities. The very success of such adaptation, however, spells a corresponding decline in the selection. Moreover, so far as those proclivities are concerned that would tend to broaden the basis of the co-operation, by making a man really feel toward men in general as toward his brothers, there is no longer an automatic mechanism for enhancing their genetic basis. At the same time the characteristically human tendency to feel antagonistic toward those outside one's "circle" keeps seeking an outlet and is not effectively selected against. This situation has left men very imperfectly constructed to live by the utopian precept "Love one another." Yet any other basis of behavior for a form of living that depends on our modern global technologies must result in even greater disharmonies, whereby these technologies themselves become turned against their users.

We are now at a juncture where we must move forward or backward. No matter what the steps may be—whether gradually constructive or catastrophic— by which the major group divisions of our present transitional political setup become superseded by an effective world-embracing organization, it is evident that there is no longer any ultimate alternative to such union except the retrogression of modern culture—that is, the virtual abandonment of the benefits of science. The latter contingency would be one that few of those aware of what it would involve would willingly choose if they could make the decision. In effect, it would mean the failure of civilization and the frustration of the rationality which, limited though it is, has been the most distinctive and creative characteristic of humanity. Assuming, however, that men do win out in their efforts to achieve a universal community, this question must be faced: What effects will the universalization and enhancement of modern culture have on the genetic constitution of man and thereby on his conditions of life?

So far as the adaptive differentiations of present human geographical groups are concerned, it is evident that their inevitable swamping-out, through merger aided by relaxed selection, should give no grounds for serious concern. For the lack of these specialized features can readily be compensated for, in the given situations, by such artificial contrivances as specially constructed clothing, shelters, means of transport, heating, cooling, special food supplies, optical equipment, medicaments, insecticides, germicides, vaccines, and so forth. Thus, far greater stretches become open to comparatively dense habitation than formerly, without the requirement of distinctive genetic endowment.

One sometimes hears the assertion that similar considerations apply to all inherited variations in man: that is, with the progress of technology and more especially of medical, general biological, and biochemical methods, it will become increasingly possible to compensate for all kinds of genetic abnormalities and deviations and thus to raise each individual virtually to the optimum level in all respects. From this self-styled "progressive" view, eugenics is an old-fashioned and reactionary notion destined to be discarded. In the official Communist version of this view, the improvements and corrections brought about in the individual's makeup by manipulation of his physical and psychological environment, including careful training, become automatically incorporated into his inheritance so that men will become better and better equipped genetically with each generation as a result of their improved environment. It would be out of place for us here to state the overwhelming case against this naïve Lamarckian doctrine, so long discredited by the fundamental principles established through decades of genetic research. In the West it is commoner for those with strong environmentalist leanings no longer to espouse Lamarckism but simply to maintain that human hereditary defects, perhaps with relatively rare exceptions, will be rendered unimportant phenotypically by means of the consummate skills of future technology, even though they will probably tend to persist as gene differences. In addition, some who wish to appear up-to-date are bold enough to declare that even defective genes may in time be repaired or replaced by ultrafine substitutions of their nucleotide constituents.

Of course, it is indisputable that, as man's control over matter advances, more and more of his bodily structure and functioning can be amended and even replaced by artificial means. Thus, even as primitive man found his body hair largely dispensable and replaced it by coverings, future man will require less and less heat regulation, antibody production, natural hormone generation, digestive juice secretion, and so forth. He can use scooters for locomotion and computers for calculation. And he can finally do without himself!

Primitive man could replace his natural faculties by artifices only in certain limited aspects of his living, as in protection against weather, wild animals, and certain vicissitudes in food supply. The techniques needed for these purposes were not too burdensome, and they actually gave him much better means of meeting the given requirements than did his inherited specializations. Hence it was these biological endowments rather than his cultural devices which ultimately became too burdensome to be maintained. Certainly in the case of modern and future man this situation will apply in many more areas of living. But to acknowledge this fact is not the same as to say that there would, in general, be a net gain in substituting for our genetic endowment everything that would now or in the future be devised to take its place. Where should we draw the line?

A given natural endowment is better lost than retained if all the following three conditions hold. First, the artificial substitute should be more effective and dependable than the natural endowment. Second, the net burden to the community involved in maintenance and operation should, for a given return, be less for the artificial substitute than for the natural endowment. Third, the maintenance of the natural endowment as a supplement to the man-made contrivance should be more trouble than it is worth before its lapse can be considered justifiable.

Today, of course, no attempt is made to assess these balances when procedures are instituted which, in helping individuals, may contribute to the relaxation of selection in given directions. It is regarded as ethical to employ every available artificial aid to enable an individual to reproduce or to enable him to live and thereby reproduce, even when his reproduction would be likely to perpetuate the genetic condition that had occasioned the given difficulty. So far as the immediately treated generation is concerned, mutual aid of this kind is unquestionably a social obligation. Its over-all cost is very small in comparison with its benefits to the community in well-being, general efficiency, harmonious interrelations, sense of security, and enjoyment of life. The real issue is not whether society should in this way help the individuals themselves to live better, as if that were where the matter stopped. It is whether the acts of society should be so ordered as actually to facilitate the perpetuation of defective genetic equipment into later generations. Should we give with one hand while taking away with the other?

Let us be clear about the genetic processses here involved. Like a gas that tends to expand in all directions as a result of the random movements of its molecules, the genetic material is continually undergoing mutations in innumerable directions in a chaotic manner, and the vast majority of these mutations are, of course, detrimental in their effects on the organism, tending to disorganize and de-adapt it, both in regard to the general fitness of the organism as a whole for living and reproducing and in regard to the development, structure, and functioning of any given part or characteristic of the organism. It is only selection which, by holding on check the multiplication of the deleterious mutants after they have arisen and, conversely, by promoting the multiplication of the very rare superior types, allows the mutation pressure to result in increased fitness of the organism for the given conditions, even as the walls of a chamber containing a gas allow the pressure of the gas to shape it to fit its container. Relax the selection in any direction, and mutation pressure will cause disorganization and de-differentiation in that direction up to whatever limit is set, much as any recession or loosening of one or more walls of the chamber is followed by a corresponding diffusion of the contained gas.

RESULTS OF THE CONTINUATION OF PRESENT PRACTICES

On the average, the counterpressure of selection, consisting in the elimination of individuals with excess detrimental genes, almost exactly equals the pressure of mutation in producing these genes. There is evidence from more than one direction that, in man, at least one person in five, or 20 per cent, carries a detrimental gene which arose in the immediately preceding generation and that, therefore, this same proportion—one in five—is, typically, prevented by genetic defects from surviving to maturity or (if surviving) from reproducing. This equilibrium holds only when a population is living under conditions that have long prevailed. Modern techniques are so efficacious that, used to the full, they might today (as judged by recent statistics on deaths and births) be able to save for life and for a virtually normal rate of reproduction some nine-tenths of the otherwise genetically doomed 20 per cent. Assuming this to be the case, there would in the next generation be 18 per cent who carried along those defects that would have failed to be transmitted in the primitive or equilibrium population, plus another 20 per cent (partly overlapping the 18 per cent) who had the most recently arisen defects. At this rate, if the effectiveness of the techniques did not diminish as their job grew, there would, after about eight generations, or 240 years, be an accumulation of about 100 "genetic deaths" (scattered over

many future generations) per 100 persons then living, in addition to the regular "load of mutations" that any population would ordinarily carry. It can be estimated (on the supposition that human mutation rates are like those in mice) that this amount of increase in the load is about the same as would be brought about by an acute exposure of all the parents of one generation to 200 r of gamma radiation, a situation similar to that at Hiroshima, or by a chronic, low-dose-rate exposure of each of the eight generations to 100 r.

This result sounds worse than it is because most of the mutant genes would cause only a slight amount of damage in their usual heterozygous condition. Since the regular load of perhaps some scores of significantly detrimental genes per individual—nearly all in heterozygous condition but each a potential cause of some far-future genetic death—gives rise to a total risk of genetic extinction, as measured under primitive conditions, of something like (but probably exceeding) 20 per cent for any *given* individual, it is evident that the addition of just one more detrimental gene to his load would usually increase his own risk of extinction by only some tenths of 1 per cent. Thus the process of genetic decline would be exceedingly slow, thanks to the innumerable factors of safety that are built into our systems. The decline, in fact, would for a very long time consist mainly in a reduction in these factors of safety.

Let us next suppose that this sparing of genetic deaths by the aid of technology were to continue indefinitely at the assumed rate, a rate at which a genetic defect, on the average, subjects a person to only a tenth as much risk as it would if he were living under primitive conditions. Eventually, after some tens of thousands of years, a new equilibrium would be reached at which the load of mutations would be about ten times as large as at present. Thus as many extinctions as mutations would again be occurring. If we are to keep to our previously chosen figure for mutations, there would be one extinction for every five individuals, or 20 per cent. The frequency of genetic deaths would therewith return to the level which it had in primitive times and would be far above that now prevailing, in spite of all technological efforts. At the same time, the average individual of that time, carrying ten times today's genetic load, would, if tested under primitive conditions, be found to be no longer subject to a risk of extinction of only 20 per cent, but to one of 200 per cent. This means that he would carry twice as much defect as would suffice to eliminate him. Man would thereby have become entirely dependent on the techniques of his higher civilization. Yet, even with these techniques, he would be subject to as high an incidence of genetic misfortunes as had afflicted him in primitive times. That is, his weaknesses would have caught up with him.

It will rightly be objected here that we have assumed in this calculation that technical skills throughout an indefinite period remained only at their present or immediately impending level, whereas, surely, if civilization advances as we hope, medical and other skills will become capable of reducing ever further the damage done by the average genetic defect. This would cause a perpetual pushing-back of the time of attainment of equilibrium. However, as in the previous illustration, each step in saving more lives would be followed by a corresponding increase in the load eventually carried. So, for example, a saving of all but one in a hundred that would originally have been lost would lead upward toward a hundred fold increase in the load, to be attained only after some hundreds of thousands of years. At that point and for a long time before that, each individual would be endowed by nature with a unique assortment of many hundreds of cryptic, as well as conspicuous, inherent defects and would therefore constitute a special case. He would have to be given a superlatively well-chosen combination of treatments, training, and artificial substitutes just to get by. The job of ministering to infirmities would come to consume all the energy that society could muster for it, leaving no surplus for general cultural purposes. Yet, even at that stage, *most* of man's genes would still be fairly normal, so new mutations, always arising at the rate of some 20 per cent in every generation, would plague him even further.

Long before such an "advanced" stage of the genetic cul-de-sac was reached, however, this medical utopia would probably be subjected to such great strains as to throw men back toward more primitive ways of life. Many would find themselves incapable of such ways. To be sure, the difficulty then would in a sense be "self-rectifying." But so late and forced a rectification would be likely to cause the loss of much that had previously been gained.

Only on paper could techniques be advanced indefinitely to avoid ever reaching the equilibrium at which the incidence of genetic deaths equals that of new mutations. An indefinite continuance of the process would, on paper, require it to proceed until virtually every one of the ten thousand or more genes in every chromosome set had been badly damaged or incapacitated. Judging by present data on mutation rates, this would happen within a period of a few million years, provided that medical men during this period had been able to work with the kind of perfection they desire. What would this situation imply? It would imply that the then existing germ cells of what were once human beings would be a lot of hopeless, utterly diverse genetic monstrosities. Surely the refashioning of these pitiful relics into human form would be a far more difficult task than the synthesis of human beings out of raw materials selected for the purpose. It would also be more difficult than the construction of robots. The marvelous techniques that such an age would possess would hardly be used for so preposterous and fatuous a purpose as the preservation of a genetic continuity that had lost its meaning.

Returning from these fantasies, we see that it is absurd to assume that environmentalist techniques alone, dealing purely with the phenotype, can in the long run keep ahead of mutations so as indefinitely to enhance or even preserve human well-being. The assumption bears a close analogy to that made by anti-Malthusians when they suppose that means can be found of continuing to increase the earth's supply of food, goods, and living room to accommodate a population that keeps on growing at its present rate. That rate, some 1.75 per cent per year, would amount to a thousand fold increase every four hundred years. The accumulation of mutation is an inordinately slower process than the expansion of population. Yet in either case the process will inevitably come to a halt too late, as a result of the misery and disorganization which it brings about, unless it is forestalled through long-range foresight that exercises a conscious control over reproduction. In the case of the population problem, that control need be exercised only over the total quantity of reproduction, whereas, to meet the mutation problem, the control must be exercised in a qualitative way—a much more difficult and still more important matter.

A favorite cliché with those who do not understand this situation is the statement that, by definition, natural selection must always be acting and must always be favoring the fitter. This statement overlooks the fact that the degree of genetically occasioned difference in reproductive rate—that is, the intensity of selection—can be far less in some situations than in others. But the major point disregarded here is that what is fitter in the immediate acts of life is not always fitter for a group or a species as a whole in the long run. In such a case the group is running a race toward debasement and sometimes toward extinction, in this respect following the great majority of species of the past. In the case of man, the trick factor in this connection is a very unusual one: culture. Although culture did serve to sharpen salutary types of human selection in the past, as we have seen, it has now reached a point at which its very efficiency, when not yet involving foresight in regard to genetics, has placed upon society the burden of supporting almost indiscriminately the ever increasing genetic failings of its members.

If, in accordance with the above cliché, we define fitness in the narrow (but erroneous) sense, by the criterion of leaving a larger number of immediate offspring, then, of course, later generations of man must, by definition, be increasingly fit. Yet this type of fitness is no longer the same as fitness in regard to the qualities conducive to the well-being and survival of mankind in general. In fact, it seems not unlikely that in regard to the human faculties of the highest group importance —such as those needed for integrated understanding, foresight, scrupulousness, humility, regard for others, and self-sacrifice—cultural conditions today may be conducive to an actually lower rate of reproduction on the part of their possessors than of those with the opposite attributes. Is it not too often true that today, when birth control is available, those persons most lacking in perspective or dominated by superstitions taboos or unduly egotistical or unmindful of others' needs or shiftless or bungling in techniques are the very ones with the largest retinue of children, whether legitimate or otherwise? These considerations suggest the possibility that a much faster-acting and more serious cause of genetic deterioration than the previously discussed accumulation of detrimental mutations occurring in the wake of relaxed selection is an actual reversal of selection in regard to those psychological traits that are of the highest social importance. Objective data are badly needed on this question.

The relaxation of selection that I have considered, as well as its postulated reversal, have been made possible by the fact that, under modern culture, the damage done by social as well as other defects of individuals is increasingly borne by society as a whole. This is *in itself* a great step forward. However, its potential consequences for the biological evolution of man have not been considered seriously enough, even though Darwin himself called attention to them.

We need not set forth in detail here the mistakes made by many of those who in the past have taken this problem seriously: their great overestimation of the speed of the genetic processes in question, their even greater underestimation of the efficacy of cultural influences in the shaping of men's minds, and the notorious support that some of them gave to the vicious doctrines of racism. Along with the highly essential repudiation of these mistakes, there has been a tendency to go to the opposite extreme of throwing out also the hard core that is really valid. It is so easy to shrug off effects that take thousands of years to become evident. And, as in the case of erosion, they are by that time accepted as a part of the order of nature.

Statesmen, economists, social scientists, and men of affairs are seldom interested in such remote matters. Yet, as evolutionists, we know that the greatest and most creative, as well as the most destructive, operations of the living world have been of this creeping, secular character. Unless

we are willing to remain, when viewed in larger perspective, helpless creatures of circumstances, we must take these insidious operations into account, master their principles, and devise ways of dealing with them.

THE PROTECTION OF OUR GENETIC HERITAGE

The crux of the problem is the interference with salutary types of selection in man that has arisen incidentally as a by-product of the widespread and increased effectiveness of mutual aid when it utilizes the tools supplied by science. What means can be used to protect our genetic heritage from this paradoxical situation? Occasional reactionary voices are to be heard calling upon us to reduce our mutual aid in the name of "rugged individualism," "private enterprise," or the like, and others are asking for a moratorium on science and even for a return to a fancied golden age.

However, it has been exactly the combination of intelligence with co-operative behavior that has made culture possible and raised men above beasts, and these propensities brook no stopping point. The enormous advances opening to men in consequence of the further extension of science (representing intelligence) and of a world-wide social organization (representing mutual aid) so utterly overshadow, in their potential effects within the next few hundred years, the damage that may be done in that period to men's genetic constitution that none but the unbalanced would consider now giving up, for genetic reasons, the march of civilization.

It must unfortunately be conceded, however, that even tomorrow suddenly, or within the century ahead of us gradually, a return to more primitive conditions might take place. It would not represent the voluntary choice of the majority of the world's inhabitants but the consequence of miscalculation or faulty organization. And if it did occur, men would endeavor to work their way up to a stage even more rational and co-operative than our present one. If they attained it, they would once more find themselves confronted with our genetic dilemma.

Thus far, men have usually been able to find an answer to the difficulties into which the application of a little science has gotten them, and that answer has been found in better science. Similarly, they have extricated themselves from difficulties occasioned by imperfect mutual aid through the application of improved mutual aid. Both factors are involved in the present case, and the solution requires a suitable combination of the two.

The main role of science in this matter is the discovery of the situation, but it will be important to get much more information concerning its details, both qualitative and quantitative, and concerning the kinds of strategies that would be effective in meeting it. However, the choice and implementation of these strategies is largely bound up with men's attitudes in regard to mutual aid.

Although the mores of our society approve the extension of society's aid to individuals for the purpose of saving their lives and thereby enabling them to reproduce, they do not yet, reciprocally, recognize a duty on the part of individuals to exercise their reproductive functions with due regard to the benefit or injury thereby done to society. So long as illegitimacy is avoided, the individual is not considered to be under any genetic obligation but deems it his right to have as many or as few children as he personally wishes. This being the case, his choice in the matter is largely determined by irrational factors and by shortsighted aims. Such practices worked out well enough genetically only so long as, in matters of survival, the families or the small groups were in large measure on their own.

What is most needed in this area of living is an extension of the feeling of social responsibility to the field of reproduction: an increasing recognition that the chief objective in bringing children into the world is not the glorification of the parents or ancestors by the mere act of having children but the well-being of the children themselves and, through them, of subsequent generations in general. When people come to realize that in some measure their gifts, as well as their failings and difficulties—physical, intellectual, and temperamental—have genetic bases and that social approval or disapproval will be accorded them if they take these matters into account in deciding how much of a family to beget, a big step forward will have been taken in the motivation of human reproduction.

It can become an accepted and valued practice to seek advice, though not dictation, in these matters, even as it is today in matters of individual health. Although no one enjoys admitting his faults, he can learn to take pride in exercising humility and ordering the most important of his biological functions—reproduction—in such ways as to win the approbation of himself and his fellows. This is, to be sure, a higher type of mutual aid, a superior moral code, than exists at present, but it can be just around the corner for people who from early youth have had the facts of genetics and evolution made vivid to them and who have been imbued with a strong sense of their participation in the attainment of human well-being.

Those for whom it seems wiser, in the interests of the coming generation, not to play as active a part as they might in producing people plagued by the very shortcomings that they have seen bring trouble to themselves can still find plenty of meritorious and satisfying work to give them a sense of fulfilment. Nearly everyone is above average at something and should be given opportunity to exercise his aptitudes in ways that do him credit and aid society. He may be a skilled teacher or custodian of the young, although, because of some unfortunate defect or combination of weaknesses, he is less suitable than the average for personal reproduction. If instructed from the beginning regarding the nature of the human effort and the interdependence of man, he can take this realization in his stride and devote himself to kinds of activity in which he can take pride.

That is not to say, of course, that there can be hard-and-fast rules and that any one or a few known genetic defects should enjoin a person from reproduction. Everyone has many minor and some more serious inherent imperfections. In conscious decisions, as in the process of primitive natural selection, it is the total balance of these that should count, and the answer need seldom be an all-or-none one.

Contrariwise, for those clearly better endowed, this kind of social motivation should lead them to place special importance on creating children, even though in such cases especially there will be great temptation to expend disproportionately much effort in other directions. It is true that economic and other aids could be of value here. However, the underlying mores will inevitably exert the more powerful influence. The main job, if the situation is to be rectified, consists in laying the foundations for these mores.

This does not mean that we can expect ever to specify just what would be the optimal number of children for any given individual to have, in view of his genetic constitution. Natural selection would never have succeeded in the past if such precision had been necessary. Environmental influences always complicate, sometimes inextricably, the determination of developed traits. It is enough, from a long-range point of view, if only the trend is in a salutary direction. And that is the result that must be sought in the attempt to protect man's most invaluable possession—his own genetic material.

Two developments of our present period are powerful positive influences toward the needed change in motivation. One is the sudden realization of the damaging effects of radiation on heredity. This, by reason of having been made a political football, has done more to arouse the public and its leaders to the fact that our genetic constitution requires protection than all the propaganda that eugenicists have ever put forth. Characteristically, the danger has been greatly exaggerated in some quarters, for ulterior purposes quite unconnected rationally with the matter at issue, and has been just as unjustifiably dismissed or played down in other quarters, where there were other axes to grind. Nevertheless, the over-all effect of the controversy has been highly educational and has helped to make people far more genetics-conscious than they ever were before. It so happens that this same radiation problem is one of the *proper* faces of the ax which is here being ground. Thus it is fitting to take advantage of the receptivity created by political circumstances to awaken the public to the more general need for a reformation of attitudes toward reproduction.

The other relevant development of our time is the menace of overpopulation. Even publicists are at last becoming alarmed at the smothering of cultural advance and the disaster to democratic institutions that it can bring about in a generation or two if unchecked. An absolute check will require not only that birth-control techniques be made available but also that large masses of people execute an about-face in their attitudes toward having children. They must recognize that to have or not to have children, and how many, should be determined primarily by the interests of the children themselves—that is, of the next and subsequent generations. If this change in outlook is effected—as it must be sooner or later—it is a relatively short step to the realization that the inborn equipment of the children also counts mightily in their well-being and opportunity for happiness.

THE GENETIC OFFENSIVE

Thus far I have emphasized conserving the genetic goods we have. As in most defensive operations, it is a dreary, frustrating business to have to keep racing merely to stay put. Nature did better for us. Why can we not do better for ourselves? For both psychological and material reasons, the best defensive in this, as in other matters, is the offensive.

A man finds little incentive to take steps to ward off a hidden danger that is a thousand or ten thousand years away. But when there is a definite possibility of tangible improvement in the conditions of life within a period such that he or his wards can directly experience it, then a man's efforts can be enlisted far more effectively.

Why should we or anyone else who has become aware of the marvelous advances that have been made in biological evolution consider it sufficient merely to keep things as good as they are if we can do much more than that? Certainly, the majority of mankind have come, within a few generations, to set their objectives much higher in the case of cultural evolution, now that they have learned how astonishingly amenable it can be to their own contrivings. They are also making considerable progress in the genetic reshaping of organisms of service to them. It seems almost inevitable that, if civilization avoids its present opposite pitfalls of mutual extermination and overpopulation, men will in the not too distant future want to utilize also, for their own benefit, the vast, though more

unwieldy, possibilities of their own biological advancement. But, to make this advance, false gods will have to fall along the way.

It is sometimes objected that our cultural evolution has superseded our biological evolution. Nothing in either of these processes is inherently exclusive of the other, even though, as we have seen, culture is now developing in a way that does tend to run counter to biological progress. It is also asserted that biological progress is no longer necessary, since so much more rapid, radical, and diverse improvements can be effected by cultural means—not only with physical and chemical techniques and educational and, sociological methods but ultimately too, no doubt, in ways of modifying embryological, including neurological, patterns.

The vast potentialities of cultural advance (subject to the mutational limitations previously discussed) are not to be denied. On the contrary, they need to be emphasized even more. But we should not think of phenotypic and genotypic operations as rivals. They can do best when they proceed in the same direction, even as they did in the formative days of our species. It is culture that chiefly distinguishes the scientist from the witch doctor, but it is genes that distinguish man from protozoön or virus and make his mastery of culture possible. In fact, the genetic and the cultural advances cannot even be considered additive; they are related more like the factors in a product formed by multiplying one by the other. Thus a small improvement in the genes may, in effect, work out as an enormous advance when there is already a high type of culture. Conversely, when acting with a high genetic endowment, a relatively small cultural advance can attain far more significance than otherwise.

The same change in attitude toward reproduction that is needed to insure the preservation of our genetic heritage is also the necessary basis for its improvement. If once it is accepted that the function of reproduction is to produce children who are as happy, healthy, and capable as possible, then it will be only natural for people to wish each new generation to represent a genetic advance, if possible, over the preceding one rather than just a holding of the line. And they will become impatient at confining themselves to old-fashioned methods if more promising ones for attaining this end are available. As the individualistic outlook regarding procreation fades, more efficacious means of working toward this goal will recommend themselves. In time, children with genetic difficulties may even come to be resentful toward parents who had not used measures calculated to give them a better heritage. Influenced in advance by this anticipation and also by the desire for community approval in general, even the less idealistic of the parental generation will tend increasingly to follow the genetic practices most likely to result in highly endowed children.

But before discussing these questions of biological means, it is important to consider ends—or, rather, objectives. We may start by a brief dismissal of the contention sometimes raised that one cannot recognize merits higher than one's own or lift one's self by one's bootstraps. If this were true, there would be no use in self-criticism, and persons of exceptionally high ability would never be identified except by each other. However, given the thesis that men can come to realize in some measure their own limitations and can conceive of beings superior to themselves, this question must be faced: By what criteria should they decide what changes would be desirable? For without some consensus on this ultimate question of values, men's efforts in biological—and, for that matter, also in cultural—directions can only be at cross-purposes.

VALUES

In the past, questions of values were passed upon for men, first, as a result of the natural selection of mutations that gave them their native predilections and the capability of having these modified by association; second, as a result of the natural selection of those developing cultures that led to the most dependable survival and multiplication. As we have seen, the combination of these processes resulted in a great increase in men's proclivities for communication and other types of co-operation and in the intelligence that made the co-operation more effective. At the same time, cultures were selected in such wise as to stress, although with very varied forms of expression, men's sense of the desirability of these functions and the attitudes lying behind them. We still have these feelings today and have a better realization than ever of their primacy for us subjectively and of their objective utility in survival. At the same time, of course, we also value many subsidiary motivations, such as those stemming from zest in the meeting of challenges, joy in accomplishment, the urge to solve problems, the desire for approval, sexual and familial love, the appreciation of different kinds of beauty, and so forth. All these overlapping propensities, as well as others, contribute to the success of the rationally guided co-operative activities that promote the survival and expansion of the group, a group that is coming ever more to comprise the species as a whole.

Despite the carpings and quibblings of some philosophers, the most generalized rational formulation of human aims that most persons concerned with the subject can agree upon is the promotion of the greatest over-all happiness. We need not define happiness more precisely here than as the sense of fulfilment derived from the attainment, or from approaching the attainment, of whatever is deeply desired.

(Any one of a number of other terms might, of course, be substituted for "happiness" here, provided that it be defined in this way.) Granted that in given cases one man's meat can be another's poison and that some find fulfilment in actually giving pain to others, most men recognize that, from a longer-range standpoint, these interpersonal disharmonies are undesirable, in that they allow less over-all happiness. In the same class would come a one-sided attachment to subsidiary aims —such as the satisfaction of pride in the building of pyramids or in the unlimited accumulation of luxuries—that reduces the capacity to contribute to the over-all welfare and thereby hinders the survival, expansion, and long-term happiness of the group.

The will to self-development—hedonism, the urge to achieve—functionalism, the ideal of service—altruism, and a spiritual attitude toward existence—consecration, all these modes of approach to living, when followed up logically, become finally resolved into the pursuit of the same objective. The reason that self-development can be included among these orientations is that man is a naturally social animal in whose individual personality a major role is played by his regard for others. The final objective, likewise, may be thought of and designated in different ways, such as human happiness, richness, of life, welfare, increasing survival, or advancement, since these are all diverse aspects of one great combination that in practice remains inseparable.

All this by no means implies that men ordinarily carry the remote, abstract-seeming goal of the common good in sight in their day-by-day activities. It is human to have very varied interests and desires—in fact, to crave variation, curiosity being one form of this craving—and to take the satisfaction of each kind of desire as an end in itself. This exceptional versatility in strivings, complemented by diverse capabilities, has been a highly important factor in man's success, for it has fostered development along many lines, and so varied opportunities could be taken advantage of and adapted to. More than any other creature, man's genius is generalized and his intelligence and potentialities protean. This dispersal of his efforts works out in the end to enhance his control over his own affairs and over his environment, in both his individual interest and that of his species.

Naturally, however, there are many points at which the pursuit of some personal desire as an end seems to lead (or actually does lead) to a different course of action from that which would be followed by directly navigating according to the distant North Star of over-all human happiness. In such a case, we are likely to say that there are conflicts between individual and social aims. But when we take into account the way a man is built, we see that he can render better service to his group if he is well-rounded and not plagued too much by deprivations and repressions. Moreover, a man's intelligence and his devotion to more distant aims are never sufficient, by themselves, to lead him into all the by-ways that he will find by trial to be fruitful. He must therefore compromise between aims and activities that seem more purely personal and those that are more obviously social and thus attain a harmonious balance among them. Yet, provided that his personality is intelligently integrated and strongly social, his over-all gratification will be especially deep if, in general, his life follows a course that appears to him to be in line with the highest welfare of mankind. Then, even if circumstances prevent the objective success of his endeavors, he may nevertheless, by this touchstone, attain a sense of personal achievement.

As this discussion implies, the balance reached by different people can be very different, and some may not acknowledge, at least to themselves, any social obligations at all. The form and level of the balance will depend not only on the very complex genetic basis provided by the given individual but also on his particular training and experiences and the culturally based attitudes that he has derived from his social group. Moreover, the groups themselves still differ widely in their degrees and kinds of socialization.

This question must then be raised: What genetic and cultural backgrounds are conducive to the highest success, as judged by the ulterior criterion of their promotion of over-all happiness? First, it is evident that the distribution of relative strengths of different drives that was most appropriate to the success of people when they were divided into many small, nearly autonomous groups is far from that most suitable for men organized into a vast society engaged in scientific and technological advances, mechanized production, transportation and communication, predominantly common interests, and rational, democratically guided decisions. Surely in this society most of us could do better if, by nature as well as by training, we had less tendency to quick anger, blinding fear, strong jealousy, and self-deceiving egotism. At the same time we need a strengthening and extension of the tendencies toward kindliness, affection, and fellow feeling in general, especially toward those personally far removed from us. These impulses should become sufficiently dynamic to issue in helpful action. As regards other affective traits, there is much room for broadening and deepening our capacity to appreciate both natural and man-made constructions, to interpret with fuller empathy the expressions of others, to create ever richer combinations of our own impressions, and to communicate them to others more adequately.

Another direction in which an advance is needed is in those traits of character that lead to independence of judg-ment and its necessary complement, intellectual honesty. We need to strengthen the drive to see things through to as near the bottom as possible and also the drive to co-ordinate the elements rationally. Just as important are the will and ability to take fair criticism with good grace and, further, to search and criticize ourselves until we recognize and discard, if need be publicly, judgments based on wishful or faulty thinking or on defective data. Of course, a great deal of all this may be taught, but there seem also to be great inborn differences in the facility and degree with which such emotion-fraught mental operations are learned and in the strength of feeling behind them.

Turning now to more purely intellectual matters, it is obvious that tomorrow's world makes desirable a much greater capacity for analysis, for quantitative procedures, for integrative operation, and for imaginative creation. With more and more of the daily grind taken over by automation, the human being will be increasingly freed for higher mental jobs; yet most of our population today would be by nature ill-adapted for such activities, even if they had the desire to pursue them.

How ignoble and inadequate for its potentialities is a society in which the material operations are conducted by the utilization of the equations of Willard Gibbs, Rutherford, Einstein, and Planck, while most of the human beings who are served thereby have hardly a glimmering of what is involved—while seeking to turn these forces chiefly to such purposes as broadcasting television commercials, football games, burlesque shows, and revival meetings, or seeing Europe in a week or accurately dropping H-bombs nine thousand miles away. Missed are the opportunities for those profound stirrings which would be theirs if they could and would follow the inner workings of these forces that the combined efforts of a relatively few among them have put at their disposal. Missed also is the thrilling awareness of what vastly enlarged possibilities a more rational use of these and other powers could open up to everyone. If men are not to be mere cogs in their work and pawns in their play, they must have deeper and broader vision, as well as a more virile, broadly based comradeliness. Then their machines and science can give them increasing freedom for further achievement and further savoring of the bounties of our exapnding universe instead of deeper enslavement in routines.

How are men to attain the higher intelligence and enhanced fellow feeling and sensitivity that will better fit them to the modern world? Certanly there can and must be reforms in the ways and mores of society, and especially in the bringing-up and teaching of children, that will work major improvements. Some enthusiasts for biological techniques even hope that some day, by means of suitable elixirs, the growing brain may be influenced favorably during its embryonic development. But we cannot rest in the precarious hope of such a miracle. And it would be beyond reason to expect that cultural methods alone, powerful though they are, could bring to the average man that ability to understand, appreciate, and exploit the forces of nature and artifice which is today reserved for specialists in their respective fields. Yet a considerable measure of that ability, in every field at once, must become the property of the common man if he is to enter into the great cultural inheritance that will make him a really voluntary agent, led by the mind and not by the nose.

Correspondingly, a man's nature must also have at its very core a genuine warmth of feeling for his fellows if, despite the personal difficulties, compromises, and renunciations that inevitably beset everyone, he is to derive an adequate sense of fulfilment from his and their joint day-by-day efforts and achievements and also from the larger contemplation of grand-scale human progress. This, too, is a situation which calls for not only cultural methods but also genetic ones.

That genetic methods could be effective is illustrated by the vast individual differences in native intellectual capacity, temperament, and emotional pattern that exist among human beings, even as among other higher animals. Studies of twins and people brought up in institutions and foster homes have shown clearly the high, though far from absolute, importance of their heredity in the determination of psychological, as well as so-called physical, traits. Undoubtedly, even seemingly minute features of the personality can be strongly influenced by the genes. More important, there are abundant instances of extremely high mental ability, of a generalized kind, reappearing conspicuously in some members of families while missing other members. Certainly, there is already genetic material on hand, recognizable through its expressions, which, if conferred on the population at large, could enable men in general to find freedom and release by engaging in great co-operative, as well as individual, assualts against the seeming inexorabilities of the outer world and their own stubborn natures and by giving the feelings thus engendered creative and artistic expressions.

For achieving this end, which, after all, would be only another beginning, it is imperative that men think through their values to the point at which they recognize the primary importance for themselves of these two essentials: deeper mental insight and the feelings that give them joy in common action and in individual creation that can be shared. At present they are likely to place equal or greater emphasis on nonessentials. If genetic methods are to be used, men must come to realize that at this stage of their development they still have many divisive tendencies, provincial attachments to styles, features, and peculiarities of their own particular group. They must learn that such predilections, about which they could now wrangle endlessly, must be discounted and set as much in the background of their thoughts as possible, in order that emphasis may be placed on the key faculties mentioned— which, after all, count the most for everyone. No people, no caste or class, has a monopoly on these essentials. But there is everywhere a dearth of them, in relation to present needs. Let men become more conscious of this dearth and, conversely, of the richer life that later generations may have in proportion to the degree to which that dearth is remedied. In the meantime, no one need fear that there will be a danger of men's really salutary diversities becoming wiped out. And later, in a wiser, kindlier age, men may more safely and calmly consider how this spice of life—variety—can be turned to better account.

MOTIVATIONS IN REPRODUCTION

It cannot be denied that the technological and social innovations of our age, combined with the influence of the scientific world view, are weakening the hold of ancient taboos and superstitions, loosening the rigidities of the family system, and greatly liberalizing the attitude of large numbers of people in regard to matters of sex. Within the twentieth century, in fact, the change has been so pronounced as to justify the application of the term "sexual revolution" to this situation, even though the ostensible, officially proclaimed standards are still much the same as in Victorian times. As yet this revolution has been of a predominantly individualistic kind. It has con-

cerned itself chiefly with making people freer of the natural reproductive consequences of sex and therefore less rigorously bound sexually, as well as less burdened with excessive childbearing and child-rearing. But it has not concerned itself with the converse matter— allowing the decisions leading to parenthood to become more rational from a genetic viewpoint and to be guided in greater measure by the type of native endowment that would be valuable for the children themselves. A further break with tradition is necessary before such a viewpoint can lead to perceptible changes in this respect.

The way to such a reform in viewpoint is paved by several groups of circumstances. One of these is the sexual revolution itself. A second is the trend toward a more social outlook in general, brought about by the increasing degree of co-operation in our society consequent upon the impact of scientific and technological advances on our economic and political system. A third, more specific, influence is brought to bear as the pressure of too rapidly increasing population causes increasing numbers of people to realize that the interests of the potential children themselves must be taken into account in decisions whether to reproduce and that the implementation of these decisions requires their using artificial controls for preventing reproduction where advisable. At the same time, sterility is becoming increasingly remediable. Finally, and still more pertinent, although not yet operative, will be the realization that artificial means are already at hand, and others nearly at hand, whereby the likelihood of the child's receiving a superior genetic endowment can be greatly improved without individual sex practices being thereby interfered with. It is this fourth factor that must increasingly turn the scales.

Nevertheless, it remains true that

some long-intrenched attitudes, especially the feelings of proprietary rights and prerogatives about one's own germinal material, supported by misplaced egotism, will have to yield to some extent. This feeling does not represent a natural instinct, since there are primitive tribes yet alive who do not have even the concept of biological fatherhood and others that, although having it, readily and without their parental relationships being affected thereby, adopt, confer, or exchange infants. That is, their egotism does not extend to their stirps. Actually, they are more logical in this respect than are most of the persons in more advanced societies who pride themselves on their ancestry or inborn constitution. For that is the one thing they themselves have been least—in fact, not at all—responsible for. Moreover, paradoxically, this kind of pride is today likely to be more intense in persons who are less, rather than more, fortunately endowed.

To more than balance the necessary weakenings of this time-worn vanity in regard to one's stirps, other feelings will tend to develop that are of equal or greater potency. Among them will be justifiable pride in accomplishment of a far more exacting and laudable kind than that of procreation: namely, having made children of especially high endowment possible and having brought them up. Deep attachments to these children will develop and a justified sense of identification. These new reproductive mores will come into being only very gradually. At first, only those with freer and more daring spirits will venture on these alien-seeming paths (to be indicated in the following two sections). There will be no clear break, and in the same family children of choice and children of tradition will grow up side by side in mutually helpful familial association. But "nothing succeeds like success," and the successes in these instances will often be outstanding.

PRESENTLY AVAILABLE GENETIC TECHNIQUES

Long before this point is reached, many warning voices—even among geneticists, or perhaps among them more especially—will be raised, protesting that we cannot predict the results of any matings in such heterogeneous material as an existing human population. We have, for such purposes, the merest smattering of knowledge regarding the genes concerned; and what the more important ones—those concerned with the traits we are here the most interested in—will do in new combinations is anyone's guess. We could not proceed according to the principles governing simple Mendelian differences, and we should be practicing not genetics but a dangerous hoax.

This argument sets up straw men and then knocks them down with straw swords. The multifactorial basis of most phenotypic differences in human and other natural cross-breeding populations is undisputed—especially in regard to differences in traits of importance and therefore long subject to natural selection—although, of course, some gene differences produce major effects, along with many more that produce minor ones. We can seldom hope, in practice, to know just what genes are concerned, nor, even if we knew them, could we say just what their effects in postulated combinations would be. Nor can we control or predict what combination a given zygote will have. We will readily admit, moreover, that the effects are seldom exactly additive. We are well aware that sometimes, in genetic effects, $2 + 2$ makes -3 or even -6.

Now if that were the whole story, natural selection would not have been more effective in sexually reproducing organisms than in asexual ones, and the method of sexual reproduction would not have been retained in animals or plants. It is unlikely that life could have advanced even as far as the stage of triploblastic animals. (The points involved are discussed in my various 1958 papers.) But if the world had somehow been supplied with wild animals, plants, and primitive men anyway, then these men, without knowledge of genetics, would never have succeeded in producing the races of domestic animals and cultivated plants highly adapted to their purposes that they transmitted to us. Even modern breeders, if supplied with these improved races, would never have been able to develop the still more improved strains that we have today, despite their knowledge of Mendelian principles.

What made all these advances possible was, for one thing, the fact that in the great majority of cases a given gene difference exerts a similar effect (e.g., the increase or the decrease of a given trait) in one genetic combination as in another one. In other words, although the effects are not accurately additive, they do work out, on the whole, in the expected directions. Second, in the comparatively rare instances in which they fail to do so, longer-term selection usually eliminates the "four-flushers" (the seemingly helpful variants that turn out to be detrimental when in otherwise desirable combination) long before these frauds have become irrevocably established. For these reasons, selection carried out on a purely empirical basis does work.

It works in spite of the frequent impossibility of discriminating between genetically and environmentally based effects. It is true that where selection has "mistakenly" favored a merely phenotypic deviant—one that was occasioned only by environmental circumstances—no genetic progress is made thereby, but no consistent harm is done either; for these "mistakes" occur in diverse directions so as ultimately to cancel one another. This situation leaves the determination of the over-all result to the remaining cases—those in which some genetic basis did exist for their having been selected. By the accumulation of many such steps, the genetic composition is caused to move significantly in the direction of selection.

Even primitive man was intelligent enough to do much better than nature usually did, inasmuch as he effected changes in his domestic races, in the directions sought, at a pace much faster than that at which species ordinarily change when under natural conditions of breeding. This was because his manner of selecting was less haphazard and more single-tracked than nature's. The selection practiced by modern man, especially in the present century, has been much more rapid and effective still, even though it likewise has in the main had to proceed without analysis of the individual genes concerned. Where the inherited differences are multifactorial, as they usually are in the case of traits of importance in any organism, such as milk yield in cattle, gene identification is seldom feasible. Neither has it been necessary in order to achieve decided results from selection. Nevertheless, knowledge of the genetic principles at work has helped greatly in the guidance of selection processes, especially in their later stages.

General genetic knowledge has discredited futile practices based on such mistaken beliefs as the inheritance of acquired characters, telegony, etc. It has proved invaluable by supporting such useful practices as progeny testing; taking the environment into account and, where possible, controlling it more rigorously; being guided by measurements made among different classes of relatives and measurements of the correlation between different traits; making judicious use of both outbreeding and inbreeding; and so on. However, even these methods seldom play much part in the earlier generations of selection, which is when the most rapid progress is usually made, despite the selection being based mainly on superficial phenotypic evidence. Since the hereditary mechanism is known to be the same in man as in sexually reproducing organisms in general, there is no reason to doubt, on purely genetic grounds, the potential efficacy of an empirical type of selection for man also—consistent with general genetic considerations but not, at least in the early stages, based on knowledge of the particular genes concerned.

It should be mentioned again that in all selectional work in which the potentialities of the individual genes in further combinations are not known, some chosen for multiplication will later turn out, when in homozygous condition or in given groupings, to have undesirable or even lethal effects. This happens also in natural matings. To be sure, careful progeny testing could reduce such events to an even lower than natural frequency. But, in any case, over-all progress will take place in the direction of selection and can, especially in the earlier stages, be very rapid. Then, in later stages, the delicate task of screening for the most dependable and precisely suited genes can be better carried out, after the general level has been raised and a plentiful supply of promising genetic material has become available. In the meantime, the favorable phenotypic effects of this rise in the level can be enormous.

What now are the means that would make such positive selection possible in man? The most effective method presently feasible is, of course, artificial insemination. Many thousands of people have already been begotten in the United States by this procedure—a considerable proportion of them, although not most, by sperm of donors other than the husband when the husband was sterile. Here is an excellent opportunity for the entering wedge of positive selection, since the couples concerned are nearly always, under such circumstances, open to the suggestion that they turn their exigency to their credit by having as well-endowed children as possible.

Unfortunately, most of the physicians in such cases, deterred by the fear of public and legal censure and having little appreciation of genetic matters, seem to be chiefly concerned with hiding their operations and avoiding a conspicuous result or failure that they might be blamed for, and they furtively attempt to produce a child as nearly as possible like that which might have been born if the father had been fertile. With this aim, they choose a donor resembling the husband in physique and even in religion, free from readily detectable defects, of course, and they are careful to keep the identity of this donor as secret as possible. Often a medical student or intern, if he is discreet and close at hand, serves, for a consideration, as a multiple donor, without regard for the fact that U.S. Army I.Q. tests have indicated this group to have the lowest mental ratings of all professions tested. But cases have even been reported of out-of-work men, originally picked up in bars, who make an easy living by regularly selling their semen on what amounts to a mass scale. Thus opportunities for introducing a substantial genetic leaven into the population at large are flouted.

Insemination by an outside donor has now gone on for so long and become so prevalent that it is high time for it to come out into the open, even in individual instances. A judge in Chicago branded the procedure "adultery," but a number of precedents in which the children were begotten by consent of both husband and wife have been held to be legal. It is highly important for the genetic paternities of the children thus produced to be properly recorded. Not only would invaluable data be provided in human genetics and selection, but, more specifically, better judgments could thereafter be made concerning the genetic potentialities of the given donors and their descendants. It should be recognized that the couple concerned in such a case, as well as the physician, has performed a service to mankind meriting not disgrace but honor. With such an outlook, even before it was generally held, both physician and couple would be armed with better incentives to take genetic considerations into account. They would be encouraged to make the best use possible of such a chance to engender the most precious thing we know of: a worthy human being.

Perhaps university teachers in scientific subjects are, through their personal experiences, better aware than any other large group of persons of the enormous differences in over-all intelligence between the average and the best endowed and of the fact that training, though essential, cannot be an adequate substitute for high native endowment. For real competence in understanding and dealing with the world as known by science, only a mind that is truly exceptional in terms of the now existing distribution will suffice. However, general intelligence is complex and multifactorial, despite the existence of rare genes that individually have a decidedly enhancing influence on intelligence (shown by cases of long-persisting, sharply segregating effects in given pedigrees). Because of this complexity, the progeny of individuals of exceptionally high intellectual endowment tend to exhibit considerable regression and variability, even among the better-endowed segregants. This by no means signifies that selection in this area is futile—it can, in fact, have a high over-all degree of success. Rather, it underlines the importance of choosing as donors individuals of the most outstanding native mental ability—that is, those at the extreme end of the positive tail of the distribution—so far as possible, and when they do not have serious defects in other directions. Moreover, those individuals should be preferred as donors

whose relatives give considerable evidence that the superior qualities are highly inheritable.

Fortunately, such a high degree of selection as here indicated is made possible by the method of artificial insemination, by reason of the large number of spermatozoa that each individual usually produces. Recently the technique of freezing spermatozoa to very low temperatures was introduced into practice, and, thanks to the accumulation of sperm thus made possible, the frequency of successful conceptions has been raised considerably above that following either natural insemination or artificial insemination of the more usual type. The deep-frozen spermatozoa can be stored virtually indefinitely without deterioration. Thus a considerable supply can in time be gathered from a chosen donor and preserved for any desired length of time. For purposes of selection, there would in such cases be enormous advantages in postponing the use of most of this supply until, say, twenty years after the donor's decease. In retrospect, after the personal attachments and animosities aroused during the donor's life had faded, much less biased judgments could be made concerning his actual merits as well as shortcomings. During this "probationary period," a limited but significant amount of progeny testing could be carried out to support a sounder estimate of the donor's genetic potentialities.

Such a procedure would also afford considerable psychological advantages, for it would eliminate that bane of present-day gynecologists who practice artificial insemination—the fear of intrigue arising between the donor and the woman concerned if either one learns the identity of the other. The motivation for possible jealous reactions of the husband would at the same time be greatly diminished. Moreover, both members of the couple, as well as all other persons, would be much more likely to recognize the donor's exceptional worth, a worth that would usually put him out of a class with living competitors. Finally, the chief present objections to having the identity of the donor known would be removed. Instead, all interested persons would wish to have the relationships concerned entirely above-board.

As was recently pointed out by Dr. Richard Meier, of the Mental Health Research Institute of the University of Michigan, another method of genetic upgrading is the outright adoption of children by those who otherwise cannot or do not wish to bear children or wish to have less than the average quota of their own genetic progeny. Since such practice does not involve as radical a departure from present-day customs and attitudes as does artificial insemination, it might recommend itself more readily in wide circles. This procedure presupposes, of course, that couples of high native endowment would be willing to bear more children than they could bring up and to give them out for adoption. Those consenting to do so would truly be socially minded.

Perhaps in the long run, though, this method would interfere more with people's personal lives and occasion more risk of undesirable personal entanglements than the half-adoption represented by artificial insemination. Certainly the outright adoption method here suggested would not allow selection to be as rigorous, even though the eggs as well as the sperm are to some extent specially selected. Then, too, this method would lack the psychological advantage, operative in the earlier transitional period of feelings on the subject, of at least half the genetic material having been derived from those who are to bring up the child. But there is no doubt that the method would be better adapted than artificial insemination for some situations and could thus serve a useful function.

TECHNICAL ADVANCES IN THE OFFING

We are surely just around the corner from other advances in artificial techniques concerned with reproduction that might extend the possibilities of positive selection much further. For example, there have as yet been only a few abortive attempts to cultivate either male or female germ cells outside the body. An energetic program of research on the subject would probably be successful within a few years in enabling spermatogonia, at least, to be multiplied indefinitely in vitro and to be induced, when desired, to undergo the processes of maturation into spermatozoa. If this could be done, then spermatogonia instead of spermatozoa might be preserved in the deep-frozen state, a technique that has already proved successful with some types of somatic cells. Later, at any desired date, the spermatogonia could be multiplied and caused to mature so as to furnish an unlimited supply of mature spermatozoa from an originally small amount of material derived from any given donor. Only our present superstitious attitudes prevent such research from being actively pursued today.

As for the female germ cells, means are already known whereby the multiple release of mature eggs can readily be effected within the female with the aid of pituitary hormones. Only a little research would be required to develop methods of flushing out these eggs from the female reproductive tract, to be fertilized in vitro with chosen sperm and then implanted in selected female hosts at the appropriate stage of their reproductive cycle. This procedure is parallel to artificial insemination. It permits the multiple distribution of eggs of a highly selected female into diverse recipient females, yet allows the child to be derived, on its paternal side, from the recipient's husband.

It is not unlikely that techniques involving mature eggs could be combined with deep freezing to allow indefinitely prolonged storage. Thus similar advantages, selectional as well as psychological, might be gained for the female germ cells as are already available, even though not yet in use, for spermatozoa.

Such techniques applied to the eggs could, of course, be combined with artificial insemination by sperm of a donor other than the recipient's husband when the couple desired it. This would be another method equivalent to outright adoption. However, it would afford the opportunity for far more powerful selection than adoption of the relatively primitive sort previously discussed and would avoid the possible psychological and social difficulties that might attend such adoption.

Still another possible development, perhaps somewhat further off technically, is parthenogenesis. It is not commonly realized that Gregory Pincus some twenty years ago succeeded in producing several vigorous, fertile female rabbits by artificial parthenogenesis. Genetic "markers" were present that showed these rabbits to be of purely maternal origin, although (as proved by breeding tests of them) heterozygous for at least some of the genes for which the mother also had been heterozygous. The inference could be drawn from this situation that in these cases diploidization had occurred through the union of the egg nucleus with one that would normally have passed off in a polar body. The great majority of the eggs that had been stimulated to begin parthenogenetic development, however, had remained haploid and, obviously in consequence of this, failed to give viable embryos. Unfortunately, the induction of diploidization had not been brought under control when research along this line was discontinued.

A more promising type of parthenogenesis might be achieved by an extension of the technique used by Briggs and King with frogs' eggs. They succeeded in obtaining normal development after implanting nuclei from cells of frog blastulae and gastrulae into recently fertilized eggs whose own nuclei had been extirpated by micromanipulation. Before this method, which affords many interesting possibilities for embryological research, could become of eugenic importance, it would, of course, have to be extended to mammalian and eventually human fertilized eggs. Methods would have to be developed of successfully implanting into them, with subsequent development, diploid nuclei derived not from embryos but from the immature germ cells—spermatogonia or oögonia—of adults, or possibly even from certain generalized types of somatic cells of adults. On theoretical grounds, this extension does not seem at all far-fetched.

This type of parthenogenesis would make possible the production of multiple progeny that resemble their genetic parent and one another about as closely, phenotypically, as identical twins reared apart resemble one another and that are about as alike genetically as identical twins. Here, then, there would be an extremely high order of predictability regarding the nature of the children and virtually no regression except that occasioned by environmental factors, such as the manner of bringing up the children. Of course, the high general intelligence of the progenitor would in most cases be capable of being applied in very diverse directions in his separate manifestations, as we might term them. Yet in the rearing of such children and in the later decisions of their lives, despite the diversity of the situations, invaluable guides would be available in the already existing knowledge concerning the progenitor's proclivities, character traits, and modes of reaction to different circumstances. Often he would himself have been able to give pertinent advice along such lines. All this would usually make it possible to avoid, in these individuals' upbringing and later career, many of the mistakes inadvertently made the first time. Thus, far better opportunity could be provided to these outstanding persons for making the most of their unusual potentialities.

When one considers how much the world owes to single individuals of the order of capability of an Einstein, Pasteur, Descartes, Leonardo, or Lincoln, it becomes evident how vastly society would be enriched if they were to be manifolded. Moreover, those who repeatedly proved their worth would surely be called upon to reappear age after age until the population in general had caught up with them. In this way, then, mankind would be able to reap the benefit of that alternation of asexual reproduction (for reliably multiplying types of tested worth) with techniques of sexual reproduction (for trying ever new combinations), an alternation that has been so advantageous in some other classes of organisms. Later generations will look with amazement at the pitifully small amount of research now being carried on to open up such possibilities, even though for years specialists have realized that they lie just around the corner.

Just as our economic and political system is inevitably, although too slowly, being modified to fit our present technological capabilities of large-scale automatic production, despite the fervor with which men try to cling to their ancient preconceptions of how business and government should operate, so too on the biological side of human affairs the time-honored notions of how reproduction should be managed will gradually give way before the technological progress that is opening and will further open up new and more promising possibilities. Practices that today are confined to couples afflicted with sterility will be increasingly taken up by people who desire to improve their reproductive lot by bestowing on themselves children with a maximal chance of being highly endowed, and thereby to make an exemplary contribution to humanity. Making some sacrifice in the matters of traditional feelings of vainglory about the idiosyncrasies of their personal stirps and braving the censure of the old-timers about them, they will form a growing vanguard that increasingly feels more than repaid by the day-by-day manifestations of their solid achievements as well as by the profound realization of the value of the service they are rendering.

But recently there has been a tendency in some circles to by-pass the arguments for positive selection by countering that, instead, means will be found of making direct alterations or substitutions of a desired kind in the genetic material itself while leaving it in the main unchanged. Such proposals range from the idea of substituting individual chromosomes or parts of chromosomes, derived from selected donors, in the chromosome set of a given person's germ cell to the idea of inducing by a mutagenic agent or ultra-fine manipulative process a given chemical change in a given gene. It would be very rash to deny that some day such extraordinary feats may be possible, but they are definitely not around the corner in the sense that the developments discussed above are.

Dismissing for the moment the unparalleled advances in technique that would here be necessary, we must take into account that such procedures would also require the most minute knowledge of the role played by individual genes in the inordinately complex economy of the human organism, including its highest, most multifactorial functions, such as general intelligence. It would also be necessary to know the locations of these genes in the genetic map. And if mutations were actually to be induced or nucleotide substitutions made, we should have to know the internal constitution of these genes and the functions in them of each of their tens or hundreds of thousands of nucleotides. Though the nucleotides are of only four kinds, it is their precise arrangement in line that counts. It is not likely that all this will be worked out before men are on a much higher genetic, as well as cultural, level than they are today.

Present evidence indicates that there are something like four billion nucleotides exactly ordered like the letters in enormous words in each haploid chromosome set. Any of these, by having a different nucleotide, of the remaining three possible types, substituted for it, might cause a change, sometimes significant and sometimes not, in the individual's phenotype. It is preposterous to suppose that, in the foreseeable future, knowledge would be precise enough to enable us to say what substitution to make in order to effect a given, desired phenotypic alteration—not that this would *never* be possible. But to suppose that, after it had become possible, men would still be bound by the reproductive traditions of today, preferring this ultra-sophisticated method of improvement to the readily available one of selecting donor material free from the given defect or already possessing the desired innovation—that would be a calumny on the rationality of the human race. It would be like supposing that in some technically advanced society elaborate superhighways were constructed to carry vehicles on enormous detours to avoid defiling hallowed domains reserved in perpetuity for their millions of sacred cows.

If human superstitions are really so unchangeable and subject to such inviolable taboo, then it is very unlikely that humanity will succeed in progressing to the stage where it understands that otherwise most marvelous organization under the sun—its own constitution. But many customs and attitudes *have* changed, and

today we see them changing rapidly. It would be very strange if in this age of exploding knowledge and technique our reproductive practices remained immune to reformation.

MORE DISTANT PROSPECTS

Evolution in the past has been for the most part a matter of millions of years. In this larger view, what we have been discussing is but a matter of today—the step we are just about to take. So great are the present psychological impediments to this step, arising out of our traditions, that we have not had time to consider the enormous vistas beyond.

The rapid upgrading of our general intelligence must be accompanied and co-ordinated as closely as possible with a corresponding effort to infuse into the genetic basis of our moral natures the springs of stronger, more genuine fellow feeling. At the same time, especially interested groups will see to it that diverse abilities and proclivities of specific types will here and there be multiplied, both those of a more purely intellectual nature and those making possible more far-reaching and poignant appreciation of the varied kinds of experiences that life may offer. As all these genetic resources of mankind grow richer, they will increasingly be combined to give more of the population many of their benefits at once. Observation shows that these faculties are not antagonistic but rather mutually enhancing. Finally, increasing attention can be paid to what is called the physical side: bettering the genetic foundations of health, vigor, and longevity; reducing the need for sleep; bringing the induction of sedation and stimulation under better voluntary control; and increasing physical tolerances and aptitudes in general.

In many physical respects there are optimal degrees of development for given types of organisms, beyond which other functions tend to be too much interfered with. Yet these optima are seldom absolute, for there are often ways of breaking through the seeming limits by means of novel developments that open new directions for solving the old problems. These directions of inquiry are so advanced that we may leave them to the more competent minds of the future to tackle.

But, at least so far as intelligence is concerned, there are no indications that we are now approaching any physiologically set limit or optimum. It is quite evident that we could benefit indefinitely by a continued increase in our mental powers: to enable us to analyse more profoundly; to recognize more readily common features when they lie deeply buried; to grasp more and more elements of a situation at once and co-ordinately; to see more steps ahead; to think more multidimensionally; and to imagine more creatively. Here, too, it is to be hoped that new breakthroughs will eventually be found; otherwise, limits will in time appear. If only we take the first, most obvious steps that we have here been considering, we shall be preparing the way for making our successors capable of planning ahead much further and more soundly than we ourselves of this fumbling generation can.

It is so easy to sit smugly back in the conceit that we have now reached nearly the acme of biological evolution and that, except for eventually bestowing on everyone the genetic advantages already enjoyed by the most favored, we can hereafter confine our advances to cultural evolution, including the manipulation of things outside our own genetic constitutions. It is true that cultural evolution, in this broad sense, is far more diversified, rapid, and explosive, both figuratively and literally, than biological evolution can be. There is every reason to extrapolate, along with "science-fiction" enthusiasts (despite their frequent unbalance!), that if men do not destroy one another,

they will cultivate the deserts, jungles, poles, and oceans, extend their domain successively to ever more distant worlds, and perhaps even, as first suggested by Bernal, build colonies in empty space. Along with the increasing understanding and mastery over physicochemical forces that such expansion implies, there will be corresponding advances in the biological and social realm. That is, there will be spectacular progress in means of reshaping and controlling bodily structures and functions by operations repeated in each generation anew and also in means of interrelating people psychologically to achieve higher, more harmonious, and more constructive interactions of their feelings, thoughts, and doings. Yet all this does not mean that genetic advances beyond the stage represented by the happiest possible combinations of the best endowed of present-day humanity would be either supererogatory, unimportant, or relatively limited.

If their genetic constitution is so unimportant for beings with such advanced means of extragenic control as envisaged for our successors of, say, five hundred years from now, why could they not just about as well use apes or even lowlier creatures instead of men and duly reconstruct and train them? Or, if the genetic difference between apes and men is really so important in determining their amenability to profit by culture and to contribute to it, why would not beings as far beyond present-day men genetically as we are beyond the apes be inordinately better suited still for exploiting the benefits of culture? The biological distance from apes to men is a relatively slight one, yet how potent! And do we hastily-made-over apes really believe that, having attained this makeshift form, further steps of this kind are to be despised? Our imaginations are woefully limited if we cannot see that, genetically just as well as culturally, we have by our recent turning of an evolutionary corner set our feet on a road that stretches far out before us into the hazy distance.

Of course, the genetic changes that would be desirable for us in the future are not, in the main, developments like fur, wings, photosynthetic ability, or anything else that would be less effective or less adaptable than our own artifices. They would not be replacements for cultural devices but the very opposite: means of better gearing together the biological and the cultural, of making still more out of our culturally enhanced propensities, and of more effectively advancing our culture. As we have seen, this evolutionary trend actually began with the advent of man, although he was unaware of it as a long-term phenomenon. But now we may carry it forward consciously and with ever longer foresight.

Although the most important genetic advances for any creature who creates a culture are obviously those that suitably extend and enhance his psychological faculties, it is a mistake to conclude that corporeal changes of diverse kinds would be of little account—such as, for example, further developments of the senses, on the one hand, or of effector organs, on the other hand. Unfortunately, spelling out radical possibilities along these lines is likely to provoke more ridicule than understanding at the present stage of purblindness in this field. For evolutionary biological developments would, in general, appear utterly fantastic to a group in whom they had not yet occurred, whereas, of course, after the event they are taken for granted as being the only reasonable arrangement.[2]

It would be presumptuous to try to specify here just what form the long-

[2] For this reason I will give only one illustration of how a biological, genetically based series of developments could be important to a species with an already highly advanced culture. This example has to do with the means of personal communication. At present these are largely confined, in man, to gestures and to some form of speech (including its derivative, writing). Speech, marvelously effective though it has been in the long run, is pitifully slow and plodding compared with the inner flow of ideas. It has special tendencies to be misleading, and it requires forcing everything into an inappropriate one-dimensional order. Wishful thinkers, mystics, and pseudo-scientists have long dreamed of telepathy to escape from the bondage of spoken forms. However, telepathy is a species of magic for which, so far as can be seen, no biological possibility exists. It might therefore appear unlikely that any biological kind of communication better than speech could arise in evolution.

Yet such a development, involving a combination of already known biological phenomena, is in fact conceivable. Many different types of organisms have developed light-emitting tissues. In some, such as the squid, the spatial and temporal pattern of the luminescence may be very complex and subject to considerable voluntary control. In some fish the light is projected through a special lens with reflector. However, a more eyelike structure, if its retinal surface were provided with luminous cells, might serve even better. The main development, then, would be the suitable connection of the visually imaginative portion of the brain, point by point, with the luminescent layer in such wise that the visual patterns imagined in the cerebrum become transferred into luminescent patterns that can be seen by other individuals. In effect, this would be the reverse of the transference that occurs in seeing, when the image produced by light focused on the retina is transmitted, via impulses in the fibers of the optic nerve, so as to give rise to a corresponding pattern of stimulated cells in the occipital cortex. Now the actively radiating pattern in the luminescent layer could either be projected onto a screen in a darkened inclosure outside, where it might in turn be subject to amplification or recording, or, alternatively, it could be seen directly by a close-up inspection of the transmitting "eye" by the receiving eye.

In addition to direct visual representations of things, subject to motion as in a cinema, there would doubtless be diverse symbolizations of conceptual thoughts. All in all, such communication could be raised to a level of facility, directness, speed, multidimensionality, comprehensiveness, and precision so much higher than is afforded by speech as to inaugurate far more advanced processes of communing, of learning, of thinking itself, of appreciation, and of resulting action. But for bringing these potentialities to fruition, further improvements of a neurological and psychological nature would be in order, even as was the case with speech.

range developments are likely to take and in what sequence they will occur. Intellectual and moral developments of the types mentioned as most important now will probably continue to occupy the center of the stage for a long time to come, if not indefinitely. The faculties here concerned could probably be extended and enhanced in many ways which our present ignorance of their structure does not permit us even to guess at.

Only after we humans have advanced considerably toward the higher level to which the rough-and-ready empirical methods now available can raise us, will we be in a position to make firmer, more definite plans envisaging longer-range possibilities. Only then, when we have developed superior intelligence and greater co-operativeness, can we expect to reach a workable degree of agreement on these plans. Only then can we begin to use more exact methods and to coordinate them better. It is too early for blueprints.

If we are to preserve that self-determination which is an essential feature of human intelligence, success, and happiness, our individual actions in the realm of genetics must be steps based on our own personal judgments and inclinations. They should be as voluntary as our other major decisions of life. Although these decisions are all conditioned by the mores about us, these mores can be specifically shaped and channelized by our own distinctive personalities. The immediate job, then, is to make a start at getting this genetic "Operation Bootstrap" incorporated into our mores, by precept and, where feasible, by example. But we must remember that the highest values to be sought in it are, in essence, those so long proclaimed but seldom actualized: wisdom and brotherhood, that is, the pursuit of "the true and the good." When it is realized that the genetic method offers simply an additional but indispensable approach toward this ancient ideal, then our voluntary genetic efforts, scattered and disjointed though they must now be, will tend in a common direction.

There are sure to be powerful attempts to pull in diverse directions, in genetic just as in other matters, but we need not be afraid of this. The diversities will tend to enrich the genetic background, increasing the resources available for recombination. These partial attempts can then be judged by their fruits, and these fruits, where sound, will be added to our bounty.

It seems highly unlikely that, in a world-wide society at an advanced level of culture and technology, founded on the recognition of universal brotherhood, such diversities would proceed so far and for so long as again to split humanity on this shrunken planet into semi-isolated groups and that these groups would thenceforth undergo increasing divergence from one another. It is because man is potentially master of all trades that he has succeeded. And if his culture is to continue to evolve indefinitely, he must retain this essential plasticity and with it the feeling that all men are, at bottom, of his own kind.

Through billions of years of blind mutations, pressing against the shifting walls of their environment, microbes finally emerged as men. We are no longer blind; at least, we are *beginning* to be conscious of what has happened and of what may happen. From now on, evolution is what we make it, provided that we choose the true and the good. Otherwise, we shall sink back into oblivion. If we hold fast to our ideal, then evolution will become, for the first time, a conscious process. Increasingly conscious, it can proceed at a pace far outdistancing that achieved by trial and error—and in ever greater assurance, animation, and enthusiasm. That will be the highest form of freedom that man, or life, can have.

HUMAN VARIATION

The members of our species differ considerably in appearance from individual to individual and from group to group. Variations in factors such as facial features, skin color, hair quality, and physique largely result from variant genetic heritage. Unless an individual happens to be somebody's monozygotic twin, his genetic heritage will be specifically unique. He will not have quite the same genotype or phenotype as anyone else. But he will resemble rather closely his relations and, more generally, the members of his community—that is, all those with whom he shares a common gene pool.

Compared with persons whose genetic constitution is different, the members of his own group will look a lot alike. Essentially, that is all there is to human variation—relative differences in heredity, some of which are manifested in distinctions in appearance. Environmental conditions also affect human variation, but in a minor way.

When group differences in appearance are very marked, they are frequently referred to as "racial." And the groups are described as constituting separate "races." Objectively, that is about all there is to "race."

As scientists, scholars, and citizens, we must give thoughtful attention to the processes of human variation and their relation to ideas about race.

1. The Study of Race [1]

Discussion of the races of man seems to generate endless emotion and confusion. I am under no illusion that this paper can do much to dispel the confusion; it may add to the emotion. The latest information available supports the traditional findings of anthropologists and other social scientists—that there is no scientific basis of any kind for racial discrimination. I think that the way this conclusion has been reached needs to be restated. The continuation of antiquated biological notions in anthropology and the oversimplification of facts weakens the anthropological position. We must realize that great changes have taken place in the study of race over the last 20 years and it is up to us to bring our profession into the forefront of the newer understandings, so that our statements will be authoritative and useful.

This paper will be concerned with three topics—the modern concept of race, the interpretation of racial differences, and the social significances of race. And, again, I have no illusion that these things can be treated briefly; I shall merely say a few things which are on my mind and which you may amplify by turning to the literature, and especially to Dobzhansky's book, *Mankind Evolving*. This book states the relations between culture and genetics in a way which is useful to social scientists. In my opinion it is a great book which puts the interrelations of biology and culture in proper perspective and avoids the oversimplifications which come from overemphasis on either one alone.

The races of man are the result of human evolution, of the evolution of our species. The races are open parts of the species, and the species is a closed system. If we look, then, upon long-term human evolution, our first problem must be the species and the things which have caused the evolution of all mankind, not the races, which are the results of local forces and which are minor in terms of the evolution of the whole species. (A contrary view has recently been expressed by Coon in *The Origin of Races*. I think that great antiquity of human races is supported neither by the record nor by evolutionary theory.)

The evolution of races is due, according to modern genetics, to mutation, selection, migration, and genetic drift. It is easy to shift from this statement of genetic theory to complications of hemoglobin, blood groups or other technical information. But the point I want to stress is that the primary implication of genetics for anthropology is that it affirms the relation of culture and biology in a far firmer and more important way than ever in our history before. Selection is for reproductive success, and in man reproductive success is primarily determined by the social system and by culture. Effective behavior is the question, not something else.

Drift depends on the size of population, and population size, again, is dependent upon culture, not upon genetic factors as such. Obviously, migration depends on clothes, transportation, economy, and warfare and is reflected in the archeological record. Even mutation rates are now affected by technology.

Genetic theory forces the consideration of culture as the major factor in the evolution of man. It thus reaffirms the fundamental belief of anthropologists that we

[1] S. L. WASHBURN, from the "Study of Race," a paper first delivered as the Presidential Address at the Annual Meeting of the American Anthropological Association, November 16, 1962, Chicago, Ill.; later published in the *American Anthropologist*, 65 (1963), pp. 521–531, © American Anthropological Association. Reprinted by permission of the author and the publisher.

must study man both as a biological and as a social organism. This is no longer a question of something that might be desirable; it must be done if genetic theory is correct.

We have, then, on the one hand the history of genetic systems, and on the other hand the history of cultural systems, and, finally, the interrelation between these two. There is no evolution in the traditional anthropological sense. What Boas referred to as evolution was orthogenesis—which receives no support from modern genetic theory. What the geneticist sees as evolution is far closer to what Boas called history than to what he called evolution, and some anthropologists are still fighting a nineteenth-century battle in their presentation of evolution. We have, then, the history of cultural systems, which you may call history; and the history of genetic systems, which you may call evolution if you want to, but if you use this word remember that it means selection, migration, drift —it is real history that you are talking about and not some mystic force which constrains mankind to evolve according to some orthogenetic principle.

There is, then, no possibility of studying human raciation, the process of race formation, without studying human culture. Archeology is as important in the study of the origin of races as is genetics; all we can do is reconstruct as best we can the long-term past, and this is going to be very difficult.

Now let me contrast this point of view with the one which has been common in much of anthropology. In the first place, anthropology's main subject, the subject of race, disregarded to an amazing degree the evolution of the human species. Anthropologists were so concerned with the subdivisions within our species and with minor detailed differences between small parts of the species that the physical anthropologists largely forgot that mankind is a species and that the important

thing is the evolution of this whole group, not the minor differences between its parts.

If we look back to the time when I was educated, races were regarded as types. We were taught to go to a population and divide it into a series of types and to re-create history out of this artificial arrangement. Those of you who have read *Current Anthropology* will realize that this kind of anthropology is still alive, amazingly, and in full force in some countries; relics of it are still alive in our teaching today.

Genetics shows us that typology must be completely removed from our thinking if we are to progress. For example, let us take the case of the Bushmen. The Bushmen have been described as the result of a mixture between Negro and Mongoloid. Such a statement could only be put in the literature without any possible consideration of migration routes, of numbers of people, of cultures, of any way that such a mixing could actually take place. The fact is that the Bushmen had a substantial record in South Africa and in East Africa and there is no evidence that they ever were anywhere else except in these areas. In other words, they are a race which belongs exactly where they are.

If we are concerned with history let us consider, on the one hand, the ancestors of these Bushmen 15,000 years ago and the area available to them, to their way of life, and, on the other hand, the ancestors of Europeans at the same time in the area available to them, with their way of life. We will find that the area available to the Bushmen was at least twice that available to the Europeans. The Bushmen were living in a land of optimum game; the Europeans were living close to an ice sheet. There were perhaps from three to five times as many Bushmen ancestors as there were European ancestors only 15,000 years ago.

If one were to name a major race, or a primary race, the Bushmen have a far better claim in terms of the archeological record than the Europeans. During the time of glacial advance more than half of the Old World available to man for life was in Africa. The numbers and distributions that we think of as normal and the races whose last results we see today are relics of an earlier and far different time in human history.

There are no three primary races, no three major groups. The idea of three primary races stems from nineteenth-century typology; it is totally misleading to put the black-skinned people of the world together—to put the Australian in the same grouping with the inhabitants of Africa. And there are certainly at least three independent origins of the small, dark people, the Pygmies, and probably more than that. There is no single Pygmy race.

If we look to real history we will always find more than three races, because there are more than three major areas in which the raciation of our species was taking place.

If we attempt to preserve the notion of three races, we make pseudo-typological problems. Take for example, again, the problem of the aboriginal Australian. If we have only three races, either they must be put with the people of Africa, with which they have nothing in common, or they must be accounted for by mixture, and in books appearing even as late as 1950, a part of the aboriginal Australian population is described as European, and listed with the Europeans, and the residue is listed with the Africans and left there.

The concept of race is fundamentally changed if we actually look for selection, migration, and study people as they are (who they are, where they are, how many they are); and the majority of anthropological textbooks need substantial revision along these lines.

Since races are open systems which are intergrading, the number of races will depend on the purpose of the classification. This is, I think, a tremendously important point. It is significant that as I was reviewing classifications in preparing this lecture, I found that almost none of them mentioned any purpose for which people were being classified. Race isn't very important biologically. If we are classifying races in order to understand human history, there aren't many human races, and there is very substantial agreement as to what they are. There are from six to nine races, and this difference in number is very largely a matter of definition. These races occupied the major separate geographical areas in the Old World.

If one has no purpose for classification, the number of races can be multiplied almost indefinitely, and it seems to me that the erratically varying number of races is a source of confusion to student, to layman, and to specialist. I think we should require people who propose a classification of races to state in the first place why they wish to divide the human species and to give in detail the important reasons for subdividing our whole species. If important reasons for such classification are given, I think you will find that the number of races is always exceedingly small.

If we consider these six or nine geographical races and the factors which produced them, I think the first thing we want to stress is migration.

All through human history, where we have any evidence of that history, people have migrated. In a recent article appearing in the *American Anthropologist* there is a suggestion that it took 400,000 years for a gene that mutated in China to reach Europe. We know, historically, that Alexander the Great went from Greece into Northern India. We know that Mongol tribes migrated from Asia into Europe. Only a person seeking to believe that the races are very separate could possibly believe such a figure as that cited.

Migration has always been important in human history and there is no such thing as human populations which are completely separated from other human populations. And migration necessarily brings in new genes, necessarily reduces the differences between the races. For raciation to take place, then, there must be other factors operating which create difference. Under certain circumstances, in very small populations, differences may be created by genetic drift, or because the founders are for chance reasons very different from other members of the species.

However, the primary factor in the creation of racial differences in the long term is selection. This means that the origin of races must depend on adaptation and that the differences between the races which we see must in times past have been adaptive. I stress the question of time here, because it is perfectly logical to maintain that in time past a shovel-shaped incisor, for example, was more efficient than an incisor of other forms and that selection would have been for this, and at the same time to assert that today this dental difference is of absolutely no social importance. It is important to make this point because people generally take the view that something is always adaptive or never adaptive, and this is a fundamental oversimplification of the facts.

Adaptation is always within a given situation. There is no such thing as a gene which has a particular adaptive value; it has this value only under set circumstances. For example, the sickle-cell gene, if Allison and others are right, protects against malaria. This is adaptive if there is malaria, but if there is not malaria it is not adaptive. The adaptive value of the gene, then, is dependent on the state of medicine and has no absolute

value. The same is true of the other characteristics associated with race.

I would like to go over some of the suggestions which have been made about the adaptive values of various structures in human beings, because I think these need to be looked at again.

I have stressed that the concept of race which comes from population genetics is compatible with what anthropologists have thought. I think that this concept represents great progress. But when I read the descriptions of the importance of adaptive characteristics, I am not sure that there has been any progress since the nineteenth century.

In this connection I should like to speak for a moment on the notion that the Mongoloids are a race which are adapted to live in the cold, that these are arctic-adapted people.

In the first place, in marked contrast to animals which are adapted to live in the arctic, large numbers of Mongoloids are living in the hot, moist tropics. Altogether unlike animal adaptation, then, the people who are supposed to be adapted to the cold aren't living under cold conditions, and I think we should stress this. For thousands of years the majority of this group have not been living under the conditions which are supposed to have produced them. They are presumed, as an arctic-adapted group following various laws, to have short extremities, flat noses, and to be stocky in build. They are, we might say, as stocky as the Scotch, as flat-nosed as the Norwegians, and as blonde as the Eskimos. Actually, there is no correlation, that is, none that has been well worked out, to support the notion that any of these racial groups is cold-adapted.

Let me say a few more words on this lack of correlation. If one follows the form of the nose, in Europe, as one moves north, narrow noses are correlated with cold climate; in Eastern Asia low noses are correlated with cold climate. In neither case is there the slightest evidence that the difference in the form of the nose has anything whatsoever to do with warming the air that comes into the face. Further, if we look at these differences expressed in this way, we see that they are posed in terms of nineteenth-century notions of what a face is all about.

Let us look at it differently. The nose is the center of a face. Most of a face is concerned with teeth, and bones, and muscles that have to do with chewing. The Mongoloid face is primarily the result of large masseter muscles and the bones from which these muscles arise (malar and gonial angles). This is a complex structural pattern related to the teeth, and a superficially very similar pattern may be seen in the Bushman, whose facial form can hardly be attributed to adaptation to cold.

The face of the Neanderthal man has recently been described also as cold-adapted, though it does not have the characteristics of the Mongoloid face. We are told that the blood supply to the Neanderthal face was greatly increased because the infraorbital foramen was large, bringing more blood to the front of the face. In actual fact, most of the blood to our face does not go through that artery. The artery that carries most of the blood to the face comes along the outside, and even our arteries are far too large to go through the mental or infra-orbital foramen of Neanderthal man. This kind of statment, as well as the statement that the maxillary sinus warmed the air and that the function of a large orbit was to keep the eyes from freezing, seems to me an extraordinary retrogression to the worst kind of evolutionary speculation—speculation that antedates genetics and reveals a lack of any kind of reasonable understanding of the structure of the human face.

The point I wish to stress is that those who have spoken of the cold-adaptation of the Mongoloid face and of the Nean-

derthal face do not know the structure of the human face. We have people writing about human faces who are anatomically illiterate. I am genetically illiterate; I do not know about the hemoglobins. I am not asserting that all of us should be required to be literate in all branches of physical anthropology. As Stanley Garn points out, the field has become complicated, but people who are writing about the structure of the human face should learn the elements of anatomy.

The adaptive value of skin color has been repeatedly claimed, but recently Blum has indicated that the situation is more complicated than it appeared. In the first place, he points out the melanin in the skin doesn't do what anthropologists have said it has done. The part of the skin which mainly stops ultraviolet light, the short-wave length light, is a thickened *stratum corneum,* rather than melanin.

Again, the chimpanzee and the gorilla live in precisely the same climatic conditions in Uganda, but the gorilla has one of the blackest, most deeply pigmented skins of the primates and the chimpanzee has a very light skin. It simply is not true that skin color closely parallels climate. The point here is that racial classification tells us very little. The classification poses problems; it does not solve them.

In scientific method, as I see it, one looks at relevant data and when these data are laid out, as in, say, the classification of races, one may then find a correlation which is helpful. But after that, one has to do an experiment; one has to do something that shows that the correlation has validity. And it's no use continuing to correlate nose-form or skin color with climate. The crude correlations were made many years ago, and to advance the study of race requires new methods and more sophisticated analyses.

When I was a student, there were naive racial interpretations based on the metrical data. When these became unacceptable politically the same people used naive constitutional correlations to reach the same conclusions of social importance. Today we have naive concepts of adaptation, taking the place of the earlier interpretations, and a recrudescence of the racial thinking.

All along the line there have been valid problems in race, valid problems in constitution, and valid problems in adaptation. What I am protesting against strongly is the notion that one can simply take a factor, such as a high cheekbone, think that it might be related to climate, and then jump to this conclusion without any kind of connecting link between the two elements—without any kind of experimental verification of the sort of material that is being dealt with. If we took really seriously this notion that a flat face with large maxillary sinuses, deep orbits, and big brow ridges is cold-adapted, it is clear that the most cold-adapted animal in the primates is the gorilla.

Race, then, is a useful concept only if one is concerned with the kind of anatomical, genetic, and structural differences which were in time past important in the origin of races. Race in human thinking is a very minor concept. It is entirely worth while to have a small number of specialists, such as myself, who are concerned with the origin of gonial angles, the form of the nose, the origin of dental patterns, changes in blood-group frequencies, and so on. But this is a very minor, specialized kind of knowledge.

If classification is to have a purpose, we may look backward to the explanation of the differences between people —structural, anatomical, physiological differences—and then the concept of race is useful, but it is useful under no other circumstances, as far as I can see.

When the meaning of skin color and structure is fully understood, it will help us to understand the origin of races, but this is not the same thing as understanding the origin of our species. It will help in the understanding of why color was important in time long past, but it will have no meaning to modern technical society.

I turn now to a brief statement on the influence of culture upon race. Beginning with agriculture and continuing at an ever-increasing rate, human customs have been interposed between the organism and the environment. The increase of our species from perhaps as few as five million before agriculture to three billion today is the result of new technology, not of biological evolution. The conditions under which the races evolved are mainly gone, and there are new causes of mutation, new kinds of selection, and vast migration. Today the numbers and distribution of the peoples of the world are due primarily to culture. Some people think the new conditions are so different that it is better no longer to use the word race or the word evolution, but I personally think this confuses more than it clarifies.

All this does not mean that evolution has stopped, because the new conditions will change gene frequencies, but the conditions which produced the old races are gone. In this crowded world of civilization and science, the claim has been made repeatedly that one or another of the races is superior to the others. Obviously, this argument cannot be based on the past; because something was useful in times past and was selected for under conditions which are now gone, does not mean that it will be useful in the present or in the future.

The essential point at issue is whether the abilities of large populations are so different that their capacity to participate in modern technical culture is affected. Remember in the first place that no race has evolved to fit the selective pressures of the modern world. Technical civilization is new and the races are old. Remember also that all the species of *Homo* have been adapting to the human way of life for many thousands of years. Tools even antedate our genus, and our human biological adaptation is the result of culture. Man and his capacity for culture have evolved together, as Dr. Dobzhansky has pointed out. All men are adapted to learn language—any language; to perform skillful tasks—a fabulous variety of tasks; to cooperate; to enjoy art; to practice religion, philosophy, and science.

Our species only survives in culture, and, in a profound sense, we are the product of the new selection pressures that came with culture.

Infinitely more is known about the language and culture of all the groups of mankind than is known about the biology of racial differences. We know that the members of every racial group have learned a vast variety of languages and ways of life. The interaction of genes and custom over the millenna has produced a species whose populations can learn to live in an amazing variety of complex cultural ways.

Racism is based on a profound misunderstanding of culture, of learning, and of the biology of the human species. The study of cultures should give a profound respect for the biology of man's capacity to learn. Much of the earlier discussion of racial inferiority centered on the discussion of intelligence; or, to put the matter more accurately, usually on that small part of biological intelligence which is measured by the IQ. In the earlier days of intelligence testing, there was a widespread belief that the tests revealed something which was genetically fixed within a rather narrow range. The whole climate of opinion that fostered this point of view has changed. At that time animals were regarded as primarily instinctive in their behavior, and the genes were supposed to exert their effects in an almost mechanical way, regardless of the environment. All this intellectual climate

has changed. Learning has proved to be far more important in the behavior of many animal species, and the action of the complexes of genes is now known to be affected by the environment, as is, to a great degree, the performance that results from them. For example, Harlow has shown that monkeys learn to learn. Monkeys become test wise. They become skillful in the solution of tests—so monkeys in Dr. Harlow's laboratories are spoken of as naive or as experienced in the use of tests. To suppose that humans cannot learn to take tests is to suppose that humans are rather less intelligent than monkeys.

Krech and Rosenzweig have shown that rats raised in an enriched environment are much more intelligent and efficient as maze-solvers than rats that have been given no opportunity to learn and to practice before the testing. To suppose that man would not learn through education to take tests more efficiently, is to suppose that our learning capacities are rather less than those of rats.

The human is born with less than a third of the adult brain capacity, and there is tremendous growth of the cortex after birth. There is possibly no mammalian species in which the environment has a longer and more direct effect on the central nervous system than man. We should expect, then, that test results are going to be more affected by the environment of man than in the case of any other animal. Deprivation studies of monkeys and chimpanzees and clinical investigations of man show that the lack of a normal interpersonal environment may be devastating to the developing individual.

Today one approaches the study of intelligence expecting to find that environment is important. The intellectual background is very different from that of the '20's. The general results on testing may be briefly summarized as follows:

The average IQ of large groups is raised by education. I believe the most important data on this are the comparisons of the soldiers of World War I and of World War II. More than 80 percent of the soldiers tested in World War II were above the mean of those tested in World War I. This means a wholesale massive improvement, judged by these tests, in the sons of the people who fought in World War I.

In the states where the least educational effort is made, the IQ is the lowest. In fact, as one looks at the review in Anastasi, it is exceedingly difficult to see why anyone ever thought that the IQ measured innate intelligence, and not the genetic constitution as modified in the family, in the schools, and by the general intellectual environment.

I would suggest that if the intelligence quotients of Negroes and Whites in this country are compared, the same rules be used for these comparisons as would be used for comparisons of the data between two groups of Whites. This may not seem a very extreme thing to suggest, but if you look at the literature, you will find that when two groups of Whites differ in their IQ's, the explanation of the difference is immediately sought in schooling, environment, economic positions of parents, and so on, but that when Negroes and Whites differ in precisely the same way the difference is said to be genetic.

Let me give you but one example of this. Klineberg showed years ago in excellent studies that the mean test scores of many Northern Negro groups were higher than those of certain groups of Southern Whites. When these findings were published, it was immediately suggested that there had been a differential migration and the more intelligent Negroes had moved to the North. But the mean of Northern Whites test results is above that of Southern Whites. Are we to believe that the intelligent Whites also moved to the North?

There is no way of telling what the IQ would be if equal opportunity were given to all racial and social groups. The group which is sociologically classified as Negro in the United States, about one-third of whose genes are of European origin, might well test ahead of the Whites. I am sometimes surprised to hear it stated that if Negroes were given an equal opportunity, their IQ would be the same as the Whites'. If one looks at the degree of social discrimination against Negroes and their lack of education, and also takes into account the tremendous amount of overlapping between the observed IQ's of both, one can make an equally good case that, given a comparable chance to that of the Whites, their IQ's would test out ahead. Of course, it would be absolutely unimportant in a democratic society if this were to be true, because the vast majority of individuals of both groups would be of comparable intelligence, whatever the mean of these intelligence tests would show.

We can generalize this point. All kinds of human performance—whether social, athletic, intellectual—are built on genetic and environmental elements. The level of all kinds of performance can be increased by improving the environmental situation so that every genetic constitution may be developed to its full capacity. Any kind of social discrimination against groups of people, whether these are races, castes, or classes, reduces the achievements of our species, of mankind.

The cost of discrimination is reflected in length of life. The Founding Fathers were wise to join life, liberty, and the pursuit of happiness, because these are intimately linked in the social and cultural system. Just as the restriction of social and economic opportunity reduces intelligence so it reduces length of life.

In 1900 the life expectancy of White males in the United States was 48 years, and in that same year the expectancy of a Negro male was 32 years; that is a difference of 50 per cent, or 16 years. By 1940 the difference had been reduced to ten years, and by 1958 to six. As the life expectancy of the Whites increased from 48 to 62 to 67 years, that of the Negroes increased from 32 to 52 to 61 years. They died of the same causes, but they died at different rates.

Discrimination, by denying equal social opportunity to the Negro, made his progress lag approximately 20 years behind that of the White. Somebody said to me, "Well, 61, 67, that's only six years." But it depends on whose six years it is. There are about 19 million people in this country sociologically classified as Negroes. If they die according to the death rate given above, approximately 100 million years of life will be lost owing to discrimination.

In 1958 the death rate for Negroes in the first year of life was 52 per thousand and for Whites 26. Thousands of Negro infants died unnecessarily. The social conscience is an extraordinary thing. A lynching stirs the whole community to action, yet only a single life is lost. Discrimination, through denying education, medical care, and economic progress, kills at a far higher rate. A ghetto of hatred kills more surely than a concentration camp, because it kills by accepted custom, and it kills every day in the year.

A few years ago in South Africa, the expectation of life for a Black man was 40 years, but it was 60 at the same time for a White man. At that same time a White woman could expect 25 more years of life than a Black woman. Among the Blacks the women lived no longer than the men. People speak of the greater longevity of women, but this is only because of modern medicine. High birth rates, high infant mortality, high maternal mortality—these are the hallmarks of the history of mankind.

Of course there are biological differences between male and female, but

whether a woman is allowed to vote, or the rate that she must die in childbirth, these are a matter of medical knowledge and of custom. Biological difference only expresses itself through the social system.

Who may live longer in the future—Whites or Negroes? There's no way of telling. Who may live longer in the future—males or females? There is no way of telling. These things are dependent on the progress in medical science and on the degree to which this progress is made available to all races and to both sexes.

When environment is important, the only way genetic difference may be determined is by equalizing the environment. If you believe in mankind, then you will want mankind to live on in an enriched environment. No one can tell what may be the ultimate length of life, but we do know that many people could live much longer if given a chance.

Whether we consider intelligence, or length of life, or happiness the genetic potential of a population is only realized in a social system. It is that system which gives life or death to its members, and in so doing changes the gene frequencies. We know of no society which has begun to realize the genetic potential of its members. We are the primitives living by antiquated customs in the midst of scientific progress. Races are products of the past. They are relics of times and conditions which have long ceased to exist.

Racism is equally a relic supported by no phase of modern science. We may not know how to interpret the form of the Mongoloid face, or why Rh° is of high incidence in Africa, but we do know the benefits of education and of economic progress. We know the price of discrimination is death, frustration, and hatred. We know that the roots of happiness lie in the biology of the whole species and that the potential of the species can only be realized in a culture, in a social system. It is knowledge and the social system which give life or take it away, and in so doing change the gene frequencies and continue the million-year-old interaction of culture and biology. Human biology finds its realization in a culturally determined way of life, and the infinite variety of genetic combinations can only express themselves efficiently in a free and open society.

Scientific terms should serve to facilitate rather than to obfuscate the perception and efficient study of reality. Although it is obvious that there are physical differences between human groups—and that the reasons for their occurrence need to be understood—it is not at all certain that these differences are best defined as "racial."

2. On the Nonexistence of Human Races

I LIVINGSTONE :[1]

In this paper I would like to point out that there are excellent arguments for abandoning the concept of race with reference to the living populations of *Homo sapiens.* Although this may seem to be a rather unorthodox position among anthropologists, a growing minority of biologists in general are advocating a similar position with regard to such diverse organisms as grackles, martens, and butterflies. Their arguments seem equally applicable to man. It should be pointed out that this position does not imply that there is no biological variability between the populations of organisms which comprise a species, but just that this variability does not conform to the discrete packages labelled races. The position can be stated in other words as: There are no races, there are only clines.

The term, race, has had a long history of anthropological usage and it can be generally defined as referring to a group of local or breeding populations within a species. Thus, it is a taxonomic term for subspecific groupings greater than the local population. Most anthropologists today use a genetic definition of races as populations which differ in the frequency of some genes.

The term, race, or its newer synonym, geographical race, is used in a similar way with reference to biological species other than man. Where the term is used, it can be considered as approximately synonymous with the term, subspecies. In 1953 Wilson and Brown first suggested discarding the concept of subspecies since it did not accord with the facts. Their main argument was that the genetic variation among the local populations of a species was discordant.

Variation is concordant if the geographic variation of the genetic characters is correlated, so that a classification based on one character would reflect the variability in any other. Such a pattern of variation is almost never found among the local populations of a wide-ranging species, although it is usually found among related relatively allopatric species.

Thus, although it is possible to divide a group of related species into discrete units, namely the species, it is impossible to divide a single species into groups larger than the panmictic population. The causes of intraspecific biological variation are different from

[1] FRANK B. LIVINGSTONE, "On the Nonexistence of Human Races," in *Current Anthropology,* 3 (1962), p. 279, © *Current Anthropology.* Reprinted by permission of the author and the publisher.

those of interspecific variation and to apply the term subspecies to any part of such variation not only is arbitrary or impossible but tends to obscure the explanation of this variation. If one genetic character is used, it is possible to divide a species into subspecies according to the variation in this character. If two characters are used, it may still be possible, but there will be some "problem populations," which, if you are an anthropologist, will be labelled composite or mixed. As the number of characters increases it becomes more nearly impossible to determine what the "actual races really are."

In addition to being a concept used to classify human variability, race has also been overworked as an explanation of this variability. When a particular blood group gene or hair form is found to be characteristic of the populations of a particular region, it is frequently "explained" as being a "racial" character. This type of explanation means, in other words, that this particular set of human populations possesses this character, while it is absent in the rest of humanity, because of the close common ancestry of the former. At times many characteristics which were thought to be racial have been found in many widely separated populations, so that the explanation in terms of race required the assumption of lengthy migrations. In this way race or common ancestry and migration have been used to explain much of the genetic variability among human populations. Unfortunately such explanations neither accord with our knowledge of the population structure and movements of hunters and gatherers, nor take into consideration the basic cause of biological variation, natural selection.

The incompatibility between race and natural selection has been recognized for a long time; so that if one's major aim was to discover the races of man, one has to disregard natural selection. Thus, nonadaptive characters were sought for and, in some instances, considered found. But the recognition of the role of natural selection has in the past ten years changed the course of research into human variability; or at least it has changed the thinking of the "aracial ultrapolymorphists."

If a central problem of physical anthropology is the explanation of the genetic variability among human population—and I think it is—then there are other methods of describing and explaining this variability which do not utilize the concept of race. This variability can also be described in terms of the concepts of cline and morphism. The variability in the frequency of any gene can be plotted in the same way that temperature is plotted on a weather map. Then one can attempt to explain this variability by the mathematical theory of population genetics. This is a very general theory and is capable of explaining all racial or gene frequency differences, although of course for any particular gene the exact magnitudes of factors, mutation, natural selection, gene drift, and gene flow, which control gene frequency differences are not known. All genes mutate, drift, flow, and for a given environment have fitnesses associated with their various genotypes. Hence differences in the frequency of any gene among a series of populations can be explained by these general factors which control gene frequency change. Gene frequency clines can result from many different types of interaction between the general factors which control gene frequencies. For example, a cline may be due to: (1) the recent advance of an advantageous gene; (2) gene flow between populations which inhabit environments with different equilibrium frequencies for the gene; or (3) a gradual change in the equilibrium value of the gene along the cline. The theoretical analysis of clines has barely begun but there seems to be no need for the concept of race in this analysis.

II DOBZHANSKY COMMENTS:[2]

I agree with Dr. Livingstone that if races have to be "discrete units," then there are no races, and if "race" is used as an "explanation" of the human variability, rather than vice versa, then that explanation is invalid. Races are genetically open systems while species are closed ones; therefore races can be discrete only under some exceptional circumstances. Races arise chiefly as a result of the ordering of the genetic variability by natural selection in conformity with the environmental conditions in different territories; therefore the variability precedes race and serves as a raw material for its formation.

The difficulties with the race concept arise chiefly from failure to realize that while race differences are objectively ascertainable biological phenomena, race is also a category of biological classification. Since human population (and those of other sexually reproducing species) often, in fact usually, differ in the frequencies of one or more, usually several to many, genetic variables, they are by this test racially distinct. But it does not follow that any racially distinct populations must be given racial (or subspecific) labels. Discovery of races is a biological problem, naming races is a nomenclatorial problem. There is nothing arbitrary about whether race differences do or do not exist, but whether races should or should not be named, and if they should, how many should be recognized, is a matter of convenience and hence of judgment. Names are given to races, species, and other categories because names are convenient in writing and speaking about the populations or the organisms discovered or investigated.

If all racial variation formed clines (geographic gradients), if all clines were uniform, and if the clines in different characters (and genes) were absolutely independent and uncorrelated, then race differences would still exist. But racial names would not be conveniently applicable, and we would have to get along without them. But this is not the situation in the human species and in many animal and plant species. The clines are not uniform; they are steeper where natural, or social, impediments to travel and intermarriage interpose obstacles to gene exchange, and more gradual where the gene exchange is unobstructed. For the same reason, different variable characters, and the gene frequencies underlying them, are often correlated. This does not make the races any more or less "natural"; but it does make them more easily nameable.

The multiplication of racial or subspecific names has gone beyond the limits of convenience in the human and in some animal species. This was bound to provoke a reaction, and up to a point this was salutary. But if the reaction goes too far in its protest it breeds confusion. To say that mankind has no races plays into hands of race bigots, and this is least of all desirable when the "scientific" racism attempts to rear its ugly head.

III LIVINGSTON REPLIES:[3]

Professor Dobzhansky appears to disagree with the major point of my article and puts forward several arguments against it. His final argument that my

---

[2] THEODOSIUS DOBZHANSKY, "Comment," in *Current Anthropology*, 3 (1962), pp. 279–280, © *Current Anthropology*. Reprinted by permission of the author and the publisher.

[3] FRANK B. LIVINGSTONE, "Reply," in *Current Anthropology*, 3 (1962), pp. 280–281, © *Current Anthropology*. Reprinted by permission of the author and the publisher.

position "plays into hands of race bigots" is irrelevant and immaterial. The fact that some crank may make political hay of a biological fact, concept, or theory is no criterion of the validity of any of these in biological science. I also fail to comprehend how a position which denies the validity of a concept supports anyone using that concept.

With regard to the biological arguments, Dobzhansky employs two different concepts for the term, race. Races exist as biological entities which are discoverable, but we should only label some of these races. In this way Dobzhansky distinguishes between races and race differences. Racial differences do not necessarily mean differences in race. Dobzhansky states, and I would agree with him, that just about all human populations differ in the frequency of some gene. He then concludes that all human populations are racially distinct, which should imply that each is a separate race. I have come to much the same conclusion but think that the term, race, is therefore inapplicable. Race as a concept has been, and still is, used to classify or group together human populations. Since any grouping differs with the gene frequency used, the number of groupings is equal to the number of genes. Thus, one population could belong to several different races. These different kinds of races have been emphasized by Garn, but I don't think they accord with the general use of the term race as a concept within the Linnean system of biological nomenclature. Any particular animal population cannot belong to several different genera, species, or any other taxonomic level within the Linnean system; such a usage is inconsistent with the assumptions of the system.

By definition, races are populations which differ in the frequency of some genes; but according to Dobzhansky all differences in gene frequency between populations are racial differences. Thus, the difference in the frequency of thalassemia between the town of Orosei in the lowlands of Sardinia and the town of Desulo in the highlands fifty kilometers away is a racial difference. With this definition, there is also a high sickle cell gene frequency race consisting of some Greeks, Italians, Turks, Arabs, Africans and Indians, and a low sickle cell race consisting of the rest of humanity. One could also speak of a high color-blind and a low color-blind race. Since Dobzhansky stresses that it may not be convenient to distinguish some racially different populations as races, these may be cases which he wouldn't want to distinguish. But someone else may find it convenient to distinguish them. However, the confusion arises from the fact that these similarities and differences are not "racial" in the sense that they are not due to closeness of common ancestry but to the operation of natural selection, a factor which I think Dobzhansky neglects.

At first, Dobzhansky agrees that natural selection is the major factor determining gene frequency differences. But later when Dobzhansky discusses the nature of genetic variability among human populations, his statements imply that gene exchange is the sole factor responsible for the shape of clines in gene frequency or, in other words, for the genetic differences between human populations. I attempted to show how natural selection and gene flow can interact in several ways to determine the shape of a cline. Although the study of clines in gene frequency among human populations has scarcely begun, surely the clines in the sickle cell gene are the result of more than gene flow. Indeed it is impossible to explain clines solely in terms of gene flow.

Finally, I think our disagreement hinges to a great extent on different views of the nature of scientific concepts and theories. To Dobzhansky races and race differences are things which exist "out there" as biological phenomena, but race is also a label by which we describe "out there." I disagree. No science can divorce its concepts, definitions, and theories so completely from its subject matter, so that Dobzhansky's dichotomy between biological and nomenclatorial problems is impossible. The names, labels, concepts, and definitions of a science are not simply conveniences, and their function is not just to serve as vehicles of communication. The concepts are also not just a set of labels by which we attempt to classify or divide up reality or our observations of it. Of course, there has to be a set of commonly accepted labels so that we can communicate, but the concepts of a science are also logically interconnected and form a coherent, consistent theory or system. The concepts of such a system are defined in terms of one another and certain primitive terms, and then the formal, mathematical, or logical properties of the system derived. For example, in the field of human biology, the concept of breeding population when considered as part of the mathematical theory of population genetics pertains to nothing in reality. But when combined with the concepts of gene frequency, random mating, etc., further concepts such as the Hardy-Weinberg Law or the principle of random gene drift can be logically derived. The latter are more or less the theorems of population genetics and are the logical outcomes of the more basic concepts or axioms. The science of population genetics then attempts to apply this theory to bodies of data and to attempt to determine which group of individuals in a particular area fits most closely the concept of breeding population, but the function of this concept or the theory is not to divide up or label reality, but to explain it. Of course, the concepts of the mathematical theory of population genetics have been developed from the data and findings of a particular sphere of reality and are approximations to these data. But they can also be considered solely as logical concepts and studied as a formal system with no reference to this reality. As Medawar has remarked, this theory has great generality in biology and in that science occupies a position analogous to Newton's Laws in physical science. An infinite population randomly mating without selection, mutation, or gene flow is analogous to Newton's body moving without friction at a constant velocity.

In applying the theory of population genetics to humanity, the species is divided into breeding populations although for any area or group of people this concept may be difficult to apply. It is likely that each breeding population will prove to be genetically unique, so that all will be racially distinct in Dobzhansky's terms. But this is not the general use of the concept of race in biology, and the concept has not in the past been associated with this theory of human diversity. Race has instead been considered as a concept of the Linnean system of classification within which it is applied to groups of populations within a species. To apply a concept of the Linnean system to a group of populations implies something about the evolutionary history of these populations, and it also implies that these populations are similar in whatever characters were used to classify them together because of close common ancestry. It is this implied explanation of whatever genetic variability is used to group populations into races which I consider to be false.

Since we *Homo sapiens* wandered out of the Old World and over the earth to become the most widely distributed of any single animal species, we have grown—superficially—somewhat apart.

3. The Distribution of Man [1]

Men with chins, relatively small brow ridges and small facial skeletons, and with high, flat-sided skulls, probably appeared on earth in the period between the last two great continental glaciers, say from 150,000 to 50,000 years ago. If the time of their origin is blurred, the place is no less so. The new species doubtless emerged from a number of related populations distributed over a considerable part of the Old World. Thus *Homo sapiens* evolved as a species and began to differentiate into races at the same time.

In any case, our direct ancestor, like his older relatives, was at once product and master of the crude pebble tools that primitive human forms had learned to use hundreds of thousands of years earlier. His inheritance also included a social organization and some level of verbal communication.

Between these hazy beginnings and the agricultural revolution of about 10,-000 years ago *Homo sapiens* radiated over most of the earth, and differentiated into clearly distinguishable races. The processes were intimately related. Like the forces that had created man, they reflected both the workings of man's environment and of his own invention. So much can be said with reasonable confidence. The details are another matter. The when, where and how of the origin of races puzzle us not much less than they puzzled Charles Darwin.

A little over a century ago a pleasingly simple explanation of races enjoyed some popularity. The races were separate species, created by God as they are today. The Biblical account of Adam and Eve was meant to apply only to Caucasians. Heretical as the idea might be, it was argued that the Negroes appearing in Egyptian monuments, and the skulls of the ancient Indian moundbuilders of Ohio, differed in no way from their living descendants, and so there could have been no important change in the only slightly longer time since the Creation itself, set by Archbishop Ussher at 4004 B.C.

With his *Origin of Species,* Darwin undid all this careful "science" at a stroke. Natural selection and the immense stretch of time provided by the geological time-scale made gradual evolution seem the obvious explanation of racial or species differences. But in his later book, *The Descent of Man,* Darwin turned his back on his own central notion of natural selection as the cause of races. He there preferred sexual selection, or the accentuation of racial features through long-established ideals of beauty in different segments of mankind. This proposition failed to impress anthropologists, and so Darwin's demolishing of the old views left something of a void that has never been satisfactorily filled.

Not for want of trying. Some students continued, until recent years, to insist that races are indeed separate species, or even separate genera, with Whites descended from chimpanzees, Negroes from gorillas and Mongoloids from orangutans. Darwin himself had al-

[1] WILLIAM W. HOWELLS, "The Distribution of Man" in *Scientific American*, 203, No. 3 (1960), pp. 113–127. Reprinted with permission of the author and the publisher. Copyright © 1960 by Scientific American, Inc. All rights reserved.

ready argued against such a possibility when a contemporary proposed that these same apes had in turn descended from three different monkey species. Darwin pointed out that so great a degree of convergence in evolution, producing thoroughgoing identities in detail (as opposed to, say, the superficial resemblance of whales and fishes) simply could not be expected. The same objection applies to a milder hypothesis, formulated by the late Franz Weidenreich during the 1940's. Races, he held, descended separately, not from such extremely divergent parents as the several great apes, but from the less-separated lines of fossil men. For example, Peking man led to the Mongoloids, and Rhodesian man to the "Africans." But again there are more marked distinctions between those fossil men than between living races.

Actually the most reasonable—I should say the only reasonable—pattern suggested by animal evolution in general is that of racial divergence within a stock already possessing distinctive features of *Homo sapiens*. As I have indicated, such a stock had appeared at the latest by the beginning of the last glacial advance and almost certainly much earlier, perhaps by the end of the preceding glaciation, which is dated at some 150,000 years ago.

Even if fossil remains were more plentiful than they are, they might not in themselves decide the questions of time and place much more accurately. By the time *Homo sapiens* was common enough to provide a chance of our finding some of his fossil remains, he was probably already sufficiently widespread as to give only a general idea of his "place of origin." Moreover, bones and artifacts may concentrate in misleading places. (Consider the parallel case of the australopithecine "man-apes" known so well from the Lower Pleistocene of South Africa. This area is thought of as their home. In fact the region actually was a geographical *cul-de-sac,* and merely a good fossil trap at that time. It is now clear that such prehumans were widespread not only in Africa but also in Asia. We have no real idea of their first center of dispersion, and we should assume that our earliest knowledge of them is not from the actual dawn of their existence.)

In attempting to fix the emergence of modern races of man somewhat more precisely we can apply something like the chronological reasoning of the pre-Darwinians. The Upper Paleolithic invaders of Europe (*e.g.,* the Cro-Magnons) mark the definite entrance of *Homo sapiens,* and these men were already stamped with a "White" racial nature at about 35,000 B.C. But a recently discovered skull from Liukiang in China, probably of the same order of age, is definitely not Caucasian, whatever else it may be. And the earliest American fossil men, perhaps 20,000 years old, are recognizable as Indians. No other remains are certainly so old; we cannot now say anything about the first Negroes. Thus racial differences are definitely older than 35,000 years. And yet—this is sheer guess—the more succesful *Homo sapiens* would probably have overcome the other human types, such as Neanderthal and Rhodesian men, much earlier if he had reached his full development long before. But these types survived well into the last 50,000 years. So we might assume that *Homo sapiens,* and his earliest racial distinctions, is a product of the period between the last two glaciations, coming into his own early during the last glaciation.

When we try to envisage the causes of racial development, we think today of four factors: natural selection, genetic drift, mutation and mixture (interbreeding). With regard to basic divergence at the level of races, the first two are undoubtedly the chief determinants. If forces of any kind favor individuals of one genetic complexion over others, in the sense that they live and reproduce more successfully, the favored individuals will necessarily increase their bequest of genes to the next generation relative to the rest of the population. That is selection; a force with direction.

Genetic drift is a force without direction, an accidental change in the gene proportions of a population. Other things being equal, some parents just have more offspring than others. If such variations can build up, an originally homogeneous population may split into two different ones by chance. It is somewhat as though there were a sack containing 50 red and 50 white billiard balls, each periodically reproducing itself, say by doubling. Suppose you start a new population, drawing out 50 balls without looking. The most likely single result would be 25 of each color, but it is more likely that you would end up with some other combination, perhaps as extreme as 20 reds and 30 whites. After this population divides, you make a new drawing, and so on. Of course at each subsequent step the departure from the then-prevailing proportion is as likely to favor red as white. Nevertheless, once the first drawing has been made with the above result, red has the better chance of vanishing. So it is with genes for hereditary traits.

Both drift and selection should have stronger effects the smaller and more isolated the population. It is easy to imagine them in action among bands of ancient men, living close to nature. (It would be a great mistake, however, to imagine that selection is not also effective in modern populations.) Hence we can look upon racial beginnings as part accident, part design, design meaning any pattern of minor change obedient to natural selection.

Darwin was probably right the first time, then, and natural selection is more important in racial adaptation than he himself later came to think. Curiously, however, it is extremely difficult to find demonstrable, or even logically appealing, adaptive advantages in racial features. The two leading examples of adaptation in human physique are not usually considered racial at all. One is the tendency among warm-blooded animals of the same species to be larger in colder parts of their territory. As an animal of a given shape gets larger, its inner bulk increases faster than its outer surface, so the ratio of heat produced to heat dissipated is higher in larger individuals. It has, indeed, been shown that the average body weight of man goes up as annual mean temperature goes down, speaking very broadly, and considering those populations that have remained where they are a long time. The second example concerns the size of extremities (limbs, ears, muzzles). They are smaller in colder parts of the range and larger in warmer, for the same basic reason—heat conservation and dissipation. Man obeys this rule also, producing lanky, long-limbed populations in hot deserts and dumpy, short-limbed people in the Arctic.

This does not carry us far with the major, historic races as we know them. Perhaps the most striking of all racial features is the dark skin of Negroes. The color of Negro skin is due to a concentration of melanin, the universal human pigment that diffuses sunlight and screens out its damaging ultraviolet component. Does it not seem obvious that in the long course of time the Negroes, living astride the Equator in Africa and in the western Pacific, developed their dark skins as a direct response to a strong sun? It makes sense. It would be folly to deny that such an adaptation is present. But a great deal of the present Negro habitat is shade forest and not bright sun, which is in fact strongest in the deserts some distance north of the Equator. The Pygmies are decidedly forest dwellers, not only in Africa but in their several habitats in southeastern Asia as well.

At any rate there is enough doubt to have called forth other suggestions. One is that forest hunters needed protective coloration, both for stalking and for their protection from predators; dark skin would have lowest visibility in the patchy light and shade beneath the trees. Another is that densely pigmented skins may have other qualities—*e.g.,* resistance to infection—of which we are unaware.

A more straightforward way out of the dilemma is to suppose that the Negroes are actually new to the Congo forest, and that they served their racial apprenticeship hunting and fishing in the sunny grasslands of the southern Sahara. If so, their Pygmy relatives might represent the first accommodation of the race to the forest, before agriculture but after dark skin had been acquired. Smaller size certainly makes a chase after game through the undergrowth less exhausting and faster. As for woolly hair, it is easy to see (still without proof) as an excellent, nonmatting insulation against solar heat. Thick Negro lips? Every suggestion yet made has a zany sound. They may only be a side effect of some properties of heavily pigmented skin (ability to produce thick scar tissue, for example), even as blond hair is doubtless a side effect of the general depigmentation of men that has occurred in northern Europe.

At some remove racially from Negroes and Pygmies are the Bushmen and Hottentots of southern Africa. They are small, or at least lightly built, with distinctive wide, small, flat faces; they are rather infantile looking, and have a five-cornered skull outline that seems to be an ancient inheritance. Their skin is yellowish-brown, not dark. None of

this has been clearly interpreted, although the small size is thought to be an accommodation to water and food economy in the arid environment. The light skin, in an open sunny country, contradicts the sun-pigment theory, and has in fact been used in favor of the protective-coloration hypothesis. Bushmen and background blend beautifully for color, at least as human beings see color.

Bushmen, and especially Hottentots, have another dramatic characteristic: steatopygia. If they are well nourished, the adult women accumulate a surprising quantity of fat on their buttocks. This seems to be a simple storehouse mechanism reminiscent of the camel's hump; a storehouse that is not distributed like a blanket over the torso generally, where it would be disadvantageous in a hot climate. The characteristic nicely demonstrates adaptive selection working in a human racial population.

The Caucasians make the best argument for skin color as an ultraviolet screen. They extend from cloudy northern Europe, where the ultraviolet in the little available sunlight is not only acceptable but desirable, down to the fiercely sun-baked Sahara and peninsular India. All the way, the correspondence with skin color is good: blond around the Baltic, swarthy on the Mediterranean, brunet in Africa and Arabia, dark brown in India. Thus, given a long enough time of occupation, and doubtless some mixture to provide dark-skinned genes in the south, natural selection could well be held responsible.

On the other hand, the Caucasians' straight faces and often prominent noses lack any evident adaptive significance. It is the reverse with the Mongoloids, whose countenances form a coherent pattern that seems consistent with their racial history. From the standpoint of evolution it is Western man, not the Oriental, who is inscrutable. The "almond" eyes of the Mongoloid are deeply set in protective fat-lined lids, the nose and forehead are flattish and the cheeks are broad and fat-padded. In every way, it has been pointed out, this is an ideal mask to protect eyes, nose and sinuses against bitterly cold weather. Such a face is the pole toward which the peoples of eastern Asia point, and it reaches its most marked and uniform expression in the cold northeastern part of the continent, from Korea north.

Theoretically the Mongoloid face developed under intense natural selection some time during the last glacial advance among peoples trapped north of a ring of mountain glaciers and subjected to fierce cold, which would have weeded out the less adapted, in the most classic Darwinian fashion, through pneumonia and sinus infections. If the picture is accurate, this face type is the latest major human adaptation. It could not be very old. For one thing, the population would have had to reach a stage of advanced skill in hunting and living to survive at all in such cold, a stage probably not attained before the Upper Paleolithic (beginning about 35,000 B.C.). For another, the adaptation must have occurred after the American Indians, who are Mongoloid but without the transformed face, migrated across the Bering Strait. (Only the Eskimos reflect the extension of full-fledged, recent Mongoloids into America.) All this suggests a process taking a relatively small number of generations (about 600) between 25,000 and 10,000 B.C.

The discussion so far has treated human beings as though they were any mammal under the influence of natural selection and the other forces of evolution. It says very little about why man invaded the various environments that have shaped him and how he got himself distributed in the way we find him now. For an understanding of these proc-

esses we must take into account man's own peculiar abilities. He has created culture, a milieu for action and development that must be added to the simplicities of sun, snow, forest or plain.

Let us go back to the beginning. Man started as an apelike creature, certainly vegetarian, certainly connected with wooded zones, limited like all other primates to tropical or near-tropical regions. In becoming a walker he had begun to extend his range. Tools, social rules and intelligence all progressed together; he learned to form efficient groups, armed with weapons not provided by nature. He started to eat meat, and later to cook it; the more concentrated diet widened his possibilities for using his time; the hunting of animals beckoned him still farther in various directions.

All this was probably accomplished during the small-brained australopithecine stage. It put man on a new plane, with the potential to reach all parts of the earth, and not only those in which he could find food ready to his hand, or be comfortable in his bare skin. He did not actually reach his limits until the end of the last glaciation, and in fact left large tracts empty for most of the period. By then he had become *Homo sapiens,* with a large brain. He had tools keen enough to give him clothes of animal skin. He had invented projectiles to widen the perimeter of his striking power: bolas, javelins with spear throwers, arrows with bows. He was using dogs to widen the perimeter of his senses in tracking. He had found what could be eaten from the sea and its shores. He could move only slowly, and was probably by no means adventurous. But hunting territory was precious, and the surplus of an expanding population had to stake out new preserves wherever there was freedom ahead. So this pressure, and man's command of nature, primitive though it still was, sent the hunters of the end of the Ice Age throughout the Old World, out into Australia, up into the far north, over the Bering Strait and down the whole length of the Americas to Tierra del Fuego. At the beginning of this dispersion we have brutes barely able to shape a stone tool; at the end, the wily, self-reliant Eskimo, with his complicated traps, weapons and sledges and his clever hunting tricks.

The great racial radiation carried out by migratory hunters culminated in the world as it was about 10,000 years ago. The Whites occupied Europe, northern and eastern Africa and the Near East, and extended far to the east in Central Asia toward the Pacific shore. Negroes occupied the Sahara, better watered then, and Pygmies the African equatorial forest; south, in the open country, were Bushmen only. Other Pygmies, the Negritos, lived in the forests of much of India and southeastern Asia; while in the open country of these areas and in Australia were men like the present Australian aborigines: brown, beetle-browed and wavy-haired. Most of the Pacific was empty. People such as the American Indians stretched from China and Mongolia over Alaska to the Straits of Magellan; the more strongly Mongoloid peoples had not yet attained their domination of the Far East.

During the whole period the human population had depended on the supply of wild game for food, and the accent had been on relative isolation of peoples and groups. Still close to nature (as we think of nature), man was in a good position for rapid small-scale evolution, both through natural selection and through the operation of chance in causing differences among widely separated tribes even if selection was not strong.

Then opened the Neolithic period, the beginning of a great change. Agriculture was invented, at first inefficient and feeble, but in our day able to feed phenomenally large populations while freeing them from looking for food. The limit on local numbers of people was gradually removed, and with it the necessity for the isolation and spacing of groups and the careful observation of boundaries. Now, as there began to be surpluses available for trading, connections between communities became more useful. Later came a spreading of bonds from higher centers of trade and of authority. Isolation gave way to contact, even when contact meant war.

The change was not speedy by our standards, though in comparison with the pace of the Stone Age it seems like a headlong rush. The new economy planted people much more solidly, of course. Farmers have been uprooting and displacing hunters from the time of the first planters to our own day, when Bushman survivors are still losing reservation land to agriculturalists in southwestern Africa. These Bushmen, a scattering of Australian aborigines, the Eskimos and a few other groups are the only representatives of their age still in place. On the other hand, primitive representatives of the Neolithic level of farming still live in many places after the thousands of years since they first became established there.

Nevertheless mobility increased and has increased ever since. Early woodland farmers were partly nomadic, moving every generation following exhaustion of the soil, however solidly fixed they may have been during each sojourn. The Danubians of 6,000 years ago can be traced archeologically as they made the same kind of periodic removes as central Africans, Iroquois Indians and pioneer Yankee farmers. Another side of farming —animal husbandry—gave rise to pastoral nomadism. Herders were much lighter of foot, and historically have tended to be warlike and domineering. With irrigation, villages could settle forever and evolve into the urban centers of high civilizations. Far from immobilizing man, however, these centers served as fixed bases from which contact (and conflict) worked outward.

The rest of the story is written more clearly. New crops or new agricultural methods opened new territories, such as equatorial Africa, and the great plains of the U. S., never successfully farmed by the Indians. New materials such as copper and tin made places once hopeless for habitation desirable as sources of raw material or as way stations for trade. Thus an island like Crete rose from nothing to dominate the eastern Mediterranean for centuries. Well before the earliest historians had made records, big population shifts were taking place. Our mental picture of the aboriginal world is actually a recent one. The Bantu Negroes moved into central and southern Africa, peoples of Mongoloid type went south through China and into Japan, and ancient folk of Negrito and Australoid racial nature were submerged by Caucasians in India. Various interesting but inconsequential trickles also ran hither and yon; for example, the migration of the Polynesians into the far Pacific.

The greatest movement came with the advent of ocean sailing in Europe. (The Polynesians had sailed the high seas earlier, of course, but they had no high culture, nor did Providence interpose a continent across their route at a feasible distance, as it did for Columbus.) The Europeans poured out on the world. From the 15th to the 19th centuries they compelled other civilized peoples to accept contact, and subjected or erased the uncivilized. So today, once again, we have a quite different distribution of mankind from that of 1492.

It seems obvious that we stand at the beginning of still another phase. Contact is immediate, borders are slamming shut and competition is fierce. Biological fitness in races is now hard to trace, and even reproduction is heavily controlled by medicine and by social values. The racial picture of the future will be determined less by natural selection and disease resistances than by success in government and in the adjustment of numbers. The end of direct European dominance in Africa and Asia seems to mean the end of any possibility of the infiltration and expansion of the European variety of man there, on the New World model. History as we know it has been largely the expansion of the European horizon and of European peoples. But the end in China of mere absorption of Occidental invention, and the passionate self-assertion of the African tribes, make it likely that racial lines and territories will again be more sharply drawn than they have been for centuries. What man will make of himself next is a question that lies in the province of prophets, not anthropologists.

Of itself "race mixing" is neither good nor bad—nor new. The biological desirability of the outcome depends on the genes of the individuals involved. Although no people is or can be racially pure, Americans are more mixed up than most.

4. Race Mixture: The African Ancestry of White Americans [1]

Defining a racial group generally poses a problem to social scientists. A definition of a race has yet to be proposed that is satisfactory for all purposes. This is particularly true when the racial group has minority group status as does the Negro group in the United States. To many persons, however, the matter of race definition is no problem. They view humanity as being divided into completely separate racial compartments. A Negro is commonly defined as a person having any known trace of Negro ancestry or "blood" regardless of how far back one must go to find it. A concomitant belief is that all whites are free of the presumed taint of Negro ancestry or "Blood."

The purpose of the research reported here was to determine the validity of this belief in the non-Negro ancestry of persons classified as white. Current definitions of Negro may have serious limitations when used as bases for classifying persons according to ancestry. The terms *African* and *non-African* will be used rather than *Negro* and *white* when discussing the ancestry of an individual. Each of the former pair of terms has a more specific referent which is the geographic point of origin of an individual. At the same time, the two pairs of terms are closely related. Hence, this paper describes an attempt to estimate the percentage of persons classified as white that have African ancestry or genes received from an African ancestor.

This raises a question concerning the relationship between having an African ancestor and receiving one or more genes from this ancestor. Since one half of an individual's genetic inheritance is received from each parent, the probability of a person with one African ancestor within the previous eight generations receiving any single gene from this ancestor is equal to or greater than $(0.5)^8$ or 3.9063×10^{-3}. It has been estimated that there are approximately 20,000 gene loci on the 23 chromosome pairs of man (Stern, 1960). The probability that an individual with one African ancestor has *one or more* genes derived from this ancestor is equal to

$$1 - (1 - 3.9063 \times 10^{-3})^{10,000}$$

or almost 1.0. Having more than one African ancestor increases this probability. One final remark needs to be made. Some degree of African ancestry is not necessarily related to the physical appearance of the individual. Many of the genes possessed by virtue of descent from an African do not distinguish the bearer from persons of non-African ancestry. They are the genes or potentials for traits which characterize the human race. Nevertheless, these genes represent an

[1] ROBERT P. STUCKERT, "African Ancestry of the White American Population," specially revised by the author for publication in this book; an earlier version appeared in the *Ohio Journal of Science*, 58 (1958), pp. 155–60. As several citations made here do not appear in the original article all references have been retained. Printed by permission of the author and the original publisher.

Dr. Stuckert is Associate Professor of Sociology at the University of Wisconsin, Milwaukee.

element in the biological constitution of the individual inherited from an African.

RESEARCH METHODOLOGY

The research methodology of this study involved constructing a genetic probability table. The primary function of this type of table is to ascertain the distribution within a known population of a variable that can not be observed directly. It is frequently used to estimate the changes that occur in the genetic composition of a population over a period of time. There are three basic steps in the computation of a genetic probability table.

1. A series of assumptions which serve as a basis for the table is made. These assumptions may refer to the initial distribution of the variable within the population, the effect of biological and nonbiological factors on the distribution, or the interrelationships of these factors. In some cases, these assumptions may be derived from available empirical data.

2. On the basis of these assumptions, the probability distributions of the variable within the population for successive time intervals are computed. This is done by applying the rules of probability relevant to the principles of biological inheritance to the changes that are known to have occurred in the observable characteristics of the population.

3. The validity of the probability table is determined by comparing the probability values included in the table with data obtained from empirical studies based on other research methods. The extent to which these values correspond is a measure of the validity of the table.

Sources of Data. The best data available for use in estimating the biological background of Americans are those dealing with the population of this country. Official records have been kept of the white and Negro population since 1790 by the Bureau of the Census and of

the influx of foreign population to this country since 1820 by the Immigration and Naturalization Service. Numerous estimates of population and immigration figures have been made for the period 1660 to 1820. There is general agreement among historians, statisticians, and population analysts on the relative reliability of the data for the years since 1750 only, (Carey, 1853; Bromwell, 1856; Bancroft, 1891; Greene, 1932; U.S. National Resources Committee, 1938). Estimates have been made of the volume of illegal smuggling of slaves into this country between 1808 and 1860 (U.S. Bureau of the Census, 1909; Dublin, 1928). Thus, it was possible to obtain usable data for each decennial period since 1750.

Assumptions. In this study, all persons were classified into four racial-ancestral categories: white persons with no African ancestry, white persons with some degree of African ancestry, Negroes with some degree of non-African ancestry, and Negroes with African ancestry only. The following assumptions were used as bases for statistically estimating the probability of African and non-African ancestry. The use of these assumptions tends to underestimate the proportion of the white population that would have African ancestry.

1. The white population of the American colonies in 1750 contained no persons of African ancestry. Any African element introduced into the background of supposedly white persons prior to 1750 was regarded as unimportant since the probability of possessing genes from any given ancestor decreases rapidly after twelve generations from the introduction of these genes.

2. All individuals classified as Negro have some degree of African ancestry.

3. The probability of a male member of any of the four racial-ancestral categories being a partner in a fecund mating during a given period of time is equal to the proportion of the total population in

the category at the beginning of the time period. In other words, if one tenth of the total population are white persons of non-African ancestry, one tenth of all fecund sexual contacts involve white males of non-African ancestry. The same is assumed for females.

4. The probability of persons classified as white mating with persons classified as Negro is one twentieth of what would be expected if mating were random. To illustrate, if 90 per cent of the population were white and 10 per cent were Negro and *mating were random,* 18 per cent of all fecund matings would involve a white and a Negro. According to this assumption of *selective mating,* the percentage of fecund matings involving members of different racial categories would be nine tenths of 1 per cent in this case. It should also be remembered that virtually all of the offspring of these mixed matings would be classified as Negro.

5. The proportion of the increase in population due to causes other than immigration from Africa and Europe during a given period that can be assigned to a racial-ancestral category is equal to the probability of a live birth being a member of that category. These causes include natural increase, emigration, and immigration from racially mixed areas (West Indies, Mexico, Central and South America). If one third of the live births during a given period are white persons of non-African ancestry, one third of the increase due to these causes is comprised of white persons of non-African ancestry.

6. All persons immigrating to the United States from Europe are of non-African ancestry only. Due to the small number of African Negroes in Europe, the incidence of African ancestry among Europeans is relatively small.

7. All persons immigrating to the United States from areas in Africa are of African ancestry and one tenth of them have some degree of non-African ancestry.

Two equations were used in computing the probability of an individual drawn at random from the population being a member of each of the four racial-ancestral categories. The derivation of these equations is presented in detail in the original article. The first equation was used to estimate the number of white persons with only non-African ancestry. The crucial problem was estimating the portion of the population increase due to causes other than immigration from Europe and Africa during a censual period that had no African ancestry. The second equation was used to estimate the number of individuals that are Negro with African ancestry only for a given censual year. The number of persons in each racial category having some degree of mixed ancestry was obtained by subtracting the estimated number having unmixed ancestry from the total in that racial category. The probability values for a given censual year needed to complete the genetic probability table were obtained by dividing these four sets of numerical estimates by the total white and Negro population at that time.

Criteria of Validity. Three types of empirical studies were used in determining the validity of the genetic probability table based upon the above assumptions. These included studies of the mixed ancestry of Negro groups, the frequency of children born of mixed parentage, and the frequency of passing.

RESEARCH RESULTS

A genetic probability table was constructed on the basis of the above data and assumptions. This table included the probabilities of an individual drawn at random from the population of the United States being a member of the four racial-ancestral categories. These probabilities were computed for every tenth year from 1750 through 1780 and each censual year since 1790. In order to high-light the relative size of the two groups with mixed ancestry, the probability values in this table were converted to absolute numbers. Table 1 includes these data for successive censual years. The percentages of the two racial categories that have both African and non-African ancestry are also included.

tively stable. Between 1900 and 1930, the percentage declined slightly. These two shifts were primarily the result of large-scale immigration from Europe. With the curtailing of this immigration, the percentage values began increasing again in 1930.

One final question pertains to the validity of these data. As mentioned

TABLE 1. TOTAL WHITE AND NEGRO POPULATION, WHITE POPULATION WITH AFRICAN ANCESTRY AND NEGRO POPULATION WITH NON-AFRICAN ANCESTRY, UNITED STATES, 1790–1960 *

| | White Population | | | Negro Population | | |
| | Total | African Ancestry | | Total | Non-African Ancestry | |
Year	(000's)	Number (000's)	Per Cent	(000's)	Number (000's)	Per Cent
1790	3,172	62	2.0	757	144	19.0
1800	4,306	164	3.8	1,002	209	20.9
1810	5,862	303	5.2	1,378	450	32.7
1820	7,887	623	7.9	1,772	620	35.0
1830	10,537	1,134	10.8	2,329	842	36.2
1840	14,196	1,939	13.7	2,874	1,041	36.2
1850	19,553	2,975	15.2	3,639	1,389	38.2
1860	26,923	4,508	16.7	4,442	1,738	39.1
1870	33,589	6,035	18.0	4,880	1,935	39.7
1880	43,403	7,961	18.3	6,581	3,248	49.4
1890	55,101	10,383	18.8	7,489	3,902	52.1
1900	66,809	13,020	19.5	8,834	5,002	56.6
1910	81,364	14,150	17.4	9,828	6,050	61.6
1920	94,120	16,703	17.7	10,463	6,780	64.8
1930	108,864	20,120	18.5	11,891	8,086	68.0
1940	118,215	36,038	22.8	18,860	14,605	77.4
1950	134,942	28,366	21.0	15,042	10,980	73.0
1960	158,455	23,035	19.5	12,866	8,993	69.9

* Excluding Alaska and Hawaii.

The data in Table 1 indicate that approximately 23 per cent of the persons classified as white in 1960 have an African element in their inherited biological background. The percentage of persons classified as white having some degree of African ancestry was extremely small in 1790. The percentage figures for successive censual years increased most rapidly between 1790 and 1850. Although this is partly a function of the computational methods used, it is characteristic of inter-breeding populations. The figures for the period 1850 to 1890 were compara-

above, three criteria were used to ascertain the validity of the probability values used in deriving Table 1. Two of the criteria involved the incidence of mixed ancestry among persons classified as Negro. First, the percentage of Negroes that had some degree of non-African ancestry was computed for each censual year. Table 1 shows that from 68.0 to 77.4 per cent of Negroes had some degree of non-African ancestry in the last four censual years. These figures correspond closely to those included in studies of Negro groups made by Hrdlicka (1928),

Herskovits (1930), and Hooton (1939). Second, estimates of the percentage of Negroes born of mixed parentage were made on the basis of the probability values included in the genetic probability table. The percentage born of mixed parentage varied between 7.9 per cent in 1850 and 8.4 per cent in 1920. These computed values do not conflict with any of the data cited by Herskovits (1928), Day (1932), and Frazier (1939). Furthermore, these values are almost the exact values needed to account for the rates of gene transfer computed by Glass and Li (1953).

The third criterion centered around the phenomena of passing. The increase in the number of persons classified as white having some degree of African ancestry given in Table 1 could have occurred only if there were a continuing influx of persons into the white group from the Negro group. The magnitude and rate of passing needed to account for the indicated increase were computed for the period 1860 to 1960. These data are given in Table 2. They fall well within the range of frequency of passing as empirically estimated by Hart (1921), Burma (1946), and Eckard (1947). The data in Table 2 also indicate that the rate of passing declined during 1951–1960 after a fairly steady increase since 1860.

TABLE 2. ESTIMATED EXTENT AND RATE OF PASSING, UNITED STATES, 1861–1960

Period	Estimated Number of Persons Passing	Annual Mean	Annual Rate*
1861–1890	90,900	3,030	0.68
1891–1910	101,300	5,065	0.68
1911–1930	183,200	9,160	0.93
1931–1940	42,700	4,270	0.36
1941–1950	155,500	15,550	1.21
1951–1960	96,900	9,690	0.64

*Rate per 1,000 Negro population per year.

CONCLUSIONS

The data presented in this study indicate that the popular belief in the non-African background of white persons is invalid. Over thirty-six million white persons are descendants of persons of African origin. Furthermore, the majority of the persons with African ancestry are classified as white. Finally, if the volume of immigration remains at the present relatively low level, the percentage of persons having mixed ancestry will increase in the future. One conclusion stands out from these data. The belief in the racial uniformity of an individual's ancestors may be the basic myth of the white man's past.

LITERATURE CITED

Bancroft, G. 1891. *History of the United States*. Vol. 2. D. Appleton and Co., New York. 565 pp.

Bromwell, W. 1856. *History of Immigration to the United States*. Redfield, New York. 225 pp.

Burma, J. H. 1946. "The measurement of Negro 'passing.'" *Amer. Jour. Sociol.* 52:18–22.

Carey, H. C. 1853. *The Slave Trade*. A. Hart, Philadelphia. 426 pp.

Day, C. B. 1932. *A Study of Some Negro-White Families in the United States*. Harvard African Studies. Vol. 10. Harvard University, Cambridge. 126 pp.

Dublin, L. I. 1928. *Health and Wealth*. Harper and Brothers, New York. 361 pp.

Eckard, E. W. 1947. "How many Negroes 'pass'?" *Amer. Jour. Sociol.* 52:498–500.

Frazier, E. F. 1939. *The Negro Family in the United States*. The University of Chicago Press, Chicago, 686 pp.

Glass, B. and C. C. Li. 1953. "The dynamics of racial intermixture—an analysis based on the American Negro." *Amer. Jour. Human Genet.* 5:1–20.

Green, E. B. 1932. *American Population Before the Federal Census of 1790*. Columbia University Press, New York. 228 pp.

Hart, H. 1921. *Selective Migration as a Factor in Child Welfare in the United States*, with Special Reference to Iowa. University of Iowa, Iowa City. 137 pp.

Herskovits, M. J. 1928. The American Negro: A Study in Racial Crossing. Alfred A. Knopf, New York. 92 pp.

———. 1930. The Anthropometry of the American Negro. Columbia University Press, New York. 283 pp.

Hooton, E. A. 1939. Crime and the Man. Harvard University, Cambridge. 403 pp.

Hrdlicka, A. 1928. "The full-blood American Negro." Amer. Jour. Phys. Anthro. 12:15–33.

Stern, C. 1960. Principles of Human Genetics. W. H. Freeman and Co., San Francisco. 753 pp.

U.S. Bureau of the Census. 1909. A Century of Population Growth from the First Census of the United States to the Twelfth, 1790–1900. Government Printing Office, Washington. 303 pp.

U.S. National Resources Committee. 1938. The Problems of a Changing Population. Government Printing Office, Washington. 28 pp.

When a factually baseless contention persists—despite its thorough scientific disrepute—there must be a reason. Some people find the idea of "racial inferiority" a useful means of justifying unpleasant attitudes and unfair actions.

5. Racism [1]

COLOR PREJUDICE

Our own civilization attaches special importance to the color of the skin and relatively dark pigmentation is a mark of difference condemning many human groups to contempt, ostracism and a debased social status.

Nevertheless, however unfounded the basis for color prejudice may be, the importance of the attitudes and behavior proceeding from it in many countries, is indisputable.

The exploitation of agriculture and mining by the whites in the newly-discovered countries from the fifteenth century on created slavery, particularly the enslavement of Negroes and American Indians. There were many who sought to maintain this situation on the grounds that the Negro was "inferior" to the white man. For instance, in 1772 the Reverend Thomas Thompson published a monograph, The Trade in Negro Slaves on the African Coast in Accord-

ance with Humane Principles and with the Laws of Revealed Religion. In 1852 the Rev. Josiah Priest published A Bible Defence of Slavery, while C. Carroll in his work The Negro as a Beast or In the Image of God? includes a chapter (Biblical and Scientific Proofs that the Negro is not a Member of the Human Race) in which he asserts that "all scientific research confirms his typically simian nature."

Despite the proclamation in the Declaration of Independence of the United States of equal rights for all men and the explicit provision of the Fifteenth Amendment that "the rights of citizens of the United States shall not be denied or abridged by the United States or by any state on account of race, colour or previous condition of servitude," and despite the inclusion of equivalent provisions in the Constitutions of most countries and the solemn agreement to the same effect in Article 2 of the Universal Declaration of Human Rights signed by

[1] JUAN COMAS, from Manual of Physical Anthropology, pp. 172–186, 1960. Courtesy of the author and Charles C. Thomas, Publisher, Springfield, Ill.

the United Nations on December 10, 1948, it is all too obvious in practice how widespread throughout the world is social, economic and political discrimination against Negroes in particular and colored races in general, based mainly on false racial concepts.

One of the major absurdities of color prejudice in the United States is the classification of anyone, regardless of his physical appearance, as a Negro who admits to having an African ancestor. In this case "Negro" is not a biological term but denotes membership in a particular cultural, economic and social group. Some "Negroes" are indistinguishable from white men and pass themselves off as such to escape anti-Negro discrimination. The lack of logic in this attitude becomes still clearer if we reflect that if a person with the smallest proportion of "Negro blood" can be classified as a Negro, it is just as logical and fair to classify everyone with one drop of "white blood" as white.

The humiliations suffered daily by Negroes, in the socio-economic and political fields, the restrictions and personal affronts and indignities, the exclusion of Negroes from certain trains and busses, the provision of restricted vehicles, waiting rooms, schools, prohibited restaurants and hotels, etc. are all insulting and ridiculous to the Negro. In South Africa, color prejudice is so strong that there was an instance in 1944 of several officials being dismissed from their posts for refusal to obey Government instructions that the same polite forms be used in official documents addressed to colored persons as in those to whites.

Ironically enough, one of the groups apparently most insistent on discrimination against Negroes are the so-called "poor whites" themselves the objects of discrimination because of lack of education and social and economic possibilities. As they are the first to fear Negro competition in the economic field and have no other argument on which to base their attitude of superiority, they fall back on skin pigmentation to which, given the circumstances, they attach an exaggerated importance.

Assumptions about psychological and social characteristics based on skin color are not only false but vary absurdly with the circumstances. As an example, we may take the changes in attitude towards the Japanese. In 1935 the majority of North Americans thought of them as "progressive," "intelligent," and "industrious." In 1942 they had become "cunning" and "treacherous." In 1950 things changed again. When there was a shortage of Chinese laborers in California they were described as "frugal," "sober" and "law-abiding." The moment competition became severe and it was necessary to exclude them, they were described as "dirty," "repulsive," "unassimilable" and even "dangerous." The same lack of objective criteria might later be found in India. While North American troops described the natives as "dirty," "uncivilized," the Hindu intellectuals characterized the Americans as "boorish," "materialistic," "unintellectual" and "uncivilized."

Regarding the supposed inferiority of the Negro's psychosomatic attributes to those of the white man, Hankins claims that the bulk of the brain is less in the Negro and deduces from this that the Negro is mentally inferior. H. L. Gordon asserts that congenital cerebral deficiency is a characteristic of the Negroes of Kenya, also as a result of lesser cranial volume and differences in conformation of the Negro brain.

However, it is in the psychological field above all that the most sustained effort has been made to prove the superiority of the white man over the Negro. It is true that Negro and white are in no respect identical either physically, intellectually or emotionally, but this does not warrant any assertion that the differences imply the superiority of one or the other.

The investigations of Leakey in Africa and Steggerda among the Negroes of Jamaica have shown that their cranial capacity is not inferior, and in some cases is even superior, to that of the white man. This is confirmed by the work of J. Huxley and A. Keith, but further corroboration of this view may be found in the work of J. H. F. Kohlbrugge on brain formations, based on earlier research by such eminent anthropologists and doctors as Retzius, Weinberg, Sergi and Kappers, which arrives at the following important conclusions:

1. The weight of the frontal lobe, regarded as the seat of the intellect, averages 44% of the total weight of the brain in men and women, black or white.

2. No racial differences are observable as regards the weight of the brain; there are however, marked variations between individuals within each human group or "race."

3. Men of marked intellectual powers have not necessarily possessed brains greater in weight or volume than the average.

4. Comparison of the incisures and convolutions of the brain afford equally little support for the view that there are discernible differences between the races. All variations are found in all "races," and concludes that if the specimens available were mixed up, there is no one who could distinguish the brains of Australians from those of Europeans nor those of people of high intelligence from those of average mentality.

Admittedly prognathism, frequently found in Negroes is a primitive somatic trait. However, the lack of body hair, the thickness of the lips, and the texture of the hair of the head, etc., in the Negro, are all consistent with a more advanced stage of evolution than in the white man. We can say with Ruth Benedict that "No race has an exclusive claim to represent the final stage in human evolution; there

is no valid argument to confirm that certain selected traits may indicate the superiority of the white race."

In this connection the qualifications of "good," "bad," "superior" and "inferior" are meaningless as they are all subjective terms. In every case they should be used in a specific connection, e.g., "the majority of Negroes are superior to white people in their resistance to malaria"; or "the majority of white people are superior to the majority of Negroes in resistance to tuberculosis," etc. The result would be to show that every human group is superior in some respects and inferior in others.

In comparisons of the position of the white and Negro races today there is a tendency to assume that the latter are inferior from the fact that their economic, political and cultural evolution is far behind that of the whites. This, however, is not due to an "innate racial inferiority," but is purely the result of circumstances and of the condition of exploitation under which almost all Negroes live today as a result of white colonization and of the existence, if not of legal slavery, of situations equivalent to it in practice.

Too often the Negro is still in a position of economic semislavery, enmeshed in a network of restrictions, partly legal and partly illegal. Poverty, contempt and disease have all contributed to his actual condition.

Regarding the supposed laziness of the Negro (as also of the American Indian) the cause may well be lack of incentive. As Burns rightly points out, the vast yield of the West African colonies, where some land is still in Negro hands, shows that the Negro is not lazy by nature. Booker T. Washington holds that the greatest harm inflicted on the Negro by slavery was to deprive him of the sense of personal independence, method and the spirit of initiative.

The contributions of Negroes as a race,

to world civilization from the XVth century to the present day, are not an adequate basis for prognostication of what they may be able to achieve in the future in terms of their own aptitudes and under more satisfactory environmental, social and economic conditions. It should not be forgotten among other facts, that the twelfth century Negro university of Timbuctoo could stand comparison with its contemporary European schools, and the same is true with regard to the respective levels of civilization in Europe and in the three great Negro kingdoms of that period. Moreover, it is probable that the working of iron, fundamental to all modern technology, was a Negro discovery.

ANTI-JEWISH PREJUDICE

Anti-Semitism, as a social and political attitude, infecting whole nations in some instances, and extensive sectors of the population in others, and defended to a greater or lesser extent on religious and economic grounds, is a long-standing antagonism examples of which can be found far back in history.

Today, however, anti-Semitism has resorted to the myth of a Jewish race in an attempt to justify and provide a pseudo-scientific cloak for its political and economic motives.

The fact that some Jews can be identified as such is due less to inherited physical traits than to certain cultural manifestations, the results of Jewish custom and the treatment inflicted on Jews by non-Jews. If the Nazis had had genuine distinctive "Jewish" characteristics to go on, why were Jews obliged to display the Star of David on their clothing to permit their identification by Aryans?

Jews of Spanish origin are dolichocephalic whereas Russian Jews are brachycephalic. A similar general observation may be made regarding the Jews of Poland, Germany and Austria. Of English Jews, 28.3% are dolichocephalic, 24.3% mesocephalic and 47.4% brachycephalic, while of the Jewish population of Daghestan (Caucasus), 5% are dolichocephalic, 10% mesocephalic and 85% brachycephalic.

It is not possible in this *Manual* to quote the detailed statistics proving the variability of all the other somatic characteristics in the misnamed "Jewish Race." However, it may be mentioned that 49% of Polish Jews are light haired and 51% dark haired, while there are only 32% blonds among German Jews. Thirty per cent of the Jews of Vienna have light colored eyes. Even the hooked nose, incorrectly considered a typical Jewish trait, occurs in 44% only of the individuals of certain groups, while straight noses are found in 40%, the so-called "roman" nose in 9% and tiptilted in 7%. All the above is clear proof of the variability and lack of morphological unity of the Jewish people.

As the eminent anthropologist F. Boas notes, "the assimilation of Jews by the groups among which they are established is much deeper than would appear. An impressive parallelism exists in stature, head shape and other traits between the physical appearance of the Jews and that of the other people among whom they live." In confirmation of this view R. N. Salaman says: "The purity of the Jewish race is imaginary. The widest variety of ethnic types is found among Jews, ranging, as regard cranial conformation only, from brachycephalics to hyperdolichocephalics. More particularly in Germany and Russia, there are Jews who do not display the smallest Semitic characteristics."

Thus, despite the view usually held, the Jewish people is racially heterogeneous. Its constant migrations and its relations, voluntary or otherwise, with the widest variety of nations and peoples have brought about such a degree of intermixture that the so-called people of Israel can produce examples of traits typical of all groups. For proof it will suffice to compare the rubicund, sturdy, heavily-built Rotterdam Jew with his co-religionist, say, in Salonika, with thin, frail physique, pale skin and dark eyes. Hence, so far as our knowledge now goes, we can assert that Jews as a whole display as great a degree of morphological disparity among themselves as could be found between members of two or more different nations.

This raises a problem. If, scientifically speaking, it can readily be demonstrated that the Jewish people is heterogeneous and that there is no such thing as a Jewish race, how is it that in fact some Jews can be identified as such? The probable explanation is that individuals professing the same religion or pertaining to a closely-knit group, attain a degree of similarity in gestures, habits, dress, etc., which facilitates their identification. Among the Jews, whose rites and customs are extremely rigid, this outward similarity arising from their ethnographic, linguistic and religious affinities, is strongly marked though quite unconnected with the variety of morphological types making up that people.

Proof of this is the fact that we fail to notice and identify a much larger number of Jews who have taken on the traits of the people among whom they live and thus pass unnoticed.

There is therefore, no foundation for the claim that there is a Jewish race, and consequently no anti-Semitic attitudes can find a valid basis for support in such a biological myth.

THE MYTH OF ''ARYAN'' OR ''NORDIC'' SUPERIORITY

Racists were not content with proclaiming the "superiority" of white over colored races nor with discriminating against Jews nor even with combatting miscegenation and asserting *a priori* that it led to racial degeneration. They also felt it necessary to erect biological and psychological hierarchies within the white race itself in an attempt to justify new rights of conquest, domination and overlordship vested in a still more exclusive caste.

That is the origin of "Aryanism" or "Nordicism" as a basic doctrine of racial superiority. The Aryan myth is the common source of other secondary myths, Germanism, Anglo-Saxonism, and Celticism, which evolved concurrently in Germany, England, the United States and France.

The first to propound the theory of an aristocracy of "German blood" was Count Henri de Boulainvilliers (1658–1722), but it was Arthur de Gobineau who laid down the doctrine of "Aryanism" in all its fullness and proclaimed the superiority of the "Aryan race" over the other white strains. His ideas had a considerable influence on philosophical and political thought in Europe and from the first he was well known in Germany, where he made contact with Richard Wagner who helped spread his ideas.

Gobineau is not very definite as to the characteristics or traits of "Aryans." They may be brachycephalic or dolichocephalic; the eyes are usually light in color, but may be dark or even black (it should be remembered that he himself was a dark-eyed Frenchman). It is his followers who ascribe to the exclusively "Aryan" type, tallness, blue eyes, fair hair and long heads with the following psychic qualities as well: virility; innate nobility; natural aggressiveness; imperturbable objectivity; dislike of useless words and vain rhetoric; distaste for the amorphous mass; precise intelligence; spirit of independence; sternness towards themselves and others; well-developed sense of responsibility; great foresight;

tenacity of will; qualities of a race of leaders, men of great undertakings and large and well-thought-out ideas, etc.

Houston S. Chamberlain, a pro-German Englishman and son-in-law of Richard Wagner, was the keenest supporter of the racist theory of the "blond, dolichocephalic Nordic." He adopted the terms "Teutonic race" and "Teuton blood," thus giving a frankly nationalistic twist to Gobineau's class thesis. He goes on to assert, "where the Germanic element has not penetrated, there is no civilization in our sense."

Anthroposociology and Social Selection. This school of thought, introduced by G. Vacher de Lapouge in France and Otto Ammon in Germany, is a special variant of "racial determinism" based on statistical research of considerable interest in itself, but the results of which were interpreted in conformity with the preconceived idea of "the superiority of the blond dolichocephalic type." Certain of the conclusions may be summed up as follows:

1. In countries of mixed blood, wealth increases in inverse ratio to the cephalic index, i.e., individuals with a lower cephalic index (dolichocephalics) are richer.

2. City-dwellers are predominantly dolichocephalic whereas brachycephalics are dominant in rural areas.

3. Urban life exercises a selective influence unfavorable to brachycephalic elements.

4. There is a greater tendency to dolichocephalism in the higher than in the lower classes. Competition for the higher social positions tends to eliminate brachycephalics, who are more frequently found among workmen.

5. Since prehistoric times there has been a steady increase in the cephalic index in Europe. Lapouge, accordingly, forecast the extinction of the "blond dolichocephalic" and a subsequent Dark Age in the world.

All the above hypotheses are based simply and solely on the so-called Ammon's Law which asserts the concentration of dolichocephalics in the city and their social "superiority" to brachycephalics.

The work of Livi in Italy, Olóriz in Spain, Beddoe in England and Houzé in Belgium demonstrated the falsity not only of Ammon's Law but also of the over-hasty deductions made by its supporters.

In fact, somatic study of people classed as intellectuals in the different countries would show the utmost variety of combinations of the anthropological traits attributed to the different so-called primitive races. We accordingly see that the theories and data put forward by anthroposociologists are obviously contradictory and prove nothing as to the alleged "intellectual superiority of the dolichocephalics." Nor have they been able to confirm that the alleged selective influence of the great cities on newcomers operates according to the shape of the skull, and even less that the proportion of dolichocephalics is higher in the "superior classes."

In 1894, belief in the God-ordained superiority of Germany became a quasireligious cult with the foundation in Freiburg under the chairmanship of L. Schemann of the "Gobineau Vereinigung." Hence the doctrines of "race purity" and "race superiority" attained much greater importance in Germany than elsewhere, and finally became a credo, already dangerous by the time of the first world war. While the German leaders stirred up popular frenzy for the defence of Teutonic culture and its propagation among the other "less civilized" races of Europe, these replied in turn that the German "blonds" were not Europeans but of Asiatic origin and descendants of the Huns, who lacked all the elements of true culture, were without the slightest notion of the concept of liberty and democracy, and deserved extermination to the last man.

In connection with the non-existence of the "Aryan" or "Nordic" type, there is an historical anecdote worth recalling. Before 1914, William II wished a racial map of Germany to be produced displaying the incidence of the "Aryan" element. When the data were assembled they could not be published because heterogeneity was so marked, and in entire regions such as Baden there were no Nordics.

One of the theorists of Hitlerite racism, F. K. Günther described the Alpine type as psychologically "specially fitted to end up as the muddle-headed owner of a cottage and a patch of garden," while the Alpine woman will turn into a "faded little creature growing old in a debased and narrow world"; Alpines according to him are "petty criminals, small-time swindlers, sneak-thieves and sexual perverts." Nordics on the other hand are "capable of the nobler crimes." However, there are racist fanatics even wilder than Günther. According to H. Gauch, the difference in anatomical and histological structure (hair, bones, teeth and tegument) between man and animals is less than that between Nordics and other human races; only Nordics possess perfect articulate speech; only in Nordics do we find the correct biped position, etc. He ends by suggesting that a strict line should be drawn between "Nordic" man and the animal world, the latter comprising all non-Nordic humanity.

The alleged somatic uniformity of the Anglo-Saxon race can be as readily exploded. If North Americans were direct descendants of the Pilgrim Fathers, and if England at that period could be considered an exclusively Anglo-Saxon country, there might be some basis for a thesis as to this type's "purity." It has been said that "the Teutonic invaders exterminated all the native inhabitants of England in a glorious universal slaughter." The truth is, however, that the Teuton conquerors were no more than a new element in the racial complex of the British Isles, and they themselves were very far from being morphologically homogeneous.

As far as the United States is concerned, there is no doubt whatsoever that the original settlers in New England were drawn from many different strata of English society and accordingly presented great physical differences. Both height and cephalic index present a considerable degree of variability in the English people. F. G. Parsons proved statistically that while over 25% showed the combination of dark eyes and brown or black hair, no more than 20% had light eyes and blond hair, and the most frequent combination was light eyes and dark hair, though there were individuals with dark eyes and blond hair. No evidence is to be found in the British Isles, and *a fortiori* even less in the United States, to justify the alleged identification of the "Anglo-Saxon" race with either nation.

"Celticism," another variant of "Aryanism," is one of the fruits of strong nationalist tendency which developed in France after the war of 1870. It asserts that France was inhabited by the Celtic type to which distinctive somato-psychic characteristics are ascribed that make it "superior" to the rest of the white groups.

A. de Quatrefages holds that the racial descent of the Prussians is entirely different from that of the French and concludes: "There is nothing Aryan about the Prussians." In 1871, Broca affirmed that France was a nation of brachycephalic (Alpine) Gauls and maintained the superiority of that strain over the dolichocephalic German "Nordic." Isaac Taylor, was another scientist who held that the Celts were a tall, brachycephalic race and the only Aryans.

Numerous investigators recognize that

"Celt" is a historical term used to designate peoples speaking related languages and presenting every morphological variety from short, dark dolichocephalics through moderately fair brachycephalics of medium height, to tall blond dolichocephalics. However, these entirely correct observations have had little influence on mentalities imbued with "racism." To sum up, if the shape of the skull, stature and color of eyes, hair and skin are taken into account, it becomes evident that morphologically, the French people were and are amazingly heterogeneous. The fundamental error of "Aryanism" or "Nordicism" in all its forms stems from a general confusion of ideas which is very widespread but unscientific by any reckoning. The term race is used by them indifferently as a synonym for language and nation.

It has already been pointed out that the term "race" has an exclusively biological significance. Nevertheless, the terms "Latin race," "Slav race," "German race" and of course "Aryan race" are in common use, and thus, men fall into the error of regarding human groups that are only linguistically homogenous, as anthropologically uniform.

F. Max Müller himself, who was one of the first to use the term "Aryan race," abjured its biological interpretation and reemphasized its purely linguistic significance. He wrote: "To me, an ethnologist who speaks of Aryan race, Aryan blood, Aryan eyes and hair, is as great a sinner as a linguist who speaks of a dolichocephalic dictionary or a brachycephalic grammar." However, the concept of the "Aryan race" had become so widespread that Müller's retraction was without practical effect.

The best illustration of this is to be found in the United States, whose 170 million citizens are a new type to which a multitude of races from all points of the world have contributed. The main strains of the population range from tall, long-skulled blonds (Nordic), through short, subbrachycephalic blonds (Eastern European), to tall, dark-skinned dolichocephalics (Atlantic-Mediterranean), all speaking English. Thus, there are a number of somatically distinct groups with a common language, to say nothing of the large numbers of citizens of Negro, Amerindian and Chinese stock.

In other words, a nation may consist of more than one race, while, conversely, biologically similar groups may be subdivided into separate nations. The inhabitants of North Germany bear more resemblance to the people of Denmark and Sweden than to the people of South Germany, while the latter are physically akin to parts of the population of France, Czechoslovakia and Yugoslavia. How then is it possible to speak of German, Aryan or Anglo-Saxon "races?"

It is in the strictly morphological field that the incongruities are greatest. Research into skull shape and other characteristics of individuals or groups regarded as authentic "Aryans," "Teutons," "Anglo-Saxons" and "Celts" has shown considerable variation throughout history as well as in our own day. Contradictions reached their peak when Chamberlain, who had described the "blond Teuton" type, concluded by denying that anthropometry had any value because it could give no indication of superiority. He admits that "the Teutons of antiquity were not all dolichocephalic giants," but . . . "a careful examination would show us that all of them possess the specific characteristics of the German people both physically and mentally." He then asserts that this subjective observation "teaches more than can be learned in an anthropological congress."

In view of the physical heterogeneity of the supposed "Nordic" or "Aryan" (a good example of this would be an individual "as tall as Goebbels, as blond as Hitler and as slim as Goering"), Nazism cast aside every pretence of biological justification for its imperialistic doctrine of economic subjugation of other peoples and reached the conclusion that "a Nordic soul may be joined to a non-Nordic body," and that "the Nordic man may be recognized by his deeds and not by the length of his nose or the color of his eyes." [2]

It is clear that in racism the physical criterion is a mere smoke screen, abandoned as useless when the circumstances of the moment require. Racism then says, "the differentiation of the human races is not a matter of science; it is by immediate perception that we recognize emotionally the differences we call racial." In the view of W. Gross: "Politics cannot wait until science has worked out a racial theory; politics must outstrip science with the intuitive basic truth of the diversity of blood between peoples and with its logical consequence, the principle of rule by the most gifted."

Thus the origin of racism is not scientific but political. Ruth Benedict put it in correct terms when she said: "No distortion of anthropomorphic facts is too absurd to be used by propaganda backed by force and the concentration camp."

The existence of individual somatic and psychic differences is a fact. In every race, nation, class or community, better and worse endowed individuals can be found. This is a biological reality to which there are no exceptions. However, such variations are completely unconnected with alleged superiority or inferiority of specific human groups.

The growing discontent of the peoples of India, the development of racial feeling among the Negroes of Africa, and the self-confidence displayed by the Japanese, Chinese and Indonesian peoples, are among the many proofs that the races hitherto despised for their supposed inferiority are every day less ready to accept judgments on their qualities passed by certain elements in the white race.

Democracy recognizes the existence of differences among men, but considers that they all possess the same inalienable rights, and seeks to afford them equal political, social and economic opportunities.

Totalitarianism also accepts the differences between men and peoples as inevitable but holds that they imply the principle of obedience to the will of a "master race" expressed through "superior men." Its concern is to enslave all who are capable of falling in with the will of the "masters" and to exterminate all those who resist being made units in a totalitarian world.

The racist myths of the twentieth century must give the appearance that they are based on science even though, according to M. Prenant, it may be "at the price of the most shameless falsifications." Racism has sought to take over anthropology, the physiology of the blood, the laws of heredity, etc., and use them for its own ends. But all its efforts have been in vain.

Race prejudice may arise from economic and political causes, from a particular race's superiority or inferiority complex, from biological differences or from combinations of various of these. In every case it is always abetted by the tendency to accept theories and hypotheses without the slightest critical examination.

It is necessary to demonstrate the absurdity of regarding human groups en bloc as "completely good" or "completely bad." Science, democratic beliefs and humanitarian feeling are at one in rejecting the condemnation of any man on grounds of race, color or social condition.

Racism is quite a different matter from mere observation of the facts about race and the present inequality of human groups or from the objective, scientific study of the subject. Racism implies the

[2] *Nationalsozialistische Korrespondenz*, June, 1936.

affirmation that this inequality is absolute and unconditional, i.e., that one race is inherently and by its very nature superior or inferior to others quite independently of the physical conditions of environment and social factors.

The last half century has seen the development of exaggerated nationalism. The horrors of war and the anxieties of an armed peace are doing much to maintain it. The elimination of racial myths through individual and collective conviction can exert a powerful influence toward bringing about a better spirit of understanding in human relations.

PART TWO

ARCHAEOLOGY

Probably because of the fascination of its subject matter, archaeology is, popularly, the best known field in anthropology. Many people think of the two terms as synonymous—that digging up the past in some remote part of the world is what all anthropologists do. Although this is not correct, it is true that the task of the archaeologist is frequently fascinating, not because of the romantic appeal of the artifacts themselves or of the exotic places they are uncovered, but because of the questions they help to answer. All the digging and the analysis of what is dug up must be related ultimately to a single profoundly simple question: how does culture work? What have been the processes of cultural development in the past? How does understanding this relate to a comprehension of the way cultures are developing at present? And what basis does all this provide for predicting the course of cultural development in the future?

The crude stone hatchet, the old Indian arrowhead, or the dusty remnant of broken pot are not of interest in themselves. It is rather the significance of the disinterred artifacts of ancient peoples that is of final importance, that is, what such objects can tell us about the rest of the culture of which they were a material part.

An important basic premise underlies the effort to answer questions such as these. It is that the aspects of culture are not related as random pieces of

207

a haphazard collection, but as historically connected functioning components of an integrated whole. This means that significant correlations are assumed to exist between a people's material goods, their technology, and the other aspects of their culture, both tangible and intangible. The old stone hatchet, the Indian arrowhead, or the broken remnant of pottery are clues. The archaeologist tries to ascertain how the hatchet was made and what it was used for. This will help to indicate how the people who used it made a living. Then, through careful analysis, he can often develop a reasonably accurate picture of their economic, social, and political systems, and of their religion and art.

THE STUDY OF THE PAST

The job of excavation has just begun. The dusty remains of ancient ways of life still have much to tell us. Uncovering them and piecing together their stories is the archaeologist's arduous, but intriguing, task.

1. The Dimensions of Archaeology [1]

This paper is an attempt to describe clearly the fundamental operations of archaeology on its empirical data. Behavioral inferences may creep in, but they will be evidence of weak-mindedness. The goal is most definitely not a lecture on how archaeology ought to be done; it is rather a description of what is done when exposition is incisive, economical, and convincing. The topic is particularly suitable for a volume honoring Leslie White, whose major work has been the systematic exposition of interrelationships of cultural phenomena. A great gain

---

[1] ALBERT C. SPAULDING, "The Dimensions of Archaeology," in *Essays in the Science of Culture*, Gertrude E. Dole and Robert L. Carneiro (eds.) (New York: 1960), pp. 437–456. Reprinted by permission of the author and the publisher, © 1960 by Thomas Y. Crowell Company.

Dr. Spaulding is Professor of Anthropology at the University of Oregon.

would result if my purpose could be realized fully: questions of fact would be sharply separated from questions of theory, thus pointing accurately to those topics on which factual data are needed and providing a guide for research along the most effective lines. Since all the matters discussed here are essentially common·knowledge I have not provided any references.

METHOD OF ANALYSIS

I assume that on an elementary level we cannot improve on the concepts that are successful in other branches of science, especially in the physical sciences, which enjoy a long tradition of enviable precision and clarity, at least when viewed from the outside. These sciences can be thought of as studying the interrelationships of the dimensions appropriate to their specified subject matter. The subject of mechanics, for example, is physical objects, and the dimensions in terms of which the objects are considered are length, mass, and time. Classical mechanics can be defined economically as the study of the interrelationships of length, mass, and time exhibited by physical objects. Thermodynamics, on the other hand, can be considered a more complicated science because it deals with temperature in addition to the three dimensions of mechanics. A dimension can be thought of as an aspect or property of the subject matter which requires its own special measuring device. There are invariable rules for operating with dimensions (the examples given are not logically independent), of which we can mention:

1. The units of discrete dimensions do not possess additive properties. Any formulation of the type $L + T = x$ or $L = T$ (feet plus minutes equals x, or feet equals minutes) or "the artifact is older than it is heavy" is meaningless.

2. Ratios of discrete dimensions, usually called rates, are meaningful, famiilar examples being miles per hour or pounds per cubic foot.

3. Concepts involving more than one application of the measuring instrument can be meaningful. Thus area is length squared, and volume is length cubed.

4. Dimensional equations must be homogeneous, that is, the same dimensions must appear on both sides of the equation. However, dimensionless numbers may be introduced into such equations.

DIMENSIONS OF ARCHAEOLOGY

It seems quite clear that the subject matter of archaeology is artifacts, using this term in its broadest sense as any material expression of human cultural activity and adding the qualification that I am concerned here with prehistoric artifacts. Although deciding whether or not a particular object is an artifact may be difficult, I will treat the artifact as given in this discussion for reasons of economy. The dimensions of artifacts which will be considered here are form (in the sense of any physico-chemical property of the artifact), temporal locus (meaning the dating of prehistoric events as inferred from atrifacts, specifically the time of manufacture, period of use, and time of deposition of an artifact or a class of artifacts), and spatial locus (the position of the artifact in the three-dimensional world). There is, I believe, general agreement that archaeologists are always concerned with these properties of artifacts and there is an implication that archaeology can be defined minimally as the study of the interrelationship of form, temporal locus, and spatial locus exhibited by artifacts. In other words, archaeologists are always concerned with these interrelationships, whatever broader interests they may have, and these interrelationships are the special business of archaeology.

All of the rules for operation with dimensions apply to form, time, and space, and certain theoretical formulations can be dismissed at once on this basis. A statement of the type "the focus concept contains more of form than it does of time (or space)" is equivalent to the dimensional equation $F + T = x$, which is dimensionally heterogeneous and hence meaningless. Presumably what is involved here is a statement of the idea that a group of artifact assemblages having a high degree of formal resemblance to each other will usually or invariably show a compact clustering in time and in space, or in dimensional terms:

$$\left[\frac{F_1}{T_1} = \frac{F_2}{T_2} \right]$$

The dimensional equation (put in brackets to indicate that it is not algebraic) states that a systematic relationship holds between degree of formal resemblance and length of time span; since form and time appear on both sides of the equation, it is homogeneous and can be given a determinate meaning. This illustration is intended to show that reasoning in terms of dimensional analysis can be something more than a sterile formality: it can be a safeguard against unclear thinking or exposition. The dimensional equation also points directly to a very real archaeological problem: if we are to substitute real data for the symbols of the equation, then we must develop objective scales for our dimensions.

The Formal Dimension. It is plain that the formal dimension cannot be dealt with by the application of any simple kind of scale, although it is a useful concept for broad theorizing. In practice formal descriptions and comparisons are made by analyzing artifact form into a number of discrete attribute systems: color, chemical composition, weight, various lengths (and the length relationships which describe shape), and so on. These attribute systems can be treated as dimensions in their own right, and from this point of view the formal dimension is a class of dimensions. I will not attempt more than a glance at some of the obvious characteristics of formal attributes.

Formal attributes can be divided into two classes, quantitative attributes (or measurements) and qualitative attributes. Quantitative attributes, weight and length for example, vary continuously, and they can be measured by ordinary scaling devices divided into equal units. Artifacts can be compared absolutely in terms of these measurements, that is, the difference between two artifacts can be expressed in equal units of the appropriate scale (x is 25 pounds heavier than y). Relative comparisons are also possible (x is twice as long as y) if the zero point of the scale is not arbitrary. To borrow an example from another dimension, it cannot be said that Hopewell is twice as old as Middle Mississippi because the age relationship is merely a function of an arbitrarily chosen reference point in time. Quantitative attributes can be described neatly in scale units, and the numerical properties of the measurements lend themselves to straightforward statistical description and inference.

Qualitative attributes cannot be described and compared by means of any familiar scaling device. They are thought of as discrete properties of artifacts, and the scale applied is no more than a notation of presence or absence. Recognition of the qualitative attributes of an artifact seems to be largely intuitive. The observer has a personal knowledge of human musculature and sensory apparatus and of the properties of materials, and he can judge at once that the addition of a pair of side notches to a flint projectile point represents a discrete segment of the total behavior involved in making the point. Qualitative attributes which are mutually exclusive can be grouped into a dimension; thus the projectile point may be made from white flint, argillite, or some other material. This grouping provides a three-position scale within the dimension of material for describing the point and for classifying a collection of points.

In an ultimate sense, the distinction between quantitative and qualitative attributes tends to break down because any real measuring instrument must be divided into discrete steps, however small they may be. Nevertheless, the distinction remains in practice; the fineness of recorded measurements is limited only by the precision of the measuring instrument and the nature of the number system in which the records are kept, but the nature of the attribute itself limits the observation of the qualitative attribute. It is sometimes possible to transform ostensibly qualitative attributes into continuously variable properties, as when personal judgments of shades of color are replaced by measurements with physical appartus, and the resulting gain in objectivity may prove to be valuable. However, the essentially discrete nature of many attributes is plain enough to make such a translation superfluous for many purposes, and a wholesale attempt to replace with measurements the current presence-or-absence observation of recognized attributes would have no utility. No one questions the reasonableness or objectivity of describing a vessel as having four strap handles and contrasting it with other vessels having two or no strap handles.

The distinction between quantitative and qualitative attributes is operationally relevant in a fundamental archaeological problem, the preparation of an attribute list for the formal description of a collection of artifacts. The very nature of quantitative attributes ensures that no two artifacts will yield exactly the same measurement, but it is necessary to discriminate between the unimportant and presumably random variation expected

of products made by hand from materials which are not uniform and the culturally meaningful variation resulting from significantly differing models held by the makers of the artifacts. The problem can be attacked by listing in order the individual values of some measurement (say projectile point length) in a collection. If the list seems to show a pronounced clustering of values around a central point with progressively fewer values toward the extremes of the observed range, the conclusion ordinarily reached will be that the variation is of the random type. If, on the other hand, there are two or more values around which the measurements cluster, then two or more categories will be distinguished, and each can be thought of as a separate qualitative attribute such as "large" and "small." The problem is purely statistical, although in many instances it can be solved by inspection rather than by formal statistical curve fitting.

Qualitative attributes are by definition those properties of artifacts which are already recognized as representing discrete segments of behavior, and accordingly they can be placed on the attribute list without further analysis. Subsequent study may show that a supposed qualitative attribute can in fact be split into two or more meaningful classes; for example, a description of a motif as an incised triangle may disguise a significant difference between large and small or scalene and isosceles triangles. Conversely, some distinctions may be quite objective but turn out to have a sharply limited utility for the purpose of describing significant variations in patterns of attribute association. Thus triangles, rectangles, or circles might appear as decorative elements on a group of otherwise identical pots, and on this basis it would make sense to group them as a class of geometrical decorative elements. These qualifications are essentially secondary, however, and do not override the basic distinction of continuity *versus* discontinuity which is the root of the quantitative-qualitative division.

Techniques for recognizing formal attributes logically precede the next problem, that of studying artifact interrelationships in terms of formal attributes. For this problem, the recognized attributes serve as linking constants from artifact to artifact: they are the units whose presences and absences constitute similarity or difference. In some respects attributes are analogous to linguistic phonemes. They represent minimal units of meaningful behavior; they are taken to be constant for comparative and descriptive purposes; and they are articulated to form the artifact, which can be regarded as the minimal independent unit of material culture. In the simplest terms, the problem is what to do with a collection of artifacts and a list of formal attributes which the artifacts exhibit. There appear to be three possibilities in ordering a collection of artifacts with respect to their formal attributes:

1. The collection can be characterized by tallying each appearance of every attribute recognized.

2. The particular combination of attributes exhibited by each artifact can be listed, and the list can be condensed by grouping and tallying identical combinations.

3. The artifacts can be classified in terms of attribute clusters; this is accomplished by mathematical manipulation of the data provided by Types 1 and 2. This process is referred to here as cluster analysis.

Classification of Type I results in a number of classes having no relationship to one another except that imposed by the nature of the attribute systems. The description offered by such a classification is of the general type: red pots, 50; other colors, 50; grit tempered pots, 35; sand tempered pots, 65; bowls, 30; jars, 30;

plates, 40; and so on. Tallies in sets of mutually exclusive attributes must sum to the total number of artifacts, but no other relationship is expressed. The information on relationships furnished by the physical association of attributes on the individual artifacts is wasted; we are told in the example that 35 of the 100 pots are grit tempered, but we do not know how many grit tempered pots are red.

Classification of Type 2 requires a list of all observed attribute combinations as the categories within which the individual specimens are tallied. It contains all the information presented by the attribute count plus full information on attribute association. The categories of combinations divide the entire collection according to one principle so that there is no question of which of two or more possible piles a specimen belongs to. In short, it is a complete descriptive classification which wastes no information, although its completeness is, of course, relative to the adequacy of the underlying attribute list. However, some unexploited analytic possibilities involving the relationships of attribute and attribute combination frequencies remain, and these are dealt with by the Type 3 classification.

Classification of the third type, cluster analysis, is dependent on the data of the second, and it is specifically concerned with such questions as how many of the red jars are grit tempered. Its basic feature is the comparison of the observed count for each attribute combination with the count expected on a hypothesis of attribute independence. These comparisons result in a rating on a continuous scale for each attribute combination along the lines of less than expected, about the same as expected, and more than expected. The reasoning involved is more easily exemplified than stated abstractly. Calculation of the expected tally for a particular combination under the hypothesis of independence uses only the attribute frequencies. In the example given, we can ask how many red grit tempered jars can be expected if these attributes are independent. In the total of 100 pots, 50 are red, 35 are grit tempered, and 30 are jars; if these attributes have no tendency to stick together, we can calculate that $(50/100) \times (35/100) \times (30/100) \times 100 = 5.25$ red grit tempered jars will be expected. The observed tally for the combination can range from 0 to 30 pots under the conditions specified. If the tally is actually 0, it would appear that the combination was avoided by the maker of the pots; a tally of 5 or 6 would suggest that the combination was neither avoided nor sought after; and a tally of 25 or 30 would indicate a strong tendency to group the three attributes. The last case illustrates what is meant here by an attribute cluster—a strong positive association of two or more attributes. I have ignored for the sake of clarity the sampling uncertainties which are so troublesome in real problems.

So far as I can see, classification with respect to attribute clusters exploits fully the formal information presented by a collection of artifacts since it interrelates the entire list of discriminated attributes in terms of both attribute frequency and attribute combination frequency. In my opinion, it also offers an explicit, operationally useful model of the relationships comprised under the concept of artifact type. A distinctive cluster of attributes is the consistent pattern central to the idea of type in both ordinary usage and discussions in archaeological literature. Cluster analysis is simply a full-dress exposition of the reasoning implied in the shorthand statement that type classifications are accomplished by putting together the artifacts that look alike. It is important to note that cluster analysis does not create clusters when they are not implied by the empirical data, it does not of itself explain the cultural meaning of the clusters (or lack of them) revealed by the analysis, and it will not necessarily assign every artifact to a typological pigeon hole: some artifacts may be genuinely intermediate between two clusters and others may be aberrant hangers-on of a reasonably well-defined type. It is equally important to realize that artifact types are not necessarily the most convenient and economical units for investigating possible systematic formal relationships in a set of collections; for this purpose simple attribute or attribute combination relative frequencies may serve as well.

When a formal analysis of two or more collections has been completed, comparisons in terms of the attribute list, the attribute combination list, and the type list are possible. These orders of comparison provide increasingly sensitive scales of similarity. Thus on a presence-or-absence basis two components may have identical attribute lists but not identical attribute combination lists, and they may have identical attribute combination lists but not identical artifact types.

Still more sensitive comparisons are possible when category frequencies (reduced to proportions so as to provide standard values for collections of varying sizes) are considered. Obviously it may be possible to detect valid differences between two collections on the basis of attribute frequencies even though both possess the same list of attributes. Somewhat less obvious is the fact that two collections may differ in attribute combination frequencies although they have the same attribute list, identical attribute frequencies, and identical attribute combination lists. This situation is illustrated in Table 1, in which three sets of attributes are symbolized by letters and subscripts with a total of 100 specimens and the following frequencies assumed for two collections:

A_1	35	B_1	50	C_1	25
A_2	65	B_2	50	C_2	75
	100		100		100

Comparison of attribute combination frequencies is, in fact, the most sensitive possible because the combination tallies are a complete enumeration of the formal empirical data. Comparisons of type frequencies in the sense of the type concept used here would not add information to the formal likeness scale because any difference in the attribute clusters must be a reflection of differences in combination frequencies. The artifact type has no special value for formal combination, although it does express objectively relationships inherent in or implied by the data. The attribute associations (or lack of them) revealed by cluster analysis are already contained, so to speak, in the attribute combination tallies. Cluster analysis brings into the open relationships which in many cases do not by any means leap to the eye from a simple inspection of the combination tallies; its purpose is to provide a basis for a culturally significant interpretation of differences in combination frequencies by ordering already existing data in a new way. It provides an escape from the dilemma of regarding everything as arbitrary (in which case "arbitrary" is robbed of any definite meaning) or neatly packaged (which is manifestly not true).

blage is more complex than a Lamoka assemblage is usually not the result of a formal calculation, but it is plain that a simple comparison of the number of attributes, attribute combinations, or types in the two entities would support the judgment. If one were willing to assume that any attribute has about the same complexity as any other attribute, an attribute count would offer an objective measure of formal complexity. A second kind of over-all characterization can be made in terms of the degree of attribute clustering shown by a collection. This sort of characterization in non-mathematical idiom takes the form of describing a collection in some such terms as rigidly stylized as opposed to unconstrained or imaginative. Possible mathematical devices to objectify judgments of this sort need not concern us in detail. A very simple example would be the ratio of observed attribute combinations to possible attribute combinations, and more complex statements based on contingency tables could be worked out.

The Spatial Dimension. Scaling of artifact loci is a familiar operation. It means no more than the application of a yardstick in the three ordinary direc-

TABLE 1. VARIATION IN ATTRIBUTE COMBINATION FREQUENCIES IN TWO COLLECTIONS

	Collection I						Collection II				
	A_1		A_2				A_1		A_2		
	B_1	B_2	B_1	B_2	Total		B_1	B_2	B_1	B_2	Total
C_1	15	8	1	1	25	C_1	3	2	9	11	25
C_2	10	2	24	39	75	C_2	15	15	23	22	75
Total	25	10	25	40	100	Total	18	17	32	33	100

Over-all characterization and comparison of collections of artifacts can be conducted at a still more generalized level at which the entire body of empirical formal data is replaced by a single number. Ranking in terms of complexity is a familiar example. The basis for judging that, for example, a Hopewell assem-

tions of space to produce the latitude, longitude, and depth measurements which define a point uniquely. Spatial attributes in this sense are given; the measuring instrument can be applied directly to the artifact *in situ,* and the resulting measurements can be recorded and analyzed with the aid of all the techniques appropriate to a continuous variable.

There are, however, certain circumstances under which spatial units are given special meaning. These are the cases where artifacts occur in some sort of container, and there is consequently a relationship between them which goes beyond mere propinquity. The container may be culturally produced, examples being the grave goods of a single burial, a group of artifacts in a cache or storage pit, or the contents of a room in a pueblo. Here the entire collection of associated artifacts becomes a descriptive and comparative unit, and the spatial interrelationships of the component artifacts are presented in a formal description of the unit as a sort of superartifact. The container may be provided by natural action —a single gravel lens in a stream deposit, a stratum of debris sealed by a layer of volcanic ash, and so on—or it may be the result of combined cultural and natural activity, as in the case of strata produced by the abandonment of a site, development of an erosion surface, and reoccupation. These situations do not differ theoretically from that of the culturally produced container; the component artifacts again become a special unit of association, and for many purposes the significant spatial measurement may be simply whether a given artifact is within or outside of the container. When these special association units are present, spatial observations are interpreted in the light of the physical laws of superposition and intrusion applied to the contents of the entire unit. On the other hand, when visible strata or other boundaries yielding association units within an archaeological deposit are not present, the analysis of spatial relationships becomes an example of the general case. Thus the interpretation of vertical relationships in a massive deposit is a function of the actual vertically scaled position of each artifact.

Aside from these examples of special association, space scaling yields a set of coordinates on a continuously variable scale as another sort of attribute for each artifact, and collections of artifacts are characterized by lists of coordinate sets. One of the primary results of the analysis of such data is so obvious that it is usually thought of as simple observation rather than analysis. This result is the recognition of the very strong tendency for artifacts to occur in tight spatial clusters, that is, in archaeological sites. The site is ordinarily taken to be a given, and the assemblage of artifacts from a site is the customary unit of description and comparison. In many cases the vertical component is treated as if it were negligible; indeed, there is no other course for surface collections or thin deposits. If adequate vertical segregation is present, however, the site may be divided into two or more assemblages.

Actual techniques for analysis of the spatial coordinates of artifacts need not be described in full detail for the purposes of this paper. When strata or other boundaries giving immediately observable units are not present, the deposit can be divided into arbitrarily defined blocks for cluster analysis along the general lines discussed earlier. Excavations are often arranged to give such blocks immediately on the assumption that measuring the individual artifact coordinates would produce needlessly refined data. Such techniques in effect transform the quantitative space attributes into qualitative attributes for ease of control and statistical manipulation. It is possible to work directly with the individual coordinates treated as continuous variables if the underlying information is available and if it is judged that the expected gain in precision justifies the additional work. Finally, assemblages can be described and compared in terms of over-all size and configuration.

The Temporal Dimension. Time itself is a continuum sensed as a succession of events. There are two types of time scales, relative and absolute. Relative time scaling is simply ranking an event as before or after some other event. Absolute time scaling means placing an event with respect to a sequence of events which are thought to occur at regular intervals and which are given a standard designation by reference to an arbitrarily chosen initial point. Our absolute scale is, of course, the calendar. As I noted above, all calendars are reckoned from an arbitrary starting period so that in a strict sense relative comparisons in terms of the calendar (x is twice as old as y) are not possible, although absolute comparisons (x is 500 years older than y) are. We can also make absolute and relative comparisons of time intervals between events and in consequence can make rate-of-change comparisons in relative terms. These aspects of chronology suggest that some confusion might be avoided if we adopt the term "time ranking" for the major type of time scale called "relative" above and generally referred to as relative chronology.

Since time scaling refers to events, not things, it is apparent that the temporal attributes of a prehistoric artifact must be prehistoric events whose occurrence is implied by the formal and spatial attributes of the artifact. The prehistoric events usually thought of as archaeologically significant—the targets of chronological inference—are the manufacture and primary deposition of the artifact. In most instances no serious question is asked about the time interval separating these two events; the general uncertainties of chronological scaling are such that the interval can be treated as negligible without serious difficulty. When the unit considered is a spatial cluster (an assemblage) of artifacts, as is usually the case, the question becomes still more complicated because a large number of events is involved. Here the goal is to define the assemblage so that the events represented by the component artifacts form a sufficiently tight cluster in time to permit the inference that no marked cultural changes took place during the time interval between the first and last events implied.

An equally plain consequence of the nature of chronological attributes is the fact that they cannot be observed directly in the way that formal and spatial characteristics can. All chronological judgments are inferences made by interpreting spatial and formal attributes in the light of physical, biological, or cultural principles. We have mentioned above the physical principles of superposition and intrusion, which allow spatial attributes to be transformed into temporal ranking. Similarly, measurement of radioactivity permits an estimate of absolute chronology based on a formal property of the artifact. These and other noncultural principles are of the highest importance because they provide a method of studying culture change over time without prior assumptions about the nature of cultural change. In short, they offer raw material for the construction of cultural theories. On the other hand, chronological judgments obtained by application of culturally derived theories of change merely illustrate what is meant by the theories; the judgments will be sound if the theories are sound and are applied correctly, but they will not be independent contributions to cultural theory. Thus one can arrange a group of assemblages in order of formal complexity of some class of artifacts common to all and infer that this arrangement is also a chronological ordering, but this procedure demonstrates nothing about formal changes in time because the ordering is a product of a prior theory about such changes.

A few remarks about chronological periods are probably in order here because of some apparent confusion in the literature and in archaeological discussions. It seems plain enough that a chronological period can be defined uniquely only by specifying unique sequent events for its boundaries in time. Nevertheless, examples of time periods defined by criteria which are actually an ambiguous succession of events are by no means unknown, and they have led to misunderstandings. Such "cultural periods" seem to have their origin in the observation that a number of assemblages in some geographical area have several artifact types in common while a number of other assemblages are characterized by quite different sets of types. In symbolic terms, there are *ABCD* sites (letters standing for types) and *EFGH* sites, and, since the spatial factor is limited, the observer falls into the habit of thinking of an *ABCD* period and *EFGH* period without further analysis. Sooner or later, however, a *CDEF* assemblage turns up, and it becomes apparent that something is wrong with the supposed chronological division. The new assemblage belongs to both or neither of the two original periods, and a new scheme is called for. This difficulty could have been avoided at the outset by more careful definition delineating a true division of time. If it is known that type *A* appeared before type *E*, then the periods could have been defined as: (1) from the appearance of type *A* to the appearance of type *E*, and (2) after the appearance of type *E*. Any assemblage having either *E* or *A* (or both *E* and *A*) can be placed in this scheme without ambiguity, and the periods can be subdivided if accumulating information makes it desirable.

INTERRELATIONSHIPS OF DIMENSIONS

The study of the interrelationship of the formal, spatial, and temporal properties of artifacts presupposes an independent scaling of each dimension considered. I have discussed in a very general way the characteristic scales and some of the scaling problems associated with each dimension, and I wish to consider now how the result of simultaneous classification in two or more dimensions leads to certain familiar archaeological concepts. The possible relationships are form-space, form-time, space-time, and form-space-time.

Form-Space. In the discussion of the formal characterization of collections of artifacts, it was asserted that artifact types could be defined solely on the basis of clusters of formal attributes. A minimum cluster is a close association of two formal attributes. But if we replace the intentionally vague concept of collection with the more restricted idea of assemblage (a spatial cluster of artifacts thought to represent something approaching a point in time), it may be possible to show a close association of a formal and a spatial attribute. Suppose that the problem at hand is a typological description of a group of vessels which are substantially identical except for the presence or absence of incised decoration on the lip, and suppose further that the collection consists of a number of assemblages. If an assemblage tally shows that plain and incised lips rarely or never occur in the same assemblage, then it would appear reasonable to recognize the two classes of vessels as distinct entities, and there is no objection to calling them artifact types. A cluster of a formal and a spatial attribute exists when the assemblage is treated as a unit of association.

Even within a single assemblage, it might be possible to show formal-spatial clustering and hence types if the special association units are considered as, for example, when the vessels with incised lips appear only as grave furnishings. Moreover, examination of the actual coordinates of the spatially segregated form variants can yield information for further inferences about the prehistoric behavior underlying the empirical data. The two types of vessels could be northern and southern or upstream and downstream variants, for example. Even the absence of any systematic arrangement of coordinates has definite implications for inferential reconstructions of behavior. A systematic time difference can be treated in the same manner, a cluster of a formal and a temporal attribute also provides satisfactory evidence for an artifact type.

A second level of form-space synthesis results from treating the assemblage as a unit of association of artifact types. The reasoning is very similar, perhaps identical, to that employed in discussing the concept of artifact type, with the assemblage playing the part of the artifact and the artifact type that of the attribute. The problem is to classify a group of assemblages with respect to their formal attributes (artifact types) so as to reveal the degree of clustering of artifact types, that is, to investigate the problem of assemblage typology. The essential raw material is a list of the artifact type combinations exhibited by each of the assemblages of the group being investigated. The method of investigation involves the familiar computing of an expected number of assemblages for various artifact type combinations under a hypothesis of independence and comparing the expected tally with the observed tally. As before, a substantial excess of observed over expected indicates a strong association of at least two artifact types, and this strong association defines a type of assemblage—a culture type. The culture type defined in this manner—as a group of assemblages possessing in common two or more artifact types having a strong positive association —seems very close to the old archaeological concept of "a culture," and it has the same faults and virtues. Specifically, it is noncommittal as to the number or nature of the artifact types forming the characterizing cluster. In fact, it implies no more than the existence of some sort of distinctive cultural entity, and the component assemblages might be virtually identical through a long list of complicated artifact types or they might barely fulfill the minimum requirements. It is plain that subclasses or subculture types can exist within a culture type. There is useful work for such concepts as the phase or the ranked (according to complexity of identifying criteria) scale of the McKern system.

A higher order of space-form relationship can be derived from the spatial position and formal typology of assemblages. If the loci of the assemblages comprising a culture type form a geographical cluster, then the area occupied by the cluster is a culture type area. Repeated examples of such culture type areas would lead to recognition of a principle of spatial coherence of the component assemblages of a culture type. Finally, the spatial clustering of culture type areas themselves can be investigated to discover whether or not there is repeated association of such areas with one geographical region. A geographical region that does show such a cluster of clusters can be considered an archaeologically defined culture area, one in which some factor is at work to produce a culturally distinct region independently of the particular types of culture characteristic of any given time period. The possibility of this kind of analysis has apparently never occurred to the archaeologists who argue that the culture area concept has no value to archaeology because variation in time inevitably produces more than one culture type in any area.

The foregoing discussion of space-form relationships is a more or less mechanical approach to some possible formulations in keeping with aims of this paper. I think it safe to hazard, however, that all archaeologists would agree to the general proposition that artifact form does in fact vary systematically in space. The relationship is a direct one: artifacts or assemblages which are formally close tend strongly toward spatial closeness. The explanation for this phenomenon is obvious, but it is drawn from observations of living cultures, not from the data of archaeology: most formal similarities are the result of person-to-person transmission of ideas and objects, and space is a barrier to this transmission. The converse of the relationship, that artifacts or assemblages which are formally distant tend strongly to be spatially distant, is no better than half true. Space is not the only barrier to transmission; time is equally effective. Hence, we expect two assemblages that are very much alike formally to be close both in space and in time. Two assemblages that are very different formally are expected to be distant in space, distant in time, or distant in both space and time.

The existence of a systematic relationship between formal similarity and spatial locus does not necessarily imply that there is any simple ratio of formal likeness to spatial distance (the time effect having been removed) which can describe the relationship adequately. If such a relationship did exist, cluster analysis would not indicate any special relationship of formal similarity to any bounded area. Similarities across all possible boundaries would be as great as similarities within boundaries. Indexes of likeness between assemblages would simply decrease at a regular ratio from any arbitrarily chosen starting point, or, if one conceded the spatial coherence of the component assemblages of a culture type, indexes of likeness of culture types would decrease at a regular rate. I am quite willing to argue that such a simple relationship does not represent adequately the empirical data. Formal similarities do tend to knot up in space, and culture areas are objectively demonstrable phenomena, not arbitrary descriptive conveniences. The explanation is again

obvious, and again it is drawn from outside the limits of strictly archaeological observations. From the standpoint of human behavior, space is not a simple matter of x and y coordinates, of barriers to communication completely described in terms of miles. The real world not only presents special impediments to communication in the form of mountains, oceans, and the like, it also poses special problems of technological and social adaptation in the form of distinctive ecological areas.

Form-Time. Since time is not a directly observable artifact attribute, form-time relationships have necessarily been dealt with to some extent in the remarks on time scaling. The discussion here will consist of listing some assertions about the nature of form-time relationships and examining the empirical implications of the assertions. These assertions are that artifact form exhibits serial correlation, that formal innovations tend to cluster on the time scale, and that formal change through time tends to be unidirectional.

The principle of serial correlation of form implies that, other things being equal, there is an inverse relationship between the formal resemblance between two artifacts, assemblages, or culture types and the amount of time separating them. Put in a slightly different way, the best prediction of the formal characteristics of the material culture of a society for next year is that they will not differ much from the situation this year. The archaeological technique of seriation is a direct application of this principle; when a group of assemblages is arranged in order of formal likeness, the assemblages are also ranked in time. If a simple, consistent ordering in an index of likeness matrix or a graphic representation is not achieved, it is taken to mean that some factor other than time (sampling difficulties, spatial variation, and so on) is also represented. Evidence from living societies and stratified archaeological deposits offers ample testimony of the general correctness of the principle, and, so far as I know, there is no serious question of its applicability to time ranking.

The existence of clustering of formal innovations on the time scale is not so easily demonstrated, although the idea seems to be widely accepted and is implicit in many formulations. In the context of historic and proto-historic studies, the concept of cultural revolutions is a clear example. The view of cultural dynamics underlying the concept is that a typical mode of cultural change is the achievement of a key invention—a sort of quantum advance—followed quickly by a number of functionally related auxiliary innovations. The short periods of rapid change would be separated by relatively long periods of comparative quiescence, although not of total cultural stagnation, of course. If one accepts the view that social systems are devices for operating technological systems (as I do), there is a clear implication that the character of key inventions is technical; they are directed toward the natural environment and have a generative relationship to change in social organization. This view is important to archaeology because archaeological data yield much fuller information on technological matters than they do on social systems. The empirical implications of such a developmental theory are clear enough: assemblages formally transitional between sequent and sharply distinctive culture types should be rare, and assemblages well within the formal boundaries of culture types should be relatively abundant. I think that the actual data do show this condition, and I suspect that the principle holds good for relationships of less spectacular dimensions than those of the grand culture types. It is this clustering tendency which makes the ambiguously defined "culture period" a useful concept in spite of its logical imperfections. The several events marking the opening or closing of the period are in fact clustered in time so that most assemblages do not seem to belong to two periods.

Unidirectionality of formal changes through time is simply the idea of cultural evolution. In strictly archaeological terms, sequent culture types in one region would be expected to show greater numbers of artifact types, not only through more formalized and more varied combinations of some stock of attributes but also through the addition of new attributes to the available list. One would also expect the sites of later culture types to be more numerous (or at any rate larger) than those of the earlier ones. These expectations are a translation into formal evidence of the behavioral concept that culture change is in the main rational: technological devices are modified and reorganized so as to increase productivity, and innovations are accepted if they are demonstrably superior with respect to productivity. Hence change tends strongly to be unidirectional. It is quite true that backsliding can occur, but it would be expected only under unusual circumstances such as climatic change. A change from an agricultural to a hunting and gathering economy in a restricted area can be imagined easily and it would not be difficult to suggest plausible explanations, but it is practically impossible to imagine circumstances short of total world disruption which would cause the abandonment of agriculture everywhere. The concept of a stage of cultural development is a combination of the ideas of unidirectionality and the key invention mode of change; there are stair-steps in culture change, and the steps lead consistently upward.

Space-Time. Time to space relationships, form being constant, are not the subject of much analysis in archaeology. Probably the most familiar generalization is that underlying the age-area concept. It is expected that the area of distribution of an artifact type will increase through time, and under some conditions a more widely distributed type is judged to have been invented earlier than a less widely distributed type. Judgments of this sort are necessarily precarious because of ecological and other conditions which can limit the spread of a type. No one expects snowshoes to be as widely spread as the use of fire, whatever their respective dates of first appearance may be. A few other remarks can be made about space-time relationships. If we consider the time-space distribution of artifacts as such, it is apparent that distribution increases in space through time, at least until the entire world is inhabited, and that space is more thickly studded with artifacts as time goes on. In short, both the quantity and the area of distribution of artifacts increases through time.

Form-Space-Time. The interrelationships of form, space, and time taken together have been foreshadowed by the discussion of the relationships of pairs of these dimensions. In a very broad sense, space and time are both expressible in terms of formal distance; the formal differences between two assemblages may be associated with either spatial distance or temporal difference or with both. If we assume that the rate of formal change has been constant in both dimensions, the interrelationship would be another example of the Pythagorean theorem. Plotting time on the vertical and space on the horizontal axis, the formal distance between a pair of points (representing two assemblages) on the graph would be the square root of the sum of squares of the time and space scales. From a dimensional point of view, such an operation implies that we have re-

duced time and space to the same dimension measured by a common scale calibrated in units of formal distance.

CONCLUSION

I have tried to make the common operations of archaeology somewhat more explicit than is frequently the case in archaeological discussions. The method used has been a translation of customary terminology into that of technically simpler and more elegant sciences, and the result has been a gain in precision and generality at the expense of realism. Certainly, to take an obvious example, there is a substantial discrepancy between my facile assumption of objective formal scales and the actual job of comparing the collections of artifacts from two assemblages. The question is whether or not such ideal formulations serve any useful purpose.

The answer is that these ideal formulations are implicit in actual archaeological research in any case, and there is no useful purpose served by not making them explicit. Indeed, failure to analyze the dimensional implications of statements about relationships has permitted formulations that are manifestly meaningless. Similarly, one may deny the possibility of objective formal scales, but the universally accepted judgment that Middle Mississippi culture is more complex than that of Indian Knoll inescapably implies that such scales are employed, however imperfect they may be. The sterile argument as to whether or not such scales exist can be replaced by a profitable discussion of ways and means to increase the sensitivity of formal scaling. The measure of success of any archaeological formulation is the degree to which it approaches the ideal, and the ideal is indispensable as an indicator of the direction and distance of the goals of archaeological research.

When faced with what is sometimes no more than a meager assembly of crumbled bricks and cracked pots, the archaeologist finds that his task of interpretation is precarious. It demands great methodological sensitivity and a theoretical frame of reference that is suggestive yet supple.

2. On the Interpretation of Archeological Evidence in Historical and Sociological Terms [1]

INTRODUCTION

Hawkes has rightly remarked that archeology belongs to "History not only in operational practice, but in philosophical theory likewise." In practice, however, history is based on documentary evidence and is highly personalized in the sense that we can usually see the individual person playing his part. On the other hand, archeological evidence is limited to the portions of material culture which time and circumstance have permitted to survive until at least the moment of discovery, and because of its medium archeology tends to be impersonal since the individual, as a person, can but very rarely be discerned. Professional historians, forgetting that philosophically, as Devoto reminds us, history is coterminous with mankind, tend to limit themselves to the study of literate societies. From the various sources of documentary evidence, of which some like inscriptions, papyri, etc., are also archeological in the manner of their discovery, we can learn about the nonmaterial aspects of that society's culture, such as language, social organization, religion, historical events, and even the personal reactions of its members to the problems of life as expressed in myth, chronicle, tale, prayer, poetry, or drama. The archeology of these societies is, to use Hawkes' term, "text-aided": in German it is sometimes called *archäologie,* as distinct from *Vor-* and *Ur-geschichte,* which is "text-free." Hawkes' cognitional system of nomenclature for prehistory serves as an excellent instrument whereby we can measure the validity of applying inferences based on documentary evidence, in practice mainly philological, to predocumentary periods. Such inferences can sometimes be extended back through protohistoric to parahistoric times but with decreasing validity. But in these periods we are mostly, and in the purely text-free zones of human history we are completely, dependent on archeological evidence and archeological reasoning for our knowledge of human activity and achievements.

During the past century archeology has developed a rather impressive form of reasoning, usually garbed in a specialist jargon, in which most of the terms are borrowed from other sciences ranging from geology to ethnology, but often with altered meanings. Most archeologists tend to take their modes of interpretation for granted but the recent studies of Willey, Phillips and Willey, and Hawkes undertake a critical re-examination of archeological methods and theory, which is a healthy symptom of scientific maturity. In this study I propose to examine further some of the problems raised by Willey, Phillips, and Hawkes in regard to the archeology of predocumentary periods, reviewing both European and American methods of interpretation. The

[1] EÓIN MACWHITE, "On the Interpretation of Archaeological Evidence in Historical and Sociological Terms," in *American Anthropologist,* 58, (1956), pp. 3–25, © American Anthropological Association. Reprinted by permission of the publisher.

hope is that we shall eventually find exact research tools of universal application, which the pressure of specialization tends to obscure, and point to certain methodological weak points and potential sources of error in archeological theory which must be corrected before archeology can claim to be founded on an unimpeachably solid scientific base.

LEVELS OF ARCHEOLOGICAL INTERPRETATION

To illustrate the processes of archeological reasoning I have constructed Table 1 showing the more frequent archeological problems treated in the published work of the last century in a graded series of levels indicating the plane of interpretation involved. In constructing this table I have followed Hawkes in taking the complexity of the logical processes involved as the basic criterion, and I have incorporated his illustrative sequence. I have also been influenced by the scheme put forward by Willey. The distinction between IIA, "Chronological," and IIIB, etc., "Historical," is essentially the distinction between "chronicle" and "historiography" emphasized by Taylor. As in Taylor's work the general concept of culture used is Sorokin's, and the distinction between the terms "sociological" and "historical" in levels III to VI is roughly parallel to his differentiation between structural and dynamic sociology.

For the most part Table 1 is self-explanatory, and only a few words of supplementary explanation are required here. Level I includes under "specific forms or types" not only types of museum articles such as flints, pots, bronzes, etc., but also tomb types, forms of habitation sites, ritual monuments, or any surviving structure or other human impingement on nature which can be described, surveyed, or excavated. The field or non-museum form of archeological evidence is usually more complex and frequently

of greater importance than museum objects, but in many areas it cannot be used to full advantage because of the relative scarcity of such evidence as compared to museum articles (even if many of these in turn came from habitation sites or other excavations).

In some cases the differentiation among levels, as, for instance, levels I, IV(3) and VII, is only a matter of degree. Thus the deduction that site X is a ritual monument, probably a temple, is level I; the inference that X was a sanctuary of a fertility cult and as such served as center for a wide area would be IV(3), and the further inference that X was also the scene of the inauguration of local chieftains together with an attempt to integrate the role of the fertility cult into the totality of the religious beliefs of the people who built X brings us up to level VII. Or the conclusion that Y is a burial monument of an important person, perhaps a chief, is likely to be an easy deduction and is level I; a comparative study of tombs of the same region and period, which show similarities to Y, might lead to the conclusion that Y is the tomb of a warrior chief who ruled over a stratified society of warriors, priests, smiths, peasants, and slaves, which would be level IV(3). A deeper analysis with ethnological comparisons leading to the conclusion that the society over which the chief buried at Y ruled was divided into moieties, practiced exogamy, and notwithstanding this and the importance of the warrior class had a strong tendency toward matriarchy raises us again to the ethereal heights of level VII.

In practice the efficacy of archeological interpretation is governed by factors of cognition which are more frequently accidental than incidental to the problems under study. In extreme cases these factors can reverse part of our gradation of interpretative levels and make a problem of even level VII simpler than one

TABLE 1. LEVELS OF ARCHEOLOGICAL INTERPRETATION FOR PREDOCUMENTARY PERIODS

I. Taxonomic and mechanical	Identification of specific forms or types, use interpretation, technique of production
IIA. Chronological	(1) Establishing contemporaneity of groups of types through stratigraphy, association, typology, etc.
	(2) Determination of local period sequences
	(3) Determination of absolute chronology by methods of natural science or through historical links to documentarily dated cultures
IIB. Ecological	Establishing physical environment and other natural determinants affecting individual sites, series of related sites or local periods
IIIA. Economic	(1) Functional study of material equipment in relation to IIB
	(2) Determination of subsistence and trade economics applied to individual sites, series of related sites or local periods
IIIB. Historical (simple)	(1) Tracing development and diffusion of types and their interrelations in time and space
	(2) Tracing developments in IIIA(2) in time and space
IV. Sociological stage I	(1) Identification of meaningful group patterns within local periods
	(2) Establishing graded series of group patterns covering different degrees of cultural differentiation
	(3) Simple inferences from material to behavioral and ideological culture: e.g., determination of social and political institutions, simple inferences regarding religious beliefs within group patterns
V. Historical complex) stage I	(1) Tracing origins, development, and spread of group patterns in time and space
	(2a) Tracing cultural continuity and change within group patterns
	(2b) Tracing interrelations of group patterns and influences of one upon another
	(3a) Tracing origin and diffusion of elements of behavioral and ideological culture as identified in IV(3)
	(3b) Reorientation of IIIB caused by viewing group pattern as logical unit
VIA. Sociological stage II	(1) Determining significance of IV(1) and (2) in sociological terms
	(2) Determining sociological conditions in which the events outlined in V(1)–(3) took place
VIB. Historical (complex) stage II	(1) Interpretation of V(1)–(3) in historical terms
	(2) Linking VIA and VIB(1) to documentary or other linguistic evidence which can be projected back to proto- or parahistoric times
VII. Psychological	Complex inferences from material culture to the behavioral and ideological culture of a social group or of an individual person

of IV or V when the range of the pertinent material vehicles used to express and socialize the immaterial aspects of culture is exceptionally rich, well preserved, and well studied. In analyzing what we might call the epistemology of archeological theory we must therefore bear in mind the varying patterns of cognitional factors involved in addition to the levels of interpretation. These patterns vary according to period, geographical and climatic conditions, and modern circumstances of discovery, as well as according to factors inherent in the culture under examination, such as presence or absence of writing, coinage, or a realistic art which may throw light on the daily life of the people.

Table 1 distinguishes seven levels, and it must be observed that in the lower three levels the reasoning used is mainly of a deductive nature and the results obtained are probably as secure and certain as any *post factum* reconstruction can be. Here the margin of error is due more to the incompleteness of the physical evidence than to errors of interpretation. On the higher levels the modes of reasoning become more reductive, to use the terminology of modern logicians, and less deductive, and also become increasingly hypothetical as we ascend the scale. On the highest or psychological plane it must be admitted that intuition (in the popular sense of the word) often replaces the more logical processes of deduction and reduction, which includes induction.

THE PROBLEM OF THE ARCHEOLOGICAL CULTURE CONCEPT

The shift from deductive to reductive thinking is not the only significant difference between levels I–III and IV–VII, which are partly parallel to the "lower" and "higher criticism" of biblical scholars. The infusion of what are described in Table 1 as "group patterns" changes the whole fabric of archeological interpretation. These group patterns are generally described by archeologists as "cultures," but in our table we have purposely avoided the term because it not only takes too much for granted but it also may cover a number of quite distinct sociocultural entities. But despite the imperfections of the present concept, which has become an almost unquestioned postulate of archeological thinking, the application of this fundamentally ethnological concept to the historical study of predocumentary periods represents the most important heuristic advance in modern archeology.

Although the idea of an archeological culture was already inherent in some of the theories of turn-of-the-century scholars such as Sophus Müller and Lord Abercomby and in practice its roots go back to De Mortillet's classifications, the current European application of the concept is largely the result of the personal teachings and publications of Kossinna. This scholar's exposition of his method bears the misleading title of *Siedlungsarchäologie* despite the fact that most of the distinctions made by him were based on burials rather than on habitations. Since 1911 his equation *Kultur = Volk* has won wide, if not general, acceptance in archeological teaching and practice.

It is almost fashionable to be derogatory about Kossinna's theories, but his methods were perhaps not as bad as the way in which he himself misused them. It is remarkable how few archeologists have ever expressly committed themselves on the basic problems of method behind the culture concept and how extremely rare are those who have tried to define the concept. This can readily be seen from Kroeber and Kluckhohn's survey, which, however, is rather incomplete on European definitions. Of course, the archeological culture is a specialized concept dealing with only fragments of the totality of culture, a point which is sometimes forgotten. Of the few who have expressed their ideas on this subject we may perhaps take the opinions of Childe as representing a consensus of opinion which (less some of the Marxist overtones in his application of the concept) is generally accepted. Childe's view of culture has not changed greatly since his first definition except for a certain shift away from the rigidity of the Kossinna equation. Childe's general approach, which is very different from that of Kossinna, lays heavy emphasis on culture as a social adaptation to physical environment, an emphasis which impresses itself on the archeologist more readily than on students of nonmaterial aspects of culture. For Childe an archeological culture is,

an assemblage of artifacts that recur repeatedly associated together in dwellings of the same kind and with burials by the same rite. The arbitrary peculiarities of the implements, weapons, ornaments, houses, burial rites and ritual objects are assumed to be the concrete expressions of the common social traditions that bind together a people.

In the heading of the chapter in which Childe gives this definition, he uses the word "society" instead of "people." Childe has emphasized that such a culture,

is not an *a priori* category elaborated in the studies of philosophers and then imposed from the outside upon working archaeologists. Cultures are observed facts. . . . The interpretation of the observed phenomenon is supplied by ethnology. The traits of a culture are thus presented together to the archaeologist because they are the creations of a single people, adjustments to its environment, approved by its collective experience; they thus express the individuality of a human group united by common social traditions.

As an example of an extreme point of view we may cite the recent theories of Pittioni who, in elaborating the Kossinna theory, has pushed it well beyond its logical conclusions. He presents us with a complicated scheme wrapped up in somewhat unorthodox terminology, which we have summarized in Table 2. I regret that it is not possible without a long explanation to translate most of the terms from German into English, but the general meaning will be grasped easily enough. Pittioni begins with a reclassification of the Three Period System into *Lithikum* (Paleo- and Mesolithic), *Keramikum* (Neolithic and Aeneolithic) and *Metallikum* (Bronze and Iron Ages). We are then given an ascending graded sequence of archeological groupings from *Lokalfacies* through *Typus, Gruppe,* and *Kultur* to *Welt* which represents a series of related *Kulturen*. It will be observed that the sociological and linguistic connotations of some of these groupings differ in each of Pittioni's three periods.

The approach of American archeologists to the concept of culture in their own field owes more to the ideas of Wissler and Kroeber than to Kossinna or Graebner. This independent line of research has been intensified in a number of American universities during the last two decades, yielding important contributions to our knowledge of the archeological aspects of culture. Many of the differences between the results of American and European research are naturally due to differing raw material, but much is due also to the different approaches. While, owing to the scarcity of certain forms of evidence, a good deal of American work on problems of level IIA has in most regions yielded results of limited value compared to the detailed results obtained by intensive research on European chronology, some of the American approaches to cultural analysis on level IV are, if not always spectacular, far more firmly based and more mature in conception than European thinking on the problem. The time is now ripe for a conjoined attack on the problems of archeological culture and its significance in terms of social and intellectual culture. Here we shall discuss briefly two important streams of American thought which have been crystallizing over the last twenty years, one associated with the Human Relations Area Files (HRAF) and the other with the Midwestern Taxonomic System (MWTS).

As an example of the HRAF school, which grew out of the Yale Cross-Cultural Survey, we may cite the scheme of correlations put forward by Murdock

TABLE 2. SOCIOLOGICAL AND LINGUISTIC CORRELATIONS OF ARCHEOLOGICAL CULTURE
GROUPS ACCORDING TO PITTIONI

I. Sociological Correlations

Archeological Group	Lithikum	Keramikum	Metallikum
Welt	Allgemeinheit des Kulturwillens	Einheit des Kulturwillens	Volk
Kultur	Einheit des Kulturwillens	Stammhafte Einheit	Stamm
Gruppe	Sippenverbandsgruppe	Sippenverbandsgruppe	Sippenverbandsgruppe
Typus	Gebundener Sippenverband	Gebundener Sippenverband	Gebundener Sippenverband
Lokalfacies	Sippe	Sippe	Sippe
Unknown	Family	Family	Family

II. Linguistic Correlations

Archeological Group	Lithikum	Keramikum	Metallikum
Welt	Linguistic stock of the first type	Linguistic stock of the second type	Linguistic family: sometimes linguistic stock as a survival
Kultur	Linguistic family	Linguistic family	Individual language
Gruppe	Individual language	Individual language	Special modification of individual language
Typus	Possibly special modification of a single language	Beginning of a dialectally orientated modification of a single language	Dialectical specializations
Lokalfacies	—	—	—

and reproduced in Table 3. The series of equations of archeological groups with sociological groups reminds us of Pittioni's theories, but biological classifications have been substituted for linguistic correlations.

The MWTS, which is allied in conception to the University of California Culture Element Distribution Survey, does not use any abstraction of culture or of culture elements but archeological habitation sites. It can, indeed, be truly described as a *Siedlungsarchäologie*. In the MWTS as originally constructed by McKern the term "component" is applied to the evidence from individual sites and habitation units and the term "focus" to the forms of culture presented by a series of related components. The foci are, in turn, grouped into an ascending series of larger units, "aspects," "phases," and "patterns."

Phillips and Willey have recently put forward some modifications of the MWTS in which they substitute for the McKern term "focus" the word "phase," which they define as "a space time unit possessing traits sufficiently characteristic to distinguish it from all other units similarly conceived, whether of the same or other cultural traditions, geographically limited to a *locality* or *region* and chronologically limited to a relatively brief span of time." It can, they hold, be anything from "a thin level in a site reflecting no more than a brief encampment to a protracted occupation represented in a large number of sites over a region of

TABLE 3. SOCIOLOGICAL CORRELATIONS OF CULTURE (AFTER MURDOCK)

Culture-Bearing Social Unit	Corresponding Cultural Unit	Analogous Biological Unit
Community	Local culture variant	Subvariety
Subtribe	Subculture	Variety
Tribe	Culture	Species
Nation	Culture cluster	Genus
Region	Culture area	Family

very elastic proportions. . . . " The sociological equivalent of the component is the community, as defined by Murdock— "the maximal group of persons who normally reside together in a face to face association." In practice they consider that component and phase are sometimes identical since "on the lower levels of cultural development society likewise frequently consists of one community." Phillips and Willey adopt a flexible attitude toward equating their phase with society; they consider the present chances to be against phase's having a definite sociological connotation but are not prepared to deny that in the future phase may be analyzed in sociological terms.

The Kossinna theory, which Zambotti described as a dangerous *petitio principii*, has not passed without raising solid opposition. Tallgren warned against the tendency to see a uniform population group behind forms of material culture and gave ethnographic examples demonstrating the weakness of this hypothesis; so did Wahle who used a strict historical approach, with special reference to the old problem of identifying Germans, Illyrians, and Celts in northern and central Europe. The often overlooked but obvious fact that behind what archeologists call "Hallstatt" lie not only Celts but also Illyrians shows clearly that ethnic groups with distinct, even if related, linguistic affinities may possess the same culture. To attach a definite ethnic signification to archeological cultures as delineated by Kossinna and his imitators without reference to documentary sources is therefore imprudent, and Wahle like Tallgren

pleads for a reorientation of archeological aims and methods to avoid the errors and narrowness of approach which Kossinna's methods inevitably force upon us. In considering the slant which Kossinna gave to the application of his concept of culture we must remember, as Wahle's study clearly shows, that Kossinna's ideas were influenced more by modern concepts of European nationalities than by ethnological views of modern cultures.

Turning to Childe's definition of an archeological culture, Phillips and Willey express views similar to those of Tallgren and Wahle. They consider that,

an archaeological culture is an arbitrary division of the space-time continuum defined by reference to its imperishable content. . . . An archaeological culture conceived of as a sliced out section of the space-time continuum corresponds to the observed facts of cultural continuity but, as with the empirical "designed" artifact types it may or may not parallel the reality of the past social unit *as this might have been conceived by the peoples who composed it.* [author's italics.]

However, Phillips and Willey hold out the hope that eventually archeological-sociological correlations may be possible.

As implied in Childe's definition, an archeological culture is based on *types*— types of pots, weapons, tools, ornaments, houses, and tombs. While modern methods of inferring sociological and economic data from archeological evidence play some part, and undoubtedly will play a still greater part in the future, in defining cultural patterns, the archeological culture, like MWTS foci and phases, is fundamentally based on the typological method, which, from De Mortillet to Montelius, was primarily a time-measuring instrument but in recent times, as indicated by the increased use of the distribution map, is now equally important on the spatial plane. Typological theory is founded on two basic assumptions: (1) that types exist and are significant, and (2) that the changes which they undergo on the time scale and on the spatial plane indicate cultural change.

Phillips and Willey point out that there are two ways of looking at the problem, one envisaging "culture change as a continuous stream to be segmented into types as this best suits the archeologist's purpose," the other tending "to conceive of types as once existent realities." In the first case the definition of types is "a purely arbitrary procedure, entirely imposed on the prehistoric phenomena by the classifier," while in the second view the task of typology is the recognition of something which once existed. Phillips and Willey do not regard these two opinions as mutually exclusive. From the point of view of a generalizing law of human behavior the two views would appear to be mutually antagonistic, but it must be agreed that both concepts are needed to face the situations presented to us by archeological evidence.

Most lithic types are probably functional types, but the greater number of the subclassifications of the functional types such as Acheulian hand-axes, Levallois flakes, Upper Paleolithic and Mesolithic blade forms, to mention a few flint forms, may represent a developing series where each object differs but slightly from the next, the classifications based on the differences between them being founded on dividing lines drawn by modern observers. Thus Movius acutely pointed out in connection with Irish Mesolithic material that,

as long as it can be understood that such groupings of the fieldworker . . . are *not* rigid, but rather consist of a series of completely subjective categories for which no very precise definition can be given, and which are intended to help clarify and interpret the present data, progress can and will be made.

The same can be said of the style sequences presented by most art-forms in archeological material on which so many regional and chronological distinctions have been elaborated. On the other hand, we can cite Nordic flint daggers, Cypriote bronze daggers, Hallstatt swords, or Irish bronze trumpets in which we find consistent repetitions of forms and even of subforms, which must represent deliberate and conscious efforts to satisfy the social and traditional requirements, stronger often than mere fashion, of their users. Between these two extremes many archeological classifications are probably a mixture of observer-imposed and real types; in this mixed category we can place some of the more elaborate typologies of both European and American prehistoric pottery, and, in Europe, megalithic tombs and Bronze and Early Iron Age fibulae have been the subjects of complicated typologies in which it is difficult to distinguish between differentiations which are observer-imposed and those which are real or inherent in the material itself.

In the last analysis, the definition of types, beyond functional distinctions, is essentially the same as the definition of certain categories in linguistics, both ultimately being bound up in the *Gestalt* framework of the human brain. The problem of real and observer-imposed distinctions exists also in linguistics, especially in phonetics, and in the realm of material culture reaches its highest refinement in the study of fine-art products. The resemblances to archeological reasoning are patent in the researches of a Strygowski, but the techniques of a Berenson or of a Venturi in identifying the works of Renaissance painters are not essentially different but only more delicately, and perhaps more intuitively, applied.

As Kroeber shows, the type concept is applicable also to institutions and aspects of behavioral or social culture. Whether we are dealing with material or non-material culture we can discern a significant patterning in the arrangement of types; sometimes this patterning is clear and simple but in other cases the rules we describe as governing the patterns are perhaps mnemonic rather than truly analytical. In either case it is not so much the actual data, whether an Acheulian hand-ax, a La Tène fibula, a Picasso painting, a word or a grammatical form, which really forms the basis of cultural delineations but the "patterns of significance" which they show. It must, however, be emphasized that we cannot begin to interpret the patterns of significance presented by archeological material in either historical or sociological terms unless we first distinguish carefully among patterns, especially group patterns such as archeological cultures, which are based on observer-imposed, real, or mixed types. In the last case we must decide, whenever possible, whether the mixed types are weighted more heavily in the direction of real types or of observer-imposed types.

The contention of Phillips and Willey that an archeological culture could not "be said to have existed as an entity until the archeologist named and defined it" is probably an overstatement, even if valid in some cases. But their warning that these units may not have been felt as in-groups is of more general validity. Some of the entities which archeologists call cultures very probably were discrete units. But in Europe, especially, the much abused word "culture," leaving aside semantic confusions, frequently covers a number of quite different group patterns representing very different sociological situations. Indeed, we can ask how many assemblages so named in any recent textbook of European archeology or in contemporary monographic studies can live up to the twenty-two simple words of Childe's definition quoted above. A large number are based on a small sector of the "imperishable content" of culture. In many cases the interrelations of these distinctions based on quite different sectors of material culture are far from clear. For instance, in a number of areas and periods in Europe, like the Early Bronze Age in Ireland or the Late Bronze Age in the Iberian Peninsula, the link between the burial material and the habitation material is very weak. In a number of groupings at present labeled "cultures," it is quite difficult to integrate the sequence of metallic types with ceramic forms, a difficulty which is frequently a reflection of the problem of linking burials with habitations.

Due possibly to the influence of Kroeber's skepticism on the cultural significance of burial rites and funerary customs, the MWTS and its cognates are inclined to play down the importance of burials. In European archeology our knowledge of habitation material frequently lags behind our knowledge of burial monuments and their contents. Although in some cases the burial material may reflect a reasonably accurate picture of daily life, it often consists of cult objects including its own pottery forms which have relatively few parallels in habitation material. Even when burial material gives a fairly clear picture of daily life, as, for instance, in the Iberic Iron Age, we may, as Prof. Julian San Valero pointed out to me, have a certain archaistic tendency which can upset our preconceived synchronisms. This may be due partly to the conservative tendencies of cult practices, the presence of heirlooms, or the fact that a person is buried with objects of personal significance which were manufactured during his youth but quite out of fashion at the time of his death.

The European tendency to concentrate on burial material is in part due to cognitional factors such as the fact that burial monuments are often more easy to recognize on the surface than are habitation sites, and, unless the ritual is architecturally complicated, they are easier to excavate. More than a century of collecting, both private and institutional, has resulted in the accumulation of a large mass of material consisting of single finds, now mainly preserved in museums, and these single objects, when we are fortunate enough to know the find-place, together with sporadic associated material, such as hoards, form a body of evidence almost equal in importance, when the quantity permits, to strictly excavation material, whether habitation or burial. We are thus faced with a more uneven pattern of discovery than that which underlies the MWTS. It is always necessary to ask if the basic material is a valid sampling of the "imperishable content" of culture or a distortion caused by accidental features of discovery, e.g., preservation of some types of monuments in nonagricultural areas, the ease of conservation of some types of habitations such as cave sites as distinct from "open" habitations, or peculiar factors of preservation arising from something inherent in the past culture, e.g., the use of an easily decomposable material for much of the material equipment, like bamboo in the Far East, or settlement habits such as in the case of nomads who dwelt in temporary tents but buried in more permanent structures versus a settled village folk who practiced water burial or tree exposure, etc. Many of the cognitional factors which distort our present picture of predocumentary archeological groupings will eventually disappear with future research and improved techniques of excavation or be recognized as a distor-

tion due to some peculiarity of the culture under study. When our knowledge of habitations in Europe catches up to our knowledge of the burial record, we may be presented with a very different picture on levels V and VI from that presented in contemporary interpretations, even if the broad outlines of present thinking on level IV remain.

Pittioni's complex scheme contains more wishful thinking than scientific analysis and has had a skeptical reception in archeological circles. However, it does contain some features which merit serious consideration. The sequence of *Lithikum, Keramikum,* and *Metallikum* is a useful didactic reminder that in these periods cultural distinctions are generally based on stone, pottery, and metal types, respectively, although it should be remembered that in the last period in Europe a large number of cultures are distinguished on the basis of pottery rather than metal types. Like the series of Murdock and McKern, Pittioni's sequence from *Lokalfacies* to *Welt* is at least an attempt to come to grips with the too often ignored problem of differentiating between varying degrees of cultural groups. While Daniel suggested a fourfold sequence of site, industry, culture, and civilization, it is perhaps significant that McKern, Murdock, and Pittioni have independently arrived at a fivefold sequence, although the center of gravity of each of the series is quite distinct.

Pittioni's insistence that the sociological equivalents of the archeological group classifications were often different in each of his three periods is fundamentally sound even if his equations are not. Patterson has acutely observed that,

the further back in time the fewer are the cultural elements found, and so the fewer the implied logical complexes, therefore the less justification for the use of the word "culture" in the anthropological sense. It is exceedingly doubtful if the word can be applied to any archaeological group of complexes prior to historical times. To these earlier groups of complexes the word "industries" has been given, in order, presumably, to get over this difficulty, though it does not seem that the real crux of the matter has been appreciated since, generally, it is to the Palaeolithic groups that the word is usually applied, and "culture" is used for every assemblage of Post-Pleistocene age.

But the relative scarcity of culture elements is not the only feature which differentiates the cultural patterns of groups in the Pleistocene and postglacial periods; the most striking feature, which can be noted to a lesser degree in later periods, is in the tempo of culture change.

While Sorokin decries the theory of the "law of acceleration" in sociocultural processes, as put forward by Novicov, Hart, Ogburn, Ogburn and Nimkoff, etc., it cannot be denied that, when we apply the perspective afforded to us by archeology, there has been a definitive and consistent increase in the rate of change of material culture forms from the Paleolithic to the present day. Viewed comprehensively we have a rising graph, although when we examine various periods more closely we can discern some ups and downs, which, however, do not change the general pattern of the upward trend. The time-span of the shortest recognizable cultural space-time unit can serve as a rough index of the tempo of culture change. Thus Abbevillian and Clactonian I appear to have had a span of *ca.* 114,000 years on Zeuner's figures based on the Milankovič chronology, and the three first phases of Acheulian cover *ca.* 200,000 years. Even if current calculations for the Upper Paleolithic are reduced, we cannot think in smaller time units than of 10,000 to 5,000 years. Our time measurement units shrink further during the postglacial Mesolithic, and by the parahistoric Neolithic we can begin to think in units of 500 years and less. The time unit can in certain restricted spheres of culture, like art, come down to

a generation in the Iron Age. Indeed it is noteworthy that in Attic figured vases of the middle of the sixth century B.C. the individual can be recognized by stylistic methods even when he does not sign his work, as has been shown by Beazley and other classical archeologists. This is probably the earliest point in Europe where we can apprehend individual personal expression through material culture.

Sorokin is, however, probably right in denying the existence of a *law* of acceleration. To explain the increasing tempo of culture change we must have recourse to a number of factors, of which progressive accumulation is only one. While it is outside the scope of this study to examine the causes of the increasing tempo of culture change, two factors, generally ignored, may be mentioned. The first is physical and the second psychological. These are the means of communication which condition the speed, frequency, and duration of culture contacts through which change may be effected and the resistance/receptivity factor, which may be religious, social, or economic, that results in a new culture element's being adopted or rejected.

But whatever the factors underlying the tempo of change in material culture, it is reasonable to suppose that both culture change and the resultant new configurations will have quite different social significations to the individuals concerned, according to the varying rates. We have two extremes: one in which change is not perceptible to the individual and the other in which the individual is keenly aware of the change. In the former case which certainly holds good at least for the Paleolithic, we must ask whether it is valid to assume that change in material culture reflects change in nonmaterial culture. If, for example, the contention of the glottochronologists that in a fixed sector of vocabulary considered to be relatively stable there is a constant retention rate of *ca.* 81 per cent per millennium "for all languages, at all times" is correct, then in a given theoretical genetically descended group in Paleolithic times, language would have changed basically a number of times within the same culture. Thus for the earliest periods linguistic-archeological identifications may never be verifiable, and, likewise, it is not possible to ascertain whether or not the rate of linguistic drift was actually constant or whether it, too, increased in tempo together with technological change.

Since the contrasts through the time scale are not so violent as in the Old World, it is not surprising that American archeology has not faced the problem of the possible variation of sociological correlations of archeological culture according to period. On a modified scale an increasing rate of change can be noted from Folsom to the Amerind groups of the early colonial period which roughly parallels the rates of the European groups from the Upper Paleolithic and Mesolithic to the Chalcolithic. In the Andes we have a rate comparable to that of the full European Bronze Age in what Willey calls the "Florescent" and "Expansionist" periods.

The Murdock sequence of equations is almost as arbitrary as Pittioni's, although as unconnected series the elements are better thought out sociologically. The equations show a serious lack of a consistent *fundamentum divisionis* in that the first four members of his cultural series are genetically conceived while the fifth is a geographical concept which can in no way be made analogous to the biological concept of family.

Although the MWTS was specifically devised to meet problems of the North American Midwest, it contains a number of concepts of universal application even though the choice of words to describe them leaves much to be desired. It can, in fact, be applied to any relatively unexplored region as a basis on which the results of a survey combined with a series of strategic excavations could be integrated quite quickly into a solid structure. Since Europe has a different pattern of find material which has already been intensively worked on, it would be uneconomical to try to apply the whole scheme, but in some areas its application could serve as a useful check on the results obtained by the conventional European approach. Furthermore, the use of some term like "component" for the culture of an individual site or a period of a site would avoid some of the abuse which the word "culture" too often receives from archeologists.

The Phillips and Willey phase is a basic concept, and, modified to allow of the full integration of single finds, hoards, and burials, could be made into the basis of a more precise definition of an archeological culture, which might now be described as a significant group of space-time units consisting of possibly one but generally a number of phases, whose basic traits belong to the same tradition.

INVASIONS AND ACCULTURATION

Parallel to the problem of the definition and demarcation of culture groups on a static plane there is the dynamic aspect of culture change. Over the last half-century archeologists in both Europe and America have succeeded in reducing the chaos of the old battle cries of diffusion versus independent invention, and the debate of *ex oriente lux* versus *mirage orientale* has been reduced to a reasonable semblance of ordered history. While the major problems up to level III and at least the outlines of level IV are now fairly clear, the processes involved in the spread of various types and forms, inventions, and ornaments from one group to another are but hazily perceived.

Faced with certain forms of culture change we frequently have varying historical explanations ranging from a full-scale invasion to "culture-contacts" of a rather tenuous ad undefined nature. Thus Thus the Kossinna-style archeologists see cultural movements mainly as tribal migrations, but their excesses have brought about a reaction in practice as well as in theory which we may exemplify by Raftery's arguments against postlithic invasions of Ireland. In all cases the fact of diffusion is admitted but the form which it took is debated. Hawkes divides diffusion into two processes, (1) primary diffusion, which comprises "actual folk movements or migrations of peoples, or human groups of whatever size or character," and (2) secondary diffusion, in which culture elements are "transmitted from one group to another without group migration." It may be said in criticism that any form of diffusion entails a migration of some sort, whether it be a visiting trader or a hunter returned after a chance encounter with a neighboring people or a foreign wife captured as part of the booty in a raid on another tribe. If we have a group of traders, a party of hunters, or a number of captured women, we would, following Hawkes' scheme closely, have to class it as primary diffusion, which I doubt was Hawkes' intention. Hawkes' primary and secondary diffusion represent two extreme poles, but as in the case of most extremes in human affairs the majority of cases fall in between. Hawkes makes a timely plea that archeologists make an effort to avoid such vague terms as "culture-contact," "transmission of elements," etc. Possibly the best basis for a closer definition and analysis of diffusion processes lies in the recent studies of acculturation beginning with the American Social Science Research Council Memorandum. Although the idea of acculturation without any significant movement of population is inherent in so many discussions in European archeology of "influences" and "contacts," it has not, except for Fox's "absorption," been scientifically applied.

Ultimately the question of invasion or acculturation has to be reduced to demographic terms. In Table 4 we summarize the main demographic situations which underlie most examples of diffusion, whether primary or secondary. In this table "invasion" means an immigration of organized groups and can be peaceful or otherwise: "immigrations" differ wherein the immigrant groups do not enter as part of an organized group. In the second half of the table we have made a distinction between "insular" and "contiguous" situations: these are, of course, again two extremes, but the intermediary situations are too varied to allow of inclusion. Where we have two cultures occupying neighboring territory, assuming peaceful conditions and a reasonable degree of receptivity, the processes of acculturation listed for insular situations (which can be applied to culture groups isolated by desert, mountain, jungle, or any other difficult geographical barrier as well as by sea) become highly intensified, and at present the results are very difficult to analyze through archeological evidence. Thus visitors can merge imperceptibly into immigrants. If these immigrants then gain the leadership and control of the group which they have joined, and if the immigration is continued, the original language might eventually be displaced by that of the newcomers. As so frequently happens in the archeology of the Highland Zone of Britain we may be faced with a situation in which culture B is absorbed by the more indigenous culture A which modifies the B types in its own way, but we are at a loss to know how far this situation extended to behavioral and social culture and, if so, to determine whether or not A kept its own language.

TABLE 4. PROCESSES OF PRIMARY AND SECONDARY DIFFUSION IN DEMOGRAPHIC TERMS

I. Invasions	(1) Migration of whole sociopolitical (ethnic) group
	(2) Migration of a large section of an ethnic group
	(3) Migration of organized groups of family units of an ethnic group
	(4) Migration of organized groups of males of an ethnic group
II. Immigrations	(1) Sporadic settling of family units of same ethnic group
	(2) Entry on permanent basis of specialist groups, usually predominantly male, e.g., traders, smiths, craftsmen, missionaries, etc.
	(3) Importation of foreign wives
	(4) Importation of foreign slaves
III. Foreign agents of acculturation	
A. Insular situations	(1) Visits of specialist groups, as II(2), of greater or less duration but who do not settle permanently
	(2) Foreign raiders
B. Contiguous situations	(1) Visits of specialist groups
	(2) Visits from all levels of population of neighboring group (the result can be the same as II(1))
	(3) Hostile incursions
IV. Native agents of acculturation	
A. Insular situations	(1) Specialist groups, e.g., fishermen, hunters, traders, smiths, etc., returned after visits to foreign lands
	(2) Warriors returned after raids in foreign lands
B. Contiguous situations	(1) Specialist groups, who usually become bilingual, who have specially close contacts with neighboring group
	(2) Whole of population which has contact with neighboring group

ARCHEOLOGY AND LINGUISTIC PROBLEMS

Some theorists like Menghin, who conceives of a special "linguistic archeology," lay much importance on the interpretation of archeological evidence in what are, strictly speaking, philological terms. This, as Tovar shows in his survey of archeology and linguistics, is due to the historical problem of identifying in the archeological record the peoples and tribes mentioned in classical texts and the need to corroborate some of the cultural data obtained about Indo-European groups through linguistic methods, together with the interest in the problem of the Indo-European *Urheimat*. Tovar notes a certain negative attitude on the part of a number of philologists regarding archeology. Indeed, in Europe this attitude is stronger than Tovar's study would lead us to believe, since so many philologists content themselves with disparaging remarks in the classroom and in the lecture hall but do not commit themselves to cold print. Apart from Trubetskoi and his school, this negative attitude is largely the monopoly of philologists of a rigid neogrammarian outlook, and it perhaps reaches a peak of invective in connection with Celtic problems where the failure of archeologists and linguists to appreciate each other's problems and methods has frustrated the development of a Celtic *archäologie*. On the whole, the American approach to these matters is quite free of such prejudices which result from a total divorce of language from culture, as can be seen from the linguistic section in Kroeber and Kluckhohn and in the papers of scholars such as Hoijer, due, as Tovar points out rightly, to the fact that American linguistics are closely bound up with ethnology.

From the point of view of method and theory, linguistic-archeological correlations pose two important questions. (1) Can an archeological culture or any other group pattern be interpreted in linguistic terms? And (2) Can we establish some basis on which the value of linguistic and archeological evidence may be assessed?

Without reliable indications from documentary evidence we cannot, at present, answer the first question with an unqualified affirmative. The controversies which rage over the applications of equations of archeological cultures with language groups are ultimately reflections of the incompleteness of our understanding of the delicate interrelations of language and culture, combined, it must be admitted, with an over-eager desire on the part of archeologists to invest their cultures with more significance than is warranted by the evidence. In some cases, however, as with archeologists who have tried to make their material comply with Schleicher's *Stammbaum* theory in tracing Indo-European movements, the fault lies in the error of the philologists, who have produced so much deadwood instead of a valid linguistic thesis.

The archeological problem of setting limits to culture forms is paralleled in linguistics by the problem of defining such entities as language (in the sense of De Saussure's *langue*) and dialect. While, as Lounsbury emphasizes, mutual intelligibility, despite the subjective nature of this criterion, must ultimately be the basis on which we mark off linguistic frontiers, the problem of defining a language is rarely easy. Bloch avoids the linguistic problem, which has led to such definitions as "a system of isoglosses," by defining language by its speakers, and he introduces the useful concept of the speech community. Before equating an

archeological subgroup with a dialect, we should at least determine which, if any, of the "sociolinguistic patterns" that word used to describe, as outlined by Martinet.

While many aspects of the language-culture relationship are far from clear, a few points are reasonably certain. Thus, as Kroeber states, "so far as the process of their transmission is concerned and the mechanism of their development, it is clear that language and culture are one." It must also be agreed that "a decisive change of speech without some change of culture seems impossible." Language, which Sorokin and others have called the vehicle of culture, must obviously play an important role in any acculturation situation, and this must be better studied before we can interpret in linguistic terms archeological material produced by an acculturation situation.

Our reply to the second question must vary according to the nature of the problem which is to be solved and according to the nature of the evidence presented by archeology and linguistic science for the solution of the problem. If a problem is posed in linguistic terms, its solution in those terms must be based primarily on linguistic methods and evidence, which then take precedence over archeological evidence. Thus Koppers limits the role of archeology in the Indo-European problem to taking one position or another based on its own evidence *vis-à-vis* the philological theories on the problem. This relationship holds good while we have problems which are framed in linguistic terms and on which there is a sufficiently large body of positive linguistic evidence. When a disagreement between archeology and philology is occasioned by the dependence of the linguistic theory on negative evidence or an *argumentum ex silentio,* the validity of the linguistic argument decreases according as we depart from a fully documented context into Hawkes' proto- or parahistoric periods. The validity of an archeological *argumentum ex silentio* depends on (1) the degree of exploration of the area concerned and (2) the absence of cognitional factors which might produce an *apparent* absence in the phenomenon in question.

Recently glottochronology has begun to receive attention from archeologists and, indeed, if the method underlying it proves sound, it will provide us with a framework on which archeological theories can be more securely attached than anything we have at present. But the theory of vocabulary retention on which it is based must stand or fall on linguistic grounds and not on the presence or absence of corroborative archeological evidence. Instead of looking to European archeology to support Indo-European time-depths, as Swadesh does, it is European archeology that must look to the results of glottochronological research on time-depths between all Indo-European languages for a time frame to guide their researches. At present glottochronology is based on word counts in thirteen languages and the results are remarkably consistent, but before we can establish it as a sort of linguistic C14 the system must be checked on all languages which give us sufficient records of 500 years or more.

DIAGNOSIS AND PROGNOSIS

While archeological reasoning on levels I–III may be considered sound and scientific, most of the theorizing carried out on levels IV–VI depends on the archeological culture concept or is inevitably influenced by it. There is a pressing need to clarify this concept further, to establish a consistent series to cover varying degrees of cultural relationship on spatial and temporal planes, and to determine how far the basic unit, whether a culture in Childe's sense or the more precise phase of Phillips and Willey, is based on observer-imposed as distinct

from real typological distinctions, and to what extent it may suffer from distortion due to cognitional features. Eventually more research on economic, religious, and social factors may enable us to make more significant cultural distinctions, but at present most of our delineations are based on typology. When the basic types are real and not observer-imposed, we are probably dealing with once existent realities, and the distinctions based on them can be interpreted in sociological terms.

But the blind application of the traditional methods of European archeology, even of approaches more refined than Kossinna's, are in need of a critical re-examination before we can generalize on sociological interpretations of archeological group patterns and their history. The linguists have their problems in regard to language frontiers, which must be solved before linguistic archeological correlations can really be put on a sound basis. For the solution of these problems we must look not to the neogrammarians but rather to the neolinguists or to American linguistics. European archeology tends, perhaps, to look to documentary history as a goal, and American archeology is more closely bound up with cultural anthropology. The time is ripe for a fusion of methods and a critical examination of theory in order to arrive at concepts of universal application. In many cases both share the same problems but have arrived at different answers.

If our approach in this study has been rather negative, it is because our purpose has been to suggest questions rather than to supply ready-made answers. As an eminent philosopher, who took up archeological research as a laboratory in which to check his philosophical ideas, the late R. G. Collingwood, never tired of emphasizing, both the meaning of a proposition and its truth are relative to the question it answers. In short the questions must be framed before the answers.

THE PALEOLITHIC

All but the last ten thousand of our nearly two million years as men were spent as Stone Age men, wandering hunters and gatherers of food, not too bright at first, and possessing only a few rudimentary tools and weapons of stone, bone, and wood. Although these tools were simple, they made all the difference; they helped to keep us alive and fed, thus—gradually—making us more cultured.

As the archaeologist deals with the Paleolithic his principal attention is focused on those simple tools and their evolution—a record of the slowly increasing technological proficiency of our ancestors and ourselves. The natural fascination of this record is increased enormously when it is perceived as parallel to the physical anthropologists' chronicle of our emergent humanness. At the outset of the Paleolithic we were beginning to become men; by the end we were fully *Homo sapiens* and on the threshold of a discovery that would change our lives forever.

1. The Old Stone Age [1]

During the last twenty-five years, our knowledge of the Paleolithic period has been greatly extended beyond the confines of western Europe. This has not resulted in the establishment of as coherent a picture of man's early attempts to develop a material culture as was originally expected. For, when we examine the bewildering array of primitive Stone Age assemblages that are constantly being augmented by fresh discoveries, we can hardly compose them into anything even remotely approaching the ordered general scheme conceived by the early workers. This is certainly not due to the fact that, in reaction against the doctrine of direct typological evolution, we have gone too far in the opposite direction but rather because, once De Mortillet's original scheme was rightly abandoned as provincial and inapplicable outside western Europe, no really adequate alternative approach has been proposed. As a matter of fact, most of the original terms developed by De Mortillet for his "classificatory system" are still in use, and they are now employed in several different senses—chronologic, typologic, technologic, and cultural—sometimes in the same breath. Instead of getting bogged down in questions pertaining to terminology at this point, however, I propose to pass on to a brief consideration of some problems of a more fundamental nature. In this paper an attempt has been made to present a synthesis of the various sequences of Paleolithic cultures within the framework of the larger continental areas. Throughout, the major trends as indicated by the most recent results have been stressed.

EUROPE

Paleolithic research, cradled and developed in Europe during the last century, has made many significant contributions during recent years. Only certain of the more important aspects of the field as a whole can be considered here; the selection has been made partly on the basis of new materials and partly on the basis of new methods that have been and are being developed. In view of the overwhelming mass of data, it is very difficult to present a consecutive account covering the region as a whole, although the major trends can be discerned.

Lower and Middle Paleolithic. As is well known, the very simple developmental scheme of Abbevillian (formerly Chellian)-Acheulian-Mousterian for the various Lower and Middle Paleolithic assemblages in western Europe was replaced early in the 1930's as the result of Breuil's investigations in the Somme Valley of northern France. According to Breuil's so-called "parallel phyla concept," there was a flake-tool tradition (Clactonian-Levalloisian) which developed in a parallel and more or less independent manner to the core-biface tradition (Abbevillian-Acheulian). This has been widely accepted, certain authors even going so far as to conceive of the flake tools as being introduced by a paleoanthropic stock of fossil man, and the core-biface complex as attributable to men of neanthropic (or *sapiens*) group. Those who implicitly accept the evidence conceive of "mixed" assemblages when hand-axes and flakes occur together, even suggesting that such mixtures resulted from contacts and migrations of different

[1] HALLAM L. MOVIUS, JR., "Old World Prehistory: Paleolithic" in *Anthropology Today,* A. L. Kroeber (ed.), (Chicago, University of Chicago Press copyright 1953), pp. 163–192. Reprinted by permission of the author and the publisher.
Dr. Movius is Professor of Anthropology at Harvard University.

racial elements. Although the parallel phyla concept is not supported by the field evidence, it is still generally accepted by the majority of workers in the field of Paleolithic archeology.

On purely a priori grounds there is something fundamentally unsound with this hypothesis. As early as 1906, Commont described a large series of flake tools from his classic Acheulian locality at St. Acheul, and in 1908 Déchelette clearly stated that flake implements occurred in intimate and direct association with hand-axes at all the main localities in the Somme region. Later, in 1925, the view was further propounded by Obermaier, who remarked that, although the materials from the Somme gravel pits were collected by the workmen and not obtained during the course of controlled excavation, it was impossible to deny the existence of well-made flake tools side by side with hand-axes. This situation was further defined by Kelley in 1937, and the evidence has made some authorities suspicious of the existence of a clear-cut differentiation between the two traditions.

Now the parallel phyla concept has encountered rather considerable difficulties in those parts of the Old World where Lower Paleolithic hand-ax assemblages and advanced flake industries of Levalloisian type have been recognized. As will be discussed presently, these two traditions constitute inseparable components of one and the same complex throughout Africa, the Middle East, and India. Nowhere in this vast region has a vertical division between the essentially flake and core techniques been reported. On the basis of this overwhelming mass of unanimous evidence, one is perhaps justified in asking whether the concept of a Levalloisian tradition as an entity separate and distinct from an Acheulian tradition has any real validity in western Europe.

Recent investigations in the demonstrably Second Interglacial gravels of the Amiens region (Somme) indicate that the parallel phyla hypothesis is based on an assumption which is not borne out in the field. For three independent investigators, Breuil, Bordes, and Kelley, have described flakes of characteristic Levalloisian type, together with tortoise cores, in direct and indisputable association with Early-Middle Acheulian materials. Therefore, the Lower Paleolithic of western Europe can no longer be considered aberrant with respect to the Great Hand-Axe Complex as a whole in other parts of the Old World. However, the Clactonian flake industry, mainly restricted to England, can be regarded as a separate and distinct entity that has not been defined as yet outside northwestern Europe.

A typological comparison of the various hand-ax assemblages from widely separated areas will reveal that, with the exception of the material from which they are manufactured, the specimens themselves exhibit a striking degree of uniformity. This applies not only to form but also to the technical processes involved in their manufacture, both of which appear to be alarmingly constant. But this observation does not apply to the accompanying flake tools, including the cores from which the latter were struck, which suggests that it is the technique resorted to in the production of flake implements that is of prime importance. In that this is both a manifestation of tradition, on the one hand, and either diffusion of ideas or possible movements of peoples, on the other, it offers a possible solution to the present dilemma. In any event, the application of detailed typology as a means of studying Lower Paleolithic assemblages is getting us absolutely nowhere, and such elaborate sequences as the seven-fold Acheulian succession in northern France is incomprehensible except for the geological basis on which it has been established.

Recently, Van Riet Lowe has convincingly argued that one of the possible lines of escape from the present stalemate of Lower Paleolithic typology is by paying less attention to the form of the finished tools and attempting to reconstruct the process of their manufacture from the very beginning. Other workers are becoming convinced of the validity of this approach. Indeed, as Watson has observed, it is likely that a Stone Age community quite readily adopted "the shape of a tool it found in use by alien tribes, once its advantages were manifest, but much less likely that it should have the opportunity of learning, or be prepared, to revolutionize its industrial technique in order to reproduce the precise method of manufacture practiced by the original users of the tool." But the real difficulty with this approach is obvious: one should be familiar with the techniques themselves in order to detect them and assess their significance. In order to acquire the requisite insight into working methods, one should actually be able to reproduce them experimentally. Such technical ability is rare, and there are very few Paleolithic archeologists who can lay claim to it. Nevertheless, it is quite likely that when such an analysis of the Lower Paleolithic hand-ax assemblages can be made, we may discover the existence of just as complex an interplay of techniques as that which exists between the various Middle and Upper Paleolithic traditions of the Old World.

In general, Paleolithic archeologists have not recognized the fact that early men had at their disposal not just one but several different techniques for flaking stone, as Breuil has rightly insisted. In the majority of instances these are common to a whole group of cultural developments at one and the same time, although in different frequencies. But when the finished tools are examined, the degree of typological uniformity within a given complex is indeed astonishing. Apparently this is due in large measure to the fact that approximately 95 per cent of the collections from open sites (i.e., gravel or sand pits) in western Europe have been made by workmen who save only the best hand-axes, flake tools, and nuclei. It is probable that this has given us a completely false picture of many of the assemblages in question. Nevertheless, even in these highly selected series it is possible to recognize the existence of certain specialized techniques which are limited to only one or possibly two kinds of assemblages and hence provide a fairly reliable and distinctive basis for descriptive purposes. These have been intensively studied by François Bordes, himself an exceedingly skilful artificer of stone artifacts; and the provisional results of his work indicate that a new approach to problems of the Paleolithic is now being developed. Since this is regarded as of fundamental importance, the results of Bordes's investigations will be considered here in some detail.

The evidence of the occurrence of flakes of Levalloisian type in the Second Interglacial gravels of the Somme Valley, previously discussed, demonstrates that in western Europe, as in Africa, the Middle East, and India, the so-called "prepared" striking-platform/tortoise-core technique, or faceted platform technique, first appears in the middle of the Acheulian stage of development, continues during the Upper Acheulian, and reaches its final expression in the Mousterian of Levalloisian facies. In western Europe, however, the situation seems to be somewhat more complicated than elsewhere (South and East Africa, for example), owing to the fact that we also have to consider other traditions, such as the Clactonian and the Tayacian, which are only sporadically found elsewhere. As regards the Clactonian, Hazzledine Warren has recently shown that it is by no means comprised exclusively of flakes. Indeed, many of the pieces described as nuclei are nodules of flint alternately worked on one end to a zigzag chopping-tool edge. In reality, the developmental pattern of these various assemblages is extremely complex and can be unscrambled only by an intensive investigation of: (*a*) the flaking techniques employed in the manufacture of the tools, (*b*) the nature of the raw material available for the production of implements, (*c*) the typology of the artifacts, and (*d*) the exact stratigraphic position of each site. The latter problem, of course, belongs in the realm of the natural sciences, and here there is still much basic field work to be done. For our present purposes, however, we can broadly group the localities into the various glacial and interglacial stages, although in many instances it would be very desirable if a more precise relative chronology could be determined.

From a typological point of view, the main criterion for subdividing the Lower and Middle Paleolithic rests on the presence or absence of hand-axes, or *bifaces,* to use a term that does not imply function. Technologically, it is the presence or absence of flakes with faceted striking-platforms and the characteristic Levalloisian preparation of these flakes on the core prior to detachment that are of fundamental importance. But, contrary to generally accepted opinion, these two features are not necessarily related. Therefore, it is necessary to define in a much more precise manner than has previously been attempted exactly what is meant by the "Levalloisian flaking techinque," on the one hand, and the discoidal nucleus or "Mousterian flaking technique," on the other. From a historical point of view a Levallois flake is a type of flake first recognized from the gravels at Levallois, a suburb of Paris. Its form has been predetermined on the nucleus by special preparation prior to detachment. For the nucleus an oval-shaped nodule of flint is selected, gener-

ally of flattened form, which is roughly flaked along its borders to remove the irregularities. Next the cortex is removed from the upper surface by the detachment of centrally directed flakes, thus forming a surface which recalls the back of a tortoise, the flake scars representing the plates. On one end, perpendicular to the long axis, a striking-platform is prepared by the removal of very small flakes, thereby producing a faceted or scarred surface. A blow delivered by percussion technique (possibly with an intermediate tool) on this surface will yield a flat, oval flake which exhibits on its upper surface the traces of the centrally directed core preparation flakes. These flakes may also be round, triangular, or rectangular, depending on the shape of the nucleus. In the case of the latter, i.e., a rectangular flake, if the length is more than double the width, one has a flake blade, which, if it has been detached from a nucleus that exhibits a series of parallel rather than centrally directed scars, will resemble very closely true blades of the Upper Paleolithic. The Levalloisian point is a particular type of Levallois flake of elongated triangular form, the shape of which has been predetermined by special preparation of the nucleus.

Now the flakes struck from a certain type of core, known as the "discoidal core" and very typical of Mousterian assemblages, are commonly mistaken for true Levalloisian flakes, as Bordes rightly maintains. The discoidal nucleus also exhibits careful trimming around its edges, as well as the scars of a series of centrally directed flakes. But the objective of the Mousterian knapper was to obtain these centrally directed flakes rather than to prepare the core for the removal of a special type of product. Normally, the discoidal nucleus is more markedly convex (although in certain instances flat or even slightly concave) than the Levalloisian form, and it may be alternately worked on the two faces, giving it a bipyramidal section. In both cases, once the first series of flakes has been removed, the craftsman proceeds by selecting the base of the ridges separating the scars of two previously detached flakes as the striking-platform. According to Bordes, a triangular flake, which resembles a Levalloisian point but with a thick butt and a clumsy appearance, is often produced in this manner. Also in the Mousterian there are flakes with plain, unprepared striking-platforms, frequently inclined toward the lower surface, in which case they are sometimes classed as "Clactonian." But this results from the techinque employed—a hammer stone struck on a plain surface—and should not be taken to imply a connection with the true Clactonian assemblages of England. For these pseudo-Clactonian flakes are found in various contexts ranging from the Abbevillian to the Neo-lithic, including the Upper Paleolithic, and hence the term "Clactonian" should be reserved for the well-known Lower Paleolithic complex in which chopping-tools and choppers constitute the core-tool increment in place of hand-axes. In any case, nothing is yet known to demonstrate a transitional stage between the Clactonian and the typical Mousterian.

After defining the technological processes employed during Middle Paleolithic times in the production of flakes, Bordes applies this to various homogeneous assemblages from different parts of France on a statistical basis. These all come from localities that have produced 100 or more objects that have been selected neither by the workmen nor by collectors for museum display purposes. Of the various indices, four seem to be of fundamental significance, as follows:

1. *Levalloisian index (LI)*:

$$\frac{\text{Total no. of Levalloisian flakes, points, and blades} \times 100}{\text{Total no. of flakes and blades of all types}}$$

2. *Index of faceting (IF)*:

$$\frac{\text{Total no. of flakes with faceted butts} \times 100}{\text{Total no. of flakes on which the butt is recognizable}}$$

3. *Index of Levalloisian typology (ILty)*:

$$\frac{\text{Total no. of Levalloisian flakes, points, and retouched points} \times 100}{\text{Total no. of retouched forms of all types}}$$

4. *Bifacial (hand-ax) index (BI)*:

$$\frac{\text{Total no. of bifaces} \times 100}{\text{Total no. of bifacial} + \text{unifacial tools}}$$

The preliminary results of Bordes's study, including those recently published in a joint paper with Bourgon, demonstrate the existence of a broad Mousterian Complex, the fundamental characteristics of which can be expressed statistically for the first time. For all practical purposes, this is comprised of the following two main groups that are further broken down into two categories each of two subdivisions:

Group I: Mousterian with bifaces (hand-axes):
1. Levalloisian technique (LI > 25–30)
   A. With faceted butts (IF > 45)
      a. Micoquian of Levalloisian facies (ILty > 30)
      b. Mousterian of Acheulian tradition: Levalloisian facies (ILty < 30)

2. Non-Levalloisian technique (LI < 25–30)
   A. With faceted butts (IF > 45)
      a. Mousterian of Acheulian tradition: non-Levalloisian facies
   B. With unfaceted butts (IF < 45)
      b. Micoquian of non-Levalloisian facies
Group II: Mousterian without or with very few bifaces (hand-axes):
1. Levalloisian technique (LI > 25–30)
   A. With faceted butts (IF > 45)
      a. Mousterian of Levalloisian facies (ILty > 30)
      (= Levalloisian III, IV, VI, and VII of Breuil's scheme)
      b. Typical Mousterian (ILty < 30)
2. Non-Levalloisian technique (LI < 25–30)
   A. With faceted butts (IF > 45)
      a. Proto-Mousterian and Moustero-Tayacian
   B. With unfaceted butts (IF < 45)
      b. Tayacian and Mousterian of La Quina type (= *Charentian*)

Until recently it was maintained that the presence or absence of small, triangular, roughly cordiform or lanceolate hand-axes at sites referable to the Mousterian Complex was of chronological significance. But manifestly this is not true. They may be fairly frequent at one site but completely absent at several others, while the associated flake assemblages remain basically the same. Thus it may well be that, in instances where their occurence is extremely sporadic, we are dealing with intermittent or occasional settlement by hand-axusing groups rather than with a true component of the technological tradition of the region in question. It is likewise possibly attributable to seasonal factors; for, as is well known, the material traits of one and the same group of hunting peoples may differ very profoundly in different places during different seasons. Furthermore, as McBurney points out, such a group habitually travels over several hundred miles of territory during the annual cycle of specialized activities connected with hunting, fishing, and collecting. Certainly in southwestern France hand-axes commonly occur at both Mousterian open-air sites, as well as at the cave and rock-shelter stations, and in both cases the associated flake assemblages are invariably characterized by the faceted striking-platform/disk-shaped core technique. In other words, the pres-

ence or absence of these tools has no apparent chronological significance, and may be purely a manifestation of specialized activity. It is also possible that it is due to geographical factors.

Now the application of the geographical approach to Paleolithic problems was first attempted by Charles McBurney two years ago. But a study of this type can be undertaken only when the data are sufficiently numerous and adequate, a situation that has come about in certain sections of Europe only during the postwar period. Since this approach has been demonstrated to be fundamentally sound, especially for the Mesolithic complexes of northwestern Europe, there is no reason to doubt that it will ultimately prove of great value in interpreting Paleolithic problems. McBurney's preliminary work has a direct bearing on the question of hand-axes at Mousterian localities in western and central Europe as a whole. Thus the sites with hand-axes appear to be mainly confined to the maritime lowlands of western Europe, while in the hilly and mountainous districts of the interior an entirely different tradition is encountered. Although the former region lies in the tundra belt immediately south and west of the margins of the last ice sheets, it nonetheless formed a uniform ecological territory, offering a "maritime forest climate without perennially frozen ground." In the upland regions and in the territory between the limits of the northern and Alpine ice sheets, on the other hand, extreme arctic conditions prevailed, with frozen-soil phenomena; this was the true treeless forest tundra. But the available data are not of a sufficiently precise nature to permit a more detailed consideration of the significance of this observation. Nevertheless, it is important, in that it points the direction that will be followed in the future by research on the Paleolithic cultures of the Old World.

One of the facts that emerged in the late 1920's as the result of Breuil's investigations in the Somme Valley is that the Levalloision technique is characteristic of sites in the north of France, whereas at contemporary localities of the south (Dordogne region in particular) non-Levalloisian workmanship is more common. Bordes (1951) attributes this in large measure to the nature of the raw material. Certainly, it is a self-evident fact that, in dealing with any Stone Age assemblage, this plays a major role. In any case, the large-sized and more or less flat nodules of flint that occur in the chalk country of northern France lend themselves to the Levalloisian method of preparation of the core, thereby facilitating the detachment of a flake of predetermined form. On the other hand, in the south the majority of the nodules of flint are too small to work in this manner. Furthermore, they are often of globular or irregular outline, and there is nothing to be gained by employing the Levalloisian technique. Here we can only state that we agree completely with Bordes in maintaining that the quality and shape in which the raw material occurs have been factors of prime consideration. But, since the non-Levalloisian facies likewise occurs in regions where large-sized nodules of flint exist, it is certainly not the only one involved.

In order to formulate a possible explanation of this situation, it is necessary to consider such additional matters as: (*a*) the enormous length of time involved, which may well represent several tens of millenniums; (*b*) such geographic (i.e., environmental) conditions as those mentioned above; and (*c*) the type of social unit with which we are dealing. In this connection McBurney has very aptly stated:

It may be an archaeological truism, but it is nevertheless a point of the utmost practical importance, that assemblages of human artifacts require, as evidence, basically different interpretation to samples of organic fossils such as say, shells or pollen. Whereas the latter may be taken to indicate a semi-permanent biological population, the former, from what we know of modern primitive peoples, may well represent communities who ranged sporadically over wide areas outside their main habitat. An Eskimo tribe, for instance, has been described as making an annual trek of over 200 miles across hostile territory to obtain a much-needed raw material.

This concept is borne out by Bordes's conclusion based on considerations of a purely technological nature, namely, that the only significant difference between the materials from the open-air loess sites of northern France and the cave and rock-shelter stations of the south referable to the Mousterian of Levalloisian facies lies in what he has defined as the "Index of Levalloisian Typology" (ILty). In the case of the former, the percentage of Levalloisian flakes which have remained in mint condition or which have been very little retouched does not fall below 40. On the other hand, the average of the Lty for five typical horizons in the Dordogne which have produced Mousterian of Levalloisian facies is less than 10. Although the significance of this fact is not as yet altogether apparent, the various series under consideration cannot be differentiated on any other basis. Indeed, as Bordes suggests, one wonders if the Dordogne localities should not be regarded as the winter camps of the groups who hunted in the loess regions of the north during the summer season. On this basis the discrepancy in Levalloisian flake utilization may well reflect environmental differences of a seasonal nature but produced in both cases by groups which were basically identical. Surely, even if this interpretation cannot be proved until evidence of a much more refined nature is available, it seems a great deal more plausible than the taxonomic approach that was in vogue until recently; for the latter based its conclusions solely on the form and characteristic retouch exhibited by a selected series of the finished pieces.

In their recent joint paper Bordes and Bourgon, employing Bordes's statistical approach, have published a detailed treatise based on their analysis of a large series of sites—caves and rock-shelters, as well as loess stations—referable to the newly defined Mousterian Complex. The graphs indicate that, regardless of the technique(s) employed in the production of flakes, the typology of the fundamental categories of implements is surprisingly constant, with the exception of the recently defined Charentian. This can only mean that the basic way of life during the time span under consideration was broadly similar over very wide areas, but the problem of the particular functions of a given type of scraper or point is just as obscure as ever.

Although still in its infancy, the geographical or environmental approach, as advocated by McBurney and others, will doubtless contribute to an understanding of the range of possibilities concerning what tools were used for. But before it can be tested we urgently need new and reliably documented materials from undisturbed sites. In the meantime, by eliminating the Levalloisian in a cultural sense and defining it as one of two basic flaking techniques

in use at one and the sime time, Bordes has made a fundamental contribution to the methodology of Paleolithic archeology. It certainly helps materially to clarify the situation with respect to the Lower and Middle Paleolithic succession in western Europe. Furthermore, it removes one very grave difficulty in working in this field, namely, the complete lack of anything approaching truly objective criteria in the study of the materials available from the early hunting and gathering levels. Up to now, much of the work has been completely subjective; therefore, the effect of providing a definitive method for assessing the technological increment in any given assemblage will certainly be far-reaching. It will be interesting to follow the more widespread application of this principle in such areas as the Near East, India, North Africa, Egypt, East and South Africa, for example, where problems of the same kind exist. As the method is more broadly applied, it will inevitably be improved, for it is still somewhat cumbersome. Nonetheless, it offers the only recourse yet devised for analyzing a given assemblage in terms of its several components. When combined with chronological and environmental studies, it is reasonably certain that significant results will accrue.

Upper Paleolithic. Until the middle 1930's the Upper Paleolithic sequence in western Europe seemed fairly straightforward: Aurignacian, Solutrean, and Magdalenian, just as set forth in all the standard textbooks. According to this concept, the "Aurignacian," as originally defined by Breuil, could be subdivided into Lower, characterized by large curved points with blunted backs and known as "Châtelperron points"; Middle, with the split-base bone point, the busked graver or burin, and various types of steep scrapers; and Upper, of which a straight point with blunted back, apparently evolved from the Châ-

telperron type and known as the "Gra-
vette point," was typical. This latter
stage immediately preceded the Final
Aurignacian with its tanged point, known
as the "Font Robert type." However,
discoveries of the last fifteen or twenty
years have shown that, in reality, the
Aurignacian succession is very much
more complex than was originally suspected.

Formerly the only Upper Paleolithic
complex known outside Europe was the
Capsian of North Africa, and, since
points with blunted backs are characteristic of the Capsian assemblages, the old
Lower and Upper Aurignacian could
be conveniently derived from this source.
The Middle Aurignacian was supposed
to have developed *in situ* during an interval when contact with North Africa
was temporarily broken. But recent work
has shown that (*a*) from a chronological
point of view the Capsian is very late in
North Africa; (*b*) it is absent in Spain;
(*c*) in North Africa it is essentialy an inland development, the coastal region
everywhere being an Ibero-Maurusian
(Oranian) province; and (*d*) many of
the forms most characteristic of the Early
Capsian (e.g., microburins and lunates)
are completely absent in the Early-Upper
Paleolithic assemblages of western Europe. On this basis, the claim of Africa
as the homeland of the Lower and
Upper Aurignacian has been pretty well
ruled out.

But the problems of just what constitutes the Aurignacian and where its
various components originated still remain obscure. At the only two really adequately excavated Upper Paleolithic localities in the entire Dordogne region—
La Ferrassie and Laugerie-Haute—M.
Denis Peyrony has found evidence which
seems to suggest that the Aurignacian
(as conceived in 1912 by Breuil) is an
infinitely more complicated series of assemblages than was originally suspected
by the creator of the old threefold

scheme. In fact, Peyrony recognizes two
separate traditions:

Périgordian = Lower (Châtelperronian)
and Upper Aurignacian (Gravette/Font
Robert) of the old system
Aurignacian = Middle Aurignacian of the
Breuil classification

Peyrony's fundamental thesis is that
in its later stages the former coexisted
with the latter, a situation which can
best be shown in the form of a table
(Figure 1).

At this juncture the writer does not
intend to present a critique of Peyrony's
scheme. Suffice it to say, however, that
his scheme is in part supported by the
stratigraphic evidence, although certain
of the substages should doubtless be regarded as local variations. This very
fundamental and important problem is
urgently in need of further investigation;
certainly, it is not possible to interpret
the data on the basis of the evidence
available at present.

As to Upper Paleolithic origins, Professor Garrod believes that, when sections of Europe other than France are
considered, it becomes apparent that the
French sequence is the result of successive influences superimposed one on the
other. According to this view, on the periphery of its distribution the Upper Paleolithic becomes a more or less heterogeneous mass of successive levels which
lack meaning. It is only when we trace
these influences back along the main
routes of their supposed diffusion that the
situation can be in some measure unscrambled. For here we should find
definite geographical regions where relatively pure manifestations of given culture complexes can be recognized.

The argument that the very specialized blade technique—the hallmark of
the Upper Paleolithic—originated outside western Europe is based on two
significant facts: (*a*) the lack of a developmental sequence between the Mous-

Breuil's Classification	Garrod's Classification	Peyrony's Classification	
		Périgordian	Aurignacian
Upper Aurignacian	Font Robert stage	*5th phase:* Tanged points; leaf-like points; Noailles burins	*5th phase:* Bone points with simple beveled base
	Gravettian stage	*4th phase:* Gravette points; small-backed blades; female statuettes	*4th phase:* Bone points with biconical section
			3d phase: Bone points with oval section
Middle Aurignacian	Aurignacian	*3d phase:* Truncated or obliquely backed blades; backed blades of misc. types	*2d phase:* Bone points with diamond-shaped section; steep scrapers
		2d phase: Châtelperron points (evolved types); blades with inverse retouch	*1st phase:* Split-base bone points; steep and carinated scrapers
Lower Aurignacian	Châtelperronian	*1st phase:* Châtelperron points (basal Périgordian)	

Figure 1.

terian and the earliest phase of the Upper Paleolithic (indeed, no instance of stratigraphic overlap is known in this entire region) and (*b*) the equally sudden appearance in western Europe at this time of men of developed *sapiens* type. As McBurney points out, it is considered very unlikely from a biological standpoint that Neanderthal could have evolved into a fully modern form within the time span suggested by the geological evidence, a fact which has convinced most workers that the concept of the rapid immigration into Europe at this time of blade-using modern man should be accepted as a plausible assumption. Nevertheless, it must be frankly admitted at the outset that there is no geological or archeological proof clearly supporting such a postulated earlier occurrence of *Homo sapiens* in association with a blade industriy outside the region under consideration.

As to what Garrod has called "Châtelperronian" (= Peyrony's Early Périgordian; Lower Aurignacian of the old

scheme), this is claimed to have already had an independent existence in early Upper Pleistocene times in the Near East: Palestine (Mount Carmel Caves) and Syria (Jabrud). Although its precise center is still unknown, it appears in western Europe during the closing stages of the Mousterian as the earliest identifiable blade complex. Possibly it came from central Europe or South Russia, since it is found there at an early date. In any case, nothing has thus far come to light in central Asia to suggest that it originated farther to the east.

The Aurignacian (= Middle Aurignacian of the old system) is also well represented in central Europe, especially in lower Austria and Hungary, as well as through Rumania, the Crimea, and Transcaucasia to the Near East, where it is very widespread and covers a considerably longer time span than in the west. Apparently this manifestation is absent on the South Russian Plain. Although Garrod suggested the Iranian plateau as a possible center where the Aurignacian developed, Coon's recent excavations have certainly contributed nothing to support this hypothesis.

Turning now to Garrod's Gravettian/Font Robert Complex (= Peyrony's Late Périgordian; Upper Aurignacian of the old scheme), which extends into Spain and Italy, this has a wide distribution in central and eastern Europe and is considered by some authorities to be the classic Upper Paleolithic culture of the South Russian Plain, where true Aurignacian elements seem to be absent. A strong supporting argument for this concept is the fact that in South Russia, central Europe, and the west female statuettes of the Willendorf type are associated with the so-called "Gravettian" complex. Since this stage is absent in the Near East, it is possible that further excavations in the plains region of southern Russia will reveal that the Gravettian was derived from this source. It is also possible, however, that Peyrony is essentially correct in suggesting France for the main center of this development. In any case, on the basis of what we know at present concerning the materials found at stations on the South Russian Plain, this seems to be just as defensible a working hypothesis as any other. Certainly, both Peyrony and Garrod are fully aware that the discoveries of the next generation will, in turn, make further extensive revisions necessary.

In connection with future investigations, it is now generally admitted by Paleolithic archeologists that problems pertaining to the origin and development of the Upper Paleolithic will have to be dealt with on a regional basis. This is certainly a very great step in the right direction. For, in the past, work in this field has been very materially hampered by what may be termed the "index fossil concept"—i.e., approaching central Europe, South Russia, or the Near East (or any other area outside France, for that matter) as if they were some sort of typo-logical appendages of western Europe. In focusing attention on the so-called "pre-Solutrean problem" in central Europe in his recent book, Lothar Zotz, in fact, has advocated this point of view, although the net result is only to complicate further rather than to simplify the problems. For the pre-Solutrean must henceforth be regarded as yet another independent tradition that has to be considered in connection with Early-Upper Paleolithic problems. Zotz notes that bifacial leaf-shaped points, in some instances extremely reminiscent of true Solutrean forms, actually occur sporadically in central Europe in various Late Acheulian, Micoquian, and Mousterian contexts, and he believes that it is from these early developments that the pre-Solutrean is basically derived. The evidence from the most important sites for this development shows that the pre-Solutrean dates from the time of the Würm I/II Interstadial, overlapping and paralleling the Châtelperronian (Early Périgordian). According to Zotz, the pre-Solutrean (also known as the Szeletian or Altmühlian) is a separate cultural manifestation heavily influenced from contemporary Upper Paleolithic sources. In fact, at certain sites it actually underlies Aurignacian horizons. Finally, during Gravettian (Late Périgordian) times, this blossoms out into the true Solutrean of central Europe assigned to the Würm II/III Interstadial on the basis of the evidence from the Czechoslovakian stations of Předmost and Moravany-Dlha.

This evidence certainly opens up a new perspective on Old Stone Age developments in central Europe, made possible only by recognizing and admitting the existence of regional cultural specializations during Middle and Upper Paleolithic times rather than by trying to force the data to fit the strictures of a taxonomic scheme established for an entirely different region over half a century ago. But, at the same time, it makes the problem of where the Solutrean originated even more obscure than ever. Once it was an accepted fact that this complex had reached France from somewhere to the east, presumably from Hungary. But when the Soviet archeologists failed to find any traces of Solutrean beyond the Dniester, the claim of Hungary began to subside. Then in 1942 Professor Pericot Garcia published the results of his excavations at the Cave of Parpalló near Gandia (south of Valencia in southeastern Spain), where he had discovered a well-developed Solutrean culture with tanged and barbed projectile points, in addition to bifacial leaf-shaped types. The fact that certain of the former were strikingly close to examples known in the Late Aterian of North Africa (Tangier: Mugharet el'Aliya) led many Paleolithic archeologists to suspect that possibly the main focus of the European Solutrean lay in this southwesterly direction. Thus, if Zotz's pre-Solutrean has validity—and there is no reason to suspect otherwise —we now have two centers from which to derive the Solutrean—central Europe and southeastern Spain, where the inspiration apparently came from a Middle Paleolithic derivative known as the Aterian of North Africa. Although in central Europe the pre-Solutrean can also be traced back to Middle Paleolithic sources, this manifestly gets us nowhere with regard to the solution of the problem. In view of the new evidence, however, the development of such a specialized technique as pressure-flaking from complexes on an entirely different technological level from that of the Upper Paleolithic of Europe does not present inherent difficulties of the same magnitude as was true fifteen years ago. Indeed, most workers are quite prepared to accept the Solutrean as due to a diffusion of certain specialized ideas rather than an invasion of new peoples with superior weapons.

By the final stage of the Upper Pale-

olithic, regional cultural developments can be discerned very clearly. For the Magdalenian, centered in France, is limited in its distribution to western Czechoslovakia, southern Germany, Switzerland, Belgium, and Spain. Elsewhere we have such cultures as the Hamburgian of northwestern Germany, the Creswellian of England, and various evolved Gravettian (in the broad sense) complexes in Italy, parts of central Europe, and South Russia. Because of its truly magnificent naturalistic art, especially that of the Franco-Cantabrian Province, priority here clearly belongs to the Magdalenian, although the discovery of Lascaux some ten years ago has revealed an unexpected richness belonging to an earlier cycle. Now, as is well known, Magdalenian art includes painting in monochrome and polychrome in a wide variety of styles and techniques, engravings on stone, bone, and ivory, and sculptures in both high and low relief. The recent discoveries, especially at Angles-sur-l'Anglin, have emphasized the importance of local centers of artistic development. The real point of issue, however, is whether or not the pictures and drawings were done for purely decorative purposes. It does not seem at all likely that a primitive hunting community, living under the conditions of a rigorous and exacting environment, could have supported a specialized class of professional artists, such as some authorities have suggested. Nevertheless, it is patently clear that certain individuals lived during the Upper Paleolithic who were endowed with a highly developed artistic ability and a true appreciation of aesthetic values. Otherwise, there could not have been such a high development of art. In any case, the whole development clearly owes its existence to the magico-religious idea, especially the custom of hunting magic, as practiced today by living primitive peoples. This is one of the very few problems facing Paleolithic archeologists upon the solution of which ethnological studies would doubtless throw new light.

AFRICA

The Paleolithic of Africa is characterized by a variety of assemblages, some of which are purely local, whereas others are surprisingly similar to, if not identical with, certain of those found in Europe. It is only during recent years that geological investigations on a really adequate basis have been undertaken in this continent, and the results to date indicate that, owing to fluctuations in rainfall, the Pleistocene epoch throughout most of Africa can be subdivided on the basis of a succession of pluvial and interpluvial stages. Perhaps eventually these may be broadly correlated with the successive glacial and interglacial episodes of Europe. The cultural sequences are well established in certain areas, as indicated below, but this does not apply as yet to the continent as a whole.

Egypt. Even in Paleolithic times Egypt already seems to have been almost as self-sufficient as she was in the dynastic period. Nothing of the rich and complex Upper Paleolithic development of the Near East is found here, but the cause of this cultural isolation from the north and east cannot be explained on the basis of the existing data. The geologic history of the Nile Valley during Late Cenozoic times is well known as the result of the intensive field work done there in the 1920's by Sandford and Arkell for the Oriental Institute of the University of Chicago.

The Abbevillian–Early Acheulian series of the 30-meter terrace calls for no special comment. Some of the very heavily rolled forms may be derived from the 45-meter terrace, although no *in situ* specimens have ever been found there. With the exception of a special form with a triangular section, known as the "Chalossian," these forms are indistinguish-

able from early Lower Paleolithic materials from western Europe. In association with these early types of hand-axes, very primitive flake tools with plain, high-angled striking-platforms occur. The Late Acheulian of the 15-meter terrace includes pointed hand-axes of Micoquian type, together with developed forms of flake implements; and in the Acheulio-Levalloisian of the 9-meter terrace there are oval or pointed flakes with faceted striking-platforms associated with tortoise-type cores and a few subtriangular hand-axes. In the 3-meter terrace there is a Middle Levalloisian industry in which a reduction in size and an increase in the delicacy of the flakes may be noted. The next series of deposits—the basal aggradational silts—yield an Upper Levalloisian assemblage, including several specialized types of points, as well as a bifacial lanceolate that suggests Aterian examples. The associated cores show a wide variety of form; in general, they are narrower than in the preceding stage.

Up to this point the main lines of development in the Kharga oasis and the Fayum follow the same basic pattern as outlined above for the Nile Valley. Subsequent to the time of the deposition of the basal aggradational silts, however, this is no longer true, since in each region there was a gradual industrial differentiation. These are: the Sebilian in Upper Egypt and Nubia; the Epi-Levalloisian in Lower Egypt and the Fayum; and the Khargan and the Aterian in the Kharga oasis. All are basically derived from the Late Levalloisian and perpetuate the same technological tradition. Thus Egypt developed along indigenous lines almost completely undisturbed by contemporary developments from outside the area, except for the appearance of the Aterian in the Kharga oasis, as discussed in the section on North Africa. Here only one of these three specialized complexes—the Sebilian—will be briefly considered.

Typical of the Lower Sebilian are

flakes of Levallois type of reduced size, often with steeply retouched edges. One characteristic form exhibits a deliberately shortened striking-platform, giving the flake a squat appearance. In the Middle Sebilian backed lunates made on small flakes rather than on microblades, as well as certain subgeometric forms, appear. True Levalloisian flakes now almost completely disappear, although technologically the industry is clearly in the prepared striking-platform/tortoise-core tradition. The Upper Sebilian, which is probably later in time than the last major pluvial episode, approaches the Lower Natufian of Palestine and the Late Capsian of North Africa—both Mesolithic complexes—in many respects. In fact, at Helwan in Upper Egypt a true microlithic industry occurs, which is very like the Natufian of Palestine. But in the Upper Sebilian the occurrence of highly evolved and much reduced flakes and tortoise cores of basic Levalloisian facies serves to link this Mesolithic assemblage with the ancient flaking tradition of the Lower and Middle Paleolithic.

East Africa. Actually, Paleolithic materials have been reported throughout the entire region intervening between Egypt and British East Africa, including the Anglo-Egyptian Sudan, Ethiopia, and Somaliland, the affinities of which have been assessed on a typological basis. But, since almost none of the horizons can be fitted into any of the established Pleistocene chronologies, there is little to be gained by presenting a regional summary of these materials. Now British East Africa—Kenya, Uganda, and Tanganyika—is bisected by the Great Rift Valley, on the walls of which excellent sections of Pleistocene deposits are exposed. The Paleolithic assemblages from sites to the west of this feature show that in prehistoric times this region belonged in equatorial Africa, just as it does at present. Therefore, it will be considered in a subsequent section; here the materials

from the definitely savannah country of most of Kenya and Tanganyika will be described.

The earliest-known and most primitive tools from this area, known as the "Kafuan," consist of pebbles with a single edge, flaked on one side only. The Kafuan implements come from definitely Lower Pleistocene deposits and are regarded as one of the oldest archeological manifestations from anywhere in the world. At the classic Middle Pleistocene locality of Olduvai, in northern Tanganyika, a series of beds covering the range of time represented by the Second (Kamasian) Pluvial, the Second Interpluvial, and the Third (Kanjeran) Pluvial are exposed. During the ensuing interpluvial, severe rifting movements occurred, accompanied by erosion and valley-cutting, which mark the close of the Middle Pleistocene in this area. From the basal beds at Olduvai a pebble-tool industry, more evolved than the Kafuan and known as the "Oldowan," has been described by Leakey. These include true chopping tools with edges alternately flaked in two directions, producing a jagged cutting edge. In the immediately overlying beds, pointed chopping tools appear which are regarded as the forerunners of the true bifacial hand-axes that have been reported from the next series of deposits, in association with various types of massive flake tools. At the horizon of the upper-middle part of Bed II at Olduvai, hand-axes of unmistakably Early Acheulian type appear. In Bed III the pointed hand-axes of Middle Acheulian type are associated with cleavers, made on "side-blow" flakes, and proto-Levalloisian flakes. This developmental sequence culminates in the Late Acheulian of Bed IV, where, in addition to finely made pointed hand-axes, there are rectangular-shaped cleavers and a fully developed Levalloisian flake industry. No other single locality discovered to date can compare with Olduvai in providing a complete and unbroken record of the entire cycle of Lower Paleolithic cultural development.

Contemporary with the widespread geographical changes marking the close of the Middle Pleistocene in East Africa, two distinct types of tool-making traditions are found: (*a*) the Early Kenya Stillbay, a Levalloisian derivative in which some surviving Acheulian elements are present, and (*b*) the Kenya Fauresmith, which is basically of Acheulian inspiration and very similar to the Fauresmith of South Africa. In addition to varous types of scrapers and points made on Levalloisian-type flakes, the former is characterized by small- to medium-sized bifacially flaked points that resemble minute hand-axes. This complex is very widespread in South Africa, where it shows a number of regional specializations. The Kenya Fauresmith also extends into Ethiopia; carefully shaped round stone balls constitute part of the assemblage. Since these normally occur in groups of twos or threes at the camp sites, they are regarded as bolas weights for use in hunting.

Following the post-Kanjeran interpluvial, the climate once again became markedly humid, and this interval is known as the "Gamblian Pluvial Period," which is of Upper Pleistocene age. The main cultural development known from deposits of this age is the Kenya Stillbay. Its bifacially flaked points often have secondarily retouched edges; and, in the final stages of the development, leaf-shaped forms appear, apparently worked by the technique of pressure-flaking. In the post-Gamblian dry phase, microlithic tools appear for the first time, and the earliest assemblage in which they are found is known as the "Magosian." From a chronological point of view the Magosian must belong to a fairly late horizon, since certain sites of this complex have yielded pottery. In addition to pottery, a true blade technique now appears in East Africa—called the "Kenya Capsian"—which is the immediate forerunner of the Elmenteitan in many of its most distinctive elements. Apparently contemporary with the latter manifestations there occurs a typical microlithic assemblage, the Kenya Wilton; but, since this has a widespread distribution in South Africa, it will be referred to in the next section.

South Africa. The Pleistocene succession in the basin of the Vaal River from near Johannesburg to the confluence with the Orange River has been worked out in great detail. This is also true of the sequences in northern and southern Rhodesia, but within the compass of the present paper, these latter areas cannot be considered. The oldest gravels of the Vaal, probably laid down during basal Pleistocene (Early Kageran) times, have not yielded any artifacts as yet, but in the next younger series of deposits pebble tools occur. These artifacts, which are called "pre-Stellenbosch" and which recall both the Kafuan and the Oldowan of East Africa, are found in a series of gravel terraces that range from 300 to 50 feet above the stream. A lower terrace at +50 feet contains Abbevillian types of hand-axes, in many cases made on pebbles, together with primitive flakes. This assemblage is called "Stellenbosch I." Following the interval of heavy rainfall during which these gravels were accumulated, there was a prolonged dry interval, marked by earth movements, for which there is no record of human occupation in South Africa. This is considered to mark the close of the Lower Pleistocene.

A new series of gravels, aggraded at relatively low elevations, are referable to a sequence of geologic episodes probably related to the Kamasian and Kanjeran pluvial periods of the Middle Pleistocene. Three terraces forming distinct levels at +40 feet, +25 feet, and river-bed level carry deposits which not only yield a very rich fauna, but also five stages representing the entire development of the South African Hand-Axe, or Stellenbosch, Complex. Stage I, in which roughly made Abbevillian-like types and primitive flake artifacts predominate, still contains some pebble tools, but these disappear in Stage II. The hand-axes and cleavers of the latter are now more refined and recall Early Acheulian forms of Europe. Together with the developed hand-axes and cleavers made on "side-blow" flakes of Stage III, the Levalloisian, or prepared striking-platform/tortoise-core technique (also called the "faceted platform technique"), has its inception. Also found in groups of twos and threes are faceted polyhedral stones, regarded by some authorities as bolas stones. The cleavers of Stage IV are characteristic, in that they are now made on end-struck flakes with a trapezoidal- rather than a parallelogram-shaped section. This stage corresponds with the Late Acheulian of East Africa, and during it the prepared striking-platform technique continued to develop. The finely made hand-axes of Stage V are comparable to the Micoquian of Europe; these are associated with cleavers that have flared edges and a variety of tools made for special functions on flakes produced by the Levalloisian technique. The climax of the long, uninterrupted Stellenbosch development was brought to a close by a second interval of earth movements and by a dry climate.

The next series of gravels was laid down during an Upper Pleistocene wet phase, probably corresponding to the Gamblian of East Africa. These sediments contain the Fauresmith assemblage, characterized by a marked refinement in the flake tools of Levalloisian facies and the development of small, relatively slender hand-axes and cleavers. In view of the overwhelming proportion of flake artifacts in the Fauresmith, Van Riet Lowe has suggested the possibility

that stabbing and throwing spears, as well as hafted tools and weapons of various sorts, now began to replace the earlier hand implements of the Stellenbosch. Following these aggradations, there was an arid interval when semidesert conditions prevailed. The ensuing wet phase, correlated with the Makalian of East Africa, witnessed the development of a series of assemblages referred to the Middle Stone Age of South Africa. Hand-axes and cleavers no longer occur, the characteristic tools being made on flakes produced by a developed Levalloisian technique (Stillbay, Pietersburg, Mossel Bay, etc.). These include slender unifacial and bifacial spear and lance points, presumably for stabbing or throwing. In the final stages of the Middle Stone Age, known as the "South African Magosian," microlithic elements appear, just as they do in East Africa.

Wind-blown deposits of the post-Makalian dry interval buried the Middle Stone Age sites. A final minor wet phase, presumably paralleled by the Nakuran of East and equatorial Africa, witnessed the introduction of the so-called "Later Stone Age" cultures—Smithfield and Wilton—which are characterized by (a) small tools, including a large number of microliths, (b) the absence of the old Levalloisian technique, (c) parallel rather than convergent flaking, and (d) the widespread use of indurated shale in the manufacture of tools. Smithfield and Wilton are closely related and reveal varying degrees of influence as the result of contact with the culture introduced by the ancestors of the Bantu-speaking peoples. Since both were still extant at the time the first Europeans arrived in South Africa, the area constitutes one of the few places in the Old World where there exists a direct link between archeology and ethnology.

Central or Equatorial Africa. A very clear demonstration of response in Paleolithic cultural development to environmental conditions can be seen in the case of central or equatorial Africa, as recently pointed out by Goodwin. Here in what Frobenius has called the "Hylaean Area," or the region of the Selva, a special evolution in material culture took place, which is characterized by the occurrence of (a) the bifacial gouge or chisel, (b) the elongated pick—possibly an adze, (c) the tranchet type of ax, and (d) the elongated lance or spearhead. That this very distinctive assemblage, known as the "Sangoan" (formerly Tumbian) culture, was developed in response to environmental conditions has been established on the basis of distribution studies. These show that everywhere it occurs it is included within the 40-inch isohet, or contour of equivalent rainfall, which roughly delimits the tropical forest or equatorial region of central Africa. In addition to an unusually dense vegetation, typical of this area, are widespread deposits of soft alluvium and humus, the present distribution of which suggests very strongly that during the pluvial periods of the past the 50-inch or even the 60-inch isohet expanded to cover the areas adjacent to this zone. Today these are characterized by parklands and open bush country. With this expansion, the Hylaean area likewise expanded, and with it new types of tools developed to cope with the daily exigencies of life under such conditions. But what the latter actually were cannot as yet be determined.

Now the Lower Paleolithic development of the area is essentially a repetition of what has already been outlined for East and South Africa. From a horizon corresponding with the beginning of Middle Stone Age times in the South African sequence, however, the artifactual development of central Africa contrasts very strikingly with the regional assemblages found to the east and south of it. In the latter regions various types of points, flakes, and blade implements predominate in all the so-called "Middle Stone Age" complexes thus far brought to light. Although certain basic tool types overlap to some extent, it is the environmental background of the Sangoan culture that is of prime importance. Possibly when more is known concerning the scope and limitations imposed on human activities by such environmental conditions, we shall be able better to assess the significance of this and interpret the possible function(s) of the various very specialized types of tools. Since the Sangoan is found in deposits laid down after the Kanjeran pluvial, it is of Upper Pleistocene age. Just as in the case of the Fauresmith of South Africa, this development had its origin in the Great Hand-Axe Complex and carries on the same basic tradition. Indeed, the Sangoan is now generally accepted as a direct derivative of the Acheulian complex, which survived in the Hylaean area well down into Upper Pleistocene times. But in the present state of our knowledge it must be accepted as a fact that the radically different ecological conditions in the "retreat area" resulted in an equally radically different cultural development, since we do not even pretend to understand the dynamics involved.

North Africa. North Africa's geographic position places it outside the area of direct contact with glacial and periglacial phenomena, which provide the keystone for chronologic studies in Eurasia. But this is in part offset by the existence of circum-Mediterranean marine phenomena linked with world-wide fluctuations of sea-level during Pleistocene and later time. Also there are indications here of arid and pluvial phases corresponding with interglacial and glacial episodes of the north. The only demonstrably Villafranchian (= basal Pleistocene) locality to yield human artifacts is situated at St. Arnaud, near Setif (Algeria). These consist of very crudely worked pebble tools of roughly spherical form and are the oldest implements ever found in the Old World. Lower Paleolithic hand-axes of both Abbevillian and Acheulian type associated with flake tools have been reported in great numbers throughout the entire area, including the Sahara, which was apparently less arid during Middle Pleistocene times than it is at present. The most important Lower Paleolithic sites are in the vicinity of Casablanca, Palikao (southeast of Mascara), Tabelbala, and Gafsa. Although the relative duration of the Lower Paleolithic is unknown in North Africa, the main developmental sequence seems to coincide broadly with that found elsewhere, and in a few isolated instances geological reference points have been established.

The Middle Paleolithic was very widespread, and it persisted in the North African area at least as late as the time of the Würm I/II Interstadial in terms of the Alpine sequence. A wide range of flake-tool assemblages, the most distinctive feature of which is the prominent role played by the prepared striking-platform/tortoise-core technique, is grouped here. Included in this category is the Mousterian, as well as the Aterian, a specialized Mousterian development characterized by tanged points made on flakes and bifacially worked in some instances. In general, the Mousterian seems to follow the Acheulian and to precede the Aterian, and several regional variations of it are claimed. But at two sites in the western part of the area (Morocco and Tangier) a simplified Mousterian follows the Aterian, while at Sidi-Zin, a recently investigated locality in Tunisia, two Acheulian horizons are separated by one yielding characteristically Mousterian tools. Hence contemporaneousness or noncontemporaneousness of similar morphological assemblages has not been demonstrated for the Middle Paleolithic of North Africa, and the various chronological schemes that have been proposed tend to degenerate into purely typological assessments.

The Capsian and Mouillian (formerly known as the "Oranian" or "Ibero-Maurusian"), both blade-tool complexes distinctive of this area, follow the Mousterian/Aterian development. Both date from the end of Upper Paleolithic times, but their main effervescence was during early postglacial (or postpluvial) times. The Capsian distribution is essentially inland and is centered around Gafsa in southern Tunisia and Tebessa in southeastern Algeria, while the Mouillian occurs everywhere along the coast from southern Tunisia to the Atlantic seaboard of Morocco. The Capsian is characterized by backed blades and points, scrapers, burins, and a very wide range of microlithic forms, the latter occurring almost exclusively at the youngest sites. The Mouillian is likewise a microlithic complex, in which the tools, on the whole, are smaller. Both the Capsian and the Mouillian persisted well after the introduction of Neolithic traits into this area.

ASIA

Recent work on the Paleolithic archeology of Asia indicates that during Middle Pleistocene times this vast region was divided into two major culture provinces, each of which has yielded a distinctive sequence. The first of these, which is in the south and east, includes China, Burma, northwestern India, and Java, where the characteristic implement types consist of choppers and chopping tools that are often made on pebbles. None of the well-known Paleolithic complexes of Europe and western Asia seem to be represented. The second major province includes the Near East, Russian Turkestan, and peninsular India, and here a developmental sequence closely paralleling that of Europe, as well as Africa in its early stages, has been reported. Indeed, during Paleolithic times the entire western portion of Asia apparently was mainly inspired by the same technological innovations that motivated contemporary developments in Europe. In fact, many of the same fundamental techniques and types of tools are common to both regions. On this basis, the region encompassed by the Near Eastern lands may be considered in a sense as a southeasterly extension of a very much larger province. Finally, north-central Asia, which apparently was not occupied until toward the close of the Upper Pleistocene, has produced materials the affinities of which can be traced to both of the major provinces. Although the "Western" increment is dominant, the occurrence of pebble tools at sites in this region attests the extremely late survival of the ancient pebble-tool tradition of the Far East.

The Chopper/Chopping-Tool Tradition of Southern and Eastern Asia. Uninfluenced by contemporary innovations in Africa, Europe, and western Asia, the archaic and very primitive tradition of making implements of the chopper and chopping-tool varieties either on pebbles or roughly tabular blocks persisted in the Far East as long as the practice of making stone tools survived. In Africa, as previously stated, such pebble-tool developments as the Kafuan, the Oldowan, and the pre-Stellenbosch are widespread and first appear in deposits laid down before the close of the Lower Pleistocene. Although human remains from Java show that man was extant at this time in Asia, no artifactual materials older than the Middle Pleistocene have yet come to light. Now the distinguishing feature of the various regional assemblages found in several sections of southern and eastern Asia is not the presence of a limited range of certain very old and fundamental types of tools; rather it is the absence of the two most distinctive features of the various Lower and Middle Paleolithic assemblages of

the west. These are (*a*) the Abbevilleo-Acheulian cycle of hand-ax development and (*b*) the intimately associated prepared striking-platform/tortoise-core, or Levalloisian, technique. In such intermediate regions as northwestern India a certain degree of overlap and fusion of the two basic technological patterns occurs, since bifacial core implements and Levalloisian-type flakes of Western type are found together with numerous pebble tools reminiscent of those from China and Burma. Below is presented a summary of the sequences in the several regions of southern and eastern Asia under discussion.

Burma.   In the terrace gravels of the Irrawaddy Valley of upper Burma a complex known as the "Anyathian" has been recognized, in which hand-axes are absent. Throughout, the Anyathian is characterized by single-edged core implements made of fossil wood and silicified tuff: choppers, chopping tools, and hand-adzes. In addition, there is a series of large crude flake implements with plain high-angle striking-platforms, comparable with those found in other parts of the world at the same general time horizon, but normally associated with early types of hand-axes. For the Early Anyathian is present in three distinct horizons of the gravels exposed on the two highest terraces of the ancestral Irrawaddy, which are of Middle Pleistocene age. The Late Anyathian, a direct development from the earlier assemblages, is characterized by smaller and better-made core and flake artifacts, including such specialized types as true scrapers and points. It is found *in situ* in the fourth Irrawaddy terrace and is Upper Pleistocene in date.

China.   Current information concerning early man in China during the Middle Pleistocene is based exclusively on the evidence from the well-known site of Choukoutien, a village at the base of a small limestone hill some 37 miles southwest of Peking. This hill contains an enormously rich series of fissure deposits, three of which were occupied during the interval of time roughly corresponding with the Second Glacial (Mindel), Second Interglacial (Mindel-Riss), and Third Glacial (Riss) stages in terms of the Alpine sequence. These are known as localities 13, 1, and 15. The single artifact from locality 13 is a small pebble tool and is the oldest evidence thus far discovered of human occupation in this part of the world. Associated with the remains of Peking Man (*Sinanthropus*) at the important locality 1 site, a large series of choppers and chopping tools has been described. These are of archaic type and made on river pebbles or other natural pieces of stone; they are associated with a quartz flake industry which includes smaller types of implements, especially scrapers and points. Large hearths occur throughout the deposits, demonstrating that *Sinanthropus* was familiar with the making and use of fire. The third Lower Paleolithic locality, No. 15 of the Choukoutien fissures, has yielded a series of somewhat better-made artifacts than those from locality 1, but nonetheless manufactured by employing the same basic techniques of stone-working which resulted in the production of pebble tools, on the one hand, and quartz flakes, on the other. It is apparent that this complex, known as the "Choukoutienian culture," forms an integral part of the chopper/chopping-tool tradition of eastern Asia.

Java. In addition to the famous discoveries of *Pithecanthropus* and other very primitive types of hominids, the former presence of early man on this island is attested by the occurrence of a large number of crude stone artifacts of Lower Paleolithic type from a site just north of Patjitan in south-central Java. Hence this assemblage is known as the "Patjitanian." The main types of imple-

ments consist of single-edged choppers, chopping tools, and hand-adzes, manufactured from various silicified rocks, that can scarcely be distinguished from those found in Burma and China. Primitive flakes, with unprepared striking-platforms at a high angle with the long axis of the implement, also occur here. In addition, there is an interesting series of pointed artifacts, including proto-hand-axes and crude hand-axes, the former being unifacial tools (i.e., worked on only one surface), whereas the latter are true bifacial implements. The presence of this hand-ax series in the Patjitanian may be accounted for as either (*a*) the independent development of tools of this type in Java or (*b*) some sort of diffusion or influence from peninsular India, where tools of this type are very common. The absence of hand-axes in Burma and Malaya tends to rule out the latter as a possibility. In defense of the former, all one can say is that a convincing argument can be put forward on typological grounds suggesting that tools of the hand-ax type were independently evolved in Java. But until there is something approaching stratigraphy to go on, it is only possible to speculate. It is a cardinal fact, however, that, to date, nothing has been reported from Java attributable to the Levalloisian prepared striking-platform/tortoise-core technique. This evidence shows that the Patjitanian should be included in the larger culture province of southern and eastern Asia which existed during Middle Pleistocene times.

Malaya. In the Middle Pleistocene tin-gravels of Perak, northern Malaya, a large series of Lower Paleolithic types of implements made of quartzite was discovered in 1938. These occur at a place called Kota Tampan and therefore are referred to as the "Tampanian" culture; they are almost indistinguishable from those found near Patjitan in Java, briefly discussed above.

India. Certain of the Paleolithic

assemblages from this vast region demonstrate that during Paleolithic times it was a marginal area intermediate between the two main provinces of western Asia, on the one hand, and southern and eastern Asia, on the other, from the point of view of the fundamental traditions employed in the manufacture of stone tools. In the Punjab Province of northwestern India assemblages of implements characteristic of both the chopper/chopping-tool and the hand-ax/Levalloisian flake complexes are found. In this latter area the earliest tools, which are of Second Glacial age (the so-called "Punjab Flake Industry"), consist of large, crude, heavily worn flakes. This development is followed in the Second Interglacial stage by the Early Soan culture, on the basis of the evidence from a series of sites in the Indus and Soan valleys. Pebble tools, including choppers and chopping tools, as well as flake implements, are characteristic. The latter, massive and crude in the early phases of the Soan, develop into forms described as "proto-Levalloisian." In part contemporary with this fundamentally "Eastern" complex is a series of hand-axes of Abbevillian and Acheulian type that recall not only European and African examples but also those of the Madras region of peninsular India. To date, no clearly stratified site has been found in northwestern India to indicate which of the two basic complexes —the Abbevilleo-Acheulian or the Soan —was the earlier in the Punjab. During Upper Pleistocene time the Late Soan is found. Evolved types of pebble tools and a wide range of flake artifacts produced by the prepared striking-platform/tortoise-core technique are typical. In addition, a few parallel-sided flake blades occur in the Late Soan.

Peninsular India is extremely prolific of Paleolithic localities, and invariably the artifactual materials include hand-axes, cleavers, and flake tools that are very reminiscent of assemblages from South and East Africa. But the actual dating and relative chronology of these sites is very little known; indeed, here Pleistocene geology has lagged far behind archeological discovery. As the result of field investigations undertaken during recent years, reports on collection from some eight or nine main areas are available. Admittedly, this is an impressive beginning, but a very great deal more basic work remains to be done. Since the sequence in the Madras region is reasonably well known, a brief summary of the evidence from Vadamadurai and Attirampakkam—the two richest sites—will be presented.

The oldest material comes from Vadamadurai, where the entire sequence is represented. It includes a series of heavily rolled and patinated flakes and Abbevillian-type hand-axes of crude outline and exhibiting deep, irregular flake scars. These are found in a deposit of boulder conglomerate. On typological grounds the next series may be compared with the Early Acheulian; it also comes from the boulder conglomerate horizon but is far less patinated than the Abbevillian group. The flakes in this series exhibit less cortex on the upper surface and more primary flaking on the core prior to detachment than is true of the older specimens. From detrital laterites overlying the boulder conglomerate a typical Middle Acheulian assemblage has been described. Some of the associated flakes show definite signs of retouch. The next younger materials are found in the nonlaterized deposits carried on three terraces, which were formed during Upper Pleistocene times but cannot be more precisely dated on the basis of the available evidence. Evolved forms of flat-sectioned hand-axes of Upper Acheulian type with more pronounced secondary working of the edges are found in these terraces at both Vadamadurai and Attirampakkam, together with cleavers, tortoise cores, and flakes with faceted butts. The typical cleavers have parallelogrammic cross-sections produced by the so-called "side-blow" technique; these are practically identical with examples from Stellenbosch V of the Vaal Valley in South Africa and from the site of Tashenghrit in North Africa. Hand-axes with an S-twist also merit special mention. The cores exhibit very regular and even working, while the flake tools have faceted striking-platforms with much primary flaking on the upper surface in the best Levalloisian tradition. Among the types of flake implements, there are some side-scrapers and triangular points definitely retouched for use.

More northerly sites, such as those in the Narbada Valley, in Mayurbhanj, and the Gujarat, have yielded hand-axes associated with cleavers and flakes, similar to the Madras localities. And, together with these characteristic Lower Paleolithic forms, there are pebble tools reminiscent of the Soan complex of the Punjab. In other words, the ancient tool-making tradition of the Far East persisted here, just as it did in northwestern India. On this basis it seems likely that old deposits will ultimately be found in this area containing only choppers and chopping tools made on pebbles.

One problem concerning Old Stone Age developments in India that still remains obscure is what happened here during Upper Paleolithic times. From the Krishna Valley, Kurnool District, Madras, and from Khandivili, near Bombay, true blade industries with burins and other characteristically Upper Paleolithic types have been described. But, as yet, all one can say with regard to dating these assemblages is that they appear to be younger than the last pluvial episode and older than the earliest microlithic assemblages, which have a wide distribution in India in association with deposits of sub-Recent age. In many respects the latter situation is very reminiscent of that found in the Near East, Europe, and Africa; in fact, some of the Indian microlithic assemblages are very suggestive of the Wilton. In any case, before any consecutive picture of Paleolithic developments in India can be presented, much intensive work remains to be done. It is therefore encouraging to note that an active research program has been implemented which will inevitably yield substantial results.

The Near East. In the western portion of Asia a Paleolithic succession very closely paralleling that of Europe has been reported, but no synthesis of the materials as a whole has ever appeared. The best stratigraphy thus far reported in detail is that revealed at a series of three caves in the Mount Carmel range, south of Haifa in northern Palestine, excavated in the early 1930's under the direction of Dorothy Garrod in the Wadi el-Mugharet, the Valley of the Caves. Three other very fine stratified sites have been dug subsequently—Ksâr 'Akil (near Beirut, Republic of Lebanon), Jabrud (north of Damascus, Syria) and Umm Qatafa (in the Judaean Desert of southern Palestine), but only the Mount Carmel sites can be considered within the compass of the present paper.

The oldest horizon yields a crude flake industry reminiscent of the Tayacian of western Europe. This, in turn, is overlain by an Upper Acheulian assemblage, including typical pear-shaped hand-axes and a large series of flake tools. A small proportion of these flakes exhibits prepared striking-platforms, just as in the case of the Upper Acheulian of the Nile Valley and the Kharga oasis. The next younger horizon is 7.10 meters thick, and it yielded over 44,500 artifacts of developed Acheulian or Micoquian type, hand-axes comprising 16 per cent of the total. The flake tools consist of a wide range of scraper types, and some of them were struck from tortoise cores with characteristically prepared striking-platforms. A surprising discovery in this horizon is the presence of a small number of blade points of the Châtelperron and Audi types of Europe, together with an increment of other types of true blade tools. The associated fauna indicates that a warm, almost tropical, climate with a heavy rainfall prevailed, which gives way to relatively drier conditions in the following level. The latter contains the Lower Levalloiso-Mousterian, in association with which a series of Neanderthaloid burials was discovered by Mc-Cown at the Mugharet es-Skhūl, the smallest of the three Mount Carmel caves. On the basis of the available dating evidence, these can be correlated with the Würm I/II Interstadial in terms of Alpine chronology.

Although a few hand-axes exist in the Lower Levalloiso-Mousterian, the industry is definitely in the prepared striking-platform/tortoise-core tradition. In Europe it would be called Mousterian of Levalloisian facies, on the basis of Bordes's terminology. The overlying Upper Levalloiso-Mousterian yields a somewhat more developed assemblage, but the two subdivisions are basically the same, the leading types being side-scrapers and points. This complex, recently reported by Coon from several localities in Iran, is very widespread throughout the Near East, including Anatolia, Iraq, and Arabia. Furthermore, it presents close analogies with contemporary developments in Egypt.

Next in the Mount Carmel sequence, the next level, called "Lower Aurignacian," yields various types of small, delicate blade tools, including points of Châtelperron type. This is overlain by two horizons of fully developed Middle Aurignacian of classic type. Here steep, keeled, and nose scrapers, small spiky points, end-of-blade scrapers, and a variety of burin types predominate. Comparable industries occur at several sites in the Caucasus and from the middle horizon of Siuren I in the Crimea. At the Mugharet el-Wad the true Middle Aurignacian is overlain by Atlitian, which represents a specialized development based on the Middle Aurignacian tradition. Then there is a break in the sequence, the next occupants of the site being the Natufians, who introduced a microlithic technique, including multi-hafted sickle blades, presumably used for harvesting wild grains.

In addition to Palestine, industries very reminiscent of the Middle Aurignacian of Europe are found in Syria, the Lebanon, and Anatolia. But no true blade complex has yet been identified in Iran, although Coon's material from the Hotu Cave on the southern shore of the Caspian Sea apparently dates from terminal Pleistocene times, and presumably the same is true of Garrod's "extended Gravettian" from Zarzi in eastern Iraq. In any case the Upper Paleolithic materials thus far brought to light in the Near East give one the impression that at this horizon this region should be regarded as a southerly extension of the Eurasiatic blade-using complex rather than as one of the centers where the latter developed. Indeed, no convincing developmental sequence has been found, and the complex as a whole is entirely lacking in Egypt until Mesolithic times.

Central Asia. In central Asia significant Paleolithic discoveries have been made in recent years. In Turkmenia surface finds of Acheulian-type hand-axes have been announced from a site 25 miles east of Krasnovodsk, while in Uzbekistan several Mousterian localities have been excavated, the most important of which is Teshik-Tash. This cave is in the Gissar Mountains, near Baisun, approximately 90 miles south of Samarkand. Here a Neanderthal child's burial was discovered associated with five (possibly six) pairs of horns of the Siberian mountain goat. The occurrence of a fully developed Mousterian assemblage, including a few flakes of classic Levalloisian type, in this remote area demonstrates how very widely this complex was distributed during Upper Pleistocene times. No justification whatsoever, on the basis either of the geological or of the paleontological evidence, can be found to support the claim put forward by the Russians that the Teshik-Tash occupation dates from Middle Pleistocene (Mindel-Riss) times.

Siberia. Between the Ob Valley, near Tomsk, on the west and the Baikal region on the east (including Transbaikalia and the upper Lena Valley) over 65 localities of Late Glacial and Early Postglacial age have been investigated. Probably the oldest group of these is later than the maximum of the Würm III (Bühl) substage in terms of the Alpine glacial sequence, and hence roughly corresponds in age with the Magdalenian of western Europe. But the age of the youngest group, classed as Mesolithic by the Russian archeologists, is unknown; very likely they belong to the Boreal or even the Early Atlantic interval of the Baltic succession, since associated with them occurs a modern type of fauna. On the other hand, the wooly rhinoceros and the mammoth are present at the oldest stations, together with other cold forms. The former becomes extinct in the next stage, and the reindeer is very abundant. At the third group of localities the mammoth is extinct, while such tundra forms as the arctic fox and the Saiga antelope have now migrated from the region. Finally, only modern forms are found at the youngest sites, as stated above.

The archeological material from the Siberian loess stations is a curious mixture of (*a*) blade tools, together with antler, bone, and ivory artifacts, of classic Upper Paleolithic type; (*b*) points and scrapers made on flakes of "Mousterian" aspect; and (*c*) pebble tools representing a survival of the ancient chopper/chopping-tool tradition of the Far East. At certain sites the *a* and *b*, or archaic, forms may run as high as 65 per cent of the total series, although found in direct association with such specialized types of bone tools as awls and needles, as well as beads and pendants of bone and ivory. Remains of semisubterranean dwellings with sloping sides and centrally located hearths occur here, just as at Upper Paleolithic sites on the South Russian Plain. Another "Western" feature is the female statuary in bone; twenty of these objects were found at one site—Mal'ta (about 54 miles from Irkutsk). At Verkholenskaia Gora (near Irkutsk) several large bifacially flaked laurel-leaf points were found, together with a typical assemblage of stone, bone, and antler tools, including barbed bone points, in association with an essentially modern type of fauna. Indeed, the most striking feature of this Siberian Paleolithic is the fact of its relatively late survival. In some localities it actually occurs in the uppermost layers of the loess immediately below a horizon of humus containing Neolithic camp sites.

Ordos Region of Northern China. In the very north of Mongolia a few late Upper Paleolithic stations belonging to the Siberian complex have been reported, but from elsewhere in this vast territory there are only sporadic surface finds doubtfully referable to the Paleolithic on a typological basis. Immediately to the south, however, in the great bend of the Yellow River, several very prolific localities were investigated in the 1920's. These materials are associated with demonstrably Upper Pleistocene deposits. Originally classified as "Moustero-Aurignacian," it is now quite apparent that the Paleolithic of the Ordos has much in common with that of the Yenisei-Baikal region of Siberia; for comparable examples of blade implements are found here in direct association with points and scrapers of Mousterian-like appearance and pebble tools of Choukoutienian tradition. But the actual dating and relative chronology of these sites involve many problems, and a great deal more intensive work of a joint archeological-geological nature is needed before it will be possible to reach final conclusions. Also the problem of terminology will have to be considered sooner or later, for the Ordos and Siberian materials simply do not conform with any Upper Paleolithic assemblages thus far described from other regions of the Old World.

GENERAL CONSIDERATIONS

On the basis of the foregoing, one is perhaps justified in asking how the data pertaining to the nature of the relationships between the various tool-making traditions of the Old World Paleolithic can ever be composed into any sort of a rational scheme. It is obvious that this problem is of basic importance, since it strikes at the shackles of several subjective and completely unwarranted assumptions that have been and are being made by workers in the field of Paleolithic archeology. The most fundamental of these concerns the significance of the various complexes with which we are dealing. Are we, in point of fact, actually studying extinct cultures, for is not our material inevitably reduced to the most imperishable vestiges of the material equipment of the different groups of very primitive hunting peoples which occupied various regions of the globe during Pleistocene times? In the light of this approach, one may indeed wonder if we can ever compose our meager data into a pattern which can be dignified by the term "culture." The time has come, however, to recognize the fallacy in the thinking of the school which seeks some sort of biological interpretation for the bewildering new array of primitive Stone Age assemblages of tools that are being constantly augmented by fresh discoveries. Those who champion this approach attribute changes registered in a particular tool-making tradition at a given point in its development or evolution to contact, or even to the actual merging of two or more divergent evolutionary lines. One could even quote instances in which it has been assumed that two totally distinct tool-making traditions have fused in some sort of a matrimonial alliance. The results of these instances of hybridization are, of course, manifest in the literature by various hyphenated terms, some of which have been mentioned in this paper. Although in many instances an extremely plausible case can be made in defense of the latter practice, it is simply begging the issue, for, causally, the arguments may be simply reduced to typological flimflam. Indeed, identification and definition by the typological approach alone ignore every possible cultural interpretation, and we are left with the curious spectacle of tools interacting among themselves. But, in the final analysis, it must be admitted that, except in very broad terms, we know as yet virtually nothing concerning (a) the origin and diffusion of the technological entities with which we are dealing, (b) the kind and degree of interplay that occurs when and if two specific tool-making traditions seem to come into contact with each other in a given region, and (c) the relationships of the main technological processes employed in the manufacture of stone tools and weapons by early men to one another in time and space. In this connection, it is of significance to note that all the fundamental processes used by Paleolithic man in Europe to produce tools are being used today, or have been employed during recent times, by the Australian aborigine, although admittedly the forms of the completed artifacts are quite different.

It is clearly apparent that the principles involved in the diffusion and continuity of a certain tool-making tradition cannot be conceived of in terms of the laws of heredity in the genetic sense of the biologist. For they are not passed on from one generation to another by procreation but by instruction and education. Possibly in some instances the intellectual capacity of a given group of Paleolithic hunters may not have been equal to mastering a certain technological development, but this seems very unlikely. In regions where a specific tool-making tradition of an archaic type persisted, such as in the case of the chopper/chopping-tool tradition of southern and eastern Asia, it is very much more likely that this occurred because of a failure of more advanced techniques to diffuse into the area than because the primitive types of mankind who lived there during Middle Pleistocene times were incapable of understanding the new and improved methods that had been and were being developed elsewhere in the Old World. Broadly speaking, Paleolithic archeology is a study of man's progressive ability to utilize and manufacture tools from raw materials supplied by nature, regardless of what tool-making tradition is dominant. Since there is at present no evidence available to indicate that differences in the material culture and behavior of different racial groups is in any sense of biologic origin, it follows that there is no justification for making an exception to this principle in the case of studies relating to fossil man.

A healthy science is one in which there is continuous re-evaluation of the problem in the light of present evidence and application of this re-evaluation to practice and terminology. As humans we think in terms of the labels we put on things. But if the labeling system does not keep up with thought, it is demonstrably a short time before thought ceases. Paleolithic archeologists are neither the only nor the worst offenders in this respect; however, the shortcomings of such fields as mammalogy need not concern us here. Because we deal with concrete physical entities—the stone artifacts made by men who lived many thousands of years ago—there is always a strong temptation to let the objects fascinate us today, just as they did the nineteenth-century collectors. Putting the label on is only half the game; taking it off again is the other half.

Notwithstanding the fact that their field is a humanistic discipline, Paleolithic archeologists must resort to the natural sciences both for chronological evidence and for indications of past conditions. For during prehistoric times, just as in the historic range, environmental and geographical factors played a dominant role in conditioning the behavior of various early (or primitive) groups of mankind. Indeed, from the point of view of the development of man's material culture in the archeological sense of the term, these factors, including climate, soil, flora, fauna, natural resources, and topography, should be considered as having provided the stage —scenery, backdrops, lighting, etc.—on which the human drama has been played ever since the emergence of the first primitive hominids from the ancestral primate stock. In a sense, therefore, typology is the joint product of cultural tradition and environment, both of which are constantly changing factors. However, the picture is far more complex, since the rate of change and the degree of interplay between man's cultural achievements and the environment to which he was ever struggling to adapt himself and on which he was dependent for his livelihood have been far from constant. The fact that these variables exist only serves as a further reminder that Paleolithic archeology always is to be regarded as a humanistic discipline.

A survey of the available literature from a historical point of view will demonstrate clearly that the reaction of early man to fundamental changes in stage and setting, which repeatedly occcurred during Pleistocene time, has not proceeded at a uniform or even predictable rate. The sum total of the data thus far brought to light bearing on the various Middle and Upper Paleolithic complexes of the Old World makes the basis for this observation abundantly clear. Certain significant facts bearing on this problem have been discussed in this paper; here the question of the possible extent of environmental influence on cultural developments during the earlier periods will be briefly considered. In this regard Dixon's observation that "the dependence of culture on environment and the closeness of correlation between them is greatest in the lower stages of cultural growth" is directly applicable. Indeed, this is the very essense of the problem: Paleolithic archeology cannot be divorced from its background of the natural sciences without denying it the key to the reconstruction and interpretation, in so far as possible, of human activities of the past. Although few Paleolithic archeologists today would disagree with this concept, it was not appreciated by the early workers in the field, who seem to have felt that their job had been completed as soon as they had produced an orderly classification and description of their material and compared it in a superficial and completely subjective manner with analogous collections from elsewhere in the region. Thus the underlying cause of the dilemma in which the subject finds itself at present is the direct result of the shortcomings of the purely formal taxonomic approach. Indeed, many instances could be cited demonstrating how the data have been abstracted from their real context in order to comply with the preconceptions of those who adhere to this system.

In that Paleolithic archeology is dependent on the natural sciences in several fundamental respects, the dividing line between the two fields cannot be clearly defined. Admittedly, man himself is both a natural and a social being. Along with the higher apes, he has inherited certain physical attributes from a common paleo-anthropoidal ancestral stock, but no one can deny that the degree of divergence between man and apes is tremendous. One of the basic reasons for this has been the capacity of the human organism to invent and develop a material culture—to conceive of and manufacture a varied assortment of tools to assist him in his struggle for survival. The archeological record demonstrates that no other single factor has played a comparably fundamental role in the emergence of man as the only mammal which today has become almost entirely liberated from the limiting factors imposed by environmental and geographical conditions. It is therefore the direct result of his ability to apply common sense and reason to the solution of a given problem and, once having arrived at this solution, to be able to impart the knowledge and experience thus obtained to others of his kind which sets the study of early man in a realm apart from the disciplines governing the natural sciences. But, by forming an alliance with the latter, Paleolithic archeologists can relate their materials not only in time but also to the total environmental picture. Ultimately it may even be possible to postulate within certain limits how the objects from the older horizons could have been employed. Certainly, there is much to be found out regarding what they were not used for, especially on the Lower Paleolithic level of development. In any case, owing to the very generalized nature of these earlier assemblages, direct typological comparison for historical purposes seems to be a completely sterile approach.

In addition to environment, there are other basic factors to be considered, three of which have been interacting throughout the entire span of Paleolithic development: (*a*) the need for a given type of tool, which may have been invented in several places at different times or abandoned if it became useless; (*b*) the inherent properties of the raw material available for implement manufacture; (*c*) the extreme degree of conservatism of early man with regard to the technological traditions that he followed in his daily routine, which, in the final analysis, is the sole basis on which the various assemblages in question can be defined objectively, as Bordes has shown. But it is clear that actual cultural connections cannot be studied in a satisfactory manner until the relative dating can be determined through the medium of tech-

niques far more refined than those now available. Since at present it is extremely difficult to establish the relative age of localities only a few miles apart, it is apparent that we are still far from this goal. Although certain broad-scale chronological tie-ups have been proposed, we are still a very long way from objectivity in any historical reconstruction of the Paleolithic cultures of the Old World. Indeed, those who have attempted such syntheses during recent years must admit that, regardless of the validity of certain basic concepts, the assumptions on which the entire structure is erected are extremely fragile.

The ability to make use of heat, and finally to harness it, has had a profound effect on man. Heat helped to make man human and provided warmth at his hearth for millennia. Now it can carry him to the stars, or destroy us all.

2. Fire [1]

Man, it is well to remember, is the discoverer but not the inventor of fire. Long before this meddling little Prometheus took to experimenting with flints, then matches and finally (we hope not too finally) hydrogen bombs, fires had burned on this planet. Volcanoes had belched molten lava, lightning had struck in dry grass, winds had rubbed dead branches against each other until they burst into flame. There are evidences of fire in ancient fossil beds that lie deep below the time of man.

Man did not invent fire but he did make it one of the giant powers on the earth. He began this experiment long ago in the red morning of the human mind. Today he continues it in the midst of coruscating heat that is capable of rending the very fabric of his universe.

Man's long adventure with knowledge has, to a very marked degree, been a climb up the heat ladder, for heat alone enables man to mold metals and glassware, to create his great chemical industries, to drive his swift machines. It is our intention in this article to trace man's manipulation of this force far back into its ice-age beginnings and to observe the part that fire has played in the human journey across the planet. The torch has been carried smoking through the ages of glacial advance. As we follow man on this journey, we shall learn another aspect of his nature: that he is himself a consuming fire.

At just what level in his intellectual development man mastered the art of making fire is still unknown. Neanderthal man of 50,000 years ago certainly

[1] LOREN C. EISELEY, "Man the Fire-Maker," in *Scientific American*, 191, No. 3 (1954), pp. 52–57. Reprinted with permission of the author and the publisher. Copyright © 1954 by Scientific American, Inc. All rights reserved.
Dr. Eiseley is University Professor of Anthropology at the University of Pennsylvania.

knew the art. Traces of the use of fire have turned up in a cave of Peking man, the primitive human being of at least 250,000 years ago who had a brain only about two thirds the size of modern man's. And seven years ago Raymond Dart of Witwatersrand University announced the discovery in South Africa of *Australopithecus prometheus,* a man-ape cranium recovered from deposits which he believed showed traces of burned bone.

This startling announcement of the possible use of fire by a subhuman creature raised a considerable storm in anthropological circles. The chemical identifications purporting to indicate evidence of fire are now considered highly questionable. It has also been intimated that the evidence may represent only traces of a natural brush fire. Certainly, so long as the South African man-apes have not been clearly shown to be tool users, wide doubts about their use of fire will remain. There are later sites of tool-using human beings which do not show traces of fire.

Until there is proof to the contrary, it would seem wise to date the earliest use of fire to Peking man—*Sinanthropus.* Other human sites of the same antiquity have not yielded evidence of ash, but this is not surprising, for as a new discovery the use of fire would have taken time to diffuse from one group to another. Whether it was discovered once or several times we have no way of knowing. The fact that fire was in world-wide use at the beginning of man's civilized history enables us to infer that it is an old human culture trait—doubtless one of the earliest. Furthermore, it is likely that man used fire long before he became sophisticated enough to produce it himself.

In 1865 Sir John Lubbock, a British banker who made a hobby of popular writing on science, observed: "There can be no doubt that man originally crept over the earth's surface, little by little, year by year, just, for instance, as the weeds of Europe are now gradually but surely creeping over the surface of Australia." This remark was, in its time, a very shrewd and sensible observation. We know today, however, that there have been times when man suddenly made great strides across the face of the earth. I want to review here one of those startling expansions—a lost episode in which fire played a tremendous part. To make its outlines clear we shall have to review the human drama in three acts.

The earliest human-like animals we can discern are the man-apes of South Africa. Perhaps walking upright on two feet, this creature seems to have been roaming the East African grasslands about one million years ago. Our ancestor, "proto-man," probably emerged from the topics and diffused over the region of warm climate in Eurasia and North Africa. He must have been dependent upon small game, insects, wild seeds and fruits. His life was hard, his search for food incessant, his numbers were small.

The second stage in human history is represented by the first true men. Paleoanthropic man is clearly a tool user, a worker in stone and bone, but there is still something of the isolated tinkerer and fumbler about him. His numbers are still sparse, judging from the paucity of skeletal remains. Short, stocky and powerful, he spread over the most temperate portions of the Afro-Eurasiatic land mass but never attempted the passage through the high Arctic to America. Through scores of millennia he drifted with the seasons, seemingly content with his troglodyte existence, making little serious change in his array of flint tools. It is quite clear that some of these men knew the use of fire, but many may not have.

The third act begins some 15,000 or

20,000 years ago. The last great ice sheet still lies across northern Europe and North America. Roving on the open tundra and grasslands below those ice sheets is the best-fed and most varied assemblage of grass-eating animals the world has ever seen. Giant long-horned bison, the huge wild cattle of the Pleistocene, graze on both continents. Mammoth and mastodon wander about in such numbers that their bones are later to astonish the first American colonists. Suddenly, into this late paradise of game, there erupts our own species of man— *Homo sapiens*. Just where he came from we do not know. Tall, lithe, long-limbed, he is destined to overrun the continents in the blink of a geological eye. He has an excellent projectile weapon in the shape of the spear thrower. His flint work is meticulous and sharp. And the most aggressive carnivore the world has ever seen comes at a time made for his success: the grasslands are alive with seemingly inexhaustible herds of game.

Yet fire as much as flesh was the magic that opened the way for the supremacy of *Homo sapiens*. We know that he was already the master of fire, for the track of it runs from camp to buried camp: the blackened bones of the animals he killed, mute testimony to the relentless step of man across the continents, lie in hundreds of sites in the Old and the New Worlds. Meat, more precious than the gold for which men later struggled, supplied the energy that carried man across the world. Had it not been for fire, however, all that enormous source of life would have been denied to him: he would have gone on drinking the blood from small kills, chewing wearily at uncooked bone ends or masticating the crackling bodies of grasshoppers.

Fire shortens the digestive process. It breaks down tough masses of flesh into food that the human stomach can easily assimilate. Fire made the difference that enabled man to expand his numbers rapidly and to press on from hunting to more advanced cultures. Yet we take fire so much for granted that this first great upswing in human numbers, this first real gain in the seizure of vast quantities of free energy, has to a remarkable degree eluded our attention.

With fire primitive man did more than cook his meat. He extended the pasture for grazing herds. A considerable school of thought, represented by such men as the geographer Carl Sauer and the anthropologist Omer Stewart, believes that the early use of fire by the aborigines of the New World greatly expanded the grassland areas. Stewart says: "The number of tribes reported using fire leads one to the conclusion that burning of vegetation was a universal culture pattern among the Indians of the U. S. Furthermore, the amount of burning leads to the deduction that nearly all vegetation in America at the time of discovery and exploration was what ecologists would call fire vegetation. That is to say, fire was a major factor, along with soil, moisture, temperature, wind, animals, etc., in determining the types of plants occurring in any region. It follows then, that the vegetation of the Great Plains was a fire vegetation." In short, the so-called primeval wilderness which awed our forefathers had already felt the fire of the Indian hunter. Here, as in many other regions, man's fire altered the ecology of the earth.

It had its effect not only on the flora but also on the fauna. Of the great herds of grazing animals that flourished in America in the last Ice Age, not a single trace remains—the American elephants, camels, long-horned bison are all gone. Not all of them were struck down by the hunters' weapons. Sauer argues that a major explanation of the extinction of the great American mammals may be fire. He says that the aborigines used fire drives to stampede game, and he contends that this weapon would have worked with peculiar effectiveness to exterminate such lumbering creatures as the mammoth. I have stood in a gully in western Kansas and seen outlined in the earth the fragmented black bones of scores of bison who had perished in what was probably a man-made conflagration. If, at the end of Pleistocene times, vast ecological changes occurred, if climates shifted, if lakes dried and in other places forests sprang up, and if, in this uncertain and unsteady time, man came with flint and fire upon the animal world about him, he may well have triggered a catastrophic decline and extinction. Five thousand years of man and his smoking weapon rolling down the wind may have finished the story for many a slow-witted animal species. In the great scale of geological time this act of destruction amounts to but one brief hunt.

Man, as I have said, is himself a flame. He has burned through the animal world and appropriated its vast stores of protein for his own. When the great herds failed over many areas, he had to devise new ways to feed his increase or drop back himself into a precarious balance with nature. Here and there on the world's margins there have survived into modern times men who were forced into just such local adjustments. Simple hunters and collectors of small game in impoverished areas, they maintain themselves with difficulty. Their numbers remain the same through generations. Their economy permits no bursts of energy beyond what is necessary for the simple age-old struggle with nature. Perhaps, as we view the looming shadow of atomic disaster, this way of life takes on a certain dignity today.

Nevertheless there is no road back; the primitive way is no longer our way. We are the inheritors of an aggressive culture which, when the great herds disappeared, turned to agriculture. Here

again the magic of fire fed the great human wave and built up man's numbers and civilization.

Man's first chemical experiment involving the use of heat was to make foods digestible. He had cooked his meat; now he used fire to crack his grain. In the process of adopting the agricultural way of life he made his second chemical experiment with heat: baking pottery. Ceramics may have sprung in part from the need for storage vessels to protect harvested grain from the incursions of rats and mice and moisture. At any rate the potter's art spread with the revolutionary shift in food production in early Neolithic times.

People who have only played with mud pies or made little sun-dried vessels of clay are apt to think of ceramics as a simple art. Actually it is not. The sun-dried vessels of our childhood experiments would melt in the first rain that struck them. To produce true pottery one must destroy the elasticity of clay through a chemical process which can only be induced by subjecting the clay to an intense baking at a temperature of at least 400 or 500 degrees centigrade. The baking drives out the so-called water of constitution from the aluminum silicate in the clay. Thereafter the clay will no longer dissolve in water; a truly fired vessel will survive in the ground for centuries. This is why pottery is so important to the archaeologist. It is impervious to the decay that overtakes many other substances, and, since it was manufactured in quantity, it may tell tales of the past when other clues fail us.

Pottery can be hardened in an open campfire, but the results can never be so excellent as in a kiln. At some point the early potter must have learned that he could concentrate and conserve heat by covering his fire—perhaps making it in a hole or trench. From this it was a step to the true closed kiln, in which there was a lower chamber for the fire and an upper one for the pottery. Most of the earthenware of simple cultures was fired at temperatures around 500 degrees centigrade, but really thorough firing demands temperatures in the neighborhood of 900 degrees.

After man had learned to change the chemical nature of clay, he began to use fire to transform other raw materials— ores into metals, for instance. One measure of civilization is the number of materials manipulated. The savage contents himself with a few raw materials which can be shaped without the application of high temperatures. Civilized man uses fire to extract, alter or synthesize a multitude of substances.

By the time metals came into extended use, the precious flame no longer burned in the open campfire, radiating its heat away into the dark or flickering on the bronzed faces of the hunters. Instead it roared in confined furnaces and was fed oxygen through crude bellows. One of the by-products of more intensified experiments with heat was glass—the strange, impassive substance which, in the form of the chemist's flask, the astronomer's telescope, the biologist's microscope and the mirror, has contributed so vastly to our knowledge of ourselves and the universe.

We hear a good deal about the "Iron Age," or age of metals, as a great jump forward in man's history; actually the metals themselves played a comparatively small part in the rise of the first great civilizations. While men learned to use bronze, which demands little more heat than is necessary to produce good ceramics, and later iron for tools and ornaments, the use of metal did not make a really massive change in civilization for well over 1,500 years. It was what

Leslie White of the University of Michigan calls the "Fuel Revolution" that brought the metals into their own. Coal, oil and gas, new sources of energy, combined with the invention of the steam and combustion engines, ushered in the new age. It was not metals as tools, but metals combined with heat in new furnaces and power machinery that took human society off its thousand-year plateau and made possible another enormous upswing in human numbers, with all the social repercussions.

Today the flames grow hotter in the furnaces. Man has come far up the heat ladder. The creature that crept furred through the glitter of blue glacial nights lives surrounded by the hiss of steam, the roar of engines and the bubbling of vats. Like a long-armed crab, he manipulates the tongs in dangerous atomic furnaces. In asbestos suits he plunges into the flaming debris of hideous accidents. With intricate heat-measuring instruments he investigates the secrets of the stars, and he is already searching for heat-resistant alloys that will enable him to hurl himself into space.

How far will he go? Three hundred years of the scientific method have built the great sky-touching buildings and nourished the incalculable fertility of the human species. But man is also *Homo duplex,* as they knew in the darker ages. He partakes of evil and of good, of God and of man. Both struggle in him perpetually. And he is himself a flame— a great, roaring, wasteful furnace devouring irreplaceable substances of the earth. Before this century is out either *Homo duplex* will have learned that knowledge without greatness of spirit is not enough for man, or there will remain only his calcined cities and the little charcoal of his bones.

As Paleolithic time passed the efficiency of our "savage" European ancestors' skills increased, preparing them for a radical technological innovation that came from outside, where it was warmer.

3. Hunters and Fishers in Ice-Age Europe [1]

European civilization and European societies undoubtedly owe something of their distinctive qualities to the privileged position of the continent between the 35th and 60th parallels, to its long indented coastline conferring on the whole a more moderate and genial climate than is enjoyed by any comparable land mass, and to a wealth of mineral resources. It is needless to recapitulate here what can be learned from any handbook of geography beyond emphasizing certain factors that were peculiarly favorable to cultural development in its earliest stages. Note first the contrast between the Mediterranean Zone with warm, dry summers but mild, wet winters and the Temperate Zone of deciduous forests and evenly distributed annual rainfall. These contrasted ecological zones demanded divergent adaptations from, and opened up distinct opportunities to, societies separated by not too impassable barriers. The Mediterranean, an enclosed but relatively narrow island-studded sea, like the Baltic and the Irish Sea, was an ideal school for navigators and soon served as a link rather than a bar to the movement of goods and persons and the diffusion of ideas. A comprehensive system of perennial rivers and streams, navigable, albeit with frequent porterages, by light craft, ensured communications throughout the forests of the Temperate Zone. The mountain barrier of the Pyrenees, the Alps, and the Balkans indeed sunders the Mediterranean from the Temperate

Zone. But it can be circumvented near both ends, while near its center a short porterage across the low Brenner Pass leads from the Danube system to the Adige and the Mediterranean. Finally generous supplies of flint and rock salt, of gold, copper, and above all tin, to which must be added the magic amber of Jutland and Sammland, exerted a potent stimulus to intertribal intercourse even in prehistoric times.

No doubt already during the Pleistocene Ice Ages distinctively European cultures were crystallizing and racial types were becoming genetically adapted to the changing environments. But till the Last Ice Age—the Würm glaciation—we can recognize no peculiarly European culture, still less a European race. Even then the direct contributions of Upper Paleolithic development to subsequent culture are not at all obvious, while the proportion of native genes carried over by European neolithic societies from the Pleistocene is quite uncertain. Hence for our purposes the Old Stone Age can be dismissed rather summarily.

It must be remembered that while vast ice sheets from the Scottish Highlands and the Scandinavian mountains covered most of Britain north of the Thames and Germany as far as the Saale and glaciers radiated far from the Alps and Pyrenees, beyond the margins of the ice tundras and steppes supported vast herds of large gregarious mammals—mammoths, woolly rhinoceros, bison, wild horse, reindeer.

[1] V. GORDON CHILDE, "Hunters and Fishers in Ice-Age Europe," in *The Prehistory of European Society* (Baltimore: 1958); pp. 15–33. Reprinted by permission of the publisher, © 1958 by Penguin Books, Inc.

The late Dr. Childe was Professor of Archaeology at the University of London.

This game, especially the bulky pachyderms, offered an easy and very rewarding prey even to poorly equipped paleolithic hunters. These created cultures adapted to the pursuit of such game which, however, decayed when the special opportunities that had evoked them passed away. For the Ice Ages were separated by three long warm intervals, termed Interglacials, during which the ice sheets and glaciers melted completely, while each Ice Age was interrupted by one or more Interstadials during which the ice retreated without vanishing altogether.

During the first advance of the Last Ice Age, that is, during Würm 1, the continent was populated apparently exclusively by "men" of Neandertal stock sheltering only in caves and living by hunting, mammoths by preference, with the aid of flint-tipped thrusting spears, heavy missiles, and perhaps simple traps. *Homo neandertalensis* is supposed to be specifically distinct from *Homo sapiens,* the species to which all modern men are assigned. If this be correct, Neandertal men can have made no contribution to the genetic constitution of Europe's population. It would then be hard to see how traditions of the Mousterian culture, with which Neandertalers were equipped for mammoth hunting during Würm 1, could have been incorporated in the traditions of later European cultures.

Yet some types of Mousterian equipment and some peculiarities of Mousterian flint technique do seem to re-emerge in later Upper Palaeolithic cultures. But not all Mousterian tools were made by Neandertalers in the strict sense. During the Last Interglacial such tools in Italy and Germany were being made by men who, though definitely Neandertaloid, much more like Neandertalers than you or I, were less highly specialized than their successors during the subsequent Würm Ice Age. It is by no means impossible that such could have communicated with, or perhaps even interbred

with, people of modern, *sapiens,* type. It is even conceivable that such an unspecialized Neandertaloid type might have evolved into *Homo sapiens.* Flint industries are known in Palestine that are transitional between the Mousterian and the classical Upper Palaeolithic, and an equally transitional status has been claimed for the "Audi culture" in France. The latter claim is not now regarded with favor by prehistorians, and moreover men of a type ancestral to *Homo sapiens* were living in England and France before the Last Ice Age.

In any case modern men (of *sapiens* type) appear in force in Europe during the interstadial climatic amelioration that interrupted the Last Ice Age and is labelled Würm 1/11. They arrived with a novel culture ready made, or at least with a vastly superior technique of flint-knapping. They had learned to make more efficient flint tools, blades, by a more economical process. With the new tools they could utilize for industrial purposes also bone, antler, and ivory. So they could fashion and arm light missile weapons whose employment augmented almost catastrophically the productivity of hunting and therefore the food-supply, and so permitted and encouraged a rapid expansion of population. Much the same kinds of superior flint implements appear about the same time in North and East Africa and parts of south-western Asia.

In Europe the lucky hunters equipped with the new armory were able to develop several distinct but rich cultures. Even during the Interstadial the Aurignacians had specialized a variety of bone, antler, and flint tools, including a very rudimentary wood-worker's kit. They pursued cave bears and woodland game more systematically than mammoth and other grass-eaters from the steppes and tundras. Moreover the Aurignacians are the first Europeans known to have taken advantage of the fish with which our rivers were well stocked; Mousterians had conspicuously neglected this valuable source of food. In France the Aurignacians began to develop the magical art that in the subsequent glacial phases culminated in world-famous cave paintings and engravings. They indeed discovered how to represent in two dimensions what they perceived as three-dimensional. The oldest datable applications of this epochal discovery certainly come from Western Europe. That is not to say that the discovery was made in Europe alone and diffused thence, that all pictorial art springs from the childish efforts of the French Aurignacians; but all European palaeolithic and mesolithic pictures probably do.

With the return of the Ice Age, as Würm ii, woodlands gave place once more to steppes or tundras even in Western Europe. There and in Central Europe, the Ukraine and South Russia too the Gravettian culture emerges as an adjustment to glacial conditions. The Gravettians pursued by preference gregarious game—mammoth, bison, wild horse —on steppes where every summer bitter winds blowing off the ice were depositing a layer of dust to form the younger loess. They tipped their missiles with points of flint instead of bone. The Gravettians had learned to construct artificial shelters without which the pursuit of mammoth on the open steppe would have been impossible. The huts were dug out in the loess to a depth of a couple of feet, roofed with hides supported on a frame of tusks or saplings, and half buried in heaped up earth to exclude the icy blasts. Gravettians too produced works of art—not of course just for art's sake alone but also for magico-religious ends. Best known are little figures of women, carved out of mammoth ivory or soft stone or even molded in clay and ash. The sexual characters are always emphasized while the faces are literally featureless. (On only two out of over sixty statuettes have

any facial features been indicated.) The figures were supposedly used in some ritual to promote the fertility of nature. Inevitably the ceremonies and the beliefs that inspired them, or were generated by them, remain unknown. But similar female figurines were manufactured by nearly all early peasant societies in Southwestern Asia and Southeastern Europe. So were little models of animals, but peasants modelled bulls and cows, Gravettians mammoths and other game.

During the same glacial phase the development of Upper Palaeolithic blade traditions seems interrupted by the spread of the celebrated "Solutrean culture." This culture should strictly be termed an industry; it is nothing more than a new method of thinning flint flakes and the superior spear- and missile-tips made by its application. Since the types thus produced are not everywhere identical and are associated with other different types in each province, prehistorians are today inclined to regard this "culture" or industry rather as a cycle of cultures, confining the term Solutrean to West European assemblages and designating Szeletian their analogues in Central Europe. A further group may be recognized in Eastern Europe from the Don to the Kuban, while the North African Aterian and the East African Still Bay cultures exhibit "Solutrean" forms and techniques, but have never been called Solutrean. The innovations on the common Upper Palaeolithic blade tradition in all these assemblages include a revival of some Mousterian types and techniques. All might therefore have arisen independently at several places and denote a fusion of Mousterian traditions with local Upper Palaeolithic ones. Yet in South Russia the innovations in question are detectable in the mild Interstadial, whereas further west they do not appear before the succeeding cold Würm ii phase. At the same time both in South Russia and in Spain and, though less explicitly, in North Africa too some of the products look like arrow-heads. If appearances be not deceptive, they would then be the first indications of the invention of a bow. The likelihood of some sort of contact between the various societies that adopted "Solutrean" techniques certainly cannot be ruled out. In particular mutual agreements between Spain and North Africa appear so striking that direct communications across the Mediterranean and therefore some sort of boat seem fair deductions.

Be that as it may, in Western and Central Europe the "Solutrean" seems a brief episode that exercised no recognizable influence on subsequent developments. In Eastern Europe on the contrary Solutrean techniques were applied at times to the later East Gravettian flintwork and survived locally even in the Mesolithic Swiderian industry to which we return later.

During the long and discontinuous retreat of the ice sheets and glaciers, the successful pursuit of reindeer and bison herds and the systematic exploitation of salmon runs in North Spain, France, South Germany, and Bohemia, supported what seems the richest and most brilliant culture ever created by food-gatherers in any part of the world—the Magdalenian. Its claim to this unique distinction rests primarily on the high quality of the naturalistic art expressed in engravings and paintings in the remote recesses of dark and inaccessible caverns, in bas-reliefs in shallow rock-shelters, and in innumerable carvings and engravings in mammoth ivory, bone, and antler, on pebbles and even on lumps of amber and ochre. This art was of course rooted in the older Aurignacian and Gravettian, but culminates in the Magdalenian. It appeals to contemporary Europeans in virtue of its direct naturalism and immediacy. Animals are represented with marvellous sympathy and accuracy as they were seen, undistorted by conceptual thought. Each picture or sculpture is the portrait

of an individual beast. The rare representations of the human form on the contrary appear to us as grotesque caricatures—a phenomenon not due to any incompetence of Magdalenian artists, but to a peculiarity of the perceptual equipment of all savages and barbarians. Nothing deserving the title of human portraiture is older than the Narmer palette, than the Urban Revolution!

Magdalenian art and the magic rituals it served were by-products of a material culture beautifully adapted to the peculiarly propitious circumstances of late glacial Europe. With the end of the Ice Age that culture collapsed, and with it the art and ceremonial it had supported vanished leaving no trace. Items of Magdalenian hunting equipment and fishing tackle no doubt survived; no comparable survival of artistic or ceremonial traditions is detectable. In the present context that fact justifies the cursory treatment of a glorious episode.

In Eastern Spain and Sicily and in North Africa too hunters painted or engraved pictures on rocks. These also may be inspired by the Aurignacian tradition, but in style they diverge widely from the Magdalenian. The East Spanish paintings are lively impressionistic scenes, not indeed conventionalized symbols, but still somewhat conceptualized. In general style and sometimes even in points of detail they are absurdly like some paintings from round the Sahara and even the Bushman paintings of Rhodesia. The series may begin during the Spanish Gravettian or Solutrean phase. It certainly went on till herdsmen with tame sheep had reached the Peninsula. North African artists too depicted herdsmen as well as hunters. In the rest of Europe Gravettian traditions, occasionally modified by "Solutrean," persisted during the late glacial period without producing any significant modification as far as archaeologists can tell. We may just mention a camp of mammoth-hunters, buried in the loess at Mezin in the Ukraine, because of the unusual decorative art illustrated there. Ivory bracelets and other small articles were engraved all over with continuous maeanders used as a repetition pattern, i.e. repeated in all directions so as to blanket the whole surface. The motive thus employed, though easily produced in basketry, is surprisingly rare in ancient art, but was systematically used by early neolithic farmers precisely on the Southeast European loess lands.

At last the long Ice Age drew to its close. The glaciers retreated towards the high mountains; the vast Scandinavian and Scottish ice sheets gradually melted and shrank. Forest trees invaded the steppes and tundras of what was henceforth to be Temperate Europe. The fauna changed with the climate and vegetation. The mammoth was already extinct; the reindeer followed the ice margins northward. The herds of gregarious herbivores that had grazed on the steppes were replaced by more solitary game—red deer, roe deer, wild oxen, wild boars—the pursuit of which required more arduous tactics and a new equipment. That spelt the end of the cultures that had brought prosperity to Upper Palaeolithic hunters. Adaptations to the novel and really sterner conditions are represented by so-called mesolithic cultures. All are equally based on hunting, fishing, and collecting, although in each the huntsmen were assisted by more or less domesticated dogs.

A few descendants of the Magdalenians, termed Azilians, lingered on in France, sheltering in caves and securing a meager subsistence by collecting wild food, fishing, and catching small game. They do not seem to have possessed a bow any more than the Magdalenians.

Interspersed among the Azilians, but ranging much further—all around the Western Mediterranean, northward to Britain and Northern Europe and again

on the steppe hinterland of the Black Sea —lived bands of archers who encamped generally on sandy tracts in the forests or on windswept coasts. They are known almost exclusively from the "pigmy flints" or "geometric microliths" with which they armed their darts and arrows. (Their microliths are qualified as "geometric" because many of these minute blades have been neatly trimmed to regular geometric shapes—triangles, trapezes, crescents.) All these archers used to be lumped together under the blanket title "Tardenoisian," but closer study and statistical analyses have revealed the shadowy outlines of several distinct cultures— an Epigravettian in the Iberian Peninsula, a Grimaldian in Italy, a Sauveterrian in France and Britain have so far been provisionally identified. Curiously similar microlithic industries occur far beyond the frontiers of Europe—even in India and Australia, but above all in Africa. These far-flung geometric industries, peculiar though they seem, can hardly all be derived from a single tradition. Indeed in Europe later Gravettian flintworkers showed an inclination to reduce their blades to pigmy size and to give them geometrical outlines, particularly round the Mediterranean but also in central France. On the other hand West European microlith assemblages seem to resemble so closely the North African Capsian that an immigration of African hunters has been assumed. African connections must certainly be admitted for the Spanish Epigravettians if these painted the pictures mentioned previously, albeit without prejudice to the question of their direction.

Finally in the forest zone of Eastern Europe roamed other archers—Swiderians—whose arrow-armament, though microlithic, was not geometric. The traditions of their flint-work which alone are known might well be traced back to the East Gravettian of Kostienki.

Really very little is known of these

early holocene hunters. Geometric micro-liths have been found in caves both in Western Europe and the Crimea, in ir-regular hut-foundations in Western Eu-rope, and in midden heaps along the Atlantic coasts. Certain Sauveterrian burials in a Ligurian cave and on islets off the coast of Brittany seem to indicate differences of rank within the band, and there is one unambiguous case of homi-cide. From the interment together in the Crimea of a mature man and a female half his age might be inferred a patri-archal family and the practice of satî. Boats of some sort were available for short voyages. Presumably all these arch-ers hunted, fished, collected snails, berries, and other wild food. But some may have kept a few sheep or goats whose milk or blood might have supplemented the products of hunting and collecting; a very few stray bones of these animals have been found with Sauveterrian relics far beyond their natural habitat even in Brittany and Devon. So some Sauveter-rian food-gatherers may rank as food-producers too. To that extent some meso-lithic cultures might be termed neolithic too. But none of the communities so far mentioned is known to have devised any equipment for dealing effectively with the most prominent item in the post-glacial European environment—the tim-ber of the temperate forests. That was developed among descendants of palaeo-lithic Europeans who had spread north-wards, perhaps in the wake of the reindeer herds, to colonize lands newly freed from ice.

The retreating ice sheets had laid bare a wide stretch of marsh and tundra on the North European plain round the Baltic depression and extended westward to England by "Northsealand"; for the ocean waters had not yet inundated the North Sea basin so that dry land, inter-rupted by a swollen Thames and Rhine and many channels from the shrinking Scandinavian ice sheet, still united Eng-land with the Continent. What was hap-pening in Northsealand can only be guessed, since all remains of human ac-tivity are buried in mud and silt below that sea. Bands of reindeer-hunters, we know had penetrated as far north as Hamburg while the edge of the ice sheet still ran across Denmark and north-east Germany. They encamped on the tundra only in summer and autumn for seasonal hunting and fowling, retiring south to winter among the advancing woods. These pioneers, termed Hamburgians, combined some Magdalenian traditions with others derived from Central or Eastern Europe. So, unlike the Mag-dalenians, they used some kind of bow. Later, when the whole Continent was ice-free, they were followed by other bands who at first encamped in the north only in summer, but subsequently were able to winter as far north as Jutland.

Eventually when birch woods and a vanguard of pines had colonized the tundras we find societies beginning to develop a distinctive and highly efficient equipment for the exploitation of the rich natural resources of the plain that then extended from the Pennines to the Urals; for Northsealand had not yet been submerged and land bridges across the Belts and the Sound left the Baltic a brackish lake—the Ancylus Lake of geol-ogists. The development of the appropri-ate culture can be followed through three successive phases that are defined by changes of climate reflected in the local vegetation. These climatic phases can in turn be provisionally dated by radio-car-bon estimates.

During the first or Pre-Boreal phase the climate of eastern England as well as of Denmark and southern Scandinavia was still very cool and continental. A lakeside encampment of four households at Star Carr near Scarborough (York-shire) reveals already the essential out-lines of the Maglemose culture-cycle that in its mature shape is so well known in the succeeding Boreal phase—arrows armed with geometric microliths for hunting, antler-pronged leisters for spearing fish, heavy flint adze-blades, sharpened ingeniously by the so-called *tranchet* blow for wood-chopping.

A thousand years later in the Boreal phase the climate had grown milder—indeed the mean annual temperature was higher than today, though the winters in Denmark, southern Sweden, and Britain were more severe and snowy. Dense coniferous forests extended from the Pennines to the Urals to join up there with the Siberian pine woods to form a continuous belt of *taiga*—to use a familiar Russian term—girdling Europe from the Atlantic to the Pacific and extending across North America to meet the Atlantic again. But during the latter half of the genial Boreal phase oaks with elms, limes, and other trees that usually accompany them began to mingle with the pines till in the end mixed oak woods became the dominant vegetation of England and Denmark. No North Sea as yet interrupted the continuity of the forest. Northsealand was doubtless largely fen, but beyond it the only gaps in the endless forest were the Ancylus Lake in the Baltic depression and a myriad smaller lakes, meres, marshes, and sluggish streams. Their waters were well stocked with fish, while their banks were frequented by game and innumerable birds. Combined with wild berries and nuts the fish, fowl, and game provided a generous diet for an expanding population of hunter-fishers. The latter are best known from the refuse dropped at temporary summer camps on the edges of meres that have since become covered with preservative peat and so are aptly termed Maglemoseans after Maglemose —the Big Moss—near Mullerup in Zealand where a seasonal camp was first excavated.

The Maglemoseans had discovered all the main resources useful to man in Northern Europe and had devised or inherited an equipment for their exploitation so ingenious that much of it survives unaltered to the present day. Hunters and fowlers were armed with bows, some reinforced with sinews, and a variety of arrows specialized for the slaughter of particular game; arrows with conical tips of wood or bone were presumably used, as they still are, for killing fur-bearing animals with minimum damage to pelts. Fish were caught with hook and line and in nets or ingenious wicker traps or weels, while large species were speared with bone-pronged leisters. For tree-felling or wood-working the Maglemoseans possessed an efficient carpenters' kit of adzes, chisels, and gouges of flint edged by a *tranchet* blow, or of fine-grained stone sharpened by grinding, supplemented by chisels and wedges of bone and antler. They had even devised a way of mounting a flint blade in a transversely perforated section of antler beam to produce the effect of a modern iron axe- or adze-head. (The reader must remember that stone and even copper axe-heads were normally stuck into the handle instead of being fitted on to it with the aid of a hole or eyelet through the head.)

Thanks to these primary tools the Maglemoseans could build transport devices. Runners survive to represent sledges, probably drawn by men, but capable of development into dog-sledges such as were actually used quite early in post-Atlantic times. On water, paddles, preserved in the peat, must have been used to propel canoes of skin or birch bark that have perished. Finally the Maglemoseans had learned how to make a good adhesive from birch bark by the application of heat—the oldest artificial substance to be made by man at least in Europe. Yet the Maglemoseans must have led a nomadic existence, and certainly shifted their habitations seasonally from winter quarters to summer camps.

Only the latter are known; they are represented by a couple of flimsy huts of birch bark and hides. Still a more sedentary version of the Maglemosean culture may have been developing on the sea coasts. Any settlements on the shores of Northsealand are of course now under water, but collections of flint implements from high strand lines in Norway may belong to such a population already pursuing the marine mammals of the Arctic Ocean.

During the millennium 6000 to 5000 B.C. this Maglemose culture, although differentiated into several local variants, is recognizable all over the former plain from Southern Britain to Finland and the East Baltic republics. Further east most Maglemose types recur in the coniferous zone of Northern Russia as far as the Urals; many reappear still further east all through the taiga belt of Northern Eurasia and North America. But none has been found even in North Russia in contexts dated to the Boreal phase by pollen analysis or radio-carbon, and many indubitably remained current much later; not a few are still in use today. Hence the distribution of the Maglemose culture east of the Baltic before 4000 B.C. remains dubious. What is certain is how much of the folk culture of Northern Eurasia is directly inherited from the Maglemosean of that epoch; birch pitch, the ingenious wicker fish-traps, nets secured with the same fast, but by no means self-evident, knots, leisters—though iron has replaced bone—to mention only a few outstanding examples, are still employed among the coniferous forests today. That means that both the techniques for their manufacture and prescriptions for their use have been handed down among local populations by oral tradition for a full 8,000 years over more than 300 generations. Other devices such as conical-headed arrows, sledge-runners, still employed by circumpolar peoples, are just as directly derived from Maglemosean models, though slightly more modified. Here we have a striking demonstration both of the excellence of the Maglemoseans' adaptation to their environment and of the debt we owe to preliterate European savages!

Towards 4000 B.C. a general rise in ocean levels finally separated Great Britain from the Continent, Scandinavia from Denmark and North Germany. As a result the climate of Northern Europe became moister, but no colder, than in the Boreal phase; Denmark and Southern Sweden enjoyed, or endured, an Atlantic climate, comparable to that of Brittany or Cornwall today, so that the term Atlantic is employed, rather confusingly, to designate this phase throughout Northern Europe. In response to the heavier and more frequent rainfall oak woods spread further than before and were now interspersed with beeches. The deciduous forests interposed more serious obstacles to communications than the Boreal pine woods, while the new North Sea and Channel put an end to dryland traffic between England and the Continent. At the same time the North Sea and the Litorina Sea that now filled the Baltic depression offered fresh opportunities to hunters and fishers.

So the relatively homogeneous Maglemosean culture-cycle broke up into a multiplicity of local cultures, each adapted to the peculiarities of the local environment. None is so well known as the Maglemosean, since few encampments were located where a subsequent growth of peat ensured the preservation of wood, bone, and other organic materials. Most have to be inferred from collections of far from distinctive stone implements. It will suffice to mention here the Ertebølle culture of Denmark, derived probably from the hypothetical coastal version of the Maglemosean and certainly adapted to take advantage of the food supplies offered by the Litorina Sea. It was the creation of strand-loopers whose encampments are represented by the Kitchen Middens—huge heaps of shells along that sea's ancient shore. The reliable supplies of food offered by the salt waters and the great oyster banks of the Sound, the Belts, and the Kattegat allowed of more permanent settlements occupied all the year round. In them are found the oldest pottery vessels known from Northern Europe. Perhaps the sedentary hunter-fishers themselves had discovered how by heat to effect the chemical change that converts plastic clay into solid water-tight vessels. But they may have been taught this art by immigrant farmers, who certainly introduced cereals and sheep and goats—plants and animals quite alien to the North European flora and fauna. By 4000 B.C. at latest (according to radio-carbon estimates) Danubian peasants had spread as far north as Magdeburg on the Elbe. The subsequent prehistory of European societies save in the taiga zone was conditioned by the new food-producing economy based on cultivation and stock-breeding. However much this was adopted by aboriginal stocks, however much its adaptation was accomplished in Europe, however far the social organization within which it worked was elaborated in that continent, the basis of the new way of life—the actual cereals and the domestic stock—were introduced from outside.

By the end of the Pleistocene we were fully *Homo sapiens*, old residents of Asia, and on our way to the Americas—across a land bridge 1,300 miles wide.

4. The Bering Strait Land Bridge [1]

The New World was already an old world to the Indians who were in residence when Europeans took possession of it in the 16th century. But the life story of the human species goes back more than a million years, and there is no doubt that man came only recently to the Western Hemisphere. None of the thousands of sites of aboriginal habitation uncovered in North and South America has antiquity comparable to that of Old World sites. Man's occupation of the New World may date back several tens of thousands of years, but no one rationally argues that he has been here even 100,000 years.

Speculation as to how man found his way to America was lively at the outset, and the proposed routes boxed the com-pass. With one or two notable exceptions, however, students of American anthropology soon settled for the plausible idea that the first immigrants came by way of a land bridge that had connected the northeast corner of Asia to the northwest corner of North America across the Bering Strait. Mariners were able to supply the reassuring information that the strait is not only narrow—it is 56 miles wide—but also shallow: a lowering of the sea level there by 100 feet or so would transform the strait into an isthmus. With little else in the way of evidence to sustain the Bering Strait land bridge, anthropologists embraced the idea that man walked dry-shod from Asia to America.

Toward the end of the last century,

[1] WILLIAM G. HAAG, "The Bering Strait Land Bridge," in *Scientific American*, 206, No. 1 (1962), pp. 112–123. Reprinted with permission of the author and the publisher. Copyright © 1962 by Scientific American, Inc. All rights reserved.

Dr. Haag is Professor of Anthropology at the Louisiana State University.

however, it became apparent that the Western Hemisphere was the New World not only for man but also for a host of animals and plants. Zoologists and botanists showed that numerous subjects of their respective kingdoms must have originated in Asia and spread to America. (There was evidence also for some movement in the other direction.) These findings were neither astonishing nor wholly unexpected. Such spread of populations is not to be envisioned as an exodus or mass migration, even in the case of animals. It is, rather, a spilling into new territory that accompanies increase in numbers, with movement in the direction of least population pressure and most favorable ecological conditions. But the immense traffic in plant and animal forms placed a heavy burden on the Bering Strait land bridge as the anthropologists had envisioned it. Whereas purposeful men could make their way across a narrow bridge (in the absence of a bridge, Eskimos sometimes cross the strait in skin boats), the slow diffusion of plants and animals would require an avenue as broad as a continent and available for ages at a stretch.

The expansion of the Bering Strait land bridge to meet these demands is a task that has intrigued geologists for many years. Although their efforts have not completely satisfied zoologists and botanists, it is apparent that the Old and New worlds were once one world, joined by a land mass that now lies submerged beneath the seas on each side of the Bering Strait. The clues to the appearance and disappearance of this land mass are to be found both on the bottom of these waters and in such faraway places as the coral atolls of the South Pacific and the delta of the Mississippi River.

Today the maximum depth in the Bering Strait is about 180 feet. On a clear day from the heights at Cape Prince of Wales in Alaska one can look across the strait and see land at Cape Dezhnev in Siberia. St. Lawrence Island, Big Diomede Island, Little Diomede Island and smaller islands make steppingstones between. South of the strait is the Bering Sea. Its floor is one of the flattest and smoothest stretches of terrain on the entire globe. With a slope of no more than three or four inches to the mile, it reaches southward to a line that runs from Unimak Pass in the Aleutians to Cape Navarin on the Asiatic shore. Along this line—the edge of the continental shelf—the sea floor plunges steeply from a depth of about 450 feet down 15,000 feet to the bottom of the ocean. The floor of the Chukchi Sea, north of the Bering Strait, is not quite so smooth; the depth varies from 120 to 180 feet, and irregularities of the terrain bring shoals upward to depths of only 45 feet and lift the great granite outcrops of Wrangell and Herald islands above the surface of the sea. Along a line that runs several hundred miles north of the Bering Strait, from Point Barrow in Alaska to the Severnaya Zemlya off Siberia, the sea floor plunges over the northern edge of the continental shelf to the bottom of the Arctic Ocean.

Sounding of the Bering and Chukchi seas thus depicts a vast plain that is not deeply submerged. At its widest the plain reaches 1,300 miles north and south, 600 miles wider than the north-south distance across Alaska along the Canadian border. The granitic islands that rise above the water testify that the plain is made of the same rock as the continents.

David M. Hopkins of the U.S. Geological Survey has shown that this great plain sank beneath the seas somewhat more than a million years ago as a result of the down-warping of the crust in the Arctic region that began with the Pleistocene epoch. Before that, Hopkins calculates, most of the area was above sea level throughout most of the 50-million-year duration of the preceding Tertiary period.

The continuity of the land mass of Asia and North America during the Tertiary period helps to solve a major portion of the biologist's problem. The paleontological evidence indicates that numerous mammals, large and small, moved from Asia to America during that time. With the subsidence of the land, however, the flow must have stopped. Nor is there any chance that the land rose up again during the million-year Pleistocene period. It is true that the Pacific region along the Aleutian and Kurile island chains is geologically active. But by comparison the Bering Strait region is rather stable, studies of ancient beach terraces on the islands in the surrounding seas indicate that the vertical movement of the land could not have exceeded 30 feet in the course of the Pleistocene. The smoothness of the Bering Sea floor is another indication of prolonged submergence. Deep layers of marine sediment have smoothed out whatever hills and valleys it acquired when it was dry land and exposed to erosion.

Fossil evidence for the origin and geographic distribution of North American mammals nonetheless shows that numerous animals, large and small, came from Asia during the Pleistocene. Beginning early in the Pleistocene, several genera of rodents arrived; such small mammals breed more rapidly than, say, elephants, and they spread far southward across North America, although not into South America. Later came the larger mammals: the mastodon and mammoth, musk oxen, bison, moose, elk, mountain sheep and goats, camels, foxes, bears, wolves and horses. (The horses flourished and then died out in North America; the genus was not seen again in the New World until the conquistadors brought their animals across the Atlantic.) Evidence from botany as well as from zoology requires a substantial dry-land connection between Asia and North America throughout the Pleistocene.

At this point it is well to remember that the sea level at any given place on the globe depends not only on the height of the land but also on the depth of the ocean. The depth of the ocean in this sense is a question of the volume of water in the ocean. With the Pleistocene began the ice age that has apparently not yet run its course. During this million-year period, for reasons subject to warm debate, at least four great ice sheets have built up, advanced and retreated on the Northern Hemisphere. That the ice can lock up considerable quantities of water on the land is evident even in the present interglacial period. The abrupt melting of the Greenland and Antarctic icecaps would, according to various estimates, raise the present world-wide sea level by as much as 300 feet.

To estimate the volume of water locked up on the land in the great continental glaciers of the Pleistocene one begins with the measurement of the land area covered by the glaciers. The great ice sheets gathered up sand, gravel and larger rubble and, when the ice proceeded to melt, deposited a mantle of this "till" on the exposed ground. From such evidence it is calculated that ice covered 30 per cent of the earth's land area during the glacial maxima of the Pleistocene.

To arrive at the volume of water in the glaciers, however, one must have some idea of the thickness of the ice as well as the area it covered. The Greenland icecap is more than a mile deep, and in Antarctica the rock lies as much as three miles below the surface of the ice. It is clear that the Pleistocene glaciers could have been thousands of feet thick. Multiplication of the area of the glaciers by thicknesses predicated on various assumptions has shown that the freezing of the water on the land may have reduced the ancient sea level by 125 to 800 feet. Such calculations are supported by evidence from coral atolls in tropical seas. Since the organisms that build these atolls do not live at depths greater than 300 feet, and since the limy structures of such islands go down several thousand feet, a lowering of the sea level by more than 300 feet is necessary to explain their existence.

By all odds the best evidence for the rise and fall of the ancient sea level is offered by the Mississippi Valley, its delta and the adjoining shores of the Gulf of Mexico. In Pleistocene times about a dozen major streams entered the Gulf. As ice accumulated in the north, lowering the level of the sea, the streams followed the retreating shore line downward. On the steeper gradient the water flowed faster, cutting deeper and straighter valleys. Then, as the ice retreated, the sea rose and again moved inland, reducing the velocity of the streams and making them deposit their burdens of gravel and silt at their mouths and farther inland. Consequently during the glacial minima the rivers built up great flood plains over which they wore meandering courses. Each glacial advance brought a withdrawal of the Gulf and quickened the rivers; each retreat raised the level of the Gulf and forced the rivers to build new flood plains.

Had the earth's crust in this region remained stable, all traces of the preceding flood plain would have been erased by the next cycle of cutting and building. But the rivers, particularly the Mississippi, deposited vast quantities of sediment in their lower valleys, building "crowfoot" deltas like that of the Mississippi today. (Many large rivers, such as the Amazon, have never built such deltas because coastwise currents distribute their sediments far and wide.) The accumulating burden of offshore sediments tilted the platform of the continent, pressing it downward under the Gulf and lifting it inland. In succeeding cycles, therefore, the build-up of the flood plain started farther downstream.

Evidence of the succession of flood plains remains today in the terraces that descend like a flight of steps down both flanks of the Mississippi Valley toward the river. Near Memphis, Tenn., the highest and oldest terrace lies about 350 feet above the plain of the present river and slopes toward the Gulf with a gradient of about eight feet per mile. The terrace below lies 200 feet above the plain and slopes about five feet per mile; the third terrace lies 100 feet above the plain, with a slope of about 18 inches; the fourth, only 40 feet above, with a slope of only six inches. The present flood plain has a gradient of about three inches per mile. Out in the Gulf, where the river has buried the older deposits under the younger, the successive slopes of the river bed are steeper.

In this setting geologists have been able to measure with great confidence the degree to which each of the glacial advances of the Pleistocene lowered the level of the sea. Borings along the axis of the old stream channels reveal the gradient of the bottom. The terraces show the slope of the alluvial plain associated with the successive streams. From these data the elevations of the earlier river mouths and consequently the sea level can be determined. The Rhine and Rhone rivers have yielded similar information, and on the Kamchatka Peninsula in Siberia it has been observed that the streams flowing into the Bering Sea are flanked by steeply sloping terraces.

The Mississippi-Gulf region has provided especially secure and precise information about the course of the last great Pleistocene glaciation, the so-called Wisconsin stage of the Pleistocene. In no other area of the globe have oil prospectors drilled so many test holes through the recent sediments into the Pleistocene; the number of holes runs into the thousands, and they dot the map 30 miles out into the Gulf. In accordance with the law, the records of these wells show the types of material brought up by the drills at fairly evenly spaced intervals. The undersea sediments that were uncovered by the retreat of the sea at the maximum advance of the Wisconsin glacier mark a horizon familiar to all well drillers. Where these sediments were exposed to the air long ago they became oxidized and show as a bright reddish-orange zone. From the examination of many well records one can tell where, geographically, these sediments were exposed to air and where they remained underwater, and so fix the coast line at the time the sea reached its lowest level. In addition, numerous samples of formerly living matter have been recovered from well borings at known depths and from archaeological sites. The dating of these by carbon-14 techniques permits accurate plotting of the course of events in time.

From this rich supply of evidence it has been determined that the Wisconsin glacier reached its maximum 40,000 years ago and lowered the sea level by as much as 460 feet. As the glacier grew and the oceans receded, an ever broader highway was revealed at the Bering Strait. With a sea-level fall of only 150 feet, the bridge connecting the two continents must have been nearly 200 miles wide. Because the slope of the sea floor is so gentle, a further fall in the sea level uncovered much larger regions. At 450 feet the entire width of the undersea plain from one edge of the continental shelf to the other must have been exposed, providing a corridor 1,300 miles wide for the flow of biological commerce between the no longer separate continents. During the peak periods of the earlier glaciations the Bering Strait land bridge would have

presented much the same appearance.

Because the maximum exposure of the land bridge necessarily coincided with a maximum of glaciation, one might think the bridge would have been blocked by ice. Geological evidence shows, however, that neither the Chukchi Peninsula in Siberia nor the westward-reaching Seward Peninsula of Alaska were glaciated during the Wisconsin period. Even large areas of central Alaska remained ice-free throughout the period. As for the now submerged plain on the floor of the Bering Strait and the adjoining seas, it seems clear that the rocky rubble, found where currents clear away the silt, was "rafted" there by icebergs; no part of this accumulation is attributed to glacial till deposited by the melting of glacial ice on the surface.

Conditions are made the more propitious for life on the bridge by the latest theory on the causes of glaciation. Paradoxically, this demands a warm Arctic Ocean over which winds could become laden with moisture for subsequent precipitation as snow deep in the Hudson Bay area, where the glacier had its center of gravity. Western Alaska would have had little snowfall and no accumulation of ice. This deduction is supported by the finding of trees in the Pleistocene deposits on Seward Peninsula. It is not thought, however, that the land bridge was ever anything but tundra.

It must be admitted that the Bering Strait land bridge of the geologist, appearing only intermittently above sea level, does not fully serve the purposes of the zoologist and botanist. Most zoologists find no evidence in the movement of animals that requires alternate opening and closing of the passage between the continents, and they argue for a broad bridge available throughout nearly all of the Pleistocene. What is more, the animals that came across the bridge were not typically cold-climate animals (none of the true cold-climate animals, such as the woolly rhinoceros, ever reached America). On the contrary, the animals were the ones that would prefer the warmer interglacial times for their spread. They may, of course, have made the crossing just as the climate was warming up and conditions on the American side were increasingly favorable to population increase and diffusion.

The botanists find even more compelling evidence for a broad land bridge throughout most of the Pleistocene. Eric Hultén of the University of Lund in Sweden recently calculated that a bridge 700 miles wide is necessary to account for the distribution of plants in Alaska and northeastern Siberia.

Giving full weight to the biological evidence, it seems amply demonstrated that a bridge wider than present-day Alaska joined the Old and New worlds during a large part of the Pleistocene. There is much to suggest that the land surface of this bridge was smooth and unbroken. And it appears that large animals moved freely across it during the 80,000 years of the Wisconsin stage and probably throughout much of the preceding interglacial stage.

Before the end of the Wisconsin period the first men must have crossed the bridge. It seems almost a truism that Asiatic man would have followed the slow spread of Asiatic animals into the New World. The men would most likely have come along the coastal margins and not across the interior that lies under the present-day strait. Their remains are covered, therefore, not only by 300 feet or more of water but also by as much as 100 feet of sediment laid down in the Recent period as the sea encroached on the continental shelf. Archaeologists need not be surprised in the future to discover evidence of man here and there in North America 50,000 years old and even older.

SECTION **III**

THE NEOLITHIC

During the last part of the Upper Paleolithic man's technology became increasingly efficient. He put his tools to a new use, one that changed his life more drastically than anything that had happened to him in more than a million years: he prepared to harvest his first crop.

Reaping wild grasses, with a sickle of wood and bone or stone, was probably the first step in learning how to grow the food our ancestors had wandered about gathering. At about the same time they learned to domesticate some of the animals they had hunted. It was then no longer necessary for them always to move on in search of fresh stands of wild plants whenever the supply was exhausted in a particular region; or endlessly to pursue wild game in its migrations. Gradually man could become sedentary.

Once food production was under way, population began to grow, and there was more time available for activities unrelated to the quest for food, for example, building more permanent and comfortable dwellings, fabricating more and better utensils and clothing—and making social life more complicated. Increases in cultural complexity such as these were primarily the consequence of revolutionary innovations that had occurred in technology—and the manner in which these innovations facilitated an increasingly productive adjustment to the natural environment.

1. Prelude to Civilization [1]

WHAT TO EXPECT OF PREHISTORY

The focus of interest of the present symposium lies with events which began to take place as prehistory came to an end. With the appearance of *civilization* or "the urban revolution"—by whatever criteria this may manifest itself in the primary documents of archeology—the range of conventional "history" has begun. Usually the criteria include writing, although the instance of the Inca civilization suggests it need not always be included. While the philological imponderability of most early writing leaves much to be desired, if the goal is full-bodied cultural interpretation, the boundary line between prehistory and conventional ancient history is generally set at the point where writing makes its appearance.

The function of this paper is taken to be a consideration of how the stage was set for the appearance of civilization (including most if not all of the criteria inferred above). Understanding of the prehistoric past depends entirely upon elucidation of the very incomplete archeological record of half a million years of preliterate human development. Much of this development took place in remote and relatively unexplored—for prehistoric purposes—parts of the world. Clark and Wheeler have recently considered the factors of the accidents of discovery, the variables affecting the preservation of antiquities, the difficulties of establishing a chronology, and the human element of the competence of the excavator himself,

all of which must be taken into account in the assessment of the relative incompleteness of the archeological record.

For Henri Frankfort, archeology's goal was "the reclamation *and interpretation* of the material remains of man's past" [author's italics]. The interpretation of a very incomplete collection of material remains, representing most of the habitable world and a very great depth of time, presents exasperating difficulties. It is dangerous to assume that a "primitive" archeological assemblage or catalogue of material remains may be given direct explication by reference to the culture pattern which includes some apparently similar assemblage possessed by one of our remaining primitive contemporaries, for example the South African Bushmen or the Australian aborigines. And it cannot be assumed that reference to some unilinear evolutionary scheme makes the most reliable basis for interpretation. It has been maintained that the conventional neo-Grecisms "paleolithic," "mesolithic," and "neolithic" show the dead hand of Gabriel de Mortillet's first two "laws," the "loi du progrès de l'humanité" and the "loi du développement similaire." Given what we have learned and are learning about the natural and cultural environments of the last half-million years, it is quite clear that human progress has not been evenly progressive and universally similar.

Throughout their prehistory, men had to adjust to the fluctuations of climates and natural environments which were sometimes worse than those of today and sometimes better. The title of Reginald

---

[1] ROBERT J. BRAIDWOOD, "Prelude to Civilization," in *City Invincible,* Carl H. Kraeling and Robert M. Adams (eds.) (Chicago: 1960). Reprinted by permission of The University of Chicago Press, © 1960 by The University of Chicago Press.

Dr. Braidwood is Professor of Anthropology at the University of Chicago.

Daly's classic account of the Pleistocene period, *The Changing World of the Ice Age*, very aptly describes what was going on. But part of the gratifying increase in the attention being given to the details of at least late-glacial/early-post-glacial climatic and environmental history is a growing realization that all our present climatic and vegetational zones did not simply shift southward, in consecutive order, as glaciers built up in the northern latitudes and shift neatly back into their present positions as the glaciers disappeared. A more variable and irregular picture is beginning to appear. The field of human "paleo-environment" is only now being developed as a serious cross-disciplinary effort; its success will depend on the establishment of easy intercommunication and field co-operation between archeologists and natural scientists.

To biologists man is an organism, an animal, a vertebrate, and a mammal, subject to strict ecological ties with the organic world about him. In a recent article Edward Deevey thoughtfully considered man's low efficiency as an organism, with vivid examples. But man became man by acquisition of culture. I believe that even if the major theme of all human prehistory were conceded to be primarily an ecological one (which I will not concede), three important variations on that ecological theme would appear, which could be paralleled in the history of no other organism. These variations would be additive and much less divisive than their separate listing makes them appear at first sight. A long overview of the details of man's prehistoric past—however incompletely known these details may be—would suggest the following as the three variations on an ecological theme:

1. Evolving subsistence patterns showed an increasing extractive efficiency through time and an increasing ability to "live into" a given environment.

2. But with the passage of time (especially during the last 50,000 years—since the appearance of anatomically modern man) increasing technological complexity made possible adjustments to variable environments and began to free men from painful dependence on one given type of environment; with increased technological complexity, regional ways of doing things came more to the fore.

3. Increasing sociocultural complexity gradually tended to mitigate the necessity for an immediate ecological balance for an increasing number of—but not all —people of any given group.

This view is no doubt both a cumbersome and a trite way of saying that man's prehistory is the history of the species' acquisition of culture and of the increasing dimensions of culture. In this sense, Kroeber's description of culture as "the superorganic" is apt. There were obviously two themes during the prehistoric prelude to civilization. The first concerns the natural history of the species, its biological evolution, and the success with which it adapted itself ecologically. The second theme concerns the cultural history of the species and sets man apart from all other organisms. It would be satisfying to assert that the second and peculiarly human theme superseded the first, but dust bowls, exhausted lands, polluted streams, and the ever necessary war on insects and on disease and famine constantly remind us that this is not so.

Thus, to a prehistorian—whose raw data very seldom show him traces of the individual—human history appears as a struggle for the establishment of adequate checks and balances between the two themes of natural and cultural history as well as the attempts of men to cope with or take advantage of forces inherent in each of these themes. The archeologist's training makes the reclamation and interpretation of the documents of cultural history congenial to him, and there are some hopeful signs that the field of human paleo-environmental study will increasingly gain respectability among the natural scientists. Only by means of a joint effort will the whole story be unfolded.

THE FIRST NINE TENTHS OF HUMAN HISTORY

For present purposes, the first approximately 450,000 of the half-million years of prehistoric time need not hold us long. Many animals *utilize* tools, but it now appears that the australopithecines—of lower Pleistocene times and at least in Africa if not in southeastern Asia—were already beginning to *fashion* tools. In several charming essays, Kenneth Oakley has developed the idea that "Tools Makyth Man," and it is generally conceded by human paleontologists that the fashioning of tools for use by the earlier fossil men forced the biological pace of human evolution.

For middle Pleistocene times, the *standardization* of at least chipped stone tool types is assured. This means that men had developed notions of an ideal standard form of tool for some particular job (or jobs) and could reproduce it at will—often in much more intractable materials than flint. It also means no doubt that tools were made in anticipation of some need in the immediate future. I have suggested elsewhere, although of course I cannot demonstrate it, that the notion of standard tool types or "perfect tool for good job" already suggests symbol-making, with all its broad cultural consequences. An impressive thing is the apparent uniformity, over vast areas of the middle latitudes of the Old World, of essentially the same tool-preparation traditions.

Nevertheless, subsistence appears to have been at a most basic level of gathering and scavenging alone. From conversation with Clark Howell, who in 1957

in Tanganyika made the most extensive exposure yet available of a "living site" with Acheulean tools, I gather that the word "hunting" would be somewhat too dignified for what the evidence suggests of subsistence. Only with the onset of upper Pleistocene times do we have traces of such suggestions of human activity beyond subsistence alone as intentional burials and the "bear cults" (purposeful arrangements of the skulls of bears). And it would be only toward the end of this long range of time that we could guess that extractive efficiency and the "living into" an environment was beginning to increase.

My own preference for a name for this long range of beginnings is "the food-gathering era," the first era in the overall "food-gathering stage." The era did not come to an end at exactly the same moment in all parts of the then habitable world. Contrary to De Mortillet's second "law," we also know that not all the tool-preparation traditions of the era were exactly similar, although the broad distribution of the core-biface and the flake traditions in southwestern Eurafrasia is impressive.

ANATOMICALLY MODERN MAN AND CULTURAL DIVERSITY

About forty or fifty thousand years ago, there begin to appear in the available prehistoric record the traces of two significant events. One of these is the appearance of anatomically modern man, the other a new tool-preparation tradition. It is not impossible, on present indications, that both these events had their beginnings in southwestern Asia. There is not, however, anything yet—in the admittedly very restricted evidence—to suggest that the two events were interconnected, save for their coincident occurrence.

Current understanding of the details of this time range—the latter half of the upper Pleistocene and all of what is conventionally called "upper paleolithic" —is best for western Europe and especially France. The word "hunting" may now certainly be used advisedly; the suggestions of organized drives or stampedes (such as the mass of horse bones at Solutré) indicate impressive increases in extractive efficiency. It is usual, and no doubt somewhere near the mark, to interpret the magnificent Franco-Cantabrian cave art as "increase magic," although that old phrase certainly over-simplifies the broad functional dimensions which the art must have had in Franco-Cantabrian culture of that time. The type names and the sequence established in France are so well known and broadly borrowed and the heritage of De Mortillet's "loi du développement similaire" is still so strong that the true nature of this era is ofen missed.

As a name for this era I prefer simply "the food-collecting era." It, also, did not begin at the same moment everywhere, nor did it end abruptly at the same moment everywhere. In fact, certain derivatives of the era still persist in a few out-of-the-way parts of the world. The blade-tool tradition, one of the two events which announces the appearance of the new era in western Eurasia, apparently did not spread over the whole habitable world. Anatomically modern man, the other hallmark of the era, did presently spread over the globe. During the development and spread of the era, the New World and the higher latitudes were occupied.

Cultural diversification seems to be the thing which distinguishes the era of food-collecting from the much longer era of food-gathering. Even within the great area of western Eurasia, where the blade-tool tradition was itself at home, the catalogues of the regional industries produced on blades show considerable regional variability. This was clearly in Dorothy Garrod's mind when she wrote:

The speeding-up of change and development which begins to show in this period is reflected in some areas, not only in the greater number of industries having enough individual character to be classified as distinct cultures, but in their restriction in space, since [cultural] evolution now starts to outstrip diffusion.

What seems to be involved here is the coming into play of our second—as well as an intensification of our first—variation on an ecological theme, namely that increasing technological complexity made adjustments to new environments possible. A vividly instructive example, were there space to document it, could be made by reference to the remains from latest Pleistocene times on the plains of central Europe and Russia. Here, at least thirty thousand years ago, lived groups of accomplished mammoth-hunters. They had certainly discovered how to "live into" a bitter environment, with sewn skin clothing and subsurface huts. Architecture is conventionally assumed to have begun at the time of the appearance of the settled village-farming community. Actually, the origins of constructed shelters in encampments of some degree of permanence go back well into the food-collecting era.

I have little to say regarding the biological aspects of the appearance of anatomically modern man beyond S. L. Washburn's idea that the important differentiation of biological races has happened since fifty thousand years ago. In this view, a "race" is a population of genetically similar composition, more or less geographically restricted, but integraded about the edges of its area with its neighbors. Culture allowed the geographical "restriction" (or, better, "localization") and seems still to have been setting the pace for biological evolution.

There is increasing evidence that, *for*

the more northerly latitudes of both the Old and the New World, the date of the late-glacial/early-postglacial time boundary can be placed at about ten thousand years ago. What followed—in the northerly latitudes—was a cultural readjustment to the sequence of early postglacial environments, *on a food-collecting level*. In fact, this level often shows traces of very intensified extractive efficiency. Such traces are usually classified under the rubrics "mesolithic" for northwestern Europe and "archaic" for North America. I am not myself of the opinion that an entirely new era had begun. There appear to have been climatic and environmental changes within the preceding thirty or forty thousand years which must have been just as traumatic as those which happened ten thousand years ago (in the regions where we are sure they happened!). But there might be value in considering a terminal "sub-era of intensified food-collecting."

I believe it is important to bear in mind that this sub-era—quite contrary to De Mortillet's second "law"—may not have taken place everywhere. The implication of radioactive-carbon chronology is increasingly that it did not take place everywhere and, in fact, that in certain favored regions of the world a new era of potentially greater importance for what was to follow replaced it. This new era is that of "incipient cultivation," the first era of the new "food-producing stage," which is considered briefly below. It is probably worth remarking here, however, that there may have been some as yet very poorly understood linkage between the sub-era of intensified food-collection and the era of incipient cultivation. Both appear to have commenced at about the same time, roughly ten thousand years ago. Both imply an increasing "living into" a given environment and a technology-bound increase in extractive efficiency in utilizing it. The understanding of this range very particularly demands the close co-operation of archeologists and natural scientists.

Grahame Clark has given much attention to the sub-era of intensified food-collecting in northwestern Europe, and Joseph R. Caldwell is one of the Americanists who has attempted its delineation in the New World. It is to this sub-era that the traces of really specialized and concentrated collection of smaller animals and plants pertain (the more "important" ones usually of a rather restricted number of species). The great shell mounds of both the Old and the New World begin at this level, as does adequate tackle for the taking of fish and waterfowl. It is probable that the first constructed dugout canoes are no older than this level, as are skis and the use of the dog as a hunting companion and possibly even the first general use of the bow and arrow. Ground stone tools and crude vessels for the crushing and preparation of seeds or acorns are also evidenced. In drier portions of North America, Willey and Phillips note ". . . widespread seed-gathering . . . which . . . tended to anchor populations in favored localities, and, by conditioning them to greater dependence on vegetal foods, prepared the way for the adoption of agriculture at a later time." The traces of settlements in the earlier phases of this sub-era suggest small seasonal encampments, whose inhabitants had at best only a relatively efficient level of extraction. It could be maintained, however, that the classic "salmon-reapers" of the northwest coast of British Columbia represented the ultimate in intensified food-collection.

There is one factor which needs to be taken into account in considering the scheme at this point. The instance of the Northwest Coast peoples suggests that intensified food-collection persisted in some places well into the ethnological present, and it is usually granted that some of the more spectacular of the

Northwest Coast traits may have been based on borrowing. No culture in the world ever lived in a complete vacuum. It is likely that we shall find earlier cases of peoples, still at a level of intensified food-collecting, who borrowed traits from neighboring contemporaries with more developed extractive efficiencies. For example, I suspect such may have been the case with Carleton Coon's "meso-lithic"and earlier "neolithic" cave dwellers at Belt and Hotu on the Caspian coast.

THE FOOD-PRODUCING STAGE

It is my thesis that in certain regions of the world which were blessed with potentially domesticable animals and/or plants, the subsistence aspect of human culture took a new and alternate direction about ten thousand years ago. The result was the development of the food-producing stage. It is not conceivable to me that civilization could have appeared without a fairly well-developed level of food-production. However "intensified" food-collection might have become, it does not seem possible that civilization and true urbanization could have eventually attended it.

There are exquisite difficulties in delineating the first era of the food-producing stage, that of incipient cultivation. In the first place, as suggested above, there must have been some subtle linkage between the sub-era of food-collection and that of incipient cultivation. It is only reasonable to suppose that incipient cultivators also did a great deal of food-collecting. Such was certainly still the case in the next era, that of "the settled village-farming community," for which our documentation is much clearer. In fact, such is still the case, however industrialized our fisheries become—to take one example. It must also have been the case during the era of incipient cultiva-

tion that the morphologies of both the plants and the animals being taken under domestication were little different from those of their wild contemporaries. Moreover, the artifacts—which were eventually developed to cope with the whole new subsistence pattern—were in their most elemental forms at best. A fair amount of "making-do" with older items of the tool kit must have obtained. Hence it is understandable that both the archeologists and the natural historians may have some difficulty in recognizing what they deal with during this era.

One clear implication of the notion of an era of incepient cultivation is that it would only be manifested within the natural habitat of the potentially domesticable animals and/or plants. Karl Narr has also considered this implication independently. Here again it should be obvious that increase in our knowledge depends as much on the interest of natural scientists as on that of archeologists.

With the study of human paleo-environments only in its infancy, it is not at all clear how many pertinent natural habitats there may have been nor even whether all the possibilities actually were the scenes of independent experiments in domestication. Carl Sauer has championed the case for an early development and spread of the domesticated vegetatively reproductive plants in southeastern Asia and has also considered many of the factors which must have conditioned the appearance of cultivation in the New World. G. P. Murdock makes a case for an early center of cultivation in the great bend of the Niger River in West Africa. Both the Southeast Asian and the West African cases seem to me quite reasonable, but there is neither archeological nor paleo-environmental documentation for their reality. The same is true of China, for which it would certainly not be completely unreasonable to expect a range of incipient cultivation, and it is not yet clear whether a separate case will eventually be made for peninsular India—as distinct from both southwestern and southeastern Asia.

For the New World, much attention has been given to the history of maize, and the pollen of one of its possible antecedents has been found in an early geological context in Mexico, but maize does not appear in the typologically earliest "village" sites so far available. Both Irving Rouse and Gordon Willey are sensitive to Sauer's suggestion for the early development of a premaize root-crop "horticulture" in lowland South America. R. S. MacNeish's earliest "incipient agricultural" horizon in Tamaulipas appears to have been a combination of squash and bean cultivation along with food-collection. The "preceramic agricultural period" mound sites of coastal Peru, which probably pertain to the beginning of the next era in any case, were inhabited by people who depended on such cultivated plants as squash, aji peppers, and canavalia beans as well as on collected wild plants and fish. It is my present understanding that from the point of view of maize as the most potentially effective New World food crop, the location (or locations?) of the natural habitat of the eventually domesticated form (or forms?) is not yet known.

The New World situation is further complicated by the fact that on various occasions in the area of what is now the United States, at least, there were prehistoric attempts at the cultivation of such seeds as pigweed, giant ragweed, sunflower, and so on. M. L. Fowler has reconsidered this evidence and concludes that these local cultivations refer to the level of the "archaic" or our sub-era of intensified food-collection. Apparently the yield from these plants was not sufficiently impressive from the point of view of extractive efficiency to lead to a truly new subsistence pattern. It is of course possible that the same sort of thing happened at various times and places in the Old World and may correspond in part to a recently postulated level of "vegeculture," the conception of which probably overemphasizes the matter of vegetatively reproductive plants and semitropical situations.

It is southwestern Asia that provides what little substance the era of incipient cultivation—as a true prelude to food-production—now has beyond pure theory. Within the biotic zone of the hilly flanks of the Fertile Crescent, a beginning has been made in a sophisticated study of the paleo-environment and suggests that the hilly-flanks zone was in fact a natural habitat of great potential. While the exact boundaries of the zone and the details of its climate and environment some ten thousand years ago are far from fixed, the zone does appear to have been the home of the wild wheats, barleys, and certain legumes and of the important food animals of the basic Western cultural tradition. Within this zone also appear the archeological traces known in Palestine as the "Natufian" and other traces found in Iraqi Kurdistan at Karim Shahir, M'lefaat, and Zawi Chemi Shanidar. These are the materials which I take to manifest the era of incipient cultivation. They show modest indications of architecture and settlement, the first flint sickle blades, perhaps the domesticated dog, and a variety of ground stone tools reasonably implying digging, grinding, and food-preparation. At the same time, implements implying food-collection also appear in the assemblages. The implications for incipient cultivation gain some force from the fact that the sites occur in the zone of the natural habitat and also by extrapolation backward from the earliest known phases of the next era—that of the settled village-farming community.

Clearly, a great deal more of both archeological and paleo-environmental study is needed before the era of incipient cultivation gains fully acceptable substance. But the place, the implications, and even the time seem to be about right. While there is as yet no radiocarbon determination for the Natufian (*senso stricto*), the termination of the Zarzian levels at Shanidar cave and determinations for the open site of Zawi Chemi Shanidar itself both fall at about 8750 B.C. This is, in fact, somewhat before the conventional date for the late-glacial/early-postglacial time boundary (and for the beginning of the "mesolithic"—our sub-era of intesified food-collection—in northwestern Europe).

Unsatisfactory as its documentation remains for the moment, the conception of an era of incipient cultivation is taken to be useful as a model for further research in prehistory. It emphasizes a clean break from De Mortillet's "loi du développement similaire" and also the proposition that a new set of culture patterns (implying with it a new type of subsistence pattern) may have been developing at the same time as was the sub-era of intensified food-collection in other regions. It emphasizes the necessity for the reclamation of evidence in the realms of both archeology and paleo-environment if real understanding of the prehistoric past is to be achieved.

The next era, that of the established village-farming community, is somewhat more generally familiar (often under the rubric "neolithic"), although its beginnings are being pushed backward in time in both hemispheres. Since the era had intensifications in favored regions as time went on, we have sometimes referred to its earlier phases as "primary."

The beginnings of this level of extractive efficiency are difficult to characterize simply and in a world-wide sense. If any definition of the "neolithic" were to be acceptable (though to me none would be,

for the word has had too many meanings ever to regain precision), it would be in Childe's sense of "'a self-sufficing food-producing economy.'" But the presence of great bulks of snail shells and traces of pistachio and acorn hulls as well as the bones of wild animals would make me uncomfortable about the possibility of self-sufficiency on the basis of *produced* food alone at the site of Jarmo. Even my choice of a name for the era, that of "the village-farming community," no doubt shows my predisposition toward the materials of southwestern Asia. There, architecturally well-expressed villages of fair permanency (as their depths of deposit show) seem to have been present from the beginning of the era. But it is not yet completely clear whether the roughly equivalent level in Mesoamerica followed the same type of settlement pattern, although the early mound sites of coastal Peru apparently do so. The presence of pottery as a "standard" trait for identifying the appearance of the "neolithic" has now clearly gone by the board in both the Old and the New World. There are even traces of pre-ceramic village communities in Thessalian Greece and in Baluchistan, which suggest that expansion away from the zone of the natural habitat had already begun before the era witnessed the appearance of pottery.

The fact is that, while the names of many of the sites of this era in both the Old and the New World are generally familiar, in no case—within the areas of potential nuclearity for the appearance of the recognized ancient civilizations—are we really well informed in either culture-historical or natural-historical terms. It would be almost pure guesswork and extrapolation to attempt to answer the question: What was the subsistence pattern of the people of a Halafian village in the upper Tigris-Euphrates basin? There are actually few enough sites, although the names of the known sites may be familiar. I grow increasingly uncomfortable because we archeologists who deal with later prehistory have also been in the clutch of De Mortillet's dead hand. We make our chronological tables as bar diagrams, never dreaming that some of the Hassunah phase, some of the Halaf phase, and perhaps even some of the Ubaid phase may have been in fact contemporaneous.

I do not take it to be my business here to detail the known sequences of the era. This has been done fairly recently for southwestern Asia and for the New World. Max Loehr's short account of China is probably the best available. The new implications of radiocarbon determination for southwestern Asia have been briefly considered recently, but there do remain a few points of interest for our present purposes.

It is my understanding of the situation in southwestern Asia, at least, that the transition from the era of incipient cultivation to the era of the primary village-farming community took place within the zone of the natural habitat of the potentially domesticable plants and animals. Soon after this, presumably, the "permissive mutations" and/or "introgressive hybridizations" allowed expansion of peoples (with their plants and animals) outside the zone of the natural habitat. Probably one important aspect of this expansion was the "fingering down the mud flats" of the Tigris and Euphrates toward alluvial Mesopotamia. Very presently, and no doubt most importantly in southern Mesopotamia although not exclusively so, the era began to take on intensified dimensions. We begin to find, for example, the remains of town-sized establishments with temples of some degree of monumentality.

It is here that I become uncomfortable with my attempt to delineate further eras or sub-eras on the primary basis of subsistence patterns and extractive efficiencies. I believe my difficulty lies with

the fact that by about this time, our third variation on an ecological theme, namely that increasing sociocultural complexity gradually tended to mitigate the necessity of an immediate ecological balance for an increasing number of people, began to become effective.

This does not mean that the natural-historian, working with the culture-historian, no longer has a role in the elucidation of events at the very threshold of civilization's appearance. The recent work of Adams and Jacobsen in southern Iraq merely serves to emphasize how important it is that we understand the natural (as well as the social) ecology of ancient Mesopotamia. Jean Perrot has convinced me of the importance of his conception of a "submarginal" culture pattern of rather mobile farmer-traders, as seen in the Beersheba-Ghassul type sites in Israel and Jordan—a culture pattern which seems to have achieved a neat balance with life well below the 200-mm. rain line. But the point remains that increasingly, as we move nearer the time of established civilizations, a scheme of classification based primarily on subsistence tends to blur rather than aid understanding.

As for the archeology of Mesopotamia in the threshold range, we still know far too little of it. In terms of Delougaz's very reasonable reclassification, we have a fair grasp of portions of the Ubaid assemblage on a few sites but know precious little of the Warka phase and certainly not yet enough of the Protoliterate phase from a full-bodied culture-historical (and natural-historical!) point of view. We do, very fortunately, begin to benefit by such extrapolations backward from "historical" times as those of Jacobsen and Wilson. Childe gives a relatively good account of the archeology of both Mesopotamia and Egypt, but it must not be read alone or without Jacobsen and Wilson and certainly Frankfort. Adams makes his own very important contribution to our understandings, especially in playing down *irrigation* as a determinate factor in the early formation of civilization.

SUMMARY

Any prehistoric reconstruction must, given the nature of the available data, remain a thing of threads and patches. It will also be quite idiosyncratic and depend on the experiences and opportunities for observation which the particular prehistorian has had as well as on the degree to which he allows himself imaginative flights with respect to his data. Should Gordon Willey attempt to trespass into the Old World, as I have into the New (and I certainly hope he will attempt it!), he would be bound to come out differently. I myself am quite unashamed of a tendency to make imaginative models as a framework against which to set problem-oriented field research. I trust I am just as ready to abandon them when the data show them to be in error; I have already had to cease, with apologies, my scolding of Miss Kenyon for her preference for a "long" chronology. I also have a tendency to think in terms both of multilinear evolution and of diffusion, as Richard Pittioni has noticed! If I understand Pittioni correctly, he does not believe diffusion took place effectively until a considerable cultural potential was built up, but not all anthropologists demand that the word "diffusion" refer to such an accomplished level. For some curious reason, one of Carl Sauer's misconceptions of our general position is that American anthropologists do not find diffusion "reputable."

To the degree in which the reader agrees or disagrees with my tendencies, he may find this brief reconstruction acceptable or unacceptable. It seems to me that the long view of prehistory taken here suggests an obviously more direct man-nature relationship at the beginning. As time went on and technology gave man more control of nature, the relationship began to acquire more "human" proportions. As time went still farther and most importantly, although not necessarily exclusively, with the appearance of food-production, the increasingly complex sociocultural aspects of life further altered the man-nature relationship. Given the biological nature of man, the relationship must obviously continue to exist, and its balance, however subtle, must be maintained if the species is to survive. Perhaps a great part of human history could be said to be concerned with the developing subtleness of balance between man and nature as the dimensions of culture increase.

Man's marvelous new skill was gradually diffused around the Mediterranean and into Europe, adapted everywhere to the varying requirements of differing natural conditions. Just as gradually the Paleolithic way of life was put aside.

2. Neolithic European Peasants [1]

THE STATUS OF EUROPEAN "NEOLITHIC" CULTURES

The beginnings of settled life in Europe and the possibility of a distinct European civilization depended in the first instance on the spread of farming from the focal territories in which cultivated forms were first elicited and on the adoption in due course of this new and alien way of life by indigenous hunter-fishers. The only part of Europe in which possible prototypes of cultivated cereals have been found in a wild state extends from Greece to Yugoslavia and even here it is only with wild forms of einkorn and millet that we have to do: over the continent as a whole, up to the northern margin of the temperate zone that formed the boundary of cereal cultivation during early times, all cultivated cereals had to be introduced into environments differing to some extent from those in which they were originally domesticated.

Even in those parts of Europe first colonized by farmers, settled life began much later than in Palestine, Cilicia, Syria and northern Mesopotamia; though to judge from radio-carbon dates no more recently than in the Nile Valley. Although the earliest peasant communities in Europe were "Neolithic" in the sense that they were ignorant of metallurgy and that their technology was governed by the possibilities inherent in the utilization of flint and stone tools, they were contemporary with societies in western Asia conversant from the latter part of the fifth millennium b.c. with the casting of copper and from the middle of the fourth with that of bronze. Even more to the point, early in the third millennium the Minoan civilization had already begun to develop in Crete along independent lines, though under the influence of those of Asia Minor, Syria and Egypt; and active centers of culture were established in the Cycladic islands and on the mainland of Greece. Already during the latter half of the third millennium b.c. both central Europe and the Mediterranean were permeated by a knowledge of copper metallurgy, and even in western and northern Europe, where Neolithic communities were unable to afford metal tools, flint and stone axes might be influenced by metal prototypes. Another striking illustration of the status of these northern "Neolithic" peoples is that they adopted the rite of collective burial from the technologically more advanced Aegean world and felt impelled, despite their comparative poverty, to share the funerary customs of peoples much richer than themselves and to erect megalithic chamber tombs.

The basic reason why parts of southwest Asia were so far in advance of Europe in adopting farming is the differ-

[1] GRAHAME CLARK, from "The Foundations of Europe Civilization: Neolithic Peasants and Arctic Hunter-Fishers," in _World Prehistory: An Outline_ (New York: 1961), pp. 119–134. Reprinted by permission of the author and the publisher, © 1961 by the Cambridge University Press.

Dr. Clark is Disney Professor of Prehistoric Archaeology at Cambridge University.

ing conditions to which the rather drastic transition from Late Pleistocene to Neothermal times give rise in the two areas: whereas in the former the desiccation of hitherto rich hunting grounds presented a challenge to people now fitted biologically and culturally to respond by a fundamental change of outlook towards their environment, in the latter a gradual increase of temperature, while bringing ecological changes in its train, offered no comparable challenge to prehistoric man. Thus an environmental change which precipitated the so-called Neolithic Revolution in one, encouraged in the other the persistence under progressively more genial conditions of old ways of life stemming from the Old Stone Age and expressed in Mesolithic culture.

The new farming economy, giving a hitherto unknown degree of control over the supply of food, was inherently expansive, but it was not until the return of wetter conditions in the neighborhood of the focal region during Altithermal times that the Neolithic way of life was able to spread to North Africa, southeastern Europe and Inner Asia. As a field for colonization by farmers, Europe fell into three major ecological zones. The first was a Mediterranean zone which formed an extension, progressively modified as one moves west, of that in which the basic discoveries were made and into which in consequence they were able to penetrate without the need for major changes. The second was a temperate zone, differing more or less markedly in climate, vegetation and soils and into which the new economy was only able to penetrate selectively and sometimes with difficulty. The third was a circumpolar zone into which only certain elements of Neolithic culture were able to filter and over which the old hunting and fishing economy continued to reign supreme.

Since men learned to farm in parts of western Asia long before they began to make pottery vessels, the question arises to what extent agriculture was introduced into Europe in advance of pottery-making. The only certain evidence for this comes from Thessaly, where traces of huts and fire-places were found at the base of mounds at Argissa near Larissa and at Sesklo, stratified below the earliest pottery-levels, but belonging to farmers who grew cereals and pulse, kept sheep or goats and presumably made do with baskets or other nonceramic containers. These pre-pottery farmers had a flint industry producing blades and trapeze-shaped points, together with stone palettes and simple bodkins and skin-working tools of bone. Similar blade and trapeze industries from the Mediterranean area may indicate a wider extension of a pre-pottery Neolithic and it is significant that remains of sheep or goats have been found with industries of similar type in France known as Tardenoisian: decisive evidence might well be obtained by an exhaustive study of the organic refuse from a site like Châteauneuf-les-Martigues, near Marseilles, where a blade and trapeze industry underlay early Neolithic impressed pottery. Another reason for thinking that agriculture may have been introduced to Europe by people ignorant of pottery is that few of the earliest pottery vessels from most of Europe can plausibly be traced to specific Asiatic sources.

THE BALKANS, CENTRAL AND EASTERN EUROPE

Nevertheless, the first farmers certainly verifiable over any extensive tract of Europe made hand-built pottery, comprising bowls and flasks with round bases, simple rims and handles in the form of lugs perforated so that the pots could be carried or suspended. The most important region settled during this early phase was the Balkan peninsula, which formed as it were a funnel, the narrow end open

TABLE 1. SEQUENCE OF EARLY PEASANT CULTURES IN PARTS OF EUROPE DOWN TO c. 1200 B.C.

South Britain	Denmark	Danube	Greece	Southeast Balkans	Ukraine
		VI			Black burnished
Bronze Age (Wessex)	Bronze Age	V	Late Helladic (Mycenaean)	Karanovo	
Secondary Neolithic	Late Neolithic	IV	Middle Helladic (Minyan)		Tripolje
	Middle Neolithic	III			
Primary Neolithic	Early Neolithic	II	Early Helladic	Gumelniţa	
			Late Neolithic (Dimini)		Izvoare
		I (Spiral-meander ware)		Boian	
			Middle Neolithic (Sesklo)		
			Early Neolithic (Impressed; Otzaki)	Starčevo	
			Proto-Neolithic		

to western Asia and the broad one to the expanses of central and eastern Europe. The earliest pottery-using farmers to penetrate the Balkans were shifting agriculturists who cultivated temporary clearings in the forest and moved on after cropping the initial fertility of the virgin land. The Starčevo people, named after the site on the north bank of the Danube near Belgrade, seem to have spread north from the Aegean coast mainly by the Vardar–Morava route into what is now eastern Yugoslavia and on into the Middle Danube valley. Western Bulgaria may have been colonized partly by way of the Struma Valley, in part from the Morava Valley by way of the Nišava, and in part by following the Danube downstream. Further north they pressed into Hungary where they concentrated on the Tisa and Körös rivers. It may prove

significant that the Starčevo people cultivated einkorn and millet, the wild prototypes of which are known from the south Balkans; and it is noteworthy that they had reaping-knives with flint insets and querns like those from western Asia; in addition they kept livestock and did some hunting. Some of their pottery vessels were more specialized in form, including bows with ring feet and, more particularly in the Körös Valley, lop-sided flasks with perforated lugs, probably designed for slinging on the back. Impressed decoration was common, though cardium shells were not used for this purpose as they were in parts of the Mediterranean area, and other favored varieties included roughening of the surface and plastic relief, including representations of animals and men; and footed bowls in fine ware might be decorated by painting. The widespread use of the Aegean mussel *Spondylus gaederopus* as a material for beads and bracelets shows that contact was maintained with the south. Clay seals, apparently barbaric versions of stone stamp seals of ultimately Asiatic origin, marble vessels, bone and clay idols and four-footed pottery stands that may have served some cult purpose are among enrichments which may well have been acquired from the more settled villagers whose settlement mounds had begun to accumulate in Greece and the south Balkans.

Immediately north of the Starčevo province, over a territory which extended from south of Lake Balaton to near the estuary of the Oder—a distance of nearly six hundred miles—and laterally from the Rhine and the Maas to the Vistula and the Upper Dniester—a span of a thousand miles—the earliest peasants made pottery decorated with spiral-meander patterns and exhibited a cultural uniformity so great as only to be explained if we suppose that the whole area was colonized comparatively rapidly. From the Middle Danube region, comprising much of central Hungary, Lower Austria and Bohemia, the pioneer farmers pushed along the great rivers, east to the Vistula and the Upper Dniester; north down the Vistula, Oder and Elbe; and west by way both of the Upper Danube and overland across Saxony and Hesse to the Rhineland and the Maas. The rapidity of their spread—according to radio-carbon dating they had reached South Germany and Dutch Limburg before the end of the fifth millennium B.C.—was due in part to their extensive system of agriculture, in part to the discontinuous distribution of the fertile and easily worked loess on which they settled, and in part to the lack of opposition. Emmer and barley were grown, as well as einkorn, peas, beans and flax, and the common farmyard animals were kept.

Material equipment remained very simple during this first phase in the settlement of the Danubian zone. There is no evidence either for weaving or for metallurgy. The pottery was made from carefully prepared clay that required neither slip nor burnish, and took the form of the standard early Neolithic shapes, round-based bowls and flasks, the latter sometimes flattened on one face, having plain rims and no handles other than lugs. Plastic ornament, like that on Starčevo ware, was used, especially in the Middle Danube area, but the most characteristic form of ornament consisted of bands defined by two or three more or less parallel incised lines and conforming to spirals or meanders; in addition designs were sometimes painted on the surface after firing. Where flint was readily available it was flaked into the form of blades which might be inserted into slots to provide cutting-edges for reaping-knives, or worked into end-scrapers and trapeziform arrowheads. The commonest stone tool, a polished stone adze-blade of D-section with a slightly hollow-ground working edge, was probably used mainly for dressing the timbers needed for building. The peasants lived in large houses, generally of rectangular plan, but in parts of Germany and in Poland often wedge-shaped with one end markedly broader than the other. They were commonly of twenty or thirty and might be up to fifty meters in length and it is thought that they must have provided space for storage and possibly for sheltering livestock as well as for the peasant family. The Danubian I peasants seem to have lived in fair-sized villages, which at first they found no need to defend by more than a palisade; but the nature of their economy caused them to shift their cultivations at frequent intervals, though commonly rebuilding on the same site. Like the Starčevo people they continued to import *Spondylus* shells from the far distant

Aegean and to deposit with the dead, interred in cemeteries of single graves, ornaments that more vividly than anything else recalled their southern origin.

Permanent settlement that gave rise to tells on the Asiatic model was confined to the Balkans. In Greece settlement mounds began to accumulate immediately over the encampments of pre-pottery peasants and it is significant that two layers, the lower of which yielded a primitive painted ware, had been formed at Otzaki before the appearance of cardial-impressed and Starčevo pottery. After the Starčevo culture had passed north, Thessaly was the scene of the flowering of a culture named after the site of Sesklo, a culture which, though having Syrian analogies, is distinctively Thessalian and may have developed there from an earlier Neolithic spread. The Sesklo potters made a fine burnished ware which they baked to reddish color in kilns. Many of the finer pots, which included flat-bottomed dishes with flaring sides, footed bowls, and mugs with well-made handles, were painted by hand before firing with red paint on a white slip or alternatively with white on a red ground. The designs were geometrical in character: these included a variety of multiple linear chevrons; and in the 'block-painted' ware rectangles, lozenges and triangles, probably inspired by the ornament on birch-bark vessels. In addition to the use of the kiln for firing painted pots, mud-bricks, stone button seals and the use of the sling all point to Asia as an ultimate source; but shoe-last adzes, the use of *Spondylus* shell for bracelets and portable clay altars were among features widely spread in the Balkans. Late Neolithic layers containing a local ware named after the site of Dimini commonly overlie Sesklo ones in the Thessalian mounds. The distinctive pottery is more elementary in form, bases being flat and lugs replacing the handles,

but designs painted on the surface now included spirals and meanders.

Outside Greece the kind of settlement that gave rise to tells did not begin until the basis of a farming economy had been laid by pioneers who moved their corn-plots and their livestock at frequent intervals and occupied no more than temporary villages. Thus the mound at Vinča near Belgrade, type site of a culture that extended over much of Yugoslavia and parts of western Roumania and Bulgaria, overlay traces of Starčevo people. Again, the Gumelniţa mound-culture of central and eastern Bulgaria replaced a pioneer peasant culture that took its name from the Boian lake near the head of the Dobrudža.

The Boian pioneers cultivated einkorn and millet and occupied rectangular houses with matting on the floor. For felling and working timber they used a variety of stone tools, including polished adze-blades of bevelled and shoe-last form. Their pottery, which included bowls with ringed-feet, biconical jars and large pear-shaped storage jars, was decorated by several different methods, but most commonly by incising or excising the surface to form in the first case either spiral or other curvilinear patterns and in the second rectilinear ones, each of which were emphasized by encrusting with red or white paint. The Boians were of more than local interest because they initiated the spread of peasant economy over much of Roumania and the Ukraine as far east as the river Dnieper. The first stage in their expansion, well exemplified at the site of Izvoare in Moldavia, penetrated the Alt valley on the west of the Carpathians and on the east extended as far as the Bug; it was only during the developed or classical phase of the culture, commonly named after Cucuteni on the Pruth or Tripolje near Kiev, that the full extent was attained. The excised technique continued to be fashionable during the Izvoare stage, but this was replaced by painting before firing, a technique already practised by the Starčevo peasants, or by U-sectioned grooves designed to hold encrustation. The spiral, a motive already exploited by the Starčevo and Danubian peasants and one that may well have been suggested originally by making coiled basketry, continued to play a leading part in decorating pottery. As regards the forms of pots, the simple rims, flat bases and absence of handles other than lugs are all persistent features. Other Balkan elements include polished stone adzes, a lithic industry based on blades, and clay stamps and female figurines made from baked clay. Like the Danubians, whom they dispossessed on the Upper Dniester, the Tripolje peasants shifted their settlements at frequent intervals as they took into cultivation fresh areas of the fertile black earth that directly overlay the loess. Likewise they lived in substantial rectangular houses, up to 30 meters in length, but they differed at least in the Ukraine in arranging these in circles or even in concentric rings, as at Kolomiishchina or Vladimirovka. It seems likely that this circular arrangement may have been designed for security against their warlike pastoral neighbours of the steppe who decorated their pots with cord imprints.

In the Middle Danube area there is evidence for the penetration, possibly as early as the beginning of the third millennium B.C., of renewed impulses from the south-east. The pottery ascribed to the Danubian II stage of settlement in this cortical area is more sophisticated in form than that of the Danubian I stage, having flat bases and including footed bowls. It was also much more diversified and one may distinguish even in Hungary between the monochrome ware of Lengyel and the encrusted ware, painted after firing, of the Theiss Valley. Apart from the painting of pottery, southern traits include female figurines and model houses of fired clay, clay stamps reminiscent of stone seals, cubical clay block vases recalling Early Minoan ones of stone, and spiral ornaments made of copper wire.

While these innovations were making themselves felt in the Middle Danube area and spreading thence over Czechoslovakia and into Germany, the heirs of the original colonists occupying the extensive outer tracts of the Danubian I territory were undergoing a certain degree of barbarization. In default of any more intensive occupation of the loess soil, such as might be implied by the growth of settlement mounds, the peasants were driven to spread on to poorer soils and develop hunting as an accessory source of food, both processes that brought them into contact with Mesolithic hunter-fishers. Among the leading features of this time was the disappearance of the spiral and meander from the decorative motives used by potters and the substitution of horizontal lines and chevrons—designs that reproduced the webbing in which round-based pots were commonly carried; and further the incised line was replaced or at least supplemented by impressions made by toothed stamps or combs, producing the so-called stroke-ornamented ware. Other more specialized wares included that named after the cemetery of Rössen near Merseberg in Saxo-Thuringia, which spread over much of the Middle and Upper Rhineland and beyond, and was decorated by broader furrowed lines apparently made by a jabbing motion and intended to secure white incrustation. Wild animal bones show that the Rössen people went in for hunting on a considerable scale and it is significant that the arrowheads belonging to the younger phases of the Danubian were of devolved Tardenoisian type, trapeziform and triangular and commonly with flat flaking. A final point to mention is that on the margin of their distribution in the west the Danubian peasants in their later phase began to come into contact with others of alien culture. No doubt it is this which explains why in its last period the great settlement at Köln-Lindenthal was defended and why in South Germany the Rössen people chose to occupy such a natural fortress as the Goldberg. What is certain is that Rössen pottery occurs on settlements of the earliest peasants of Switzerland, whose cultural affinities lie in the west.

THE MEDITERRANEAN AND WESTERN EUROPE

The earliest pottery from western Europe is that from the islands and shores of the Mediterranean, simple bowls and flasks with round bases and lugs, plain or decorated by impressions of cardium shells. Closely similar pottery has been recovered from western Asia, for example from the lowest levels in the tells at Mersin in Cilicia and Ras Shamrah (Ugarit) in Syria. The distribution of cardial impressed ware in the Mediterranean area strongly suggests that it was transmitted by sea: it is found on the islands of Leukas and Corfu; on the coast of Yugoslavia and the Adriatic coast of Italy, including the Tremiti islands; on Malta, Sicily, Elba and Sardinia; on the coast of Liguria; in the French provinces of Languedoc and Provence; and on the east and south-east coasts of Spain and the south coast of Portugal. The impressions, which were frequently made by toothed stamps and other objects as well as by cardium shells, were most commonly arranged as horizontal or vertical lines, zig-zags or hanging arcs. Most of the settlement material has come from caves or rock-shelters and represents what appear to have been temporary occupations. The lithic industries of these early farmers were based on the production of blades, from sections of which trapeze and transverse arrowheads were made;

hunting evidently played some part in a mainly pastoral economy. Polished stone axes and adzes testify to the felling of trees and the working of wood. Among the simple objects made from bone the most noteworthy were spatulae used, in all probability, for eating cereal food. For personal ornamentation perforated animal teeth, shells and foot-bones of hare were used as beads, and bracelets were made from polished stone or shell.

Whether the predominantly plain, round-based wares associated with Neolithic farmers in France, parts of Iberia and beside the Swiss lakes stemmed from the same source as the impressed wares or whether they represent a distinct and to some extent parallel tradition remains uncertain. Although the pottery from the Camp de Chassey in the French department of Saône-et-Loire was frequently plain it was sometimes decorated by geometrical patterns incised before firing or scratched on afterwards, and the pots of the younger stage of the Swiss Cortaillod ware, named after the locality on Lake Neuchâtel, might be ornamented by patterns cut out of birch-bark and applied to the surface of the pot by means of resin. Plain western ware is found with flint blades, trapeziform arrowheads and polished stone axes and adzes on settlements like El Garcel in Almeria and with collective burials in southern Iberia. The Chassey culture spread extensively over France from the Mediterranean, by the valley of the Rhone and Saône to the Paris basin and west of the Massif Central to the Atlantic coast of Brittany; and it is significant that fired clay female figurines have been found as far north as Fort-Harrouard, Eure-et-Loire. The makers of the Cortaillod pottery, which has a counterpart to the south of the Alps in the Lagozza culture of North Italy, occupied rectangular wooden houses resembling those made by the Rössen and other Danubian II groups from whom they may well have derived them. The lakeside locations of their settlements favored the survival of a much greater range of material equipment than is normally available from Neolithic sites and has shown that the Cortaillod people made an extensive use of wood and bark for containers and other things, as well as making baskets, nets and a great variety of linen textiles. Yet the Alpine countryside set limits to agriculture, and the proportion of wild animal bones shows that hunting contributed in a significant way to the supply of food; moreover, stag antler played a conspicuous role as a raw material for making a wide range of objects, such as mattock-heads, holders for adze- and axe-heads, harpoon-heads and personal ornaments.

THE WEST BALTIC AREA

Meanwhile a distinctive culture, characterized by beakers with flaring, funnel-shaped necks, was beginning to develop on the North European Plain beyond the frontiers of the Lengyel and Rössen groups of the Danubian II tradition. In spite of many differences of detail between its various sub-groups, the Northern culture was marked by features common to its whole extent from Mecklenburg to the Vistula and from central Prussia to Denmark and South Sweden. Its distinctive character rules out the possibility that its appearance can have been due solely to the expansion of any of the Neolithic cultures previously established in territories further south; and yet, at the same time, the appearance of basic Neolithic traits, notably stock-raising, cereal-growing and the making of pottery containers, can only be attributed to impulses from the south. On geographical grounds the most likely source is the Danubian province, and indeed pottery of Danubian II–III character has commonly been found in the same graves as Northern forms in Silesia and Poland.

Quite plainly the northward spread of Neolithic civilization was accomplished by means of acculturation rather than of colonization. The North European Plain supported in the Maglemosian culture and its successors the most vigorous Mesolithic settlement in Europe. The hunter-fisher populations of the region were correspondingly selective in their borrowings: thus, the coast-dwelling Ertebölle people, while adopting the arts of domestication, continued to rely substantially on hunting, fishing and the gathering of shellfish, and, in taking over the art of potting, applied to the manufacture of their larger, coarse vessels the technique of coiling used in basketry; similarly, the stone shoe-last adze failed to penetrate in face of flint forms evolved over millennia in a territory lavishly provided with the essential raw-material, though flint celts were now for the first time in this region finished by polishing. The vigor of the indigenous "Mesolithic" heritage is shown in other ways, for example in the lavish use of amber, but the adoption of rectangular houses as far north as the Vrå culture of middle Sweden shows the force of the intrusive impulses. In burying their dead in single graves, the Funnel-neck Beaker people conformed to the general Danubian practice, but in constructing stone monuments they were making the most of their own habitat and giving expression to their own genius. Definition of individual graves by means of the glacial boulders so widely distributed on the North European Plain was practiced by the Danubian groups north of the Sudeten mountains as well as by the Funnel-neck Beaker people, but the use of thin stone slabs or large blocks of megalithic proportions to form closed cists was peculiar to the northerners. Still more was this the case with the mounds erected over the graves and frequently themselves defined by boulders: in Denmark these mounds might be circular, but over the

North European Plain in general they were built like the houses of the living on the elongated plan, which in the west was generally rectangular, but in the east, again corresponding with the local house-plan, was characteristically wedge-shaped.

The primary Neolithic culture of southern and more particularly of south-western Britain drew some elements from French sources, but it is becoming increasingly evident that much of its inspiration came from the North European Plain to the east, a conclusion which in view of the common Maglemosian heritage should hardly occasion surprise. The earthen long barrows, occasionally parallel-sided, but more often wedge-shaped in plan, have been notoriously difficult to parallel in France, but find analogues as far east as the Kujavian graves of Poland, even though, apart from the Medway group, their structural elements are of timber and turf rather than stone. The causewayed camps, for which again no adequate parallel has been adduced from France, have been wrongly compared with the fortified sites of Urmitz and Mayen in the Middle Rhineland; a more significant, if rather loose, analogy lies with enclosures formed by radial settings of houses noted at Kolomiishchina and other Tripolje sites in South Russia. Again the flint-mines for which parallels admittedly exist in North France and the Low Countries, can be matched by the examples with vertical shafts and radiating galleries at Krzemionkach Opatowskich and other sites in Poland.

On its western margins the Northern culture came into contact with the Western province both in the Middle Rhenish and Alpine zones. From these contacts arose the Michelsburg and Pfyn cultures respectively, the former named after a hill-fort overlooking the Rhine plain a few miles north of Karlsruhe and the latter designated by the locality to which it is confined in the eastern part of Switzerland. The Michelsberg culture, typified by the tulip beaker and a series of ceramic forms, was centered on the Main, the Middle Rhine and the Neckar, whence it spread east into Bohemia, south into Alsace-Baden and north into the Koblenz area and Belgium.

COPPER-WORKING IN CENTRAL EUROPE

Meanwhile impulses emanating ultimately from the East Mediterranean had already begun to carry exotic burial rites, metallurgy and the use of metal tools over wide zones of Europe. Several central European groups of the Danubian III stage, notably the Bodrogkeresztur of northeast Hungary, the Jordansmühl of Bohemia and Silesia and the Baden of Austria and much of Czechoslovakia, fabricated copper artifacts, including perforated axe-adzes and a variety of ornaments. The sources of the copper ores used by these early smiths are still not fully known, but it is likely that the copper ores of the eastern Alps and of central Germany were already being worked, and certain that flat axes made from copper won in the latter region were being traded to the peasants of the Northern Neolithic culture before this had emerged from its early phase. The replacement of the flint axe with pointed butt and lozengé section by one polished all over and having a thin butt and flattened sides, which took place towards the end of the Northern Early Neolithic, was almost certainly inspired by the flat copper axe that was too costly for general use.

In Pakistan and China, and later in Japan, the first efforts at food production had similarly revolutionary consequences for man's way of life.

3. The Emergence of the Chinese Neolithic [1]

In China, prehistoric archeology is only just beginning. It may be said to have started in 1920 with the discovery of a neolithic site at Yang-shao-ts'un, in Miench'ih Hsien, Honan Province, by J. G. Andersson, and a paleolithic implement near Chao-chia-chai, in Ch'ing-yang Hsien, Kansu, by Pére Émile Licent. During the subsequent decade and a half, through the efforts of Chinese and Western scientists, information concerning the stone ages and the initial bronze age began to accumulate at a moderate rate, until 1937, when the outbreak of the Sino-Japanese War put a stop to the scientific field researches in China. Systematic archeological field work in this part of the world was not resumed until 1949, when Communist archeologists began to unearth materials with bewildering rapidity. Thus, what scientific information we have on the formative stage of Chinese civilization was gathered during a mere twenty-seven years (1920–37, 1949–59). The brevity of this period of work, the shifting personal, national, and ideological biases of the Chinese, Western, and Communist workers during its various stages, and the complete absence (with a handful of exceptions) of collaboration with natural scientists, all help to explain the tentativeness of the interpretation of the formation of the Chinese civilization that is to follow.

It is apparent that a complete areal coverage of China, as large in area as the whole of Europe or most of either of the Americas, with ecological zones no less

varying, is next to impossible to achieve in a short essay. We shall therefore focus our attention here upon the area where Chinese cultural tradition emerged and developed, the area of the middle and lower Huangho (or the Yellow River). The northern peripheries of the area in Mongolia and Manchuria and, to the south, the part of the Huaiho, the Yangtze, and the Pearl River valleys into which the Chinese civilization and its formative phases radiated will also be briefly treated.

The temporal coverage of our subject matter is, on the other hand, not difficult to define. Since our interest, in this symposium, lies mainly in the process and mechanism of cultural and social development, suffice it here to delineate our time range, simply on the basis of developmental concepts, as stretching from the terminal stage of the paleolithic food-gathering cultures to the emergence of urban life in China. This time span, furthermore, can be pinned down in absolute dates. In spite of the fact that in China none of the modern techniques of dating have so far been utilized, we can date the termination of our developmental sequence in the nuclear area of Chinese culture to the middle part of the second millennium B.C., when historic records began with the emergence of urban life, and place its commencement at the late glacial period, which probably is synchronous with the Würm glacial in Europe in geological terms.

[1] KWANG-CHIH CHANG, "China," in *Courses Toward Urban Life*, Robert J. Braidwood and Gordon R. Willey (eds.) (New York: 1962), pp. 177–191. Reprinted by permission of the author and the publisher, © 1962 by the Wenner-Gren Foundation for Anthropological Research.

Dr. Chang is an Instructor in Anthropology at Yale University.

THE TERMINAL FOOD-GATHERERS

After the stage of Choukoutien sedimentation, on the eroded surface of the reddish clay (*terra rossa*) in north China, a variety of zonal loessic facies accumulated during the climatic interval that has been correlated with the fourth Glaciation of the Himalayas and the Würm glacial in Europe. The climate over north China during the loessic stage was cool and dry—continental—with a prevailing wind from the northwest, though neither cooling nor desiccation is regarded as having then reached a higher peak than now exists in northeastern Asia. The various regional facies of the loess in north China have been grouped by Pére Teilhard de Chardin into two distinct subcycles: A, the true Malan loess with slope deposits dominant; and B, the Mongolian-Manchurian Sands with lake or *nor* deposits dominant.

The human industry of subcycle A is represented by the paleolithic assemblage at the site of *Shui-tung-kou* in northwest Ordos in the province of Ninghsia, and that of subcycle B by the finds at *Sjara-osso-gol* in the southernmost part of Suiyuan. According to Movius, "the geological and palaeontological evidence shows that broadly speaking the two sites are contemporary, although Shui-tung-kou may be slightly older than Sjara-osso-gol." Both assemblages are characterized by a blade-and-flake tradition and were presumably hunting cultures, as judged from the associated fauna (wild ass, rhinoceros, bison, ostrich, elephants, antelope, horse) and the presence of projectile points. But unlike Shui-tung-kou, which is a blade industry par excellence (blade cores, blades, burins, end scrapers) with a high percentage of "Mousterian" flakes (perforators, points, side scrapers), the Sjara-osso-gol assemblage is, above all, characterized by the predominance of a microblade tradition,

which, together with the abundance of bone and antler implements and the apparent increase of the microfauna (insect-eaters, rodents, birds), seems to indicate that, on the one hand, in addition to the hunting of big game the small-game collecting pattern also played an important role and, on the other, the importance of the composite tools apparently increased.

Subsequent to the loessic facies in north China began the recent period, which started with a land movement (and *Panchiao* erosion) and a climatic amelioration that intensified the lacustrine-riverine facies of the loessic stage and extended it to all north China. In other words, the post-Pleistocene started off there with the extinction of the Pleistocene fauna, a rise in temperature and precipitation, an increase of vegetation cover, and a gradual continental uplift and stage of general erosion. This was a moist and warm period, well covered by forests in the loessic highlands in western north China and Manchuria ("the Black Earth stratum") and by *nors,* swamps, marshes, and lakes in the eastern alluvial plains. The woods were inhabited by a variety of animals (including many southern and warm-climate species), but deer were the predominant inhabitants.

If the beginning of the Recent period intensified the lacustrine-riverine facies of the loessic landscape and witnessed its distribution all over north China, it did the same thing with the culture of this interval—the mesolithic stage of north China in general witnessed a general spread and upsurge of the microblade tradition and of composite tool manufacture. But the stage did not spread all over north China. Remains of the early post-Pleistocene hunter-fishers are found only in Mongolia (along the oases where they primarily fished) and in Manchuria and the eastern fringes of the western north China highlands (in the woods and by the water where they hunted and fished; e.g., the Upper Cave of Chou-koutien and the Sha-yüan assemblages in central Shensi and northern Shansi). Such remains are not noted in the eastern plains, which may possibly have been too wet to be habitable at that time. The environment chosen by the post-Pleistocene hunter-fishers was a favorable one, and their culture was fairly intensified, specialized, and elaborated. Aside from these broad generalizations, we are ill-informed concerning these terminal food-gatherers as regards the other aspects of their life.

EMERGENCE OF FOOD PRODUCTION IN THE HUANGHO BASIN

We have little evidence on which to base a conclusion about the earliest dates of food production in China. Speculation is rife in the matter, but the paucity of reliable data forces us to refrain from commenting on the origin of food production in this part of the Old World in any positive manner. We do not even know whether it was spontaneously invented or introduced from the outside as the result of stimulus diffusion. The available archeological record, furthermore, is regrettably lacking in evidence on the transitional stage from food-gathering to food-producing, and as yet we are substantially ignorant of the when, the where, and the how of this important event in China.

We can, however, legitimately make some well-grounded guesses. If the important event that Gordon Childe has termed the "neolithic revolution" took place in China at all, it probably did so in the region that I have tentatively called the "north China nuclear area," that is, the region around the confluences of the three great rivers, Huangho, Fenho, and Weishui, or the joining place of the three provinces Honan, Shansi, and Shensi. The north China nuclear area is in fact a small basin encircled on the north, west, and south by the Shansi plateau, the Shensi-Kansu loessic plateau, and the Tsinling Mountains, but open to the eastern plains. The speculative role of this region as a cradle for the food-producing cultures of north China has been based on a number of considerations. In the first place, as described above, during the "climatic optimum," the nuclear area was located on the border between the wooded western highlands and the swampy eastern lowlands, and thus it had both the "hilly flanks" and the habitat for the sedentary waterside fishermen that Robert Braidwood and Carl Sauer consider, respectively, as the birthplace of farmers and herders. It had, first, rain and warmth enough to be comfortably off and herds of game and fish shoals enough to sustain its inhabitants. It was also conveniently located at the intersection of natural avenues of communication. Second, it is in the nuclear area that the only Huangho basin mesolithic assemblage was found in the Sha-yüan (sand-dune) region in Chao-i and Ta-li Counties in eastern Shensi of the lower Wei-shui valley. Third, the only stratigraphically suggested pre-Yangshao neolithic evidence was found in Pao-chi Hsien in the middle Wei-shui valley, peripheral to the nuclear area. In the fourth place, the importance of fishing, as shown during the subsequent Yangshao stage in this area, is highly suggestive. In the fifth place, archeological evidence is ample to demonstrate that the nuclear area played a leading role in the transition from the Yangshao to the Lungshan. Finally, during most of the four thousand years of historic China, the nuclear area had always been one of the strategically vital regions that have controlled the destiny of the entire Empire to a considerable extent.

It is thus conceivable that at a few millennia B.C. the terminal food-gatherers in the nuclear area, having possibly already settled down and having a well-developed culture, switched to food production by inventing or adopting plant cultivation and animal domestication. Although in the subsequent neolithic stages there were still a handful of items of a mesolithic woodland heritage (e.g., pressure-flaked projectile points and arrowheads, chipped-stone discs, microblades, prismatic arrowheads, semisubterranean dwellings, and semilunar and rectangular stone knives), and the possibility cannot yet be entirely ruled out that the first idea of food production was introduced rather than invented, yet—from what we know of it—Chinese neolithic culture assumed a distinctive pattern from the very beginning that shows independence and originality. The following traits, considered either singly or totally, have been enumerated as being characteristic of the Chinese neolithic culture tradition.

1. The cultivation of millet, rice, and kaoliang (and possibly the soybean)

2. The domestication of pig, cattle, sheep, dog, chicken, and possibly horse

3. The *hang-t'u* (stamped earth) structures and the lime-plastered house floors

4. The domestication of silkworms and the loom (?)-weaving of silk and hemp

5. Possible use of tailored garments

6. Pottery with cord-mat-basket designs

7. Pottery tripods (especially *ting* and *li*) and pottery steamers (*tseng* and *yen*) and the possible use of chopsticks

8. Semilunar and rectangular stone knives

9. The great development of ceremonial vessels

10. The elaborate complex of jade artifacts; a possible wood-carving complex

11. Scapulimancy

In addition to these, the Chinese language presumably had a neolithic basis. Such a cultural tradition was not accumulated overnight, but of its initial stages there is as yet scarcely any evidence in the archeological record. That the earliest ceramic phases in north China were probably characterized by the cord-mat-basket-marked wares has been speculated upon, on the ground of geographic distribution, and is meagerly substantiated by some stratigraphical evidence. But of the general cultural configuration of the earliest ceramic phases we know next to nothing. An era of incipient cultivation has been assumed on the ground of necessity; whether this era can be equated with the Shengwen horizon is a big question.

From this point on we are on surer ground. From a small part of north China, the part with the nuclear area as a center and including northern and western Honan, southern and central Shansi, southwestern Hopei, central Shensi, and eastern Kansu, still largely confined within the drainages of the middle Huangho, Fenho, and Wei-shui, there have been found hundreds of prehistoric sites that are grouped together by their similar stratigraphic position and by the presence of a number of common distinctive horizon markers—painted pottery, some pottery forms (pointed-bottomed jars, flat- and round-based cups and bowls, thin-necked and big-belly jars, and possibly *li*-tripods), and some characteristic stone forms (rectangular knives and round axes, mostly symmetrically edged). In terms of cultural style this was the Yangshao horizon—which as a horizon had a solid functional basis, as will be presently seen—and in terms of ecosocial development this was the stage of the establishment of the farming villages and effective food production.

Archeological remains of the Yangshao horizon indicate the appearance of moderate-sized (200–300 meters to a side) nucleated villages. Approximately a dozen round or rectangular semisubterranean dwellings, or sometimes a few long, partitioned communal houses, comprised the village, which, according to the community patterning, might have sheltered one or several lineages or clans. The inhabitants engaged in farming, cultivating millet (*Setaria* and *Panicum*), kaoliang (*Andropogon*), and rice (*Oryza*), and in animal husbandry (dog, pig, and possibly sheep-goat and cattle). The cultivating implements included the hoe, spade, digging stick, and weeding knife. According to the shifting and repetitive pattern of settlement—indicated by the multiple components of the sites and the brevity of occupation of each component—it seems reasonable to assume that these early farmers engaged in slash-and-burn cultivation. Stone axes with a round or lentoid cross section and a symmetrical edge were manufactured, presumably for clearing fields in the woods. Stone implements were chipped, pecked, or ground, and pottery of a variety of paste was manufactured, by hand (often coiled) or with the aid of a mold. Most of the ceramic wares were of a domestic nature, cooking pots, water jars, storage jars, and bowls and cups; some of them (especially the cooking pots) were impressed with cord-mat-basket patterns, and others were beautifully painted in monochromic or bichromic decorations. Hunting and fishing took place, sometimes on a considerable scale, but these activities remained of a supplementary nature. The bow and arrow, harpoons, spears, and fishhooks were among the principal implements. Silkworms were raised, and hemp was possibly cultivated; the fabrics were spun (spindle-whorls), woven (loom?), and sewed (eyed needles).

Each village of Yangshao farmers was apparently a self-contained "little community," consisting of a dwelling area, an incorporated or separate quarter with kilns, and a village cemetery. Considering that the decorative art was focused upon domestic activities, that the evidence of a religious nature points to a fecundity cult and a fertility ritual that was presumably performed on behalf of the whole community rather than for a selected portion of the inhabitants, and that the community pattern shows no symbolic orientation of outstandingly privileged personnel, one tends to conclude that the internal status-and-role differentiation of the village inhabitants was not significantly developed; presumably, such distinctions as existed were based on age, sex, and personal achievement. The tenor of life seems to have been peaceful in the main, since evidence of both defensive measures and offensive weapons is scanty.

Presumably during this stage the Yangshao farmers were only beginning to become established, and the process of their expansion, within the limited region of the nuclear area and its peripheral surroundings, was largely confined to the gradual reclamation of immediately accessible and cultivable land by the descendant villages, which had split from their relatively overpopulated parent villages. Evidence from the Pan-shan hills in eastern Kansu and from a group of settlements in Hua Hsien in eastern Shensi shows that several neighboring villages shared a common cemetery, and this can best be interpreted in terms of the split-village situation rather than in terms of the formation of alliances of many discrete villages. The argument for this kind of expansion is also supported by the uniformity of style over the entire area of distribution of the Yangshao horizon. Though there were minor regional variations and two possible micro-horizons (Honan and Kansu), the stage shows striking stylistic uniformity over a wide area, as compared with the stage that was to follow.

EXPANSION OF THE
HUANGHO FARMING
VILLAGES AND THE
FORMATION OF
REGIONAL TRADITIONS

Since the transition from food-gathering to food-producing is not documented in the archeological record of north China, the consequences of the emergence of food production in the Huangho basin are not directly observable in the brief account we have presented so far; but from what followed, one is able to extrapolate and examine certain highly probable consequences.

The rate of growth of productivity brought about by the introduction of agriculture and animal husbandry can hardly be exaggerated. Two immediate consequences were the growth of population density and the potentiality for the elaboration of culture owing to the reserve energy released by surplus. Further consequences consisted of the fixity of settlements, the internal status-and-role specialization of communities, the frequency of warfare, the general spread of farming villages into the hitherto unexplored and underexplored areas, and the formation of a number of regional traditions that were synchronized in a widespread Lungshanoid horizon. Let us examine each of these phenomena in turn.

The Lungshanoid settlements were spread over most of China proper, but they can be grouped together on the basis of stratigraphy and a horizon style that was distinctive of this stage. These horizon-markers include the following:

1. A great variety of pottery forms, particularly tripods (*li, ting, chia, kui*) and ring-footed vessels (*tsun, p'o,* and *tou* or fruit-stand). These forms characterize not only the Lungshanoid of north China but also areas far beyond it, and they may, together with scapulimancy, reflect the complexity of rituals in this stage.

2. A distinctive ceramic style. One of the most striking features of the pottery of this horizon is the sharpness of the curves on every part of the body, in great contrast to the "roundness" of the pottery shapes of the Yangshao horizon.

3. The perforated-ring feet of fruitstands and other forms of vessels.

4. The decline of the art of ceramic painting, the increase of incisions and combed marks and the appearance of checker impressions.

5. Certain edged tools of stone, which are often square or rectangular in cross section and which have assymmetrical edges.

The ecosocial basis of these stylistic expressions is not hard to find. The Lungshanoid settlements were considerably larger than the Yangshao ones in areal dimensions and were often of longer duration. The repetitive settlement occupation pattern had given way to settled, permanent villages, as indicated by the conditions of continuous deposition, the permanent earthen village walls, the predominance of adzes and chisels (woodworking complex) over axes (for forest-clearance primarily), and the general configuration of the settlement culture, among other things. Besides noting some basis in ecology (the wet and fertile land provided by the eastern low countries into which the farmers had expanded), we are still uncertain as to the basic factors that brought about the tendency toward permanent settlement in north China as a whole. Irrigation, the use of fertilizer, the fallowing of fields, and the improvement of cultivating implements and techniques are all possible innovations of this stage, but we have no substantial evidence of any one of them. Metals might have been used to a small extent (a few metal objects have been found from a Lungshan-stage site in Kansu and from one in Hopei, and the sharp curves of pottery are suggestive of a metallic fashion), but it seems extremely unlikely that metal was used for making agricultural implements at this time. In fact, metal does not seem to have been widely employed for this purpose in ancient China until iron came into use in the middle first millennium B.C. From the little we do know about status-and-role differentiation and the presence of public works (the village wall), it is not

altogether unreasonable to assume that
the fixity of settlements during this stage
resulted, to a certain extent, from a kind
of organized management of manpower
that could have achieved a greater efficiency than heretofore. But there is a
good deal of speculation in this statement.

In the Huaiho valley, remains of rice
and wheat grains were found in a Lungshanoid context, but it seems proper to
assume that millet remained a leading
staple in the north. Hoes, spades, dig-
ging-sticks, and sickles are the principal
farming tools that are known archeologically; and stone, clay, bone and antler,
shell and presumably wood constituted
the raw materials of artifact manufacture. Livestock varieties remained unchanged, but cattle and sheep-goats may
have gained in importance, and the horse
may have been added at this time. Hunting and fishing were locally important.
In a word, the basic technology does not
seem to have undergone any considerable
improvement during this stage, and the
growing productivity can be accounted
for only in terms of social organization
and management. The significant novelty
of this stage seems to lie in its increasing
population density and the growth of
internal specialization and differentiation
among the populace.

The internal specialization and differentiation of the villages are shown by a
number of indications. In several of the
Lungshan traditions the potter's wheel
was now in use. This, plus the fact that
some of the black pottery was extremely
finely and delicately manufactured,
points to the fact that by this time pottery-making was already a full-time job.
Metallurgy, as was suggested above, may
have begun in this stage; what metallurgy implies in terms of craft specialization is common knowledge.

There is also some evidence of a differentiation of personnel in other terms at
this stage. At the Liang-ch'eng-chen site

in Jih-chao on the coastal Shantung, there
was one spot where finely made jade
objects were concentrated. Also at this
settlement and at a site at Ta-ch'eng-shan
near T'ang-shan in Hopei, the burials
were both face up and prone, a sure indication of status differentiation, according to the Yin-Shang mode of interment.
Furthermore, during this stage the art of
scapulimancy appeared, seen all over
north and central China in Hopei, Shantung, Honan, Shansi, Shensi, Kansu,
Anhwei, and Kiangsu, which was presumably handled by a specialized class
of shamans or priests. In this regard, the
prevalence and variety of ceremonial
vessels is highly suggestive. Taken together, such indications support the
conclusion that in the Lungshanoid settlements there were specialized craftsmen,
full-time administrators, and priest-sha-
mans, and that there were also a theocratic art and a theocratically vested
ceremonial pattern, which, no longer the
common property of the entire village,
was focused upon a selected portion of
the villagers. From what we know of the
later (Yin-Shang) practices, the basis of
selection might have been founded on
kinship.

Each of the Lungshanoid villages,
however, seems to remain self-contained
in the basic ecosocial and religious affairs,
as indicated by the completeness of the
functional network of the settlement culture. Relationships among settlements
might have been more frequent than
previously, but not infrequently the relationship was rather hostile and took the
form of warfare. The earth walls of the
Lungshanoid settlements at Hou-kang in
northern Honan and at Ch'eng-tzu-yai in
central Shantung appear too high and too
thick to have served as decorations or
boundary markers in time of peace.
Arrowheads, daggers, spears, halberds,
and clubs were among the offensive weapons. Skeletons were found at a site near
Han-tan, Hopei, that show evidence of

violent death, some having even been beheaded or scalped. This is hardly unexpected, for as population grew, taxing the land's capacity, people either reclaimed more land or fought for the field that was already available.

The transition from the Yangshao stage to the Lungshan stage seems to have started somewhere in the nuclear area. There are some two dozen sites now where the Lungshan-over-Yangshao-with-a-break-in-between stratigraphy has been observed, sites distributed all over the middle Huangho valley, from Kansu to northern Honan. On the other hand, in the nuclear area, in western Honan, southern Shansi, and eastern central Shensi, there are a number of sites of the transitional stage that show a mixture of the markers of both horizons, although the Yangshao markers predominate in quantity in the lower portions of the deposit, as the Lungshanoid ones do in the upper. The famed site at Yang-shao-ts'un itself, for instance, belongs to this transitional category, though for the sake of convenience the name Yangshao has been temporarily maintained for the horizon stage that preceded the Lungshan. Moreover, it is in the nuclear area that an early form of the Lungshan-stage horizon has been found that seems to be the prototype from which the other peripheral Lungshanoid traditions radiated.

Following the lead of the nuclear area, the Lungshan settlers gradually developed upon the basis of the Yangshao shifting-farmer level into the entire area on the western highlands of north China. Population pressure, among other factors, might have been responsible for causing the north China farmers to spread into the formerly unexplored or underexplored riverine, lacustrine, wooded and hilly regions in the east, north, and south. The distribution of Yangshao sites indicates that the eastern plains, the Huaiho valley, and the Shantung uplands were not at this time significantly occupied by the farmers, if at all, possibly owing to the swampy environment. The Lungshan settlers, however, began to penetrate into this area and build earth mounds on which village sites were located. To the north, agricultural settlements began to appear in the southern fringes of the Jehol mountains, the Liao-Sungari plains, and the southeastern Manchurian uplands. Remains of these settlements show a clear mixture of the Lungshanoid elements and the woodland and maritime mesolithic and subneolithic hunting-fishing inventories.

South of the Tsinling mountains and the Huaiho valley, insofar as we know at present, evidence of agriculture and animal husbandry begins with the widespread appearance of the Lungshanoid horizon. Prior to this horizon, the evidence indicates that only the southwestern portion of south China was inhabited by mesolithic food-collectors, whom some scholars have labeled the "Hoabinhian" because of the similarity of their cultural inventory to that of their Indochinese contemporaries. Subsequent to the nonceramic phase of this sheet of culture and prior to the appearance of the Lungshanoid farmers there was probably an intermediate ceramic stage, characterized by the appearance of cord-marked pottery and some polished-stone implements. These remains have been located in scatters in the southwest, on the coasts of Kwangtung, and on the island of Formosa. But evidence of both agriculture and its cultural affinities is still wanting. At any rate, the extensive exploration—at an early agricultural level—of the central and south China jungles, hills, and swampy valleys was the achievement of the Lungshanoid farmers spreading from the north. When these farmers had moved into a new ecological zone, they were forced to perform a series of important adaptive changes, which led to the predominance of rice and presumably fruit-and-root crops over millet, and the abandonment of stamped-earth structures and of lime-plastered floors. Mounds or pile-dwellings were built along the eastern coasts, and there is a generally pioneer aspect to their settlement and culture. These southern Lungshanoid farmers then began to settle down and, after receiving considerable stimulation (primarily in connection with metallurgy and decorative patterns) from the urban civilization subsequently developed in the north, a southern geometric horizon developed that was assimilated shortly before the time of Christ by the Ch'in and Han empires.

On account of the wide expanse of the area; the great environmental differences that the settlers encountered in moving into it; the hostility between settlements, with a resultant semi-isolation; and the different groups of hunter-fishers assimilated by the settlers in the new environment, the Lungshanoid horizon —although unified by its constituents' common heritage, by their similar developmental situation, and by far-reaching trade—was divided into a number of regional stylistic traditions. The most easily distinguished of these are the Honan, the Shansi-Shensi, the Kansu, the Shantung, the southern Manchurian, the Huaiho, the Hanshui, and the southeastern coastal traditions. It was with one of these regional Lungshanoid traditions (Honan, Shensi-Shansi, or Hanshui, according to different advocates) as a base that the first Chinese civilization eventually came into being.

EMERGENCE OF
CIVILIZATION IN THE
HUANGHO BASIN

The Lungshan horizon of the formative stage of ancient Chinese culture in the alluvial plains of the lower and middle Huangho valley and in the Huaiho valley, in the provinces of Honan, western Shantung, southwestern Hopei, eastern Shensi, northern Anhwei, and northern Kiangsu, was followed by the first civilization in Chinese history that has been amply substantiated by archeology, the Yin-Shang Dynasty. The Yin-Shang civilization has all the essential ingredients that a civilization is supposed to contain—writing, a fully developed bronze metallurgy, palaces and temples, science and the calendar, chariots and squads of warriors, a political and religious hierarchy of a royal house, class differentiation, far-reaching trade, a centralized management and redistribution of agricultural produce and other scarce goods, and a great artistic tradition. There are two settlement groups of this period that are relatively well known archeologically, Anyang and Chengchow, both in northern Honan. Each was composed of a number of small farming and handicrafting communities, whose close ties are indicated by their clustering within eye-sight distances and their sharing of a common administrative and ceremonial center. This was Hsiao-t'un in the case of Anyang and an earth-walled town in the case of Chengchow.

The emergence of such a highly developed civilization in the Huangho basin appears to have been in itself relatively sudden and new, and most archeologists believe that there must have been a transitional period between the Lungshan and the Yin-Shang horizons. It must be stressed, however, that from the neolithic Lungshan to the bronze-age Yin-Shang there was a developmental continuation rather than a cultural break. Table 1 shows in a preliminary manner the neolithic heritage of the Yin-Shang bronze-age culture and its innovations.

From the mere enumeration given in the chart it becomes apparent that in the past the "suddenness" of the emergence of the Yin-Shang civilization has been unduly exaggerated. Even the new items in the right-hand column mostly indicate a process of intensification and a change

TABLE 1

Continuities	Discontinuities
A. Formation of village aggregates B. Raids and warfare C. Status differentiation and prone burials D. The elaborate ceremonial complex (more lineage-ancestral than community-agricultural) E. Cultivation of millet, rice, kaoliang, wheat, hemp F. Use of domesticated dog, pig, cattle, sheep, horse, chicken G. Stamped-earth structures H. Semisubterranean houses and lime-plastered floors I. Industrial specialization J. Scapulimancy K. Some pottery forms (especially ritual forms with ring-feet and lids) L. The Shengwen (corded ware) tradition M. Some decorative motifs N. Some stone implements and weapons O. Shell and bone craft P. Silk Q. The jade complex R. Language(?)	a. Mature urbanism and related institutions (especially the formation of differentiated groups) b. Class differentiation c. New government and economic patterns (conquest, tribute, redistribution) d. Wider trade, currency e. New war patterns (capture of slaves and use of the chariot) f. Chamber burials and human sacrifice g. Domestication of water buffalo; possible use of wooden plow h. Highly developed bronze metallurgy i. Writing j. Advanced stone carvings k. New pottery forms

in degree. It is apparent, however, that civilization in China started with the Yin-Shang and not, as is sometimes asserted, with the Lungshan stage and that these two are decisively different. First of all, the Yin-Shang witnessed the intensifications of all aspects of Chinese culture—more advanced technology, greater population density, more intensified status-and-role differentiation, greater centralization of government and economy, more frequent warfare, and more institutionalized communication in the form of writing and trade.

The developmental change of society culture during the Yin-Shang is, furthermore, most distinctively marked off by the formation of the differentiated settlement groups and the specialization of the various settlements in a settlement group in ecosocial functions. The Lungshan communities, as previously stated, were self-contained "little communities," in spite of their sometimes large size and some degree of internal specialization and differentiation. But the Yin-Shang settlements had become specialized externally in ecosocial functions. Each community no longer worked only for its own survival and wealth, but worked for other communities and was worked for by others as well. The new horizon was marked by the appearance of centers of administration, redistribution, and ceremony, which one may call towns or cities, where officials and priests managed rather than labored. There were also farming and handicrafting hamlets, the inhabitants of which engaged in organized labor co-ordinated under a central control. This phenomenon, the ecosocial interdependence among specialized communities, is to this author one of the most decisive criteria of urbanization, which in turn was brought about by a change of the total social-cultural structure. Insofar as one can see from the archeological record of this part of the world, no single factor alone makes a civilization appear.

COMMENT

The tentative nature of the foregoing synthesis is most readily admitted. Indeed, it will be astonishing if, within a decade, new information that is now accumulating does not force an amplification and amendment of our scheme —perhaps even its drastic alteration. At the present time the scheme given above is the most we can do, but this is an attempt that has to be made if a world-wide consideration of cultural alternatives is to be made. Alfred Whitehead once observed that China "forms the largest volume of civilisation which the world has seen." Any consideration of the nature of civilization's growth in general cannot afford to leave China out, and China must be dealt with in the theoretical terms that anthropologists all over the globe are at home with. These theoretical terms are not those of the traditional doctrine in Chinese archeology. It is the traditional viewpoint that in neolithic China (and, for some obscure reason, only in a late aspect of it) there were two (or possibly three) distinctive cultural strains. The Yangshao (or "Painted Pottery") and the Lungshan (or "Black Pottery") are the main suggested strains, the former in the west and the latter along the eastern coast. Yin-Shang civilization was derived—the traditional viewpoint holds—from a third strain, which came to China fully devel-

oped from some source not yet fully specified. It is only now that, equipped with a good deal more data, we can begin to consider some of the major premises afresh and adopt a holistic, configurational, and functional approach that a new and probably truer picture has emerged. The prehistoric cultures in China are no longer regarded as a conglomeration of indigenous and exotic traits each of which had a separate history of development. Rather, the structural covariations and efficient causes are being stressed in terms of social mechanism and cultural pattern.

In the same manner, the problems regarding the "origins" of cultural elements in ancient China, which were the focusing point of many archeologists and sinologues, have also received some basically fresh reappraisal. The origin and history of the development of various and sundry objects are highly interesting and instructive matters, no doubt; but it is becoming clear that the basic issues of cultural and social growth do not necessarily rely upon their solutions. It is this writer's profound conviction that ancient China owed much of her riches to loans from the outside, just as many outsiders owed their riches to loans from her. But, to the writer, the important issue lies primarily in the functional context of the development sequence itself, without an understanding of which one will never understand how and why China received outside help at a certain point of time and how and why she had such things to offer in return.

On the other side of the earth, in temporal, spatial, and historical isolation from the Old World, the same technological transformation occurred. The Neolithic Revolution took place somewhat later in the Americas, possibly about 2000 B.C., but under familiar circumstances.

4. The Rise of the Seed-Planters [1]

Men first entered the New World in the Upper Pleistocene (27,000 years ago), across Bering Strait, at the northwestern-most corner of Alaska. Today the Strait is covered by water; then it was probably still spanned by a land bridge. The great northern glaciers—which at one time extended as far south as Illinois—had begun to recede, but they still held in their grip enough of the world's water supply to lower the surface of the sea significantly below present levels. The first immigrants to America were hunters, in pursuit of food. Equipped with darts tipped with projectile points and spear-throwers to lend added strength to their throwing arm, they followed in the wake of wild mammoth, horse, and llama. We have seen that it did not take these hunters long to reach the tip of South America. Around 7000 B.C. they were feasting on wild horses in southern Chile.

The presence of these men is also attested in Middle America. Huge bone-beds, containing the remains of mammoth, llama, bison, and wild horses, have been discovered at Tequixquiac, just north of the valley of Mexico. Among the unquestionable human artifacts which have come to light in this animal graveyard are a chalcedony graver, a point carved from the tibia of a bison, and a vertebra of a species of extinct llama carved in the shape of a coyote. The carved vertebra comes from a geo-logic layer dated Terminal Pleistocene, probably around 11000 B.C. The same date was assigned to the remains of a human skeleton, excavated near the town of Tepexpan, close to the western outskirts of Mexico City. Unfortunately, the skeleton itself was not associated with the remains of prehistoric animals, though the layer in which it was found is heavily shot through with fossil bones of mammoth. Its dating therefore must remain problematical. But more recent finds have definitely established the presence of man in the valley of Mexico during the Late Pleistocene. In 1952 and 1954, human projectile points were found in association with mammoth remains at Santa Isabel Iztapan, close to Tepexpan. The points show distinct similarities to game-hunter projectile points encountered in North America.

The big-game hunters were not, however, the only settlers in Middle America. In the southwestern United States archeologists have discovered remains of people of quite a different cultural orientation. Instead of relying on large game, they hunted small game and obtained most of their food from wild plants and their seed. Still today, Indians in the arid Southwest use one or another tree-borne fruit that can be stored easily and for a long period of time: piñon, mesquite, or acorns. Archeologically, these people left behind their querns and mullers, the grinding platforms and the milling

[1] ERIC R. WOLF, "Rise of the Seed-Planters," in Sons of the Shaking Earth (Chicago: 1959). Reprinted by permission of the author and The University of Chicago Press, © 1959 by The University of Chicago Press.

Dr. Wolf is Professor of Anthropology at the University of Michigan.

stones, on which they ground their plant food into a palatable meal. These seed-gatherers appear to have lived between 15000 and 2500 B.C. For some eight thousand years they lived alongside the hunters of large game but essentially independent of them. Around 7500 B.C. environmental conditions began to favor their chances of survival, while lessening the survival opportunities of the big-game hunters. This date marks the onset of a great change in climate. Over a wide area extending from Utah to the southern highland of Middle America large tracts of grassland became waste desert; large game and plants requiring a lot of water gave way to small game and desert-adapted plants. The seed-gatherers survived, because their hardy basic staple survived. The big-game hunters disappeared, as their food supply declined and finally vanished.

Like all living organisms, the game hunters and their game depend, ultimately, on plants. To live and to survive, organisms require fuel—energy. The ultimate source of energy is the sun. To tap this energy, we must as yet rely on plants; plants are the only organisms capable of synthesizing significant amounts of organic material in the photosynthetic process. We can also eat animals and animal products, but animals in turn depend on plant food for their energy supply. Plant food is thus the strategic element in the chain of life, and man's chances for survival hang upon his success in obtaining that food. The big-game hunters lost the battle for survival; the seed-gatherers won it.

Seed-gathering proved more viable also in another way. Around 6000 B.C. some seed-gatherer somewhere began to interfere successfully in the planting, germination, and fruition of wild plants. Anthropologists have long recognized this technological achievement as a milestone in the evolution of human culture. V. Gordon Childe, the British archeolo-

gist, speaks of it as the first major revolution in man's existence. It is certainly a major step toward giving man greater control of his environment, toward making him its master rather than its slave. For a hunter and gatherer of wild food is a slave to his food supply: if his game or wild food crop is abundant, he may live the life of a savage Riley; if it decreases or vanishes, he may face extinction with it. In controlling the growth and maturation of plants and animals, man still makes use of natural processes. But he assumes some of the functions of nature himself, replacing the natural controls over plant maturation and growth with his own.

The origins of cultivation in Middle America, as in the entire New World, are still shrouded in mystery, though we are getting closer to an understanding of its beginnings. Many different disciplines contribute to this search. The archeologist digs for material objects which would indicate the presence or absence of cultivation and looks for plant remains which are now—thanks to the C-14 method—datable. The linguist attempts to trace the presence or the absence of terms denoting cultivation and cultivated plants in the reconstructed vocabularies of extinct and reconstructed languages. Similarities and differences in the names of plants from one language to another may also tell him how the plants diffused from one linguistic group to another. The botanist attempts to define the ancestors and the relatives of the present cultivated varieties and to trace their distribution, as well as the distribution of the cultigens. Frequently, he will seek to define the area in which they achieved their greatest diversity, on the hypothesis that such diversity occurs where the plant has been cultivated for the longest period of time.

To date, the earliest evidence for plant domestication in the Middle American area does not come from Middle America proper but from its northern periphery, from New Mexico in the northwest and from Tamaulipas in the northeast. There is also a promise of more to come from the valley of Mexico, where in 1958 Helmut de Terra and Arturo Romano located a burial associated with grinding stones and mullers, traceable perhaps to an early seed-gathering population and dated tentatively at between 8000 and 6000 B.C. Such finds will close the gap which now exists between the disappearance of the big-game hunters around 11000 B.C. and appearance of the first full-fledged farmers around 1500 B.C. Until then, however, we are still largely reduced to guesswork on the basis of such meager information as we now possess.

Taking our departure from such uncertain bases, we would say that New World cultivation developed practically independently of agriculture in the Old World. Its techniques and its cultivated plants both differ sufficiently from those of the Old World to make this statement more than probable. Within the body of New World cultivation, we find essentially two divergent traditions. The first of these is found largely to the south of Middle America. It was based on vegetative reproduction, that is, reproduction through cuttings. The crops which belong to this tradition of cultivation yield mostly starches and sugar and are low in proteins and fats. The chief of these is a root crop, manioc (*Manihot utilissima*: Nahuatl, *quauhcámotl;* Maya, *tsin*) which has been cultivated so long that it has nearly lost its abiilty to set seed. The older maniocs are sweet and non-poisonous. They are distributed more widely than the bitter or poisonous variety grown in the Caribbean and in Brazil but unknown in Middle America, in Colombia, and along the Pacific drainage of South America. Another such crop is the sweet potato (*Ipomoea batatas*: Nahuatl, *camotli;* Maya, *iz;* Spanish, *batata*). For some time scientists thought that this food complex once dominated also the Gulf coast in Middle America, largely because querns and griddles, characteristically associated with maize-processing, are absent from early archeological deposits in the coastal area. But this is based on a misconception. Maize can be eaten without grinding, and griddles are used to prepare dishes other than maize. All evidence goes to show that even on the Gulf coast vegetative reproduction always remained of secondary importance.

Middle American cultivation belongs basically to the other major tradition of New World cultivation, to the tradition based on seed-planting. This complex does not involve setting out cuttings: each year seed is harvested, stored, selected for desirable qualities, and resown. It is notable that seed-planting remained dominant even on the coastal lowlands where the tuber complex might have achieved greater importance. Nor was Middle America lacking in wild plants which could be reproduced through cuttings; such plants (like *camotes del cerro*) are still collected wild and sold in the market place, but they are not cultivated. The seed-planting tradition probably had an origin wholly different from the tradition based on vegetative cuttings. Its inventors were probably the same hardy seed-gatherers who outlived and outlasted the more dramatic big-game hunters after the great climatic change of 7500 B.C.

Several factors may have predisposed them to such an invention. They used seeds, and after the climate grew increasingly arid they probably began to concentrate their existence around certain well-watered and favored spots where wild seed crops appeared with regularity, even when other areas failed. This semi-sedentary existence attracted plants in turn. Many of the plants used later in cultivation were once common weeds which —attracted by human refuse—grew up around habitation sites. Weeds and men were bound together by mutual advantages: human beings provided the disturbed soils in which these plants could grow; the plants provided seeds which men required for their diet. We know that plants throw up new varieties all the time. Many of them die out, often because they cannot find room in the environment, some unoccupied niche where they might take root and flourish. Human habitation sites, however, represent a radical change in the environment, new niches with new opportunities for plant adaptation and growth. Similarly, men burned over the land to speed the taking of game, and burned-over ground furnished a similar ecological haven.

Nor are men the only agents in plant growth and dispersal. Rivers often change their courses, eat into mountainsides, and deposit the acquired sediment, thus furnishing environmental opportunities for plants seeking a new home. Once such plants develop, men can contribute to their propagation by aiding their geographic spread. Old varieties get an opportunity to meet new variants with which they can exchange hereditary characteristics. Thus new offspring are born, possessed of the great vigor which usually comes with hybridization. This process continues even today, when cultivated plants are often hybridized with weeds to produce new and hardier offspring.

Some of the earliest weeds selected for increased attention and cultivation may have been plants like amaranth and chenopodium, which are improved relatives of the common pigweed of farm and field. Amaranth (*Amaranthus lescarpus* and *A. cruentus:* Nahuatl, *huauhtli;* Maya, *xtez;* Spanish, *bledo*) seems to have been especially important, up to the time of the Spanish Conquest. The annual food tribute of the Mexica state consisted of 200,000 bushels of amaranth, compared with 280,000 bushels of maize and 230,000 bushels of beans. In pollen profiles from the valley of Mexico, corresponding in time to the beginnings of cultivation, a marked rise in amaranth pollen precedes the rise in maize pollen. The Spaniards forbade its cultivation, because it was heavily associated with ritual practices; this association would again suggest a certain antiquity. Needless to say, they did not succeed in stamping it out. It is still grown as a minor adjunct to peasant diet throughout Middle America. Similarly, chenopodium (*Chenopodium Nuttalliae* Safford: Nahuatl, *cuauhzontli, epazote;* Maya, *lucum xíu*) is still cultivated, eaten, or used in folk medicine. It is closely related to the Andean quinoa and may even be the same plant. In the Andes, quinoa is characteristically a high-altitude plant which takes the place of maize in the higher mountains and is either ground into a meal or fermented into beer (*chicha*).

By 1400 B.C. cultivation was no longer peripheral to Middle America but an integral aspect of its existence. Looking at the scattered relics of these full-fledged cultivators, we are conscious of the big gap which separates them from their pioneering ancestors. They were fully sedentary; they lived in villages; fragments of burned clay, bearing the imprint of sticks or poles, tell us that their houses were made of wattle, daubed with clay or mud and probably thatched with reeds or straw, in the manner of Indian huts or *jacales* (Nahuatl, *xacalli*) to this day. By this time, they possessed maize and squash, and a little later they added the bean, thus completing the trinitarian basis of the Middle American diet. Their equipment for processing maize was the same as that of any modern Indian household: the stone quern or *metate* (Nahuatl, *metlatl*) on which maize was ground to a meal, the stone muller or *mano* (Nahuatl, *metlapil,* or "son of the metate"), the circular clay griddle or *comal* (Nahuatl, *comalli*) on which maize cakes were baked over the fire. In the highlands of Guatemala they stored their crops in rectangular and bottle-shaped pits, which they filled afterward with trash and often used to bury their dead. Deer bones and bird bones are numerous, tell-tale remnants of food obtained with dart points made of obsidian and carved with stone and bone scrapers. Where people lived near lakes, as in the valley of Mexico, or along rivers, as in northern Veracruz, fish provided a vital source of protein.

The main tools employed in cultivation were the stone ax and probably the wooden digging stick, its point treated in the fire. The wooden digging stick or *coa* is still in use today. Most people probably still made their other tools as they needed them, but a concentrated group of obsidian workshops with large refuse pits from highland Guatemala shows that specialization had set in at least in this one important region. A simple kind of pottery was made and traded to adjacent localities. Cloth was woven; a fragment of cotton cloth mixed with apocynum fiber has been found in the valley of Mexico. The cotton (*Gossypium hirsutum* L.: Maya, *tamán;* Nahuatl, *izcatl*) must have come from the lowlands, since cotton will not grow in the altitude of Mexico City. Perhaps it came from Morelos or from northern Veracruz. Snails and shells were traded inland from the coastal country, from the Pacific shore first, later from the Atlantic. Salt was probably an important item of trade, vital to people who were beginning to rely increasingly on a plant-derived diet.

When people died, they were interred in scattered graves and given offerings to accompany them on their journey. These offerings do not vary greatly from grave to grave; they indicate a rough equality of wealth and power among the dead. At the same time, some men were buried with companions—either members of their family or perhaps servants whose involuntary death provided aid for their master in the world of the spirits. In such multiple burials, the male occupied the central position. Perhaps people were interred near their house, or even under the floors of their house, as was the custom in much of Middle America in later days. At any rate, the unity of the community was not yet symbolized by grouping the village dead into a common burial ground.

Plentiful everywhere (but in the lowland Maya area after about 500 B.C.) are small clay figurines which represent women, women with swelling thighs and heavy breasts, or women with narrow hips and braided hair of a type called "pretty lady" by the archeologist. Holding one of these little works of art in the palm of our hand—they are rarely longer than three or four inches—we can only wonder about their meaning. Are they portraits of individuals who once walked the earth? They are indeed strongly individualized, as if the artist had been trynig to capture in clay the features of some person he knew. Are they representative of some form of erotic art? Their nudity, together with the careful exaggeration of their generative organs and the secondary characteristics of their sex would lend support to this view. Yet, by and large, there is little erotic art among American Indians (Peruvian Mochica art of A.D. 600–900 is the striking exception), and what is erotic art to a modern beholder may simply be conventional stylization to the native artist. Do the figurines then embody some general concept of fertility, magically expressed in their emphasized organs of reproduction? Many archeologists incline to this view, but the individualized faces of the figurines speak rather against it. We should expect a generalized concept to find expression in more stereotyped form.

The same objection can be raised against the idea that the figurines depict a "corn mother," a female generative principle which makes the corn grow, as a "'rice mother" is thought to be responsible for the growth of rice throughout Southeast Asia. Are they perhaps representations of ancestors who bring fertility and happiness to the living, just as the kachina dolls of the Hopi and Zuñi Indians of our Southwest represent the collective rain-giving supernatural ancestors of the tribe? But the kachina cult is not attested before the thirteenth or fourteenth century among the southwestern Pueblos, and, anyway, why would all the ancestors depicted be females? Are we dealing with a culture in which descent through females provided the main organizing principle of social life? This is not impossible; women carry the burden of agriculture among many simple farmers and are the strategic sex in the production of food for such a society. Under such circumstances, property in houses, goods, and crops frequently passes in the female line. Yet the evidence of the figurines is contradicted here by the central position of the male in those burials which contain multiple occupants. In Guatemala, however, we also find figurines of monkeys, animals later associated with the deities of the dance and fertility.

We have no systematic knowledge of the ways in which these early farmers grew their crops, but the major system of cultivation was probably slash-and-burn farming, still practiced in many parts of Middle America today. Tourists traveling along the Pan-American Highway into northern Veracruz in the summertime can see fields cultivated in this manner without getting out of their cars. Under this system, fields are carved out of the forest by cutting back and burning off the vegetative cover. Occupation of a field is temporary. After the first two years, yields usually decrease sharply. The modern Totonac and the Yucatec Maya abandon their cultivated clearings after two years; the Huastec after two to

three years. The farmer will then cut and burn over another strip of forest or brush land to obtain a new clearing; and he will repeat this process every two years until his initial clearing has reverted to forest and regained its fertility. He may then return to the point of origin in his circuit. It is important to recognize that yields may be very high during the brief period of years that a field is under cultivation. In Tepoztlán, a modern Nahuatl-speaking village in Morelos, yields from slash-and-burn clearings run on an average twice as high as those obtained on land plowed year after year; among the modern Totonac yields run 100:1 per unit of seed put into the ground, and a farmer can obtain two crops a year.

One limiting factor in this kind of cultivation is, however, the availability of land. As long as the farmer has access to new land, he can maintain his yield; when his access to land is restricted, he may have to farm his old clearings before they regain their fertility, and his yields will suffer accordingly. It follows that a man needs a rather large area of land to produce at a constant rate of productivity year after year. Among the modern Totonac of the Gulf coast a family of five members needs thirty acres to feed itself on the basis of such field-forest rotation without declining yields; among the Maya of Yucatán a family of the same size may need as much as seventy-two acres. Lack of land may ultimately cause a population to abandon this system of cultivation; but as long as land is available, its advantages outweigh its disadvantages. We know from other areas of the world that people have even abandoned sedentary agriculture based on careful terracing if presented with new land frontiers. On the other hand, the disadvantages of the system may be heavily increased by any means that limits the amount of available land. A Dutch scholar has even worked out a mathematical formula expressing the amount of land which must be taken from a slash-and-burn population to force them to work on European-owned plantations.

The system is thus ultimately predicated on a very lavish use of natural resources, on a situation in which only a few men use a great deal of land. It thus contributes to low population densities: men must live apart if they are to feed themselves today and their increasing generations tomorrow. At the same time, the system is strongly centrifugal. It inhibits tendencies toward population concentration, as well as the reach and effectiveness of secular and sacred rulers. The inherent mobility of its component units would make it rather unlikely that a strong state based on tribute and labor drafts could arise under such circumstances. Just such an unlikely combination of circumstances has been alleged for the ancient Maya of the Theocratic period (900 B.C.–A.D. 750). There are only two logical possibilities under which a Mayalike system could arise with such a system of cultivation as we have been discussing here. One possibility is that Maya society, with its priestly centers, stabilized itself through the use of some other system of cultivation, yet unknown. The other possibility is that the Maya priestly center was the product of population increase and increased occupation of the land, that it served as the centralized control needed to allocate land and to regulate shifts in cultivation. Both possibilities are present, and we shall return to both later.

Another system of cultivation which may have originated early is the two-field system familiar to economic and social historians from accounts of medieval Europe. In this system, one field is planted in crops, while the other is left fallow one or two years until it regains its former fertility. This can be done only where climatic conditions do not completely destroy the mineral content of the soil after tillage. In Middle America this system has been described for the highland Totonac and for the Tarascan area. In all cases, it is associated with permanent residence of the cultivator in a house, with the use of a kitchen garden. Among the highland Totonac only 6.25 acres are needed to feed one family each year, and such a family needs only 16.25 acres to maintain productivity. This is in sharp contrast with the figures reported for the lowland Totonac, who carry on slash-and-burn farming. Under the two-field system associated with a permanent kitchen garden, then, many more people can live off the same amount of land than in slash-and-burn cultivation. Where a slash-and-burn community of 100 families of 5 members each needs 7,200 acres in northern Yucatán, only 1,625 acres are required to feed a similar community among the highland Totonac with the two-field system.

From the beginning of cultivation, Middle American farmers opened fields on the hillsides and the slopes of mountains in preference to cultivating the valley floors. In many areas, this preference was due to the mountainous nature of the terrain: there were simply not enough level lands to cultivate. Often, however, the valley soils look better than they are in reality. They may be covered with silt, sand, and gravel but recently washed down from the heights by mountain streams and torrential rains and insufficiently weathered to offer good nutriment for plants. Frequently such sterile deposits cover highly productive soils and render them unusable for agricultural purposes. Yet even good and easily available valley soils presented serious obstacles to primitive farmers: their pointed wooden digging sticks frequently could not destroy the web of grass roots in the soil. Not until the Spaniards introduced the plow did some of the plain areas become accessible to cultivation. The lighter soils of the hillsides did not represent such a barrier.

At the same time, hillside farming has a positive advantage: frost hazards are less severe along the lower slopes than they are along the floors of valley basins, a fact of which modern Indian cultivators are keenly aware.

Slash-and-burn clearing and hillside farming had, however, unrecognized side-effects which acted in turn to make food production less viable. As a cultivator, man controls his environment, and yet he may in the very process, all unknowingly, unleash environmental forces which threaten his survival. The ax and the torch of the cultivator cut back the forest but opened the way to invasion of the former forest floor by tough competitive grasses. Such an invasion by grass is a menace to the tropical cultivator. Forest floors after burning are soft and easily worked and fertile because of the soluble minerals contained in the ashes; but grass creates a tough network of rhizomes and roots which is very difficult to uproot without iron tools. Grassland, in turn, may reduce rainfall: it reflects the rays of the sun and evaporates moisture, while stands of forest bind water and reduce evaporation.

In the uplands of Middle America, cultivation also set free other forces which men are still fighting to contain. Mountains are precarious repositories of cultivable soils; gravity and the flow of water speed the soil on its way to lower altitudes. Soil is a temporary product, a stage in the process of dissolution that carries rocks and minerals to the sea. Plants feed upon this process of dissolution; it is essential to them. Yet if man is to survive, he must regulate its speed and intensity. When he cuts down the trees that stand guard over the deposits of soil in the mountains, he also undercuts his chances of survival. Today, deserted villages, barrens thickly sown with potsherds that bespeak the dense settlement of past eras, canals and terraces laid out many feet above present water levels, provide mute testimony to a process which began four thousand years ago or more. The modern Indian who lets the dry soil of his meager field run through his hand to test its moisture and organic content sees in his dry land the sign that the present world is approaching its appointed ruin. He, however, is but the heir of men who first ravaged the crust of the earth in the hope of increasing their chances of survival, their own and also that of their sons.

By 900 B.C., the Middle American diet had in all probability achieved the standardized form which it still possesses today. It rests essentially on the consumption of plant food, in contrast to the diets of Europe and North America, which combine the consumption of cereals with meat-eating and milk-drinking. Domesticated animals, however, played and still play a very minor role in the Middle American diet. In pre-Hispanic times, small dogs were raised and fattened for eating; together with the turkey (Nahuatl, *totolli;* Maya, *tso;* today called *guajolote* in Middle American Spanish after the Nahuatl *uexólotl,* "male turkey") they constituted the only inhabitants of the barnyard. The people of the lowlands, like the Maya and the Totonac of the Gulf, kept bees, and the Maya mixed fermented honey with the bark of the balche tree (*Lonchocarpus longistylus* Pittier) to make a fermented drink, but the highland people obtained part of their supply of sugar from the sweet juice of the century plant. There were none of the many burden-carrying food animals of the Old World which played such a vital role by lending mobility in transportation and warfare to masses of men. In Middle America burdens were always carried by men, and troops moved on foot, until the Spanish Conquest presented the Indians with the spectacle of armed centaurs whose nostrils breathed hot metal and fire.

If the Middle American diet indeed

began with the pigweeds, its mainstay became the staple combination of maize, beans, and squash, sometimes called the Trinity of the American Indian. The earliest evidence for cultivated maize (*Zea mays:* Nahuatl, *centli;* Maya, *ixim*) comes from Bat Cave in New Mexico, where layers dated as early as 4000 B.C. yielded a maize with cobs the size of strawberries which united the characteristics of both popcorn and podcorn. Similar kinds of maize have come to light in southeastern Tamaulipas, where they are dated at 3000 B.C. Yet it is clear that maize has existed in Middle America as a wild weed since Pleistocene times; pollen of wild maize has been found in the valley of Mexico to a depth of some 200 feet. Somewhere in Middle America—though we still do not know where—some group of seed-planters must have domesticated this weed. At some later time, probably in the southeastern highland of Guatemala and Chiapas, the domesticated maize plant hybridized with a weed called *teocentli,* itself a hybrid between maize and a weed called *Tripsacum.* From here it spread into South America, but it arrived late—after the system based on cuttings had a secure hold—and always remained a secondary food. Its earliest appearance in Peru is dated at 900–700 B.C.; its use as food was as corn on the cob—low in efficiency when compared to the Middle American manner of using it—or as the basis for maize beer (*chicha*).

The plant is possessed of an astonishing variability and is extraordinarily adaptable to different environments. It grows at altitudes ranging from sea level to 12,700 feet at Lake Titicaca in the high Andes; in regions with short summers and cool climates, as well as in deserts with an annual precipitation of less than 8 inches. In Middle America, maize kernels are toasted, ground into a meal, and eaten either dry or as a gruel (modern Mexican, *pinole;* Nahuatl, *pinolli;*

Maya, *ƙah*); or mixed and left to stand in a lime solution, later finely ground, patted into round cakes, and cooked rapidly on a griddle to make tortillas (Nahuatl, *tlaxcalli;* Maya, *uah*). The tortilla can be eaten as such, or wrapped around meat, beans, and chili to make tamales or tacos. Tortilla dough can be mixed with water to make *pozole* (Nahuatl, *pozolli;* Maya, *ƙeyem*) or cooked slightly with an added flavoring of some sort to make *atole* (Nahuatl, *atolli;* Maya, *za*). It is safe to say that at least 75 per cent of the daily energy intake of people in Middle America today is based on maize prepared in one of these several guises.

The second member of the Trinity of American seed plants is the bean, high in proteins and fat content, usually eaten boiled. Again, the center of distribution of most New World beans seems to be in Middle America, but the different species are adapted to quite different climatic conditions. Thus the common kidney bean (*Phaseolus vulgaris:* Nahuatl, *ayacotl;* Maya, *buul;* Spanish, *frijol*) which forms a mainstay of Mexican diet, is mainly an upland bean which does not prosper in lowlands or at very high altitudes. The tepary bean (*Phaseolus acutifolius,* var.) is a desert-adapted plant. The lima bean (*Phaseolus lunatus:* Maya, *ib;* Spanish, *frijol*) is a hot-country crop, usually found in tropics with a marked dry season, and only rarely encountered above 4,000 feet. The earliest Middle American evidence of the bean comes from southeastern Tamaulipas, dated at 2500 B.C. Yet while some of the earliest known farming communities in the valley of Mexico possessed maize, about 1350 B.C., they did not get beans until somewhat later. This would mean that at one time they lacked a most important source of protein to supplement the carbohydrates furnished by maize.

Ralph Linton argues persuasively that any group of people must control an adequate source of protein to maintain stable life. Hunters and gatherers can obtain proteins by hunting game or wild fowl, or by fishing. Cultivators, on the other hand, find it increasingly difficult to fill their protein quota if they do not also possess domesticated animals. Middle America, as all America before Columbus, possessed only a scant number of domesticated animals, when compared with the large inventory of such animals in the Old World. The bean may therefore have been an important strategic addition to the developing diet of the Middle American farmer.

The third major type of plant included in the American Trinity are the squashes and pumpkins (*Cucurbita:* Spanish, *calabaza;* Nahuatl, *ayotli;* Maya, *ḳum*) and the gourds (*Lagenaria siceraria:* Spanish, *calabaza;* Nahuatl, *tecomatl;* Maya, *bux, leḳ*). These are among the oldest agricultural remains found, both in southeastern Tamaulipas and in Peru in South America; in both places, they preceded beans and maize. They were undoubtedly first protected and then cultivated for their oily, protein-bearing seeds rather than for their flesh; the seeds still form an important part of the Middle American diet. Flowers and leaves are also eaten. The wild varieties have no flesh; human control, however, has produced a wide range of large starchy and sugary varieties.

An inevitable companion of the Middle American meal is the chili pepper (*Capsicum annum* L., and *C. frutescens* L.: Nahuatl, *chilli;* Maya, *ic;* Mexican Spanish, *chile*). It occurs in innumerable varieties; the areas of greatest diversification—Middle America and Brazil—may also be the areas where the species originated. Some varieties are eaten raw, some in sauces. They are a valuable source of vitamins and serve as an aid in the digestion of foodstuffs high in cellulose. Another necessary addition to such a diet is salt. Meat-eaters and milk-drinkers do not seem to need salt in the same amounts as plant-eaters, who seem to crave added quantities of sodium chloride. Salt deposits thus played a strategic role in Middle American historical development. The valley of Mexico was especially blessed in that salt could be obtained from its saline lakes by evaporation. Elsewhere it had to be transported overland or across the sea: the salt trade was an important factor in linking the Gulf coast of Mexico with Yucatán from early times.

So standardized is this diet and so invariable its adherence to maize, squash, beans, and chili that many observers have concluded that it must produce serious dietary deficiencies. Meat-eaters and milk-drinkers are, however, apt to pass uninformed judgments on the dietary norms of other cultures. Middle American Indians ate and still eat many foods in addition to the above, foods which may not suit the palates of people whose tastes derive from a tradition of animal husbandry coupled with grain agriculture. Laboratory analysis has discovered considerable quantities of protein, vitamins, and minerals in such Middle American foods as *axayacatl,* a highland moth, and its eggs (*ahuauhtli*), a very elegant caviar; in *malva,* a wild highland plant which tastes like spinach; in cactus (*nopal*); in sesame and squash seeds; in peanuts and piñon nuts; in the red-and-white worms that infest the century plant; in the iguana, the large lizard of the tropical lowlands that tastes like frogs' legs, and its roe; in turtles, snakes, triatomas (*chumil*), rats, and many other occasional additions to the daily diet. Furthermore, in the highlands, the Indians also drink considerable quantities of pulque (Nahuatl, *octli*), the fermented and unfiltered juice of the century plant (*Agave atrovirens:* Nahuatl, *metl*), which possesses an alcohol content of from 3 to 5 per cent. In many areas, the drink provides significant daily amounts of minerals and of vitamins C and B. Often confined in pre-Conquest times to nobles or old people and taboo to commoners or to the young and able-bodied, pulque is today drunk by everyone. Discoveries of scrapers used to increase the flow of juice from the heart of the century plant have been made at Teotihuacán; the use of pulque is thus at least as old as the Theocratic period and very probably much older.

In the second half of the second millennium B.C., then, we witness throughout Middle America the growth of a life centered upon villages maintained by farmers with simple tools, bent upon winning the basic crops of a standardized diet from the earth, and with an approach to the powers of the supernatural that seems to involve some projection of the female generative principle into the world of the sacred. Ties between communities are still tenuous; they are based on occasional commercial contacts, and the communities are not yet subordinate to an authority which has its seat outside their limits. These seed-planters are thus still primitive farmers, not yet peasants in the strict sense of the word, because a peasantry is no longer an isolated segment of society, sufficient unto itself; it is a functional part of a larger social whole, in which the society has become dichotomized into a center of power and control and a rural hinterland of dependent cultivators. Such a society comprises three levels of organization: the individual household; the community which embraces the individual households; and the emergent state which embraces the communities and dictates to them.

Until 900 B.C., however, there was no sign of this last phenomenon. The community was the autonomous unit of social life; and the growth of ties beyond its limits was still to come. And when we look at this unit in long-term perspective, we find that in Middle America it was never obliterated. The simple inventory of farm tools and kitchen equipment, the tasks of farming, the religious concepts geared to the cycle of planting and harvesting, the style of life centered upon the community of one's birth—these have remained basic and stable until today. Empires and conquests sweep over the land, cities arise, new gods announce salvation, but in the dusty streets of the little villages a humble kind of life persists, and rises again to the surface when the fury of conquest is stilled, when the cities crumble into ashes, and when the new gods are cast into oblivion. In the rhythm of Middle American development we recognize phases of great metabolic construction, followed by catabolic processes which gnaw at the foundations of temples and citadels until they collapse of their own weight or vanish in a fury of burning and destruction. Yet until today the community of cultivators has retained its capacity to turn in upon itself and to maintain its integrity in the face of doubt and disaster—until today and perhaps not much longer, because the modern world is engaged in severing once and for all the ties which bind people into local unity, in committing them to complete participation in the Great Society. This is a one-way street, along which there is no return. The Middle American world has survived many destructions; our present cycle of time is now approaching its nadir.

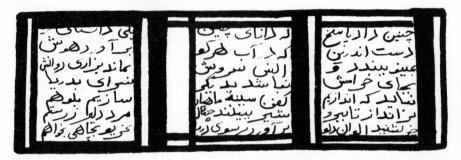

THE RISE OF CIVILIZATION

Civilization is a term that is too often misused as an ethnocentric appellation for our own way of life. For the anthropologist it serves only as an objectively descriptive term to define a general stage, or level, of cultural development, that is, one characterized by relative complexity.

Cultures defined as civilized are always built upon a relatively advanced technological base, one that can support a fairly large, and usually dense, population. The accompanying economic systems tend to be more complicated and diverse than those of the technologically less "advanced" peoples; social, political, and ideological systems are also likely to be more intricate and complex.

When we say that such cultures are more advanced than their "primitive" antecedents or contemporaries, no normative connotation is intended. As a matter of fact, we can state that one people is civilized and another not on the basis of the objective criteria of greater over-all cultural complexity. But we cannot state this on the basis of absolute betterness. We, for example, are civilized. The decision as to whether or not we are "better off" for being so is wholly a question of culturally acquired taste.

As with the earlier emergence of the Neolithic Age, the rise of civilization was marked almost everywhere by the presence of a number of analytically comparable circumstances and consequences.

1. Early Civilizations, Subsistence, and Environment [1]

This symposium has accepted as its central problem the cumulative, if hardly constant, tendency of human society to grow in size and complexity. Its major substantive foci, of course, are the roots of our own Western tradition in the early civilizations of Egypt and western Asia. At the same time, it is clear that processes and institutions appearing first in the ancient Orient subsequently have recurred, with varying degress of similarity, in widely separated regions and at different times. A better understanding of some of these recurrent features may help to clarify not only the picture of developing Egyptian and Sumero-Babylonian societies but also the cumulative development of society at large.

My task is to describe briefly some of the major ecological relationships which sustained the growth of civilizations in a number of "nuclear" areas. In addition to Mesopotamia and Egypt, the choice of pre-Spanish Mesoamerica and Peru seems most appropriate. It is supported not only by the volume and historical-archeological depth of relevant data that are available from the latter two areas but also by the likelihood that extreme geographic separation reduced their dependence on Old World precursors to a minimum. In spite of this separation there is a striking similarity, in scope and form, of nuclear American sociopolitical attainments to those of the Fertile Crescent area at a much earlier time.

J. H. Steward has argued convincingly that even the demonstrated fact of dif-

fusion between two cultural traditions is insufficient to "explain" their likenesses. "One may fairly ask," he maintains, "whether each time a society accepts diffused culture, it is not an independent recurrence of cause and effect." From this point of view, it is possible to regard all four areas as historically distinct examples regardless of the ultimate "origins" of particular traits. This is especially true for our purposes, since cultural-environmental relationships within an area are pre-eminently a matter of independent adjustment to local conditions and resources.

Moreover, the substantive evidence in these cases for the presence of diffusion from some outside source as a determinative factor is either lacking or at best equivocal. Each of the four areas stood out over its surroundings as a highly creative rather than a passively receptive center. While the complete absence of trans-Pacific stimuli for New World high cultural development cannot be assured, the conclusion of Willey like most Americanists today is that the latter "stands clearly apart and essentially independent from the comparable culture core of the Old World." There is certainly no suggestion of any New World–Old World contact as important as the relatively brief but catalytic influence of Mesopotamia on Egypt at about 3000 B.C., yet in the latter case Frankfort took pains to point out the selective, qualified, and generally transient character of the borrowing. With respect to interrelations

[1] ROBERT M. ADAMS, "Early Civilizations, Subsistence, and Environment," in *City Invincible*, pp. 269–294. Carl H. Kraeling and Robert M. Adams (eds.) (Chicago: 1960). Reprinted by permission of the author and The University of Chicago Press, © 1960 by The University of Chicago Press.

Dr. Adams is Associate Professor of Anthropology at the University of Chicago.

between Peru and Mesoamerica, it is sufficient to state that not a single object or record of influence or contact between these areas has been accepted as authentic from the long time span between the Formative (or Early Village) period and the coming of the Spaniards, although the over-all tempo of development in each is remarkably similar. In short, it is both reasonable on a priori theoretical grounds and justified by present evidence to use Mesopotamia, Egypt, Mesoamerica, and Peru as essentially independent examples for a discussion of their internal ecological relationships.

Within the limits of this discussion it is neither possible nor necessary to explore fully the similarities in cultural development among these four areas. All clearly became civilizations, in the sense in which that term is defined here as a functionally interralated set of social institutions: class stratification, marked by highly different degrees of ownership or control of the main productive resources; political and religious hierarchies complementing each other in the administration of territorially organized states; a complex division of labor, with full-time craftsmen, servants, soldiers, and officials alongside the great mass of primary peasant producers. Each was a complex, deeply rooted cultural tradition displaying most or all of V. G. Childe's more inclusive civilizational criteria as well: monumental public works, the imposition of tribute or taxation, "urban" settlements, naturalistic art, the beginnings of exact and predictive sciences, a system of writing suitable at least for rudimentary records and accounts. The attainment of civilization, from a diachronic point of view, was expressed in each of the four areas by a series of parallel trends or processes: urbanization, militarization, stratification, bureaucratization, and the like. Of course, these processes were truncated in the New World by the Spanish Conquest—as a plausible ap-

proximation, after a level of development had been reached which was functionally equivalent to Old Kingdom Egypt or southern Mesopotamia under the Dynasty of Agade. However, this does not affect our comparisons here, which will be limited to earlier periods in the Near East for which New World equivalents are available.

It thus seems possible to group the four civilizations as representatives of a single type or class of social system. (Other members of the class would include the unknown Indus Valley polity of Harappa and Mohenjo Daro, Shang China, and perhaps certain West African city-states.) To be sure, this stress on structural and functional similarities needs supplementing by the traditional humanistic emphasis on the unique and relatively timeless qualities of each civilization for a properly balanced view. One example of the latter emphasis is the invocation of particular environmental features of different civilizations to account in part for their differing views of the natural world as reconstructed from works of ancient literature or art, for the distinctive structuring of their formal cosmologies, and perhaps even for dominant psychological attitudes. A typological approach necessarily neglects, although certainly cannot deny, the unique total patterning of every culture irrespective of what proportion of its constituent elements may have close parallels elsewhere. Probably this patterning is expressed most systematically, concisely, and impersonally in stylistic or configurational terms. But in any case these widely ramifying, largely ideational, aspects of the interrelations between man and the natural world are beyond the scope of this paper. Here we are concerned only with the generalized social order common to a group of autochthonous civilizations and with its relations to the environment.

CLIMATE, PHYSIOGRAPHY, RESOURCES, AND POPULATION

Beyond the limitation of each of the nuclear areas to subtropical latitudes, the combined gross catalogue of environmental features is characterized mainly by its diversity. If Egyptian and Sumero-Babylonian civilization are restricted to great arid or semi-arid river valleys, no such uniform description holds for the zones occupied by either Mesoamerican or Peruvian civilization. Both of the latter range from sea level to high mountain slopes, with tropical, temperate, or even cold-temperate climates corresponding to their altitudes. If coastal Peru and much of highland Mesomerica are sufficiently dry to be closely comparable with the Old World centers, this is progressively less true in the Peruvian sierra with increasing altitude and distance from the Pacific coast and not true at all in the Gulf Coastal lowlands of Middle America.

Both of the New World areas lack great inclusive river systems comparable to Egypt and the Nile or Mesopotamia and the Tigris-Euphrates. Instead, short, steeply descending watercourses that drain relatively small watersheds are common, and many of the largest of these are reduced in their pre-Hispanic importance by geographic factors. The main valley of the Rio Balsas and the intermontane basins of the Bajío on the Rio Lerma in Mexico, for example, were lightly occupied before the Spanish introduction of draft animals and the iron-tipped plow made it possible for agriculturalists to deal with heavy soils and sod. The Amazon headwaters in the eastern sierra and Montaña of Peru may be found to provide a more significant exception when they have been explored more adequately, but at least the lowland rain forest of the Amazon basin proper acted as a major ecological barrier to the expansion of Peruvian civilization. Since the potentialities of the Old World rivers for disastrous floods, for large-scale irrigation, and as arteries of commerce are often thought to have promoted political unification and the growth of trade in the ancient Orient, it is worth noting that the same cultural phenomena appeared independently in regions where these potentialities were absent or at least far less important.

With respect to natural resources, it is sufficient to recall the absence of even stone in the alluvial soil of southern Mesopotamia, as well as the extremely poor quality for building of the soft and quick-growing woods that alone were available locally. In contrast, parts at least of the New World nuclear regions were well favored, although with great altitudinal variation local self-sufficiency was often replaced by patterns of regional specialization and exchange. As with climate and terrain, then, we cannot identify a fixed constellation of raw materials which acted as a necessary precondition (much less as a "cause"!) for the emergence of civilization in every area.

While relatively continuous settlement in linear patterns coinciding with the positions of the watercourses was possible in southern Mesopotamia and Egypt, enclaves of dense occupation separated by stretches of relatively inhospitable terrain were more characteristic of Mesoamerica and Peru. The best known and largest of the Mesoamerican enclaves is the interior drainage basin called the Valley of Mexico, which has provided the bulk of population and subsistence resources successively for the great religious center of Teotihuacan, the Toltec realm with Tula as its capital, the widespread conquests and incipient empire formation of the Aztecs, and present-day Mexico City. Yet in spite of the unparalleled importance of this region its area does not exceed 8,000 sq. km. In Peru the areas of intensive settlement and cultivation were all still smaller. Perhaps the largest of the mountain basins able to support a concentrated population is that of Huancayo, in the central highlands, with an area of only 1,200 sk. km. The arable area of the Chicama Valley, the largest in the North Coastal lowlands, is approximately the same.

In all of nuclear America, only along the Gulf Coast and on the low-lying Yucatan Peninsula were the conditions suitable for relatively uniform and continuous settlement. There, too, the rivers most nearly resemble the Nile or the Euphrates in regularity of flow and ease of control. But the lateritic soils and heavy rain-forest vegetation impose a very long recovery period after brief use for slash-and-burn agriculture, which materially reduces population density and perhaps helped to postpone for a considerable time the onset of urbanization processes which had been initiated in adjacent Mesoamerican highlands. A sharper contrast would be hard to imagine than that between Sumerians clustering in cities and Classic Mayans living in dispersed, essentially rural, hamlets while only a small elite permanently inhabited the elaborate religious centers. Yet both were civilized. In short, the distribution of population and settlements within the nuclear areas appears to have been as variable as the general environmental conditions within which they occurred, although average density in each case was surely much higher than in surrounding areas.

VARIATIONS IN AGRICULTURAL SUBSISTENCE PATTERNS

While the essential basis for subsistence in every civilization is obviously to be found in sedentary agriculture, this rubric covers impressive technical, botanical, and zoological differences when it is applied to the high cultures of both the New and the Old World. Largely following C. O. Sauer, we may summarize these differences briefly.

New World agriculture, in the first place, essentially did not involve stock-breeding or the utilization of such animal products as dung fertilizer or milk. Domesticated Andean camelids such as the llama were used mainly for transport and were largely confined to the higher slopes; hence they cannot be regarded as important exceptions. Also missing in nuclear America, therefore, is the unique and powerful ambivalence of relations between herdsman and farmer, involving both symbiosis and hostility, which has shaped the social life, tinctured the history, and enriched the literature of the civilizations of the Fertile Crescent.

Second, nuclear American agriculture involves an entirely different range of cultivated plants, which nonetheless seem to have provided as balanced and adequate a diet as the cereal-date-vegetable-livestock complexes of the ancient Orient.

Third, basically different methods of cultivation were employed in the New World. In the absence of draft animals, the major implements were the digging stick and the hoe instead of the plow. Instead of a definite brief harvest season, crop-gathering was prolonged by the use of the major food crops also as green vegetables during earlier stages of their growth and by the widespread practice of interspersing different crops within a single field.

Finally, corresponding to the greater variations in climate because of altitude, New World agriculture was far more variable. There is little difference in at least the potential yields of the Assyrian uplands and the Mesopotamian alluvial plain other than that due to the inability of the date palm to flourish beyond the northern limit of the alluvium and to the greater (but not exclusive) reliance on barley rather than wheat south of that limit. By contrast, coastal Peruvian agriculture essentially revolved around a maize-beans-squash-cotton-fruits complex, while in the sierra subsistence depended on an entirely different complex composed of root crops like potatoes, oca, and quinoa. Similarly, maize, beans, and squash were the staple foods in both highland and lowland Mesoamerica, but they had been differentiated very early into altitudinally specialized varieties. Moreover, the cultivation of cotton, cacao, and many fruits was restricted to the lowlands.

SIMILARITIES IN SUBSISTENCE PATTERNS

In spite of these profound differences, common features are not lacking. Perhaps something can be learned of the general place of subsistence in the growth of civilizations by outlining three common elements which seem to be of greatest importance.

One such significant common feature is that "farmers were persuaded or compelled to wring from the soil a surplus above their own domestic requirements and [that] this surplus was made available to support new economic classes not directly engaged in producing their own food." It must be understood that the notion of a surplus is related to fixed biological needs and the level of productive efficiency only in very general terms and that both the kinds and the quantities of available surpluses were determined to a considerable degree by the broad social contexts—"non-economic" as well as "economic"—within which they occurred. Yet the institutional forms for the concentration and redistribution of surpluses show a high degree of uniformity among the early civilizations and serve to distinguish the latter sharply from societies in which no full-time activity other than primary food production finds sanction. Although it is impossible to quantify, it is only reasonable to assume that the proliferation of nonagricultural specialists common to all the early civilizations was correlated with a general increase in agricultural efficiency. It is, of course, quite another matter to assume that improved efficiency was independent of and prior to the whole ramifying network of concurrent social changes. Even purely technological advances, which in most instances these increased surpluses probably do not reflect, are usually linked with the social and cultural milieu, as Kroeber's study of independent and relatively simultaneous inventions was first to show.

A second common feature of some importance may be the complexity of the subsistence base on which each of the civilizations seems to have rested. We are dealing in no case with a single-crop economy or with one in which the bulk of the population normally could supply the entire range of agricultural produce for themselves. Perhaps the diversity of resources is partly to be understood as the protection against natural calamity necessary for long-term cultural growth. But also in part it must have been responsible for the development of trade, exchange, and resdistributive institutions which in turn enhanced the growth of some form of centralized authority.

Mesopotamia is perhaps the best-documented example. The complementarity of dates and grain finds symbolic expression in the alabaster "Uruk vase," of late Protoliterate date, where alternate palm and cereal shoots in the bottom register figuratively support the abundant ceremonial life illustrated above. Fishing was another essential subsistence pursuit; of the 1,200 or so members of the Baba temple community in Girsu in the mid-third millennium B.C., more than 100 were fishermen. The precise role of fishing in earlier times is difficult to ascertain, but quantities of fish offerings found in a late Ubaid temple at Eridu may indicate that it had already attained considerable importance by that remote period. Slightly less numerous than the Baba temple fishermen were its shepherds and herdsmen, but their numbers in that specific case do not adequately reflect the crucial position of sheep, donkeys, and oxen in the mixed economy of ancient Mesopotamia for plowing, transport, wool, and fertilizer as well as meat. Surely the prominence of the shepherd-and-byre motif in Protoliterate glyptic art reflects a high antiquity for husbandry as an essential part of the configuration of subsistence activities. In all of these cases it is interesting to note that the temple and state institutions played a vital part in the collection and redistribution of the agricultural produce.

To the far more limited degree to which there are pertinent data on diversification and specialization of subsistence in Old Kingdom Egypt, the picture is at least not inconsistent with what has been described for Mesopotamia. The idealized representations in the tombs of life on the estates of court officials record a great variety of craft activities and subsistence pursuits; since an organization of the work under foremen is sometimes illustrated, there must have been at least a partial specialization of function in the real world as well. While the great bulk of the peasant's caloric intake may always have been derived from grain, the cultivation of vegetables and fruits and fowling, fishing, and animal husbandry also play a substantial part in the tomb scenes of Old Kingdom officials. The importance of herding, in particular, may have been obscured by its limited modern role under very different conditions of land use. For obvious reasons the main center of husbandry was in the Nile Delta, and the close concern of the state for husbandry is clearly to be seen in the emphasis on

livestock in lists of claimed tribute and loot, in periodic censuses of the herds, and in the appointment of numerous officials charged with responsibility of one kind or another for domestic animals.

In the New World the differentiation of subsistence pursuits seems to have been mainly on a regional basis, perhaps as a consequence of the greater environmental diversity that has previously been alluded to. But the necessity for a wide interchange of agricultural products remained the same, and the organization of this interchange similarly must have helped to expand and consolidate the positon of centralized social authority. In North Coastal Peru, for example, llamas from the sierra were already being ceremonially buried in a community shrine or public building in Late Formative times. In another case, the only llama bones from a contemporary site of the same period were found in association with the burial of an individual whose relatively elaborate *Beigaben* suggest a priestly status. By the succeeding Florescent era, the relative abundance of llama bones, wool, and droppings indicates that trading contacts with the highland centers of domestication for these animals had been regularized and enlarged. Presumably cotton, maritime products, peppers, fruits, and coca were among the commodities moving in the reverse direction, as they were at the time of the Conquest. To some degree, regional specialization with regard to subsistence extended into craft production as well, as is implied by the importation of a colony of Chimu craftsmen to work for the Inca government in Cuzco. It is interesting to note that a high degree of specialization still characterizes the Quechua community.

Similar patterns of differentiation in specialized production can be identified in Mesoamerica. Cotton from the lower-lying valleys of Puebla and Morelos was already being interchanged with the Valley of Mexico in Early Formative times, and the securest archeological dating horizons of later periods are provided by distinctive pottery wares that were traded widely from their different centers of manufacture. For the Conquest period these traces of evidence can be greatly amplified with eyewitness accounts of, for example, the great and diversified market at Tlatelolco with its separate vendors for many varieties of fruit, meat, maize, vegetables, and fish and with a reputed daily attendance of 60,000 persons. From a different point of view, the heterogeneity of native resources is also underlined by the *matricula de tributos*. Although it accounts for tribute levied by the Aztecs rather than for trade, the general concentration of assignments for particular kinds of produce (other than the ubiquitous mantles) to a very few provinces surely reflects earlier patterns for the interchange of normal regional surpluses. And by Aztec times, if not earlier, the integration of interregional trading with the needs and policies of the expanding state is well known.

A third significant feature common to the agricultural pursuits of the early civilizations was the development of some degree of intensive land use. Whether or not this was accompanied by a general increase in agricultural efficiency (output/labor input), certainly it must have increased at least the total agricultural output. However, the point of current interest is not so much the effect of intensive methods of cultivation on the volume of available surplus as their effect directly on social organization. The argument, following Ralph Linton's lucid portrayal of the introduction of wet rice cultivation in Madagascar, is that under conditions of intensive cultivation plots of land acquire different values based, for example, on cumulative improvements and the availability of

water. Since water, or good bottom land, or some other similar resource was almost always relatively scarce, well-favored and improved plots came to be regarded as capital investments. While unimproved land was allotted equitably among all members of the village or extended kin group, under conditions of intensive cultivation the cohesiveness of the older social units broke down and tended to be replaced by a small number of individual families as the hereditary landholding units. The emergence of an authoritarian "king," of rudimentary social classes including nobles, commoners, and war-captive slaves, and increasing expenditures on warfare are some of the further consequences which Linton traces to the basic shift in cultivation practices. Under at least some circumstances, in other words, the social processes we have identified with the beginnings of civilization are closely interconnected with the beginning of intensive agriculture. No necessary distinction into "cause" and "effect" is implied, be it understood, between subsistence change and institutional change. The investment of labor in land improvement and the adoption of intensive cultivation techniques were as much influenced by contemporary social forms as they influenced the latter.

Intensive agriculture, in the case of the earlier civilizations, usually is taken to be roughly synonymous with irrigation. Indeed, without some kind of irrigation arriculture is and probably always was impossible in southern Mesopotamia, Egypt, and coastal Peru. But we shall attempt to show that in most cases irrigation was part of a broader range of intensive techniques and that some of the assumed implications of irrigation as a single, gross category are misleading when applied to the four nuclear areas where the civilizations with which this paper is concerned had their beginnings. Here, then, irrigation is subsumed under the general rubric of intensive cultivation rather than equated with it.

It is important to distinguish between the functional significance of different kinds of irrigation if we are to understand better the relations between ecology and cultural growth. Small-scale irrigation, including flood-water techniques and the construction of short lengths of canal serving small landholdings, does not seem essentially different in its social effects from those observed by Linton in Madagascar. It may make available for agricultural purposes only a fraction of the potentially irrigable land surface, since it will seldom extend very far from the streams and since short canals will not be sufficient everywhere to bring the water to fields at a high enough level. Alluvial situations, in which rivers tend to raise their beds above the level of the surrounding land, are particularly favorable for small-scale irrigation. For the same reason, they invite destruction of existing canals by silting and flooding, although this is not critical where canals do not represent a heavy investment in labor and can be quickly replaced. The construction and maintenance of this kind of irrigation, we submit, requires no elaborate social organization and does not depend on labor resources larger than those at the disposal of the individual community, kin group, or even family— or, at most, those easily available locally through patterns of reciprocity. To the extent that this kind of irrigation is important, its chief influence on social development would seem to arise from its encouragement of stratification based on differentiation of landholdings. Perhaps also it encouraged the growth of militarism associated with increasing competition for developed canal networks and the most fertile and easily irrigated lands.

Large-scale irrigation, on the other hand, imposes technical and social demands of a different order. Masses of labor must be mobilized from many scattered communities, and their activities need close co-ordination. The problem of maintenance and supervision is a continuous one and again demands a superordinate authority. Some kind of equitable distribution of the available irrigation water must be imposed on many competing communities, and disputes must be adjudicated. Since downstream users are inherently at the mercy of those higher up, large-scale irrigation networks are only durable where the entire area they serve is a politically integrated unit. As has often been observed, large-scale canal networks can only be associated with formal state superstructures in which the ultimate authority rests with an administrative elite.

The problem for us is an absolutely basic one, however sparse, refractory, and ambiguous most of the present evidence may be. To the extent that large-scale irrigation is found to have begun very early, its social requirements may be adduced as a convincing explanation for the origin of primitive states in the ancient civilizations. Processes of class stratification associated with intensive agriculture then might be a secondary and derivative phenomenon on this reconstruction; because of its monopoly over hydraulic facilities, the state bureaucracy is identified as the strongest social force. Largely following Karl Wittfogel, Julian Steward took this position in a recent symposium with respect to Mesopotamia and Peru although not to Mesoamerica. Our view is firmly to the contrary. It is beyond the scope of a paper dealing with cultural ecology to argue that the primitive state is mainly linked instead with the emergence of a stratified society, but at least it will be suggested here that the introduction of great irrigation networks was more a "consequence" than a "cause" of the appearance of dynastic state organizations—however much the requirements of large-scale irrigation subsequently may have influenced the development of bureaucratic elites charged with administering them. The admittedly still inadequate evidence for this proposition now needs to be briefly summarized.

Our present understanding of the antiquity of irrigation in Mesopotamia is derived mainly from surface reconnaissance in Akkad and the Diyala basin and is obscured by the heavy and continuous alluviation with which the northern part of the alluvial plain has been particularly affected over the millenniums intervening since Sumerian times. At least in this region, however, there appears to have been little change in settlement pattern between the beginning of widespread agricultural occupation in the Ubaid period (*ca.* 4000 B.C.) and the end of the third millennium B.C. or even later. There is historical documentation for the construction of occasional large canals and irrigation works as early as the Protoimperial period, but on the whole the settlements followed closely the shifting, braided channels of the major rivers.

In other words, for a long time irrigation seems to have been conducted principally on an *ad hoc* and small-scale basis, which would have involved periodic cleaning and perhaps straightening of clogged natural channels, adjusting the location of fields and settlements in the closest possible conformity with the existing hydraulic regime, and for the most part constructing and maintaining only relatively small-scale field and feeder canals that were wholly artificial. Where the king explicitly claims credit for initiating dredging operations on either a canal or a natural watercourse (as in modern Iraq, the same word is used for both!), it is noteworthy that the aspect of canals as providers of irrigation water is entirely unmentioned. Moreover, whatever the rhetoric of the king's claimed responsibilities, the necessary labor forces for the maintenance work were apparently organized and directed by the individual temples. No Early Dynastic or Protoimperial record has survived of the mode of allocation of irrigation water, but at least in Ur III times this was separately handled in each temple constituency by a special official in charge of sluice gates. In short, there is nothing to suggest that the rise of dynastic authority in southern Mesopotamia was linked to the administrative requirements of a major canal system.

There are very few data yet available on the character or extent of Egyptian irrigation during the period for which it might be compared with New World equivalents, that is, up to the beginning of the Middle Kingdom. Prior to the opening of the Fayyum depression to irrigation in the Twelfth Dynasty, there is nothing less ambiguous to demonstrate state responsibility for irrigation than the statement of a Sixth-Dynasty royal architect that he had dug two canals for the king. Unfortunately, the inscription fails to make clear whether the canals were intended for irrigation or only for the movement of royal supplies like building stone, as was the case with five contemporary canals dug to bypass the First Cataract of the Nile. Still another possible explanation of the significance of the passage is that it refers to land reclamation by swamp drainage, much as a very late (and therefore doubtful) tradition credits Menes with having drained the territory around Memphis. Yet swamp drainage began long before any pharaoh appeared on the scene—if the obvious meaning is attached to the claim of a Third-Dynasty official that he "founded" twelve estates in nomes of Lower Egypt and continued afterward without the necessity of royal initiative. In considering alternatives other than irrigation we are also confronted with a protodynastic scorpion macehead ostensibly showing the king breaking ground for a waterway of some kind. Again, an immunity charter of Pepi I protects the priesthood of the two pyramids of Snefru against any obligation for labor service on what may be a canal; here it is neither clear that the putative canal was for irrigation nor that the pharaoh was responsible for its construction. Interestingly enough, the same charter continues with an injunction against enumerating canals, lakes, wells, hides, and trees belonging to the priesthood for tax purposes and thus suggests that all of those categories were under purely local jurisdiction.

In short, considering the number of known records of royal building activity in the Old Kingdom, it seems only fair to regard their silence on the construction of irrigation works as strange if the demands of large-scale irrigation had indeed been responsible for the initial emergence of a pharaoh at the head of a unified state. On the assumption of a centrally administered irrigation system, the failure of officials with long and varied careers of public service to refer to administrative posts connected with canal maintenance or water distribution is equally puzzling. To the degree that an *argumentum ex silentio* ever carries conviction, the Egyptian case parallels that of Mesopotamia.

Although there is serious danger of overgeneralizing from it, the data on Peruvian irrigation are reasonably consistent with what has been adduced from Mesopotamia and Egypt. Drawing principally from Gordon Willey's pioneer study of settlement patterns in a typical small valley transecting the arid North Coastal strip, we cannot presently trace large-scale irrigation earlier than the Florescent era (beginning probably at about the time of Christ). The distribution of Late Formative sites suggests, however, that small-scale experimentation with canal-building had begun in a few advantageous locales several centuries prior to this time, and some success

with at least flood-water irrigation on the river flats is implied by the slow expansion inward from the valley mouth which began a millennium earlier. The Early Florescent (Gallinazo) canals, it is interesting to note, were built as integral parts of an elaborate and impressive complex of monumental construction which included fortifications and ceremonial pyramids as well; on present evidence, both of the latter types of monumental construction antedated the large canals. By mid-Florescent times at least, valley-wide systems of irrigation were in use on the North Coast (although our particular example comprises only 98 sq. km. of arable land!), and some individual canals are large by any standards: the canal of La Cumbre in the Chicama Valley, for example, is 113 km. long. A subsequent development, probably dating only from the Militaristic era (beginning after A.D. 700), was the still more extensive reshaping of natural drainage patterns through the introduction of intervalley irrigation systems in which urban zones occupied by a governing elite were set off from areas for agricultural exploitation.

Irrigation apparently developed more slowly in highland Peru than on the North Coast, although the sharpness of the contrast may be a reflection in part of the lesser amount of archeological attention that the sierra has received. Terraces for soil conservation have been reported first for the Tiahuanaco horizon, at the outset of the Militaristic era. In the characteristically steep and narrow Andean valleys rapid runoff was perhaps a more serious problem than paucity of rainfall, but in general the later terraces seem to have been associated with irrigation channels as well. The elaborate, well-cut, and extensive terrace-irrigation systems for which Peru is famous all were products of the labor-service obligation imposed by the Inca state as a tax in the final century or so of its successful expansion before the coming of the Spaniards.

Even the Early Inca terraces, probably postdating the onset of the Tiahuanaco horizon by four or more centuries, have been described as "small and irregular, and probably the work of individual family groups." As in North Coastal Peru, Egypt, and southern Mesopotamia, we seem to have evidence here of a very gradual evolution of irrigation practices beginning with local and small-scale terracing which emphatically did not require political organization embracing a large group of communities. Large-scale, integrated programs of canalization and terracing apparently were attempted only after the perfection of the Inca state as a political apparatus controlling the allocation of mass-labor resources. They are consequences, perhaps, of the attainment of a certain level of social development; we repeat that they cannot be invoked to explain the processes by which that level was attained.

For Mesoamerica the situation is more complex and not a little contradictory. The traditional view is that "there is little evidence that irrigation was of basic importance anywhere in Mexico, in pre-Spanish times, and that it is erroneous to speak of maize culture as having flourished most in arid or subarid regions of that country." Recently this conclusion has been controverted effectively by a number of investigators, although the full significance of their empirical findings is still open to dispute. On the whole though, the situation seems to be quite similar to that described for the other nuclear areas; in fact, it was primarily the recent findings in Mesoamerica which stimulated the reconsideration of irrigation that this paper represents.

The question of the role of irrigation in the formation of Mesoamerican civilization takes us back at least to the beginning of the Classic era (*ca.* A.D. 100?), if not earlier, and revolves particularly around the population and ceremonial center of Teotihuacan in the Valley of Mexico. The Pyramid of the Sun there, one of the largest pre-Hispanic structures in Mesoamerica, apparently antedates that era. It has been estimated that before its abandonment in Late Classic times (*ca.* A.D. 700) the site occupied 750 hectares or more of religious and civic buildings, residential "palaces," workshops, and clusters of ordinary rooms and patios housing "at least" 50,000 inhabitants. True, the observed limits of surface debris may reflect only the aggregate area of the center over a period of several centuries and not its maximum size at any one period. Moreover, the proportion of residential units within the built-up area of the site is still not at all clear. But even if the estimate is scaled down considerably, it certainly reflects an urban civilization in being. To what extent, if at all, did it depend on irrigation agriculture? No direct evidence for canal irrigation has yet been reported. Instead, we have the observations that irrigation is necessary today for cultivation of even a single yearly crop in the subregion of which Teotihuacan is a part, that according to paleoclimatic studies based on pollen analysis and fluctuating lake levels it was even more necessary during the time of emergence of Teotihaucan as a great center, and hence that the use of irrigation must be assumed. The difficulty is that a center of the enormous size of Teotihuacan must have developed on a sustaining area far larger than its immediate subregion and that a major contribution from its immediate surroundings cannot be assumed to have been indispensable for the growth of the site. Monte Alban, Xochicalco, and other examples can be found which approach Teotihuacan in size but which lie at some distance from their main agricultural hinterland. A second argument is still less conclusive. It consists of the suggestion that irrigation is implied by representation of cacao and fruit trees along the banks of streams or canals in a mural from a

Teotihuacan "palace." Even if the identification of cacao is accepted as correct, the location of the scene is unknown and the crucial question of whether the waterways are natural or artificial is unanswered. There remains only a distributional argument, based on the wide extent of Mesoamerican irrigation practices at the time of the Conquest. Like all distributional arguments, it is loaded with presuppositions and provides no real clue to the antiquity of the trait in question. And so for Formative and Classic times the existence of canal irrigation still remains to be demonstrated.

For the final, or Historic, era (beginning ca. A.D. 900 with the founding of Tula), on the other hand, the evidence for large-scale irrigation agriculture and other hydraulic works is incontrovertible. Perhaps such works are already implied by the legendary account of the formation of Tula in the Codex Ramirez which describes the damming-up of a river in order to form an artificial lake stocked with fish and waterfowl. In any case, the Spanish conquerors were full of admiration for the scale and intricacy of the system of dikes and aqueducts that by 1519 was both supplying Tenochtitlan with potable water and controlling fluctuations in the salt- and fresh-water levels of the lakes surrounding the city. The sequence of construction of these works can be traced in some detail in historical sources, and the conclusion seems justified that they should be viewed "not so much as the result of many small-scale initiatives by small groups, but as the result of large-scale enterprise, well-planned, in which an enormous number of people took part, engaged in important and prolonged public works under centralized and authoritative leadership." Elsewhere in the Valley of Mexico, an irrigation complex in the Old Acolhua domain has been described that was roughly contemporary with the Aztec construction and also seems to have been initiated by a dynastic authority and carried out as a planned large-scale enterprise. Finally, an impressive list of places, with a wide distribution throughout Mesoamerica outside the Maya area, can be assembled for which irrigation is definitely identified or can reasonably be inferred in Spanish contact sources. In short, the position that irrigation was not important anywhere or at any period in pre-Spanish Mexico no longer seems tenable.

It needs to be stressed again, however, that distribution is a highly unreliable index to antiquity and that even the examples from the Valley of Mexico appertain only to the final century before the Conquest. Moreover, with the exception of the above-mentioned Aztec system all the known Mesoamerican irrigation networks are quite small in comparison with those of the Old World and Peru. On present evidence, then, Wolf and Palerm rightly tend to regard planned large-scale canal irrigation not as a primary cause of Mesoamerican civilization but merely as its culminating activity in the economic sphere. They recognize, to be sure, that political controls in turn probably were centralized and intensified by the introduction of major irrigation works.

But if large-scale canalization is late in Mesoamerica, there are indications that other forms of irrigation and intensive cultivation—as in Peru and Mesopotamia also—can be traced to a more remote antiquity. Canal irrigation probably never became as important a technique in the Valley of Mexico as chinampa agriculture, that is, the cultivation of artificial islands made out of plant debris and mud scooped from the lake beds. Modern chinampas are largely devoted to truck gardening, but, since the tasks of construction and maintenance do not require extensive organization and capital, they may have been used aboriginally as highly productive subsistence plots for kin groups or even families. The only example of an apparent chinampa so far subjected to archeological scrutiny contained occupational refuse dating to about the beginning of the Classic period and suggests that the technique is sufficiently old to have been a factor in the subsistence of Teotihuacan. The means were at hand early enough, in other words, for differential returns from specialized farming to have provided the material basis for the growth of a stratified society.

Since chinampas were unknown elsewhere in Mesoamerica (or depended on conditions not repeated elsewhere), their high and perennial productivity may not have been a direct factor in the development of civilization throughout the whole area. At the same time, the Valley of Mexico was in many other respects the key area of development for the greater part of Mesoamerica, for a very long time the center of its most advanced political forms, its widest and most closely intercommunicating trade network, its densest population. To a degree, then, it may have set the course of development which elsewhere was merely followed with more or less local innovation. To that degree, chinampa agriculture may far exceed in importance its highly circumscribed geographical limits. Unfortunately, having largely set aside simple diffusion studies, anthropologists are only beginning to develop more functional approaches to the analysis of interregional relations, through which the supposed primacy of the Valley of Mexico might be understood and evaluated.

Another, and broader, aspect of intensive cultivation in Mesoamerica is perhaps to be seen in the maintenance of dooryard garden plots in close symbiosis with individual houses, which augment the production of foodstuffs through the use of leavings as fertilizer and encourage stability of residence. Although not subject to archeological confirmation at present, this practice was apparently well established at the time of the Conquest and is possibly very old. Again, crudely made terraces for erosion-control purposes have been observed at many places in highland Mesoamerica and in at least one instance in the lowland rain forest of the Yucatan Peninsula. Certainly in many cases of considerable pre-Spanish antiquity, they suggest agricultural regimes of greater intensity than the milpa system as it is practiced today. Although at present impossible to document for pre-Conquest times, a more intensive application of labor in the form of hand-weeding would have prolonged cultivation and increased output, particularly in the tropical lowlands. This might make less inexplicable or even "explain" the extraordinary cultural achievements of the Classic Maya in the lowlands.

By assisting in the establishment of residential stability and in the production of surpluses, all the above-mentioned practices would have provided at least a receptive hinterland within which the new and more complex social forms could expand and consolidate. The origin of innovations such as the primitive state might then be sought in a few small strategic regions such as the Valley of Mexico where the inducements to accumulate surpluses and institutionalize class differences were probably greatest. In a wider sense, it may be granted, the florescence of the state could only take place where conditions in the hinterland were also propitious, so that the pinpointing of precise points of origin is probably misleading.

Briefly to recapitulate, we have attempted to show that developments in modes of subsistence within Mesoamerica were substantially similar to those in Mesopotamia, Egypt, and Peru in that large-scale canal irrigation was a culminating, rather than an early and persistent, form of intensive cultivation. It is conceded that differences in the rate of development existed, probably in large part because of the fewer inducements and opportunities to depend on irrigation that Mesoamerica offered. But these, we suggest, are quantitative and not qualitative differences. In North Coastal Peru the culmination came in the mid-Florescent era—or even later, in the Militaristic era, if the introduction of intervalley irrigation systems is accepted as a significant later innovation. In Mesoamerica it came in late Historic or Militaristic times, as it also seems to have done in *highland* Peru. According to our Mesopotamian data, admittedly inadequate in detail and based on a possibly retarded Akkad instead of Sumer, the onset of large-scale artificial canalization did not occur until after the time of Hammurabi. Even in Sumer itself there is no justification for supposing that this process began any earlier than the late Early Dynastic or the Protoimperial period—a sound equivalent for the New World Historic or Militaristic era. In *no* area, then, at least on present evidence, was large-scale irrigation early enough to "explain" the emergence of the great theocratic centers of the Classic era or the dynastic states which closely followed them. The concern of Wolf and Palerm, and latterly of Steward, over the distinction between "Theocratic Irrigation States" (Protoliterate Mesopotamia and Florescent Peru) and "Ceremonial Trade States" (Classic Mesoamerica) thus seems groundless.

RECIPROCAL EFFECTS OF HUMAN CULTURE ON ENVIRONMENT

This discussion so far has assumed that the natural physiography and resources of the four nuclear areas were relatively stable. The different cultural traditions have been regarded implicitly as evolving successive patterns of ecological adjustment and land use entirely according to

some internal dynamic of their own. The effect of environment, in these terms, is merely that of providing a fixed framework of potentialities and limiting conditions which somehow is then exploited selectively by the creative cultural growth within it. Such a view is obviously an oversimplification of the processes of interaction between man and the natural world, even if decisive climatic shifts no longer are regarded as likely to have occurred during the span of time that led to the emergence of any civilization.

Unfortunately the reciprocal effects of changing patterns of human activity on the land and flora cannot be traced continuously for any area. Perhaps the clearest and best-documented example is provided by recent work in central Mexico, where it has been shown that intensive hill-slope cultivation during the last centuries of Aztec dominance had gone far to destroy the capacity of the soil to sustain agriculture even before the arrival of the Spaniards. But the more remote history of occupance in even this relatively well-studied region is still insufficiently known for its environmental effects to be understood. The abandonment of the central Peten region by the lowland Classic Maya furnishes an even more dramatic case, with ecological processes such as sheet erosion, the silting-up of fresh-water sources, and the gradual replacement of forest vegetation by uncultivable savanna in the course of slash-and-burn agriculture all having been suggested as contributing factors. But in spite of a generation of speculation and interest these factors still exist only as hypotheses, and in a recent general work on the Maya it is interesting to note that they are largely rejected in favor of an explanation of the collapse of at least the elaborate ceremonial life in purely historical terms.

In the alluvial valleys of the Old World civilizations, processes of erosion are less likely to have affected directly the course of cultural development. It is not impossible, however, that deforestation at the headwaters of the Tigris and Euphrates increased both the silt loads carried by those rivers and their flooding potential. In turn, this would have affected the continuity of occupation in the alluvium and and the problems associated with constructing and maintaining irrigation systems. But, although deforestation undoubtedly went on, there are no empirical data at present on its rate nor on its consequences for the alluvial plain as a whole. Even the traditional assumption that the area of the plain has been continuously enlarged by the deposition of silt along the margin of the Persian Gulf has now been challenged by evidence that extensions of the land have been roughly counterbalanced by subsidence.

On the other hand, a group of different and important reciprocal effects is likely to have been initiated directly by the introduction of various techniques of intensive cultivation. Depletion of soil nutrients by inadequate crop rotation or fallowing cycle is one example. Salinization of poorly drained land as a result of continuous irrigation is another. Still a third may be the disturbance of natural patterns of drainage by the slow rise of canal beds and banks as a result of silting. To some degree all of these processes must have gone on, but their importance can only be gauged against the background of a far better understanding of ancient agriculture than we have at present for any area. To begin with, empirical studies are necessary of changes in the intensity of land use and of the exact nature of the full agricultural cycle over a long period in the past. At the time of this writing, a study along these lines has been undertaken for a small section of the Mesopotamian plain but not for any other nuclear area.

For the present, therefore, the distortions of a picture in which cultures are conceived as having evolved within a static environmental framework must remain uncorrected. If several possible types of correction have been mentioned, their effects cannot even be demonstrated satisfactorily with the evidence available from most areas, and in any case they are virtually impossible to quantify. One can only conclude that attempts to invoke changing ecological factors as "causes" of cultural development—however convenient they may appear as heuristic hypotheses—are still no more than a priori speculations.

In a broader sense, the lack of data on population density and land use underlies the purely speculative character of all those heuristic hypotheses which regard cultural change as an adaptive response to direct environmental forces. One account of the rise of militarism, for example, sees it as a consequence of the displacement of a population surplus, although there is absolutely no evidence of a concurrent reduction in the sustaining capacity of the environment or of a trend toward overpopulation in any of the nuclear areas. Another recent synthesis, going still farther, attributes not only the rise of large-scale warfare but also the cyclical character of the early empires in large part to population pressure. How population "pressure" can be defined usefully except by reference to real patterns and intensities of land utilization and settlement pressing against clearly defined ecological limits—for which, we must emphasize again, the evidence is still almost entirely lacking—is not apparent.

There is always an attraction for explanations of historical and cultural phenomena that stem from "outside" the immediate field of study. They have the advantage of providing fixed points from which analysis may proceed in a straightforward chain of cause-and-effect processes. But on closer inspection many such fixed points will be found to dissolve into shifting relationships which are not as separate and distinct from cultural influences as they may appear. Premature dependence upon explanations in terms of the external environment only diverts the historian or anthropologist from unraveling the complex stresses within human institutions. In all but the simplest societies, it is forces within the social order rather than direct environmental factors which have provided the major stimulus and guide to further growth.

CONCLUSION

In retrospect, the significant common features of land use among the early civilizations of the Old and the New World are so general that they are almost trite. If we have attempted to define the terms more closely than is usual, there is certainly nothing unusual about finding that all the great civilizational traditions rested on surpluses made available through sedentary, diversified, intensive agriculture. In addition, of course, it is implicit in this discussion that the common social institutions and processes of development identified in each of the four civilizations were bound up together with this general constellation of subsistence practices in a functionally interact-

ing network which characterizes early civilization as a sort of cultural type.

Against this simple and limited finding of regularity, the diversity of other environmental subsistence features and the huge proliferation of cultural forms stand in sharp contrast. History is not a mathematical exercise in the application of "laws," and the meaning of human experience is not to be found by suppressing its rich variety in the search for common, implicitly deterministic, denominators. From this point of view, perhaps the lack of closer specificity in the ecological relationships that are common to the early civilizations is the single most important point to be made. Much of sociocultural development seems to proceed very largely on its own terms, including even some important aspects of ecological adjustment. Societal growth is a continuously creative process, conditioned far more by past history than by directly felt environmental forces. On the whole, then, one may reasonably conclude that for an understanding of the meaning of the early civilizations—both in their own terms and for the modern world—the natural environment serves as no more than a backdrop.

Early "rural" farming communities were isolated, homogeneous, and largely self-sufficient. Life was monotonous. With the advent of urbanization—a classic characteristic of civilization—man's simple social life was radically transformed.

2. The Cities of Mesopotamia [1]

The differences between the various groups of prehistoric farmers are insignificant beside the overriding similarity of their mode of life, relatively isolated as they were and almost entirely self-

sufficient in their small villages. But by the middle of the fourth millennium B.C. this picture changed, first in Mesopotamia and a little later in Egypt; and the change may be described in terms of

[1] HENRI FRANKFORT, "The Cities of Mesopotamia," in *Birth of Civilization* (Bloomington, Ind.: 1951), pp. 49–77. Reprinted by permission of the publisher, © 1951 by the Indiana University Press.
The late Dr. Frankfort was Research Professor of Archaeology at the University of Chicago.

archaeological evidence. In Mesopotamia we find a considerable increase in the size of settlements and buildings such as temples. For the first time we can properly speak of monumental architecture as a dominant feature of sizable cities. In Egypt, too, monumental architecture appeared; and in both countries writing was introduced, new techniques were mastered, and representational art—as distinct from the mainly decorative art of the preceding period—made its first appearance.

It is important to realize that the change was not a quantitative one. If one stresses the increased food supply or the expansion of human skill and enterprise; or if one combines both elements by proclaiming irrigation a triumph of skill which produced abundance; even if one emphasizes the contrast between the circumscribed existence of the prehistoric villagers and the richer, more varied, and more complex life in the cities—one misses the point. All these quantitative evaluations lead to generalizations which obscure the very problem with which we are concerned. For a comparison between Egypt and Mesopotamia discloses, not only that writing, representational art, monumental architecture, and a new kind of political coherence were introduced in the two countries; it also reveals the striking fact that the purpose of their writing, the contents of their representations, the functions of their monumental buildings, and the structure of their new societies differed completely. What we observe is not merely the establishment of civilized life, but the emergence, concretely, of the distinctive "forms" of Egyptian and Mesopotamian civilization.

It is necessary to anticipate here and to substantiate the contrast. The earliest written documents of Mesopotamia served a severely practical purpose; they facilitated the administration of large economic units, the temple communities. The earliest Egyptian inscriptions were legends on royal monuments or seal engravings identifying the king's officials. The earliest representations in Mesopotamian art are preponderantly religious; in Egyptian art they celebrate royal achievements and consist of historical subjects. Monumental architecture consists, in Mesopotamia, of temples, in Egypt of royal tombs. The earliest civilized society of Mesopotamia crystallized in separate nuclei, a number of distinct, autonomous cities—clear-cut, self-assertive polities—with the surrounding lands to sustain each one. Egyptian society assumed the form of the single, united, but rural, domain of an absolute monarch.

The evidence from Egypt, which is the more extensive, indicates the transition was neither slow nor gradual. It is true that towards the end of the prehistoric period certain innovations heralded the coming age. But when the change occurred it had the character of a crisis, affecting every aspect of life at once but passing within the space of a few generations. Then followed—from the middle of the First until the end of the Third Dynasty—a period of consolidation and experiment, and with this the formative phase of Egyptian civilization was concluded. Few things that mattered in Pharaonic Egypt were without roots in that first great age of creativity.

In Mesopotamia a parallel development possessed a somewhat different character. It likewise affected every field of cultural activity at once, but it lacked the finality of its Egyptian counterpart. It cannot be said of Mesopotamia that its civilization evolved in all its significant aspects from the achievements of one short period, decisive as that had been. Mesopotamian history shows a succession of upheavals, at intervals of but a few centuries, which did more than modify its political complexion. For instance, the Sumerian language, which was dominant throughout the formative phase of Mesopotamian civilization, was replaced by Semitic Akkadian during the second half of the third millennium. And the shift of the center of power, in the third millennium, from Sumer in the extreme south to Babylonia in the center, in the second millennium to Assyria, in the extreme north, brought with it important cultural changes. Yet notwithstanding all the changes, Mesopotamian civilization never lost its identity; its "form" was modified by its turbulent history, but it was never destroyed.

We shall now desist from comparisons and consider the formative age of Mesopotamia, which is called the Protoliterate period since it witnessed the invention of writing. To this period the earliest ruins of cities belong. Now one may say that the birth of Mesopotamian civilization, like its subsequent growth, occurred under the sign of the city. To understand the importance of the city as a factor in the shaping of society, one must not think of it as a mere conglomeration of people. Most modern cities have lost the peculiar characteristic of individuality which we can observe in cities of Renaissance Italy, of Medieval Europe, of Greece, and of Mesopotamia. In these countries the physical existence of the city is but an outward sign of close communal affinities which dominate the life of every dweller within the walls. The city sets its citizens apart from the other inhabitants of the land. It determines their relations with the outside world. It produces an intensified self-consciousness in its burghers, to whom the collective achievements are a source of pride. The communal life of prehistoric times became civic life.

The change, however, was not without its disadvantages, especially in a country like Mesopotamia. The modest life of the prehistoric villager had fitted well enough into the natural surroundings, but the city was a questionable institution, at variance, rather than in keeping,

with the natural order. This fact was brought home by the frequent floods and storms, droughts and marsh-fires with which the gods destroyed man's work. For in Mesopotamia, in contrast with Egypt, natural conditions did not favor the development of civilization. Sudden changes could bring about conditions beyond man's control. Spring tides in the Persian Gulf may rise to a height of eight to nine feet; prolonged southerly gales may bank up the rivers for as much as two feet or more. Abnormal snowfalls in Armenia, or abnormal rainfall farther to the south, may cause a sudden rise of level in the rivers; a landslide in the narrow gorges of the two Zabs or of the Khabur may first hold up, then suddenly release, an immense volume of water. Any one of these circumstances, or the simultaneous occurrence of two or more of them, may create a flow which the earth embankments in the southern plain are not able to contain. In prehistoric times when primitive farmers sowed a catch crop after the inundation, it was possible to adapt human settlement to the ever-changing distribution of land and water, even though the villages were frequently destroyed. But large permanent towns, dependent upon drainage and irrigation, require unchanging watercourses. This can be achieved only through relentless vigilance and toil; for the quickly running Tigris carries so coarse a silt that canals easily get blocked. Even when cleaned annually, they rise gradually above the plain as a result of precipitation; and the risk that they, or the rivers themselves, may burst through their banks is never excluded. In 1831 the Tigris, rising suddenly, broke its embankment and destroyed 7000 houses in Baghdad in a single night.

Small wonder, then, that the boldness of those early people who undertook to found permanent settlements in the shifting plain had its obverse in anxiety; that the self-assertion which the city—its organization, its institutions, citizenship itself—implied was overshadowed by apprehension. The tension between courage and the awareness of man's dependence on superhuman power found a precarious equilibrium in a peculiarly Mesopotamian conception. It was a conception which was elaborated in theology but which likewise informed the practical organization of society: the city was conceived to be ruled by a god.

Theocracy, of course, was not peculiar to Mesopotamia: Egypt, too, was ruled by a god. But this god was incarnate in Pharaoh; and whatever may be paradoxical in a belief in the divinity of kings, it at least leaves no doubt as to the ultimate authority in the state and subjects the people unreservedly to the ruler's command. In Mesopotamia no god was identified with the mortal head of the state. The world of the gods and the world of men were incommensurate. Nevertheless, a god was supposed to own the city and its people. The temple was called the god's house; and it functioned actually as the manor-house on an estate, with the community laboring in its service. We shall describe the organization of the temple community at the end of this chapter. It is necessary first to survey the actual remains of the Protoliterate cities —the earliest cities in Mesopotamia.

In Protoliterate ruins the temples are the most striking feature. We have seen how, in the Al Ubaid period, temples were erected at Eridu in the south and at Tepe Gawra in the north. But the edifices of the Protoliterate period at Erech are much more impressive. The temple of the god Anu was placed upon an artificial mound forty feet high and covering an area of about 420,000 square feet. It dominated the plain for many miles around. Near its base lay another great shrine, dedicated to the goddess Inanna. Several times changed and rebuilt, it measured, at one stage, 240 by 110 feet; at another it possessed a colonnade in which each column measured 9 feet in diameter. Each of these, and also the adjoining walls and the sides of the platform supporting them, was covered with a weatherproof "skin" consisting of tens of thousands of clay cones, separately made, baked, and colored. These formed patterns of lozenges, zigzags, and triangles, and so on, in black and red on a buff ground. The cones were stuck into a thick mud plaster which covered the brickwork. The patterning in color enlivened a façade already richly articulated by complex systems of buttresses, recesses, and semi-engaged columns, and thus achieved an effect far beyond anything which the exclusive use of mud as building material would suggest as attainable.

The most characteristic feature of Mesopotamian temple architecture was the artificial mound, called a ziggurat or temple tower, the tower of Babel being the best known, that of Ur the best preserved, example. However, ziggurats were not found in connection with all temples. The Protoliterate temple at Tell Uqair, which has the same plan and even the same dimensions as the contemporary temple on the ziggurat at Erech, stands on a platform only a few meters high. I am inclined to see in this an abbreviated rendering of the ziggurat, but the possibility that the two differed in significance cannot be excluded. We cannot explain why some temples should lack ziggurats; but we can understand why so many great shrines were equipped with them, and why the staggering communal effort which their construction entailed was undertaken.

The significance of the ziggurats is revealed by the names which many of them bear, names which identify them as mountains. That of the god Enlil at Nippur, for example, was called "House of the Mountain, Mountain of the Storm, Bond between Heaven and Earth." Now "mountain," as used in Mesopotamia, is a term so heavily charged with religious significance that a simple translation does it as little justice as it would to the word "Cross" in Christian, or the words "West" or "Nun" (Primeval Ocean) in Egyptian, usage. In Mesopotamia the "mountain" is the place where the mysterious potency of the earth, and hence of all natural life, is concentrated. This is perhaps best understood if we look at a rather rough relief of terra cotta which was found at Assur in a temple of the second millennium B.C., although similar representations are known on seals of a much earlier date. The deity represented is clearly a personification of chthonic forces. His body grows out of a mountain (the scale pattern is the conventional rendering of a mountainside), and the plants grow from the mountainsides as well as from the god's hands. Goats feed on these plants; and water, indispensable to all life, is represented by two minor deities flanking the god. Deities like the main figure on this relief were worshipped in all Mesopotamian cities, although their names differed. Tammuz is the best known of them. As personifications of natural life they were thought to be incapacitated during the Mesopotamian summer, which is a scourge destroying vegetation utterly and exhausting man and beast. The myths express this by saying that the god "dies" or that he is kept captive in the "mountain." From the mountain he comes forth at the New Year when nature revives. Hence, the mountain is also the land of the dead; and when the sun god is depicted rising daily upon the mountains of the East, the scene is not merely a reminder of the geography of the country. The vivifying rain is also brought from the mountain by the weather god. Thus the mountain is essentially the mysterious sphere of activity of the superhuman powers. The Sumerians created the conditions under which communication with the gods became possible when

they erected the artificial mountains for their temples.

In doing so they also strengthened their political cohesion. The huge building, raised to establish a bond with the power upon which the city depended, proclaimed not only the ineffable majesty of the gods but also the might of the community which had been capable of such an effort. The great temples were witnesses to piety, but also objects of civic pride. Built to ensure divine protection for the city, they also enhanced the significance of citizenship. Outlasting the generation of their builders, they were true monuments of the cities' greatness.

It is in these temples that we find the first signs of a new invention without which the undertaking of works of this magnitude, or, indeed, of communal organization on a considerable scale, would not have been feasible, that is, writing. From the first it appears in the form of impressions made by a reed on clay tablets. The earliest of the tablets, found in the temple at Erech, were memoranda—aids for the running of the temple as the production center, warehouse, and workshop of the community. The simplest were no more than tallies with a few numerals. Others bear, besides the numerals, impressions of cylinder seals to identify the parties or witnesses to the transactions recorded. Still others indicate the object of the transaction. For instance, a simple inscription may consist of the entry: so many sheep, so many goats. There even occurs a more complex type, namely, a wage-list with a series of entries—presumably personal names—followed by the indication "beer and bread for one day." There is no reason to assume (as has usually been done) that these earliest tablets represent the last stage of a long development; the script appears from the first as a system of conventional signs—partly arbitrary tokens, partly pictograms—such as might well have been introduced all at once.

We are confronted with a true invention, not with an adaptation of pictorial art.

As regards the art of the Protoliterate period, the vast majority of the extant works deal with religious matters. Sometimes ritual acts were depicted, sometimes an ornamental pattern was built up of religious symbols; and occasionally it is impossible to be certain whether the one or the other was intended. But the reference is, in all cases, to the gods. Among the symbols—on seals and in the mural decoration of temples—plants and animals, especially those upon which man depends for his livelihood, were by far the most frequent. These were the emblems of the great goddess worshipped at Erech and throughout the land. They occur singly or in combination (for instance an ear of barley and a bull), the vegetable kingdom often being represented by rosettes. Friezes of sheep or cattle covered the walls of the Protoliterate temples—painted at Uqair, inlaid or carved in stone at Erech. Implements used in the cult, such as stands for offerings, were likewise decorated with animals, as were also sacred vessels: a trough, from which the temple flock was presumably fed, shows sheep near their fold —a reed structure (srefe) like those still built by the marsh Arabs in southern Iraq; and the building is crowned by two curiously bound reed bundles which correspond to the oldest form of the sign with which the name of the mother-goddess was written. Vases and seal designs showing the performance of ritual acts are also common. Like the symbols used in decorative art, these acts point consistently to the worship of deities manifest in nature.

The gods were also symbols of a collective identity. Each city projected its sovereignty into the deity which it conceived as its owner. There seems to be a contradiction here: the nature gods whom the Protoliterate monuments celebrate would seem more suitable for worship by countrymen and farmers than by townsmen as we know them. But our contrast "town versus country" is misleading. While it is true that the city in Mesopotamia was an outstanding innovation of the Protoliterate period, the great divergence between city and countryside, between rural and urban life, is, in the form in which we are familiar with it, a product of the "industrial revolution," and emphasis on this contrast mars our perspective when we view earlier situations.

About 400 B.C. roughly three-quarters of the Athenian burghers owned some land in Attica, and as recently as the European Middle Ages our contrast "urban-rural" was unknown. At that time the city was as distinct a social institution as it has ever been, but it was intimately related with the land. Trevelyan writes:

In the Fourteenth Century the English town was still a rural and agricultural community as well as a centre of industry and commerce . . . outside lay the "townfields," unenclosed by hedges, where each citizen-farmer cultivated his own strips of corn-land; and each grazed his cattle and sheep on the common pasture of the town. . . . In 1388 it was laid down by Parliamentary Statute that in harvest-time journeymen and apprentices should be called on to lay aside their crafts and should be compelled "to cut, gather and bring in the corn"; mayors, bailiffs and constables of towns were to see this done.

In Mesopotamia, then, many of the townspeople worked their own fields. And the life of all was regulated by a calendar which harmonized society's progress through the year with the succession of the seasons. A recurring sequence of religious festivals interrupted all business and routine at frequent intervals; several days in each month were set aside for the celebration of the completion by the moon of one of its phases, and of other natural occurrences. The greatest annual event in each city, which might last as long as twelve days, was the New Year's festival, celebrated at the critical point of the farmer's year when nature's vitality was at a low ebb and everything depended upon a turn of the tide. Society, involved to the extent of its very life, could not passively await the outcome of the conflict between the powers of death and revival. With great emotional intensity it participated by ritual acts in the vicissitudes of the gods in whom were personified the generative forces of nature. The mood of these urban celebrations, as late as Assyrian and Neo-Babylonian times, shows that the main issue was still the maintenance of the bond with nature.

We do not know for what reasons certain of the nature gods became connected with a given city. We only know that the city, as soon as it became recognizable, appears as the property of one god, although other deities were worshipped there as well. The city god was sometimes viewed as an absentee landlord, always difficult of approach and apt to express himself somewhat casually in signs and portents, dreams and omens of dubious meaning. Yet a misunderstanding of the commands thus conveyed was likely to provoke the calamity of divine anger.

It is in keeping with the tenor of Mesopotamian religiosity at all times that the relationship between the city and its divine owner could be conceived only as one of complete dependence. Throughout we meet with the somber conviction that man is impotently exposed to the impact of a turbulent and unpredictable universe. This feeling was rationalized in theology, which taught that man was created especially to serve the convenience of the gods. In the *Epic of Creation* man was brought into being after Marduk, the creator, had remarked casually:

Let him be burdened with the toil of the gods that they may freely breathe.

The same view is implied in an older, Sumerian, myth in which Enlil breaks the earth's crust with a pickaxe so that men may sprout forth like plants. And the other gods surround Enlil and beg him to allot to them serfs from among the Sumerians who are breaking forth from the earth.

The belief that man fulfilled the purpose of his being by serving the gods had very remarkable consequences for the structure of early Sumerian society. Since the citizens projected the sovereignty of their community into their god, they were all equal in his service. In practice this service took the form of a co-operative effort which was minutely organized. The result was a planned society, and the remains of the Protoliterate period show that it existed then, although it is better known from Early Dynastic times.

We must start by distinguishing two interlocking but distinct social institutions. The political unit was the city; the economic-religious unit the temple community. Each temple owned lands which formed the estate of its divine owners. Each citizen belonged to one of the temples, and the whole of a temple community—the officials and priests, herdsmen and fishermen, gardeners, craftsmen, stone cutters, merchants, and even slaves—was referred to as "the people of the god X." Ideally one can imagine one temple community to have formed the original kernel of each city; but whether this situation ever prevailed we do not know, since the Early Dynastic tablets acquaint us with cities comprising several temples with their estates.

Part of the temple land was actually worked by all for all, or again, to put it in the terms of the ancients, by all in the service of the god. This part of the land—not more than one-fourth of the whole in a case we can check—was called *nigenna*-land, a term which may be translated "Common," since the land involved was cultivated by the community as a whole. A second part, called *kur-land*, was divided into allotments which were assigned to members of the community for their support at a rent amounting to from one-third to one-sixth of the yield. Most of this rent could be paid in grain, but a small part had to be paid in silver.

The temple supplied the seed-corn, draft animals, and implements for the cultivation of the Common; and high and low worked every year in the "fields of the god," repairing the dikes and canals as a *corvée*. The *sangu,* or priest, who stood at the head of the temple community assigned the shares in the communal tasks. He appeared as bailiff of the god and was assisted by a *nubanda,* or steward, who supervised labor, magazines, and administration. Stores of grain which had accumulated were not merely used for seed-corn, nor were they exclusively at the disposal of the priest, to be used for sacrifices and for the sustenance of the temple personnel. The priests, like everyone else, had their allotments to support themselves, and the fruits of communal labor returned in part to the citizens in the form of rations of barley and wool, which were distributed regularly, and extra rations, supplied on feast days.

Although the amounts of rations were not equal, nor the tasks assigned to all men equally burdensome, we observe here a fact unparalleled in the ancient world, namely, that in principle all members of the community were equal. All received rations as well as allotments to support themselves; all worked on the Common and on the canals and dikes. There was no leisure class. Likewise there were no native serfs. Some foreigners and prisoners of war were kept as slaves, but private people possessed very few, if any. Slaves worked in the temple alongside free-men as porters and gardeners. Slave girls were kept in considerable numbers as spinners, and they helped in the kitchens, the brewery, and the sties where pigs were fattened.

The allotments differed in size, even when assigned to men of the same profession, and we cannot explain the differences. There is no evidence of large estates in the hands of single members of the temple community, but we may suppose that the existence of several temple communities in one city may have made it possible for some men to dispose of allotments in more than one of them. We know of a *nubanda* who had about 120 acres and a supervisor of the herb magazines who owned about 80 acres. But such conditions represent deviations from the original system. More significant is the fact that even the smallest allotment entered in the temple lists—a *gan,* or seven-eights of an acre—would suffice to keep a man. Monogamy and the scarcity of slaves would, in any case, limit the area which one family could cultivate.

Women are also listed as holders of allotments, and this means that they served the community in some function or other. For the basic rule of the temple community was that a person received land for his sustenance because he put his specialized skill at the service of all: the shepherd and the fisherman, the carpenter and the smith, provided the temple magazines with certain quantities of their produce or simply devoted all their time to work on temple property.

The magazines contained an immense variety of articles: grain, sesame seed as the raw material for oil, onions and other vegetables, beer, dates, wine (which was rare), fish (dried or salted), fat, wool, skins, huge quantities of reeds and rushes used for ceilings and for torches, temporary structures, mats for floor coverings and hangings, wood of many kinds, asphalt (used wherever anything had to be waterproof), valuable stones like marble and diorite, to be made into statues and cult objects such as offering-stands, ritual vessels, and the maceheads of the temple guards. The stone, and some of the wood, was imported by merchants, who also brought from Elam aromatics which, in the "oil house," were made into ointments with a base of animal fat. Tools were owned by the temple in great quantities and given out on loan.

All these articles and materials were checked and booked upon arrival and either stored or worked up within the temple precincts. Carpenters made ploughs and other implements, kept them in repair, and built chariots, and probably ships. Tanners prepared skins for harnesses and for leather bottles in which milk and oil were kept. Wool was prepared, and part of it spun, by slave girls; the Baba temple at Lagash employed 127 of these, with 30 of their children. But only 18 were spinners. The others cleaned and prepared the wool, of which large quantities were used in the export trade. A good deal was also distributed as rations to the members of the community. The shearing of the numerous sheep —or rather, the plucking of their wool —was done in a special compound outside the temple precincts, as was, likewise, the milling of the grain.

Barley constituted the main crop, but spelt and emmer wheat were also grown. Monthly rations of barley went from the granaries to the brewery and kitchen of the temple. The brewers also took charge of sheep and cattle to be fattened. But cattle were scarce, for there was little rich meadow land for grazing. The steppe in Iraq will sustain sheep in spring, but the sun burns the grass early in the summer; and even in antiquity the flocks had to be tided over the worst period with grain. In some local calendars there is a month "in which barley is given to the sheep."

The common protein food was fish rather than meat. We have records of private fishponds, and fifty different kinds of fishes are named in the texts. These also distinguish river fishermen, canal fishermen, coast fishermen, and fishermen of the high seas. Sheep and goats were kept for milk and wool. Oxen were used for ploughing, as were also asses. Both oxen and asses were used in teams of four head and fed on barley. The native breeds, deteriorating in the exhausting climate of the plain, were periodically invigorated by crossing with animals imported from Persia. Pigs were kept in the marshes and were also fattened.

Beside extensive cane brakes the temple owned "woods"; these consisted largely of date groves, and there, between the palms, other plants were cultivated, such as grapes, figs, pomegranates, and mulberries. Other groves consisted of timber trees, and there were apple orchards where, it seems, the blind were put to work.

The citizens, when working for the temple, were organized in groups or guilds under their own foremen. These divided the tasks among the members of the group, were responsible for the delivery of the produce, and received the rations for the group. Other lists, enumerating the citizens liable for military service, suggest that the men served guildwise with their foremen as cadre. But there were also professional soldiers, distinguished in two groups, spearmen and shield-bearers. In peace time they worked on the Common, harvested reeds in the cane brakes and assisted in building operations.

The specialization and detailed division of labor of the temple community, and especially the grouping of all kinds of laborers under foremen responsible for deliveries and receipt of rations, offered many opportunities for oppression. But too much can be made of the weaknesses of the system. To speak of the "surplus" of food which must be produced in order to maintain officials as well as merchants and craftsmen, and to imply that the officials must have been a parasitic class which kept the farmers in subjection, leaves out of account several circumstances, of which the most important is the climate of the country. Wherever there is power there is, inevitably, abuse of power. But the rich soil of Mesopotamia, if well watered, produces food in abundance without excessive or continuous toil. Labor in the fields was largely seasonal. At seed time and harvest time every able-bodied person was no doubt on the land, as was the case in medieval England. But the farmers were not a separate class or caste. Every citizen, whether priest, merchant, or craftsman, was a practical farmer who worked his allotment· to support himself and his dependents. Once the seed was sown and the harvest gathered, plenty of time remained in which special skills could be developed, taught, and exploited. There are interesting analogies in villages of our own time, where often enough a farmer or a laborer is a specialist in some branch of craftsmanship. In Europe this condition is rapidly disappearing and was never regularized; but we may quote two modern African instances which will make it easier for us to imagine how practical husbandry and the exercise of crafts and home industry can go together. The modern instances differ, of course, in important details but are instructive nevertheless. Of the Nuer, Howell said:

There are no specialized and hereditary trades though certain persons may acquire a local reputation for skill in making such things as pipes, collars for bulls, canoes or ivory bracelets. These people are not craftsmen by trade, and their activities centre round their cattle, like every other Nuer. Their services are normally accepted by others as part of the integral system of mutual aid which is the basis of every Nuer community, and they are repaid by assistance in pastoral or agricultural activities or by reciprocal gifts.

For another instance, with a rather peculiar character, Lowie states:

In West Africa the Pangwe do not make a business of carving and weaving; all such work is done on the side, in the intervals of fishing and farming. But in so far as a man does carve he is the narrowest of experts. He will manufacture tools but will leave bows to his neighbour, and a spoon carver would never attempt a ladle.

We are reminded of the many names to designate fishermen in Sumerian, even though specialization was certainly less narrow in the Mesopotamian cities. But the point I want to make is that, for all the guilds and professional skills which we find there, the population as a whole was concerned with the primary business of tillage and cannot be compared with any modern body of city dwellers.

Since a considerable proportion of agricultural and other produce passed through the temple magazines, an elaborate system of administration was set up. To illustrate the kind of careful accounts kept of the expenses, we shall quote a record of the grain used in a certain operation. To understand it, it is necessary to know that the fields were ploughed twice, first to break up the ground, then to sow and cover the seed. For the second ploughing a seed funnel was attached to the plough to ensure an even distribution along the furrow. Since the second ploughing was less heavy than the breaking of the ground, the oxen used for it got only half the fodder allotted to the teams used in the first. (The Sumerian measures can be converted by taking the *gan* at just under an acre and the *gur* at about 3⅓ bushels.) This grain came from the temple magazines which had been filled by the harvest of the Common.

In order to make it possible to draw up a budget, the yield per acre was estimated, account being taken of whether the land was good and arable, newly

TABLE 1

147 *gan* arable land, the oxen put in the plough and seed:		
Barley for food of the ploughing oxen	24½	*gur*
Barley for food of the sowing oxen	12¼	"
Seed-corn	12¼	"
Waste	1½	"
36 *gan* sown in addition:		
Seed-corn	3	"
Fodder	3	"
Together: 183 *gan* arable land. Its grain Expenditure for the Common	56½	"

reclaimed, swampy, or distant from water. The monthly allowances of functionaries were listed, as were the monthly supplies to brewery, bakery, and kitchen, and the tasks allotted to the guilds of craftsmen, shepherds, fishermen; and other specialized workers were also listed in monthly quotas. All these documents were signed by the *sangu* and the *nubanda*. But the absence of money made simplification imperative, since the accounts recorded a continual intake of all kinds of goods, and the outflow of similarly varied stores, in the form of rations, sacrifices, materials for repairs, goods for trade, and so on—which were not reduced to a common standard of value. It would have been impossible to budget from month to month and from year to year unless the book-keeping had been adapted to a somewhat simple scheme with fixed ratios prevailing throughout. The schematic character of the temple accounts can be seen in the one instance which we quoted above: the fodder for the sowing oxen was precisely the same quantity as that used for seed. The span used to break the ground received precisely twice the amount allotted to the span following after with the seed funnel. Similar simple ratios were used for valuations: one *gur* of barley was reckoned equivalent to one *gin* of silver; one *gur* of barley was likewise charged as rent for one *gan* of land. It is obvious that such equations reduced the innumerable calculations of the temple bookkeeping to manageable proportions. But it is likewise obvious that these simplified

and rigid scales never corresponded to the actual values of goods or services. The margin cannot have worked consistently to the detriment of the people, for then the system would have collapsed. Consequently, the margin must have been disadvantageous to the temple economy which could well afford it and which was, in a way, the property of the people as a whole. When in bad years deliveries of certain goods fell short of the quantities due each month to the temple magazines, debts arose and were duly booked and were expected, ultimately, to be paid off. But, on the whole, the organization of the temple economy aimed at simplicity rather than efficiency; and in the Sumerian city, although it was a "planned society," men found considerable scope for private enterprise.

The margin between the schematic values used in dealings with the temple and the actual yield of fields, flocks, and workshops must have given opportunities for some accumulation of private wealth and hence for barter. Craftsmen could utilize their special skills for private commissions as long as they used materials not supplied by the temple magazines. The shepherd could dispose of any increase in his flock beyond the statutory figure; the fisherman could dispose of the remainder of his catch after delivering to the temple his monthly quota. If, therefore, "the people of the god X"— the temple community—can be said to have lived under a system of theocratic socialism, we must add that this planned economy formed a hard core which was surrounded by an ample fringe of private enterprise that remained free.

That the accumulation of private wealth was accepted by the community as a matter of course is shown by the rule that a proportion of the rent of *uru-lal* land had to be paid in silver and not in produce. Moreover, the variety of imported articles testifies to the scope left to barter. It is true that the import and export trade was again organized at the center. Merchants travelled abroad to obtain stones, gold, silver, copper, lead, wood, and aromatics for the temple. In exchange they could offer grain, dates, onions, and similar produce. But their best opportunities were offered by the produce, not of the rich Mesopotamian soil, but of the skill of the people. Manufactured goods sent abroad included, above all (and at all times), textiles—woollen clothing, hangings, and carpets—and also, to judge by the wide distribution of Sumerian types of tools, weapons, and jewelery, metal objects fashioned in the Plain from imported materials. The merchant in those early days was concerned exclusively with export and import. He did not conduct trade among members of his own community; he exchanged locally finished goods for products of other cities in the Plain or of foreign countries like Elam. It is significant that in return for his effort he received an allotment of land—certain proof that he was in the service of the community. Moreover, he had the use of a team of donkeys belonging to the temple, no doubt in view of his travels. It seems likely enough that the merchants found opportunities for private trade on the side, and it remains uncertain to what extent they supplied directly the imported articles found in houses. In excavations, for instance, handmills consisting of flat stones with roundish grinders were found in every house. Yet the hard volcanic stones used for them must all have been imported. In the private tombs of the end

of the Protoliterate period lead tumblers and stone vases are common. At Khafajah copper vessels, and stands for stone food dishes, or drinking cups, or lamps, are found in graves of the Second Early Dynastic period. The somewhat later cemeteries at Kish and Ur show even greater luxury and refinement. There were found copper mirrors; copper and gold toilet sets—tweezers, a toothpick, and an earscoop, fastened on a ring and carried in a small conical case; pins of copper or silver with round lapis lazuli heads; beads and animal pendants of alabaster, carnelian, and lapis lazuli, and other semi-precious stones. The silversmith knew how to make filigrain pendants and girdle clasps, and even fine-linked chains.

Most of these articles were, of course, luxuries. In matters of dwelling, food, and clothing, the country was self-supporting. The houses were built of sun-dried bricks and make an entirely unpretentious impression. They do not show a regular system of planning. Rooms were fitted together as the available plot allowed. Doors were low and arched; one had to stoop to pass from one room to another. Windows were small and high up in the walls and fitted with wooden bars or with screens of baked clay. But the ruins of mud brick do not give a fair impression of the setting in which these people lived. We must imagine the floors covered with smooth, clean rush mats, the walls and benches with gaily colored rugs and blankets.

The people wore a shawl-like dress, wound round the waist, sometimes with one end pulled round the back and forward over the left shoulder. It is rendered on the monuments in a manner which suggests sheep or goatskin, but this may be a ceremonial dress only, for it is certain that textiles were worn and they are depicted from the middle of the third millennium onward.

Thus the actual remains found in the excavations demonstrate that the temple community did not impose as rigid a form of life on its members as our description may have suggested; and the texts, in proving the existence of private property and trade, corroborate the elasticity of the system. We know, moreover, that it was able to bear the strain of hard times; for it has been calculated that the temple received a great deal more grain from the *nigenna land* and as rent than was normally needed. The accumulated reserves were made available in an emergency—a better safeguard of the people's food supply than reliance on individual providence might have been. It seems also that the temple supplied rations during the interval between sowing time and harvest, when stores were low.

The accounts of the temple do not differentiate between its role as central store of the community and its religious function; goods withdrawn for sacrifices are treated exactly like those serving for rations. The distinction in function was apparently not made. The temple community was a religious institution regulating the social life of the community, and the two aspects which we distinguish were apparently experienced as one and indivisible.

The temple community seems not, however, to have been a political institution. The oldest such institutions of which traces have yet been recognized show the same equalitarian spirit as the organization of the religious community. Political authority seems originally to have rested with the citizens; sovereign power under the city god lay in an assembly—presumably consisting of all free males—guided by a group of elders who seem, moreover, to have been in charge of current affairs. Since the terms for "assembly" and "elders" occur already in the Protoliterate tablets, we can surmise that these peculiar political institutions existed as long as the cities themselves.

It is well to recognize the extraordinary character of this urban form of political organization. It represents in the highest degree the intensified self-consciousness and self-assertion which we recognized as distinctive of the innovations of the Protoliterate period. It is a man-made institution overriding the natural and primordial division of society in families and clans. It asserts that habitat, not kinship, determines one's affinities. The city, moreover, does not recognize outside authority. It may be subjected by a neighbor or a ruler; but its loyalty cannot be won by force, for its sovereignty rests with the assembly of its citizens. Thus, the early Mesopotamian cities resembled those of Greece, of the Hanseatic League, of Renaissance Italy, in many respects. In all these cases we meet local autonomy, the assumption that every citizen is concerned with the common weal, and a small group of influential men who deal with current affairs and sometimes impose an oppressive oligarchy upon the mass of the people.

We do not know whether oligarchic rule ever became a Mesopotamian institution. Our Protoliterate sources are too scanty to disclose gradations of power within the existing framework. And in Early Dynastic times, when the texts became plentiful, the framework had collapsed and the old institutions were no more than ghostlike survivals of the past. But it was single rule rather than oligarchy which had supplanted the assembly.

The reason for the change is clear; the equalitarian assembly possessed the disadvantages of freedom to an uncommon degree. Subjection to the will of the majority, as expressed in a vote, was unknown. The assembly continued deliberation under the guidance of the elders until practical unanimity was reached. This might be the result of true agreement, or of mass emotion, or due to a prudent concurrence of the opponents with a line of action advocated by a powerful group. In any case, it was not easily attained; and in an emergency when quick decision and purposeful action was required, the Mesopotamian city, like the Roman republic, put itself into the hands of a dictator. In Sumer he was called *lugal,* which means "great man" and is habitually translated "king."

Kingship was a *bala,* a "reversion," or "return to origin." In other words, the kingly office had a limited tenure; at the end of the emergency authority reverted to the assembly. But, in practice, the threat of an emergency was never absent once the cities flourished and increased in number. Contiguous fields, questions of drainage and irrigation, the safeguarding of supplies by procuring safety of transit—all these might become matters of dispute between neighboring cities. We can follow through five or six generations a futile and destructive war between Umma and Lagash with a few fields of arable land as the stakes. Under such conditions the kingship seems to have become permanent in certain cities.

Elsewhere the concentrated authority called for by the dangers to which the community was frequently exposed was conferred upon leaders who held important permanent offices. Some of these were exalted enough to enable their holders, when emergencies arose, to exercise power similar to that of the *lugal.* The *sangu* or *nubanda* in the temple of the city god was the administrative leader of the most important temple community in the city. For him to become the political leader of the city was perfectly feasible, but in such a case the official who had usurped the prerogatives of a ruler assumed, instead of the secular title *lugal,* a title emphasizing his dependence on the city god and proclaiming, by implication, the god's agreement with his rule. This title was *ensi,* best translated as "governor" (viz. of the god).

Whether *lugal* or *ensi,* the city ruler in Mesopotamia did not derive his position from any innate superiority or right of birth. He acted either on behalf of the assembly, or as steward of the real sovereign, the city god. In theology, personal rule was sanctioned by a doctrine of divine election which remained the foundation of kingship down to the end of the Assyrian empire. Divine approval could be withdrawn at any time, and the formation of a dynasty, the succession of the son to the throne of the father, although known already in Early Dynastic times, had no basis in the theory of kingship but was interpreted in each case as a sign of favor bestowed by the gods. These limiting conceptions of the monarchy reflect the preponderant influence of the city in Mesopotamian thought. Monarchy remained a problematical institution and failed, therefore, to become an instrument of unity as it did in Egypt. It carried in some degree the taint of usurpation, especially in early times.

The task of the *ensi* in the main was to co-ordinate the temple communities within the city. To each he assigned a share in the common tasks on buildings, canals, and dikes. These *corvées* were then divided among the guilds and individual members of a community by its *sangu* or *nubanda.* The *ensi* dealt, furthermore, with matters of defense and trade, in other words, with foreign affairs. The professional soldiers were under his direct and personal command and formed an important source of his power within the city. Like every other citizen, he received an allotment for his sustenance; but his fields were part of the Common and were cultivated by the people as part of their communal task. Here, again, was an opportunity for abuse of power. Moreover, it became customary to acknowledge the *ensi's* exalted position by offering him presents on the festivals of the gods. He also took a fee for making legal decisions or decreeing a divorce, and imposed certain taxes. While he administered the main temple of the city, he appointed members of his family to head other temple communities.

Although the assembly seems not to have been superseded entirely, the effective power of the *ensi* was preponderant; and what had been the original strength of Sumerian society, its integration with the temple organization, became its weakness when the leaders of the temple communities utilized the need for leadership, which the growth of the cities called forth, to oppress the people. We know, for instance, that one *ensi* sequestered fields assigned to him on the Common and used them to build up an independent "estate of the palace," modelled on that of the temple. The tablets from Fara show how varied an assortment of people had become directly dependent upon the *ensi*: scribes, chamberlains, heralds, pages, cupbearers, butlers, cooks, musicians, and all kinds of craftsmen. An equalitarian society had been thoroughly transformed, and the power assumed by the ruler was reflected in the presumptions and extortions of his officials. In fact, the Early Dynastic period ends, in Lagash, in an abortive attempt to move against the current and restore the theocratic form of its ideal prototype to Sumerian society. An *ensi*, called Urukagina, states that he "contracted with the god Ningirsu (the city god of Lagash) that he would not deliver up the orphan and the widow to the powerful man. He also put a stop to specific abuses: "he took the ships away from the master of the boatmen; he took the sheep and asses away from the head-herdsman. . . . He took away from the heralds the tribute which the *sangus* paid to the palace." These "changes," and many like them, listed in the so-called reform texts, mean that the prerogatives usurped by the foremen and officials were abolished

and that these rights were vested once more exclusively in the temple as a vital organ of the community.

Urukagina also ended abuses introduced by his own predecessors; he forbade, to use his own words, "that oxen of the god plough the onion plot of the *ensi.*" He lowered the fees for interments and for prayer services. He vindicated the right of the lowly man to his property:

> When a good donkey has been born to a royal soldier (?), and his foreman has said to him, "I will buy it from thee"—if he then lets him buy—he shall say: "Weigh out unto me silver as much as it pleasing to my heart." And if he does not let him buy, the foreman shall not molest him.

It is, of course, possible to suppose that Urukagina, by curbing the power of prominent people, was trying, not only to restore the temple communities to their original purity, but also to win the support of the common people for himself. In any case, factors outside his control interfered with his plans. He was attacked by the ruler of the neighboring city of Umma and destroyed.

The abuses Urukagina tried to abolish were, in essence, those which vitiate the realization of any political ideal. Weaknesses peculiar to Mesopotamia, however, became clear when serious attempts were made to establish a unified state comprising all the separate cities. This change was attempted by Sargon of Akkad and his successors. Sargon had been a high official under a king of Kish, and about 2340 B.C. he founded a city of his own, Akkad. He defeated Lugalzaggesi, the conqueror of Urukagina, and other city rulers who opposed him, until he was paramount throughout the country. Similar successes had been achieved before his time, but they had always been short-lived. And while Sargon's rise to power conformed entirely to the older pattern, a piecemeal subjection of other cities, he struck out a new course in consolidating his position. This time the state survived its founder for several generations. The novelty of his approach may be due to the fact that he represented a northern element in the Mesopotamian population which now became dominant for the first time. This is indicated by the inscriptions: royal inscriptions and many business documents began to be written in the Semitic language which is called Akkadian. This change, in particular, is responsible for the opinion held by some scholars that the rise of Sargon represents a foreign conquest; and it is true that the language points to the middle Euphrates and adjoining territories as its country of origin. But this region had been permeated by Mesopotamian culture for centuries, and people from that quarter cannot be called foreigners in the ordinary sense of the word. Already in Protoliterate times Sumerian civilization had moved northwards along the two rivers, as the Al Ubaid culture (probably also Sumerian) had done in prehistoric times. As Roman influence in barbaric Europe can be traced by means of coins, the influence of Protoliterate Mesopotamia throughout the ancient Near East can be traced by the distinctive cylinder seals of the period. They are found as far to the north as Troy, as far to the south as Upper Egypt, as far to the east as middle, or even north-east Persia. At Brak, on the Khabur in northern Syria, 500 miles north of Erech, has been discovered a temple built on the plan of those in the south, containing similar objects and decorated with cone mosaics. Later, in Early Dynastic times, Ishtar temples at Mari on the Euphrates and at Assur on the Tigris were equipped with statues of Sumerian style, representing men in Sumerian dress. Thus it is obvious that there existed along the two great rivers a cultural continuum within which people could move without creating a disturbance in the fabric of civi-

lization. And the change of language to which we have referred, points to a gradual but continuous drift of people towards the south, as if the cultural influences emanating from Sumer attracted those who had come under its spell. Evidence of this movement is contained in Early Dynastic inscriptions. The thoroughly Sumerianized people of Mari, who had adopted the Sumerian script, inscribed their statues in Akkadian. The same seems to have happened at Khafajah near Baghdad. At Kish, a little farther to the south, the population seems to have been bilingual.

These observations in the field of language are valuable pointers; there may have been other, intangible, differences between the northern and the southern elements in the population of Mesopotamia, differences which would distinguish two strains with distinct cultural traditions. And although the old view that the accession of Sargon of Akkad represents a foreign conquest is untenable, his reign truly marks a new beginning. In the arts a new spirit finds magnificent expression, and in statecraft an entirely new attempt is made to create a political unity which would comprise the city states but surpass their scope, and which had no precedent in the past. The house of Sargon appears as a succession of rulers consistently claiming kingship over the whole land; and it is possible that their political ideal was not unrelated with the fact that they were free, as their predecessors were not, from the traditional viewpoint which grasped political problems exclusively in terms of the city. For among most Semitic-speaking people kinship provides the supreme bond. It is possible that the Akkadian-speaking inhabitants of middle and northern Mesopotamia had always acknowledged loyalties which went beyond the city proper. In Sumer there is no sign of the existence of such loyalties, nor was there a political institution which over-arched the sovereignty of the separate cities. But of Sargon a chronicle reports: "He settled his palace folk for thirty-three miles and reigned over the people of all lands." The first part of this entry suggests that Sargon allotted parts of lands of temple communities to his own followers, thus overriding the age-old local basis of land rights. No conqueror could rely on the loyalty of the defeated cities, and it seems as if Sargon built up a personal following, perhaps exploiting kinship ties in the wide sense of tribal loyalty. Under his grandson Naramsin, governors of cities styled themselves "slave of the king."

Sargon also seems to have made a bid for the loyalty of the common people. This appears from a change in the formula for oaths. The name of the king could now be invoked alongside the gods. This had a definite practical significance: if an agreement thus sworn to was broken, or if perjury was committed, the king was involved and would make it his business to uphold the right of the injured party. This was of the utmost importance, for the judge had originally been merely an arbitrator, whose main task was the reconciliation or satisfying of both parties. He had had no power to enforce his decisions; and if a man without personal prestige did not have a powerful patron to "overshadow him," there was little chance of his finding satisfaction in court. The new oath formula put the king in the position of the patron of all who swore by his name; in practice he constituted a court of appeal for the whole land, independent of the cities—a step of the greatest importance in the development of Mesopotamian law and society. Another step towards unification of the country was the introduction of a uniform calendar. Hitherto each city had had its own, with its own month names and festivals. Finally, the existence of a single monarch, who styled himself "King of the Four Quarters of the World," served as a perpetual reminder of the unity of the state.

If pressure from the outside world could be relied upon to bring about national unity, Mesopotamia would no doubt have become a single state on the lines laid down by the kings of Akkad. For the country was at all times exposed to great dangers. Civilized and prosperous, but lacking natural boundaries, it tempted mountaineers and steppe dwellers with the possibilities of easy loot. Raids could be dealt with by the cities, but the large-scale invasions, which recurred every few centuries, required a strong central government, to be repelled. The safeguarding of the trade routes, too, went beyond the competence of individual cities, and one would expect them to have co-operated in a national effort. Indeed, we find an epic, "The King of Battle," which describes how Sargon of Akkad, at the request of Mesopotamian merchants trading in Anatolia, went there with an army to champion their cause. The story may well reflect an actual occurrence, for Sargon's grandson, Naramsin, built a strong castle at Brak on the Khabur, and the lumber used in its construction included not only poplar and plane, but also ash, elm, oak, and pine, which must have been imported. The Akkadian kings thus undertook a task which occupied all succeeding rulers of the land. Even in the first millennium, the annual sweep of the Assyrian army up into the mountains of Armenia and down towards the west was a sustained and systematic attempt to keep the mountaineers in check; for, with the unlimited possibilities of retreat into their remote valleys, it was impossible to subject them permanently. From Sargon of Akkad on, kings knew that it was necessary to maintain a unified and centralized state; it was necessary to dominate the borderlands sufficiently to meet aggression there; in short, imperialism was the only guarantee of peace.

One would expect to find the people rallying to the new order imposed by the Akkadian kings, especially since a feeling of national coherence did exist. The Sumerians had a phrase, "the black-headed people," to designate themselves as an ethnic unit; and the gods Enlil and Anu, among others, were worshipped throughout the land. But this feeling had never found expression in a political form; it remained without effect, it seems, on the country's history. The particularism of the cities was never overcome. At each new accession of a king in Akkad, the land rose in revolt. Far from rallying against the barbarians, the people attempted to revert to the local autonomy which had been the rule before the rise of Sargon. Similar conditions persisted throughout the country's history. For example, the discoveries at Tell Asmar (ancient Eshnunna) illustrate the prevalence of local over national considerations. The ruler of that city collaborated with the Amorites who ravaged the country after the fall of the Third Dynasty of Ur; the barbarians were tolerated, and perhaps even assisted in their attacks on neighboring towns, which were incorporated into the state of Eshnunna after the Amorites had looted them.

Under the Akkadian kings the tragic pattern of Mesopotamia's history became visible. About 2180 B.C. their dynasty collapsed under the onslaught of the Guti from the Zagros mountains. Combined invasions of Elamites and Amorites ended the empire of the Third Dynasty of Ur in 2025 B.C. The invasions of Hittites and Kassites ended the empire of Hammurabi's dynasty in 1595 B.C. The invasion of the Medes destroyed the Assyrian empire (611 B.C.). The attack of Cyrus the Persian ended Neo-Babylonian rule (539 B.C.).

The absence of safety and stability in the political field is entirely in keeping with the prevailing mood of the country. Mesopotamia achieved her triumphs in an atmosphere of deep disquiet. The spirit pervading her most important writings is one of disbelief in man's ability to achieve lasting happiness. Salvation might be experienced emotionally in the annual festivals of the gods, but was not a postulate of theology.

In Pakistan a rich alluvial valley, watered by the Indus and the Sarasvati, provided another extended area of natural irrigation, and, again, the environmental basis for a great civilization.

3. The Indus Valley [1]

The word "Chalcolithic" is a term which has been widely and not always very discriminately used by writers on Indian archaeology; applied alternatively to essentially stone-using communities to which copper or bronze are rare luxuries, or, less aptly, to copper- and bronze-using communities which retain a substantial though subordinate stone equipment. It may be accepted as an ugly utility-term; an alternative label, "Protometallic," is scarcely more elegant or exact.

Of the Chalcolithic phase in the Baluch hills and the Indus valley much has been

[1] R. E. M. WHEELER, "The Indus Civilization," in *Early India and Pakistan* (New York: 1959), pp. 93–117. Reprinted by permission of the author and the publishers, © 1959 by Frederick A. Praeger, Inc. and Thames and Hudson, Ltd.
Sir Richard is at the British Academy, London.

written in accessible form, and the barest summary must here suffice. In general terms, the situation is as follows, with the reminder that all dates prior to the latter half of the 3rd millennium (and many after it) are very insecure.

In the 4th and 3rd millennia, if not before, the sullen borderland where the Iranian plateau drops tumultuously to the Indus plain sheltered a hive of hidden tribal and village societies, appropriately cellular but sharing a common standard of living and technology. In their recondite valleys they were diversely reaching the cultural optimum which their rugged milieu permitted. Their pottery, modified from region to region and age to age, was by 3000 B.C. of good quality, wheel-turned and well-baked, often thin and attractively painted with geometrical or semirealistic motifs which betrayed both their own individuality and their cultural kinship with the societies of the great plateau behind them. They made stone implements amongst which simple chert blades predominated, and a little copper or bronze was beginning to come their way for use or ornament. Occasional contact between one community and another and with the outside world is manifest, but for the most part the tribes or regions, though not necessarily devoid of a nomadic element, were self-contained on the basis of the local crops which they learned to irrigate by the concentration of floodwater (with or without masonry dams), and the small flocks and herds which the children tended on the neighboring slopes. Further integration, whether political or cultural, was barred by environment.

Just so far, it may be claimed that the potential of these upland groups was not unlike that of early Greece, with its small hill-divided and independent states. There, however, the encompassing sea provided a sufficient measure of mutual contact to create, if not unity, at least an interterritorial sentiment of Greek civilization and nationhood as against the outer "barbarians" of alien speech and tradition. In the massif of Baluchistan, save at its southernmost end, this vitalizing link was missing. Instead, however, there lay along its flank the great plain of the Indus and its tributary or adjacent rivers, a plain at that time largely jungle-covered but serving, with its broad waterways, in some sense as an inland sea and as a passable means of lateral communication. Those two factors—the terminal ocean and the flanking plain—were together formative in the sudden emergence of the next cultural phase, that of the Indus Civilization, probably a little before 2500 B.C.

It is now widely familiar that, since 1921, there has been laid bare in and near the Indus valley some part of the most extensive civilization of the preclassical world. With metropolitan centers, each more than three miles in circumference, at Harappā in the Punjab and Mohenjo-daro in Sind, it stretched from Rūpar at the foot of the Simla hills to Sutkagen-dor near the shores of the Arabian Sea, a distance of 1,000 miles. But that is not all. Exploration during the past ten years has extended the reach of this vast civilization eastwards to Ukhlina, 19 miles west of Meerut in the Jumna basin, and southwards into Kāthiāwāḍ (Rangpur, Lothal, Somnāth, the Hālār district), and beyond, to the shore of the Gulf of Cambay near the estuaries of the Narbadā and the Tapti. There, 500 miles southeast of Mohenjo-daro, at three sites, Mehgam and Telod and Bhagertarar, potsherds of the Indus Civilization were found in 1957, and there for the present is the Civilization's southernmost limit. These southern extensions on or near the shores of the Arabian Sea have altered the shape of the Civilization as previously envisaged; they immensely enlarge the coastwise aspect of the problem of origins and contact, and in the new context these must be briefly reconsidered.

But first the principal characters of the Civilization may be recalled. Both at Harappā and, more clearly, at Mohenjo-daro excavation has revealed the general shape of the great cities in their prime and decadence. At the earliest period known to us, they were already rigorously planned in regular rectangular blocks, each measuring about 400 by 200 yards, divided from one another by broad main streets, and containing methodically drained lanes and buildings. So far as present evidence goes, they possessed no general system of urban fortification, though there is the possibility that at Mohenjo-daro an ancient embankment designed to restrain the Indus floods may be of this period. The recent report that Lothal in Kāthiāwāḍ, a similarly regimented coastal township of the same Civilization, had been protected after a flood-disaster by an embankment upwards of eight feet high is incorrect. On the other hand, both Harappā and Mohenjo-daro were dominated by an embattled acropolis or citadel, occupying a marginal block and built up with mud and mudbrick to a height of forty or fifty feet above the featureless plain with a revetment of baked brick. Upon this acropolis were ritual buildings and places of assembly. That at Mohenjo-daro also carried the State Granary, which must have been the economic focus of the régime; at Harappā, less known to us, equivalent or supplementary granaries were marshalled on the lower ground between the acropolis and the river. From its acropolis we may suppose that each city was regarded by rulers who may on general probability have had priestly attributes but, as their well-ordered towns and evolved dwellings imply, were essentially secular in outlook; sufficiently benevolent or far-sighted, at the least, to nurture an uncommonly high general standard of living, and at the same time sufficiently authoritative to ensure that this general standard was long maintained. In this sense the contrast with Pharaonic Egypt, where, under a totalitarian god-bound administration, civic life in any liberal usage of the phrase scarcely existed, is manifest. To the nearer analogy of Mesopotamia we shall turn in a moment.

What wider function the two outstanding cities fulfilled is more speculative. They are 400 miles apart, and between them, opposite the Sulaiman Range and the Bugti Country, the Indus valley is constricted, so that each city may be said to dominate a partially defined and unitary province. The overriding facts remain, however, that they are situated upon the same river-system, and are culturally identical. That identity extends throughout the immense territory— nearly half a million square miles— wherein the Indus Civilization has now been recognized. It is tempting to infer something like an imperial status for so uniform a civilization, perhaps with the metropolitan duality which was later to mark the Kushān, Arab, and Mogul régimes in northern India and seems indeed to be endemic in that spacious land. If at any rate the underlying inference is correct, as it may be, then the Indus Civilization exemplifies the vastest political experiment before the advent of the Roman Empire.

But whatever the political implications, the cultural unity of the Civilization is itself a sufficiently imposing phenomenon, and the problem of its origins, as of its ultimate fate, commands attention.

How far was the Indus Civilization a product of the *genius loci?* How far, if at all, was it indebted to outside influence? One's thoughts, encouraged by the new coastal bias of the Indus distribution, turn naturally to Mesopotamia as a source. Certainly Mesopotamian civilization was a going concern several centuries before the earliest date to which we can ascribe that of the Indus. Certainly, too, there is much in what we know of the Mesopotamian urban way of life that matches our Indus evidence: the suggestion of middle-class well-being, of effective civic consciousness, to which the Mesopotamian records give a definition that is absent from the Indus evidence. The indication is that the citizen in the streets of Mohenjo-daro must have had much the same sort of interests as his contemporaries in the streets of Sumerian Ur. Of the two cities, indeed, Mohenjo-daro with its admirable public sanitation and its comprehensive planning suggests an even more evolved civic intelligence. True, we cannot there point to an artistry that might rival the elaborate polychromy of the Mesopotamian temples or the dramatic extravagance of Sir Leonard Woolley's "Royal Tombs." But then we have as yet found nowhere in the Indus valley the corresponding tombs of the ruling class, and cannot guess what awaits us when chance shall deliver them to us, if, as may be suspected, they somewhere exist. Nor can we guess the quality of the vanished Indus woodwork, though the skill of later Indian wood-carvers suffices to remind us of the possible magnitude of our loss. We can find some consolation in the superb carving of miniature animal forms on the famous steatite seals of the Indus, and reflect that to these at least Mesopotamia can offer no native equivalent.

In brief, analogies between the two civilizations are of a general kind and cannot be pushed into detail. Even general analogy fails in an important respect if the inferred political unity of the Indus Civilization approximates to fact, as against the basic trend in Mesopotamia towards nucleation in city-states; though even here, in the 24th century B.C., when commercial contacts show that the Indus Civilization was in its prime, an imperialistic régime had emerged in Akkad and may have influenced, or even been

influenced by, contemporary political development on the Indus. But if we stick to material evidence the differences are emphatic enough. Neither in its ceramic industry nor in its tools and armory does the Indus Civilization suggest a remotely foreign origin. Its pottery, though specifically individual, is as generically akin to that of some of the village communities in or below the Baluch hills as to that of Sumer. The thin, rather feeble knives and spears and the flat axes, of copper or bronze poor in tin, run counter to the types prevailing in Iran or Mesopotamia. The unread Indus script is unlike any other in the ancient world. The baked bricks of which the two largest and several of the smaller Indus towns were mostly built (doubtless in response to a relatively rainy climate), though not without precedent in early Mesopotamia, are exceptional there. The normal Mesopotamian building material was unbaked brick or plain mud.

Now this last consideration does in fact raise an interesting issue at Mohenjo-daro. The two earliest buildings at present known on the acropolis, the State Granary and the first of a succession of peripheral towers near the southeast corner, are built of baked brick but were reinforced superficially and internally with timbers in a mode natural to mud-brick structures, but alien to baked-brick construction. Inevitably in the Indus climate these timbers quickly decayed, causing local collapses of the brickwork and necessitating brick reinforcement. The lesson was learned and the experiment was not (so far as we know) repeated; but its occurrence in the early phase suggests that the master-builder concerned had been a foreigner accustomed to methods appropriate to a drier climate and inexperienced in Indus conditions. Here if anywhere we have a hint of direct intrusion from abroad. Of its wider implication, if any, nothing can be affirmed without much further excavation.

If, apart from this reservation, we now review the comparison between the two civilizations as a whole, it is fair to recognize a general affinity with recurring and important differences in detail which are at least sufficient to set aside any likelihood of immediate or wholesale colonization of the Indus region from Sumer. For the physical structure of the Indus Civilization we must look to more local sources and causes. But that is not to rob Mesopotamia of a close responsibility in the matter. Mesopotamia, and none other, retains her world-priority, not to the "invention" of town-life (in which at present Jericho in Jordan is far in the lead), but to the production of a mature and literate civilization, with organized accounts and archives: in other words, to the essential *idea* of civilization. Thanks to Mesopotamia, by the end of the 4th millennium the *idea* of civilization was in the air of the Middle East; and, as I have remarked before, ideas have wings. Archaeology, in its proper pursuit of material evidence, is liable to understress the intangibles which may have been, and in some circumstances certainly were, the true agents of diffusion, penetrating more surely and significantly than pence and potsherds. So from Mesopotamia, by easy land-routes, the idea of civilization penetrated shortly to Egypt, where the ideas of writing and of certain architectural modes were adopted and adapted in a local idiom. From Mesopotamia, we may be sure, the mature idea of civilization, always including that of writing, later reached the Indian coast and the Indus valley by an easy sea-route and perhaps by land, to be adapted there to local taste and circumstance. The alternative postulate, that in each of three lands so accessible to one another the immensely complex idea of an evolved civilization should, within the narrow space of some five or six centuries, have emerged spontaneously and without cross-reference, is too absurd to merit argument.

In this connection it is no doubt significant that the later (19th century B.C.) town-plan of Ur, mostly laid out in orderly rectilinear fashion, incorporated devious and casual main streets, obvious survivals from an amorphous small-town beginning, just as in New York the ancient suburban Broadway trundles carelessly across the modern grid-plan. In other words, Ur evolved from 4th-millennium village to 3rd-millennium city, learning as it went; whereas the later foundation, Mohenjo-daro, came into being (as it seems) in full awareness of the evolved civil idea—an idea which it can only have received from an adult Mesopotamia.

But it stands equally to reason that an idea can only take root in prepared and congenial soil. By the middle of the 3rd millennium, something very important was happening in the Indus valley, and happening probably at great speed. Then or rather earlier, certain of the little communities in the Baluch foothills were emboldened to experiment. Who the first leaders were who led their people, however hesitantly, down to the wide and jungle-ridden plain we shall never know, nor why they ventured; but they were bold men, pioneers in the fullest sense, no mere ejects from the highland zone. Some, perhaps many of them, led forlorn hopes and perished. Imperfect though our knowledge be, we know enough to recognize here and there on the Indus plain the débris of villages or small towns which antedate the full-blown civilization and were superseded by it. For example, at Kot Diji, fifteen miles south of Khairpur and twenty-five miles east of Mohenjo-daro, excavation in 1955–7 revealed a town of pre-Indus date with a strongly walled citadel armed with rectangular towers of stone and mud brick. About 2400 B.C. (the central figure, as Dr. F. A. Khan tells me, of a C 14 dating by the University of Pennsylvania of some of the latest pre-Indus material) this town was covered with a burnt deposit upon which was built an unfortified settlement of Indus Civilization type. The pottery of the pre-Indus town was partially comparable with that found under the Harappā fortifications in 1946, but already included, by borrowing or anticipation, some Harappān elements.

Seemingly the attempted colonization of the valley continued intermittently, failure succeeding failure, until at last a leader, more determined and far-sighted and fortunate than the rest, won through. To appreciate his qualities and those of his associates and successors, it is necessary to glance a little more closely at his problems.

Amongst the favorable factors confronting him was, of course, the great river-system itself, flanked by wide expanses of fertile alluvium which was renewed by the annual flood. Its broad jungles and intermittent marshes were indeed infested with elephant, tiger, buffalo, rhinoceros, and crocodile, familiar to us from their exquisite representations on the Indus seals. But the rivers themselves were full of fish that are still the livelihood of whole floating villages and were both netted and hooked by the Indus people, in whose script they became one of the most recurrent symbols. Those same rivers were arterial routes to the sea and the Persian Gulf on the one hand and to the timber-producing Himālayas on the other. Along them, and along the trackways which would shortly flank and feed them, metals and gemstones foreign to their alluvium could be brought by long-range traffic. And by the same token intellectual interchange, a currency in ideas, now became feasible with unprecedented ease and scope. In contrast to the upland valley with its scanty soil, uncertain water-supply, and close horizon, the prospect was a spacious one indeed.

But there was a debit side to this account. The annual snow-melt flood fertilizes but, unrestrained, is also an angry destroyer. The extensive irrigation demanded by a large city of the plain involves tireless planning and coordination, and readily succumbs to indifferent control. Fevers are endemic to marsh and jungle. The arterial waterways which may carry trade may equally carry invasion. The benefits offered on so formidable a scale by an environment at the same time so vast, so exuberant, and so menacing are dependent, and *dependent from the outset,* upon the power of man to master and constrain. The situation was one which can have brooked no pusillanimity, no piecemeal compromise. A society strong in heart, disciplined, numerous and imaginatively led grasped the problem and, we may be sure, simultaneously solved it; else it had perished. Here if anywhere may we fairly discern in human affairs an example of that swift adaptation and progression which biologists know as "explosive."

From this explosively successful beginning, from the lightning subugation of the huge valley and the adjacent coast, the Indus citizens seem to have drawn the penalty of early success: a complacency, even a self-satisfaction, which impeded further effort. Our admittedly incomplete knowledge does not suggest any trend towards new social or aesthetic horizons. The Indus Civilization settled down for perhaps a thousand years to the exploitation of its environment with an equanimity disturbed only by unceasing struggle with its essential but implacable rivers. With the aid of some sort of irrigation system, which is now deeply buried by post-Indus aggradation but may, in principle, be assumed, it grew food-crops and cotton; it kept considerable herds; and, as a scatter of Indus seals and other trifles in the Mesopotamian cities shows, it traded with its neighbors of the Persian Gulf from the 800 miles of coastline which we must now allot to it. And here it may be that certain cuneiform texts of Old Babylonia help to fill out the picture.

Inscribed clay tablets from the city of Ur, which served as the principal port of entry into Mesopotamia in the time of the Dynasty of Larsa (c. 1950 B.C.), show that sailors returning at that time from Telmun or Dilmun—that is, with little doubt, the island of Bahrain in the Persian Gulf—offered a share of their cargoes at the temple of the goddess Ningal. Gold, silver, much copper, lapis lazuli in lumps, stone beads, ivory combs and ornaments and inlays, eye-paint, certain kinds of wood, and perhaps pearl ("fish-eyes") are mentioned. But in this period Telmun was merely an intermediate market at which the Ur shippers bartered their stocks for goods brought to the island from "Makkan" and "Meluhha," two places of which the identity is conjectural. This practice had not always prevailed. In the time of Sargon of Akkad (c. 2350 B.C.) we hear of ships from or destined for Meluhha, Makkan, and Telmun as moored in the harbor outside the capital. Some at least of the trade with these places was then direct, using Telmun doubtless for revictualing purposes rather than as a commercial intermediary. Later, under the 3rd Dynasty of Ur (c. 2100 B.C.), we find that trade was still sustained with Makkan and Telmun, but that Meluhha was now out of direct reach, although copper, stone, wood, ivory objects, and certain breeds of animals were still somehow obtained from there. Later again, under the Dynasty of Larsa, Telmun monopolizes the role of middleman; and sometime between the fall of the Larsa Dynasty and the decline of the Hammurabi Dynasty (c. 1700 B.C.) Telmun lost contact with

the mining centers of Makkan and its ancillary sources. The implication of this record of dwindling trade is that Telmun, Makkan, and Meluhha lay at successively greater distances from Mesopotamia; and if to this inference be added the association of the ultimate Meluhha with ivory, wood, and copper, its identification with the Indus Civilization (with its forests and elephants and its sources of copper in Rājasthān) becomes probable. It matches, too, with the archaeological evidence. Ivory working was an Indus craft; one of the victims of the last massacre at Mohenjo-daro, for instance, was attempting to carry away an elephant's tusk when he was cut down. And the main stream of Indus relics recovered from identified strata in the Mesopotamian cities dates from the Sargonid period of direct contact with Meluhha, with a diminishing trickle into the Larsa period of indirect contact. With that maritime enterprise which characterized ancient Indian trade in many ages, we may imagine cargoes of woods and metals and ivory—and why not also apes and peacocks, both familiar to the Indus artist?—setting sail from the Indus ports in the heyday of the Civilization; and in the sequel, with the long-drawn-out decline which, as will be seen, is evident in later civic standards, it is easy to visualize a corresponding decline in the scope and volume of overseas traffic. Inference from the records and the material evidence are at one.

Consistent too are the results of the excavations recently carried out by Dr. P. V. Glob's Danish expedition on the island of Telmun or Bahrain itself. The principal ancient settlement on Bahrain was at the northern end of the island, at Ras al Qala'a, where particularly good springs are available. The excavations there exhibit a town of the competent but rather crude kind which might be expected from its function merely as a mart and servicing-station. A few links with Mesopotamia and with the Indus have been identified, notably circular steatite seals with grooved and pierced bosses at the back, variants of an Indus pattern. Since only five of these seals have been found in fairly extensive excavation at Bahrain, they are perhaps unlikely to be local. They bear animal and other designs—short-horned bull with head twisted slightly to one side, a square grid, a manger (?)—reminiscent of Indus seal-motifs but not identical with normal mid-Indus types, amongst which the circular seal is itself exceptional. They approximate more nearly to circular steatite seals found occasionally at Ur and elsewhere in Mesopotamia: there the general type is equally alien and intrusive, and since five or more of the seals bear the distinctively Indus script there is no doubt as to the origin of some of their users. Thus as a whole the Ur-Bahrain series can be ascribed neither to the great inland cities of the Indus, such as Mohenjo-daro, nor yet to Sumerian invention. Rather must we associate them in some more general fashion with the coastal entrepôts which we are beginning to identify between the Gulf of Cambay and the head of the Persian Gulf. To distinguish them from the Indus seals proper, as we know them, I propose to name them the "Persian Gulf seals."

How did the Indus Civilization end? Certainly, at the center it declined and fell, as has already been hinted, though how universal its decline and how precipitous its fall cannot at present be affirmed in general terms. It is to be anticipated that so far-flung a society decayed differentially and found death or reincarnation in varying forms from region to region. But at Mohenjo-daro at least the picture is clear enough: decline was long-drawn-out and progressive, the final fall catastrophic.

First, the decline. Everywhere in the later levels of Mohenjo-daro the excavators have found an increasing deterioration in standards of building and living. Walling and flooring tended to become more ramshackle, older buildings were subdivided, even domestic courtyards, the focus of the household, were partitioned in untidy fashion. And that this process was prolonged may be illustrated by a single example. Adjoining the northern end of the Great Granary on the side of the acropolis, the main building-level is over twenty feet below the present level of the plain, and a dozen feet below the present dry-weather water-table. In digging down to it in 1950, I passed through a continuous succession of buildings, all subsequent to the construction of the acropolis-mound and the immense brick podium of the flanking granary. The lower buildings, so far as explored, were still of tolerably good build but the upper walls, enclosing small rooms, were of increasingly shoddy aspect. The highest of them, founded upon a mass of débris, were right at the top of the podium, at least forty feet above the lowest established level of the mound. Interpreted in terms of time, this vast accumulation must be supposed to represent the lapse of several centuries.

In any interpretation of this process, however, two considerations are important. The first is the annual impact of the Indus flood which raises the flooded area and simultaneously raises the water-table. Today, the Mohenjo-daro landscape is only preserved from disastrous inundation by large annual expenditure on a series of protective banks or bunds. So, no doubt, from the outset considerable engineering was already needed when the new city rose upon its far lower flood-plain. Even so, the swollen river broke through from time to time; its alluvium has been identified at intervals in deep sections, and houses were raised to safer heights, sometimes with the help of mud-brick platforms. Any relaxation in the supervision of the bunds, any accidental weakness in their structure, any exceptional volume in the spring torrent, must have been immediately fatal. And a population harassed by this recurring enemy may well have tired a little, as human societies under continuous stress are apt to do. A convergence of causes may be thought to have induced an increasingly rapid decline.

The other factor is this. Millions of well-baked bricks went to the building and rebuilding of Mohenjo-daro. Millions of tons of firewood went to the baking of them. With all allowance for the arrival of floating timber from the upper reaches, this implies a widespread deforestation of the surrounding region. This in turn, though partially compensated by growing crops, must have checked the transpiration of moisture and reduced the rainfall. If at the same time energy and discipline were flagging, and irrigation-channels and bunds inadequately maintained, the total deterioration must have been appreciable. Desert was encroaching on the sown. In rough terms, Mohenjo-daro was *wearing out its landscape,* whether by excessive zeal or by excessive indolence. Over the years it was dying long before the final blow.

That final blow has often enough been described. It is represented by groups of skeletons—men, women, and children, some bearing axe- or sword-cuts—which have been found lying on the topmost level in the sprawled or contorted positions in which they fell. They had been left there by raiders who had no further use for the city which they had stormed. In that moment Mohenjo-daro was dead.

Now what is the historical meaning of all this? We do not know but I have made a guess. The Indus Civilization is commonly and, I think, rightly regarded as non-Aryan in character. There is some material evidence that it was still in action within the first half of the 2nd millennium B.C.; and it is widely accepted that somewhere about the middle of that millennium occurred the Aryan invasion which is reflected in the earliest literature of India, the hymns of the *Rigveda.* In these hymns the invasion constantly assumes the form of an onslaught upon the walled cities of the aborigines, and the only fortifications of approximate date known to us are those of the citadels of Harappā and Mohenjo-daro and at certain of the smaller contemporary towns. It is tempting to relate the two circumstances to one another and to recognize in the destroyers of Mohenjo-daro, indifferent to the city which they had sacked, some of these heroic but barbarian nomads, to whom city-life was alien. It is not indeed impossible that the name of Harappā itself is concealed in the Hari-Yūpīyā which is mentioned in the *Rigveda* as the scene of a battle. But at present these thoughts are no more than conjectures; picturesque, perhaps probable, but not proven. It must not be forgotten that Mohenjo-daro is the only place where clear material evidence of final massacre is at present forthcoming.

What was the immediate sequel to the Indus Civilization? North Indian history first assumes definition in the time of the Buddha, about 500 B.C. If we infer provisionally that in the central Indus region the Civilization ended within a century or so of 1500 B.C., there remain a thousand years with no surer written content than that provided by the great Indian epics, which have reached us as a romantic amalgam of many ages. Happily, however, Indian archaeologists have recently been at work upon this Dark Age both in the north and in the west, and dawn is on the horizon.

In due course we shall encounter in the northern plains an Indian Bronze Age ceramic of cardinal importance known as the Painted Grey Ware, a highly distinctive fabric to which the schematic dates 1000–500 B.C. have been provisionally given, though 800–500 B.C. would be safer. This ware has been found on a number of sites (notably Rupar) which have also produced Indus valley relics, and in every case the Grey Ware overlay the Indus material with a clear intervening gap. Here in the north, therefore, we are left with the period 1500–1000 or 800 B.C. (more or less) to fill, and, as the task is still actively in hand, no detailed discussion is appropriate to the present review.

Briefly, the present position is this. On a number of Indus sites, superimposed vestiges of later cultures have been observed. At Harappā itself remains of jerry-built houses of reused brick have been found built into the débris overlying the Indus city, and the intruders buried their dead in alien fashions and in or with good but largely alien pottery, in a cemetery known to archaeology as "Cemetery H." This Cemetery H culture has at present been identified on only two other sites (in Bahāwalpur), and little is known of it save that it would appear to have postdated the Indus Civilization by an appreciable interval. Again at Chanhu-daro, some eighty miles south of Mohenjo-daro, a shoddy late Indus phase was succeeded by a squatter-culture of lower grade, named the "Jhukar" culture from another site in Sind. The Jhukar squatters made coarser pottery than their Indus predecessors, and used round button-seals, commonly bearing radiate or compartmental patterns reminiscent of 2nd-millennium types in northern Iran and the Caucasus. There would appear to have been an approximation of age between the end of the Indus Civilization here and the arrival of the squatters, though actual continuity is not implied. After an interval, more squatters (the "Jhangar" people) replaced the Jhukars. The whole succession is undated and leaves us little wiser, but is sufficient to show a continuing cultural deterioration

in this region after the end of the Civilization, and to suggest recurrent links with Iran and the Caucasus. This suggestion may be sustained into the latter part of the 2nd millennium by burial cairns at Moghul Ghundai in the Zhob valley of northern Baluchistan, from which a tripod jar, horse-bells, rings, and bangles have been thought to recall similar objects from "Cemetery B" at Sialk in central Iran, dated to 1000 B.C. or thereabouts. On the other hand, there is some evidence that these cairns may in fact be appreciably later. Again, to the bracket 1200–1000 B.C. and to a western origin Heine-Geldern would ascribe both the celebrated bronze dagger of about the 12th century B.C. found at Fort Munro in the Sulaiman Range west of the Indus, and a copper trunnion-axe from the Kurram valley on the Afghan border. These and other scattered objects, of indubitably western (Iranian or Caucasian) type but often of disputed date, are at least sufficient to suggest infiltration into northwestern India in the centuries closely following the end of the Indus Civilization, and may be associated by the temerarious with the Aryan movement from Iran and Afghanistan in the Punjab. But proof is distant.

If, however, it is clear enough that sporadic destruction and low-grade replacement marked the end of the Indus Civilization in its central region, it does not follow that the same fate attended the more southerly cities in Kāthiāwād, which probably lay beyond the Aryan impact. The evidence there is indeed of a contrary kind. Thus at Rangpur excavation revealed a basic microlithic industry without pottery, succeeded by a Chalcolithic culture containing Indus Civilization elements, which was in turn followed by a culture described as "late Chalcolithic" with red and buff pottery suggesting an organic development from the previous phase. The late phase also contained, in its top level, sherds of Black-and-red Ware which had "a technical similarity with the 'megalithic' pottery of southern India." This Black-and-red Ware, of which more will be said, is not normally earlier than 1000 b.c. and is often much later; but it certainly occurs, in small quantities, with late Indus valley material at Lothal, which is only thirty miles northeast of Rangpur, and a similar association has now been observed at Rosadi in mid-Kāthiā-wād. It is becoming increasingly clear that the more southerly towns of the Indus Civilization endured for an appreciable time after the fall of Mohenjo-daro, and that the general similarity of the early Black-and-red sherds of Rangpur and Lothal to the pottery of the southern megaliths of a later age is specific and significant. Meanwhile, the important conclusion is that here, in Kāthiāwād, the Indus culture was not obliterated but was transmuted into successor-cul-

tures which adapted Indus ceramic forms and evolved eventually, with other wares, a fine lustrous red pottery painted sometimes with schematized caprids in the old Chalcolithic tradition.

For the rest, it will suffice to add that the distinctive Painted Grey Ware, which in the north marks the lower bracket of our Dark Age (1000 b.c. or somewhat later), was preceded at Hastināpura in the upper Ganges valley by a settlement which used crude ochre-colored pottery and copper implements. An interval elapsed between the two occupations, so that the ochre pottery should carry us back well into the hiatus there. Again, this is at present merely a pointer without substantive value; but in one way and another, and particularly in the western coastlands, Indian archaeology is beginning to close in upon its Dark Age from both ends, and the gap may well have vanished by the time that these words appear in print.

As the Neolithic came to an end in the Far East many of the characteristics of classic Chinese culture were taking shape. There, in the valley of the Huangho, Shang civilization was first to arise.

4. Shang China [1]

In the later part of their development, some of the Proto-Chinese villages grew into towns and cities with industries of every description. The bronze age remains of the Shang people have always been found associated with the Grey Pottery, so it is stratigraphically clear that the Shang Chinese stemmed directly from the Grey Pottery culture. The Shang capitals at An-yang and Chêng-chou were built over Grey Pottery sites which were previously occupied by the Yang-shao Red Pottery and the Lung-

shan Black Pottery peoples at separate intervals.

The region that covers the provinces of Honan, Hopei, Shansi and Shensi was known in Chinese history as Chung-yuan or the Central Plain. It is the border of the loess highland and the flood plain of Huangho. The course of events in history indicates that it was the center of Chinese life and that any rising power which had the advantage of controlling it would eventually become the ruler of the whole of China. The same situa-

[1] CHENG TE-K'UN, from *Archaeology in China* (Toronto: 1960), pp. 242–249. Reprinted by permission of the author and the publisher, © 1960 by the University of Toronto Press.
Dr. Cheng is Lecturer in Far Eastern Art and Archaeology at Cambridge University.

tion may also be found in the prehistoric period. It is archaeologically clear that the expansion of the four Neolithic cultures, Gobi, Yang-shao, Lung-shan and Hsiao-t'un, tended to concentrate in this area, where their struggle for supremacy was most intense. As a result of their rivalry and co-existence, the archaeological sites in the area occur in a wide variety of combinations, some in successive stages while others are complicated mixtures.

The mixing of these cultures may also be noticed elsewhere in practically every province in China. To the north of the Great Wall many sites have been found with the mixing of the Gobi and the Huangho cultures. They occur always in mixed forms, some dominated by the Yang-shao, others by the Lung-shan, a great majority by the Hsiao-t'un elements, many of which are associated with bronze objects and are definitely historical in date. The same situation has also been found in the Yangtse basin and in south China. Most of the southern sites present only the Huangho Neolithic elements in various stages of advance and in various degrees of combination with other cultures and are also mostly historical in date. In view of the fact that many of the Shang traits had their roots deeply embedded in the Neolithic past and that the Shang culture was surrounded and supported by a sea of Neolithic survivals, there seems to be no reason to doubt that the rise of the Shang culture was a logical outcome of the mixing of these Neolithic cultures. The process could only have happened in a region like the Central Plain where the cultural mixing took place.

The physical characteristics of the Shang Chinese are similar to those of the Proto-Chinese. There was, however, an evident increase of the brachycephalic elements in the composition of the Shang population as compared with the inhabitants of the prehistoric period. But this must not be taken as an indication of any fundamental change in the ethnical composition of the Shang population. The limited number of measurements and traits chosen for comparison scarcely justifies any basic conclusion of this kind. There may have been some mixing of physical types, but the majority of the Shang Chinese were essentially Mongoloid, just as the inhabitants of north China in the prehistoric period had been, and as the Chinese of historical times are. It is a well-known theory that the shovel-shaped upper incisors form a physical trait distinctly mongolian in character. The almost universal presence of such a particular morphological feature among the Hou-chia-chuang skulls is sufficient to prove the racial affinity of the Shang Chinese to the Mongoloid race.

Since the fundamental stratum on which Shang culture was built was deeply rooted in the prehistoric past, a number of the Proto and Early Shang settlements were merely those of the Hsiao-t'un culture which existed side by side with the Gobi, the Yang-shao and the Lung-shan cultures. The beginning of the Shang may therefore safely be placed in the prehistoric period shortly after 2500 B.C. The stratigraphy revealed by various sites allows us to recognize at least five successive levels in the culture. They may be taken as five stages of development, namely, Proto, Early, Middle, Late and Post Shang.

The absolute dating of these five stages is still open for research. As already described at an earlier point, Tung Tsopin follows the traditional dating with some slight adjustments based on his study of the oracle records, believing that the dynastic Shang began in 1751 B.C., that the date for the moving of the capital to An-yang during the reign of P'an-kêng was 1384, and that the fall of the dynasty occurred in 1111. These figures give a total of 640 years for the duration of the dynasty. The fall of the capital at An-yang did not mean the disappearance of the Shang culture. In fact the Shang people continued to live under the Chou dynasty and kept their own identity for a long time afterwards. A period of about a century should be allowed for the continuation of the Shang culture after the fall of its political power. It seems reasonable therefore to suggest that the Shang culture was in existence approximately from 2500–1000 B.C. The proposed dating of the five stages is roughly as follows—

1. Proto Shang—Neolithic—2500–2100.

2. Early Shang—pre-dynastic—2100–1750.

3. Middle Shang—early dynastic—1750–1400.

4. Late Shang—later dynastic—1400–1100.

5. Post Shang—transitional Shang-Chou—1100–1000 B.C.

The Shang excavations prove that in the early years of its development the Shang culture did not show any fundamental difference from the other Neolithic cultures of the Huangho basin, but in the Early and Middle Shang times new features began to appear and develop, reaching their climax in the Late Shang times. The progress was noticeable in practically every aspect of their life, covering not only the material culture and social organization but also their religious, intellectual and artistic activities. A large number of new cultural traits have been described in detail in the course of the present volume. Ten of these may be picked out for special attention—

(A. Material culture—)

1. Development in the ceramic industry.

2. Development in carving.

3. Development in bronze casting.

4. Use of chariots.

5. Development of architecture and chamber burials.

(B. Social organization—)

6. Development of the feudal system.

7. Development of ancestral worship.

(C. Intellectual and artistic activities—)

8. Development of the calendar.

9. Development of the animal style.

10. Development of writing.

As far as our present knowledge goes all of these ten traits are features in which Shang culture made marked progress in advance of the four Neolithic cultures that flourished before.

There is no doubt that the greater part of the Shang ceramic wares was made in the Neolithic fashion. The Shang potter was aware of the existence of the Red and Painted Yang-shao and the Black Lung-shan wares. But while following their ways, the Shang industry experimented with some inventions of its own. Grey Stoneware which was sometimes covered with an extra coating of glaze appeared for the first time in Early Shang and continued in vogue throughout the rest of the dynasty. The White Pottery which was made of kaolin clay was first introduced in Middle Shang and its manufacture reached its height in the Late Shang period. There was a distinct change in both the style and the method of production of the more refined articles. We may safely conclude that the Shang potter was responsible for two major ceramic developments, the use of glaze and kaolin clay which set the industry on the right track and destined it to be one of the most famous Chinese contributions to art.

Carving had its beginning also in the Neolithic period when some of the basic techniques were already known. Most of the artifacts of the Proto and Early Shang periods, and a large number of those of the Middle Shang period are simple and clearly made in the Neolithic tradition; but in the Middle Shang period further development took place, the chief cause of which seems to have been the introduction of new techniques, notably the use of rotating apparatus. Many artifacts were then carved with a rotary wheel or drill. Carving reached its highest level in the Late Shang period, when bone, horn, shell, stone and jade carvings were abundantly produced. The techniques were followed and improved upon in the Chou period and the art continued to be a major means of expression throughout the Chinese history. Such is the craftsmanship of the Chinese that the carving of jade has almost become a symbol of Chinese culture.

Working in metal was a new discovery of the Shang Chinese. Articles made of almost pure metal, like copper, lead and gold have been found. Bronze articles made their first appearance, however, in the Early Shang levels. In the beginning the bronze technique was primitive and the finished products were crude and flimsy. Archaeological evidence shows that there was a gradual development not only in the use of the apparatus and the making of the alloy but also in the shapes of the objects and in the decorative patterns. This industry too reached its height in the Late Shang period, when many complicated objects, some imitating the carved woodwork, were produced. The bronze art was an unique achievement of the Shang Chinese, since wine vessels in the shapes of the *chueh, chio, chia, ku* and *chih,* and cooking vessels such as the *ting, li* and *hsien* tripods are all unique forms. The decorative patterns of these bronzes are always unmistakably Shang in composition and in spirit. Many of these continued in use and were further developed in the Chou and later dynasties.

The same sequence of invention, use and improvement was true of the evolution of military weapons. The development of the *ko* dagger-axe furnishes a good example, lasting more than a thousand years from the Shang period, through the long Chou dynasty, down to the third century B.C. The weapon finally merged with the spear-head and developed into the *chi* halberd, a characteristic weapon of the Han period. Li Chi traced the evolution of this particular fighting weapon and found that the *ko* of the Shang period was typologically the simplest, with a crude hafting technique, a blunt posterior part and no necking at all. The first development of the *hu* necking took place in the early Chou times and it gradually lengthened till it finally reached the standard type as recorded in the *K'ao kung chi,* which may be dated from the fourth to the third centuries B.C. Li is convinced that the morphological development of the *ko* throughout the Shang and Chou times indicates a systematic endeavor to improve the weapon through trial and error and a firm effort to achieve perfection. The weapon was thus invented by the Shang people and continuously developed by the Chou people without any interruption. The typological evolution of this weapon serves to link the Shang and the Chou culture together on a common foundation, which had never been so clear before the excavations.

The continuation of Shang industrial art into the Chou period may again be illustrated by reference to the bronzes and jades produced in the Post Shang period. It is well known that without adequate archaeological data it is most difficult to draw a line between the bronzes and jades of the Late Shang and the Early Chou periods. Nothing illustrates better the essential continuity of the arts of these two periods than this difficulty experienced by connoisseurs. In fact with the exception of a few inscriptions there are hardly any criteria to distinguish the bronzes and jades of the Shang period from those of the Chou period between 1100 and 1000 B.C. Most of the Shang artisans continued to supply the remaining Shang nobility and the new rulers with their wares. The style of art began to change gradually about 1000 B.C.

The fauna of the Yang-shao remains had consisted of pigs, dogs and cattle; neither sheep nor horses were found. In the Lung-shan culture the list of animal bones had included those of pigs, dogs, sheep, oxen and horses. In both cases deer were also found, but on the whole bones of wild animals had been rare in the Neolithic sites. This indicates a quiet life devoted entirely to agriculture and the keeping of a few domesticated animals. If there had been any game hunting it was limited to the hunting of a few deer. But the faunistic assemblage of the Shang culture, especially towards the later periods, is much more remarkable; the whole list of the mammalian collection being no fewer than twenty-nine in number. In the Middle Shang period we notice an increased use of the horse not only for riding but also for pulling chariots. The Late Shang chariot was drawn by either two or four horses in a team. The number gradually increased and in an early Chou tomb, twelve chariots were found together with seventy-two horses, which means an average of six in a team. It is well known that King Mu in the eleventh century B.C. used a chariot in his western expedition which enjoyed a team of eight selected horses. The Chinese chariot was invented by the Shang people and it continued to be improved upon in the Chou period. Towards the end of the Chou dynasty the power of a feudal state was counted by the number of war chariots which it possessed.

The development of architecture and of the structure of burial chambers also shows a steady improvement in the Shang period. In the beginning the people lived in underground dwellings in the Neolithic fashion, but in the Early Shang period we notice a gradual development until large ancestral temples and palaces were constructed according to prepared plans. Drainage systems and the careful preparation of the foundations with the *hang-t'u* technique came into use.

The same may be said of the burial chamber. In the early days, most of the tombs were small and simple, but gradually the burial pit with a *yao-k'êng* and tomb passages was introduced. It became larger and more and more elaborate until it reached its climax in the royal burials of Hou-chia-chuang and Wu-kuan-ts'un. These set the style for the burial of royal personages in later dynasties.

The Shang political and social organization was based primarily on the emergence of two social institutions, ancestral worship and the feudal system. We have no way of knowing how these began, but judging from the elaborate accounts in the oracle records there seems no doubt that they had long histories before the Late Shang period, and must have developed simultaneously with the expansion of the Shang kingdom. They exercised a strong influence on Chinese religious beliefs and social institutions in subsequent Chinese history. The organization of Shang society into two clearly defined strata, the warrior-nobility and the common people, was the beginning of the bifurcated society which has been the fundamental characteristic of the Chinese society ever since.

The rise and fall of the Conservative and the Progressive Schools in the Late Shang period shows clearly that the keeping of the calendar was a living institution and it was being improved with the passage of time. The basic elements of the Shang calendar, including the naming and counting of the hours, days, weeks, months and years were all faithfully followed though with some improvements in later generations.

Although the use of animal shapes as decorations and ornaments in art may be noticed in the prehistoric times, the development of the Shang animal style from realistic to composite was unique. Although not very prominent in the earlier stages, in Late Shang this composite animal style exploded like a gigantic force to dominate the entire field of art. It is essentially symbolic, dominated by animal motifs, at the same time still retaining a number of geometric patterns. The achievement of this style may be attributed to the artist's freedom to take advantage of the experiences of others and to express himself according to his own will and imagination. The outcome was the creation and development of an artistic tradition, balanced in composition and highly individualistic in style, that not only led to further evolution in the Chou dynasty but also inspired many local developments in various regions surrounding the whole Pacific area. It was also in the same tradition that the Chinese *lung* dragon, *ch'i-lin* unicorn and fantastic animal forms were created in the later centuries to suit the Chinese fancy.

Of all the cultural developments of the Shang dynasty none was more important than writing. The oldest form of Shang writing seems to have been the pictographical script which must have had its beginning in the very early Shang period if not in the Neolithic period. By the time of Middle and Late Shang it was already regarded as an archaic form of the script and was used mainly in personal and clan names which were found in the inscriptions of bronze objects. The development of the Shang kingdom made it necessary to improve on this early form of writing which, being pictographical in nature, was clumsy and complicated to write, or more exactly, to draw. The improvement was made by simplifying the form of each character. Throughout the entire Shang period some 3,000 characters were created for use and the script proved able to deal with the complicated demands made on it by the royal court and household. The study of the oracle script shows that the writing was already in service in the time of Wu-ting in the thirteenth century B.C., the forerunner of the form of Chinese script used throughout the centuries to the present day. It is interesting to note that whenever the characters in the Chinese script have seemed too complicated and cumbersome, they have been simplified in much the same way. Such a process is almost the standard method for improving the Chinese script and a new movement along the same lines is at the present time reshaping the Chinese writing with full government backing.

The excavations of Shang remains in China may be said to have brought to light the origin of the Chinese civilization. There is plenty of evidence to show that the Shang culture had already attained some of the most fundamental Chinese characteristics. It has been abundantly verified that the early historical Chinese civilization is essentially a north China creation of the native inhabitants. The region is continental, and by the time of the Neolithic period, a series of individual cultures had been developed only to stimulate each other towards progress. Chinese culture was created by the activities of the Shang people in absorbing all the useful cultural elements within and beyond their kingdom. The Shang culture was the most prosperous as well as the most progressive one of its time, laying the foundation for an even more prosperous civilization in the following dynasties.

The material evidence left by high cultures such as those of Mesoamerica and Peru is far richer in detail than that of earlier, culturally simpler peoples. Nevertheless it is essential to avoid temptingly overeasy explanations—and pat answers—to questions about the complex factors that contributed to the first appearance of these and other civilizations.

5. The Pre-Columbian Civilizations [1]

In native America, not a great many centuries after the establishment of a village agricultural way of life, two major art styles of the first rank appear, more or less contemporaneously, in southern Mesoamerica and in northern Peru. These are known as the Olmec and the Chavín. I propose to consider these two art styles, first, and briefly, as to their content and form and, secondly, but in more detail, in their cultural settings and from the general perspective of New World culture history. For what engages our attention is that both styles occur at that point in time which might be said to mark the very first stirrings of civilization in the Mesoamerican and Peruvian areas. What role did these art styles, or the motivations of which they are the symbols, play in the rise and development of pre-Columbian civilizations? Are they, the styles themselves, the touchstones of that condition we refer to as civilization? What do we know of their origins or, if not their origins, their pre-conditions?

Like most anthropologists who are interested in culture history I am interested in origins and causes, but I am not sanguine about the possibilities of easy or early victories. Certainly the answers to the ultimate causal questions as to why the ancient American civilizations began and flourished where they did and when

they did still elude us, and what I can offer here will do little more, at best, than describe and compare certain situations and series of events.

My use of the term "great styles" is a special and intentional one. I refer to art styles and to manifestations of these generally considered as "fine arts." Their greatness is judged in their historical contexts, but it is none the less real. These great pre-Columbian art styles of Mesoamerica and Peru are expressed monumentally; they occur in settings that were obviously sacred or important in the cultures which produced them; they are also pervasive, being reproduced in a variety of media and contexts; the products are rendered with the consummate skill of the specially and long-trained artist; they conform to strict stylistic canons; their subject matter tends to be thematic; and finally, the finest monuments or creations in these styles are truly powerful and awe-inspiring. These last criteria are subjective, but I do not think we can ignore them. We see ancient art—the word "primitive" is here most inappropriate—across the millennia and with the eyes of an alien culture; yet we are not unmoved. Man speaks to man through art, and the screen of cultural difference and relativism does not strain out all emotional effect. Olmec and Chavín art measure fully to standards of greatness.

[1] GORDON R. WILLEY, "The Early Great Styles and the Rise of the Pre-Columbian Civilizations," in *American Anthropologist*, 64 (1962), pp. 1–11, © American Anthropological Association. Reprinted by permission of the author and the publisher.
Dr. Willey is Professor of Anthropology at Harvard University.

OLMEC AND CHAVÍN

The Olmec style of Mesoamerica has been known for 30 years as such. Stirling and his associates fully revealed the style in their discoveries in southern Veracruz and Tabasco. They and Caso and Covarrubias made it widely known and also opened the question of its cultural and chronological position in Mesoamerican culture history. Olmec art is rendered in life-size, or greater than life-size, full-round, and bas-relief stone monuments. These include free-standing heads, human and anthropomorphic figures, stelae, and altars. Carvings are also found on natural boulders after the manner of pictographs, but most of these are done with such skill and are so much a part of the deliberate style, that "bas-relief," rather than "pictograph," is the fitting term to describe them. Olmec sculptures also occur as small pieces: jade and serpentine figurines, celts, ornamental effigy axes, plaques, and other small ornaments. Ceramic objects in the Olmec style are less common but include figurines, pottery stamps, and vessels.

The central theme of Olmec art is a jaguar-human or were-jaguar being. The concept is nearly always expressed as more human, in total characteristics, than jaguar. The face is frequently infantile as well as jaguar-like, and in many instances actual human infant bodies are portrayed. But subtle shades of this infantile jaguarism infect almost all human or anthropomorphic representations, ranging all the way from only slightly snubbed, feline noses and down-turned drooping mouths to toothed and snarling countenances. Some stelae and monuments bear another concept, elderly men with aquiline noses and beards who are sometimes depicted with portrait realism; but there is also a fusion of the jaguar-like anthropomorph with the bearded man in Olmec iconography. Other motifs are rarer: fully animalized

jaguars, bird and duck monsters, serpents, and fish.

The formal properties of the Olmec style are highly distinctive. Although the subject matter is to a large extent in the mythological realm the portrayals are carried out with a "realistic" intent. It is thoroughly nongeometric and nonabstract; lines have a slow curvilinear rhythm, and free space balances figures. There is little fine detail. As a style it is the equivalent of any of the later great styles of Mesoamerica, and in the full-round treatment of the human body it is the superior of all.

The climax region of the Olmec style was southern Veracruz and Tabasco in such ceremonial center sites as La Venta, Tres Zapotes, and San Lorenzo. Insofar as the style is expressed monumentally there is little doubt but that this is its homeland. Elsewhere, Olmec monuments are widely scattered and occasional. Most are bas-relief figures carved on boulder outcrops, as in Morelos, Chiapas, Guerrero, Guatemala, and Salvador. Aside from these monuments, portable objects of the Olmec style, such as jade figurines, ornaments, and small manufactures, are found throughout much of southern Mesoamerica, from the Valley of Mexico and Guerrero on the northwest down through Chiapas and Pacific Guatemala. Covarrubias held the opinion that Guerrero was the ancestral home of the Olmec style, in its pre-monumental era, but it has yet to be demonstrated that the numerous Olmec figurines found in that region are earlier manifestations of the style than the great sculptures of Veracruz-Tabasco. In any event, for our present discussion, it is sufficient to note that the climax of the "great" aspects of the style are in this latter zone but that the style as a whole is spread over much of southern Mesoamerica. Wherever it can be dated, Olmec art appears in the Middle pre-Classic Period of Mesoamerican history, with an outer dating range of

1000 to 300 B.C., and a probable more specific bracketing by radiocarbon determinations of between 800 and 400 B.C.

Chavín style art is named for Chavín de Huántar, an imposing archeological site in the Marañon drainage of the north highlands of Peru. Tello, more than any other archeologist, called attention to Chavín art; subsequently, Bennett, Larco Hoyle, and Carrion Cachot made significant contributions. Like Olmec, the Chavín style is one closely adapted to sculptural forms, both monumental and small. The heroic-sized sculptures are mostly free-standing monoliths or stelae, lintels, cornices, and decorative features of buildings. These are executed with a relief-incision and champlévé technique in stone or are modelled in clay. Some full-round carving and modelling is also attempted in heads or figures tenoned or affixed to walls or buildings. Chavín small carving produced stone and bone plaques, stone and gourd vessels, ceremonial stone mortars and pestles, and ornaments. The style also appears in finely modelled and incised pottery vessels, in repoussé goldwork, and even in textile designs. In sum, it enters into more varied media than the Olmec style, but both styles are most at home in carving, particularly in large sculptures and in the work of the lapidary.

The content of Chavín art, like that of Olmec, deals with a few powerful central themes. With Chavín the dominant motif is either the feline or the fusion of feline elements, such as fangs and claws, with other beings, including humans, condors, the cayman, and the serpent. The fantastic beings of Chavín art emphasize somewhat more the animal attributes than the human, in contradistinction to Olmec. Strictly human representations are rare, and none of these have the qualities of portraiture observed in some of the Olmec sculptures. Although firmly set in a unified style, the monster or composite beings show great variations in the combinations of jaguar or puma and other animal elements.

The formal properties of the Chavín style, which are its essence, are decidedly different from those of Olmec. No one would mistake the two styles in juxtaposition. Chavín is intricate with detail in a way that Olmec is not. It does not employ free space, but seeks to fill it with such things as small secondary heads and eyes disposed over the body of the central monster figure of the sculpture. There is little mastery of realism or naturalism. It has more features that are stiff and "archaic." As styles the two have common ground only in that they rely upon slow heavy curves rather than straight lines, and both have a quality of the esoteric about them rather than the obvious.

The heartland of the Chavín style, insofar as it is monumental and in stone or sculptured adobe, is in the north highlands of Peru, at such sites as Chavín de Huántar, Yauya, and Kuntur Wasi, and in the coastal valleys of Nepeña and Casma. This is but one sector of the larger Peruvian culture area, and as such this focal concentration is comparable to the distribution of Olmec art in the Veracruz-Tabasco region within the larger sphere of Mesoamerica. The wider compass of Chavín art, as expressed in small manufactures, takes in much of the Peruvian culture area. Formerly thought to embrace only the northern part of Peru, its definite influence is now traced as far south on the coast as the Cerrillos phase of the Inca and Nazca Valleys. Thus, in its total geographic extent Chavín outstrips Olmec, the latter being confined to the southern half, or less, of its culture area setting. Chronologically, Chavín art belongs to the Formative Period of Peruvian prehistory and to either the Early or Middle subdivision of that period, depending upon one's terminology. The gross estimated dates for the Peruvian Formative Period are approximately the

First Millennium B.C. Within this range, and with the aid of radiocarbon determinations, the horizon of the Chavín art style is narrowed to between 800 and 400 B.C. As will be noted, this is identical to the dates for the time span estimated for the Olmec style in Mesoamerica. These two sets of dates, incidentally, were arrived at quite independently by different sets of archeologists.

OLMEC AND CHAVÍN IN CULTURE HISTORICAL PERSPECTIVE

As we have already observed, Olmec and Chavín styles make their first appearance on an underlying base of village agriculture. In Mesoamerica, village agriculture, defined as sedentary life based primarily upon maize cultivation, became established by about 1500 B.C., following a long epoch of incipient plant domestication. The presence of ceremonial architecture, in the form of platform mounds for temples or other buildings, in the early centuries of Mesoamerican agricultural life is probable, although not well documented. But by 800 B.C., some 700 years or so after the village agricultural threshold, the great Olmec ceremonial center of La Venta was founded in Tabasco. At the same time that these events were taking place in Mesoamerica, similar and related ones were going on in Peru. At about 1500 B.C. a well-developed variety of Mesoamerican maize appeared in coastal Peru and was rapidly assimilated into the local root-crop agricultural economies of the Peruvian coastal communities. Soon after this the Peruvians were making pottery and building ceremonial mounds, and to clinch the relationships between Peru and the north at this time, a distinctly Mesoamerican figurine has been found in one of these early Peruvian ceremonial sites known as Las Aldas. The Chavín style appears shortly after this. During its period, contact between Mesoamerica and Peru continued. For example, among the best known traits that have often been pointed to as linking the Olmec phase of Tlatilco and the Chavín Cupisnique phase are figurines, rocker-stamped pottery, incised and color-zoned wares, flat-bottomed open-bowl forms, and the stirrup-mouth jar.

In this setting of an almost exact equation in time, and with further evidences of contact in specific ceramic items, can we go further and argue that Olmec and Chavín are definitely related? Drucker, Wauchope, and I have all called attention to this possibility, and Della Santa has argued the case in earnest; but on reflection I do not think that the two styles show a close relationship. At least they do not exhibit a relationship which, in the realm of art, is a counterpart to the Mesoamerican maize in Peru or the Tlatilco-Cupisnique ceramic ties. What they possess in common, except for an addiction to sculptural and lapidaristic modes of expression, is largely the concept of the feline being, most probably the jaguar. Therefore, their relationship, if it existed, must have been on a level of concept and mythology, either an ancient undercurrent of belief on which both Peruvian and Mesoamerican societies could have drawn to develop quite different art styles or by a stimulus diffusion in which the source idea was drastically reworked in the recipient setting. In this last connection the example of Mesopotamian stimuli to the rise of early Egyptian civilization comes to mind. If this interpretation of the relationship between Olmec and Chavín is the correct one, I would, all things considered, see Mesoamerica as the source and Peru as in the role of the receiving culture.

An argument against a close, continuous Olmec-Chavín relationship on the level of style is, of course, the absence of either style, or any style definitely related to either, in the Intermediate area of

Lower Central America, Colombia, and Ecuador. The San Agustín sculptures of southern Colombia are, perhaps, the only candidates; but they are remarkably unlike either Olmec or Chavín, sharing with them only the attribute of feline-fanged beings, and they are only dubiously dated on the same time level as Olmec and Chavín. Further, as a style, San Agustín is considerably below the quality or sophistication of these great styles. This absence of stylistic linkages in the Intermediate area stands in contrast, however, to many of the significant traits of the village agricultural base out of which Olmec and Chavín seem to have developed. Evidence is rapidly accumulating from Ecuador, Colombia, and Lower Central America which shows the Intermediate area to be a common participant in early ceramic and other traits held also by Mesoamerica and Peru. A notable example of this is the striking similarity between Guatemalan Ocos pottery and that of the Ecuadorean Chorrera phase. Thus, in spite of this background of apparent intercommunication and interchange down and up the axis of Nuclear America, the entities of style which we recognize as Olmec and Chavín remain bound to their respective areas. They did not spread to the Intermediate area, nor can they reasonably be derived from there.

THE EARLY GREAT STYLES AS PRECURSORS TO CIVILIZATION

We have placed Olmec and Chavín at that point in the developmental history of the Mesoamerican and Peruvian cultures where village farming societies undergo a transformation to become temple center-and-village societies. This event is another major threshold in pre-Columbian life. It is a different kind of threshold than that of village agriculture which precedes it by a few hundred years, but it signals important changes. It is, in effect, the threshold of complex society that leads on to civilization. The economy appears much the same as earlier; it is based on maize, or maize and root crops, supplemented with other American food plants. The technology includes pottery-making, weaving, stone carving—in brief, the village agricultural neolithic arts. Houses were permanent to semi-permanent affairs disposed in small hamlets or villages. The most noticeable difference on the cultural landscape is the ceremonial center. These centers were not urban zones. Heizer has made quite explicit the nonurban nature of La Venta, and he estimates that the constructions there could have been built and sustained only by the cooperative efforts of villagers from a surrounding radius of several kilometers. Although Chavín de Huántar is situated in a radically different natural environment from La Venta, it, too, appears to have been a complex of ceremonial buildings and chambers without a large resident population in close proximity.

It is in such ceremonial centers that the outstanding monuments of the Olmec and Chavín styles are found. In Mesoamerica it is assumed that this ceremonial center-with-outlying hamlets type of settlement pattern is allied with a theocratic political structure. The assumption derives partly from the nature of the settlement and the feeling that such dispersed societies could only have been bound together by strong religious beliefs, but it derives mostly from our knowledge of the late pre- and early post-Columbian periods in Mesoamerica when lowland ceremonial centered societies were known to have a strong theocratic bias. In Peru this kind of theocratic orientation was not a feature of the Inca state; but there the archeological record shows a definite trend, from early to late times, that can best be interpreted as a movement away from religion as a dominant force and the gradual ascendance of secular power. In the light of such trends it is likely that priest leadership was more important in Chavín times than later. Thus, archeological inference is on the side of identifying the non-urban ceremonial center as primarily a sacred or religious establishment whatever other functions may have been served there. Olmec and Chavín works of art must surely, then, have been religious expressions. This concatenation of circumstances, the shift from simple village agricultural societies to complex temple-centered ones and the appearance of the two great styles, suggests that Olmec and Chavín are the symbols of two ecumenical religions. These religions lie at the base of the subsequent growth of pre-Columbian Mesoamerican and Peruvian civilizations.

This fundamental underlying nature of Olmec and Chavín art is revealed in the later cultures and styles in the two areas. For Mesoamerica, Michael D. Coe suggests that all known major art styles of the southern part of the area have an origin in the Olmec style. Most directly related among these would be the styles of the slightly later "danzante" monuments at Monte Alban and the Monte Alban I phase effigy incensarios, the Olmec-derived sculptures from the later pre-Classic Period levels at Tres Zapotes, the Izapa style stelae in Chiapas, and the closely similar Late pre-Classic monuments found recently at Kaminalijuyu. More remotely, but nevertheless showing affiliations with Olmec art, especially through the link of the Izapa style, would be the Classic Maya and Classic Veracruz styles. Further afield, the derivative influences are dimmed or uncertain. Classic Teotihuacan art stands most apart in showing little Olmec influence, and perhaps this may be correlated with the relatively slight impress of Olmec art on an earlier level in the Valley of Mexico where it is known mainly in the occasional Tlatilco ceramic objects. But that some connections, however indirect, did exist between Olmec and Teotihaucan iconography is shown by Covarrubias in his diagram of the stylistic evolution of the Teotihuacan and other rain gods from the prototype of the Olmec baby-jaguar face.

For Peru, the story is much the same. There, the distribution of the Chavín style was more nearly area-wide. Perhaps as a consequence, nearly all post-Chavín styles show some Chavín feline elements. Mochica art, of the north coast, depicts a feline or anthropomorphic feline as an apparent deity. Feline symbolism has an important part in Recuay, Pucara, and Nazca cultures. It is present in Tiahuanaco art, although not as the dominant motif.

CONSIDERATIONS OF CAUSALITY

We see Olmec and Chavín styles at the root of civilization in Mesoamerica and Peru. We also note, in the wider perspective of Nuclear America, that contemporaneous and related societies of the geographically intervening Intermediate area do not possess comparable great styles. Neither do they go on to civilization. From these facts I think we may reasonably conclude that Olmec and Chavín art are in some way involved with the rise to the status of civilization in their respective areas. But these are observations of history, or prehistory, and like all such observations it is difficult and perilous to attempt to read causality into them. In pointing to what I think is a special relationship between the early great styles and civilization, am I not merely defining civilization in terms of itself? In a partial sense I am; great art styles are one of the criteria by which the condition of civilization may be judged. But it is not, however, altogether true that many of the criteria of civilization are not yet present in either Mesoamerica or Peru at the time of Olmec and Chavín art florescence. Certainly one of the most significant of these, urbanization, is not; writing and metallurgy, if present, are only in their infancy; and the institution of the state, in any extensive territorial sense, is highly unlikely. The appearance of the first great styles, then, comes early in the growth of these American civilizations. By the time a full civilizational status has been achieved in either Mesoamerica or Peru these styles, as organized entities, have vanished, leaving only their residue in later styles. Nevertheless, styles themselves cannot be reified into civilization builders. They are, as I have said, symbols of institutions, attitudes, beliefs. Is, then, a belief system, a religion, a prime causal force as Toynbee has stated? I would think so, or at least I consider it near enough to a causal core to speculate on the proceeses whereby fundamental beliefs and their representative art may promote the growth of civilization.

In making these speculations let us consider a hypothesis about culture development in native America and particularly in the Nuclear American areas. Casting back to earlier chronological ranges than I have been talking about, it is now becoming evident that man changed from a collecting-hunting mode of existence to one of food plant cultivation by a process of introgression. The term is a botanical one, and it applies to what happened to plants over the several millennia leading up to village agriculture in Mesoamerica; but I also think it applicable to the culture change that went along with the gradual domestication of plants. The studies of Mangelsdorf and MacNeish have shown that original wild plants were found in a great many small locales where they were gathered and used and where seeds were eventually sown and plants tended by small, local populations. With contact between two such small communities, of plants and people, plant introgression and hybridization ensued with a genetically improved result. This process continued among enclaves with both hybridization and with the interchange of different species as well. Present investigations indicate that primitive maize, beans, and squashes do not follow the same sequence of occurrence in incipient agricultural stratigraphies in all parts of Mesoamerica but that the order varies from region to region. This diversity in development led, eventually, to the New World complex of food plants and to village agriculture. I would suggest that culture, too, evolved along with plants in much the same way, by introgression or interchange and by hybridization or fusion. This, I believe, is an aspect of what Lesser is saying in his concept of social fields. To follow the analogy, I think that this is what continued to happen in the development of cultures and societies after the attainment of village agriculture. Regional interchange or regional symbiosis provided an important impetus for change and growth. Sanders has detailed this process for parts of ancient Mesoamerica. It led to civilization.

In this hypothesis an obviously crucial factor is natural environmental setting and a multiplicity of varied settings in relatively close juxtaposition to one another. As has been pointed out by various authors, Mesoamerica is well suited in this regard. It is a land of climatic, altitudinal, and vegetational variety; it is rich in natural resources. Further, the archeological record shows trade and contact among distinct natural environmental and cultural regions from early times. Peru, as well, although not quite so varied, has dramatic regional differentiation, particularly between coast and highland; and the prehistory of that area may be read as a kind of counterpoint between the regional cultures of these natural zones. Contrast the potentialities of these two areas with others of the

New World which also had a basis of village agriculture. The natural environmental and cultural contours of differentiation within the Amazon basin or the Eastern Woodlands of North America are low in comparison. Products from region to region were the same or similar. Perhaps this homogeneity discouraged exchange.

Are we, now, at a nexus of causality in the rise of pre-Columbian civilizations in certain areas but not in others? Although conceding the importance of intra-areal cultural heterogeneity, and realizing that such heterogeneity must be to a large extent based in natural environment, I am not convinced. What of the Intermediate area which lies between and close to both of our areas of high civilization and which did not match them in these conditions of civilization? It is an area of spectacular regional environmental differentiation, tropical and semi-arid coasts, tropical lowlands, semitropical and temperate valleys, cool-temperate uplands. It has them all, and it is not an area poor in resources. We also know that the communities of this area were in possession of agriculture about as early as those of either Mesoamerica and Peru. These village agriculturists were similarly skilled in pottery making and, probably, the other neolithic crafts. In fact, they participated in the same technical traditions as their Mesoamerican or Peruvian contemporaries. Where then is the lack? What are the essential differences between the Intermediate area and its native cultures and those of the Mesoamerican and Peruvian areas?

I return, again, to the great styles, to Olmec and Chavín, for which there is no counterpart from Honduras to southern Ecuador. I have suggested that they, in themselves, are but the symbols for the religious ideologies of the early farming societies of Mesoamerica and Peru. I would further suggest that in these ideologies these early societies had developed a mechanism of intercommunication, a way of knitting together the smaller parts of the social universe of their day into a more unified whole than it had heretofore been or would otherwise be. In a way similar to that of the interchange of objects, plants, and techniques which had previously prepared the village agricultural threshold, the sharing of common ideologies led to the threshold of civilization by enlarging the effective social field. By this enlargement more individuals, more social segments, more local societies combined and coordinated their energies and efforts than at any time before. Regional differentiation in culture is an important precondition to cultural development insofar as differences contribute to the richness of the larger order, but without union the different parts remain isolated and in danger of stagnation. There are various ways by which man has promoted such union, but mutually and deeply held beliefs seem paramount. Such belief systems were, I think, the distinguishing features of the Mesoamerican and Peruvian societies of the first half of the First Millennium B.C., and the great Olmec and Chavín art styles are our clues to them.

Yet, even if my thesis is accepted thus far, have we done more than follow the chimaera of causality into one more disguise? Why did Mesoamerica and Peru develop early great religions and art styles and other areas not? What was the reason for their genius? I do not know. I do not think that it sprang from a seed planted by Chinese voyagers—or from two seeds brought by two such sets of voyagers—despite the facts that the Chou dynasty is replete with prowling tigers and that the time element is right for such a transference. It does us no good to deny the sudden mutation of creative change to the aborigines of America. It is no easier to explain elsewhere than it is here. What we are seeking is probably in New World soil, but genius must arise from preconditions which to our eyes do not foreshadow it. Local prototypes of Chavín and Olmec may eventually be found, although these will only carry the story back a little in time and leave the startling florescences unexplained.

I do not reject in their entirety any of the factors or forces we have been discussing as having had possible important influence in the growth of New World civilization. Climate, soil, agricultural potential, natural regional variety, all undoubtedly were significant. I am hesitant, however, to pinpoint any one of them as *the cause*. I am equally hesitant to advance my thesis of an early, prevailing, multi-regional ecumenical religion in either Mesoamerica or Peru as a *sole cause* of later civilizational greatness. I ask, rather, that such phenomena as I have directed attention to be considered as a step in the process of cultural development—a step which almost certainly was taken in these two areas of native America. For it may be that we phrase the problem wrong, that the search for the very well-springs of origin and cause is meaningless, and that the limits of anthropology are to appraise and understand the continuum of process as it is disclosed to us rather than to fix its ultimate beginnings.

GLOSSARY

Abbevillian: Now used to describe the European hand axe industry that is associated with the first interglacial period; formerly called *Chellian*.

Acheulian: Pertaining to the early Middle Pleistocene hand axe industry; ovate forms predominate, but flake tools also occur.

adaptive radiation: The evolutionary branching-out from a basic animal form, in following diverging lines of evolution.

adnate: Pertaining to an organism that grows partially adherent to another organism or some other body.

adze: A cutting tool like an ax, but with a cutting edge perpendicular to the plane of its movement.

Aëneolithic: Designating the transitional period between Neolithic and Bronze Ages, in which some copper was used.

allele: One pair of genes occupying corresponding loci in a chromosome pair.

allotropic species: A species that shows a variation of form.

alluvial plain: A periodically flooded lowland terrain.

altithermal times: Of or belonging to postglacial times.

alveolar prognathism: A forward jutting lower face.

ammonite: The spiraled shell of an extinct mollusk; related to the chambered nautilus.

anthropocentric: Pertaining to the assumption that man is the central and most important being in the cosmos.

anthropoid: "Manlike," usually used in referring to the anthropoid apes, to distinguish them from monkeys.

anthropoidea: Suborder of the Primates, containing all the higher primates: New and Old World monkeys, apes, fossil men and their descendants, *Homo sapiens*.

anthropometry: Measurement of the human body, including its skeleton.

Anthropos: A human being.

Aterian: Designating a specialized Mousterian culture found in northern Africa from Egypt to Morocco.

Aurignacian: Designating a widespread Upper Paleolithic stone industry characterized by increased diversity and technological refinement of tool forms.

Australopithecinae: Early Pleistocene subfamily of the family Hominidae, containing the early South African man-apes but excluding later forms.

Australopithecine: A member of the subfamily Australopithecinæ (South African "man-apes") of the family Hominidae, the family of man.

autochthonous: Indigenous; referring to the original inhabitants of a place.

axilla: A cavity beneath the junction of the arm containing the axillary artery and vein.

biasterionic breadth: The distance between points behind the ears where the parietal, temporal, and occipital bones meet.

bicipital tuberosity: A bone ending consisting of two protuberances.

biface: A stone tool chipped along the top and bottom edges of both sides.

blade tools: Stone flakes that are finely made and carefully detached from a specially prepared core.

blastula: An early Metazoan embryo.

brachiation: A type of movement in which an animal uses its arms to swing through the trees, a characteristic means of locomotion among the apes.

brachycephally: Roundheadedness.

breccia: A mass of material such as earth, broken rocks, fossils, and sand that has become consolidated by some kind of cementing matrix, often lime salts from water.

burin: An Upper Paleolithic tool with a beveled point.

calva: The upper part of the human cranium.

celt: A Neolithic implement of polished stone, round on one end with a convex cutting edge at the other.

Cenozoic: Pertaining to an era of geological history extending from the beginning of the Tertiary to the present; the Age of Mammals.

Chalcolithic: Referring to early Neolithic times, when copper was first used.

champlevé: Pertaining to a cleared field.

Chellean: Pertaining to a Lower Paleolithic stone industry site at Chelles, France; sometimes used to refer to Abbevillian culture.

chert: Impure flintlike rock.

chronology: The arranging of time in periods; the dating of events in the order of their occurrence.

chthonic forces: Forces that are spirits of the underworld; infernal deities.

conchoidal fracture: A shell-like configuration resulting from a spiral striking of a stone surface.

coprolite: Fossil excrement.

core biface: A hand ax with two opposing cutting edges.

core chopper: A tool made by chipping away flints from a piece of stone and using the core that remains.

coronoid process: A projection of the ulna in which it articulates with the coronoid fossa on the humerus.

cortex: The outer layer of gray matter of the brain, containing most of the higher nervous centers involved in sensory perception.

cortical: Pertaining to the cortex.

crural: relating to the thigh or leg.

cusp: A blunt or pointed protuberance of the crown of the tooth.

cytoplasm: The living substance or protoplasm of the cell, exclusive of the nucleus.

demography: The statistical study of the characteristics of human populations.

dendrochronology: Dating by counting tree-rings.

diabase: A basalt.

diachronic: Referring to the study of phenomena as they change through time.

diencephalic: Relating to the posterior subdivision of the forebrain.

diploe: The bony tissue between the tables of the skull.

diploid: Pertaining to that which is double or twofold in appearance or arrangement.

diploidization: The act of becoming diploid.

distal: Designating that which is remote from the point of attachment.

dolichocephaly: Long headedness.

dorsal sulcus: a shallow furrow, as on the surface of the brain, separating adjacent convolutions.

Drosophila: Fruit fly.

Dryopithecinae: A subfamily of the family Pongidae, containing a heterogeneous group of Miocene and Pliocene fossil apes related to the living great apes.

Dryopithecus: An important genus of Miocene and Pliocene fossil apes, represented by several species, especially from Europe, probably ancestral to the living apes.

dura mater: The tough, fibrous membrane that envelopes the brain and spinal cord.

ecology: The science of the balance in nature existing between the total of animal and vegetable species in any environment.

ecosocial: Referring to that which is both economic and social.

edentulous: Pertaining to the loss of teeth previously present.

emmer: An early form of cultivated wheat.

endemic: Belonging, or native, to a particular people or country.

endocranial: Referring to the inner surface of the cranium.

endogamous: Designating marriage within a specific group as required by custom or law.

endogamy: A socially enforced rule that marriages take place only between persons who are members of some defined group, such as one based on kinship or locality.

epiphysis: A joint surface or process of bone that ossifies and grows separately; uniting with the body of the bone near maturity; this is characteristic of mammals.

equid: A member of the family Equidae, consisting of the horses, asses, zebras, and various extinct related mammals.

eugenics: A science that deals with the importance of hereditary qualities in a series of generations of a race or breed; especially social control of human mating.

euhominid: Designating a member of the Homininae subfamily of the Hominidae, the family of man; can be used informally to refer to actual men as opposed to the "man-apes."

exogamy: A socially enforced rule that marriages take place only between persons who are not members of some defined group such as one based on kinship or locality.

facies: The general appearance or character of a geological or archaeological site.

femur: The thighbone.

fibula: The outer bone of the hind leg, below the knee.

flake tool: A stone tool common in

Lower and Middle Paleolithic sites in Europe, Africa, and Western Asia.

foramen magnum: The large opening in the base of the vertebrate skull, through which the spinal cord passes.

gamete: A reproductive cell capable of uniting with another to form a fertilized cell that can develop into a new plant or animal.

gastrula: An early Metazoan embryo.

generalized: Referring to the opposite of specialized, designating an animal or organ not strikingly adapted to a given environment or way of life; generally closer to ancestral forms and probably more adaptable in different directions than corresponding specialized forms.

genes: The units of inheritance, located on the chromosomes in the nuclei of cells; since the chromosomes are paired, the genes occur in pairs.

genotype: The genetic constitution of an individual.

gestation: The period from conception to birth.

Gigantopithecus: A giant fossil ape, postulated on the basis of several teeth found in Chinese drugstores by von Koenigswald.

glabella: The smooth prominence of the forehead between the eyebrows; also part of the frontal bone that lies above the root of the nose.

glottochronology: A linguistic technique used to reconstruct and date languages ancestral to known ones; age is reckoned by determining the rate at which linguistic divergence occurs.

gracile: Thin or delicate, used in describing the general character of certain bones.

heterozygous: Pertaining to two different genes making up a single gene pair.

heuristic: Pertaining to the purpose of furthering knowledge.

histology: The science of the tissues of animals and plants, especially of their microscopic structure.

Holocene: Pertaining to the geological recent.

holotype: A single specimen designated as the type of the species.

hominid: Pertaining to the family Hominidae, of man; relating to characteristics or members of this family.

Hominidae: The family of man, including modern man and fossil man (the subfamily of Homininae), the South African man-apes (Australopithecinae), and possibly the Pliocene form, Oreopithecus.

Homininae: The subfamily of the family Hominidae, containing the fossil men of the Pleistocene and living man (Java man to *Homo sapiens,* but excluding the Australopithecinae.

hominine: Pertaining to that which is euhominid.

Hominoidea: A superfamily of Anthropoidea or higher primates, containing and combining the families Pongidae (anthropoid apes) and Hominidae (man and the Australopithecines).

homologous: Describing that which exhibits homology.

homology: The correspondence in type or structure between parts of different organisms because of common evolutionary origin.

homozygous: Pertaining to a gene pair comprised of identical genes.

Hopewell: Designating a phase of Indian cultural development in the Mississippi Valley.

hyracoid: A hoofed mammal whose habitat is Africa and Southwest Asia.

ilium: The dorsal and upper one of the three bones composing either lateral half of the pelvis.

infraorbital: Pertaining to bone situated beneath the orbit.

inion: The external occipital protuberance of the skull.

innominate: Referring to that which has no name.

in situ: In place, used for paleontological or archaeological materials discovered in the original matrix in which they were deposited in antiquity.

internal pterygoid: The bony element of the vertebrate skull.

isogloss: A boundary line between places or regions that differ in a particular linguistic feature; a linguistic feature shared by some but not all speakers of a dialect.

isohet: A line indicating equal rainfall.

lacustrine: Pertaining to lakes.

Lagomorpha: An order of Eutheria comprised of gnawing mammals, such as rabbits.

lapidary: Pertaining to the art of cutting stones.

larynx: The modified upper part of the trachea; in man the organ of voice.

laterite: A residual product of rock decay, red in color; having a high content of iron oxide and hydroxide of aluminum.

leister: A pronged spear for striking fish.

Levallois: Pertaining to the stone industry typical of the European Middle Paleolithic; consisting primarily of blades struck carefully from a core.

loess: An unstratified deposit of yellowish-brown loam, consisting of tiny air- or water-borne grains of dirt.

lumbar: The part of the spinal column between the ribs and the pelvis; in man it is strongly bent back in order to straighten the upper part of the body over the legs.

lunate: Crescent-shaped.

malar: The cheekbone.

mandible: The lower jaw, in which lower teeth are rooted.

mastoid process: A nobbin of bone behind each ear to which are attached balancing muscles of the neck, used to turn the human head from side to side.

matriarchy: A state or social condition in which women rule.

maxilla: The membrane bone on each side of the face, which bears most of the upper teeth.

megalithic: Pertaining to huge stones used in some prehistoric structures; monumental.

megalocephaly: Large headedness.

Meganthropus: An ape-man known from two lower jaw bones found in Java.

mesocephaly: The head shape intermediately between long and round.

mesolithic: Designating a group of hunting and gathering cultures in Europe between the end of the Pleistocene and the beginning of Neolithic food growing.

microlithic: Pertaining to a very small stone tool; generally made on flakes.

milpa: A small field cleared from the jungle, cropped for a few years, and then abandoned.

Miocene: Designating the fourth division of the Cenozoic or Tertiary era, lasting from about 25 million to about 10 million b.c.; apes ancestral to modern forms were taking shape.

miscegenation: A derogatory term sometimes used to refer to interbreeding between "races" of men.

moiety: A kinship group comprising half the members of a society.

monogamy: Marriage with but one person at a time.

monogenesis: The theory of the development of all living things from a single cell.

monolithic: Pertaining to a single stone or block of stone, usually of great size.

monophyletic: Pertaining to a single stock, developed from a common parent form.

moraine: An accumulation of earth, stones, etc., deposited by a glacier.

mores: Standards of conduct; traditional values concerning ethically correct behavior; customs.

morphology: The form or structure of a thing or organism; or the study of that form or structure.

Mousterian: Pertaining to the stone industry located at Le Moustier, France; consisting mostly of flake tools and frequently ascribed to the Middle Paleolithic.

mutagen: An agent that tends to effect an increase in the occurrence or extent of mutation.

mutation: A permanent change in some gene carried by an individual, producing a changed effect in the trait to which the gene is related, in those of his descendants who receive the gene.

neanthropic: Pertaining to man of the surviving species, *Homo sapiens;* as distinguished from earlier hominids.

neo: New.

Neolithic: "New stone," more properly designating the period anywhere in which simple farming existed, without large communities or cities; appeared perhaps as much as 10,000 years ago in the Middle East; much later in Europe and elsewhere.

neoteny: The retention of immature characteristics in adulthood.

nucleotide: A compound that is formed by partial hydrolysis of a nucleic acid, or that occurs free in the tissues.

occipital: Pertaining to the back of the skull and hind part of the skull base, including the foramen magnum.

occlusal: Pertaining to the jaws' closure with the cusps fitting together, as upper and lower teeth.

Oldowan: Pertaining to the Lower Pleistocene stone industry of trimmed stone pebbles, among the earliest tools of deliberate manufacture.

olecranon: The process of the ulna projecting behind the elbow.

ontogenetic: Pertaining to the life history or development of an individual organism.

oögonia: Descendants of a primordial germ cell that gave rise to oöcytes, or the female gamete of certain Protozoa.

orbital: Ocular, pertaining to the eyes.

Oreopithecinae: Provisionally regarded as a subfamily of the Hominidae, containing the Pliocene fossil *Oreopithecus.*

orthogenesis: The theory that the processes of biological and cultural evolution are such that they move always in a determined direction, passing through fixed stages irrespective of external conditions.

osteology: The science of dealing with the bones of vertebrates.

paleo: Old, ancient.

paleontology: The study of the remains of extinct and ancient life as revealed in the geological record.

Paleozoic: Pertaining to the Age of Fishes, the first geological period in which fossil remains of vertebrates are found.

Paranthropus: One genus of protohuman man-apes of the Pleistocene of South Africa.

parietal bones: The "walls" of the skull vault, forming the upper part of the sides of the skull.

parthenogenesis: Reproduction by the development of an unfertilized egg.

pelagic: Pertaining to the ocean, or conducting operations under the ocean.

periglacial: Designating the time about when the glaciations occurred; usually used to refer to the period at the end of the Pleistocene and the beginning of the Recent (Holocene).

pharynx: The part of the alimentary canal between the mouth cavity and the esophagus.

phenotype: Visible characteristics, the external appearance of a trait as opposed to genotype, which refers to genetic constitution.

philology: The study of literature and language, and of culture as it is revealed in literature.

phonation: Verbal utterance.

phoneme: A minimal unit of spoken sound, change of which produces an alteration of meaning in the utterance.

phylectic: Pertaining to a phylum.

phylogeny: The evolution of a species

or order of life as opposed to ontogeny, the development of the individual.

phylum: One of the primary divisions of the animal or vegetable kingdom; all members are assumed to share descent from a common ancestor.

physiography: A general description of nature; physical geography.

physiology: The life processes of an organism, or the study of these processes.

Piltdown man: A supposed early form of man, the fossil remains of which have now been proved to have been the result of a scientific forgery; a fossil fake.

piriform: Pertaining to that which is pear-shaped.

Pithecanthropus: A genus of extinct primate ancestral to man.

Pleistocene: Pertaining to the last division of time before the Recent; the Ice Age; all fossil humans belong to this period.

Pliocene: Designating the fifth division of the Cenozoic or Tertiary era, lasting —very approximately—from 10 million to 1 million B.C.; ancestors of modern apes and early men were present; most Dryopithecus species and Oreopithecus belong to this period.

Pliopithecus: A fossil gibbon of the Miocene and Pliocene.

pluvial: Of or pertaining to rain; characterized by abundant rain.

polar body: A minute cell that separates from the egg during its maturation.

polity: A form or constitution of government; a politically organized community or state.

poly: Many.

polyandry: A condition of marriage in which a woman has more than one husband at a time.

polygamy: A state of having more than one marriage partner at a time.

polygenesis: Plurality of origin, descended from a variety of antecedents.

polygyny: A condition of marriage in

which a man has more than one wife at a time.

polymorphism: A state in which something has or assumes various forms.

polyphyletic: Pertaining to that which is derived from more than one original, or ancestral type, race or family.

pongid: Pertaining to the Pongidae.

Pongidae: The family of the anthropoid apes, living and extinct; grouped with the Hominidae, the family of man, in the superfamily Hominoidea.

post: After, later, behind.

postlamboidal: Pertaining to the region behind the suture connecting the parietal and occipital bones.

prehension: The ability of some primates to enclose an object in grasping movements with their digits; some New World monkeys also use their tails.

prehominines: Pertaining to that which is prehominid.

primate: An order of mammals, to which man, the apes, and all monkeys belong; divided into two suborders: Prosimii, the lower apes; and Anthropoidea, monkeys, apes, and man.

prismatic: Pertaining to a form with faces parallel to the vertical axis.

Proconsul: A Miocene genus of ape, known from three species from East Africa, possibly ground-running rather than brachiating.

prognathism: The prominent projection of the lower face.

proximal: Describing that which is nearest to a point.

pterygoid: Pertaining to a certain bony or cartiliginous element of the skull of vertebrates.

Quadrumana: Primates excluding man, considered as a group distinguished by hand-shaped feet.

Quarternary: The last age of the Cenozoic era; comprised of the Pleistocene and Holocene periods; first evidence of man occurs in the lower Quarternary.

quern: A simple stone milling device used for grinding grain.

raciation: The differentiation of local groups within a larger population through selection for ecologically useful variations under conditions of at least partial isolation.

repoussé: Embossed; pertaining to an ornamentally raised surface.

revetment: A facing of stone; a retaining wall.

Rhodesian man: A species of fossil men found in Rhodesia and South Africa, characterized by a low-arched skull vault and enormous brow ridges.

sagittal crest: The suture between the parietal bones of the skull.

sati: Suttee; custom of a Hindu widow willingly cremating herself on the funeral pyre of her husband as an act of devotion.

scapulimancy: Divination that uses a mammalian shoulder bone.

selva: Pertaining to tropical rain forest.

sericulture: The production of raw silk by raising silk worms.

serology: The science that treats the reactions, preparation, and use of serums.

Sinanthropus: Pekin man.

Sinologue: A student of the Chinese.

specialized: Designating an animal or organism strongly adapted to a particular environment or way of life; carrying the connotation of tending to be limited as to other, alternative possibilities.

speciation: Formation of biological species.

spermatozoa: Male sexual cells, or sperm cells whose function is the fertilization of the egg.

stadial: The period of farthest advance of a glaciation.

steatopygia: A condition characterized by the presence of a heavy deposit of fat on the buttocks, found particularly among the Bushmen and Hottentots of Southern Africa.

Steinheim man: Middle Pleistocene fossil hominid from western Germany.

stelae: Monumental stone slabs generally carrying inscriptions of a descriptive or commemorative nature.

steppe: One of the vast tracks of land in southeastern Europe and Asia that is usually level and without forest, often characterized by great temperature variations.

stirp: A line descending from a common ancestor; stock or lineage.

stratigraphy: The layers of rock and soil at an archaeological or paleontological site; the study of the sequence of such strata for the purpose of dating.

sub: Below.

subtrochanteric: Pertaining to the region below the prominent part of the upper femur.

suid: A member of the family Suidae, swine.

supraorbital torus: The bony ridge over the eyebrows.

taiga: The swampy coniferous forest of Siberia, begins where the Tundra ends.

taxonomy: Classification, especially on the basis of natural relationships.

telegony: The supposed carrying over of the influence of a sire to the offspring of subsequent matings with other males.

teleological: Pertaining to the metaphysical attitude that all things in nature are designed and moving toward some determined end; progress toward the realization of some higher principle, nonmechanistic.

tell: A mound or hill.

temporal muscle: The muscle that raises the jaw; arises as a flat sheet from a large area on the side of the skull.

Tertiary: Designating the age of mammals, earlier period of the Cenozoic era; just preceding the Quarternary, the age of man.

tibia: One of the two bones of the lower leg.

till: An unstratified glacial drift, or deposit.

triploblastic: Pertaining to that which has three primary germ layers.

tundra: A level or undulating treeless plain, characteristic of arctic and sub-arctic regions; usually supports dense growth of mosses and lichens.

ulna: The bone of the forearm that forms the hinge joint at the elbow, and on which the radius twists to rotate the wrist and hand.

ulnar diaphysis: The shaft of the ulna.

vertebra: One of the parts of the spinal column.

vertebrates: The major group of animals to which man and the backboned animals belong.

vertex: The top of the head.

Wisconsin glaciation: The fourth major glacial advance in North America, corresponding in time to the Würm advance in Europe.

Würm: The fourth major glacial advance in Europe; occurred in later Pleistocene times.

xenophobia: The hatred of foreigners.

zygote: A cell formed by the union of two gametes, matured sex cells.

INDEX

Mesag de Vallois
One Neander - Clart 100

left accidental 18 7

Montigue 177
Neander Tabun   recently intermixt
modern   Skhul
_____
Co Magnon Away 5' 11
            cave paint

Ddy rate mutation
  1 - 10, or 25,000.00

onlooon - races 171
         wash - no

Olduvai ooze 39
            _

           293
B - 7 C
Zain chemi Shan Kurdistan
Karim 5 at bog Kurdistan
Natufian - Pales